SPURGEON'S SERMONS ON THE DEATH AND RESURRECTION OF JESUS

SPURGEON'S SERMONS ON THE DEATH AND RESURRECTION OF JESUS

C. H. SPURGEON

Hendrickson Publishers, Inc.
P. O. Box 3473
Peabody, Massachusetts 01961-3473

ISBN 978-1-56563-805-1

Printed in the United States of America

Second Printing—June 2007

Table of Contents

Preface

If you ask most people today who Charles Haddon Spurgeon was, you might be surprised at the answers. Most know he was a preacher, others remember that he was Baptist, and others go so far as to remember that he lived in England during the nineteenth century. All of this is true. Yet Charles Haddon Spurgeon was so much more.

Born into a family of Congregationalists in 1834, Spurgeon's father and grandfather were both Independent preachers. These designations seem benign today, but in the mid-nineteenth century, they describe a family committed to a Nonconformist path—meaning they did not conform to the established Church of England. Spurgeon grew up in a rural village, a village virtually cut off from the Industrial Revolution rolling over most of England.

Spurgeon became a Christian at a Primitive Methodist meeting in 1850, at age sixteen. He soon became a Baptist (to the sorrow of his mother) and almost immediately began to preach. Considered a preaching prodigy—"a boy wonder of the fens"—Spurgeon attracted huge audiences and garnered a reputation that reached throughout the countryside and into London. As a result of his great success, Spurgeon was invited to preach at the New Park Street Chapel in London in 1854, when he was just nineteen. When he first preached at the church, they were unable to draw even two hundred people. Within the year, Spurgeon filled the twelve-hundred-seat church to overflowing; he soon began preaching in larger and larger venues, outgrowing each, until finally in 1861, the Metropolitan Tabernacle was completed, which seated six thousand persons. This would be Spurgeon's home base for the rest of his career, until his death in 1892, at age fifty-seven.

Spurgeon married Susannah Thompson in 1856 and soon they had twin sons, Charles and Thomas, who would later follow him in his work. Spurgeon opened Pastors' College, a training school for preachers, which trained over nine hundred preachers during his lifetime. He also opened orphanages for underprivileged boys and girls, providing educations to each of the students. And he developed a program to publish and distribute Christian literature. He is said to have preached to over ten million people in his 40 years of preaching. His sermons sold over 25,000 copies each week, and were translated into 20 languages. He was utterly committed to spreading the Gospel, through preaching and through the written word.

During Spurgeon's lifetime, the Industrial Revolution transformed England from a rural, agricultural society, to an urban, industrial society, with all the attendant difficulties and horrors of a society in major transition. The people displaced by these sweeping changes, the factory workers, the shopkeepers—these became Spurgeon's congregation. Coming from a small village himself and having been transplanted to a large and inhospitable city, Spurgeon was a common man, and he understood innately the spiritual needs of the common people. Listeners welcomed his message because he was a communicator who made the Gospel so relevant and because he spoke so brilliantly to people's deepest needs.

Keep in mind that Spurgeon preached in the days before microphones or speakers: in other words, he preached without benefit of amplifier systems. Once he preached to a crowd of over twenty-three thousand people without mechanical amplification of any sort. He himself was the electrifying presence on the platform: he did not stand and simply read a stilted sermon. Spurgeon worked off of an outline, speaking "in common language to common people." He developed his themes extemporaneously. His sermons were filled with stories and poetry, drama and emotion. He would stride back and forth across the stage, he gestured broadly, he acted out stories, he used humor, and he painted pictures using his words and himself. For Spurgeon, preaching was about communicating the truth of God, and he would use any gift at his disposal to accomplish this.

Spurgeon's preaching was anchored in his spiritual life, a life rich in prayer and Scripture study. He was not tempted by fashion, be it theological, social, or political. Scripture was the cornerstone of Spurgeon's life and his preaching. He was mostly an expositional preacher, exploring a passage of Scripture for its meanings both within the text and to his congregation. Spurgeon saw scripture as alive and specifically relevant to people's lives, whatever their social status, economic situation, or in whatever time they live.

Reading his sermons, there is a sense that Spurgeon embraced God's revelation completely: God's revelation through Jesus Christ, through Scripture, and through his own prayer and study. For him, revelation was not a finished act: God was still revealing Himself, if His people made themselves available. Some recognize Spurgeon for the mystic he was—one who was willing and eager to explore the mysteries of God, able to live with those bits of truth that do not conform to a particular system of theology, and perfectly comfortable with saying "This I know and this I don't know—yet will I trust."

This collection of sermons is Spurgeon's preaching on the passion, death, and resurrection of Jesus Christ—without question the holiest season of the Christian year and the biggest mysteries of the Christian faith.

These sermons are not a series. They were not created or intended by Spurgeon to be sequential, except in the most general way. They are instead stand-alone sermons, meant to explore specific events in the life of Jesus, focusing on specific periods of His life. The sermons were preached at different times of Spurgeon's career, and they have distinct and differing characteristics. They have not been homogenized or edited to sound as though they are all of a kind. Instead, they reflect the preacher himself, allowing the voice of this remarkable man to ring clearly as he guides the reader into a particular account, a particular event—to experience, with Spurgeon, God's particular revelation.

Listen while you read. These are words meant to be heard, not merely read. Listen carefully and you will hear the cadences of this remarkable preaching, the echoes of God's timeless truth traveling across the years. And above all, enjoy Spurgeon's enthusiasm, his fire, his devotion, and his zeal for God's gift to us in the sacrifice of Jesus Christ.

—*Patricia S. Klein*

The Lord's Supper

Communion with Christ and His People

"The cup of blessing which we bless, is it not the communion of the blood of Christ? The bread which we break, is it not the communion of the body of Christ? For we being many are one bread, and one body: for we are all partakers of that one bread."—I Cor. 10:16, 17.

I will read you the text as it is given in the Revised Version: "The cup of blessing which we bless, is it not a communion of the blood of Christ?" That is to say—Is it not one form of expressing the communion of the blood of Christ? "The bread," or as it is in the margin, "the loaf which we break," is it not a communion of the body of Christ? Seeing that we, who are many, are one loaf, one body: for we all partake of the one loaf." The word "loaf" helps to bring out more clearly the idea of unity intended to be set forth by the apostle.

It is a lamentable fact that some have fancied that this simple ordinance of the Lord's supper has a certain magical, or at least physical power about it, so that, by the mere act of eating and drinking this bread and wine, men can be made partakers of the body and blood of Christ. It is marvelous that so plain a symbol should have been so complicated by genuflections, adornments, and technical phrases. Can anyone see the slightest resemblance between the Master's sitting down with the twelve, and the mass of the Roman community? The original rite is lost in the superimposed ritual. Superstition has produced a sacrament where Jesus intended a fellowship. Too many who would not go the length of Rome, yet speak of this simple feast as if it were a mystery dark and obscure. They employ all manner of hard words to turn the children's bread into a stone. It is not the Lord's supper, but the Eucharist; we see before us no plate, but a "paten"; the cup is a "chalice," and the table is an "altar." These are incrustations of superstition, whereby the blessed ordinance of Christ is likely to be again overgrown and perverted.

What does this supper mean? It means communion: *communion with Christ, and communion with one another.*

What is communion? The word breaks up easily into *union,* and its prefix *com,* which means *with,* "union with." We must, therefore, first enjoy union with Christ, and with His Church, or else we cannot enjoy communion. Union lies at the basis of communion. We must be one with Christ in heart, and soul, and life; baptized into His death; quickened by His life, and so brought to be members of His body, one with the whole Church of which He is the Head. We cannot have communion with Christ till we are in union with *Him;* and we cannot have communion with the Church till we are in vital union with *it.*

I. *The teaching of the Lord's supper is just this—that while we have many ways of communion with Christ, yet the receiving of Christ into our souls as our Savior is the best way of communion with Him.*

I said, dear friends, that we have many ways of communion with Christ; let me show you that it is so.

Communion is ours *by personal intercourse* with the Lord Jesus. We speak with Him in prayer, and He speaks with us through the Word. Some of us speak oftener with Christ than we do with wife or child, and our communion with Jesus is deeper and more thorough than our fellowship with our nearest friend. In meditation and its attendant thanksgiving we speak with our risen Lord, and by His Holy Spirit He answers us by creating fresh thought and emotion in our minds. I like sometimes in prayer, when I do not feel that I can say anything, just to sit still, and look up; then faith spiritually descries the Well-beloved, and hears His voice in the solemn silence of the mind. Thus we have intercourse with Jesus of a closer sort than any words could possibly express. Our soul melts beneath the warmth of Jesus' love, and darts upward her own love in return. Think not that I am dreaming, or am carried off by the memory of some unusual rhapsody: no, I assert that the devout soul can converse with the Lord Jesus all the day, and can have as true fellowship with Him as if He still dwelt bodily among men. This thing comes to me, not by the hearing of the ear, but by my own personal experience: I know of a surety that Jesus manifests Himself unto His people as He doth not unto the world.

Ah, what sweet communion often exists between the saint and the Well-beloved, when there is no bread and wine upon the table, for the Spirit Himself draws the heart of the renewed one, and it runs after Jesus, while the Lord Himself appears unto the longing spirit! Truly our fellowship is with the Father, and with His Son Jesus Christ. Do *you* enjoy this charming converse?

Next, we have communion with Christ *in His thoughts, views, and purposes;* for His thoughts are our thoughts according to our capacity and sanctity. Believers take the same view of matters as Jesus does; that which pleases Him, pleases them, and that which grieves Him grieves them also. Consider, for instance, the greatest theme of our thought, and see whether our thoughts are not like those of Christ. He delights in the Father, He loves to glorify the Father: do not we? Is not the Father the center of our soul's delight? Do we not rejoice at the very sound of His name? Does not our spirit cry, "Abba, Father"? Thus it is clear we feel as Jesus feels towards the Father, and so we have the truest communion with Him. This is but one instance; your contemplations will bring before you a wide variety of topics wherein we think with Jesus. Now, identity of judgment, opinion, and purpose forms the highway of communion; yea, it is communion.

We have also communion with Christ *in our emotions.* Have you never felt a holy horror when you have heard a word of blasphemy in the street? Thus Jesus felt when He saw sin, and bore it in His own person: only He felt it infinitely more than you do. Have you never felt as you looked upon sinners that you must weep over them? Those are holy tears, and contain the same ingredients as those which Jesus shed when He lamented over Jerusalem. Yes, in our zeal for God, our hatred of sin, our detestation of falsehood, our pity for men, we have true communion with Jesus.

Further, we have had fellowship with Christ *in many of our actions.* Have you ever tried to teach the ignorant? This Jesus did. Have you found it difficult? So Jesus found it. Have you striven to reclaim the backslider? Then you were in communion with the Good Shepherd who hastens into the wilderness to find the one lost sheep, finds it, lays it upon His shoulders, and brings it home rejoicing. Have you ever watched over a soul night and day with tears? Then you have had communion with Him who has borne all our names upon His broken heart, and carries the memorial of them upon His pierced hands. Yes, in acts of self-denial, liberality, benevolence, and piety, we enter into communion with Him who went about doing good. Whenever we try to disentangle the snarls of strife, and to make peace between men who are at enmity, then are we doing what the great Peace-maker did, and we have communion with the Lord and Giver of peace. Wherever, indeed, we co-operate with the Lord Jesus in His designs of love to men, we are in true and active communion with Him.

So it is *with our sorrows*. Certain of us have had large fellowship with the Lord Jesus in affliction. "Jesus wept": He lost a friend, and so have we. Jesus grieved over the hardness of men's hearts: we know that grief. Jesus was exceedingly sorry that the hopeful young man turned away, and went back to the world: we know that sorrow. Those who have sympathetic hearts, and live for others, readily enter into the experience of "the Man of sorrows." The wounds of calumny, the reproaches of the proud, the venom of the bigoted, the treachery of the false, and the weakness of the true, we have known in our measure; and therein have had communion with our Lord Jesus.

Nor this alone: we have been with our Divine Master *in His joys*. I suppose there never lived a happier man than the Lord Jesus. He was rightly called "the Man of sorrows"; but He might, with unimpeachable truth, have been called, "the Man of joys." He must have rejoiced as He called His disciples, and they came unto Him; as He bestowed healing and relief; as He gave pardon to penitents, and breathed peace on believers. His was the joy of finding the sheep, and taking the piece of money out of the dust. His work was His joy: such joy that, for its sake, He endured the cross, despising the shame. The exercise of benevolence is joy to loving hearts: the more pain it costs, the more joy it is. Kind actions make us happy, and in such joy we find communion with the great heart of Jesus.

Thus have I given you a list of windows of agate and gates of carbuncle through which you may come at the Lord; but the ordinance of the Lord's supper sets forth a way which surpasses them all. It is the most accessible and the most effectual method of fellowship. Here it is that we have fellowship with the Lord Jesus by receiving Him as our Savior. We, being guilty, accept of His atonement as our sacrificial cleansing, and in token thereof we eat this bread and drink this cup. "Oh!" says one, "I do not feel that I can get near to Christ. He is so high and holy, and I am only a poor sinner." Just so. For that very reason you can have fellowship with Christ in that which lies nearest to His heart: He is a Savior, and to be a Savior there must be a sinner to be saved. Be you that one, and Christ and you shall at once be in union and communion: He shall save, and you shall be saved; He shall sanctify, and you shall be sanctified; and twain shall thus be one. This table sets before you His great sacrifice. Jesus has offered it; will you accept it? He does not ask you to bring anything—no drop of blood, no pang of flesh; all is here, and your part is to come and partake of it, even as of old the offerer partook of the peace offering which he had brought, and so feasted with God and with the priest. If you work for Christ, that will certainly be some kind of fellowship with Him; but I tell you that the communion of receiving him into your inmost soul is the nearest and closest fellowship possible to mortal man. The fellowship of service is exceedingly honorable, when we and Christ work together for the same objects; the fellowship of suffering is exceedingly instructive, when our heart has graven upon it the same characters as were graven upon the heart of Christ: but the fellowship of the soul which receives Christ, and is received by Christ, is closer, more vital, more essential than any other.

Such fellowship is eternal. No power upon Earth can henceforth take from me the piece of bread which I have just now eaten, it has gone where it will be made up into blood, and nerve, and muscle, and bone. It is within me, and of me. That drop of wine has coursed through my veins, and is part and parcel of my being. So he that takes Jesus by faith to be his Savior has chosen the good part which shall not be taken away from him. He has received the Christ into his inward parts, and all the men on earth, and all the devils in Hell, cannot extract Christ from him. Jesus saith, "He that eateth Me, even he shall live by Me." By our sincere reception of Jesus into our hearts, an indissoluble union is established between us and the Lord, and this manifests itself in mutual communion. To as many as received Him, to them has He given this communion, even to them that believe on His name.

II. I have now to look at another side of communion—namely, the fellowship of true believers with each other.

We have many ways of communing the one with the other, but there is no way of mutual communing like the common reception of the same Christ in the same way. I have said that there are many ways in which Christians commune with one another, and these doors of fellowship I would mention at some length.

Let me go over much the same ground as before. We commune by *holy converse*. I wish we had more of this. Time was when they that feared the Lord spake often one to another; I am afraid that now they more often speak one against another. It is a grievous thing that full often love lies bleeding by a brother's hand. Where we are not quite so bad as that, yet we are often backward and silent, and so miss profitable converse. Our insular reserve has often made one Christian sit by another in utter isolation, when each would have been charmed with the other's company. Children of one family need not wait to be introduced to each other: having eaten of this one bread, we have given and received the token of brotherhood; let us therefore act consistently with our relationship, and fall into holy conversation next time we meet. I am afraid that Christian brotherhood in many cases begins and ends inside the place of worship. Let it not be so among us. Let it be our delight to find our society in the circle of which Jesus is the center, and let us make those our friends who are the friends of Jesus. By frequent united prayer and praise, and by ministering the one to the other the things which we have learned by the Spirit, we shall have fellowship with each other in our Lord Jesus Christ.

I am sure that all Christians have fellowship together in their *thoughts*. In the essentials of the gospel we think alike: in our thoughts of God, of Christ, of sin, of holiness, we keep step; in our intense desire to promote the kingdom of our Lord, we are as one. All spiritual life is one. The thoughts raised by the Spirit of God in the souls of men are never contrary to each other. I say not that the thoughts of all professors [Christians] agree, but I do assert that the minds of the truly regenerate in all sects, and in all ages, are in harmony with each other—a harmony which often excites delighted surprise in those who perceive it. The marks that divide one set of nominal Christians from another set are very deep and wide to those who have nothing of religion but the name; yet living believers scarcely notice them. Boundaries which separate the cattle of the field are no division to the birds of the air. Our minds, thoughts, desires, and hopes are one in Christ Jesus, and herein we have communion.

Beloved friends, our *emotions* are another royal road of fellowship. You sit down and tell your experience, and I smile to think that you are telling mine. Sometimes a young believer enlarges upon the sad story of his trials and temptations, imagining that nobody ever had to endure so great a fight, when all the while he is only describing the common adventures of those who go on pilgrimage, and we are all communing with him. When we talk together about our Lord, are we not agreed? When we speak of our Father, and all His dealings with us, are we not one? And when we weep, and when we sigh, and when we sing, and when we rejoice, are we not all akin? Heavenly fingers touching like strings within our hearts bring forth the selfsame notes, for we are the products of the same Maker, and tuned to the same praise. Real harmony exists among all the true people of God: Christians are one in Christ.

We have communion with one another, too, in our *actions*. We unite in trying to save men: I hope we do. We join in instructing, warning, inviting, and persuading sinners to come to Jesus. Our life-ministry is the same: we are workers together with God. We live out the one desire—"Thy kingdom come. Thy will be done in earth, as it is in Heaven."

Certainly we have much communion one with the other in our *sufferings*. There is not a poor sick or despondent saint upon the Earth with whom we do not sympathize at this moment, for we are fellow members, and partakers of the sufferings of Christ. I hope we can say,

> *Is there a lamb in all Thy flock,*
> *I would disdain to feed?*
> *Is there a foe, before whose face,*
> *I fear Thy cause to plead?*

No, we suffer with each other, and bear each other's burden, and so fulfill the law of Christ. If we do not, we have reason for questioning our own faith; but if we do so, we have communion with each other.

I hope we have fellowship in our *joys*. Is one happy? We would not envy him, but rejoice with him. Perhaps this is not so universal as it should be among professors. Are we at once glad because another prospers? If another star outshines ours, do we delight in its radiance? When we meet a brother with ten talents, do we congratulate ourselves on having such a man given to help us, or do we depreciate him as much as we can? Such is the depravity of our nature, that we do not readily rejoice in the progress of others if they leave us behind; but we must school ourselves to this. A man will speedily sit down and sympathize with a friend's griefs; but if he sees him honored and esteemed, he is apt to regard him as a rival, and does not so readily rejoice with him. This ought not to be; without effort we ought to be happy in our brother's happiness. If we are ill, be this our comfort, that many are in robust health; if we are faint, let us be glad that others are strong in the Lord. Thus shall we enjoy a happy fellowship like that of the perfected above.

When I have put all these modes of Christian communion together, no one of them is so sure, so strong, so deep, as communion in receiving the same Christ as our Savior, and trusting in the same blood for cleansing unto eternal life. Here on the table you have the tokens of the broadest and fullest communion. This is a kind of communion which you and I cannot choose or reject: if we are in Christ, it is and must be ours. Certain brethren restrict their communion in the outward ordinance, and they think they have good reasons for doing so; but I am unable to see the force of their reasoning, because I joyfully observe that these brethren commune with other believers in prayer, and praise, and hearing of the Word, and other ways: the fact being that the matter of real communion is very largely beyond human control, and is to the spiritual body what the circulation of the blood is to the natural body, a necessary process not dependent upon volition. In perusing a deeply spiritual book of devotion, you have been charmed and benefited, and yet upon looking at the title page it may be you have found that the author belonged to the Church of Rome. What then? Why, then it has happened that the inner life has broken all barriers, and your spirits have communed. For my own part, in reading certain precious works, I have loathed their Romanism, and yet I have had close fellowship with their writers in weeping over sin, in adoring at the foot of the cross, and in rejoicing in the glorious enthronement of our Lord. Blood is thicker than water, and no fellowship is more inevitable and sincere than fellowship in the precious blood, and in the risen life of our Lord Jesus Christ. Here, in the common reception of the one loaf, we bear witness that we are one; and in the actual participation of all the chosen in the one redemption, that unity is in very deed displayed and matured in the most substantial manner. Washed in the one blood, fed on the same loaf, cheered by the same cup, all differences pass away, and "we, being many, are one body in Christ, and every one members one of another."

Now, then, dear friends, if this kind of fellowship be the best, *let us take care to enjoy it. Let us at this hour avail ourselves of it.*

Let us take care *to see Christ* in the mirror of this ordinance. Have any of you eaten the bread, and yet have you not seen Christ? Then you have gained no benefit. Have you drunk the wine, but have you not remembered the Lord? Alas! I fear you have eaten and drunk condemnation to yourselves, not discerning the Lord's body. But if you did see through the emblems, as aged persons see through their spectacles, then you have been thankful for such aids to vision. But what is the use of glasses if there is nothing to look at? and what is the use of the communion if Christ be not in our thoughts and hearts?

If you did discern the Lord, then be sure, again, to *accept Him.* Say to yourself,

> All that Christ is to any, He shall be to me. Does He save sinners? He shall save me. Does He change men's hearts? He shall change mine. Is He all in all to those that trust Him? He shall be all in all to me.

I have heard persons say that they do not know how to take Christ. What says the apostle? "The Word is nigh thee, even in thy mouth, and in thy heart." If you have something in your mouth that you desire to eat, what is the best thing to do? Will you not swallow it? That is exactly what faith does. Christ's word of grace is very near you, it is on your tongue; let it go down into your inmost soul. Say to your Savior,

> I know I am not fit to receive Thee, O Jesus, but since Thou dost graciously come to me as bread comes to the hungry, I thankfully receive Thee, rejoicing to feed upon Thee! Since Thou dost come to me as the fruit of the vine to a thirsty man, Lord, I take Thee, willingly, and I thank Thee that this reception is all that Thou dost require of me. Has not Thy Spirit so put it—"As many as received Him, to them gave He power to become the sons of God, even to them that believe on His name"?

Beloved friends, when you have thus received Jesus, fail not to *rejoice in Him* as having received Him. How many there are who have received Christ, who talk and act as if they never had received Him! It is a poor dinner of which a man says, after he has eaten it, that he feels as if he had not dined; and it is a poor Christ of whom anyone can say, "I have received Him, but I am none the happier, none the more at peace." If you have received Jesus into your heart, you *are* saved, you *are* justified. Do you whisper, "I hope so"? Is that all? Do you not know? The hopings and hoppings of so many are a poor way of going; put both feet down, and say, "I know whom I have believed, and am persuaded that He is able to keep that which I have committed unto Him against that day." You are either saved or lost; there is no state between the two. You are either pardoned or condemned; and you have good reason for the highest happiness, or else you have grave causes for the direst anxiety. If you have received the atonement, be as glad as you can be; and if you are still an unbeliever, rest not till Christ is yours.

Oh, the joy of continually entering into fellowship with Christ, in such a way that you never lose His company! Be this yours, beloved, everyday, and all the day! May His shadow fall upon you as you rest in the sun, or stray in the gardens! May His voice cheer you as you lie down upon the seashore, and listen to the murmuring of the waves; may His presence glorify the mountain solitude as you climb the hills! May Jesus be to you an all-surrounding presence, lighting up the night, perfuming the day, gladdening all places, and sanctifying all pursuits! Our Beloved is not a Friend for Lord's-days only, but for weekdays, too; He is the inseparable Companion of His loving disciples. Those who have had fellowship with His body and His blood at this table may have the Lord as an habitual Guest at their own tables; those who have met their Master in this upper room may expect Him to make their own chamber bright with His royal presence. Let fellowship with Jesus and with the elect brotherhood be henceforth the atmosphere of our life, the joy of our existence. This will give us a Heaven below, and prepare us for a Heaven above.

The Memorable Hymn

*"And when they had sung a hymn, they went out
into the mount of Olives."—Matthew 26:30.*

The occasion on which these words were spoken was the last meal of
which Jesus partook in company with His disciples before He went
from them to His shameful trial and His ignominious death. It was His
farewell supper before a bitter parting, and yet they needs must sing. He
was on the brink of that great depth of misery into which He was about to
plunge, and yet He would have them sing "a hymn." It is wonderful that
he sang, and in a second degree it is remarkable that *they* sang. We will
consider both singular facts.

I. Let us dwell a while on the fact that Jesus sang at such a time as this.

What does He teach us by it? Does He not say to each of us, His followers,

My religion is one of happiness and joy; I, your Master, by My example would instruct you to sing even when the last solemn hour is come, and all the glooms of
death are gathering around you? Here, at the table, I am your Singing-master,
and set you lessons in music, in which My dying voice shall lead you: notwithstanding all the griefs which overwhelm My heart, I will be to you the Chief
Musician, and the Sweet Singer of Israel?

If ever there was a time when it would have been natural and consistent with
the solemnities of the occasion for the Savior to have bowed His head upon
the table, bursting into a flood of tears; or, if ever there was a season when He
might have fittingly retired from all company, and have bewailed His coming
conflict in sighs and groans, it was just then. But no; that brave heart will sing
"a hymn." Our glorious Jesus plays the man beyond all other men. Boldest of

the sons of men, He quails not in the hour of battle, but tunes His voice to loftiest psalmody. The genius of that Christianity of which Jesus is the Head and Founder, its object, spirit, and design, are happiness and joy, and they who receive it are able to sing in the very jaws of death.

This remark, however, is quite a secondary one to the next: *our Lord's* complete fulfillment of the law is even more worthy of our attention. It was customary, when the Passover was held, to sing, and this is the main reason why the Savior did so. During the Passover, it was usual to sing the hundred and thirteenth, and five following Psalms, which were called the "Hallel" The first commences, you will observe, in our version, with "Praise ye the Lord!" or, "Hallelujah!" The hundred and fifteenth, and the three following, were usually sung as the closing song of the Passover. Now, our Savior would not diminish the splendor of the great Jewish rite, although it was the last time that He would celebrate it. No; there shall be the holy beauty and delight of psalmody; none of it shall be stinted; the "Hallel" shall be full and complete. We may safely believe that the Savior sang through, or probably chanted, the whole of these six Psalms; and my heart tells me that there was no one at the table who sang more devoutly or more cheerfully than did our blessed Lord. There are some parts of the hundred and eighteenth Psalm, especially, which strike us as having sounded singularly grand, as they flowed from His blessed lips. Note verses 22, 23, 24. Particularly observe those words, near the end of the Psalm, and think you hear the Lord Himself singing them,

> God is the Lord, which hath shewed us light: bind the sacrifice with cords, even unto the horns of the altar. Thou art my God, and I will praise Thee: Thou art my God, I will exalt Thee. O give thanks unto the Lord; for He is good: for His mercy endureth forever.

Because, then, it was the settled custom of Israel to recite or sing these Psalms, our Lord Jesus Christ did the same; for He would leave nothing unfinished. Just as, when He went down into the waters of baptism, He said, "Thus it becometh us to fulfill all righteousness," so He seemed to say, when sitting at the table, "Thus it becometh us to fulfill all righteousness; therefore let us sing unto the Lord, as God's people in past ages have done." Beloved, let us view with holy wonder the strictness of the Savior's obedience to His Father's will, and let us endeavor to follow in His steps, in all things, seeking to be obedient to the Lord's Word in the little matters as well as in the great ones.

May we not venture to suggest another and deeper reason? Did not the singing of "a hymn" at the supper show *the holy absorption* of the Savior's soul in His

Father's will? If, beloved, you knew that at—say ten o'clock tonight—you would be led away to be mocked, and despised, and scourged, and that tomorrow's sun would see you falsely accused, hanging, a convicted criminal, to die upon a cross, do you think that you could sing tonight, after your last meal? I am sure you could not, unless with more than earth-born courage and resignation your soul could say, "Bind the sacrifice with cords, even unto the horns of the altar." You would sing if your spirit were like the Savior's spirit; if, like Him, you could exclaim, "Not as I will, but as Thou wilt"; but if there should remain in you any selfishness, any desire to be spared the bitterness of death, you would not be able to chant the "Hallel" with the Master. Blessed Jesus, how wholly wert Thou given up! how perfectly consecrated! so that, whereas other men sing when they are marching to their joys, Thou didst sing on the way to death; whereas other men lift up their cheerful voices when honor awaits them, Thou hadst a brave and holy sonnet on Thy lips when shame, and spitting, and death were to be Thy portion.

This singing of the Savior also teaches us *the whole-heartedness of the Master in the work which He was about to do.* The patriot-warrior sings as he hastens to battle; to the strains of martial music he advances to meet the foeman; and even thus the heart of our all-glorious Champion supplies Him with song even in the dreadful hour of His solitary agony. He views the battle, but He dreads it not; though in the contest His soul will be "exceeding sorrowful even unto death," yet before it, He is like Job's war-horse, "he saith among the trumpets, Ha, ha; and he smelleth the battle afar off." He has a baptism to be baptized with, and He is straitened until it be accomplished. The Master does not go forth to the agony in the garden with a cowed and trembling spirit, all bowed and crushed in the dust, but He advances to the conflict like a man who has his full strength about him—taken out to be a victim (if I may use such a figure), not as a worn out ox that has long borne the yoke, but as the firstling of the bullock, in the fullness of His strength. He goes forth to the slaughter, with His glorious undaunted spirit fast and firm within Him, glad to suffer for His people's sake, and for His Father's glory.

> *For as at first Thine all-pervading look*
> *Saw from Thy Father's bosom to the abyss,*
> *Measuring in calm presage,*
> *The infinite descent;*
> *So to the end, though now of mortal pangs*
> *Made heir, and emptied of Thy glory a while,*
> *With unaverted eye*
> *Thou meetest all the storm.*

Let us, O fellow-heirs of salvation, learn to sing when our suffering time comes, when our season for stern labor approaches; aye, let us pour forth a canticle of deep, mysterious, melody of bliss, when our dying hour is near at hand! Courage, brother! The waters are chilly; but fear will not by any means diminish the terrors of the river. Courage, brother! Death is solemn work; but playing the coward will not make it less so. Bring out the silver trumpet; let thy lips remember the long-loved music, and let the notes be clear and shrill as thou dippest thy feet in the Jordan: "Yea, though I walk through the valley of the shadow of death, I will fear no evil: for Thou art with me; Thy rod and Thy staff they comfort me." Dear friends, let the remembrance of the melodies of that upper room go with you tomorrow into business; and if you expect a great trial, and are afraid you will not be able to sing after it, then sing before it comes. Get your holy praise-work done before affliction mars the tune. Fill the air with music while you can. While yet there is bread upon the table, sing, though famine may threaten; while yet the child runs laughing about the house, while yet the flush of health is in your own cheek, while yet your goods are spared, while yet your heart is whole and sound, lift up your song of praise to the Most High God; and let your Master, the singing Savior, be in this your goodly and comfortable example.

There is much more that might be said concerning our Lord's sweet swan-song, but there is no need to crowd one thought out with another; your leisure will be well spent in meditation upon so fruitful a theme.

II. We will now consider the singing of the disciples.

They united in the "Hallel"—like true Jews, they joined in the national song. Israel had good cause to sing at the Passover, for God had wrought for His people what He had done for no other nation on the face of the earth. Every Hebrew must have felt his soul elevated and rejoiced on the Paschal night. He was "a citizen of no mean city," and the pedigree which he could look back upon was one, compared with which kings and princes were but of yesterday.

Remembering the fact commemorated by the Paschal supper, Israel might well rejoice. They sang of their nation in bondage, trodden beneath the tyrannical foot of Pharaoh; they began the Psalm right sorrowfully, as they thought of the bricks made without straw, and of the iron furnace; but the strain soon mounted from the deep bass, and began to climb the scale, as they sang of Moses the servant of God, and of the Lord appearing to him in the burning bush. They remembered the mystic rod, which became a serpent, and which swallowed up the rods of the magicians; their music told of the plagues and wonders which God had wrought upon Zoan; and of that dread night when the first-born of Egypt fell before the avenging sword of the angel of death, while they themselves, feeding on the lamb which had been slain for them, and whose blood was sprinkled upon the lintel and upon the side-posts of the door, had been graciously preserved. Then the song went up concerning the hour in which all Egypt was humbled at the feet of Jehovah, whilst as for His people, He led them forth like sheep, by the hand of Moses and Aaron, and they went by the way of the sea, even of the Red Sea. The strain rose higher still as they tuned the song of Moses, the servant of God, and of the Lamb. Jubilantly they sang of the Red Sea, and of the chariots of Pharaoh which went down into the midst thereof, and the depths covered them till there was not one of them left. It was a glorious chant indeed when they sang of Rahab cut in pieces, and of the dragon wounded at the sea, by the right hand of the Most High, for the deliverance of the chosen people.

But, beloved, if I have said that Israel could so properly sing, *what shall I say of those of us who are the Lord's spiritually redeemed?* We have been emancipated from a slavery worse than that of Egypt: "with a high hand and with an outstretched arm," hath God delivered us. The blood of Jesus Christ, the Lamb of God's Passover, has been sprinkled on our hearts and consciences. By faith we keep the Passover, for we have been spared; we have been brought out of Egypt; and though our sins did once oppose us, they have all been drowned in the Red Sea of the atoning blood of Jesus: "the depths have covered them, there is not one of them left." If the Jew could sing a "great Hallel," our "Hallel" ought to be more glowing still; and if every house in "Judea's happy land" was full of music when the people ate the Paschal feast, much more reason have we for filling every heart with sacred harmony tonight, while we feast upon Jesus Christ, who was slain, and has redeemed us to God by His blood.

III. The time has now come for me to say how earnestly I desire you to "sing a hymn."

I do not mean to ask you to use your voices, but let your hearts be brimming with the essence of praise. Whenever we repair to the Lord's table, which represents to us the Passover, we ought not to come to it as to a funeral. Let us select solemn hymns, but not dirges. Let us sing softly, but none the less joyfully. These are no burial feasts; those are not funeral cakes which lie upon this table, and yonder fair white linen cloth is no winding sheet. "This is My body," said Jesus, but the body so represented was no corpse, we feed upon a living Christ. The blood set forth by yonder wine is the fresh life-blood of our immortal King.

We view not our Lord's body as clay-cold flesh, pierced with wounds, but as glorified at the right hand of the Father. We hold a happy festival when we break bread on the first day of the week. We come not hither trembling like bondsmen, cringing on our knees as wretched serfs condemned to eat on their knees; we approach as freemen to our Lord's banquet, like His apostles, to recline at length or sit at ease; not merely to eat bread which may belong to the most sorrowful, but to drink wine which belongs to men whose souls are glad. Let us recognize the rightness, yea, the duty of cheerfulness at this commemorative supper; and, therefore, let us "sing a hymn."

Being satisfied on this point, perhaps you ask, "What hymn shall we sing?" Many sorts of hymns were sung in the olden time: look down the list, and you will scarcely find one which may not suit us now.

One of the earliest of earthly songs was *the war-song.* They sang of old a song to the conqueror, when he returned from the battle. "Saul has slain his thousands, and David his ten thousands." Women took their timbrels, and rejoiced in the dance when the hero returned from the war. Even thus of old did the people of God extol Him for His mighty acts, singing aloud with the high sounding cymbals: "Sing unto the Lord, for He hath triumphed gloriously... The Lord is a man of war: the Lord is His name." My brethren, let us lift up a war-song tonight! Why not?

> Who is this that cometh from Edom, with dyed garments from Bozrah? this that is glorious in His apparel, traveling in the greatness of His strength? I that speak in righteousness, mighty to save.

Come, let us praise our Emmanuel, as we see the head of our foe in His right hand; as we behold Him leading captivity captive, ascending up on high, with trumpets' joyful sound, let us chant the pæan; let us shout the war-song, *"Io Triumphe!"* Behold, He comes, all glorious from the war: as we gather at this festive table, which reminds us both of His conflict and of His victory, let us salute Him with a psalm of gladsome triumph, which shall be but the prelude of the song we expect to sing when we get up—

> *Where all the singers meet.*

Another early form of song was *the pastoral.* When the shepherds sat down amongst the sheep, they tuned their pipes, and warbled forth soft and sweet airs in harmony with rustic quietude. All around was calm and still; the sun was brightly shining, and the birds were making melody among the leafy branches. Shall I seem fanciful if I say, let us unite in a pastoral tonight? Sitting round the table, why should we not sing, "The Lord is my Shepherd; I shall not want. He maketh me to lie down in green pastures: He leadeth me beside the still waters"? If there be a place beneath the stars where one might feel perfectly at rest and ease, surely it is at the table of the Lord. Here, then, let us sing to our great Shepherd a pastoral of delight. Let the bleating of sheep be in our ears as we remember the Good Shepherd who laid down His life for His flock.

You need not to be reminded that the ancients were very fond of *festive songs*. When they assembled at their great festivals, led by their chosen minstrels, they sang right joyously, with boisterous mirth. Let those who will speak to the praise of wine, my soul shall extol the precious blood of Jesus; let who will laud corn and oil, the rich produce of the harvest, my heart shall sing of the Bread which came down from Heaven, whereof, if a man eateth, he shall never hunger. Speak ye of royal banquets, and minstrelsy fit for a monarch's ear? Ours is a nobler festival, and our song is sweeter far. Here is room at this table tonight for all earth's poesy and music, for the place deserves songs more lustrous with delight, more sparkling with gems of holy mirth, than any of which the ancients could conceive.

> *Now for a tune of lofty praise*
> *To great Jehovah's equal Son!*
> *Awake, my voice, in heavenly lays*
> *Tell the loud wonders He hath done!*

The *love-song* we must not forget, for that is peculiarly the song of this evening. "Now will I sing unto my Well-beloved a song." His love to us is an Immortal theme; and as our love, fanned by the breath of Heaven, bursts into a vehement flame, we may sing, yea, and we will sing among the lilies, a song of loves.

In the Old Testament, we find many Psalms called by the title, "A Song of Degrees." This "Song of Degrees" is supposed by some to have been sung as the people ascended the temple steps, or made pilgrimages to the holy place. The strain often changes, sometimes it is dolorous, and anon it is gladsome; at one season, the notes are long drawn out and heavy, at another, they are cheerful and jubilant. We will sing a "Song of Degrees" tonight. We will mourn that we pierced the Lord, and we will rejoice in pardon bought with blood. Our strain must vary as we talk of sin, feeling its bitterness, and lamenting it, and then of pardon, rejoicing in its glorious fullness.

David wrote a considerable number of Psalms which he entitled, "Maschil," which may be called in English, "instructive Psalms." Where, beloved, can we find richer instruction than at the table of our Lord? He who understands the mystery of incarnation and of substitution, is a master in Scriptural theology. There is more teaching in the Savior's body and in the Savior's blood than in all the world besides. O ye who wish to learn the way to comfort, and how to tread the royal road to heavenly wisdom, come ye to the cross, and see the Savior suffer, and pour out His heart's blood for human sin!

Some of David's Psalms are called, *"Michtam."* which means "golden Psalm." Surely we must sing one of these. Our psalms must be golden when we sing of the Head of the Church, who is as much fine gold. More precious than silver or gold is the inestimable price which He has paid for our ransom. Yes, ye sons of harmony, bring your most melodious anthems here, and let your Savior have your golden psalms!

Certain Psalms in the Old Testament are entitled, "Upon Shoshannim," that is, "Upon the lilies." O ye virgin souls, whose hearts have been washed in blood, and have been made white and pure, bring forth your instruments of song:

> *Hither, then, your music bring,*
> *Strike aloud each cheerful string!*

Let your hearts, when they are in their best state, when they are purest, and most cleansed from earthly dross, give to Jesus their glory and their excellence.

Then there are other Psalms which are dedicated "To the sons of Korah." If the guess be right, the reason why we get the title, "To the sons of Korah"—"a song of loves"—must be this: that when Korah, Dathan, and Abiram were swallowed up, the sons of Dathan and Abiram were swallowed up, too; but the sons of Korah perished not. Why they were not destroyed, we cannot tell. Perhaps it was that sovereign grace spared those whom justice might have doomed; and "the sons of Korah" were ever after made the sweet singers of the sanctuary; and whenever there was a special "song of loves," it was always dedicated to them. Ah! we will have one of those songs of love tonight, around the table, for we, too, are saved by distinguishing grace. We will sing of the heavenly Lover, and the many waters which could not quench His love.

> *Love, so vast that nought can bound;*
> *Love, too deep for thought to sound*
> *Love, which made the Lord of all*
> *Drink the wormwood and the gall.*
>
> *Love, which led Him to the cross,*
> *Bearing there unutter'd loss;*
> *Love, which brought Him to the gloom*
> *Of the cold and darksome tomb.*

Love, which made Him hence arise
Far above the starry skies,
There with tender, loving care,
All His people's griefs to share.

Love, which will not let Him rest
Till His chosen all are blest;
Till they all for whom He died
Live rejoicing by His side.

We have not half exhausted the list, but it is clear that, sitting at the Lord's table, we shall have no lack of suitable psalmody. Perhaps no one hymn will quite meet the sentiments of all; and while we would not write a hymn for you, we would pray the Holy Spirit to write now the spirit of praise upon your hearts, that, sitting here, you may "after supper" sing "a hymn."

IV. For one or two minutes let us ask—"What shall the tune be?"

It must be a strange one, for if we are to sing "a hymn" tonight, around the table, the tune must have all the parts of music. Yonder believer is heavy of heart through manifold sorrows, bereavements, and watchings by the sick. He loves his Lord, and would fain praise Him, but his soul refuses to use her wings. Brother, we will have a tune in which you can join, and you shall lead the bass. You shall sing of your fellowship with your Beloved in His sufferings; how He, too, lost a friend; how He spent whole nights in sleeplessness; how His soul was exceeding sorrowful. But the tune must not be all bass, or it would not suit some of us tonight, for we can reach the highest note. We have seen the Lord, and our spirit has rejoiced in God our Savior. We want to lift the chorus high; yea, there are some true hearts here who are at times so full of joy that they will want special music written for them. "Whether in the body, I cannot tell; or whether out of the body, I cannot tell": said Paul, and so have said others since, when Christ has been with them. Ah! then they have been obliged to mount to the highest notes, to the very loftiest range of song.

Remember, beloved, that the same Savior who will accept the joyful shoutings of the strong, will also receive the plaintive notes of the weak and weeping. You little ones, you babes in grace, may cry, "Hosanna" and the King will not silence you; and you strong men, with all your power of faith, may shout, "Hallelujah!" and your notes shall be accepted, too.

Come, then, let us have a tune in which we can all unite; but ah! we cannot make one which will suit the dead—the dead, I mean, "in trespasses and sins"—and there are some such here. Oh, may God open their mouths, and unloose their tongues; but as for those of us who are alive unto God, let us, as we come to the table, all contribute our own share of the music, and so make up a song of blended harmony, with many parts, one great united song of praise to Jesus our Lord!

We should not choose a tune for the communion table which is not *very soft*. These are no boisterous themes with which we have to deal when we tarry here. A bleeding Savior, robed in a vesture dyed with blood—this is a theme which you must treat with loving gentleness, for everything that is coarse is out of place. While the tune is soft, it must also be *sweet*. Silence, ye doubts; be dumb, ye fears; be hushed, ye cares! Why come ye here? My music must be sweet and soft when I sing of Him. But oh! it must also be *strong*; there must be a full swell in my praise. Draw out the stops, and let the organ swell the diapason! In fullness let its roll of thundering harmony go up to Heaven; let every note be sounded at its loudest. "Praise ye Him upon the cymbals, upon the high-sounding cymbals; upon the harp with a solemn sound." Soft, sweet, and strong, let the music be.

Alas! you complain that your soul is out of tune. Then ask the Master to tune the heart-strings. Those "Selahs" which we find so often in the Psalms, are supposed by many scholars to mean, "Put the harp-strings in tune": truly we require many "Selahs," for our hearts are constantly unstrung. Oh, that tonight the Master would enable each one of us to offer that tuneful prayer which we so often sing,

> Teach me some melodious sonnet,
> Sung by flaming tongues above:
> Praise the mount—oh, fix me on it,
> Mount of God's unchanging love!

V. We close by inquiring—who shall sing this hymn?

Sitting around the Father's board, we will raise a joyful song, but who shall do it? "I will," saith one; "and we will," say others. What is the reason why so many are willing to join? The reason is to be found in the verse we were singing just now,

> When He's the subject of the song,
> Who can refuse to sing?

What! A Christian silent when others are praising his Master? No; he must join in the song. Satan tries to make God's people dumb, but he cannot, for the Lord has not a tongue-tied child in all His family. They can all speak, and they can all cry, even if they cannot all sing, and *I* think there are times when they can all sing; yea, they must, for you know the promise, "Then shall the tongue of the dumb sing." Surely, when Jesus leads the tune, if there should be any silent ones in the Lord's family, they must begin to praise the name of the Lord. After Giant Despair's head had been cut off, Christiana and Mr. Greatheart, and all the rest of them, brought out the best of their provisions, and made a feast, and Mr. Bunyan says that, after they had feasted, they danced. In the dance there was one remarkable dancer, namely, Mr. Ready-to-Halt. Now, Mr. Ready-to-Halt usually went upon crutches, but for once he laid them aside. "And," says Bunyan, "I warrant you he footed it well!" This is quaintly showing us that, sometimes, the very sorrowful ones, the Ready-to-Halts, when they see Giant Despair's head cut off, when they see death, Hell, and sin led in triumphant captivity at the wheels of Christ's victorious chariot, feel that even *they* must for once Indulge in a song of gladness. So, when I put the question tonight, "Who will sing?" I trust that Ready-to-Halt will promise, "I will."

You have not much comfort at home, perhaps; by very hard work you earn that little. Sunday is to you a day of true rest, for you are worked very cruelly all the week. Those cheeks of yours, poor girl, are getting very pale, and who knows but what Hood's pathetic lines may be true of you?

> *Stitch, stitch, stitch,*
> *In poverty, hunger, and dirt,*
> *Sewing at once, with a double thread,*
> *A shroud as well as a shirt.*

But, my sister, you may surely rejoice tonight in spite of all this. There may be little on earth, but there is much in Heaven. There may be but small comfort for you here apart from Christ; but oh! when, by faith, you mount into His glory, your soul is glad. You shall be as rich as the richest tonight if the Holy Spirit shall but bring you to the table, and enable you to feed upon your Lord and Master. Perhaps you have come here tonight when you ought not to have done so. The physician would have told you to keep to your bed, but you persisted in coming up to the house where the Lord has so often met with you. I trust that we shall hear your voice in the song. There appear to have been in David's day many things to silence the praise of God, but David was one who would sing. I like that expression of his, where the devil seems to come up, and put his hand on his mouth, and say, "Be quiet." "No," says David, "I will sing." Again the devil tries to quiet him, but David is not to be silenced, for three times he puts it, "I will sing, yea, I will sing praises unto the Lord." May the Lord make you resolve this night that you will praise the Lord Jesus with all your heart!

Alas! there are many of you here tonight whom I could not invite to this feast of song, and who could not truly come if you were invited. Your sins are not forgiven; your souls are not saved; you have not trusted Christ; you are still in nature's darkness, still in the gall of bitterness, and in the bonds of iniquity. Must it always be so? Will you destroy yourselves? Have you made a league with death, and a covenant with Hell? Mercy lingers! Longsuffering continues! Jesus waits! Remember that He hung upon the cross for sinners such as you are, and that if you believe in Him now, you shall be saved. One act of faith, and all the sin you committed is blotted out. A single glance of faith's eye to the wounds of the Messiah, and your load of iniquity is rolled into the depths of the sea, and you are forgiven in a moment!

"Oh!" says one, "would God I could believe!" Poor soul, may God help thee to believe now! God took upon Himself our flesh; Christ was born among men, and suffered on account of human guilt, being made to suffer "the Just for the unjust, that He might bring us to God." Christ was punished in the room, place, and stead of every man and woman who will believe on Him. If you believe on Him, He was punished for you; and you will never be punished. Your debts are paid, your sins are forgiven. God cannot punish you, for He has punished Christ instead of you, and He will never punish twice for one offence. To believe is to trust. If you will now trust your soul entirely with Him, you are saved, for He loved you, and gave Himself for you. When you know this, and feel it to be true, then come to the Lord's table, and join with us, when, *after supper we sing our hymn,*

> *"It is finished!"—Oh, what pleasure*
> *Do these charming words afford!*
> *Heavenly blessings without measure*
> *Flow to us from Christ the Lord:*
> *"It is finished!"*
> *Saints, the dying words record.*
>
> *Tune your harps anew, ye seraphs,*
> *Join to sing the pleasing theme;*
> *All on earth, and all in Heaven,*
> *Join to praise Immanuel's name!*
> *Hallelujah!*
> *Glory to the bleeding Lamb!*

Jesus Asleep on a Pillow

"And He was in the hinder part of the ship, asleep on a pillow: and, they awake Him, and say unto Him, 'Master, carest Thou not that we perish?' And He arose, and rebuked the wind, and said unto the sea, 'Peace, be still.' And the wind ceased, and there was a great calm."—Mark 4:38, 39.

Our Lord took His disciples with Him into the ship to teach them a practical lesson. It is one thing to talk to people about our oneness with them, and about how they should exercise faith in time of danger, and about their real safety in apparent peril; but it is another, and a far better thing, to go into the ship with them, to let them feel all the terror of the storm, and then to arise, and rebuke the wind, and say unto the sea, "Peace, be still." Our Lord gave His disciples a kind of kindergarten lesson, an acted sermon, in which the truth was set forth visibly before them. Such teaching produced a wonderful effect upon their lives. May we also be instructed by it!

In our text there are two great calms; the first is, *the calm in the Savior's heart*, and the second is, *the calm which He created* with a word upon the storm tossed sea.

I. Within the Lord there was a great calm, and that is why there was soon a great calm around Him; for what is in God comes out of God.

Since there was a calm in Christ for Himself, there was afterwards a calm outside for others. What a wonderful inner calm it was! "He was in the hinder part of the ship, asleep on a pillow."

He had *perfect confidence in God* that all was well. The waves might roar, the winds might rage, but He was not at all disquieted by their fury. He knew that the waters were in the hollow of His Father's hand, and that every wind was but the breath of His Father's mouth; and so He was not troubled; nay, He had not even a careful thought, He was as much at ease as on a sunny day. His mind and heart were free from every kind of care, for amid the gathering tempest He deliberately laid Himself down, and slept like a weary child. He went to the hinder part of the ship, most out of the dash of the spray; He took a pillow, and put it under His head, and with fixed intent disposed Himself to slumber. It was His own act and deed to go to sleep in the storm; He had nothing for which to keep awake, so pure and perfect was His confidence in the great Father. What an example this is to us! We have not half the confidence in God that we ought to have, not even the best of us. The Lord deserves our unbounded belief, our unquestioning confidence, our undisturbed reliance. Oh, that we rendered it to Him as the Savior did!

There was also mixed with His faith in the Father *a sweet confidence in His own Sonship*. He did not doubt that He was the Son of the Highest. I may not question God's power to deliver, but I may sometimes question my right to expect deliverance; and if so, my comfort vanishes. Our Lord had no doubts of this kind. He had long before heard that word, "This is My beloved Son, in whom I am well pleased"; He had so lived and walked with God that the witness within Him was continuous, so He had no question about the Father's love to Him as His own Son. "Rocked in the cradle of the deep," His Father keeping watch over Him—what could a child do better than go to sleep in such a happy position? And so He does. You and I, too, want a fuller assurance of our sonship if we would have greater peace with God. The devil knows that, and therefore he will come to us with his insinuating suggestion, "If thou be the son of God." If we have the Spirit of adoption in us, we shall put the accuser to rout at once, by opposing the Witness within to his question from without. Then shall we be filled with a great calm, because we have confidence in our Father, and assurance of our sonship.

Then *He had a sweet way*—this blessed Lord of ours—*of leaving all with God*. He takes no watch, He makes no fret; but He goes to sleep. Whatever comes, He has left all in the hands of the great Caretaker; and what more is needful? If a watchman were set to guard my house, I should be foolish if I also sat up for fear of thieves. Why have a watchman if I cannot trust him to watch? "Cast thy burden upon the Lord"; but when thou hast done so, leave it with the Lord, and do not try to carry it thyself. That is to make a mock of God, to have the name of God, but not the reality of God.

Lay down every care, even as Jesus did when He went calmly to the hinder part of the ship, and quietly took a pillow, and went to sleep.

But I think I hear someone say, "I could do that if mine were solely care about myself." Yes, perhaps you could; and yet you cannot cast upon God your burden of care about your children. But your Lord trusted the Father with those dear to Him. Do you not think that Christ's disciples were as precious to Him as our children are to us? If that ship had been wrecked, what would have become of Peter? What would have become of "that disciple whom Jesus loved"? Our Lord regarded with intense affection those whom He had chosen and called, and who had been with Him in His temptation, yet He was quite content to leave them all in the care of His Father, and go to sleep.

You answer, "Yes, but there is a still wider circle of people watching to see what will happen to me, and to the cause of Christ with which I am connected. I am obliged to care, whether I will or no." Is your case, then, more trying than your Lord's? Do you forget that "there were also with Him many other little ships"? When the storm was tossing His barque, their little ships were even more in jeopardy; and He cared for them all. He was the Lord High Admiral of the Lake of Gennesaret that night. The other ships were a fleet under His convoy, and His great heart went out to them all. Yet He went to sleep, because He had left in His Father's care even the solicitudes of His charity and sympathy. We, my brethren, who are much weaker than He, shall find strength in doing the same.

Having left everything with His Father, *our Lord did the very wisest thing possible*. He did just what the hour demanded. "Why," say you, "He went to sleep!" That was the best thing Jesus could do; and sometimes it is the best thing we can do. Christ was weary and worn; and when anyone is exhausted, it is his duty to go to sleep if he can. The Savior must be up again in the morning, preaching and working miracles, and if He does not sleep, He will not be fit for His holy duty; it is incumbent upon Him to keep Himself in trim for His service. Knowing that the time to sleep has come, the Lord sleeps, and does well in sleeping. Often, when we have been fretting and worrying, we should have glorified God far more had we literally gone to sleep. To glorify God by sleep is not so difficult as some might think; at least, to our Lord it was natural. Here you are worried, sad, wearied; the doctor prescribes for you; his medicine does you no good; but oh! if you enter into full peace with God, and go to sleep, you will wake up infinitely more refreshed than by any drug. The sleep which the Lord giveth to His beloved is balmy indeed. Seek it as Jesus sought it. Go to bed, brother, and you will better imitate your Lord than by putting yourself into ill humor, and worrying other people.

There is a spiritual sleep in which we ought to imitate Jesus. How often I have worried my poor brain about my great church, until I have come to my senses, and then I have said to myself, "How foolish you are! Can you not depend upon God? Is it not far more His cause than yours?" Then I have taken my load in prayer, and left it with the Lord. I have said, "In God's name, this matter shall never worry me again," and I have left my urgent care with Him, and ended it forever. I have so deliberately given up many a trying case into the Lord's care that, when any of my friends have said to me, "What about so and so?" I have simply answered, "I do not know, and I am no longer careful to know. The Lord will interpose in some way or other, but I will trouble no more about it." No mischief has ever come through any matter which I have left in the divine keeping. The staying of my hand has been wisdom. "Stand still, and see the salvation of God," is God's own precept. Here let us follow Jesus. Having a child's confidence in the great Father, He retires to the stern of the ship, selects a pillow, deliberately lies down upon it, and goes to sleep; and though the ship is filling with water, and rolls and pitches, He sleeps on. Nothing can break the peace of His tranquil soul. Every sailor on board reels to and fro, and staggers like a drunken man, and is at his wits' end; but Jesus is neither at his wits' end, nor does He stagger, for He rests in perfect innocence, and undisturbed confidence. His heart is happy in God, and therefore doth He remain in repose. Oh, for grace to copy Him!

II. But here notice, dear friends, the difference between the master and his disciples; for while He was in a great calm, they were in a great storm.

Here see their failure. They were just as we are, and we are often just as they were.

They gave way to fear. They were sorely afraid that the ship would sink, and that they would all perish. In thus yielding to fear, *they forgot the solid reasons for courage which lay near at hand;* for, in truth, they were safe enough. Christ is on board that vessel, and if the ship goes down, He will sink with them. The heathen mariner took courage during a storm from the fact that Caesar was on board the ship that was tossed by stormy winds; and should not the disciples feel secure with Jesus on board? Fear not, ye carry Jesus and His cause! Jesus had come to do a work, and His disciples might have known that He could not perish with that work unaccomplished. Could they not trust Him? They had seen Him multiply the loaves and fishes, and cast out devils, and heal all manner of sicknesses; could they not trust Him to still the storm? Unreasonable unbelief! Faith in God is true prudence, but to doubt God is irrational. It is the height of absurdity and folly to question omnipotent love.

And *the disciples were so unwise as to do the Master a very ill turn*. He was sadly weary, and sorely needed sleep; but they hastened to Him, and roused Him in a somewhat rough and irreverent manner. They were slow to do so, but their fear urged them; and therefore they awoke Him, uttering ungenerous and unloving words: "Master, carest Thou not that we perish?" Shame on the lips that asked so harsh a question! Did they not upon reflection greatly blame themselves? He had given them no cause for such hard speeches; and, moreover, it was unseemly in them to call Him "Master," and then to ask Him, "Carest Thou not that we perish?" Is He to be accused of such hard-heartedness as to let his faithful disciples perish when He has power to deliver them? Alas, we, too, have been guilty of like offences! I think I have known some of Christ's disciples who have appeared to doubt the wisdom or the love of their Lord. They did not quite say that He was mistaken, but they said that He moved in a mysterious way; they did not quite complain that He was unkind to them, but they whispered that they could not reconcile His dealings with His infinite love. Alas, Jesus has endured much from our unbelief! May this picture help us to see our spots, and may the love of our dear Lord remove them!

III. I have spoken to you of the Master's calm and of the disciples' failure; now let us think of the great calm which Jesus created.

"There was a great calm." *His voice produced it*. They say that if oil be poured upon the waters they will become smooth, and I suppose there *is some* truth in the statement; but there is all truth in this, that if God speaks, the storm subsides into a calm, so that the waves of the sea are still. It only needs our Lord Jesus to speak in the heart of any one of us, and immediately the peace of God, which passeth all understanding, will possess us. No matter how drear your despondency, nor how dread your despair, the Lord can at once create a great calm of confidence. What a door of hope this opens to any who are in trouble! If I could speak a poor man rich, and a sick one well, I am sure I would do so at once; but Jesus is infinitely better than I am, and therefore I know that He will speak peace to the tried and troubled heart.

Note, too, that *this calm came at once*. "Jesus arose, and rebuked the wind, and said unto the sea, 'Peace, be still.' And the wind ceased, and there was a great calm." As soon as Jesus spake, all was quiet. I have met with a very large number of persons in trouble of mind, and I have seen a few who have slowly come out into light and liberty; but more frequently deliverance has come suddenly. The iron gate has opened of its own accord, and the prisoner has stepped into immediate freedom. "The snare is broken, and we are escaped." What a joy it is to know that rest is so near even when the tempest rages most furiously!

Note, also, that *the Savior coupled this repose with faith,* for He said to the disciples as soon as the calm came, "Why are ye so fearful? How is it that ye have no faith?" Faith and the calm go together. If thou believest, thou shalt rest; if thou wilt but cast thyself upon thy God, surrendering absolutely to His will, thou shalt have mercy, and joy, and light. Even If we have no faith, the Lord will sometimes give us the blessing that we need, for He delights to do more for us than we have any right to expect of Him; but usually the rule of His kingdom is, "According to your faith be it unto you."

This great calm is very delightful, and concerning this I desire to bear my personal testimony. I speak from my own knowledge when I say that it passeth all understanding. I was sitting, the other night, meditating on God's mercy and love, when suddenly I found in my own heart a most delightful sense of perfect peace. I had come to Beulah-land, where the sun shines without a cloud. "There was a great calm." I felt as mariners might do who have been tossed about in broken water, and all on a sudden, they cannot tell why, the ocean becomes as unruffled as a mirror, and the sea-birds come and sit in happy circles upon the water. I felt perfectly content, yea, undividedly happy. Not a wave of trouble broke upon the shore of my heart, and even far out to sea in the deeps of my being all was still. I knew no ungratified wish, no unsatisfied desire. I could not discover a reason for uneasiness, or a motive for fear. There was nothing approaching to fanaticism in my feelings, nothing even of excitement: my soul was waiting upon God, and delighting herself alone in Him. Oh, the blessedness of this rest in the Lord! What an Elysium it is! I must be allowed to say a little upon this purple island in the sea of my life: it was none other than a fragment of Heaven. We often talk about our great spiritual storms, why should we not speak of our great calms? If ever we get into trouble, what a noise we make of it! Why should we not sing of our deliverances?

Let us survey our mercies. Every sin that we have ever committed is forgiven. "The blood of Jesus Christ, His Son, cleanseth us from all sin." The power of sin within us is broken; it "shall not have dominion over you, for ye are not under the law but under grace." Satan is a vanquished enemy; the world is overcome by our Lord Jesus, and death is abolished by Him. All providence works for our good. Eternity has no threat for us, it bears within its mysteries nothing but immortality and glory. Nothing can harm us. The Lord is our shield, and our exceeding great reward. Wherefore, then, should we fear? The Lord of hosts is with us, the God of Jacob is our refuge. To the believer, peace is no presumption: he is warranted in enjoying "perfect peace"—a quiet which is deep, and founded on truth, which encompasses all things, and is not broken by any of the ten thousand disturbing causes which otherwise might prevent our rest. "Thou wilt keep him in perfect peace whose mind is stayed on Thee; because he trusteth in Thee." Oh, to get into that calm, and remain in it till we come to that world where there is no more sea!

A calm like that which ruled within our Savior should we be happy enough to attain to it will give us in our measure the power to make outside matters calm. He that hath peace can make peace. We cannot work miracles, and yet the works which Jesus did shall we do also. Sleeping His sleep, we shall awake in His rested energy, and treat the winds and waves as things subject to the power of faith, and therefore to be commanded into quiet. We shall speak so as to console others: our calm shall work marvels in the little ships whereof others are captains. We, too, shall say, "Peace! Be still." Our confidence shall prove contagious, and the timid shall grow brave: our tender love shall spread itself, and the contentious shall cool down to patience. Only the matter must begin within ourselves. We cannot create a calm till we are in a calm. It is easier to rule the elements than to govern the unruliness of our wayward nature. When grace has made us masters of our fears, so that we can take a pillow and fall asleep amid the hurricane, the fury of the tempest is over. He giveth peace and safety when He giveth His beloved sleep.

Real Contact with Jesus

*"And Jesus said, 'Somebody hath touched Me:
for I perceive that virtue is gone out of Me.'"*—Luke 8:46.

Our Lord was very frequently in the midst of a crowd. His preaching was so plain and so forcible that He always attracted a vast company of hearers; and, moreover, the rumor of the loaves and fishes no doubt had something to do with increasing His audiences, while the expectation of beholding a miracle would be sure to add to the numbers of the hangers-on. Our Lord Jesus Christ often found it difficult to move through the streets, because of the masses who pressed upon Him. This was encouraging to Him as a preacher, and yet how small a residuum of real good came of all the excitement which gathered around His personal ministry! He might have looked upon the great mass, and have said, "What is the chaff to the wheat?" for here it was piled up upon the threshing floor, heap upon heap; and yet, after His decease, His disciples might have been counted by a few scores, for those who had spiritually received Him were but few. Many were called, but few were chosen. Yet, wherever one was blessed, our Savior took note of it; it touched a chord in His soul. He never could be unaware when virtue had gone out of Him to heal a sick one, or when power had gone forth with His ministry to save a sinful one. Of all the crowd that gathered round the Savior upon the day of which our text speaks, I find nothing said about one of them except this solitary "somebody" who had touched Him. The crowd came, and the crowd went; but little is recorded of it all. Just as the ocean, having advanced to full tide, leaves but little behind it when it retires again to its channel, so the vast multitude around the Savior left only this one precious deposit—one "somebody" who had touched Him, and had received virtue from Him.

Ah, my Master, it may be so again this evening! These Sabbath mornings, and these Sabbath evenings, the crowds come pouring in like a mighty ocean, filling this house, and then they all retire again; only here and there is a "somebody" left weeping for sin, a "somebody" left rejoicing in Christ, a "somebody" who can say, "I have touched the hem of His garment, and I have been made whole." The whole of my other hearers are not worth the "somebodies." The many of you are not worth the few, for the many are the pebbles, and the few are the diamonds; the many are the heaps of husks, and the few are the precious grains. May God find them out at this hour, and His shall be all the praise!

Jesus said, "Somebody hath touched Me," from which we observe that, *in the use of means and ordinances, we should never be satisfied unless we get into personal contact with Christ,* so that we touch Him, as this woman touched His garment. Secondly, *if we can get into such personal contact, we shall have a blessing:* "I perceive that virtue is gone out of Me"; and, thirdly, *if we do get a blessing, Christ will know it;* however obscure our case may be, He will know it, and He will have us let others know it; He will speak, and ask such questions as will draw us out, and manifest us to the world.

I. First, then, in the use of all means and ordinances, let it be our chief aim and object, to come into personal contact with the Lord Jesus Christ.

Peter said, "The multitude throng Thee, and press Thee," and that is true of the multitude to this very day; but, of those who come where Christ is in the assembly of His saints, a large proportion only come because it is their custom to do so. Perhaps they hardly know why they go to a place of worship. They go because they always did go, and they think it wrong not to go. They are just like the doors which swing upon their hinges; they take no interest in what is done, at least only in the exterior parts of the service; into the heart and soul of the business they do not enter, and cannot enter. They are glad if the sermon is rather short, there is so much the less tedium for them. They are glad if they can look around and gaze at the congregation, they find in that something to interest them; but getting near to the Lord Jesus is not the business they come upon. They have not looked at it in that light. They come and they go; they come and they go; and it will be so till, by-and-by, they will come for the last time, and they will find out in the next world that the means of grace were not instituted to be matters of custom, and that to have heard Jesus Christ preached, and to have rejected Him, is no trifle, but a solemn thing for which they will have to answer in the presence of the great Judge of all the earth.

Others there are who come to the house of prayer, and try to enter into the service, and do so in a certain fashion; but it is only self-righteously or professionally. They may come to the Lord's table; perhaps they attend to baptism; they may even join the church. They are baptized, yet not by the Holy Spirit; they take the Lord's supper, but they take not the Lord Himself; they eat the bread, but they never eat His flesh; they drink the wine, but they never drink His blood; they have been buried in the pool, but they have never been buried with Christ in baptism, nor have they risen again with Him into newness of life. To them, to read, to sing, to kneel, to hear, and so on, are enough. They are content with the shell, but the blessed spiritual kernel, the true marrow and fatness, these they know nothing of. These are the many, go into what church or meeting-house you please. They are in the press around Jesus, but they do not touch Him. They come, but they come not into contact with Jesus. They are outward, external hearers only, but there is no inward touching of the blessed person of Christ, no mysterious contact with the ever-blessed Savior, no stream of life and love flowing from Him to them. It is all mechanical religion. Of vital godliness, they know nothing.

But, "somebody," said Christ, "somebody hath touched Me," and that is the soul of the matter. O my hearer, when you are in prayer alone, never be satisfied with having prayed; do not give it up till you have touched Christ in prayer; or, if you have not got to Him, at any rate sigh and cry until you do! Do not think you have prayed, but try again. When you come to public worship, I beseech you, rest not satisfied with listening to the sermon, and so on—as you all do with sufficient attention; to that I bear you witness—but do not be content unless you get at Christ the Master, and touch Him. At all times when you come to the communion table, count it to have been no ordinance of grace to you unless you have gone right through the veil into Christ's own arms, or at least have touched His garment, feeling that the first object, the life and soul of the means of grace, is to touch Jesus Christ Himself; and except "somebody" hath touched Him, the whole has been a mere dead performance, without life or power.

The woman in our text was not only amongst those who were in the crowd, but she touched Jesus; and therefore, beloved, let me hold her up to your example in some respects, though I would to God that in other respects you might excel her.

Note, first, she felt that it was of no use being in the crowd, of no use to be in the same street with Christ, or near to the place where Christ was, but *she must get at Him; she must touch Him.* She touched Him, you will notice, under *many difficulties.* There was a great crowd. She was a woman. She was also a woman enfeebled by a long disease which had drained her constitution, and left her more fit to be upon a bed than to be struggling in the seething tumult. Yet, notwithstanding that, so intense was her desire, that she urged on her way, I doubt not with many a bruise, and many an uncouth push, and at last, poor trembler as she was, she got near to the Lord. Beloved, it is not always easy to get at Jesus. It is very easy to kneel down to pray, but not so easy to reach Christ in prayer. There is a child crying, it is your own, and its noise has often hindered you when you were striving to approach Jesus; or a knock will come at the door when you most wish to be retired. When you are sitting in the house of God, your neighbors in the seat before you may unconsciously distract your attention. It is not easy to draw near to Christ, especially coming as some of you do right away from the counting-house, and from the workshop, with a thousand thoughts and cares about you. You cannot always unload your burden outside, and come in here with your hearts prepared to receive the gospel. Ah! it is a terrible fight sometimes, a real foot-to-foot fight with evil, with temptation, and I know not what. But, beloved, do fight it out, do fight it out; do not let your seasons for prayer be wasted, nor your times for hearing be thrown away; but, like this woman, be resolved, with all your feebleness, that you will lay hold upon Christ. And oh! if you be resolved about it, if you cannot get to Him, He will come to you, and sometimes, when you are struggling against unbelieving thoughts, He will turn and say, "Make room for that poor feeble one, that she may come to Me, for My desire is to the work of My own hands; let her come to Me, and let her desire be granted to her."

Observe, again, that this woman touched Jesus *very secretly.* Perhaps there is a dear sister here who is getting near to Christ at this very moment, and yet her face does not betray her. It is so little contact that she has gained with Christ that the joyous flush, and the sparkle of the eye, which we often see in the child of God, have not yet come to her. She is sitting in yonder obscure corner, or standing in this aisle, but though her touch is secret, it is true. Though she cannot tell another of it, yet it is accomplished. She has touched Jesus. Beloved, that is not always the nearest fellowship with Christ of which we talk the most. Deep waters are still. Nay, I am not sure but what we sometimes get nearer to Christ when we think we are at a distance than we do when we imagine we are near Him, for we are not always exactly the best judges of our own spiritual state, and we may be very close to the Master, and yet for all that we may be so anxious to get closer that we may feel dissatisfied with the measure of grace which we have already received. To be satisfied with self, is no sign of grace; but to long for more grace, is often a far better evidence of the healthy state of the soul. Friend, if thou canst not come to the table tonight publicly, come to the Master in secret. If thou darest not tell thy wife, or thy child, or thy father, that thou art trusting in Jesus, it need not be told as yet. Thou mayest do it secretly, as he did to whom Jesus said, "When thou wast under the fig tree, I saw thee." Nathaniel retired to the shade that no one might see him; but Jesus saw him, and marked his prayer, and He will see thee in the crowd, and in the dark, and not withhold His blessing.

This woman also came into contact with Christ *under a very deep sense of unworthiness.* I dare say she thought, "If I touch the Great Prophet, it will be a wonder if He does not strike me with some sudden judgment," for she was a woman ceremonially unclean. She had no right to be in the throng. Had the Levitical law been strictly carried out, I suppose she would have been confined to her house; but there she was wandering about, and she must needs go and touch the Holy Savior. Ah! poor heart, you feel tonight that you are not fit to touch the skirts of the Master's robe, for you are so unworthy. You never felt so undeserving before as you do tonight. In the recollection of last week and its infirmities, in the remembrance of the present state of your heart, and all its wanderings from God, you feel as if there never was so worthless a sinner in the house of God before. "Is grace for me?" say you. "Is Christ for me?" Oh! yes, unworthy one. Do not be put off without it. Jesus Christ does not save the worthy, but the unworthy. Your plea must not be righteousness, but guilt. And you, too, child of God, though you are ashamed of yourself, Jesus is not ashamed of you; and though you feel unfit to come, let your unfitness only impel you with the greater earnestness of desire. Let your sense of need make you the more fervent to approach the Lord, who can supply your need.

Thus, you see, the woman came under difficulties, she came secretly, she came as an unworthy one, but still she obtained the blessing.

I have known many staggered with that saying of Paul's, "He that eateth and drinketh unworthily, eateth and drinketh damnation to himself." Now, understand that this passage does not refer to the unworthiness of those persons who come to the Lord's table; for it does not say, "He that eateth and drinketh *being unworthy.*" It is not an adjective; it is an adverb: "He that eateth and drinketh unworthily," that is to say, he who shall come to the outward and visible sign of Christ's presence, and shall eat of the bread in order to obtain money by being a member of the church, knowing himself to be a hypocrite, or who shall do it jestingly, trifling with the ordinance: such a person would be eating and drinking unworthily, and he will be condemned. The sense of the passage is, not "damnation," as our version reads it, but "condemnation." There can be no doubt that members of the church, coming to the Lord's table in an unworthy manner, do receive condemnation. They are condemned for so doing, and the Lord is grieved. If they have any conscience at all, they ought to feel their sin; and if not, they may expect the chastisements of God to visit them. But, O sinner, as to coming to Christ—which is a very different thing from coming to the Lord's table—as to coming to Christ, the more unworthy you feel yourself to be, the better. Come, thou filthy one, for Christ can wash thee. Come, thou loathsome one, for Christ can beautify thee. Come utterly ruined and undone, for in Jesus Christ there is the strength and salvation which thy case requires.

Notice, once again, that *this woman touched the Master very tremblingly, and it was only a hurried touch, but still it was the touch of faith.* Oh, beloved, to lay hold on Christ! Be thankful if you do but get near Him for a few minutes. "Abide with me," should be your prayer; but oh, if He only give you a glimpse, be thankful! Remember that a touch healed the woman. She did not embrace Christ by the hour together. She had but a touch, and she was healed; and oh, may you have a sight of Jesus now, my beloved! Though it be but a glimpse, yet it will gladden and cheer your souls. Perhaps you are waiting on Christ, desiring His company, and while you are turning it over in your mind you are asking,

> Will He ever shine upon me? Will He ever speak loving words to me? Will He ever let me sit at His feet? Will He ever permit me to lean my head upon His bosom?

Come and try Him. Though you should shake like an aspen leaf, yet come. They sometimes come best who come most tremblingly, for when the creature is lowest then is the Creator highest, and when in our own esteem we are less than nothing and vanity, then is Christ the more fair and lovely in our eyes. One of the best ways of climbing to Heaven is on our hands and knees. At any rate, there is no fear of falling when we are in that position, for:

> *He that is down*
> *need fear no fall.*

Let your lowliness of heart, your sense of utter nothingness, instead of disqualifying you, be a sweet medium for leading you to receive more of Christ. The more empty I am, the more room is there for my Master. The more I lack, the more He will give me. The more I feel my sickness, the more shall I adore and bless Him when He makes me whole.

You see, the woman did really touch Christ, and so I come back to that. Whatever infirmity there was in the touch, it was a real touch of faith. She did reach Christ Himself. She did not touch Peter; that would have been of no use to her, any more than it is for the parish priest to tell you that you are regenerate when your life soon proves that you are not. She did not touch John or James; that would have been of no more good to her than it is for you to be touched by a bishop's hands, and to be told that you are confirmed in the faith, when you are not even a believer, and therefore have no faith to be confirmed in. She touched the Master Himself; and, I pray you, do not be content unless you can do the same. Put out the hand of faith, and touch Christ. Rest on Him. Rely on His bloody sacrifice, His dying love, His rising power, His ascended plea; and as you rest in Him, your vital touch, however feeble, will certainly give you the blessing your soul needs.

This brings us to the second part of our discourse, upon which I will say only a little.

II. The woman in the crowd did touch Jesus, and, having done so, she received virtue from him.

The healing energy streamed at once through the finger of faith into the woman. In Christ, there is healing for all spiritual diseases. There is a speedy healing, a healing which will not take months nor years, but which is complete in one second. There is in Christ a sufficient healing, though your diseases should be multiplied beyond all bounds. There is in Christ an all-conquering power to drive out every ill. Though, like this woman, you baffle physicians, and your case is reckoned desperate beyond all parallel, yet a touch of Christ will heal you. What a precious, glorious gospel I have to preach to sinners! If they touch Jesus, no matter though the devil himself were in them, that touch of faith would drive the devil out of them. Though you were like the man into whom there had entered a legion of devils, the word of Jesus would cast them all into the deep, and you should sit at His feet, clothed, and in your right mind. There is no excess or extravagance of sin which the power of Jesus Christ cannot overcome. If thou canst believe, whatever thou mayest have been, thou shalt be saved. If thou canst believe, though thou hast been lying in the scarlet dye till the warp and woof of thy being are ingrained therewith, yet shall the precious blood of Jesus make thee white as snow. Though thou art become black as Hell itself, and only fit to be cast into the pit, yet if thou trustest Jesus, that simple faith shall give to thy soul the healing which shall make thee fit to tread the streets of Heaven, and to stand before Jehovah-Rophi's face, magnifying the Lord that healeth thee.

And now, child of God, I want you to learn the same lesson. Very likely, when you came in here, you said—

> Alas! I feel very dull; my spirituality is at a very low ebb; the place is hot, and I do not feel prepared to hear; the spirit is willing, but the flesh is weak; I shall have no holy enjoyment today!

Why not? Why, the touch of Jesus could make you live if you were dead, and surely it will stir the life that is in you, though it may seem to you to be expiring! Now, struggle hard, my beloved, to get at Jesus! May the Eternal Spirit come and help you, and may you yet find that your dull, dead times can soon become your best times. Oh! what a blessing it is that God takes the beggar up from the dunghill! He does not raise us when He sees us already up, but when He finds us lying on the dunghill, then He delights to lift us up, and set us among princes. Or ever you are aware, your soul may become like the chariots of Ammi-nadib. Up from the depths of heaviness to the very heights of ecstatic worship you may mount as in a single moment if you can but touch Christ crucified. View Him yonder, with streaming wounds, with thorn-crowned head, as in all the majesty of His misery, He expires for you!

"Alas!" say you, "I have a thousand doubts tonight." Ah! but your doubts will soon vanish when you draw nigh to Christ. He never doubts who feels the touch of Christ, at least, not while the touch lasts, for observe this woman! She felt in her body that she was made whole, and so shall you, if you will only come into contact with the Lord. Do not wait for evidences, but come to Christ for evidences. If you cannot even dream of a good thing in yourselves, come to Jesus Christ as you did at the first. Come as if you never had come at all. Come to Jesus as a sinner, and your doubts shall flee away.

"Aye!" saith another, "but my sins come to my remembrance, my sins since conversion." Well, return to Jesus, when your guilt seems to return. The fountain is still open, and that fountain, you will remember, is not only open for sinners, but for saints; for what saith the Scripture—"There shall be a fountain opened *for the house of David and for the inhabitants of Jerusalem,"*—that is, for you, church members, for you, believers in Jesus? The fountain is still open. Come, beloved, come to Jesus anew, and whatever be your sins, or doubts, or heaviness, they shall all depart as soon as you can touch your Lord.

III. And now the last point is—and I will not detain you long upon it—if somebody shall touch Jesus, the Lord will know it.

I do not know your names; a great number of you are perfect strangers to me. It matters nothing; your name is "somebody," and Christ will know you. You are a total stranger, perhaps, to everybody in this place; but if you get a blessing, there will be two who will know it—you will, and Christ will. Oh! if you should look to Jesus this day, it may not be registered in our church-book, and we may not hear of it; but still it will be registered in the courts of Heaven, and they will set all the bells of the New Jerusalem a-ringing, and all the harps of angels will take a fresh lease of music as soon as they know that you are born again.

> With joy the Father doth approve
> The fruit of His eternal love;
> The Son with joy looks down and sees
> The purchase of His agonies;
> The Spirit takes delight to view
> The holy soul He formed anew;
> And saints and angels join to sing
> The growing empire of their King.

"Somebody!" I do not know the woman's name; I do not know who the man is, but—"Somebody!"—God's electing love rests on thee, Christ's redeeming blood was shed for thee, the Spirit has wrought a work in thee, or thou wouldst not have touched Jesus; and all this Jesus knows.

It is a consoling thought that Christ not only knows the great children in the family, but He also knows the little ones. This stands fast: "The Lord knoweth them that are His," whether they are only brought to know Him now, or whether they have known Him for fifty years. "The Lord knoweth them that are His," and if I am a part of Christ's body, I may be but the foot, but the Lord knows the foot; and the head and the heart in Heaven feel acutely when the foot on Earth is bruised. If you have touched Jesus, I tell you that amidst the glories of angels, and the everlasting hallelujahs of all the blood-bought, He has found time to hear your sigh, to receive your faith, and to give you an answer of peace. All the way from Heaven to Earth there has rushed a mighty stream of healing virtue, which has come from Christ to you. Since you have touched Him, the healing virtue has touched you.

Now, *as Jesus knows of your salvation,* He wishes other people to know of it, and that is why He has put it into my heart to say—Somebody has touched the Lord. Where is that somebody? Somebody, where are you? Somebody, where are you? You have touched Christ, though with a feeble finger, and you are saved. Let us know it. It is due to us to let us know. You cannot guess what joy it gives us when we hear of sick ones being healed by our Master. Some of you, perhaps, have known the Lord for months, and you have not yet come forward to make an avowal of it; we beg you to do so. You may come forward tremblingly, as this woman did; you may perhaps say, "I do not know what I should tell you." Well, you must tell us what she told the Lord; she told Him all the truth. We do not want anything else. We do not desire any sham experience. We do not want you to manufacture feelings like somebody else's that you have read of in a book. Come and tell us what you have felt. We shall not ask you to tell us what you have not felt, or what you do not know. But, if you have touched Christ, and you have been healed, I ask it, and I think I may ask it as your duty, as well as a favor to us, to come and tell us what the Lord hath done for your soul.

And you, believers, when you come to the Lord's table, if you draw near to Christ, and have a sweet season, tell it to your brethren. Just as when Benjamin's brethren went down to Egypt to buy corn, they left Benjamin at home, but they took a sack for Benjamin, so you ought always to take a word home for the sick wife at home, or the child who cannot come out. Take home food for those of the family who cannot come for it. God grant that you may have always something sweet to tell of what you have experimentally known of precious truth, for while the sermon may have been sweet in itself, it comes with a double power when you can add, "and there was a savor about it which I enjoyed, and which made my heart leap for joy"!

Whoever you may be, my dear friend, though you may be nothing but a poor "somebody," yet if you have touched Christ, tell others about it, in order that they may come and touch Him, too; and the Lord bless you, for Christ's sake! Amen.

Jesus, the Great Object of Astonishment

"Behold, My Servant shall deal prudently, He shall be exalted and extolled, and be very high. As many were astounded at Thee; His visage was so marred more than any man, and His form more than the sons of men; so shall He sprinkle many nations; the kings shall shut their mouths at Him: for that which had not been told them shall they see; and that which they had not heard shall they consider."—Isaiah 52:13-15.

Our Lord Jesus Christ bore from of old the name of "Wonderful," and the word seems all too poor to set forth His marvelous person and character. He says of Himself, in the language of the prophet—"Behold, I and the children whom the Lord hath given Me are for signs and for wonders." He is a fountain of astonishment to all who know Him, and the more they know of Him, the more are they astounded at Him. It is an astonishing thing that there should have been a Christ at all. The Incarnation is the miracle of miracles; that He who is the Infinite should become an infant, that He who made the worlds should be wrapt in swaddling-bands, remains a fact out of which, as from a hive, new wonders continually fly forth. In His complex nature He is so mysterious, and yet so manifest, that doubtless all the angels of Heaven were and are astonished at Him. O Son of God, and Son of man, when Thou, the Word, wast made flesh, and dwelt among us, and Thy saints beheld Thy glory, it was but natural that many should be astonished at Thee!

Our text seems to say that our Lord was, first, *a great wonder in His griefs;* and, secondly, that He was *a great wonder in His glory.*

I. He was a great wonder in His griefs.

> As many were astounded at Thee; His visage was so marred more than any man, and His form more than the sons of men.

His visage was marred: no doubt His countenance bore the signs of a matchless grief. There were ploughings on His brow as well as upon His back; suffering, and brokenness of spirit, and agony of heart, had told upon that lovely face, till its beauty, though never to be destroyed, was "so" marred that never was any other so spoiled with sorrow. But it was not His face only, His whole form was marred more than the sons of men. The contour of His bodily manhood showed marks of singular assaults of sorrow, such as had never bowed another form so low. I do not know whether His gait was stooping, or whether His knees tottered, and His walk was feeble; but there was evidently a something about Him which gave Him the appearance of premature age, since to the Jews He looked older than He was, for when He was little more than thirty they said unto Him, "Thou art not yet fifty years old." I cannot conceive that He was deformed or ungainly; but despite His natural dignity, His worn and emaciated appearance marked Him out as "the Man of sorrows," and to the carnal eye His whole natural and spiritual form had in it nothing which evoked admiration; even as the prophet said, "When we shall see Him, there is no beauty that we should desire Him." The marring was not of that lovely face alone, but of the whole fabric of His wondrous manhood, so that many were astonished at Him.

Our astonishment, when in contemplation we behold our suffering Lord, will arise from the consideration of what His natural beauty must have been, enshrined as He was from the first within a perfect body. Conceived without sin, and so born of a pure virgin without taint of hereditary sin, I doubt not that He was the flower and glory of manhood as to His form, and from His early youth He must have been a joy to His mother's eye. Great masters of the olden time expended all their skill upon the holy child Jesus, but it is not for the colors of Earth to depict the Lord from Heaven. That "holy thing" which was born of Mary was "seen of angels," and it charmed their eyes. Must such loveliness be marred? His every look was pure, His every thought was holy, and therefore the expression of His face must have been heavenly, and yet it must be marred. Poverty must mark it; hunger, and thirst, and weariness must plough it; heart-griefs must seam and scar it; spittle must stain it; tears must scald it;

smiting must bruise it; death must make it pale and bloodless. Well does Bernard sing,

> *O sacred Head, once wounded,*
> *With grief and pain weigh'd down,*
> *How scornfully surrounded*
> *With thorns, Thine only crown;*
> *How pale art Thou with anguish,*
> *With sore abuse and scorn!*
> *How does that visage languish,*
> *Which once was bright as morn!*

The second astonishment to us must be that he could be so marred who had nothing in His character to mar His countenance. Sin is a sad disfigurement to faces which in early childhood were surpassingly attractive. Passion, if it be indulged in, soon sets a seal of deformity upon the countenance. Men that plunge into vice bear upon their features the traces of their hearts' volcanic fires. We most of us know some withered beings, whose beauty has been burned up by the fierce fires of excess, till they are a horror to look upon, as if the mark of Cain were set upon them. Every sin makes its line on a fair face. But there was no sin in the blessed Jesus, no evil thought to mar His natural perfectness. No redness of eyes ever came to Him by tarrying long at the wine; no unhallowed anger ever flushed His cheek; no covetousness gave to His eye a wolfish glance; no selfish care lent to His features a sharp and anxious cast. Such an unselfish, holy life as His ought to have rendered Him, if it had been possible, more beautiful every day. Indulging such benevolence, abiding in such communion with God, surely the face of Christ must, in the natural order of things, have more and more astonished all sympathetic observers with its transcendent charms. But sorrow came to engrave her name where sin had never made a stroke, and she did her work so effectually that His visage was more marred than that of any man, although the God of mercy knows there have been other visages that have been worn with pain and anguish past all recognition. I need not repeat even one of the many stories of human woe: that of our Lord surpasses all.

Remember that the face of our Well-beloved, as well as all His form, must have been an accurate index of His soul. Physiognomy is a science with much truth in it when it deals with men of truth. Men weaned from simplicity know how to control their countenances; the crafty will appear to be honest, the hardened will seem to sympathize with the distressed, the revengeful will mimic goodwill. There are some who continually use their countenance as they do their speech, to conceal their feelings; and it is almost a point of politeness with them never to show themselves, but always to go masked among their fellows.

But the Christ had learned no such arts. He was so sincere, so transparent, so childlike and true, that whatever stirred within Him was apparent to those about Him, so far as they were capable of understanding His great soul. We read of Him that He was "moved with compassion." The Greek word means that He experienced a wonderful emotion of His whole nature, He was thrilled with it, and His disciples saw how deeply He felt for the people, who were as sheep without a shepherd. Though He did not commit Himself to men, He did not conceal Himself, but wore His heart upon His sleeve, and all could see what He was, and knew that He was full of grace and truth. We are, therefore, not surprised, when we devoutly consider our Lord's character, that His visage and form should indicate the inward agonies of His tender spirit; it could not be that His face should be untrue to His heart. The ploughers made deep furrows upon His soul as well as upon His back, and His heart was rent with inward convulsions, which could not but affect His whole appearance. Those eyes saw what those around Him could not see; those shoulders bore a constant burden which others could not know; and, therefore, His countenance and form betrayed the fact. O dear, dear Savior, when we think of Thee, and of Thy majesty and purity, we are again astonished that woes should come upon Thee so grievously as to mar Thy visage and Thy form!

Now think, dear friends, what were the causes of this marring. It was not old age that had wrinkled His brow, for He was still in the prime of life, neither was it a personal sickness which had caused decay; much less was it any congenital weakness and disease, which at length betrayed itself, for in His flesh there was no possibility of impurity, which would, in death, have led to corruption. It was occasioned, first, by His constant sympathy with the suffering. There was a heavy wear and tear occasioned by the extraordinary compassion of His soul. In three years it had told upon Him most manifestly, till His visage was marred more than that of any other man. To Him there was a kind of sucking up into Himself of all the suffering of those whom He blessed. He always bore upon Him the burden of mortal woe. We read of Christ healing all that were sick, "that it might be fulfilled which was spoken by Esaias the prophet, saying, 'Himself took our infirmities, and bare our sicknesses.'" Yes, He took those infirmities and sicknesses in some mystical way to Himself, just as I have heard of certain trees, which scatter health, because they themselves imbibe the miasma, and draw up into themselves those noxious vapors which otherwise would poison mankind. Thus, without being themselves polluted, they disinfect the atmosphere around them. This, our Savior did, but the cost was great to Him. You can imagine, living as He did in the midst of one vast hospital, how constantly He must have seen sights that grieved and pained Him. Moreover, with a nature so pure and loving, He must have been daily tortured with the sin, and hypocrisy, and oppression which so abounded in His day. In a certain sense, He was always laying down His life for men, for He was spent in their service, tortured by their sin, and oppressed with their sorrow. The more we look into that marred visage, the more shall we be astonished at the anguish which it indicated.

Do not wonder that He was more marred than any man, for He was more sensitive than other men. No part of Him was callous, He had no seared conscience, no blunted sensibility, no drugged and deadened nerve. His manhood was in its glory, in the perfection in which Adam was when God made him in His own image, and therefore He was ill-housed in such a fallen world. We read of Christ that He was "grieved for the hardness of their hearts," "He marveled because of their unbelief," "He sighed deeply in His spirit," "He groaned in the spirit, and was troubled." This, however, was only the beginning of the marring.

His deepest griefs and most grievous marring came of *His substitutionary work,* while bearing the penalty of our sin. One word recalls much of His woe: it is, "Gethsemane." Betrayed by Judas, His trusted friend, that the Scripture might be fulfilled, "He that eateth bread with Me hath lifted up his heel against Me"; deserted even by John, for all the disciples forsook Him and fled; not one of all the loved ones with Him: He was left alone. He had washed their feet, but they could not watch with Him one hour; and in that garden He wrestled with our deadly foe, till His sweat was as it were great drops of blood falling down to the ground, and as Hart puts it—

> He bore all Incarnate God could bear,
> With strength enough, but none to spare.

I do verily believe that verse to be true. Herein you see what marred His countenance, and His form, even while in life. The whole of His manhood felt that dreadful shock, when He and the prince of darkness, in awful duel, fought it out amidst the gloom of the olives on that cold midnight when our redemption began to be fully accomplished.

The whole of His passion marred His countenance and His form with its unknown sufferings. I restrain myself, lest this meditation should grow too painful. They bound Him, they scourged Him, they mocked Him, they plucked off the hair from His face, they spat upon Him, and at last they nailed Him to the tree, and there He hung. His physical pain alone must have been very great, but all the while there was within His soul an inward torment which added immeasurably to His sufferings. His God forsook Him. *"Eloi, Eloi, lama, sabachthani?"* is a voice enough to rend the rocks, and assuredly it makes us all astonished when, in the returning light, we look upon His visage, and are sure that never face of any man was so marred before, and never form of any son of man so grievously disfigured. Weeping and wondering, astonished and adoring, we leave the griefs of our own dear Lord, and with loving interest turn to the brighter portion of His unrivaled story.

> *Behold your King! Though the moonlight steals*
> *Through the silvery sprays of the olive tree,*
> *No star-gemmed scepter or crown it reveals,*
> *In the solemn shade of Gethsemane.*
> *Only a form of prostrate grief,*
> *Fallen, crushed, like a broken leaf!*
> *Oh, think of His sorrow, that we may know*
> *The depth of love in the depth of woe!*
>
> *Behold your King, with His sorrow crowned,*
> *Alone, alone in the valley is He!*
> *The shadows of death are gathering round,*
> *And the cross must follow Gethsemane.*
> *Darker and darker the gloom must fall,*
> *Filled is the cup, He must drink it all!*
> *Oh, think of His sorrow, that we may know*
> *His wondrous love in His wondrous woe!*

II. There is an equal astonishment at His glories.

I doubt not, if we could see Him now, as He appeared to John in Patmos, we should feel that we must do exactly as the beloved disciple did, for He deliberately wrote, "When I saw Him, I fell at His feet as dead." His astonishment was so great that he could not endure the sight. He had doubtless longed often to behold that glorified face and form, but the privilege was too much for him. While we are encumbered with these frail bodies, it is not fit for us to behold our Lord, for we should die with excess of delight if we were suddenly to behold that vision of splendor. Oh, for those glorious days when we shall lie forever at His feet, and see our exalted Lord!

"Behold, My servant shall deal prudently, He shall be exalted and extolled, and be very high." Observe the three words, "exalted and extolled, and be very high"; language pants for expression. Our Lord is now *exalted* in being lifted up from the grave, lifted up above all angels, and principalities, and powers. The Man Christ Jesus is the nearest to the eternal throne, aye, the Lamb is before the throne. "And I beheld, and, lo, in the midst of the throne and of the four beasts, and in the midst of the elders, stood a Lamb as it had been slain." He is in His own state and person exalted, and then by the praise rendered Him he is *extolled,* for he is worshiped and adored by the whole universe. All praise goes up before Him now, so that men extol Him, while "God also hath highly exalted Him, and given Him a name, which is above every name; that at the name of Jesus every knee should bow, of things in Heaven, and things in earth, and things under the earth; and that every tongue should confess that Jesus Christ is Lord, to the glory of God the Father." Deep were His sorrows, but as high are His joys. It is said that, around many of the lochs in Scotland, the mountains are as high as the water is deep; and so our Lord's glories are as immeasurable as were His woes. What a meditation is furnished by these two-fold and incalculable heights and depths! Our text says that He shall "be very high." It cannot tell us how high. It is inconceivable how great and glorious in all respects the Lord Jesus Christ is at this moment. Oh, that He may be very high in our esteem! He is not yet exalted and extolled in any of our hearts as He deserves to be. I would we loved Him a thousand times as much as we do, but our whole heart goeth after Him, does it not? Would we not die for Him? Would we not set Him on a throne as high as seven Heavens, and then think that we had not done enough for Him, who is now our all in all, and more than all?

You notice what is said, concerning the Christ, as the most astonishing thing of all: "So shall He sprinkle many nations." Now is it the glory of our risen Lord, at this moment, that His precious blood is to save many nations. Before the throne, men of all nations shall sing, "Thou wast slain, and hast redeemed us unto God by Thy blood." Not the English nation alone shall be purified by His atoning blood, but many nations shall He sprinkle with His reconciling blood, even as Israel of old was sprinkled with the blood of sacrifice. We read in the tenth chapter of the Epistle to the Hebrews, at the twenty-second verse, of "having our hearts sprinkled from an evil conscience," and this is effected by that precious blood by which we have been once purged so effectually that we have no more consciousness of sins, but enter into perfect peace. The blood of bulls and of goats, and the ashes of an heifer, sprinkling the unclean, sanctified to the purifying of the flesh, and much more doth the blood of Christ purge our conscience from dead works, to serve the living God.

The sprinkling of the blood was meant also to confirm the covenant: thus Moses "sprinkled both the book and all the people, saying, 'This is the blood of the testament which God hath enjoined unto you.'" Our Lord Himself said, "This is My blood of the new covenant, which is shed for many for the remission of sins." But is it not a wonderful thing that He should die as a malefactor on the tree, amid scorn and ridicule, and yet that He is this day bringing nations into covenant with God? Once so despised, and now so mighty! God has given Him "for a covenant of the people, for a light of the Gentiles." Many nations shall by Him be joined in covenant with the God of the whole earth. Do not fall into the erroneous idea that this world is like a great ship-wrecked vessel, soon to go to pieces on an iron-bound coast; but rather let us expect the conversion of the world to the Lord Jesus. As a reward for the travail of His soul, He shall cause many nations to "exult with joy," for so some read the passage; the peoples of the Earth shall not only be astonished at His griefs, but they shall admire His glories, adore His perfections, and be filled with an amazement of joy at His coming and kingdom. I can conceive nothing in the future too great and glorious to result from the passion and death of our Divine Lord.

Listen to this, "Kings shall shut their mouths at Him." They shall see such a King as they themselves have never been; they speak freely to their brother-kings, but they shall not dare to speak to Him, and as for speaking against Him, that will be altogether out of the question.

> Kings shall fall down before Him,
> And gold and incense bring.

"For that which had not been told them shall they see." Kings are often out of the reach of the gospel, they do not hear it, it is not told to them. They would despise the lowly preacher, and little gatherings of believers meeting together for worship; they would only listen to stately discourses, which do not touch the heart and conscience. The great ones of the Earth are usually the least likely to know the things of God, for while the poor have the gospel preached unto them, princes are more likely to hear soft flatteries and fair speeches. The time shall come, however, when Caesar shall bow before a real Imperator, and monarchs shall behold the Prince of the kings of the earth. "For the Lord Himself shall descend from Heaven with a shout, with the voice of the archangel, and with the trump of God." They shall see His majesty, of which they had not even been told.

"That which they had not heard shall they consider." They shall be obliged, even on their thrones, to think about the kingdom of the King of kings, and they shall retire to their closets to confess their sins, and to put on sackcloth and ashes, and to give heed to the words of wisdom. "Be wise now, therefore, O ye kings: be instructed, ye judges of the earth." Today, the humble listen to Christ, but by-and-by the mightiest of the mighty shall turn all their thoughts towards Him. He shall gather sheaves of scepters beneath His arm, and crowns shall be strewn at His feet; and "He shall reign forever and ever," and "of the increase of His government and peace there shall be no end." If we were astonished at the marring of His face, we shall be much more astonished at the magnificence of His glory. Upon His throne none shall question His supremacy, none shall doubt His loveliness; but His enemies shall weep and wail because of Him whom they pierced; while He shall be admired in all them that believe. Adorable Lord, we long for Thy glorious appearing! We beseech Thee, tarry not!

> *Come, and begin Thy reign*
> *Of everlasting peace;*
> *Come, take the kingdom to Thyself,*
> *Great King of Righteousness!*

The Sin-Bearer

"Who His own self bare our sins in His own body on the tree,
that we, being dead to sins, should live unto righteousness:
by whose stripes ye were healed. For ye were as sheep going
astray; but are now returned unto the Shepherd and Bishop
of your souls."—I Peter 2:24, 25.

This wonderful passage is a part of Peter's address to servants; and in his day nearly all servants were slaves. Peter begins at the eighteenth verse: "Servants, be subject to your masters with all fear; not only to the good and gentle, but also to the froward [stubborn, unreasonable]. For this is thankworthy, if a man for conscience toward God endure grief, suffering wrongfully. For what glory is it, if, when ye be buffeted for your faults, ye shall take it patiently? but if, when ye do well, and suffer for it, ye take it patiently, this is acceptable with God. For even hereunto were ye called: because Christ also suffered for us, leaving us an example, that ye should follow His steps: who did no sin, neither was guile found in His mouth: who, when He was reviled, reviled not again; when He suffered, He threatened not; but committed Himself to Him that judgeth righteously: who His own self bare our sins in His own body on the tree, that we, being dead to sins, should live unto righteousness: by whose stripes ye were healed." If we are in a lowly condition of life, we shall find our best comfort in thinking of the lowly Savior bearing our sins in all patience and submission. If we are called to suffer, as servants often were in the Roman times, we shall be solaced by a vision of our Lord buffeted, scourged, and crucified, yet silent in the majesty of His endurance. If these sufferings are entirely undeserved, and we are grossly slandered, we shall be comforted by remembering Him who did no sin, and in whose lips was found no guile. Our Lord Jesus is Head of the Guild of Sufferers: He did well, and suffered for it, but took it patiently. Our support under the cross, which we are appointed to bear, is only to be found in Him "who His own self bare our sins in His own body on the tree."

We ourselves now know by experience that there is no place for comfort like the cross. It is a tree stripped of all foliage, and apparently dead; yet we sit under its shadow with great delight, and its fruit is sweet unto our taste. Truly, in this case, "like cures like." By the suffering of our Lord Jesus, our suffering is made light. The servant is comforted since Jesus took upon Himself the form of a servant; the sufferer is cheered "because Christ also suffered for us"; and the slandered one is strengthened because Jesus also was reviled.

> *Is it not strange, the darkest hour*
> *That ever dawned on sinful earth*
> *Should touch the heart with softer power*
> *For comfort than an angel's mirth?*
> *That to the cross the mourner's eye should turn*
> *Sooner than where the stars of Christmas burn?*

Let us, as we hope to pass through the tribulations of this world, stand fast by the cross; for if *that* be gone, the lone-star is quenched whose light cheers the down-trodden, shines on the injured, and brings light to the oppressed. If we lose the cross—if we miss the substitutionary sacrifice of our Lord Jesus Christ, we have lost all.

The verse on which we would now devoutly meditate speaks of three things: *the bearing of our sins, the changing of our condition,* and *the healing of our spiritual diseases.* Each of these deserves our most careful notice.

I. The first is the bearing of our sins by our Lord.

"Who His own self bare our sins in His own body on the tree." These words in plainest terms assert that our Lord Jesus did really bear the sins of His people. How *literal* is the language! Words mean nothing if substitution is not stated here. I do not know the meaning of the fifty-third of Isaiah if this is not its meaning. Hear the prophet's words: "The Lord hath laid on Him the iniquity of us all"; "for the transgression of my people was He stricken"; "He shall bear their iniquities": "He was numbered with the transgressors, and He bare the sin of many."

I cannot imagine that the Holy Spirit would have used language so expressive if He had not intended to teach us that our Savior did really bear our sins, and suffer in our stead. What else can be intended by texts like these?

> *Christ was once offered to bear the sins of many. (Heb. 9:28)*

> *He hath made Him to be sin for us, who knew no sin; that we might be made the righteousness of God in Him. (2 Cor. 5:21)*

> *Christ hath redeemed us from the curse of the law, being made a curse for us: for it is written, "Cursed is every one that hangeth on a tree." (Gal. 3:13)*

> *Christ also hath loved us, and hath given Himself for us an offering and a sacrifice to God for a sweet-smelling savor. (Eph. 5:2)*

> *Once in the end of the world hath He appeared to put away sin by the sacrifice of Himself. (Heb. 9: 26)*

I say modestly, but firmly, that these Scriptures either teach the bearing of our sins by our Lord Jesus, or they teach nothing. In these days, among many errors and denials of truth, there has sprung up a teaching of "modern thought" which explains away the doctrine of substitution and vicarious sacrifice. One wise man has gone so far as to say that the transference of sin or righteousness is impossible, and another creature of the same school has stigmatized the idea as immoral.

It does not much matter what these modern haters of the cross may dare to say; but, assuredly, that which they deny, denounce, and deride, is the cardinal doctrine of our most holy faith, and is as clearly in Scripture as the sun is in the heavens. Beloved, as we suffer through the sin of Adam, so are we saved through the righteousness of Christ. Our fall was by another, and so is our rising again: we are under a system of representation and imputation, gainsay it who may. To us, the transference of our sin to Christ is a blessed fact clearly revealed in the Word of God, and graciously confirmed in the realizations of our faith. In that same chapter of Isaiah we read, "Surely He hath borne our griefs, and carried our sorrows," and we perceive that this was a matter of fact, for He was really, truly, and emphatically sorrowful; and, therefore, when we read that "He bare our sins in His own body on the tree," we dare not fritter it away, but assuredly believe that in very deed He was our Sin-Bearer. Possible or impossible, we sing with full assurance:

> *He bore on the tree*
> *the sentence for me.*

Had the sorrow been figurative, the sin-bearing might have been mythical; but the one fact is paralleled by the other. There is no figure in our text; it is a bare, literal fact: "Who His own self bare our sins in His own body on the tree." Oh, that men would give up caviling! To question and debate at the cross, is an act near akin to the crime of the soldiers when they parted His garments among them, and cast lots for His vesture.

Note how *personal* are the terms here employed! How expressly the Holy Ghost speaketh! "Who His own self bare our sins in His own body." It was not by delegation, but "His own self"; and it was not in imagination, but "in His own body." Observe, also, the personality from our side of the question, He "bare *our* sins," that is to say, my sins and your sins. There is a sort of cadence of music here,—"His own self," "our sins." As surely as it was Christ's own self that suffered on the cross, so truly was it our own sins that Jesus bore in His own body on the tree. Our Lord has appeared in court for us, accepting our place at the bar: "He was numbered with the transgressors." Nay, more, He has appeared at the place of execution for us, and has borne the death penalty upon the gibbet of doom in our stead. *In propriâ personâ,* our Redeemer has been arraigned, though innocent; has come under the curse, though forever blessed; and has suffered to the death, though He had done nothing worthy of blame.

> He was wounded for our transgressions, He was bruised for our iniquities: the chastisement of our peace was upon Him; and with His stripes we are healed.

This sin-bearing on our Lord's part was *continual.* The passage before us has been forced beyond its teaching, by being made to assert that our Lord Jesus bore our sins nowhere but on the cross: this, the words do *not* say. "The tree" was the place where beyond all other places we see our Lord bearing the chastisement due to our sins; but before this, He had felt the weight of the enormous load. It is wrong to base a great doctrine upon the incidental form of one passage of Scripture, especially when that passage of Scripture bears another meaning.

The marginal reading, which is perfectly correct, is "Who His own self bare our sins in His own body *to* the tree." Our Lord carried the burden of our sins up to the tree, and there and then He made an end of it. He had carried that load long before, for John the Baptist said of Him, "Behold the Lamb of God, which taketh away" (the verb is in the present tense, "which taketh away") "the sin of the world" (John 1: 29). Our Lord was then bearing the sin of the world as the Lamb of God. From the day when He began His divine ministry, I might say even before that, He bore our sins. He was the Lamb "slain from the foundation of the world"; so, when He went up to Calvary, bearing His cross, He was bearing our sins up to the tree. Yet, specially and peculiarly in His death-agony He stood in our stead, and upon His soul and body burst the tempest of justice which had gathered through our transgressions.

This sin-bearing is *final*. He bore our sins in His own body on the tree, but He bears them now no more. The sinner and the sinner's Surety are both free, for the law is vindicated, the honor of government is cleared, the substitutionary sacrifice is complete. He dieth no more, death hath no more dominion over Him; for He has ended His work, and has cried, "It is finished." As for the sins which He bore in His own body on the tree, they cannot be found, for they have ceased to be, according to that ancient promise, "In those days, and in that time, saith the Lord, the iniquity of Israel shall be sought for, and there shall be none; and the sins of Judah, and they shall not be found" (Jeremiah 50:20). The work of the Messiah was "to finish the transgression, and to make an end of sins, and to make reconciliation for iniquity, and to bring in everlasting righteousness" (Daniel 9:24). Now, if sin is made an end of, there is an end of it; and if transgression is "finished," there is no more to be said about it.

Let us look back with holy faith, and see Jesus bearing the stupendous load of our sins up to the tree, and on the tree; and see how *effectual* was His sacrifice for discharging the whole mass of our moral liability both in reference to guiltiness in the sight of God, and the punishment which follows thereon. It is a law of nature that nothing can be in two places at the same time; and if sin was borne away by our Lord, it cannot rest upon us. If by faith we have accepted the Substitute whom God Himself has accepted, then it cannot be that the penalty should be twice demanded, first of the Surety, and then of those for whom He stood. The Lord Jesus bore the sins of His people away, even as the scapegoat, in the type, carried the sin of Israel to a land uninhabited. Our sins are gone forever. "As far as the east is from the west, so far hath He removed our transgressions from us." He hath cast all our iniquities into the depths of the sea; he hath hurled them behind his back, where they shall no more be seen.

Beloved friends, we very calmly and coolly talk about this thing, but it is the greatest marvel in the universe; it is the miracle of earth, the mystery of Heaven, the terror of Hell. Could we fully realize the guilt of sin, the punishment due to it, and the literal substitution of Christ, it would work in us an intense enthusiasm of gratitude, love, and praise. I do not wonder that our Methodist friends shout, "Hallelujah!" This is enough to make us all shout and sing, as long as we live, "Glory, glory to the Son of God!" What a wonder that the Prince of glory, in whom is no sin, who was indeed incapable of evil, should condescend to come into such contact with our sin as is implied in His being "made sin for us"! Our Lord Jesus did not handle sin with the golden tongs, but He bore it on His own shoulders. He did not lift it with golden staves, as the priests carried the ark; but He Himself bore the hideous load of our sin in His own body on the tree. This is the mystery of grace which angels desire to look into. I would forever preach it in the plainest and most unmistakable language.

II. *In the second place, briefly notice the change in our condition, which the text describes as coming out of the Lord's bearing of our sins: "That we, being dead to sins, should live unto righteousness."*

The change is a dying and a reviving, a burial and a resurrection: we are brought from life to death, and from death to life.

We are henceforth legally dead to the punishment of sin. If I were condemned to die for an offence, and some other died in my stead, then I died in him who died for me. The law could not a second time lay its charge against me, and bring me again before the judge, and condemn me, and lead me out to die. Where would be the justice of such a procedure? I am dead already: how can I die again? I have borne the wrath of God in the person of my glorious and ever-blessed Substitute; how then can I bear it again? Where was the use of a Substitute if I am to bear it also? Should Satan come before God to lay an accusation against me, the answer is, "This man is dead. He has borne the penalty, and is 'dead to sins,' for the sentence against him has been executed upon Another." What a wonderful deliverance for us! Bless the Lord, O my soul!

But Peter also means to remind us that, by and through the influence of Christ's death upon our hearts, *the Holy Ghost has made us now to be actually* "dead to sins": that is to say, we no longer love them, and they have ceased to hold dominion over us. Sin is no longer at home in our hearts; if it enters there, it is as an intruder. We are no more its willing servants. Sin calls to us by temptation, but we give it no answer, for we are dead to its voice. Sin promises us a high reward, but we do not consent, for we are dead to its allurements. We sin, but our will is not to sin. It would be Heaven to us to be perfectly holy. Our heart and life go after perfection, but sin is abhorred of our soul. "Now, if I do that which I would not, it is no more I that do it, but sin that dwelleth in me." Our truest and most real self loathes sin; and though we fall into it, it is a fall—we are out of our element, and escape from the evil with all speed. The newborn life within us has no dealings with sin; it is dead to sin.

The Greek word here used cannot be fully rendered into English; it signifies "being unborn to sins." We were born in sin, but by the death of Christ, and the work of the Holy Spirit upon us, that birth is undone, "we are unborn to sins." That which was wrought in us by sin, even at our birth, is through the death of Jesus counteracted by the new life which His Spirit imparts. "We are unborn to sins." I like the phrase, unusual as it sounds. Does it seem possible that birth should be reversed: the born unborn? Yet so it is. The true *ego,* the realest "I," is now unborn to sins, for we are "born, not of blood, nor of the will of the flesh, nor of the will of man, but of God." We are unborn to sins, and born unto God.

But our Lord's sin-bearing has also *brought us into life*. Dead to evil according to law, we also live in newness of life in the kingdom of grace. Our Lord's object is "that we should live unto righteousness." Not only are our lives to be righteous, which I trust they are, but we are quickened and made sensitive and vigorous unto righteousness: through our Lord's death we are made quick of eye, and quick of thought, and quick of lip, and quick of heart unto righteousness. Certainly, if the doctrine of His atoning sacrifice does not vivify us, nothing will. When we sin, it is the sorrowful result of our former death; but when we work righteousness, we throw our whole soul into it, "We live unto righteousness." Because our Divine Lord has died, we feel that we must lay ourselves out for His praise. The tree which brought death to our Savior is a tree of life to us. Sit under this true *arbor vitæ,* and you will shake off the weakness and disease which came in by that tree of knowledge of good and evil. Livingstone in Africa used certain medicines which are known as *Livingstone's Rousers;* but what rousers are those glorious truths which are extracted from the bitter wood of the cross! O my brethren, let us show in our lives what wonders our Lord Jesus has done for us by His agony and bloody sweat, by His cross and passion!

III. The apostle then speaks of the healing of our diseases by Christ's death: "By whose stripes ye were healed. For ye were as sheep going astray; but are now returned unto the Shepherd and Bishop of your souls."

We were healed, and we remain so. It is not a thing to be done in the future; it has been wrought. Peter describes our disease in the words which compose verse twenty-five. What was it, then?

First, it was *brutishness.* "Ye were as sheep." Sin has made us so that we are only fit to be compared to beasts, and to those of the least intelligence. Sometimes the Scripture compares the unregenerate man to an ass. Man is said to be "born like a wild ass's colt." Amos likens Israel to the "kine of Bashan," and he saith to them, "Ye shall go out at the breaches, every cow at that which is before her." David compared himself to behemoth: "So foolish was I, and ignorant: I was as a beast before Thee." We are nothing better than beasts until Christ comes to us. But we are not beasts after that: a living, heavenly, spiritual nature is created within us when we come into contact with our Redeemer. We still carry about with us the old brutish nature, but by the grace of God it is put in subjection, and kept there; and our fellowship now is with the Father, and with His Son Jesus Christ. We "were as sheep," but we are now men redeemed unto God.

We are cured also of the *proneness to wander* which is so remarkable in sheep. "Ye were as sheep going astray," always going astray, loving to go astray, delighting in it, never so happy as when they are wandering away from the fold. We wander still, but not as sheep wander: we now seek the right way, and desire to follow the Lamb whithersoever He goeth. If we wander, it is through ignorance or temptation. We can truly say, "My soul followeth hard after Thee." Our Lord's cross has nailed us fast as to hands and feet: we cannot now run greedily after iniquity; rather do we say, "Return unto thy rest, O my soul; for the Lord hath dealt bountifully with thee!"

> My wanderings, Lord, are at an end,
> I'm now return'd to Thee:
> Be Thou my Father and my Friend,
> Be all in all to me.

Another disease of ours was *inability to return:* "Ye were as sheep going astray; but are now returned." Dogs and even swine are more likely to return home than wandering sheep. But now, beloved, though we wandered, we have returned, and do still return to our Shepherd. Like Noah's dove, we have found no rest for the sole of our foot anywhere out of the ark, and therefore we return unto Him, and He graciously pulls us in unto Him. If we wander at any time, we bless God that there is a sacred something within us which will not let us rest, and there is a far more powerful something above us which draws us back. We are like the needle in the compass: touch that needle with your finger, and compel it to point to the east, or to the south, and it may do so for the moment; but take away the pressure, and in an instant it returns to the pole. So we must go back to Jesus; we must return to the bishop of our souls. Our soul cries, "Whom have I in Heaven but Thee? and there is none upon Earth that I desire beside Thee." Thus, by the virtue of our Lord's death, an immortal love is created in us, which leads us to seek His face, and renew our fellowship with Him.

Our Lord's death has also cured us of our *readiness to follow other leaders*. If one sheep goes through a gap in the hedge, the whole flock will follow. We have been accustomed to follow ringleaders in sin, or in error: we have been too ready to follow custom, and to do that which is judged proper, respectable, and usual: but now we are resolved to follow none but Jesus, according to His word, "My sheep hear My voice, and I know them, and they follow Me. A stranger will they not follow, but will flee from him: for they know not the voice of strangers." For my own part, I am resolved to follow no human leader. Faith in Jesus creates a sacred independence of mind. We have learned so entire a dependence upon our crucified Lord that we have none to spare for men.

Finally, beloved friends, when we were wandering we were like sheep *exposed to wolves,* but we are delivered from this by being near the Shepherd. We were in danger of death, in danger from the devil, in danger from a thousand temptations, which, like ravenous beasts, prowled around us. Having ended our wandering, we are now in a place of safety. When the lion roars, we are driven the closer to the Shepherd, and rejoice that His crook protects us. He says, "My sheep hear My voice, and I know them, and they follow Me: and I give unto them eternal life; and they shall never perish, neither shall any man pluck them out of My hand."

What a wonderful work of grace has been wrought in us! We owe all this, not to the teaching of Christ, though that has helped us greatly; not to the example of Christ, though that is charming us into a diligent copying of it; but we owe it all to His stripes: "By whose stripes ye were healed." Brethren, we preach Christ crucified, because we have been saved by Christ crucified. His death is the death of our sins. We can never give up the doctrine of Christ's substitutionary sacrifice, for it is the power by which we hope to be made holy. Not only are we washed from guilt in His blood, but by that blood we overcome sin. Never, so long as breath or pulse remains, can we conceal the blessed truth that He "His own self bare our sins in His own body on the tree, that we, being dead to sins, should live unto righteousness." The Lord give us to know much more of this than I can speak, for Jesus Christ's sake! Amen.

Redeemed Souls Freed from Fear

"Fear not: for I have redeemed thee."—Isaiah 43:1.

I was lamenting this morning my unfitness for my work, and especially for the warfare to which I am called. A sense of heaviness came over me, but relief came very speedily, for which I thank the Lord. Indeed, I was greatly burdened, but the Lord succored me. The first verse read at the Sabbath morning service exactly met my case. It is in Isaiah 43:1, "But now thus saith the Lord that created thee, O Jacob, and He that formed thee, O Israel, 'Fear not.'" I said to myself, "I am what God created me, and I am what He formed me, and therefore I must, after all, be the right man for the place wherein He has put me." We may not blame our Creator, nor suspect that He has missed His mark in forming an instrument for His work. Thus new comfort comes to us. Not only do the operations of grace in the spiritual world yield us consolation, but we are even comforted by what the Lord has done in creation. We are told to cease from our fears; and we do so, since we perceive that it is the Lord that made us, and not we ourselves, and He will justify His own creating skill by accomplishing through us the purposes of His love. Pray, I beseech you, for me, the weakest of my Lord's servants, that I may be equal to the overwhelming task imposed upon me.

The next sentence of the chapter is usually most comforting to my soul, although on this one occasion the first sentence was a specially reviving cordial to me. The verse goes on to say,—

Fear not: for I have redeemed thee.

Let us think for a few minutes of the wonderful depth of consolation which lies in this fact. We have been redeemed by the Lord Himself, and this is a grand reason why we should never again be subject to fear. Oh, that the logic of this fact could be turned into practice, so that we henceforth rejoiced, or at least felt the peace of God!

These words may be spoken, first of all, of those frequent occasions in which the Lord has redeemed His people out of *trouble*. Many a time and oft might our Lord say to each one of us, "I have redeemed thee." Out of six, yea, six thousand trials He has brought us forth by the right hand of His power. He has released us from our afflictions, and brought us forth into a wealthy place. In the remembrance of all these redemptions the Lord seems to say to us,

> What I have done before, I will do again. I have redeemed thee, and I will still redeem thee. I have brought thee from under the hand of the oppressor; I have delivered thee from the tongue of the slanderer; I have borne thee up under the load of poverty, and sustained thee under the pains of sickness; and I am able still to do the same: wherefore, then, dost thou fear? Why shouldst thou be afraid, since already I have again and again redeemed thee? Take heart, and be confident; for even to old age and to death itself I will continue to be thy strong Redeemer.

I suppose there would be a reference here to the great redemption out of Egypt. This word is addressed to the people of God under captivity in Babylon, and we know that the Lord referred to the Egyptian redemption; for He says in the third verse, "I gave Egypt for thy ransom." Egypt was a great country, and a rich country, for we read of "all the treasures of Egypt," but God gave them for His chosen: He would give all the nations of the Earth for His Israel. This was a wonderful stay to the people of God: they constantly referred to Egypt and the Red Sea, and made their national song out of it. In all Israel's times of disaster, and calamity, and trial, they joyfully remembered that the Lord had redeemed them when they were a company of slaves, helpless and hopeless, under a tyrant who cast their firstborn children into the Nile, a tyrant whose power was so tremendous that all the armies of the world could not have wrought their deliverance from his iron hand. The very nod of Pharaoh seemed to the inhabitants of Egypt to be omnipotent; he was a builder of pyramids, a master of all the sciences of peace and the arts of war. What could the Israelites have done against him? Jehovah came to their relief in their dire extremity. His plagues followed each other in quick succession. The dread volleys of the Lord's artillery confounded His foes. At last He smote all the firstborn of Egypt, the chief of all their strength. Then was Egypt glad that Israel departed, and the Lord brought forth His people with silver and gold. All the chivalry of Egypt was overthrown and destroyed at the Red Sea, and the timbrels of the daughters of Israel sounded joyously upon its shores. This redemption out of Egypt is so remarkable that it is remembered even in Heaven. The Old Testament song is woven into that of the New Covenant; for there they "sing the song of Moses the servant of God, and the song of the Lamb." The first redemption was so wonderful a type and prophecy of the other that it is no alloy to the golden hymn of eternal glory, but readily melts into the same celestial chant. Other types may cease to be remembered, but this was so much a fact as well as a type that it shall be had in memory forever and ever. Every Israelite ought to have had confidence in God after what He had done for the people in redeeming them out of Egypt. To every one of the seed of Jacob it was a grand argument to enforce the precept, "Fear not."

But I take it that the chief reference of these words is to that redemption which has been wrought out for us by Him who loved us, and washed us from our sins in His own blood. Let us think of it for a minute or two before we break the bread and drink of the cup of communion.

The remembrance of this transcendent redemption ought to comfort us in all times of *perplexity*. When we cannot see our way, or cannot make out what to do, we need not be at all troubled concerning it; for the Lord Jehovah can see a way out of every intricacy. There never was a problem so hard to solve as that which is answered in redemption. Herein was the tremendous difficulty—how can God be just, and yet be the Savior of sinners? How can He fulfill His threatenings; and yet forgive sin? If that problem had been left to angels and men, they could never have worked it out throughout eternity; but God has solved it through freely delivering up His own Son. In the glorious sacrifice of Jesus we see the justice of God magnified; for He laid sin on the blessed Lord, who had become one with His chosen. Jesus identified Himself with His people, and therefore their sin was laid upon Him, and the sword of the Lord awoke against Him. He was not taken arbitrarily to be a victim, but He was a voluntary Sufferer. His relationship amounted to covenant oneness with His people, and "it behooved Christ to suffer." Herein is a wisdom which must be more than equal to all minor perplexities. Hear this, then, O poor soul in suspense! The Lord says, "I have redeemed thee. I have already brought thee out of the labyrinth in which thou wast lost by sin, and therefore I will take thee out of the meshes of the net of temptation, and lead thee through the maze of trial; I will bring the blind by a way that they know not, and lead them in paths which they have not known. I will bring again from Bashan, I will bring up My people from the depths of the sea." Let us commit our way unto the Lord. Mine is a peculiarly difficult one, but I know that my Redeemer liveth, and He will lead me by a right way. He will be our Guide even unto death; and after death He will guide us through those tracks unknown of the mysterious region, and cause us to rest with Him forever.

So also, if at any time we are in great *poverty*, or in great straitness of means for the Lord's work, and we are, therefore, afraid that we shall never get our needs supplied, let us cast off such fears as we listen to the music of these words: "Fear not: for I have redeemed thee." God Himself looked down from Heaven, and saw that there was no man who could give to Him a ransom for his brother, and each man on his own part was hopelessly bankrupt; and then, despite our spiritual beggary, He found the means of our redemption. What then? Let us hear the use which the Holy Spirit makes of this fact: "He that spared not His own Son, but delivered Him up for us all, how shall He not with Him also freely give us all things"? We cannot have a want which the Lord will not supply. Since God has given us Jesus, He will give us, not some things, but "all things." Indeed, all things are ours in Christ Jesus. No necessity of this life can for a single moment be compared to that dread necessity which the Lord has already supplied. The infinite gift of God's own Son is a far greater one than all that can be included in the term "all things": wherefore, it is a grand argument to the poor and needy, "Fear not: for I have redeemed thee." Perplexity and poverty are thus effectually met.

We are at times troubled by a sense of our personal *insignificance*. It seems too much to hope that God's infinite mind should enter into our mean affairs. Though David said, "I am poor and needy, yet the Lord thinketh upon me," we are not always quite prepared to say the same. We make our sorrows great under the vain idea that they are too small for the Lord to notice. I believe that our greatest miseries spring from those little worries which we hesitate to bring to our heavenly Father. Our gracious God puts an end to all such thoughts as these by saying, "Fear not: for I have redeemed thee." You are not of such small account as you suppose. The Lord would never be wasteful of His sacred expenditure. He bought you with a price, and therefore He sets great store by you. Listen to what the Lord says: "Since thou wast precious in My sight, thou hast been honorable, and I have loved thee: therefore will I give men for thee, and people for thy life." It is amazing that the Lord should think so much of us as to give Jesus for us. "What is man that Thou art mindful of him?" Yet God's mind is filled with thoughts of love towards man. Know ye not that His only-begotten Son entered this world, and became a man? The man Christ Jesus has a name at which every knee shall bow, and He is so dear to the Father that, for His sake, His chosen ones are accepted, and are made to enjoy the freest access to Him. We sing truly,

> *So near, so very near to God,*
> *Nearer we cannot be,*
> *For in the person of His Son*
> *We are as near as He.*

And now the very hairs of our head are all numbered, and the least burden we may roll upon the Lord. Those cares which we ought not to have may well cease, for "He careth for us." He that redeemed us never forgets us: His wounds have graven us upon the palms of His hands, and written our names deep in His side. Jesus stoops to our level, for He stooped to bear the cross to redeem us. Do not, therefore, be again afraid because of your insignificance.

> Why sayest thou, O Jacob, and speakest, O Israel, "My way is hid from the Lord, and my judgment is passed over from my God?" Hast thou not known? Hast thou not heard, that the everlasting God, the Lord, the Creator of the ends of the earth, fainteth not, neither is weary? There is no searching of His understanding. He giveth power to the faint; and to them that have no might He increaseth strength.

The Lord's memory is toward the little in Israel. He carrieth the lambs in His bosom.

We are liable to fret a little when we think of our *changeableness*. If you are at all like me, you are very far from being always alike; I am sometimes lifted up to the very heavens, and then I go down to the deeps; I am at one time bright with joy and confidence, and at another time dark as midnight with doubts and fears. Even Elijah, who was so brave, had his fainting fits. We are to be blamed for this, and yet the fact remains: our experience is as an April day, when shower and sunshine take their turns. Amid our mournful changes we rejoice to hear the Lord's own voice, saying, "Fear not: for I have redeemed thee." Everything is not changeful wave; there is rock somewhere. Redemption is a fact accomplished.

The Cross, it standeth fast. Hallelujah!

The price is paid, the ransom accepted. This is done, and can never be undone. Jesus says, "I have redeemed thee." Change of feeling within does not alter the fact that the believer has been bought with a price, and made the Lord's own by the precious blood of Jesus. The Lord God has already done so much for us that our salvation is sure in Christ Jesus. Will He begin to build, and fail to finish? Will He lay the foundation in the everlasting covenant? Will

He dedicate the walls with the infinite sacrifice of the Lamb of God? Will He give up the choicest treasure He ever had, the chosen of God and precious, to be the cornerstone, and then not finish the work He has begun? It is impossible. If He has redeemed us, He has, in that act, given us the pledge of all things.

See how the gifts of God are bound to this redemption. "I have redeemed thee. I have called thee."

> For whom He did foreknow, He also did predestinate to be conformed to the image of His Son, that He might be the firstborn among many brethren. Moreover whom He did predestinate, them He also called: and whom He called, them He also justified: and whom He justified, them He also glorified.

Here is a chain in which each link is joined to all the rest, so that it cannot be separated. If God had only gone so far as to make a promise, He would not have drawn back from it; if God had gone as far as to swear an oath by Himself, He would not have failed to keep it; but when He went beyond promise and oath, and in very deed the sacrifice was slain, and the covenant was ratified: why, then it would be blasphemous to imagine that He would afterwards disannul it, and turn from His solemn pledge. There is no going back on the part of God, and consequently His redemption will redeem, and in redeeming it will secure us all things. "Who shall separate us from the love of Christ?" With the blood-mark upon us we may well cease to fear. How can we perish? How can we be deserted in the hour of need? We have been bought with too great a price for our Redeemer to let us slip. Therefore, let us march on with confidence, hearing our Redeemer say to us, "When thou passest through the waters, I will be with thee; and through the rivers, they shall not overflow thee: when thou walkest through the fire, thou shalt not be burned; neither shall the flame kindle upon thee." Concerning His redeemed, the Lord will say to the enemy, "Touch not Mine anointed, and do My prophets no harm." The stars in their courses fight for the ransomed of the Lord. If their eyes were opened, they would see the mountain full of horses of fire and chariots of fire round about them. Oh, how my weary heart prizes redeeming love! If it were not for this, I would lay me down, and die. Friends forsake me, foes surround me, I am filled with contempt, and tortured with the subtlety which I cannot baffle; but as the Lord of all brought again from the dead our Lord Jesus, that great Shepherd of the sheep, by the blood of the everlasting covenant, so by the blood of His covenant doth He loose His prisoners, and sustain the hearts of those who tremble at His Word. "O my soul, thou hast trodden down strength," for the Lord hath said unto thee, "Fear not: for I have redeemed thee."

The Believer Not an Orphan

"I will not leave you comfortless: I will come to you."—John 14:18.

You will notice that the margin reads, "I will not leave you orphans: I will come to you." In the absence of our Lord Jesus Christ, the disciples were like children deprived of their parents. During the three years in which He had been with them, He had solved all their difficulties, borne all their burdens, and supplied all their needs. Whenever a case was too hard or too heavy for them, they took it to Him. When their enemies well nigh overcame them, Jesus came to the rescue, and turned the tide of battle. They were all happy and safe enough whilst the Master was with them; He walked in their midst like a father amid a large family of children, making all the household glad. But now He was about to be taken from them by an ignominious death, and they might well feel that they would be like little children deprived of their natural and beloved protector. Our Savior knew the fear that was in their hearts, and before they could express it, He removed it by saying, "You shall not be left alone in this wild and desert world; though I be absent in the flesh, yet I will be present with you in a more efficacious manner; I will come to you spiritually, and you shall derive from My spiritual presence even more good than you could have had from My bodily presence, had I still continued in your midst."

Observe, first, here is *an evil averted:* "I will not leave you orphans;" and, in the second place, here is *a consolation provided:* "I will come to you."

I. First, here is, an evil averted.

Without their Lord, believers would, apart from the Holy Spirit, be like other orphans, unhappy and desolate. Give them what you might, their loss could not have been recompensed. No number of lamps can make up for the sun's absence; blaze as they may, it is still night. No circle of friends can supply to a bereaved woman the loss of her husband; without him, she is still a widow. Even thus, without Jesus, it is inevitable that the saints should be as orphans; but Jesus has promised in the text that we shall not be so; the only thing that can remove the trial He declares shall be ours, "I will come to you."

Now remember, that *an orphan is one whose parent is dead.* This in itself is a great sorrow, if there were no other. The dear father, so well beloved, was suddenly smitten down with sickness; they watched him with anxiety; they nursed him with sedulous care; but he expired. The loving eye is closed in darkness for them. That active hand will no longer toil for the family, that heart and brain will no longer feel and think for them. Beneath the green grass the father sleeps, and every time the child surveys that hallowed hillock his heart swells with grief. Beloved, we are not orphans in that sense, for our Lord Jesus is not dead. It is true He died, for one of the soldiers with a spear pierced His side, and forthwith came thereout blood and water, a sure evidence that the pericardium had been pierced, and that the fountain of life had been broken up. He died, 'tis certain, but He is not dead now. Go not to the grave to seek Him. Angel voices say, "He is not here, for He is risen." He could not be holden by the bands of death. We do not worship a dead Christ, nor do we even think of Him now as a corpse. That picture on the wall, which the Romanists paint and worship, represents Christ as dead; but oh! it is so good to think of Christ as living, remaining in an existence real and true, none the less living because He died, but all the more truly full of life because He has passed through the portals of the grave, and is now reigning forever. See then, dear friends, the bitter root of the orphan's sorrow is gone from us, for our Jesus is not dead now. No mausoleum enshrines His ashes, no pyramid entombs His body, no monument records the place of His permanent sepulcher.

> He lives, the great Redeemer lives,
> What joy the blest assurance gives!

We are not orphans, for "the Lord is risen indeed."

The orphan has a sharp sorrow springing out of the death of his parent, namely, that *he is left alone.* He cannot now make appeals to the wisdom of the parent who could direct him. He cannot run, as once he did, when he was weary, to climb the paternal knee. He cannot lean his aching head upon the parental bosom. "Father," he may say, but no voice gives an answer. "Mother," he may cry, but that fond title, which would awaken the mother if she slept, cannot arouse her from the bed of death. The child is alone, alone as to those two hearts which were its best companions. The parent and lover are gone. The little ones know what it is to be deserted and forsaken. But we are not so; we are not orphans. It is true Jesus is not here in body, but His spiritual presence is quite as blessed as His bodily presence would have been. Nay, it is better, for supposing Jesus Christ to be here in person, you could not all come and touch the hem of His garment,—not all at once, at any rate. There might be thousands waiting all the world over to speak with Him; but how could they all reach Him, if He were merely here in body? You might all be wanting to tell Him something, but in the body He could only receive some one or two of you at a time.

But in spirit there is no need for you to stir from the pew, no need to say a word; Jesus hears your thoughts talk, and attends to all your needs at the same moment. No need to press to get at Him because the throng is great, for He is as near to me as He is to you, and as near to you as to saints in America, or the islands of the Southern Sea. He is everywhere present, and all His beloved may talk with Him. You can tell Him at this moment the sorrows which you dare not open up to anyone else. You will feel that, in declaring them to Him, you have not breathed them to the air, but that a real Person has heard you, One as real as though you could grip His hand, and could see the loving flash of His eye and mark the sympathetic change of His countenance.

Is it not so with you, ye children of a living Savior? You know it is; you have a Friend that sticketh closer than a brother. You have a near and dear One, who, in the dead of the night is in the chamber, and in the heat and burden of the day is in the field of labor. You are not orphans, the "Wonderful, Counselor, the mighty God, the Everlasting Father, the Prince of Peace," is with you; your Lord is here; and, as one whom his mother comforteth, so Jesus comforts you.

The orphan, too, has *lost the kind hand which took care always that food and raiment should be provided, that the table should be well stored, and that the house should be kept in comfort.* Poor feeble one, who will provide for his wants? His father is dead, his mother is gone: who will take care of the little wanderer now? But it is not so with us. Jesus has not left us orphans; His care for His people is no less now than it was when He sat at the table with Mary, and Martha, and Lazarus, whom "Jesus loved." Instead of the provisions being less, they are even greater, for since the Holy Spirit has been given to us, we have richer fare and are more indulged with spiritual comforts than believers were before the bodily presence of the Master had departed. Do your souls hunger tonight?

Jesus gives you the bread of Heaven. Do you thirst tonight? The waters from the rock cease not to flow.

Come, make your wants, your burdens known.

You have but to make known your needs to have them all supplied. Christ waits to be gracious in the midst of this assembly. He is here with His golden hand, opening that hand to supply the wants of every living soul. "Oh!" saith one, "I am poor and needy." Go on with the quotation. "Yet the Lord thinketh upon me." "Ah!" saith another, "I have besought the Lord thrice to take away a thorn in the flesh from me." Remember what he said to Paul, "My grace is sufficient for thee." You are not left without the strength you want. The Lord is your Shepherd still. He will provide for you till He leads you through death's dark valley, and brings you to the shining pastures upon the hilltops of glory. You are not destitute, you need not beg an asylum from an ungodly world by bowing to its demands, or trusting its vain promises, for Jesus will never leave you nor forsake you.

The orphan, too, is *left without the instruction which is most suitable for a child.* We may say what we will, but there is none so fit to form a child's character as the parent. It is a very sad loss for a child to have lost either father or mother in its early days; for the most skillful preceptor, though he may do much, by the blessing of God very much, is but a stop-gap, and but half makes up for the original ordinance of Providence, that the parent's love should fashion the child's mind. But, dear friends, we are not orphans; we who believe in Jesus are not left without an education. Jesus is not here Himself, it is true. I dare say some of you wish you could come on Lord's-days, and listen to Him! Would it not be sweet to look up to this pulpit, and see the Crucified One, and to hear Him preach? Ah! so you think, but the apostle says, "Though we have known Christ after the flesh, yet now henceforth know we Him no more."

It is most for your profit that you should receive the Spirit of truth, not through the golden vessel of Christ in His actual presence here, but through the poor earthen vessels of humble servants of God like ourselves. At any rate, whether *we* speak, or an angel from Heaven, the speaker matters not; it is the Spirit of God alone that is the power of the Word, and makes that Word to become vital and quickening to you. Now, you have the Spirit of God. The Holy Spirit is so given, that there is not a truth which you may not understand. You may be led into the deepest mysteries by His teaching. You may be made to know and to comprehend those knotty points in the Word of God which have hitherto puzzled you. You have but humbly to look up to Jesus, and His Spirit will still teach you. I tell you, though you are poor and ignorant, and perhaps can scarcely read a word in the Bible; for all that, you may be better instructed in the things of God than doctors of divinity, if you go to the Holy Spirit, and are taught of Him. Those who go only to books and to the letter, and are taught of men, may be fools in the sight of God; but those who go to Jesus, and sit at His feet, and ask to be taught of His Spirit, shall be wise unto salvation. Blessed be God, there are not a few amongst us of this sort. We are not left orphans; we have an Instructor with us still.

There is one point in which the orphan is often sorrowfully reminded of his orphanhood, namely, *in lacking a defender.* It is so natural in little children, when some big boy molests them, to say, "I'll tell my father!" How often did we use to say so, and how often have we heard from the little ones since, "I'll tell mother!" Sometimes, the not being able to do this is a much severer loss than we can guess. Unkind and cruel men have snatched away from orphans the little which a father's love had left behind; and in the court of law there has been no defender to protect the orphan's goods. Had the father been there, the child would have had its rights, scarcely would any have dared to infringe them; but, in the absence of the father, the orphan is eaten up like bread, and the wicked of the Earth devour his estate. In this sense, the saints are not orphans. The devil would rob us of our heritage if he could, but there is an Advocate with the Father who pleads for us. Satan would snatch from us every promise, and tear from us all the comforts of the covenant; but we are not orphans, and when he brings a suit-at-law against us, and thinks that we are the only defendants in the case, he is mistaken, for we have an Advocate on high. Christ comes in and pleads, as the sinners' Friend, for us; and when *He* pleads at the bar of justice, there is no fear but that His plea will be of effect, and our inheritance shall be safe. He has not left us orphans.

Now I want, without saying many words, to get you who love the Master to feel what a very precious thought this is, that you are not alone in this world; that, if you have no earthly friends, if you have none to whom you can take your cares, if you are quite lonely so far as outward friends are concerned, yet Jesus is with you, is really with you, practically with you, able to help you, and ready to do so, and that you have a good and kind Protector close at hand at this present moment, for Christ has said it: "I will not leave you orphans."

II. Secondly, there is a consolation provided.

The remedy by which the evil is averted is this, our Lord Jesus said, "I will come to you."

What does this mean? Does it not mean, from the connection, this—"I will come to you by My Spirit"? Beloved, we must not confuse the Persons of the Godhead. The Holy Spirit is not the Son of God; Jesus, the Son of God, is not the Holy Spirit. They are two distinct Persons of the one Godhead. But yet there is such a wonderful unity, and the blessed Spirit acts so marvelously as the Vicar of Christ, that it is quite correct to say that, when the Spirit comes, Jesus comes, too, and "I will come to you," means—"I, by My Spirit, who shall take My place, and represent Me, I will come to be with you." See then, Christian, you have the Holy Spirit in you and with you to be the Representative of Christ. Christ is with you now, not in person, but by His Representative—an efficient, almighty, divine, everlasting Representative, who stands for Christ, and is as Christ to you in His presence in your souls. Because you thus have Christ by His Spirit, you cannot be orphans, for the Spirit of God is always with you. It is a delightful truth that the Spirit of God always dwells in believers;—not sometimes, but always. He is not always active in believers, and He may be grieved until His sensible presence is altogether withdrawn, but His secret presence is always there. At no single moment is the Spirit of God wholly gone from a believer. The believer would die spiritually if this could happen, but that cannot be, for Jesus has said, "Because I live, ye shall live also." Even when the believer sins, the Holy Spirit does not utterly depart from him, but is still in him to make him smart for the sin into which he has fallen. The believer's prayers prove that the Holy Spirit is still within him. "Take not Thy Holy Spirit from me," was the prayer of a saint who had fallen very foully, but in whom the Spirit of God still kept His residence, notwithstanding all the foulness of his guilt and sin.

But, beloved, in addition to this, Jesus Christ by His Spirit *makes visits to His people of a peculiar kind.* The Holy Ghost becomes wonderfully active and potent at certain times of refreshing. We are then especially and joyfully sensible of His divine power. His influence streams through every chamber of our nature, and floods our dark soul with His glorious rays, as the sun shining in its strength. Oh, how delightful this is! Sometimes we have felt this at the Lord's table. My soul pants to sit with you at that table, because I do remember many a happy time when the emblems of bread and wine have assisted my faith, and kindled the passions of my soul into a heavenly flame. I am equally sure that, at the prayer meeting, under the preaching of the Word, in private meditation, and in searching the Scriptures, we can say that Jesus Christ has come to us. What! have you no hill Mizar to remember?

> *No Tabor-visits to recount,*
> *When with Him in the Holy Mount?*

Oh, yes! some of these blessed seasons have left their impress upon our memories, so that, amongst our dying thoughts, will mingle the remembrance of those blessed seasons when Jesus Christ manifested Himself unto us as He doth not unto the world. Oh, to be wrapped in that crimson vest, closely pressed to His open side! Oh, to put our finger into the print of nails, and thrust our hand into His side! We know what this means by past experience.

> *Dear Shepherd of Thy chosen few,*
> *Thy former mercies here renew.*

Permit us once again to feel the truth of the promise, "I will not leave you orphans; I will come to you,"

And now, gathering up the few thoughts I have uttered, let me remind you, dear friends, that *every word of the text is instructive:* "I will not leave you orphans: I will come to you." Observe the "I" there twice over.

> I will not leave you orphans; father and mother may, but I will not; friends once beloved may turn stony-hearted, but I will not; Judas may play the traitor, and Ahithophel may betray his David, but I will not leave you comfortless. You have had many disappointments, great heart-breaking sorrows, but I have never caused you any; I—the faithful and the true Witness, the immutable, the unchangeable Jesus, the same yesterday, today, and forever, I will not leave you comfortless; *I* will come unto you.

Catch at that word, "I," and let your souls say,

> Lord, I am not worthy that Thou shouldest come under my roof; if Thou hadst said, "I will send an angel to thee," it would have been a great mercy, but what sayest Thou, "I will come unto thee"? If Thou hadst bidden some of my brethren come and speak a word of comfort to me, I had been thankful, but Thou hast put it thus in the first person, "I will come unto you." O my Lord, what shall I say, what shall I do, but feel a hungering and a thirsting after Thee, which nothing shall satisfy till Thou shalt fulfill Thine own Word, 'I will not leave you comfortless; I will come to you'?

And then notice the persons to whom it is addressed, "I will not leave *you* comfortless, you, Peter, who will deny Me; *you*, Thomas, who will doubt Me; I will not leave *you* comfortless." O you who are so little in Israel that you sometimes think it is a pity that your name is in the church-book at all, because you feel yourselves to be so worthless, so unworthy, He will not leave *you* comfortless, not even *you!* "O Lord," thou sayest,

> if Thou wouldst look after the rest of Thy sheep, I would bless Thee for Thy tenderness to them, but I—I deserve to be left; if I were forsaken of Thee, I could not blame Thee, for I have played the harlot against Thy love, but yet Thou sayest, "I will not leave you."

Heir of Heaven, do not lose your part in this promise. I pray you say,

> Lord, come unto me, and though Thou refresh all my brethren, yet, Lord, refresh me with some of the droppings of Thy love; O Lord, fill the cup for me; my thirsty spirit pants for it.
>
> > *I thirst, I faint, I die to prove*
> > *The greatness of redeeming love,*
> > *The love of Christ to me.*
>
> Now, Lord, fulfill Thy word to Thine unworthy handmaid, as I stand like Hannah in Thy presence. Come unto me, Thy servant, unworthy to lift so much as his eyes towards Heaven, and only daring to say, "God be merciful to me a sinner." Fulfill Thy promise even to me, "I will not leave you comfortless; I will come to you."

Take whichever of the words you will, and they each one sparkle and flash after this sort. Observe, too, *the richness and sufficiency of the text:* "I will not leave you comfortless: I will come to you." He does not promise, "I will send you sanctifying grace, or sustaining mercy, or precious mercy," but He says, what is the only thing that will prevent your being orphans, "I will come to you." Ah! Lord, Thy grace is sweet, but Thou art better. The vine is good, but the clusters are better. It is well enough to have a gift from Thy hand, but oh! to touch the hand itself. It is well enough to hear the words of Thy lips, but oh! to kiss those lips as the spouse did in the Song, this is better still. You know, if there be an orphan child, you cannot prevent its continuing an orphan. You may feel great kindness towards it, supply its wants, and do all you possibly can towards it, but it is an orphan still. It must get its father and its mother back, or else it will still be an orphan. So, our blessed Lord, knowing this, does not say, "I will do this and that for you," but, "I will come to you."

Do you not see, dear friends, here is not only all you can want, but all you think you can want, wrapped up in a sentence, "I will come to you"? "It pleased the Father that in Him should all fullness dwell"; so that, when Christ comes, in

Him "all fullness" comes. "In Him dwelleth all the fullness of the Godhead bodily," so that, when Jesus comes, the very Godhead comes to the believer.

All my capacious powers can wish
In Thee doth richly meet;

and if Thou shalt come to me, it is better than all the gifts of Thy covenant. If I get Thee, I get all, and more than all, at once. Observe, then, the language and the sufficiency of the promise.

But I want you to notice, further, *the continued freshness and force of the promise.* Somebody here owes another person fifty pounds, and he gives him a note of hand, "I promise to pay you fifty pounds." Very well! the man calls with that note of hand tomorrow, and gets fifty pounds. And what is the good of the note of hand now? Why, it is of no further value, it is discharged. How would you like to have a note of hand which would always stand good? That would be a right royal present. "I promise to pay evermore, and this bond, though paid a thousand times, shall still hold good." Who would not like to have a check of that sort? Yet this is the promise which Christ gives you, "I will not leave you orphans: I will come to you." The first time a sinner looks to Christ, Christ comes to him. And what then? Why, the next minute it is still, "I will come to you." But here is one who has known Christ for fifty years, and he has had this promise fulfilled a thousand times a year: is it not done with? Oh, no! there it stands, just as fresh as when Jesus first spoke it, "I will come to you." Then we will treat our Lord in His own fashion, and take Him at His word. We will go to Him as often as ever we can, for we shall never weary Him; and when He has kept His promise most, then is it that we will go to Him, and ask Him to keep it more still; and after ten thousand proofs of the truth of it, we will only have a greater hungering and thirsting to get it fulfilled again. This is fit provision for life, and for death, "I will come to you." In the last moment, when your pulse beats faintly, and you are just about to pass the curtain, and enter into the invisible world, you may have this upon your lips, and say to your Lord, "My Master, still fulfill the word on which Thou hast caused me to hope, 'I will not leave you comfortless: I will come to you.'"

Let me remind you that *the text is at this moment valid,* and for this I delight in it. "I will not leave you comfortless." That means now, "I will not leave you comfortless *now.*" Are you comfortless at this hour? It is your own fault. Jesus Christ does not leave you so, nor make you so. There are rich and precious things in this word, "I will not leave you comfortless: I will come to you, I will come to you now." It may be a very dull time with you, and you are pining to come nearer to Christ. Very well, then plead the promise before the Lord. Plead the promise as you sit where you are: "Lord, Thou hast said Thou wilt come unto me; come unto me tonight." There are many reasons, believer, why you should plead thus. You want Him; you need Him; you require Him; therefore plead the promise, and expect its fulfillment. And oh! when He cometh, what a joy it is; He is as a bridegroom coming out of his chamber with his garments fragrant with aloes and cassia! How well the oil of joy will perfume your heart! How soon will your sackcloth be put away, and the garments of gladness adorn you! With what joy of heart will your heavy soul begin to sing when Jesus Christ shall whisper that you are His, and that He is yours! Come, my Beloved, make no tarrying; be Thou like a roe or a young hart upon the mountains of separation, and prove to me Thy promise true, "I will not leave you orphans: I will come to you."

And now, dear friends, in conclusion, let me remind you that *there are many who have no share in the text.* What can I say to such? From my soul I pity you who do not know what the love of Christ means. Oh! If you could but tell the joy of God's people, you would not rest an hour without it.

> *His worth, if all the nations knew,*
> *Sure the whole world would love Him too.*

Remember, if you would find Christ, He is to be found in the way of faith. Trust Him, and He is yours. Depend upon the merit of His sacrifice; cast yourselves entirely upon that, and you are saved, and Christ is yours.

God grant that we may all break bread in the kingdom above, and feast with Jesus, and share His glory! We are expecting His second coming. He is coming personally and gloriously. This is the brightest hope of His people. This will be the fullness of their redemption, the time of their resurrection. Anticipate it, beloved, and may God make your souls to sing for joy!

> *'Mid the splendors of the glory*
> *Which we hope ere long to share;*
> *Christ our Head, and we His members,*
> *Shall appear, divinely fair.*
> *Oh, how glorious!*
> *When we meet Him in the air!*
>
> *Bright the prospect soon that greets us*
> *Of that long'd-for nuptial day,*
> *When our heavenly Bridegroom meets us*
> *On His kingly, conquering way;*
> *In the glory,*
> *Bride and Bridegroom reign for aye!*

Mysterious Visits

"Thou hast visited me in the night."—Psalm 17:3.

It is a theme for wonder that the glorious God should visit sinful man. "What is man, that Thou art mindful of him? and the son of man, that Thou visitest him?" A divine visit is a joy to be treasured whenever we are favored with it. David speaks of it with great solemnity. The Psalmist was not content barely to *speak* of it; but he wrote it down in plain terms, that it might be known throughout all generations: "Thou hast visited me in the night." Beloved, if God has ever visited you, you also will marvel at it, will carry it in your memory, will speak of it to your friends, and will record it in your diary as one of the notable events of your life. Above all, you will speak of it to God Himself, and say with adoring gratitude, "Thou hast visited me in the night." It should be a solemn part of worship to remember and make known the condescension of the Lord, and say, both in lowly prayer and in joyful psalm, "Thou hast visited me."

To you, beloved friends, who gather with me about this communion table, I will speak of my own experience, nothing doubting that it is also yours. If our God has ever visited any of us, personally, by His Spirit, two results have attended the visit: *it has been sharply searching, and it has been sweetly solacing.*

When first of all the Lord draws nigh to the heart, the trembling soul perceives clearly the searching character of His visit. Remember how Job answered the Lord: "I have heard of Thee by the hearing of the ear: but now mine eye seeth Thee, wherefore I abhor myself, and repent in dust and ashes." We can read of God, and hear of God, and be little moved; but when we feel His presence, it is another matter. I thought my house was good enough for kings; but when the King of kings came to it, I saw that it was a hovel quite unfit for His abode. I had never known sin to be so "exceeding sinful" if I had not known God to be so perfectly holy. I had never understood the depravity of my own nature if I had not known the holiness of God's nature. When we see Jesus, we fall at His feet as dead; till then, we are alive with vainglorious life. If letters of light traced by a mysterious hand upon the wall caused the joints of Belshazzar's loins to be loosed, what awe overcomes our spirits when we see the Lord Himself! In the presence of so much light our spots and wrinkles are revealed, and we are utterly ashamed. We are like Daniel, who said, "I was left alone, and saw this great vision, and there remained no strength in me: for my comeliness was turned in me into corruption." It is when the Lord visits us that we see our nothingness, and ask, "Lord, what is man?"

I do remember well when God first visited me; and assuredly it was the night of nature, of ignorance, of sin. His visit had the same effect upon me that it had upon Saul of Tarsus when the Lord spake to him out of Heaven. He brought me down from the high horse, and caused me to fall to the ground; by the brightness of the light of His Spirit He made me grope in conscious blindness; and in the brokenness of my heart I cried, "Lord, what wilt Thou have me to do?" I felt that I had been rebelling against the Lord, kicking against the pricks, and doing evil even as I could; and my soul was filled with anguish at the discovery. Very searching was the glance of the eye of Jesus, for it revealed my sin, and caused me to go out and weep bitterly. As when the Lord visited Adam, and called him to stand naked before Him, so was I stripped of all my righteousness before the face of the Most High. Yet the visit ended not there; for as the Lord God clothed our first parents in coats of skins, so did He cover me with the righteousness of the great sacrifice, and He gave me songs in the night. It was night, but the visit was no dream: in fact, I there and then ceased to dream, and began to deal with the reality of things.

I think you will remember that, when the Lord first visited you in the night, it was with you as with Peter when Jesus came to him. He had been toiling with his net all the night, and nothing had come of it; but when the Lord Jesus came into his boat, and bade him launch out into the deep, and let down his net for a draught, he caught such a great multitude of fishes that the boat began to sink. See! the boat goes down, down, till the water threatens to engulf it, and Peter, and the fish, and all. Then Peter fell down at Jesus' knees, and cried, "Depart from me; for I am a sinful man, O Lord!" The presence of Jesus was too much for him: his sense of unworthiness made him sink like his boat, and shrink away from the Divine

Lord. I remember that sensation well; for I was half inclined to cry with the demoniac of Gadara, "What have I to do with Thee, Jesus, Thou Son of God most high?" That first discovery of His injured love was overpowering; its very hopefulness increased my anguish; for then I saw that I had slain the Lord who had come to save me. I saw that mine was the hand which made the hammer fall, and drove the nails that fastened the Redeemer's hands and feet to the cruel tree.

> *My conscience felt and own'd the guilt,*
> *And plunged me in despair;*
> *I saw my sins His blood had spilt,*
> *And help'd to nail Him there.*

This is the sight which breeds repentance: "They shall look upon Him whom they have pierced, and mourn for Him." When the Lord visits us, He humbles us, removes all hardness from our hearts, and leads us to the Savior's feet.

When the Lord first visited us in the night, it was very much with us as with John, when the Lord visited him in the isle that is called Patmos. He tells us, "And when I saw Him, I fell at His feet as dead." Yes, even when we begin to see that He has put away our sin, and removed our guilt by His death, we feel as if we could never look up again, because we have been so cruel to our best Friend. It is no wonder if we then say, "It is true that He has forgiven me; but I never can forgive myself. He makes me live, and I live in Him; but at the thought of His goodness I fall at His feet as dead. Boasting is dead, self is dead, and all desire for anything beyond my Lord is dead also." Well does Cowper sing of—

> *That dear hour, that brought me to His foot,*
> *And cut up all my follies by the root.*

The process of destroying follies is more hopefully performed at Jesus' feet than anywhere else. Oh, that the Lord would come again to us as at the first, and like a consuming fire discover and destroy the dross which now alloys our gold! The word *visit* brings to us who travel the remembrance of the government officer who searches our baggage; thus doth the Lord seek out our secret things. But it also reminds us of the visits of the physician, who not only finds out our maladies, but also removes them. Thus did the Lord Jesus visit us at the first.

Since those early days, I hope that you and I have had many visits from our Lord. Those first visits were, as I said, sharply searching; but the later ones have been *sweetly solacing*. Some of us have had them, especially in the night, when we have been compelled to count the sleepless hours. "Heaven's gate opens when this world's is shut." The night is still; everybody is away; work is done; care is forgotten, and then the Lord Himself draws near. Possibly there may be pain to be endured, the head may be aching, and the heart may be throbbing; but if Jesus comes to visit us, our bed of languishing becomes a throne of glory. Though it is true "He giveth His beloved sleep," yet at such times He gives them something better than sleep, namely, His own presence, and the fullness of joy which comes with it. By night upon our bed we have seen the unseen. I have tried sometimes not to sleep under an excess of joy, when the company of Christ has been sweetly mine.

"Thou hast visited me in the night." Believe me, there are such things as personal visits from Jesus to His people. He has not left us utterly. Though He be not seen with the bodily eye by bush or brook, nor on the mount, nor by the sea, yet doth He come and go, observed only by the spirit, felt only by the heart. Still he standeth behind our wall, He showeth Himself through the lattices.

> *Jesus, these eyes have never seen*
> *That radiant form of Thine!*
> *The veil of sense hangs dark between*
> *Thy blessed face and mine!*
>
> *I see Thee not, I hear Thee not,*
> *Yet art Thou oft with me,*
> *And Earth hath ne'er so dear a spot*
> *As where I meet with Thee.*
>
> *Like some bright dream that comes unsought,*
> *When slumbers o'er me roll,*
> *Thine image ever fills my thought,*
> *And charms my ravish'd soul.*
>
> *Yet though I have not seen, and still*
> *Must rest in faith alone;*
> *I love Thee, dearest Lord! and will,*
> *Unseen, but not unknown.*

Do you ask me to describe these manifestations of the Lord? It were hard to tell you in words: you must know them for yourselves. If you had never tasted sweetness, no man living could give you an idea of honey. Yet if the honey be there, you can "taste and see." To a man born blind, sight must be a thing past imagination; and to one who has never known the Lord, His visits are quite as much beyond conception.

For our Lord to visit us is something more than for us to have the assurance of our salvation, though that is very delightful, and none of us should rest satisfied unless we possess it. To know that Jesus loves me, is one thing; but to be visited by Him in love, is more.

Nor is it simply a close contemplation of Christ; for we can picture Him as exceedingly fair and majestic, and yet not have Him consciously near us. Delightful and instructive as it is to behold the likeness of Christ by meditation, yet the enjoyment of His actual presence is something more. I may wear my friend's portrait about my person, and yet may not be able to say, "Thou hast visited me."

It is the actual, though spiritual, coming of Christ, which we so much desire. The Romish church says much about the *real* presence; meaning thereby, the corporeal presence of the Lord Jesus. The priest who celebrates mass tells us that he believes in the *real* presence, but we reply, "Nay, you believe in knowing Christ after the flesh, and in that sense the only real presence is in Heaven; but we firmly believe in the real presence of Christ which is spiritual, and yet certain." By spiritual we do not mean unreal; in fact, the spiritual takes the lead in realness to spiritual men. I believe in the true and real presence of Jesus with His people: such presence has been real to my spirit. Lord Jesus, Thou Thyself hast visited me. As surely as the Lord Jesus came really as to His flesh to Bethlehem and Calvary, so surely does He come really by His Spirit to His people in the hours of their communion with Him. We are as conscious of that presence as of our own existence.

When the Lord visits us in the night, what is the effect upon us? When hearts meet hearts in fellowship of love, communion brings first peace, then rest, and then joy of soul. I am speaking of no emotional excitement rising into fanatical rapture; but I speak of sober fact, when I say that the Lord's great heart touches ours, and our heart rises into sympathy with Him.

First, we experience *peace*. All war is over, and a blessed peace is proclaimed; the peace of God keeps our heart and mind by Christ Jesus.

> *Peace! perfect peace! in this dark world of sin?*
> *The blood of Jesus whispers peace within.*

> *Peace! perfect peace! with sorrows surging round?*
> *On Jesus' bosom nought but calm is found.*

At such a time there is a delightful sense of *rest;* we have no ambitions, no desires. A divine serenity and security envelop us. We have no thought of foes, or fears, or afflictions, or doubts. There is a joyous laying aside of our own will. We *are* nothing, and we *will* nothing: Christ is everything, and His will is the pulse of our soul. We are perfectly content either to be ill or to be well, to be rich or to be poor, to be slandered or to be honored, so that we may but abide in the love of Christ. Jesus fills the horizon of our being.

At such a time a flood of great *joy* will fill our minds. We shall half wish that the morning may never break again, for fear its light should banish the superior light of Christ's presence. We shall wish that we could glide away with our Beloved to the place where He feedeth among the lilies. We long to hear the voices of the white-robed armies, that we may follow their glorious Leader whithersoever He goeth. I am persuaded that there is no great actual distance between Earth and Heaven: the distance lies in our dull minds. When the Beloved visits us in the night, He makes our chambers to be the vestibule of His palace halls. Earth rises to Heaven when Heaven comes down to earth.

Now, beloved friends, you may be saying to yourselves, "We have not enjoyed such visits as these." You may do so. If the Father loves you even as He loves His Son, then you are on visiting terms with Him. If, then, He has not called upon you, you will be wise to call on Him. Breathe a sigh to Him, and say—

> *When wilt Thou come unto me, Lord?*
> *Oh come, my Lord most dear!*
> *Come near, come nearer, nearer still,*
> *I'm blest when Thou art near.*
>
> *When wilt Thou come unto me, Lord?*
> *I languish for the sight;*
> *Ten thousand suns when Thou art hid,*
> *Are shades instead of light.*
>
> *When wilt Thou come unto me, Lord?*
> *Until Thou dost appear,*
> *I count each moment for a day,*
> *Each minute for a year.*

"As the hart panteth after the water-brooks, so panteth my soul after Thee, O God!" If you long for Him, He much more longs for you. Never was there a sinner that was half so eager for Christ as Christ is eager for the sinner; nor a saint one-tenth so anxious to behold his Lord as his Lord is to behold him. If thou art running to Christ, He is already near thee. If thou dost sigh for His presence, that sigh is the evidence that He is with thee. He is with thee now: therefore be calmly glad.

Go forth, beloved, and talk with Jesus on the beach, for He oft resorted to the seashore. Commune with Him amid the olive groves so dear to Him in many a night of wrestling prayer. If ever there was a country in which men should see traces of Jesus, next to the Holy Land, this Riviera is the favored spot. It is a land of vines, and figs, and olives, and palms; I have called it "Thy land, O Immanuel." While in this Mentone, I often fancy that I am looking out upon the Lake of Gennesaret, or walking at the foot of the Mount of Olives, or peering into the mysterious gloom of the Garden of Gethsemane. The narrow streets of the old town are such as Jesus traversed, these villages are such as He inhabited. Have your hearts right with Him, and He will visit you often, until everyday you shall walk with God, as Enoch did, and so turn weekdays into Sabbaths, meals into sacraments, homes into temples, and Earth into Heaven. So be it with us! Amen.

Over the Mountains

"My Beloved is mine, and I am His: He feedeth among the lilies. Until the day break, and the shadows flee away, turn, my Beloved, and be Thou like a roe or a young hart upon the mountains of Bether."—Solomon's Song 2:16, 17.

It may be that there are saints who are always at their best, and are happy enough never to lose the light of their Father's countenance. I am not sure that there are such persons, for those believers with whom I have been most intimate have had a varied experience; and those whom I have known, who have boasted of their constant perfectness, have not been the most reliable of individuals. I hope there is a spiritual region attainable where there are no clouds to hide the Sun of our soul; but I cannot speak with positiveness, for I have not traversed that happy land. Every year of my life has had a winter as well as a summer, and every day its night. I have hitherto seen clear shinings and heavy rains, and felt warm breezes and fierce winds. Speaking for the many of my brethren, I confess that though the substance be in us, as in the teil-tree and the oak, yet we do lose our leaves, and the sap within us does not flow with equal vigor at all seasons. We have our downs as well as our ups, our valleys as well as our hills. We are not always rejoicing; we are sometimes in heaviness through manifold trials. Alas! we are grieved to confess that our fellowship with the Well-beloved is not always that of rapturous delight; but we have at times to seek Him, and cry, "Oh, that I knew where I might find Him!" This appears to me to have been in a measure the condition of the spouse when she cried, "Until the day break, and the shadows flee away, turn, my Beloved."

I. These words teach us, first, that communion may be broken.

The spouse had lost the company of her Bridegroom: conscious communion with Him was gone, though she loved her Lord, and sighed for Him. In her loneliness she was sorrowful; but *she had by no means ceased to love Him,* for she calls Him her Beloved, and speaks as one who felt no doubt upon that point. Love to the Lord Jesus may be quite as true, and perhaps quite as strong, when we sit in darkness as when we walk in the light. Nay, *she had not lost her assurance of His love to her,* and of their mutual interest in one another; for she says, "My Beloved is mine, and I am His"; and yet she adds, "Turn, my Beloved." The condition of our graces does not always coincide with the state of our joys. We may be rich in faith and love, and yet have so low an esteem of ourselves as to be much depressed.

It is plain, from this Sacred Canticle, that the spouse may love and be loved, may be confident in her Lord, and be fully assured of her possession of Him, and yet there may for the present be mountains between her and Him. Yes, we may even be far advanced in the divine life, and yet be exiled for a while from conscious fellowship. There are nights for men as well as babes, and the strong know that the sun is hidden quite as well as do the sick and the feeble. Do not, therefore, condemn yourself, my brother, because a cloud is over you; cast not away your confidence; but the rather let faith burn up in the gloom, and let your love resolve to come at your Lord again whatever be the barriers which divide you from Him.

When Jesus is absent from a true heir of Heaven, sorrow will ensue. The healthier our condition, the sooner will that absence be perceived, and the more deeply will it be lamented. This sorrow is described in the text as darkness; this is implied in the expression, *"Until the day break."* Till Christ appears, no day has dawned for us. We dwell in midnight darkness; the stars of the promises and the moon of experience yield no light of comfort till our Lord, like the sun, arises and ends the night. We must have Christ with us, or we are benighted: we grope like blind men for the wall, and wander in dismay.

The spouse also speaks of shadows. "Until the day break, *and the shadows flee away."* Shadows are multiplied by the departure of the sun, and these are apt to distress the timid. We are not afraid of real enemies when Jesus is with us; but when we miss Him, we tremble at a shade. How sweet is that song, "Yea, though I walk through the valley of the shadow of death, I will fear no evil: for Thou art with me; Thy rod and Thy staff they comfort me!" But we change our note when midnight is now come, and Jesus is not with us: then we people the night with terrors: specters, demons, hobgoblins, and things that never existed save in fancy, are apt to swarm about us; and we are in fear where no fear is.

The spouse's worst trouble was that *the back of her Beloved was turned to her,* and so she cried, "Turn, my Beloved." When His face is towards her, she suns herself in His love; but if the light of His countenance is withdrawn, she is sorely troubled. Our Lord turns His face from His people though He never turns His heart from His people. He may even close His eyes in sleep when the vessel is tossed by the tempest, but His heart is awake all the while. Still, it is pain enough to have grieved Him in any degree: it cuts us to the quick to think that we have wounded His tender heart. He is jealous, but never without cause. If He turns His back upon us for a while, He has doubtless a more than sufficient reason. He would not walk contrary to us if we had not walked contrary to Him. Ah, it is sad work this! The presence of the Lord makes this life the preface to the life celestial; but His absence leaves us pining and fainting, neither doth any comfort remain in the land of our banishment. The Scriptures and the ordinances, private devotion and public worship, are all as sundials—most excellent when the sun shines, but of small avail in the dark. O Lord Jesus, nothing can compensate us for Thy loss! Draw near to Thy beloved yet again, for without Thee our night will never end.

> *See! I repent, and vex my soul,*
> *That I should leave Thee so!*
> *Where will those vile affections roll*
> *That let my Savior go?*

When communion with Christ is broken, in all true hearts *there is a strong desire to win it back again.* The man who has known the joy of communion with Christ, if he loses it, will never be content until it is restored. Hast thou ever entertained the Prince Emmanuel? Is He gone elsewhere? Thy chamber will be dreary till He comes back again. "Give me Christ or else I die," is the cry of every spirit that has lost the dear companionship of Jesus. We do not part with such heavenly delights without many a pang. It is not with us a matter of "maybe He will return, and we hope He will"; but it must be, or we faint and die. We cannot live without Him; and this is a cheering sign; for the soul that cannot live without Him shall not live without Him: He comes speedily where life and death hang on His coming. If you must have Christ you shall have Him. This is just how the matter stands: we must drink of this well or die of thirst; we must feed upon Jesus or our spirit will famish.

II. We will now advance a step, and say that when communion with Christ is broken, there are great difficulties in the way of its renewal.

It is much easier to go downhill than to climb to the same height again. It is far easier to lose joy in God than to find the lost jewel. The spouse speaks of "mountains" dividing her from her Beloved: she means that the *difficulties were great.* They were not little hills, but mountains, that closed up her way. Mountains of remembered sin, Alps of backsliding, dread ranges of forgetfulness, ingratitude, worldliness, coldness in prayer, frivolity, pride, unbelief. Ah me, I cannot teach you all the dark geography of this sad experience! Giant walls rose before her like the towering steeps of Lebanon. How could she come at her Beloved?

The dividing difficulties were many as well as great. She does not speak of "a mountain," but of "mountains": Alps rose on Alps, wall after wall. She was distressed to think that in so short a time so much could come between her and Him of whom she sang just now, "His left hand is under my head, and His right hand doth embrace me." Alas, we multiply these mountains of Bether with a sad rapidity! Our Lord is jealous, and we give Him far too much reason for hiding His face. A fault, which seemed so small at the time we committed it, is seen in the light of its own consequences, and then it grows and swells till it towers aloft, and hides the face of the Beloved. Then has our sun gone down, and fear whispers, "Will His light ever return? Will it ever be daybreak? Will the shadows ever flee away?" It is easy to grieve away the heavenly sunlight, but ah, how hard to clear the skies, and regain the unclouded brightness!

Perhaps the worst thought of all to the spouse was the dread that *the dividing barrier might be permanent.* It was high, but it might dissolve; the walls were many, but they might fall; but, alas, they were mountains, and these stand fast for ages! She felt like the Psalmist, when he cried, "My sin is ever before me." The pain of our Lord's absence becomes intolerable when we fear that we are hopelessly shut out from Him. A night one can bear, hoping for the morning; but what if the day should never break? And you and I, if we have wandered away from Christ, and feel that there are ranges of immovable mountains between Him and us, will feel sick at heart. We try to pray, but devotion dies on our lips. We attempt to approach the Lord at the communion-table, but we feel more like Judas than John. At such times we have felt that we would give our eyes once more to behold the Bridegroom's face, and to know that He delights in us as in happier days. Still there stand the awful mountains, black, threatening, impassable; and in the far off land the Life of our life is away, and grieved.

So the spouse seems to have come to the conclusion that *the difficulties in her way were insurmountable by her own power.* She does not even think of herself going over the mountains to her Beloved, but she cries, "Until the day break, and the shadows flee away, turn, my Beloved, and be Thou like a roe or a young hart upon the mountains of Bether." She will not try to climb the mountains, she knows she cannot: if they had been less high, she might have attempted it; but their summits reach to Heaven. If they had been less craggy or difficult, she might have tried to scale them; but these mountains are terrible, and no foot may stand upon their lone crags. Oh, the mercy of utter self-despair! I love to see a soul driven into that close corner, and forced therefore to look to God alone. The end of the creature is the beginning of the Creator. Where the sinner ends the Savior begins. If the mountains can be climbed, we shall have to climb them; but if they are quite impassable, then the soul cries out with the prophet,

> Oh, that Thou wouldest rend the heavens, that Thou wouldest come down, that the mountains might flow down at Thy presence. As when the melting fire burneth, the fire causeth the waters to boil, to make Thy name known to Thine adversaries, that the nations may tremble at Thy presence. When Thou didst terrible things which we looked not for, Thou camest down, the mountains flowed down at Thy presence.

Our souls are lame, they cannot move to Christ, and lo! we turn our strong desires to Him, and fix our hopes alone upon Him; will He not remember us in love, and fly to us as He did to His servant of old when He rode upon a cherub, and did fly, yea, He did fly upon the wings of the wind?

III. Here arises that prayer of the text which fully meets the case.

"Turn, my Beloved, and be Thou like a roe or a young hart upon the mountains of division." Jesus can come to us when we cannot go to Him. The roe and the young hart, or, as you may read it, the gazelle and the ibex, live among the crags of the mountains, and leap across the abyss with amazing agility. For swiftness and sure-footedness they are unrivaled. The sacred poet said, "He maketh my feet like hinds' feet, and setteth me upon my high places," alluding to the feet of those creatures which are so fitted to stand securely on the mountain's side. Our blessed Lord is called, in the title of the twenty-second Psalm, "the Hind of the morning"; and the spouse in this golden Canticle sings, "My Beloved is like a roe or a young hart; behold He cometh, leaping upon the mountains, skipping upon the hills."

Here I would remind you that this prayer is one that we may fairly offer, because *it is the way of Christ to come to us* when our coming to Him is out of the question. "How?" say you. I answer that of old He did this; for we remember "His great love wherewith He loved us even when we were dead in trespasses and in sins." His first coming into the world in human form, was it not because man could never come to God until God had come to him? I hear of no tears, or prayers, or entreaties after God on the part of our first parents; but the offended Lord spontaneously gave the promise that the Seed of the woman should bruise the serpent's head. Our Lord's coming into the world was unbought, unsought, unthought of; he came altogether of His own free will, delighting to redeem.

> *With pitying eyes, the Prince of grace*
> *Beheld our helpless grief;*
> *He saw, and (oh, amazing love!)*
> *He ran to our relief.*

His incarnation was a type of the way in which He comes to us by His Spirit. He saw us cast out, polluted, shameful, perishing; and as He passed by, His tender lips said, "Live!" In us is fulfilled that word, "I am found of them that sought Me not." We were too averse to holiness, too much in bondage to sin, ever to have returned to Him if He had not turned to us. What think you? Did He come to us when we were enemies, and will He not visit us now that we are friends? Did He come to us when we were dead sinners, and will He not hear us now that we are weeping saints? If Christ's coming to the Earth was after this manner, and if His coming to each one of us was after this style, we may well hope that now He will come to us in like fashion, like the dew which refreshes the grass, and waiteth not for man, neither tarrieth for the sons of men. Besides, He is coming again in person, in the latter-day, and mountains of sin, and error, and idolatry, and superstition, and oppression stand in the way of His kingdom; but He will surely come and overturn, and overturn, till He shall reign over all. He will come in the latter-days, I say, though He shall leap the hills to do it, and because of that I am sure we may comfortably conclude that He will draw near to us who mourn His absence so bitterly. Then let us bow our heads a moment, and silently present to His most excellent Majesty the petition of our text: "Turn, my Beloved, and be Thou like a roe or a young hart upon the mountains of division."

Our text gives us sweet assurance that *our Lord is at home with those difficulties* which are quite insurmountable by us. Just as the roe or the young hart knows the passes of the mountains, and the stepping-places among the rugged rocks, and is void of all fear among the ravines and the precipices, so does our Lord know the heights and depths, the torrents and the caverns of our sin and sorrow. He carried the whole of our transgression, and so became aware of the tremendous load of our guilt. He is quite at home with the infirmities of our nature; He knew temptation in the wilderness, heartbreak in the garden, desertion on the cross. He is quite at home with pain and weakness, for "Himself took our infirmities, and bare our sicknesses." He is at home with despondency, for He was "a Man of sorrows, and acquainted with grief." He is at home even with death, for He gave up the ghost, and passed through the sepulcher to resurrection. O yawning gulfs and frowning steeps of woe, our Beloved, like hind or hart, has traversed your glooms! O my Lord, Thou knowest all that divides me from Thee; and Thou knowest also that I am far too feeble to climb these dividing mountains, so that I may come at Thee; therefore, I pray Thee, come Thou over the mountains to meet my longing spirit! Thou knowest each yawning gulf and slippery steep, but none of these can stay Thee; haste Thou to me, Thy servant, Thy beloved, and let me again live by Thy presence.

It is easy, too, for Christ to come over the mountains for our relief. It is easy for the gazelle to cross the mountains, it is made for that end; so is it easy for Jesus, for to this purpose was He ordained from of old that He might come to man in his worst estate, and bring with Him the Father's love. What is it that separates us from Christ? Is it a sense of sin? You have been pardoned once, and Jesus can renew most vividly a sense of full forgiveness. But you say, "Alas! I have sinned again: fresh guilt alarms me." He can remove it in an instant, for the fountain appointed for that purpose is opened, and is still full. It is easy for the dear lips of redeeming love to put away the child's offences, since He has already obtained pardon for the criminal's iniquities. If with His heart's blood He won our pardon from our Judge, he can easily enough bring us the forgiveness of our Father. Oh, yes, it is easy enough for Christ to say again, "Thy sins be forgiven!" "But I feel so unfit, so unable to enjoy communion." He that healed all manner of bodily diseases can heal with a word your spiritual infirmities. Remember the man whose ankle-bones received strength, so that he ran and leaped; and her who was sick of a fever, and was healed at once, and arose, and ministered unto her Lord. "My grace is sufficient for thee; for

My strength is made perfect in weakness." "But I have such afflictions, such troubles, such sorrows, that I am weighted down, and cannot rise into joyful fellowship." Yes, but Jesus can make every burden light, and cause each yoke to be easy. Your trials can be made to aid your Heavenward course instead of hindering it. I know all about those heavy weights, and I perceive that you cannot lift them; but skillful engineers can adapt ropes and pulleys in such a way that heavy weights lift other weights. The Lord Jesus is great at gracious machinery, and He has the art of causing a weight of tribulation to lift from us a load of spiritual deadness, so that we ascend by that which, like a millstone, threatened to sink us down.

What else doth hinder? I am sure that, if it were a sheer impossibility, the Lord Jesus could remove it, for things impossible with men are possible with God. But someone objects, "I am so unworthy of Christ. I can understand eminent saints and beloved disciples being greatly indulged, but I am a worm, and no man; utterly below such condescension." Say you so? Know you not that the worthiness of Christ covers your unworthiness, and He is made of God unto you wisdom, righteousness, sanctification, and redemption? In Christ, the Father thinks not so meanly of you as you think of yourself; you are not worthy to be called His child, but He does call you so, and reckons you to be among His jewels. Listen, and you shall hear Him say, "Since thou wast precious in My sight, thou hast been honorable, and I have loved thee. I gave Egypt for thy ransom; Ethiopia and Seba for thee." Thus, then, there remains nothing which Jesus cannot overleap if He resolves to come to you, and reestablish your broken fellowship.

To conclude, *our Lord can do all this directly.* As in the twinkling of an eye the dead shall be raised incorruptible, so in a moment can our dead affections rise to fullness of delight. He can say to this mountain, "Be thou removed hence, and be thou cast into the midst of the sea," and it shall be done. In the sacred emblems now upon this supper table, Jesus is already among us. Faith cries, "He has come!" Like John the Baptist, she gazes intently on Him, and cries, "Behold the Lamb of God!" At this table Jesus feeds us with His body and His blood. His corporeal presence we have not, but His real spiritual presence we perceive. We are like the disciples when none of them durst ask Him, "Who art Thou?" knowing that it was the Lord. He is come. He looketh forth at these windows—I mean this bread and wine; showing Himself through the lattices of this instructive and endearing ordinance. He speaks. He saith, "The winter is past, the rain is over and gone." And so it is; we feel it to be so: a heavenly springtide warms our frozen hearts. Like the spouse, we wonderingly cry, "Or ever I was aware, my soul made me like the chariots of Ammi-nadib." Now in happy fellowship we see the Beloved, and hear His voice; our heart burns; our affections glow; we are happy, restful, brimming over with delight. The King has brought us into his banqueting-house, and His banner over us is love. It is good to be here!

Friends, we must now go our ways. A voice saith, "Arise, let us go hence." O Thou Lord of our hearts, go with us! Home will not be home without Thee. Life will not be life without Thee. Heaven itself would not be Heaven if Thou wert absent. Abide with us. The world grows dark, the gloaming of time draws on. Abide with us, for it is toward evening. Our years increase, and we near the night when dews fall cold and chill. A great future is all about us, the splendors of the last age are coming down; and while we wait in solemn, awe-struck expectation, our heart continually cries within herself, "Until the daybreak, and the shadows flee away, turn, my Beloved, and be Thou like a roe or a young hart upon the mountains of division."

> *Hasten, Lord! the promised hour;*
> *Come in glory and in power;*
> *Still Thy foes are unsubdued;*
> *Nature sighs to be renew'd.*
> *Time has nearly reach'd its sum,*
> *All things with Thy bride say "Come";*
> *Jesus, whom all worlds adore,*
> *Come and reign for evermore!*

The Spiced Wine of the Pomegranate

"I would cause Thee to drink of spiced wine
of the juice of my pomegranate."—Solomon's Song 8:2.

"And of His fullness have all we received, and grace for grace."—John 1:16.

The immovable basis of communion having been laid of old in the
eternal union which subsisted between Christ and His elect, it only
needed a fitting occasion to manifest itself in active development. The
Lord Jesus had forever delighted Himself with the sons of men, and he
ever stood prepared to reveal and communicate that delight to His people; but they were incapable of returning His affection or enjoying His fellowship, having fallen into a state so base and degraded, that they were
dead to Him, and careless concerning Him. It was therefore needful that
something should be done for them, and in them, before they could hold
converse with Jesus, or feel concord with Him. This preparation being a
work of grace and a result of previous union, Jesus determined that, even
in the preparation for communion, there should be communion. If they
must be washed before they could fully converse with Him, He would
commune with them in the washing; and if they must be enriched by gifts
before they could have full access to Him, He would commune with them
in the giving. He has therefore established a fellowship in imparting His
grace, and in partaking of it.

This order of fellowship we have called "The Communion of Communication," and we think that a few remarks will prove that we are not running
beyond the warranty of Scripture.

The word κοινωνια, or communion, is frequently employed by inspired
writers in the sense of communication or contribution. When, in our English

97

version, we read, "For it hath pleased them of Macedonia and Achaia to make *a certain contribution* for the poor saints which are at Jerusalem" (Romans 15:26), it is interesting to know that the word κοινωνιαν is used, as if to show that the generous gifts of the Church in Achaia to its sister Church at Jerusalem was a communion. Calvin would have us notice this, because, saith he, "The word here employed well expresses the feeling by which it behooves us to succor the wants of our brethren, even because there is to be a common and mutual regard on account of the union of the body." He would not have strained the text if he had said that there was in the contribution the very essence of communion. Gill, in his commentary upon the above verse, most pertinently remarks, "Contribution, or communion, as the word signifies: it being one part of the communion of churches and of saints to relieve their poor by communicating to them." The same word is employed in Hebrews 13:16, and is there translated by the word "communicate." "But to do good, and to communicate, forget not: for with such sacrifices God is well pleased." It occurs again in 2 Corinthians 9:13, "And for your liberal *distribution* unto them, and unto all men"; and in numerous other passages the careful student will observe the word in various forms, representing the ministering of the saints to one another as an act of fellowship. Indeed, at the Lord's supper, which is the embodiment of communion, we have ever been wont to make a special contribution for the poor of the flock, and we believe that in the collection there is as true and real an element of communion as in the partaking of the bread and wine. The giver holds fellowship with the receiver when he bestows his benefaction for the Lord's sake, and because of the brotherhood existing between him and his needy friends. The teacher holds communion with the young disciple when he labors to instruct him in the faith, being moved thereto by a spirit of Christian love. He who intercedes for a saint because he desires his well being as a member of the one family, enters into fellowship with his brother in the offering of prayer. The loving and mutual service of church members is fellowship of a high degree. And let us remember that the recipient communes with the benefactor: the communion is not confined to the giver, but the heart overflowing with liberality is met by the heart brimming with gratitude, and the love manifested in the bestowal is reciprocated in the acceptance. When the hand feeds the mouth or supports the head, the diverse members feel their union, and sympathize with one another; and so is it with the various portions of the body of Christ, for they commune in mutual acts of love.

Now, this meaning of the word communion furnishes us with much instruction, since it indicates the manner in which recognized fellowship with Jesus is commenced and maintained, namely, by giving and receiving, by *communication* and reception. The Lord's supper is the divinely ordained exhibition of communion, and therefore in it there is the breaking of bread and the pouring forth of wine, to picture the free gift of the Savior's body and blood to us; and there is also the eating of the one and the drinking of the other, to represent the reception of these priceless gifts by us. As without bread and wine there could be no Lord's supper, so without the gracious bequests of Jesus to us there would have been no communion between Him and our souls: and as participation is necessary before the elements truly represent the meaning of the Lord's ordinance, so is it needful that we should receive His bounties, and feed upon His person, before we can commune with Him.

It is one branch of this mutual communication which we have selected as the subject of this address. "Looking unto Jesus," who hath delivered us from our state of enmity, and brought us into fellowship with Himself, we pray for the rich assistance of the Holy Spirit, that we may be refreshed in spirit, and encouraged to draw more largely from the covenant storehouse of Christ Jesus the Lord.

We shall take a text, and proceed at once to our delightful task. "And of His fullness have all we received, and grace for grace." (John 1:16.)

As the life of grace is first begotten in us by the Lord Jesus, so is it constantly sustained by Him. We are always drawing from this sacred fountain, always deriving sap from this divine root; and as Jesus communes with us in the bestowing of mercies, it is our privilege to hold fellowship with Him in the receiving of them.

There is this difference between Christ and ourselves, He never gives without manifesting fellowship, but we often receive in so ill a manner that communion is not reciprocated, and we therefore miss the heavenly opportunity of its enjoyment. We frequently receive grace insensibly, that is to say, the sacred oil runs through the pipe, and maintains our lamp, while we are unmindful of the secret influence. We may also be the partakers of many mercies which, through our dullness, we do not perceive to be mercies at all; and at other times well known blessings are recognized as such, but we are backward in tracing them to their source in the covenant made with Christ Jesus.

Following out the suggestion of our explanatory preface, we can well believe that when the poor saints received the contribution of their brethren, many of them did in earnest acknowledge the fellowship which was illustrated in the generous offering, but it is probable that some of them merely looked upon the material of the gift, and failed to see the spirit moving in it. Sensual thoughts in some of the receivers might possibly, at the season when the contribution was distributed, have mischievously injured the exercise of spirituality, for it is possible that, after a period of poverty, they would be apt to give greater prominence to the fact that their need was removed than to the sentiment of fellowship with their sympathizing brethren. They would rather rejoice over famine averted than concerning fellowship manifested. We doubt not that, in many instances, the mutual benefactions of the Church fail to reveal our fellowship to our poor brethren, and produce in them no feelings of communion with the givers.

Now this sad fact is an illustration of the yet more lamentable statement which we have made. We again assert that, as many of the partakers of the alms of the Church are not alive to the communion contained therein, so the Lord's people are never sufficiently attentive to fellowship with Jesus in receiving His gifts, but many of them are entirely forgetful of their privilege, and all of them are too little aware of it. Nay, worse than this, how often doth the believer pervert the gifts of Jesus into food for his own sin and wantonness! We are not free from the fickleness of ancient Israel, and well might our Lord address us in the same language:

> Now when I passed by thee, and looked upon thee, behold, thy time was the time of love; and I spread My skirt over thee, and covered thy nakedness: yea, I swear unto thee, and entered into a covenant with thee, saith the Lord God, and thou becamest Mine. Then washed I thee with water; yea, I throughly washed away thy blood from thee, and I anointed thee with oil. I clothed thee also with broidered work, and shod thee with badgers' skin, and I girded thee about with fine linen, and I covered thee with silk. I decked thee also with ornaments, and I put bracelets upon thy hands, and a chain on thy neck. And I put a jewel on thy forehead, and earrings in thine ears, and a beautiful crown upon thine head. Thus wast thou decked with gold and silver; and thy raiment was of fine linen, and silk, and broidered work; thou didst eat fine flour, and honey, and oil: and thou wast exceeding beautiful, and thou didst prosper into a kingdom. And thy renown went forth among the heathen for thy beauty: for it was perfect through My comeliness, which I had put upon thee, saith the Lord God. But thou didst trust in thine own beauty, and playedst the harlot because of thy renown. (Ezek. 8:16)

Ought not the mass of professors [Christians] to confess the truth of this accusation? Have not the bulk of us most sadly departed from the purity of our love? We rejoice, however, to observe a remnant of choice spirits, who live near the Lord, and know the sweetness of fellowship. These receive the promise and the blessing, and so digest them that they become good blood in their veins, and so do they feed on their Lord that they grow up into Him. Let us imitate those elevated minds, and obtain their high delights. There is no reason why the meanest of us should not be as David, and David as the servant of the Lord. We may now be dwarfs, but growth is possible; let us therefore aim at a higher stature. Let the succeeding advice be followed, and, the Holy Spirit helping us, we shall have attained thereto.

Make every time of need a time of embracing thy Lord. Do not leave the mercy-seat until thou hast clasped Him in thine arms. In every time of need He has promised to give thee grace to help, and what withholdeth thee from obtaining sweet fellowship as a precious addition to the promised assistance? Be not as the beggar who is content with the alms, however grudgingly it may be cast to him; but, since thou art a near kinsman, seek a smile and a kiss with every benison [blessing] He gives thee. Is He not better than His mercies? What are they without Him? Cry aloud unto Him, and let thy petition reach His ears,

> O my Lord, it is not enough to be a partaker of Thy bounties, I must have Thyself also; if Thou dost not give me Thyself with Thy favors, they are but of little use to me! O smile on me, when Thou blessest me, for else I am still unblest! Thou puttest perfume into all the flowers of Thy garden, and fragrance into Thy spices; if Thou withdrawest Thyself, they are no more pleasant to me. Come, then, my Lord, and give me Thy love with Thy grace.

Take good heed, Christian, that thine own heart is in right tune, that when the fingers of mercy touch the strings, they may resound with full notes of communion. How sad is it to partake of favor without rejoicing in it! Yet such is often the believer's case. The Lord casts His lavish bounties at our doors, and we, like churls, scarcely look out to thank Him. Our ungrateful hearts and unthankful tongues mar our fellowship, by causing us to miss a thousand opportunities for exercising it.

If thou wouldst enjoy communion with the Lord Jesus in the reception of His grace, *endeavor to be always sensibly drawing supplies from Him.* Make thy needs public in the streets of thine heart, and when the supply is granted, let all the powers of thy soul be present at the reception of it. Let no mercy come into thine house unsung. Note in thy memory the list of thy Master's benefits. Wherefore should the Lord's bounties be hurried away in the dark, or buried in forgetfulness? Keep the gates of thy soul ever open, and sit thou by the wayside to watch the treasures of grace which God the Spirit hourly conveys into thy heart from Jehovah—Jesus, thy Lord.

Never let an hour pass without drawing upon the bank of Heaven. If all thy wants seem satisfied, look steadfastly until the next moment brings another need, and then delay not, but with this warrant of necessity, hasten to thy treasury again. Thy necessities are so numerous that thou wilt never lack a reason for applying to the fullness of Jesus; but if ever such an occasion should arise, enlarge thine heart, and then there will be need of more love to fill the wider space. But do not allow any supposititious [false] /riches of thine own to suspend thy daily receivings from the Lord Jesus. You have constant need of Him. You need His intercession, His upholding, His sanctification; you need that He should work all your works in you, and that He should preserve you unto the day of His appearing. There is not one moment of your life in which you can do without Christ. Therefore be always at His door, and the wants which you bemoan shall be remembrances to turn your heart unto your Savior. Thirst makes the heart pant for the water-brooks, and pain reminds man of the physician. Let your wants conduct you to Jesus, and may the blessed Spirit reveal Him unto you while He lovingly affords you the rich supplies of His love! Go, poor saint, let thy poverty be the cord to draw thee to thy rich Brother. Rejoice in the infirmity which makes room for grace to rest upon thee, and be glad that thou hast constant needs which compel thee perpetually to hold fellowship with thine adorable Redeemer.

Study thyself, seek out thy necessities, as the housewife searches for chambers where she may bestow her summer fruits. Regard thy wants as rooms to be filled with more of the grace of Jesus, and suffer no corner to be unoccupied. Pant after more of Jesus. Be covetous after Him. Let all the past incite thee to seek greater things. Sing the song of the enlarged heart—

> *All this is not enough: methinks I grow*
> *More greedy by fruition; what I get*
> *Serves but to set*
> *An edge upon my appetite;*
> *And all Thy gifts invite*
> *My pray'rs for more.*

Cry out to the Lord Jesus to fill the dry beds of thy rivers until they overflow, and then empty thou the channels which have hitherto been filled with thine own self-sufficiency, and beseech Him to fill these also with His superabundant grace. If thy heavy trials sink thee deeper in the flood of His consolations, be glad of them; and if thy vessel shall be sunken up to its very bulwarks, be not afraid. I would be glad to feel the masthead of my soul twenty fathoms beneath the surface of such an ocean; for, as Rutherford said, "Oh, to be over the ears in this well! I would not have Christ's love entering into me, but I would enter into it, and be swallowed up of that love." Cultivate an insatiable hunger and a quenchless thirst for this communion with Jesus through His communications. Let thine heart cry forever, "Give, give," until it is filled in Paradise.

> *O'ercome with Jesu's condescending love,*
> *Brought into fellowship with Him and His,*
> *And feasting with Him in His house of wine,*
> *I'm sick of love—and yet I pant for more*
> *Communications from my loving Lord.*
> *Stay me with flagons full of choicest wine,*
> *Press'd from His heart upon Mount Calvary,*
> *To cheer and comfort my love-conquer'd soul.*
> *Thyself I crave!*
>
> *Thy presence is my life, my joy, my heav'n,*
> *And all, without Thyself, is dead to me.*
> *Stay me with flagons, Savior, hear my cry,*
> *Let promises, like apples, comfort me;*
> *Apply atoning blood, and cov'nant love,*
> *Until I see Thy face among the guests*
> *Who in Thy Father's kingdom feast.*

—"Nymphas," *by Joseph Irons.*

This is the only covetousness which is allowable: but this is not merely beyond rebuke, it is worthy of commendation. O saints, be not straitened in your own bowels, but enlarge your desires, and so receive more of your Savior's measureless fullness! I charge thee, my soul, thus to hold continual fellowship with thy Lord, since He invites and commands thee thus to partake of His riches.

Rejoice thyself in benefits received. Let the satisfaction of thy spirit overflow in streams of joy. When the believer reposes all his confidence in Christ, and delights himself in Him, there is an exercise of communion. If he forgetteth his psalm-book, and instead of singing is found lamenting, the mercies of the day will bring no communion. Awake, O music! stir up thyself, O my soul, be glad in the Lord, and exceedingly rejoice! Behold His favors, rich, free, and continual; shall they be buried in unthankfulness? Shall they be covered with a winding-sheet of ingratitude? No! I will praise Him. I must extol Him! Sweet Lord Jesus, let me kiss the dust of Thy feet, let me lose myself in thankfulness, for Thy thoughts unto me are precious, how great is the sum of them! Lo, I embrace Thee in the arms of joy and gratitude, and herein I find my soul drawn unto Thee!

This is a blessed method of fellowship. It is kissing the divine lip of benediction with the sanctified lip of affection. Oh, for more rejoicing grace, more of the songs of the heart, more of the melody of the soul!

Seek to recognize the source of thy mercies as lying alone in Him who is our Head. Imitate the chicken, which, every time it drinketh of the brook, lifts up its head to Heaven, as if it would return thanks for every drop. If we have anything that is commendable and gracious, it must come from the Holy Spirit, and that Spirit is first bestowed on Jesus, and then through Him on us. The oil was first poured on the head of Aaron, and thence it ran down upon his garments. Look on the drops of grace, and remember that they distill from the Head, Christ Jesus. All thy rays are begotten by this Sun of Righteousness, all thy showers are poured from this Heaven, all thy fountains spring from this great and immeasurable depth. Oh, for grace to see the hand of Jesus on every favor! So will communion be constantly and firmly in exercise. May the great Teacher perpetually direct us to Jesus by making the mercies of the covenant the handposts on the road which leadeth to Him. Happy is the believer who knows how to find the secret abode of his Beloved by tracking the footsteps of His loving providence: herein is wisdom which the casual observer of mere second causes can never reach. Labor, O Christian, to follow up every clue which thy Master's grace affords thee!

Labor to maintain a sense of thine entire dependence upon His good will and pleasure for the continuance of thy richest enjoyments. Never try to live on the old manna, nor seek to find help in Egypt. All must come from Jesus, or thou art undone forever. Old anointings will not suffice to impart unction to our spirit; thine head must have fresh oil poured upon it from the golden horn of the sanctuary, or it will cease from its glory. Today thou mayest be upon the summit of the mount of God; but He who has put thee there must keep thee there, or thou wilt sink far more speedily than thou dreamest. Thy mountain only stands firm when He settles it in its place; if He hide His face, thou wilt soon be troubled. If the Savior should see fit, there is not a window through which thou seest the light of Heaven which he could not darken in an instant. Joshua bade the sun stand still, but Jesus can shroud it in total darkness. He can withdraw the joy of thine heart, the light of thine eyes, and the strength of thy life; in His hand thy comforts lie, and at His will they can depart from thee. Oh! how rich the grace which supplies us so continually, and doth not refrain itself because of our ingratitude! O Lord Jesus, we would bow at Thy feet, conscious of our utter inability to do aught without Thee, and in every favor which we are privileged to receive, we would adore Thy blessed name, and acknowledge Thine unexhausted love!

When thou hast received much, admire the all-sufficiency which still remaineth undiminished, thus shall you commune with Christ, not only in what you obtain from Him, but also in the superabundance which remains treasured up in Him. Let us ever remember that giving does not impoverish our Lord. When the clouds, those wandering cisterns of the skies, have poured floods upon the dry ground, there remains an abundance in the storehouse of the rain: so in Christ there is ever an unbounded supply, though the most liberal showers of grace have fallen ever since the foundation of the Earth. The sun is as bright as ever after all his shining, and the sea is quite as full after all the clouds have been drawn from it: so is our Lord Jesus ever the same overflowing fountain of fullness. All this is ours, and we may make it the subject of rejoicing fellowship. Come, believer, walk through the length and breadth of the land, for as far as the eye can reach, the land is thine, and far beyond the utmost range of thine observation it is thine also, the gracious gift of thy gracious Redeemer and Friend. Is there not ample space for fellowship *here?*

Regard every spiritual mercy as an assurance of the Lord's communion with thee. When the young man gives jewels to the virgin to whom he is affianced, she regards them as tokens of his delight in her. Believer, do the same with the precious presents of thy Lord. The common bounties of providence are shared in by all men, for the good Householder provides water for His swine as well as for His children: such things, therefore, are no proof of divine complacency. But thou hast richer food to eat; "the children's bread" is in thy wallet, and the heritage of the righteous is reserved for thee. Look, then, on every motion of grace in thine heart as a pledge and sign of the moving of thy Savior's heart towards thee. There is His whole heart in the bowels of every mercy which He sends thee. He has impressed a kiss of love upon each gift, and He would have thee believe that every jewel of mercy is a token of His boundless love. Look on thine adoption, justification, and preservation, as sweet enticements to fellowship. Let every note of the promise sound in thine ears like the ringing of the bells of the house of thy Lord, inviting thee to come to the banquets of His love. Joseph sent to his father asses laden with the good things of Egypt, and good old Jacob doubtless regarded them as pledges of the love of his son's heart: be sure not to think less of the kindnesses of Jesus.

Study to know the value of His favors. They are no ordinary things, no paste jewels, no mosaic gold: they are every one of them so costly, that, had all Heaven been drained of treasure, apart from the precious offering of the

Redeemer, it could not have purchased so much as the least of His benefits. When thou seest thy pardon, consider how great a boon is contained in it! Bethink thee that Hell had been thine eternal portion unless Christ had plucked thee from the burning! When thou art enabled to see thyself as clothed in the imputed righteousness of Jesus, admire the profusion of precious things of which thy robe is made. Think how many times the Man of sorrows wearied Himself at that loom of obedience in which He wove that matchless garment; and reckon, if thou canst, how many worlds of merit were cast into the fabric at every throw of the shuttle! Remember that all the angels in Heaven could not have afforded Him a single thread which would have been rich enough to weave into the texture of His perfect righteousness. Consider the cost of thy maintenance for an hour; remember that thy wants are so large, that all the granaries of grace that all the saints could fill, could not feed thee for a moment.

What an expensive dependent thou art! King Solomon made marvelous provision for his household (1 Kings 4:22), but all his beeves [steers] and fine flour would be as a drop in the bucket compared with thy daily wants. Rivers of oil, and ten thousand rams or fed beasts, would not provide enough to supply the necessities of thy hungering soul. Thy least spiritual want demands infinity to satisfy it, and what must be the amazing aggregate of thy perpetually repeated draughts upon thy Lord! Arise, then, and bless thy loving Immanuel for the invaluable riches with which He has endowed thee. See what a dowry thy Bridegroom has brought to His poor, penniless spouse. He knows the value of the blessings which He brings thee, for He has paid for them out of His heart's richest blood; be not thou so ungenerous as to pass them over as if they were but of little worth. Poor men know more of the value of money than those who have always reveled in abundance of wealth. Ought not thy former poverty to teach thee the preciousness of the grace which Jesus gives thee? For remember, there was a time when thou wouldst have given a thousand worlds, if they had been thine, in order to procure the very least of His abundant mercies.

Remember how impossible it would have been for thee to receive a single spiritual blessing unless thou hadst been in Jesus. On none of Adam's race can the love of God be fixed, unless they are seen to be in union with His Son. No exception has ever been made to the universal curse on those of the first Adam's seed who have no interest in the second Adam. Christ is the only Zoar in which God's Lots can find a shelter from the destruction of Sodom. Out of Him, the withering blast of the fiery furnace of God's wrath consumes every green herb, and it is only in Him that the soul can live. As when the prairie is on fire, men see the Heavens wrapped in sheets of flame, and in hot haste they fly before the devouring element. They have but one hope. There is in the distance a lake of water. They reach it, they plunge into it, and are safe. Although the skies are molten with the heat, the sun darkened with the smoke, and the earth utterly consumed in the fire, they know that they are secure while the cooling flood embraces them. Christ Jesus is the only escape for a sinner pursued by the fiery wrath of God, and we would have the believer remember this. Our own works could never shelter us, for they have proved but refuges of lies. Had they been a thousand times more and better, they would have been but as the spider's web, too frail to hang eternal interests upon. There was but one name, one sacrifice, one blood, by which we could escape. All other attempts at salvation were a grievous failure. For,

> though a man could scourge out of his body rivers of blood, and in neglect of himself could outfast Moses or Elias; though he could wear out his knees with prayer, and had his eyes nailed on Heaven; though he could build hospitals for all the poor on earth, and exhaust the mines of India in alms; though he could walk like an angel of light, and with the glittering of an outward holiness dazzle the eyes of all beholders; nay (if it were possible to be conceived) though he should live for a thousand years in a perfect and perpetual observation of the whole law of God, if the only exception to his perfection were the very least deviation from the law, yet such a man as this could no more appear before the tribunal of God's justice, than stubble before a consuming fire. (Reynolds on the Life of Christ.)

How, then, with thine innumerable sins, couldst thou escape the damnation of Hell, much less become the recipient of bounties so rich and large? Blessed window of Heaven, sweet Lord Jesus, let Thy Church forever adore Thee, as the only channel by which mercies can flow to her. My soul, give Him continual praise, for without Him thou hadst been poorer than a beggar. Be thou mindful, O heir of Heaven, that thou couldst not have had one ray of hope, or one word of comfort, if thou hadst not been in union with Christ Jesus! The crumbs which fall from thy table are more than grace itself would have given thee, hadst thou not been in Jesus beloved and approved.

All thou hast, thou hast in Him: in Him chosen, in Him redeemed, in Him justified, in Him accepted. Thou art risen in Him, but without Him thou hadst died the second death. Thou art in Him raised up to the heavenly places, but out of Him thou wouldst have been damned eternally. Bless Him, then. Ask the angels to bless Him. Rouse all ages to a harmony of praise for His condescending love in taking poor guilty nothings into oneness with His all-adorable person. This is a blessed means of promoting communion, if the sacred Comforter is pleased to take of the things of Christ, and reveal them to us as ours, but only ours as we are in Him. Thrice-blessed Jesus, let us never forget that we are members of Thy mystical body, and that it is for this reason that we are blessed and preserved.

Meditate upon the gracious acts which procured thy blessings. Consider the ponderous labors which thy Lord endured for thee, and the stupendous sufferings by which He purchased the mercies which He bestows. What human tongue can speak forth the unutterable misery of His heart, or describe so much as one of the agonies which crowded upon His soul? How much less shall any finite comprehension arrive at an idea of the vast total of His woe! But all His sorrows were necessary for thy benefit, and without them not one of thine unnumbered mercies could have been bestowed. Be not unmindful that—

> There's ne'er a gift His hand bestows,
> But cost His heart a groan.

Look upon the frozen ground of Gethsemane, and behold the bloody sweat which stained the soil! Turn to the hall of Gabbatha, and see the victim of justice pursued by His clamorous foes! Enter the guard-room of the Prætorians, and view the spitting, and the plucking of the hair! and then conclude your review upon Golgotha, the mount of doom, where death consummated His tortures; and if, by divine assistance thou art enabled to enter, in some humble measure, into the depths of thy Lord's sufferings, thou wilt be the better prepared to hold fellowship with Him when next thou receivest His priceless gifts. In proportion to thy sense of their costliness will be thy capacity for enjoying the love which is centered in them.

Above all, and chief of all, never forget that Christ is thine. Amid the profusion of His gifts, never forget that the chief gift is Himself, and do not forget that, after all, His gifts are but Himself. He clothes thee, but it is with Himself, with His own spotless righteousness and character. He washes thee, but His innermost self, His own heart's blood, is the stream with which the fountain overflows. He feeds thee with the bread of Heaven, but be not unmindful that the bread is Himself, His own body which He gives to be the food of souls. Never be satisfied with a less communication than a whole Christ. A wife will not be put off with maintenance, jewels, and attire: all these will be nothing to her unless she can call her husband's heart and person her own. It was the Paschal lamb upon which the ancient Israelite did feast on that night that was never to be forgotten. So do thou feast on Jesus, and on nothing less than

Jesus, for less than this will be food too light for thy soul's satisfaction. Oh, be careful to eat His flesh and drink His blood, and so receive Him into thyself in a real and spiritual manner, for nothing short of this will be an evidence of eternal life in thy soul!

What more shall we add to the rules which we have here delivered? There remains but one great exhortation, which must not be omitted. *Seek the abundant assistance of the Holy Spirit* to enable you to put into practice the things which we have said, for without His aid, all that we have spoken will but be tantalizing the lame with rules to walk, or the dying with regulations for the preservation of health. O thou Divine Spirit, while we enjoy the grace of Jesus, lead us into the secret abode of our Lord, that we may sup with Him, and He with us, and grant unto us hourly grace that we may continue in the company of our Lord from the rising to the setting of the sun! Amen.

I Will Give You Rest

"I will give you rest"—Matthew 11:28

We have a thousand times considered these words as an encouragement to the laboring and the laden; and we may, therefore, have failed to read them as a promise to ourselves. But, beloved friends, we *have* come to Jesus, and therefore He stands engaged to fulfill this priceless pledge to us. We may now enjoy the promise; for we have obeyed the precept. The faithful and true Witness, whose word is truth, promised us rest if we would come to Him; and, therefore, since we have come to Him, and are always coming to Him, we may boldly say, "O Thou, who art our Peace, make good Thy word to us wherein Thou hast said, 'I will give you rest.'"

By faith, I see our Lord standing in our midst, and I hear Him say, with voice of sweetest music, first to all of us together, and then to each one individually, "I will give you rest." May the Holy Spirit bring to each of us the fullness of the rest and peace of God! For a few minutes only shall I need your attention; and we will begin by asking the question,

I. What must these words mean?

A dear friend prayed this morning that, while studying the Scriptures, we might be enabled to read between the lines, and beneath the letter of the Word. May we have holy insight thus to read our Lord's most gracious language!

This promise must mean rest to all parts of our spiritual nature. Our bodies cannot rest if the head is aching, or the feet are full of pain; if one member is disturbed, the whole frame is unable to rest; and so the higher nature is one, and such intimate sympathies bind together all its faculties and powers, that

111

every one of them must rest, or none can be at ease. Jesus gives real, and, consequently, universal rest to every part of our spiritual being.

The heart is by nature restless as old ocean's waves; it seeks an object for its affection; and when it finds one beneath the stars, it is doomed to sorrow. Either the beloved changes, and there is disappointment; or death comes in, and there is bereavement. The more tender the heart, the greater its unrest. Those in whom the heart is simply one of the largest valves are undisturbed, because they are callous; but the sensitive, the generous, the unselfish, are often found seeking rest and finding none. To such, the Lord Jesus says, "Come unto Me, and I will give you rest." Look hither, ye loving ones, for here is a refuge for your wounded love! You may delight yourselves in the Well-beloved, and never fear that He will fail or forget you. Love will not be wasted, however much it may be lavished upon Jesus. He deserves it all, and he requites it all. In loving Him, the heart finds a delicious content. When the head lies in His bosom, it enjoys an ease which no pillow of down could bestow. How Madame Guyon rested amid severe persecutions, because her great love to Jesus filled her soul to the brim! O aching heart, O breaking heart, come hither, for Jesus saith, "I will give you rest."

The conscience, when it is at all alive and awake, is much disturbed because the holy law of God has been broken by sin. Now, conscience once aroused is not easily quieted. Neither unbelief nor superstition can avail to lull it to sleep; it defies these opiates of falsehood, and frets the soul with perpetual annoyance. Like the troubled sea, it cannot rest; but constantly casts up upon the shore of memory the mire and dirt of past transgressions and iniquities. Is this your case? Then Jesus says, "I will give you rest." If, at any time, fears and apprehensions arise from an awakened conscience, they can only be safely and surely quieted by our flying to the Crucified. In the blessed truth of a substitution, accepted of God, and fully made by the Lord Jesus, our mind finds peace. Justice is honored, and law is vindicated, in the sacrifice of Christ. Since God is satisfied, I may well be so. Since the Father has raised Jesus from the dead, and set Him at His own right hand, there can be no question as to His acceptance; and, consequently, all who are in Him are accepted also. We are under no apprehension now as to our being condemned; Jesus gives us rest, by enabling us to utter the challenge, "Who is he that condemneth?" and to give the reassuring answer, "Christ hath died."

The intellect is another source of unrest; and in these times it operates with special energy towards labor and travail of mind. Doubts, stinging like mosquitoes, are suggested by almost every page of the literature of the day. Most men are drifting, like vessels which have no anchors, and these come into collision with us. How can we rest? This scheme of philosophy eats up the other; this new fashion of heresy devours the last. Is there any foundation? Is anything true? Or is it all romance, and are we doomed to be the victims of an ever-changing lie? O soul, seek not a settlement by learning of men; but come and learn of Jesus, and thou shalt find rest! Believe Jesus, and let all the Rabbis contradict. The Son of God was made flesh, He lived, He died, He rose again, He lives, He loves; this is true, and all that He teaches in His Word is assured verity; the rest may blow away, like chaff before the wind. A mind in pursuit of truth is a dove without a proper resting place for the sole of its foot, till it finds its rest in Jesus, the true Noah.

Next, *these words mean rest about all things.* He who is uneasy about anything has not found rest. A thousand thorns and briars grow on the soil of this earth, and no man can happily tread life's ways unless his feet are shod with that preparation of the gospel of peace which Jesus gives. In Christ, we are at rest as to our duties; for He instructs and helps us in them. In Him, we are at rest about our trials; for He sympathizes with us in them. With His love, we are restful as to the movements of Providence; for His Father loves us, and will not suffer anything to harm us. Concerning the past, we rest in His forgiving love; as to the present, it is bright with His loving fellowship; as to the future, it is brilliant with His expected Advent. This is true of the little as well as of the great. He who saves us from the battle-axe of Satanic temptation, also extracts the thorn of a domestic trial. We may rest in Jesus as to our sick child, as to our business trouble, or as to grief of any kind. He is our Comforter in all things, our Sympathizer in every form of temptation. Have you such all-covering rest? If not, why not? Jesus gives it; why do you not partake of it? Have you something which you could not bring to Him? Then, fly from it; for it is no fit thing for a believer to possess. A disciple should know neither grief nor joy which he could not reveal to his Lord.

This rest, we may conclude, *must be a very wonderful one,* since Jesus gives it. His hands give not by penny-worths and ounces; he gives golden gifts, in quantity immeasurable. It is Jesus who gives the peace of God which passeth all understanding. It is written, "Great peace have they which love Thy law"; what peace must they have who love God's Son! There are periods when Jesus gives us a heavenly Elysium of rest; we cannot describe the divine repose of our hearts at such times. We read, in the Gospels, that when Jesus hushed the storm, "there was a great calm," not simply "a calm," but a great calm, unusual, absolute, perfect, memorable. It reminds us of the stillness which John describes in the Revelation: "I saw four angels standing on the four corners of the earth, holding the four winds of the earth, that the wind should not blow on the earth, nor on the sea, nor on any tree"; not a ripple stirred the waters, not a leaf moved on the trees.

Assuredly, our Lord has given a blessed rest to those who trust Him, and follow Him. They are often unable to inform others as to their deep peace, and the reasons upon which it is founded; but they know it, and it brings them an inward wealth compared with which the fortune of an ungodly millionaire is poverty itself. May we all know to the full, by happy, personal experience, the meaning of our Savior's promise, "I will give you rest"!

II. But now, in the second place, let us ask, why should we have this rest?

The first answer is in our text. We should enjoy this rest *because Jesus gives it*. As He gives it, we *ought* to take it. Because He gives it, we *may* take it. I have known some Christians who have thought that it would be presumption on their part to take this rest; so they have kept fluttering about, like frightened birds, weary with their long flights, but not daring to fold their tired wings, and rest. If there is any presumption in the case, let us not be so presumptuous as to think that we know better than our Lord. He gives us rest: for that reason, if for no other, let us take it, promptly and gratefully. "Rest in the Lord, and wait patiently for Him." Say with David, "My heart is fixed, O God, my heart is fixed: I will sing and give praise."

> Now rest, my long-divided heart;
> Fix'd on this blissful center, rest.

Next, we should take the rest that Jesus gives, *because it will refresh us*. We are often weary; sometimes we are weary *in* God's work, though I trust we are never weary *of* it. There are many things to cause us weariness: sin, sorrow, the worldliness of professors [Christians], the prevalence of error in the Church, and so on. Often, we are like a tired child, who can hold up his little head no longer. What does he do? Why, he just goes to sleep in his mother's arms! Let us be as wise as the little one; and let us rest in our loving Savior's embrace. The poet speaks of

> Tired nature's sweet restorer, balmy sleep;

and so it is. Sometimes, the very best thing a Christian man can do is, literally, to go to sleep. When he wakes, he will be so refreshed, that he will seem to be in a new world. But spiritually, there is no refreshing like that which comes from the rest which Christ gives. As Isaiah said, "This is the rest wherewith ye may cause the weary to rest: and this is the refreshing." Dr. Bonar's sweet hymn, which is so suitable for a sinner coming to Christ for the first time, is just as appropriate for a weary saint returning to his Savior's arms; for he, too, can sing,

> *I heard the voice of Jesus say,*
> *"Come unto Me, and rest;*
> *Lay down, thou weary one, lay down,*
> *Thy head upon My breast."*
>
> *I came to Jesus as I was,*
> *Weary, and worn, and sad:*
> *I found in Him a resting-place,*
> *And He has made me glad.*

Another reason why we should have this rest is, that *it will enable us to concentrate all our faculties.* Many, who might be strong servants of the Lord, are very weak, because their energies are not concentrated upon one object. They do not say with Paul, "This one thing I do." We are such poor creatures that we cannot occupy our minds with more than one subject at a time. Why, even the buzzing of a fly, or the trumpeting of a mosquito, would be quite sufficient to take our thoughts away from our present holy service! As long as we have any burden resting on our shoulders, we cannot enjoy perfect rest; and as long as there is any burden on our conscience or heart, we cannot have rest of soul. How are we to be freed from these burdens? Only by yielding ourselves wholly to the Great Burden-Bearer, who says, "Come unto Me, and I will give you rest." Possessing this rest, all our faculties will be centered and focused upon one object, and with undivided hearts we shall seek God's glory.

Having obtained this rest, *we shall be able to testify for our Lord.* I remember, when I first began to teach in a Sunday-school, that I was speaking one day to my class upon the words, "He that believeth on Me hath everlasting life." I was rather taken by surprise when one of the boys said to me, "Teacher, have *you* got everlasting life?" I replied, "I hope so." The scholar was not satisfied with my answer, so he asked another question, "But, teacher, don't you *know?*" The boy was right; there can be no true testimony except that which springs from assured conviction of our own safety and joy in the Lord. We speak that we do know; we believe, and therefore speak. Rest of heart, through coming to Christ, enables us to invite others to Him with great confidence, for we can tell them what heavenly peace He has given to us. This will enable us to put the gospel very attractively, for the evidence of our own experience will help others to trust the Lord for themselves. With the beloved apostle John, we shall be able to say to our hearers,

> That which was from the beginning, which we have heard, which we have seen with our eyes, which we have looked upon, and our hands have handled, of the Word of life (for the life was manifested, and we have seen it, and bear witness, and show unto you that eternal life, which was with the Father, and was manifested unto us); that which we have seen and heard declare we unto you, that ye also may have fellowship with us: and truly our fellowship is with the Father, and with His Son Jesus Christ.

Once more, *this rest is necessary to our growth.* The lily in the garden is not taken up and transplanted two or three times a day; that would be the way to prevent all growth. But it is kept in one place, and tenderly nurtured. It is by keeping it quite still that the gardener helps it to attain to perfection. A child of God would grow much more rapidly if he would but rest in one place instead of being always on the move. "In returning and rest shall ye be saved; in quietness and in confidence shall be your strength." Martha was cumbered about much serving; but Mary sat at Jesus' feet. It is not difficult to tell which of them would be the more likely to grow in the grace and knowledge of our Lord Jesus Christ.

This is a tempting theme, but I must not linger over it, as we must come to the communion. I will give only one more answer to the question, "Why should we have this rest"? *It will prepare us for Heaven.* I was reading a book, the other day, in which I met with this expression—"The streets of Heaven begin on earth." That is true; Heaven is not so far away as some people think. Heaven is the place of perfect holiness, the place of sinless service, the place of eternal glory; and there is nothing that will prepare us for Heaven like this rest that Jesus gives. Heaven must be in us before we are in Heaven; and he who has this rest has Heaven begun below. Enoch was virtually in Heaven while he walked with God on the earth, and he had only to continue that holy walk to find himself actually in Heaven. This world is part of our Lord's great house, of which Heaven is the upper story. Some of us may hear the Master's call, "Come up higher," sooner than we think; and then, will we rest *in* Christ, there we shall rest *with* Christ. The more we have of this blessed rest now, the better shall we be prepared for the rest that remaineth to the people of God, that eternal "keeping of a Sabbath" in the Paradise above.

III. I have left myself only a minute for the answers to my third question—how can we obtain this rest?

First, by *coming to Christ*. He says, "Come unto Me...and I will give you rest." I trust that all in this little company have come to Christ by faith; now let us come to Him in blessed fellowship and communion at His table. Let us keep on coming to Him, as the apostle says, "to whom coming," continually coming, and never going away. When we wake in the morning, let us come to Christ in the act of renewed communion with Him; all the day long, let us keep on coming to Him even while we are occupied with the affairs of this life; and at night, let our last waking moments be spent in coming to Jesus. Let us come to Christ by searching the Scriptures, for we shall find Him there on almost every page. Let us come to Christ in our thoughts, desires, aspirations wishes; so shall the promise of the text be fulfilled to us, "I will give you rest."

Next, we obtain rest by *yielding to Christ*. "Take My yoke upon you...and ye shall find rest unto your souls." Christ bids us wear *His* yoke, not make one for ourselves. He wants us to share the yoke with Him, to be His true yoke-fellow. It is wonderful that He should be willing to be yoked with us; the only greater wonder is that we should be so unwilling to be yoked with Him. In taking His yoke upon us what joy we shall enter upon our eternal rest! Here we find rest unto our souls; a further rest beyond that which He gives us when we come to Him. We first rest in Jesus by faith, and then we rest in Him by obedience. The first rest He gives through His death; the further rest we find through copying His life.

Lastly, we secure this rest *by learning of Christ*. "Learn of Me, for I am meek and lowly in heart: and ye shall find rest unto your souls." We are to be workers with Christ, taking His yoke upon us; and, at the same time, we are to be scholars in Christ's school, learning of Him. We are to learn *of* Christ, and to learn *Christ;* He is both Teacher and lesson. His gentleness of heart fits Him to teach, and makes Him the best illustration of His own teaching. If we can become as He is, we shall rest as He does. The lowly in heart will be restful of heart. Now, as we come to the table of communion, may we find to the full that rest of which we have been speaking, for the Great Rest-Giver's sake! Amen.

Christ's Passion

Gethsemane

"And being in an agony he prayed more earnestly: and his sweat was as it were great drops of blood falling down to the ground."—Luke 22:44.

Few had fellowship with the sorrows of Gethsemane. The majority of the disciples were not there. They were not sufficiently advanced in grace to be admitted to behold the mysteries of "the agony." Occupied with the Passover feast at their own houses, they represent the many who live upon the letter, but are mere babes and sucklings as to the spirit of the gospel. The walls of Gethsemane fitly typify that weakness in grace which effectually shuts in the deeper marvels of communion from the gaze of ordinary believers. To twelve, nay, to eleven only was the privilege given to enter Gethsemane and see this great sight. Out of the eleven, eight were left at some distance; they had fellowship, but not of that intimate sort to which the men greatly beloved are admitted.

Only three highly favored ones, who had been with Him on the mount of transfiguration, and had witnessed the life-giving miracle in the house of Jairus—only these three could approach the veil of His mysterious sorrow; within that veil even these must not intrude; a stone's-cast distance must be left between. He must tread the wine-press alone, and of the people there must be none with Him. Peter and the two sons of Zebedee, represent the few eminent, experienced, grace-taught saints, who may be written down as "Fathers"; these having done business on great waters, can in some degree, measure the huge Atlantic waves of their Redeemer's passion; having been much alone with Him, they can read His heart far better than those who merely see Him amid the crowd.

To some selected spirits it is given, for the good of others, and to strengthen them for some future, special, and tremendous conflict, to enter the inner circle and hear the pleadings of the suffering High Priest; they have fellowship with Him in His sufferings, and are made conformable unto His death. Yet I say, even these, the elect out of the elect, these choice and peculiar favorites among the king's courtiers, even these cannot penetrate the secret places of the Savior's woe, so as to comprehend all His agonies. "Thine unknown sufferings" is the remarkable expression of the Greek liturgy; for there is an inner chamber in His grief, shut out from human knowledge and fellowship. Was it not here that Christ was more than ever an "unspeakable gift" to us? Is not Watts right when he sings

> And all the unknown joys He gives,
> Were bought with agonies unknown.

Since it would not be possible for any believer, however experienced, to know for himself all that our Lord endured in the place of the olive-press, when He was crushed beneath the upper and the nether mill-stone of mental suffering and hellish malice, it is clearly far beyond the preacher's capacity to set it forth to you. Jesus Himself must give you access to the wonders of Gethsemane: as for me, I can but invite you to enter the garden, bidding you put your shoes from off your feet, for the place whereon we stand is holy ground.

Several matters will require our brief consideration. Come Holy Spirit, breathe light into our thoughts, life into our words.

I. Come hither and behold the Savior's unutterable woe.

The emotions of that dolorous night are expressed by several words in Scripture. John describes Him as saying four days before His passion, "Now is my soul troubled," as He marked the gathering clouds. He hardly knew where to turn Himself, and cried out "What shall I say?" Matthew writes of Him, "he began to be sorrowful and very heavy." Upon the word αδημονειν translated "very heavy," Goodwin remarks that there was a distraction in the Savior's agony, since the root of the word signifies "separated from the people—men in distraction, being separated from mankind." What a thought, my brethren, that our blessed Lord should be driven to the very verge of distraction by the intensity of His anguish.

Matthew represents the Savior Himself as saying "My soul *is exceeding sorrowful,* even unto death." Here the word Περιλυπός means encompassed, encircled, overwhelmed with grief. "He was plunged head and ears in sorrow and had no breathing-hole," is the strong expression of Goodwin.

Sin leaves no cranny for comfort to enter, and therefore the sin-bearer must be entirely immersed in woe. Mark records that He began to be *sore amazed*, and to be very heavy. In this case θαμβεισθαι, with the prefix εκ, shews extremity of amazement like that of Moses when he did exceedingly fear and quake. O blessed Savior, how can we bear to think of Thee as a Man astonished and alarmed! Yet was it even so when the terrors of God set themselves in array against Thee.

Luke uses the strong language of my text—"being in an agony." These expressions, each of them worthy to be the theme of a discourse, are quite sufficient to show that the grief of the Savior was of the most extraordinary character; well justifying the prophetic exclamation, "Behold and see if there be any sorrow like unto my sorrow which was done unto me." He stands before us peerless in misery. None are molested by the powers of evil as He was; as if the powers of Hell had given commandment to their legions, "Fight neither with small nor great, save only with the king himself."

Should we profess to understand all the sources of our Lord's agony, wisdom would rebuke us with the question "Hast thou entered into the springs of the sea? or hast thou walked in search of the depths?" We cannot do more than look at the revealed causes of grief. It partly arose from the horror of His soul *when fully comprehending the meaning of sin*. Brethren, when you were first convinced of sin and saw it as a thing exceeding sinful, though your perception of its sinfulness was but faint compared with its real heinousness, yet horror took hold upon you. Do you remember those sleepless nights? Like the Psalmist, you said "My bones waxed old through my roaring all the day long, for day and night thy hand was heavy upon me; my moisture is turned into the drought of summer."

Some of us can remember when our souls chose strangling rather than life; when, if the shadows of death could have covered us from the wrath of God, we would have been too glad to sleep in the grave that we might not make our bed in Hell. Our blessed Lord saw sin in its natural blackness. He had a most distinct perception of its treasonable assault upon His God, its murderous hatred to Himself, and its destructive influence upon mankind. Well might horror take hold upon Him, for a sight of sin must be far more hideous than a sight of Hell, which is but its off-spring.

Another deep fountain of grief was found in the fact that Christ now *assumed more fully His official position with regard to sin*. He was now made *sin*. Hear the word! He, Who knew no sin, was made *sin* for us, that we might be made the righteousness of God in Him. In that night the words of Isaiah were fulfilled—"The Lord hath laid on him the iniquity of us all." Now He stood as the sin-bearer, the substitute accepted by divine justice to bear that we might never bear the whole of wrath divine. At that hour Heaven looked on Him as standing in the sinner's stead, and treated as sinful man had richly deserved to be treated. Oh! dear friends, when the immaculate Lamb of God found Himself in the place of the guilty, when He could not repudiate that place because He had voluntarily accepted it in order to save His chosen, what must His soul have felt, how must His perfect nature have been shocked at such close association with iniquity?

We believe that at this time, *our Lord had a very clear view of all the shame and suffering of His crucifixion.* The agony was but one of the first drops of the tremendous shower which discharged itself upon His head. He foresaw the speedy coming of the traitor-disciple, the seizure by the officers, the mock-trials before the Sanhedrim, and Pilate, and Herod, the scourging and buffeting, the crown of thorns, the shame, the spitting. All these rose up before His mind, and, as it is a general law of our nature that the foresight of trial is more grievous than trial itself, we can conceive how it was that He Who answered not a word when in the midst of the conflict, could not restrain Himself from strong crying and tears in the prospect of it. Beloved friends, if you can revive before your mind's eye the terrible incidents of His death, the hounding through the streets of Jerusalem, the nailing to the Cross, the fever, the thirst, and, above all, the forsaking of His God, you cannot marvel that He began to be very heavy, and was sore amazed.

But possibly a yet more fruitful tree of bitterness was this—*that now His Father began to withdraw His presence from Him.* The shadow of that great eclipse began to fall upon His spirit when He knelt in that cold midnight amidst the olives of Gethsemane. The sensible comforts which had cheered His spirit were taken away; that blessed application of promises which Christ Jesus needed as a man, was removed; all that we understand by the term "consolations of God" were hidden from His eyes. He was left single-handed in His weakness to contend for the deliverance of man. The Lord stood by as if He were an indifferent spectator, or rather, as if He were an adversary, He wounded Him "with the wound of an enemy, with the chastisement of a cruel one."

But in our judgment the fiercest heat of the Savior's suffering in the garden lay in *the temptations of Satan.* That hour above any time in His life, even beyond the forty days' conflict in the wilderness, was *the time of His* temptation. "This is your hour and the power of darkness." Now could *He* emphatically say, "The prince of this world cometh." This was His last hand-to-hand fight with all the hosts of Hell, and here must He sweat great drops of blood before the victory can be achieved.

II. Turn we next to contemplate the temptation of our Lord.

At the outset of His career, the serpent began to nibble at the heel of the promised deliverer; and now as the time approached when the seed of the woman should bruise the serpent's head, that old dragon made a desperate attempt upon his great destroyer. It is not possible for us to lift the veil where revelation has permitted it to fall, but we can form some faint idea of the suggestions with which Satan tempted our Lord. Let us, however, remark by way of caution, before we attempt to paint this picture, that whatever Satan may have suggested to our Lord, His perfect nature did not in any degree whatever submit to it so as to sin. The temptations were, doubtless, of the very foulest character, but they left no speck or flaw upon Him, Who remained still the fairest among ten thousand. The prince of this world came, but He had nothing in Christ. He struck the sparks, but they did not fall, as in our case, upon dry tinder; they fell as into the sea, and were quenched at once. He hurled the fiery arrows, but they could not even scar the flesh of Christ; they smote upon the buckler of His perfectly righteous nature, and they fell off with their points broken, to the discomfiture of the adversary.

But what, think you, were these temptations? It strikes me, from some hints given, that they were somewhat as follows—there was, first, *a temptation to leave the work unfinished;* we may gather this from the prayer—"If it be possible, let this cup pass from me."

"Son of God," the Tempter said,

. . .is it so? Art Thou really called to bear the sin of man? Hath God said, 'I have laid help upon one that is mighty,' and art thou He, the chosen of God, to bear all this load? Look at thy weakness! Thou sweatest, even now, great drops of blood; surely thou art not He Whom the father hath ordained to be mighty to save; or if Thou be, what wilt Thou win by it? What will it avail Thee? Thou hast glory enough already. See what miscreants they are for whom Thou art to offer up Thyself a sacrifice. Thy best friends are asleep about Thee when most Thou needest their comfort; Thy treasurer, Judas, is hastening to betray Thee for the price of a common slave. The world for which Thou sacrificest Thyself will cast out Thy name as evil, and Thy Church, for which Thou dost pay the ransom-price, what is it worth? A company of mortals! Thy divinity could create the like any moment it pleaseth Thee; why needest Thou, then, pour out Thy soul unto death?

Such arguments would Satan use; the hellish craft of one who had then been thousands of years tempting men, would know how to invent all manner of mischief. He would pour the hottest coals of Hell upon the Savior. It was in struggling with this temptation, among others, that, being in an agony, our Savior prayed more earnestly.

Scripture implies that our Lord was assailed by *the fear that His strength would not be sufficient.* He was heard in that He feared. How, then, was He heard? An angel was sent unto Him strengthening Him. His fear, then, was probably produced by a sense of weakness. I imagine that the foul fiend would whisper in His ear—

> Thou! Thou endure to be smitten of God and abhorred of men! Reproach hath broken Thy heart already; how wilt Thou bear to be publicly put to shame and driven without the city as an unclean thing? How wilt Thou bear to see Thy weeping kinsfolk and Thy broken-hearted mother standing at the foot of Thy cross? Thy tender and sensitive spirit will quail under it. As for Thy body, it is already emaciated; Thy long fastings have brought Thee very low; Thou wilt become a prey to death long ere Thy work is done. Thou wilt surely fail. God hath forsaken Thee. Now will they persecute and take Thee; they will give up Thy soul to the lion, and Thy darling to the power of the dog.

Then would he picture all the sufferings of crucifixion, and say, "Can thine heart endure, or can thine hands be strong in the day when the Lord shall deal with Thee?" The temptation of Satan was not directed against the Godhead, but the manhood of Christ, and therefore the fiend would probably dwell upon the feebleness of man.

> Didst Thou not say Thyself, "I am a worm and no man, the reproach of men and the despised of the people?" How wilt Thou bear it when the wrath-clouds of God gather about Thee? The tempest will surely shipwreck all Thy hopes. It cannot be; Thou canst not drink of this cup, nor be baptized with this baptism.

In this manner, we think, was our Master tried. But see He yields not to it. Being in an agony, which word means in a wrestling, He struggles with the tempter like Jacob with the angel. "Nay," saith He, "I will not be subdued by taunts of My weakness; I am strong in the strength of My Godhead, I will overcome thee yet." Yet was the temptation so awful, that, in order to master it, His mental depression caused Him to "sweat as it were great drops of blood falling down to the ground."

Possibly, also, the temptation may have arisen from a suggestion *that He was utterly forsaken.* I do not know—there may be sterner trials than this, but surely this is *one* of the worst, to be utterly forsaken. "See," said Satan, as he hissed it out between his teeth—

> . . .see, Thou hast a friend nowhere! Look up to Heaven, Thy Father hath shut up the bowels of His compassion against Thee. Not an angel in Thy Father's courts will stretch out his hand to help Thee. Look Thou yonder, not one of those spirits who honored Thy birth will interfere to protect Thy life. All Heaven is false to Thee; Thou art left alone. And as for earth, do not all men thirst for Thy blood? Lo! Thou hast no friend left in Heaven or earth. All Hell is against Thee. I have stirred up mine infernal den. I have sent my missives throughout all regions summoning every prince of darkness to set Thee this upon night, and we will spare no arrows, we will use all our infernal might to overwhelm Thee; and what wilt Thou do, Thou solitary one?"

It may be, this was the temptation; I think it was, because the appearance of an angel unto Him strengthening Him removed that fear. He was heard in that He feared; He was no more alone, but Heaven was with Him.

We think Satan also assaulted our Lord with a bitter taunt indeed. You know in what guise the tempter can dress it, and how bitterly sarcastic he can make the insinuation—

> Ah! *Thou wilt not be able to achieve the redemption of Thy people.* Thy grand benevolence will prove a mockery, and Thy beloved ones will perish. Thou shalt not prevail to save them from my grasp. Thy scattered sheep shall surely be my prey. Son of David, I am a match for Thee; Thou canst not deliver out of my hand. Many of Thy chosen have entered Heaven on the strength of Thine atonement, but I will drag them thence, and quench the stars of glory; I will thin the courts of Heaven of the choristers of God, for Thou wilt not fulfil Thy suretyship; Thou canst not do it. Thou art not able to bring up all this great people; they will perish yet. See, are not the sheep scattered now that the Shepherd is smitten? They will all forget Thee. Thou wilt never see of the travail of Thy soul. Thy desired end will never be reached. Thou wilt be forever the man that began to build but was not able to finish.

Perhaps this is more truly the reason why Christ went three times to look at His disciples. You have seen a mother; she is very faint, weary with a heavy sickness, but she labors under a sore dread that her child will die. She has started from her couch, upon which disease had thrown her, to snatch a moment's rest. She gazes anxiously upon her child. She marks the faintest sign of recovery. But she is sore sick herself, and cannot remain more than an instant from her own bed. She cannot sleep, she tosses painfully, for her thoughts wander; she rises to gaze again—"How art thou, my child, how art thou? Are those palpitations of thy heart less violent? Is thy pulse more gentle?" But, alas! she is faint, and she must go to her bed again, yet she can get no rest. She will return again and again to watch the loved one. So, methinks, Christ looked upon Peter, and James, and John, as much as to say, "No, they are not all lost yet; there are three left"; and, looking upon them as the type of all the Church, He seemed to say—"No, no; I will overcome; I will get the mastery; I will struggle even unto blood; I will pay the ransom-price, and deliver My darlings from their foe."

Now these, methinks, were His temptations. If you can form a fuller idea of what they were than this, then right happy shall I be. With this one lesson I leave the point—*"Pray that ye enter not into temptation."* This is Christ's own expression; His own deduction from His trial. You have all read, dear friends, John Bunyan's picture of Christian fighting with Apollyon. That master-painter has sketched it to the very life. He says, though

> . . .this sore combat lasted for above half a day, even till Christian was almost quite spent. I never saw him all the while give so much as one pleasant look, till he perceived he had wounded Apollyon with his two-edged sword; then, indeed, he did smile and look upward! But it was the dreadfullest sight I ever saw.

That is the meaning of that prayer, "Lead us not into temptation."

Oh you that go recklessly where you are tempted, you that pray for afflictions—and I have known some silly enough to do that—you that put yourselves where you tempt the devil to tempt you, take heed from the Master's own example. He sweats great drops of blood when He is tempted. Oh! pray God to spare you such a trial. Pray this morning and every day, "Lead me not into temptation."

III. Behold, dear brethren, the bloody sweat.

We read, that "he sweat as it were great drops of blood." This phenomenon, though somewhat unusual, has been witnessed in other persons. There are several cases on record, some in the old medicine books of Galen, and others of more recent date, of persons who after long weakness, under fear of death have sweat blood. But this case is altogether one by itself for several reasons. If you will notice, He not only sweat blood, but it was in great drops; the blood coagulated, and formed large masses. I cannot better express what is meant than by the word "gouts"—big, heavy drops. This has not been seen in any case. Some slight effusions of blood have been known in cases of persons who were previously enfeebled, but great drops never. Here He stands unrivaled. He was a man in good health, only about thirty years of age, and was laboring under no fear of death; but the mental pressure arising from His struggle with temptation, and the straining of all His strength, in order to baffle the temptation of Satan, so forced His frame to an unnatural excitement, that His pores sent forth great drops of blood which fell down to the ground. This proves how tremendous must have been the weight of sin when it was able so to crush the Savior that He distilled drops of blood! This proves too, my brethren, the mighty power of His love.

It is a very pretty observation of old Isaac Ambrose that the gum which exudes from the tree without cutting is always the best. This precious camphor-tree yielded most sweet spices when it was wounded under the knotty whips and when it was pierced by the nails on the cross; but see, it giveth forth its best spice when there is no whip, no nail, no wound. This sets forth the voluntariness of Christ's sufferings, since without a lance the blood flowed freely. No need to put on the leech, or apply the knife; it flows spontaneously. No need for the rulers to cry "Spring up, O well"; of itself it flows in crimson torrents.

Dearly beloved friends, if men suffer some frightful pain of mind—I am not acquainted with the medical matter—apparently the blood rushes to the heart. The cheeks are pale; a fainting fit comes on; the blood has gone inward, as if to nourish the inner man while passing through its trial. But see our Savior in His agony; He is so utterly oblivious of self, that instead of His agony driving His blood to the heart to nourish himself, it drives it outward to bedew the earth. The agony of Christ, inasmuch as it pours Him out upon the ground, pictures the fullness of the offering which He made for men.

Do you not perceive, my brethren, how intense must have been the wrestling through which He passed, and will you not hear its voice *to you?*—"Ye have not yet resisted unto blood, striving against sin." It has been the lot of some of us to have sore temptations—else we did not know how to teach others—so sore that in wrestling against them the cold, clammy sweat has stood upon our brow. The place will never be forgotten by me—a lonely spot; where, musing upon my God, an awful rush of blasphemy went over my soul, till I would have preferred death to the trial; and I fell on my knees there and then, for the agony was awful, while my hand was at my mouth to keep the blasphemies from being spoken.

Once let Satan be permitted really to try you with a temptation to blasphemy, and you will never forget it, though you live till your hairs are blanched; or let him attack you with some lust, and though you hate and loathe the very thought of it, and would lose your right arm sooner than indulge in it, yet it will come, and hunt, and persecute, and torment you. Wrestle against it even unto sweat, my brethren, yea, even unto blood. Pray that ye enter not into temptation, so that when ye enter into it ye may with confidence say, "Lord, I did not seek this, therefore help me through with it, for Thy name's sake."

IV. I want you, in the fourth place, to notice the Savior's prayer.

Dear friends, when we are tempted and desire to overcome, the best weapon is prayer. When you cannot use the sword and the shield, take to yourself the famous weapon of all—prayer. So your Savior did. Let us notice His prayer. *It was lonely prayer.* He withdrew even from His three best friends about a stone's cast. Believer, especially in temptation, be much in solitary prayer. As private prayer is the key to open Heaven, so is it the key to shut the gates of Hell. As it is a shield to prevent, so is it the sword with which to fight against temptation. Family prayer, social prayer, prayer in the Church, will not suffice, these are very precious, but the best beaten spice will smoke in your censer in your private devotions, where no ear hears but God. Betake yourselves to solitude if you would overcome.

Mark, too, it was *humble prayer.* Luke says He knelt, but another evangelist says He fell on His face. What! does the King fall on His face? Where, then, must be thy place, thou humble servant of the great Master? Doth the Prince fall flat to the ground? Where, then, wilt thou lie? What dust and ashes shall cover thy head? What sackcloth shall gird thy loins? Humility gives us good foot-hold in prayer. There is no hope of any real prevalence with God, who casteth down the proud, unless we abase ourselves that He may exalt us in due time.

Further, it was *filial prayer.* Matthew describes Him as saying "O my Father," and Mark puts it, "Abba, Father." You will find this always a stronghold in the day of trial to plead your adoption. Hence that prayer, in which it is written, "Lead us not into temptation, but deliver us from evil," begins with "Our Father which art in Heaven." Plead as a child. You have no rights as a subject; you have forfeited them by your treason, but nothing can forfeit a child's right to a father's protection. Be not then ashamed to say, "My Father, hear my cry."

Again, observe that it was *persevering prayer.* He prayed three times, using the same words. Be not content until you prevail. Be as the importunate widow, whose continual coming earned what her first supplication could not win. Continue in prayer, and watch in the same with thanksgiving.

Further, see how it glowed to a red-hot heat—it *was earnest prayer*. "He prayed more earnestly." What groans were those which were uttered by Christ! What tears, which welled up from the deep fountains of His nature! Make earnest supplication if you would prevail against the adversary.

And last, *it was the prayer of resignation*. "Nevertheless, not as I will, but as thou wilt." Yield, and God yields. Let it be as God wills, and God *will* will it that it shall be for the best. Be thou perfectly content to leave the result of thy prayer in His hands, Who knows when to give, and how to give, and what to give, and what to withhold. So pleading, earnestly, importunately, yet mingling with it humility and resignation, thou shalt yet prevail.

Dear friends, we must conclude, turn to the last point with this as a practical lesson—*"Rise and pray."* When the disciples were lying down they slept; sitting was the posture that was congenial to sleep. Rise; shape yourselves; stand up in the name of God; rise and pray. And if you are in temptation, be you more than ever you were in your life before, instant, passionate, importunate with God that He should deliver you in the day of your conflict.

V. As time has failed us, we close with the last point, which is, the Savior's prevalence.

The cloud has passed away. Christ has knelt, and the prayer is over. "But," says one, "did Christ prevail in prayer?" Beloved, could we have any hope that He would prevail in Heaven if He had not prevailed on earth? Should we not have had a suspicion that if His strong crying and tears had not been heard *then*, He would fail *now*? His prayers did speed, and therefore He is a good intercessor for us. "How was He heard?" The answer shall be given very briefly indeed. He was heard, I think, in three respects. The first gracious answer that was given Him was, *that His mind was suddenly rendered calm*. What a difference there is between "My soul is exceeding sorrowful,"—His hurrying to and fro, His repetition of the prayer three times, the singular agitation that was upon Him—what a contrast between all these and His going forth to meet the traitor with "Betrayest thou the Son of Man with a kiss?" Like a troubled sea before, and now as calm as when He Himself said, "Peace be still," and the waves were quiet.

You cannot know a profounder peace than that which reigned in the Savior when before Pilate, He answered him not a word. He is calm to the last, as calm as though it were His day of triumph rather than His day of trouble. Now I think this was vouchsafed to Him in answer to His prayer. He had sufferings perhaps more intense, but His mind was now quieted so as to meet them with greater deliberation.

Next, we believe that He was answered *by God strengthening Him through an angel.* How that was done we do not know. Probably it was by what the angel said, and equally likely is it that it was by what he did. The angel may have whispered the promises; pictured before His mind's eye the glory of His success; sketched His resurrection; portrayed the scene when His angels would bring His chariots from on high to bear Him to His throne; revived before Him the recollection of the time of His advent, the prospect when He should reign from sea to sea, and from the river even to the ends of the earth; and so have made Him strong. Or, perhaps, by some unknown method God sent such power to our Christ, who had been like Samson with his locks shorn, that He suddenly received all the might and majestic energy that were needed for the terrific struggle. Then He walked out of the garden no more a worm and no man, but made strong with an invisible might that made Him a match for all the armies that were round about Him.

And I think we may conclude with saying, that God heard Him in granting Him now, not simply strength, *but a real victory over Satan.* I do not know whether what Adam Clarke supposes is correct, that in the garden Christ did pay more of the price than he did even on the cross; but I am quite convinced that they are very foolish who get to such refinement that they think the atonement was made on the cross, and nowhere else at all. We believe that it was made in the garden as well as on the cross; and it strikes me that in the garden one part of Christ's work was finished, wholly finished: and that was His conflict with Satan. I conceive that Christ had now rather to bear the absence of His Father's presence and the revilings of the people and the sons of men, than the temptations of the devil. I do think that these were over when He rose from His knees in prayer, when He lifted Himself from the ground where He marked His visage in the clay in drops of blood. The temptation of Satan was then over, and He might have said concerning that part of the work—"It is finished; broken is the dragon's head; I have overcome him." If this be so, Christ was then heard in that He feared; He feared the temptation of Satan, and He was delivered from it, He feared His own weakness, and He was strengthened; He feared His own trepidation of mind, and He was made calm.

What shall we say, then, in conclusion, but this lesson. Does it not say "Whatsoever ye shall ask in prayer, believing, ye shall have." Then if your temptations reach the most tremendous height and force, still lay hold of God in prayer and you shall prevail. Convinced sinner! that is a comfort for you. Troubled saint! that is a joy for you. To one and all of us is this lesson of this morning—"Pray that ye enter not into temptation." If in temptation, let us ask that Christ may pray for us that our faith fail not, and when we have passed through the trouble, let us try to strengthen our brethren, even as Christ has strengthened us this day.

Barabbas Preferred to Jesus

"Then cried they all again, saying, 'Not this man, but Barabbas.' Now Barabbas was a robber."—John 18:40.

The custom of delivering a prisoner upon the day of the Passover was intended no doubt as an act of grace on the part of the Roman authorities towards the Jews, and by the Jews it may have been accepted as a significant compliment to their Passover. Since on that day they themselves were delivered out of the land of Egypt, they may have thought it to be most fitting that some imprisoned person should obtain his liberty. There was no warrant however in Scripture for this, it was never commanded by God, and it must have had a very injurious effect upon public justice, that the ruling authority should discharge a criminal, some one quite irrespective of his crimes or of his repentance; letting him loose upon society, simply and only because a certain day must be celebrated in a peculiar manner.

Since some one prisoner must be delivered on the paschal day, Pilate thinks that he has now an opportunity of allowing the Savior to escape without at all compromising his character with the authorities at Rome. He asks the people which of the two they will prefer, a notorious thief then in custody, or the Savior. It is probable that Barabbas had been, till that moment, obnoxious to the crowd; and yet, notwithstanding his former unpopularity—the multitude, instigated by the priests, forget all his faults, and prefer him to the Savior.

Who Barabbas was, we cannot exactly tell. His name, as you in a moment will understand, even if you have not the slightest acquaintance with Hebrew, signifies "his father's son," *"Bar"* signifying "son," as when Peter is called Simon Barjonas, son of Jonas; the other part of his name

"*Abbas,*" signifying "father"—"abbas" being the word which we use in our filial aspirations, "Abba Father." Barabbas, then, is the "son of his father"; and some mysticists think that there is an imputation here, that he was particularly and specially a son of Satan.

Others conjecture that it was an endearing name, and was given him because he was his father's darling, an indulged child; his father's boy, as we say; and these writers add that indulged children often turn out to be imitators of Barabbas, and are the most likely persons to become injurious to their country, griefs to their parents, and curses to all about them. If it be so, taken in connection with the case of Absalom, and especially of Eli's sons, it is a warning to parents that they err not in excessive indulgence of their children. Barabbas appears to have committed three crimes at the least: he was imprisoned for murder, for sedition, and for felony—a sorry combination of offences, certainly; we may well pity the sire of such a son.

This wretch is brought out and set in competition with Christ. The multitude are appealed to. Pilate thinks that from the sense of shame they really cannot possibly prefer Barabbas; but they are also so blood-thirsty against the Savior, and are so moved by the priests, that with one consent—there does not appear to have been a single objecting voice, nor one hand held up to the contrary—with a marvelous unanimity of voice, they cry, "Not this man, but Barabbas," though they must have known, since he was *a notable* well-known offender, that Barabbas was a murderer, a felon, and a traitor.

This fact is very significant. There is more teaching in it than at first sight we might imagine. Have we not here, first of all, in this act of the deliverance of the sinner and the binding of the innocent, a sort of type of that great work which is accomplished by the death of our Savior? You and I may fairly take our stand by the side of Barabbas. We have robbed God of His glory; we have been seditious traitors against the government of Heaven: if he who hateth his brother be a murderer, we also have been guilty of that sin. Here we stand before the judgment seat; the Prince of Life is bound for us and we are suffered to go free. The Lord delivers us and acquits us, while the Savior, without spot or blemish, or shadow of a fault, is led forth to crucifixion.

Two birds were taken in the rite of the cleansing of a leper. The one bird was killed, and its blood was poured into a basin; the other bird was dipped in this blood, and then, with its wings all crimson, it was set free to fly into the open field. The bird slain well pictures the Savior, and every soul that has by faith been dipped in His blood, flies upward towards

Heaven singing sweetly in joyous liberty, owing life and liberty entirely to Him who was slain. It comes to this, Barabbas must die or Christ must die; you the sinner must perish, or Christ Immanuel, the Immaculate, must die. He dies that we may be delivered. Oh! have we all a participation in such a deliverance today? and though we have been robbers, traitors, and murders yet we can rejoice that Christ has delivered us from the curse of the law, having been made a curse for us?

The transaction has yet another voice. This episode in the Savior's history shows that in the judgment of the people, Jesus Christ was a greater offender than Barabbas; and, for once, I may venture to say, that *vox populi* (the voice of the people), which in itself was a most infamous injustice, if it be read in the light of the imputation of our sins to Christ, was *vox Dei* (the voice of God). Christ, as He stood covered with His people's sins, had more sin laid upon Him than that which rested upon Barabbas. In Him was no sin; He was altogether incapable of becoming a sinner: holy, harmless, and undefiled is Christ Jesus, but He takes the whole load of His people's guilt upon Himself by imputation, and as Jehovah looks upon Him, He sees more guilt lying upon the Savior, than even upon this atrocious sinner, Barabbas. Barabbas goes free—innocent—in comparison with the tremendous weight which rests upon the Savior. Think, beloved, then, how low your Lord and Master stooped to be thus *numbered with the transgressors*. Watts has put it strongly, but, I think, none too strongly:

> *His honour and His breath*
> *Were taken both away,*
> *Join'd with the wicked in His death,*
> *And made as vile as they.*

He was so in the estimation of the people, and before the bar of justice, for the sins of the whole company of the faithful were made to meet upon Him. "The Lord hath laid upon him the iniquity of us all." What that iniquity must have been, no heart can conceive, much less can any tongue tell. Measure it by the griefs He bore, and then, if you can guess what these were, you can form some idea of what must have been the guilt which sunk Him lower before the bar of justice than even Barabbas himself. Oh! what condescension is here! The just One dies for the unjust. He bears the sin of many, and makes intercession for the transgressors.

Yet, again, there seems to me to be a third lesson, before I come to that which I want to enforce from the text. Our Savior knew that His disciples would in all ages be hated by the world far more than outward sinners. Full often the world has been more willing to put up with murderers, thieves, and drunkards, than with Christians; and it has fallen to the lot of some of the best and most holy of men to be so slandered and abused that their names have been cast out as evil, scarcely worthy to be written in the same list with criminals. Now, Christ has sanctified these sufferings of His people from the slander of their enemies, by bearing just such sufferings Himself, so that, my brethren, if you or I should find ourselves charged with crimes which we abhor, if our heart should be ready to burst under the accumulation of slanderous venom, let us lift up our head and feel that in all this we have a Comrade who has true fellowship with us, even the Lord Jesus Christ, who was rejected when Barabbas was selected. Expect no better treatment than your master. Remember that the disciple is not above his Lord. If they have called the Master of the house Beelzebub, much more will they call them of His household; and if they prefer the murderer to Christ, the day may not be distant when they will prefer even a murderer to you.

These things seem to me to lie upon the surface; I now come to our more immediate subject. First, we shall consider *the sin as it stands in the Evangelical history;* second, we shall observe that *this is the sin of the whole world;* thirdly, that *this sin we ourselves were guilty of before conversion;* and fourthly, that *this is, we fear, the sin of very many persons who are here this morning:* we shall talk with them and expostulate, praying that the Spirit of God may change their hearts and lead them to accept the Savior.

I. *A few minutes may be profitably spent in considering, then, the sin as we find it in this history.*

They preferred Barabbas to Christ. The sin will be more clearly seen if we remember that *the Savior had done no ill.* No law, either of God or man, had He broken. He might truly have used the words of Samuel—"Behold, here I am: witness against me before the Lord, and before his anointed; whose ox have I taken? or whose ass have I taken? or whom have I defrauded? whom have I oppressed? or of whose hand have I received any bribe to blind mine eyes therewith? and I will restore it you." Out of that whole assembled crowd there was not one who would have had the presumption to accuse the Savior of having done him damage.

So far from this, they could but acknowledge that *He had even conferred great temporal blessings upon them.* O ravening multitude, has He not fed you when you were hungry? Did He not multiply the loaves and fishes for you? Did He not heal your lepers with His touch? cast out devils from your sons and daughters? raise up you paralytics? give sight to your blind, and open the ears of your deaf? For which of these good works do ye conspire to kill Him? Among that assembled multitude, there were doubtless some who owed to Him priceless boons, and yet, though all of them his debtors if they had known it, they clamor against Him as though He were the worst trouble of their lives, a pest and a pestilence to the place where He dwelt.

Was it His teaching that they complained of? Wherein did His teaching offend against morality? Wherein against the best interests of man? If you observe the teaching of Christ there was never any like it, even judge of by how far it would subserve human welfare. Here was the sum and substance of His doctrine, "Thou shalt love the Lord thy God with all thy heart, and thy neighbor as thyself." His precepts were of the mildest form. Did He bid them draw the sword and expel the Roman, or ride on in a ruthless career of carnage, and rapine? Did he stimulate them to let loose their unbridled passions? Did He tell them to seek first of all their own advantage and not to care for their neighbor's weal? Nay, every righteous state must own Him to be its best pillar, and the commonwealth of manhood must acknowledge Him to be its conservator; and yet, for all this, there they are, hounded on by their priests, seeking His blood, and crying, "Let him be crucified! let him be crucified!"

His whole intent evidently was their good. What did He preach for? No selfish motive could have been urged. Foxes had holes, and the birds of the air had nests, but He had nowhere to lay His head. The charity of a few of His disciples alone kept Him from absolute starvation. Cold mountains, and the midnight air, witnessed the fervor of His lonely prayers for the multitudes who are now hating Him. He lived for others: they could see this; they could not have observed Him during the three years of His ministry without saying, "Never lived there such an unselfish soul as this"; they must have known, the most of them, and the rest might have known, had they enquired ever so little, that He had no object whatever in being here on earth, except that of seeking the good of men.

For which of these things do they clamor that He may be crucified? For which of His good works, for which of His generous words, for which of His holy deeds will they fasten His hands to the wood, and His feet to the tree? With unreasonable hatred, with senseless cruelty, they only answer to the question of Pilate, "Why, what evil hath he done?" "Let him be crucified! let him be crucified!" The true reason of their hate, no doubt, lay in the natural hatred of all men to perfect goodness. Man feels that the presence of goodness is a silent witness against his own sin, and therefore he longs to get rid of it. To be too holy in the judgment of men is a great crime, for it rebukes their sin. If the holy man has not the power of words, yet his life is one loud witness-bearing for God against the sins of his creatures. This inconvenient protesting led the wicked to desire the death of the holy and just One.

Besides, the priests were at their backs. It is a sad and lamentable thing, but it is often the case that the people are better than their religious teachers. No doubt bribery also was used in this case. Had not Rabbi Simon paid the multitude? Was there not a hope of some feast after the Passover was over to those who would use their throats against the Savior? Beside, there was the multitude going that way; and so if any had compassion they held their tongue. Often they say that "Discretion is the better part of valor;" and truly there must be many valorous men, for they have much of valor's better part, discretion. If they did not join in the shout, yet at least they would not incommode the others, and so there was but one cry, "Away with him! away with him! It is not fit that he should live." What concentrated scorn there is this fortieth verse. It is not "this Jesus," they would not foul their mouths with His name, but this *fellow*—"this devil," if you will. To Barabbas they give the respect of mentioning his name; but "this—" whom they hate so much, they will not even stoop to mention. We have looked, then, at this great sin as it stands in history.

II. But now let us look, in the second place, at this incident as setting forth the sin which has been the guilt of the world in all ages, and which is the world's guilt now.

When the apostles went forth to preach the gospel, and the truth had spread through many countries, there were severe edicts passed by the Roman Emperors. Against whom were these edicts framed? Against the foul offenders of that day? It is well known that the whole Roman Empire was infested with vices such as the cheek of modesty would blush to hear named.

The first chapter of the Epistle to the Romans is a most graphic picture of the state of society throughout the entire Roman dominions. When severe laws were framed, why were they not proclaimed against these atrocious vices? It is scarcely fit that men should go unpunished who are guilty of crimes such as the apostle Paul has mentioned, but I find no edicts against these things—I find that they were borne with and scarcely mentioned with censure; but burning, dragging at the heels of wild horses, the sword, imprisonment, tortures of every kind, were used against whom think you? Against the innocent, humble followers of

Christ, who, so far from defending themselves, were willing to suffer all these things, and presented themselves like sheep at the shambles, willing to endure the butcher's knife.

The cry of the world, under the persecutions of Imperial Rome, was "Not Christ, but Sodomites, and murderers, and thieves—we will bear with any of these, but not with Christ; away with his followers from the earth." Then the world changed its tactics; it became nominally Christian, and Antichrist came forth in all its blasphemous glory. The Pope of Rome put on the triple crown, and called himself the Vicar of Christ; then came in the abomination of the worship of saints, angels, images, and pictures; then came the Mass, and I know not what, of detestable error; and what did the world say? "Popery forever!" Down went every knee, and every head bowed before the sovereign representative of Peter at Rome. The world chose the harlot of Rome, and she who was drunk with the wine of her abominations had every eye to gaze upon her with admiration, while Christ's gospel was forgotten, buried in a few old books, and almost extinguished in darkness.

Since that day the world has changed its tactics yet again; in many parts of the Earth Protestantism is openly acknowledged, and the gospel is preached, but what then? Then comes in Satan, and another Barabbas, the Barabbas of mere ceremonialism, and mere attendance at a place of worship is set up. So long as we are as good as our neighbors, and keep the outward rite, the inward does not matter. An outward name to live is set up, and is received by those who are dead; and many of you now present are quite easy and content, though you have never felt the quickening Spirit of God: though you have never been washed in the atoning blood, yet you are satisfied because you take a seat in some place of worship; you give your guinea, your donation to an hospital, or your subscription to a good object, forgetting and not caring to remember that all the making clean of the outside of the cup and the platter will never avail, unless the inward nature be renewed by the Spirit of the living God. This is the great Barabbas of the present age, and men prefer it before the Savior.

That this is true, that the world really loves sin better than Christ, I think I could prove clearly enough by one simple fact. You have observed sometimes Christian men inconsistent, have you not? The inconsistency was nothing very great, if you had judged them according to ordinary rules of conduct. But you are well aware that a worldly man might commit any sin he liked, without much censure; but if the Christian man commits ever so little, then hands are held up, and the whole world cries, "Shame!" I do not want to have that altered, but I do want just to say this:

"There is Mr. So-and-So, who is known to live a fast, wicked, gay life; well, I do not see that he is universally avoided and reprobated, but on the contrary, he is tolerated by most, and admired by some." But suppose a Christian man, a well-known professor [of the faith], to have committed some fault which, compared with this, were not worth mentioning, and what is done? "Oh! publish it! publish it! Have you heard what Mr. So-and-So did? Have you heard of this hypocrite's transgression?" "Well, what was it?" You look at it: "Well, it is wrong, it is very wrong, but compared with what you say about it is nothing at all."

The world therefore shows by the difference between the way in which it judges the professedly religious man, and that with which it judges its own, that it really can tolerate the most abandoned, but cannot tolerate the Christian. Of course, the Christian never will be altogether free from imperfections; the world's enmity is not against the Christian's imperfections evidently, because they will tolerate greater imperfections in others. The objection must therefore be against the man, against the profession which he has taken up, and the course which he desires to follow. Watch carefully, beloved, that ye give them no opportunity; but when ye see that the slightest mistake is laid hold of and exaggerated, in this you see a clear evidence that the world prefers Barabbas to the followers of the Lord Jesus Christ.

III. I come in the third place, and O for some assistance from on high, to observe that the sin of preferring Barabbas to Christ was the sin of every one of us before our conversion.

Will you turn over the leaves of your diary, now, dear friends, or fly upon the wings of memory to the hole of the pit whence you were digged. Did you not, O you who live close to Christ, did you not once despise Him? What company did you like best? Was it not that of the frivolous, if not that of the profane? When you sat with God's people, their talk was very tedious; if they spoke of divine realities, and of experimental subjects, you did not understand them, you felt them to be troublesome. I can look back upon some whom I know now to be most venerable believers, whom I thought to be a gross nuisance when I heard them talk of the things of God. What were our thoughts about? When we had time for thinking, what were our favorite themes? Not much did we meditate upon eternity; not much upon Him who came to deliver us from the misery of Hell's torments.

Brethren, His great love wherewith He loved us was never laid to heart by us as it should have been; nay, if we read the story of the crucifixion, it had no more effect upon our mind than a common tale. We knew not the beauties of Christ; we thought of any trifle sooner than of Him. And what were our pleasures? When we had what we called a day's enjoyment, where did we seek it? At the foot of the cross? In the service of the Savior? In communion with Him? Far from it; the further we could remove from godly associations the better pleased we were. Some of us have to confess with shame that we were never more in our element than when we were without a conscience, when conscience ceased to accuse us and we could plunge into sin with riot.

What was our reading then? Any book sooner than the Bible: and if there had lain in our way anything that would have exalted Christ and extolled Him in our understandings, we should have put by the book as much too dry to please us. Any three-volume heap of nonsense, any light literature; nay, perhaps, even worse would have delighted our eye and our heart; but thoughts of *His* eternal delight towards us—thoughts of His matchless passion and His glory now in Heaven, never came across our minds, nor would we endure those who would have led us to such meditations.

What were our aspirations then? We were looking after business, aiming at growing rich, famous for learning or admired for ability. Self was what we lived for. If we had some regard for others, and some desire to benefit our race, yet self was at the bottom of it all. We did not live for God—we could not honestly say, as we woke in the morning, "I hope to live for God today"; at night, we could not look back upon the day, and say, "We have this day served God." He was not in all our thoughts. Where did we spend our best praise? Did we praise Christ? No; we praised cleverness, and when it was in association with sin, we praised it none the less. We admired those who could most fully minister to our own fleshly delights, and felt the greatest love to those who did us the worst injury. Is not this our confession as we review the past? Have I not read the very history of your life? I know I have of my own. Alas! for those dark days, in which our besotted soul went after any evil, but would not follow after Christ.

It would have been the same today with us, if almighty grace had not made the difference. We may as well expect the river to cease to run to the sea, as expect the natural man to turn from the current of his sins. As well might we expect fire to become water, or water to become fire, as for the unrenewed heart ever to love Christ. It was mighty grace which made us to seek the Savior. And as we look back upon our past lives, it must be with mingled feelings of gratitude for the change, and of sorrow that we should have been so grossly foolish as to have chosen Barabbas, and have said of the Savior, "Let him be crucified!"

IV. And now I shall come to the closing part of the sermon, which is, that there are doubtless many here who this day prefer Barabbas to our Lord Jesus Christ.

Let me first state your case, dear friends. I would describe it honestly, but at the same time so describe it that you will see your sin in it; and while I am doing so, my object will be to expostulate with you, if haply the Lord may change your will. There are many here, I fear, who prefer sin to Christ. There stands drunkenness, I see it mirrored before me with all its folly, its witlessness, its greed and filth; but the man chooses all that, and though he has known by head knowledge something concerning the beauty and excellency of Christ, he virtually says of Jesus, "Not this man, but drunkenness."

Then there are other cases, where a favorite lust reigns supreme in their hearts. The men know the evil of the sin, and they have good cause to know it; they know also something of the sweetness of religion, for they are never happier than when they come up with God's people; and they go home sometimes from a solemn sermon, especially if it touches their vice, and they feel, "God has spoken to my soul today, and I am brought to a standstill." But for all that, the temptation comes again, and they fall as they have fallen before. I am afraid there are some of you whom no arguments will ever move; you have become so set on this mischief, that it will be your eternal ruin. But oh! think you, how will this look when you are in Hell—"I preferred that foul Barabbas of lust to the beauties and perfections of the Savior, who came into the world to seek and to save that which was lost!" and yet this is the case, not of some, but of a great multitude who listen to the gospel, and yet prefer sin to its saving power.

There may be some here, too, of another class, who prefer *gain*. It has come to this: if they become truly the Lord's people, they cannot do in trade what they now think their trade requires them to do; if they become really and genuinely believers, they must of course become honest, but their trade would not pay, they say, if it were conducted upon honest principles; or it is such a trade, and there are some few such, as ought not to be conducted at all, much less by Christians. Here comes the turning-point. Shall I take the gold, or shall I take Christ? True, it is cankered gold, and gold on which a curse must come. It is the fool's pence, maybe it is gain that is extorted from the miseries of the poor; it is money that would not ever stand the light because it is not fairly come by; money that will burn its way right through your souls when you get upon your death-beds; but yet men who love the world, say, "No, not Christ, give me a full purse, and away with Christ." Others, less base or less honest, cry, "We know His excellence, we wish we could have Him, but we cannot have Him on terms which involve the renunciation of our dearly beloved gain." "Not this man, but Barabbas."

I might thus multiply instances, but the same principle runs through them all. If anything whatever keeps you back from giving your heart to the Lord Jesus Christ, you are guilty of setting up an opposition candidate to Christ in your soul, and you are choosing "not this man, but Barabbas."

Let me occupy a few minutes with pleading Christ's cause with you. Why is it that you reject Christ? Are you not conscious of the many good things which you receive from Him? You would have been dead if it had not been for Him; nay, worse than that, you would have been in Hell. God has sharpened the great axe; justice, like a stern woodman, stood with the axe up-lifted, ready to cut you down as a cumberer of the ground. A hand was seen stopping the arm of the avenger, and a voice was heard saying, "Let it alone, till I dig about it and dung it." Who was it that appeared just then in your moment of extremity? It was no other than that Christ, of whom you think so little that you prefer drunkenness or vice to Him! You are this day in the house of God, listening to a discourse which I hope is sent from Him. You might have been in Hell—think one moment of that—shut out from hope, endur-ing in body and soul unutterable pangs. That you are not there, should make you love and bless Him, who has said, "Deliver him from going down into the pit." Why will you prefer your own gain and self-indulgence to that blessed One to whom you owe so much? Common gratitude should make you deny yourself something for Him who denied Himself so much that He might bless you.

Do I hear you say that you cannot follow Christ, because His precepts are too severe? In what respect are they too severe? If you yourself were set to judge them, what is the point with which you would find fault? They deny you your sins—say, they deny you your miseries. They do not permit you, in fact, to ruin yourself. There is no precept of Christ which is not for your good, and there is nothing which He forbids you which He does not forbid on the principle that it would harm you to indulge in it. But suppose Christ's precepts to be ever so stern, is it not better that you should put up with them than be ruined?

The soldier submits implicitly to the captain's command, because he knows that without discipline there can be no victory, and the whole army may be cut in pieces if there be a want of order. When the sailor has risked his life to penetrate through the thick ice of the north, we find him consenting to all the orders and regulations of authority, and bearing all the hardships of the adventure, because he is prompted by the desire of assisting in a great discovery, or stimulated by a large reward. And surely the little self-denials which Christ calls us to will be abundantly recompensed by the reward He offers; and when the soul and its eternal interests are at stake, we may well put up with these temporary inconveniences if we may inherit eternal life.

I think I hear you say that you would be a Christian, but there is no happiness in it. I would not tell you a falsehood on this point, I would speak the truth if it were so, but I do solemnly declare that there is more joy in the Christian life than there is in any other form of life; that if I had to die like a dog, and there were no hereafter, I would prefer to be a Christian. You shall appeal to the very poorest among us, to those who are most sick and most despised, and they will tell you the same. There is not an old country woman shivering in her old ragged red cloak over a handful of fire, full of rheumatism, with an empty cupboard and an aged body, who would change with the very highest and greatest of you if she had to give up her religion; no, she would tell you that her Redeemer was a greater comfort to her than all the luxuries which could be heaped upon the tables of Dives.

You make a mistake when you dream that my Master does not make His disciples blessed; they are a blessed people who put their trust in Christ. Still I think I hear you say, "Yes, this is all very well, but still I prefer *present* pleasure." Dost thou not in this talk like a child; nay, like a fool, for what is present pleasure? How long does that word "present" last? If thou couldst have ten thousand years of merriment I might agree with thee in a measure, but even there I should have but short patience with thee, for what would be ten thousand years of sin's merriment compared with millions upon millions of years of sin's penalty.

Why, at the longest, your life will be but very short. Are you not conscious that time flies more hurriedly every day? As you grow older, do you not seem as if you had lived a shorter time instead of longer? till, perhaps, if you could live to be as old as Jacob, you would say, "Few and evil have my days been, for they appear fewer as they grow more numerous." You know that this life is but a span, and is soon over. Look to the graveyards, see how they are crowded with green mounds. Remember your own companions, how one by one they have passed away. They were as firm and strong as you, but they have gone like a shadow that declineth. Is it worth while to have this snatch space of pleasure, and then to lie down in eternal pain? I pray you to answer this question. Is it worth while to choose Barabbas for the sake of the temporary gain he may give you, and give up Christ, and so renounce the eternal treasures of joy and happiness which are at His right hand for evermore?

Many men profess to be believers in Scripture, and yet, when you come to the point as to whether they do believe in eternal woe and eternal joy, there is a kind of something inside which whispers, "That is in the Book—but still it is not real, it is not true to us." Make it true to yourselves, and when you have so done it, and have clearly proved that you must be in happiness or woe, and that you must here either have Barabbas for your master, or have Christ for your Lord, then, I say, like sane men, judge which is the better choice, and may God's mighty grace give you spiritual sanity to make the right choice; but this I know, you never will unless that mighty Spirit who alone leads us to choose the right, and reject the wrong, shall come upon you and lead you to fly to a Savior's wounds.

I need not, I think, prolong the service now, but I hope you will prolong it at your own houses by thinking of the matter. And may I put the question personally to all as you separate: whose are you? On whose side are you? There are no neuters; there are no betweenites: you either serve Christ or Belial; you are either with the Lord or with His enemies. Who is on the Lord's side this day? Who? Who is for Christ and for His Cross; for His blood, and for His throne? Who, on the other hand, are His foes? As many as are not for Christ, are numbered with His enemies. Be not so numbered any longer, for the gospel comes to you with an inviting voice—"Believe in the Lord Jesus Christ, and thou shalt be saved." God help thee to believe and cast thyself upon Him now; if and thou trustest Him, thou art saved now, and thou shalt be saved forever. Amen.

The Precious Blood of Christ

"The precious blood of Christ."—*I Peter 1:19.*

Blood has from the beginning been regarded by God as a most precious thing. He has hedged about this fountain of vitality with the most solemn sanctions. The Lord thus commanded Noah and his descendants, "Flesh with the life thereof, which is the blood thereof, shall ye not eat." Man had every moving thing that liveth given him for meat, but they were by no means to eat the blood with the flesh. Things strangled were to be considered unfit for food, since God would not have man became too familiar with blood by eating or drinking it in any shape or form. Even the blood of bulls and goats thus had a sacredness put upon it by God's decrees.

As for the blood of man, you remember how God's threatening ran,

And surely your blood of your lives will I require; at the hand of every beast will I require it, and at the hand of man; at the hand of every man's brother will I require the life of man. Whoso sheddeth man's blood, by man shall his blood be shed: for in the image of God made he man.

It is true that the first murderer had not his blood shed by man, but then the crime was new and the penalty had not then been settled and proclaimed, and therefore the case was clearly exceptional, and one by itself; and, moreover, Cain's doom was probably far more terrible than if he had been slain upon the spot: he was permitted to fill up his measure of wickedness, to be a wanderer and a vagabond upon the face of the earth, and then to enter into the dreadful heritage of wrath, which his life of sin had doubtless greatly increased. Under the theocratic dispensation, in which God was the King and governed Israel, murder was always punished in the most exemplary manner, and there was never any toleration or excuse for it. Eye for eye, tooth for tooth, life for life, was the stern inexorable law. It is expressly written, "Ye shall take no satisfaction for the life of a murderer which is guilty of death: but he shall surely be put to death."

Even in cases where life was taken in chance: melee or misadventure, the matter was not overlooked. The slayer fled at once to the city of refuge, where, after having his case properly tried, he was allowed to reside; but there was no safety for him elsewhere until the death of the high priest. The general law in all cases was,

> So ye shall not pollute the land wherein ye are: for blood, it defileth the land: and the land cannot be cleansed of the blood that is shed therein, but by the blood of him that shed it. Defile not therefore the land which ye shall inhabit, wherein I dwell: for I the Lord dwell among the children of Israel.

It is clear, then, that blood was ever precious in God's sight, and He would have it so in ours.

Now, if in ordinary cases the shedding of life be thus precious, can you guess how fully God utters His heart's meaning when He says, "Precious in the sight of the Lord is the death *of his saints?*" If the death of a rebel be precious, what must be the death of a child? If He will not contemplate the shedding of the blood of His own enemies and of them that curse Him without proclaiming vengeance, what think you concerning His own elect, of whom He says, "Precious shall their blood be in his sight?" Will He not avenge them, though He bear long with them? Shall the cup which the harlot of Rome filled with the blood of the saints, long remain unavenged? Shall not the martyrs from Piedmont and the Alps, and from our Smithfield, and from the hills of covenanting Scotland, yet obtain from God the vengeance due for all that they suffered, and all the blood which they poured forth in the defense of His cause?

I have taken you up, you see, from the *beast* to *man,* from man to *God's chosen* men, the martyrs. I have another step to indicate to you: it is a far longer one—it is to the blood of *Jesus Christ.* Here, powers of speech would fail to convey to you an idea of the preciousness! Behold here, a person innocent, without taint within, or flaw without; a Person meritorious, who magnified the law and made it honour able—a Person who served both God and man even unto death. Nay, here you have a divine Person—so divine, that in the Acts of the Apostles Paul calls His blood the "blood of God." Place innocence, and merit, and dignity, and position, and Godhead itself, in the scale, and then conceive what must be the inestimable value of the blood which Jesus Christ poured forth. Angels must have seen that matchless blood shedding with wonder and amazement, and even God Himself saw what never before was seen in creation or in providence; He saw Himself more gloriously displayed than in the whole universe beside.

Let us come nearer to the text and try to shew forth the preciousness of the blood of Christ. We shall confine ourselves to an enumeration of some of the many properties possessed by this precious blood. I felt as I was studying, that I should have so many divisions this morning, that some of you would compare my sermon to the bones in Ezekiel's vision—they were very many and they were very dry; but I am in hopes that God's Holy Spirit may so descend upon the bones in my sermon, which would be but dry of themselves, that they being quickened and full of life, you may admire the exceeding great army of God's thoughts of loving-kindness towards His people, in the sacrifice of His own dear Son.

The precious blood of Christ is useful to God's people in a thousand ways: we intend to speak of twelve of them. After all, the real preciousness of a thing in the time of pinch and trial, must depend upon its usefulness. A bag of pearls would be to us, this morning, far more precious than a bag of bread; but you have all heard the story of the man in the desert, who stumbled, when near to die, upon a bag, and opened it, hoping that it might be the wallet of some passer-by, and he found in it *nothing but pearls!* If they had been crusts of bread, how much more precious would they have been! I say, in the hour of necessity and peril, the use of a thing really constitutes the preciousness of it. This may not be according to political economy, but it is according to common sense.

I. The precious blood of Christ has a redeeming power. It redeems from the law.

We were all under the law which says, "This do, and live." We were slaves to it: Christ has paid the ransom price, and the law is no longer our tyrant master. We are entirely free from it. The law had a dreadful curse; it threatened that whosoever should violate one of its precepts, should die: "Christ hath redeemed us from the curse of the law, being made a curse for us." By the fear of this curse, the law inflicted a continual dread on those who were under it; they knew they had disobeyed it, and they were all their lifetime subject to bondage, fearful lest death and destruction should come upon them at any moment: but we are not under the law, but under grace, and consequently "We have not received the spirit of bondage again to fear, but we have received the spirit of adoption, whereby we cry, Abba, Father."

We are not afraid of the law now; its worst thunders cannot affect us, for they are not hurled at us! Its most tremendous lightening cannot touch us, for we are sheltered beneath the Cross of Christ, where the thunder loses its terror and the lightning its fury. We read the law of God with pleasure now; we look upon it as in the Ark covered with the mercy seat, and not thundering in tempests from Sinai's fiery brow.

Happy is that man who knows his full redemption from the law, its curse, its penalty, its present dread. My brethren, the life of a Jew, happy as it was compared with that of a heathen, was perfect drudgery compared to yours and mine. He was hedged in with a thousand commands and prohibitions, his forms and ceremonies were abundant, and their details minutely arranged. He was always in danger of making himself unclean. If he sat upon a bed or upon a stool, he might be defiled; if he drank out of an earthen pitcher, or even touched the wall of a house, a leprous man might have put his hand there before him, and he would thus become defiled.

A thousand sins of ignorance were like so many hidden pits in his way; he must be perpetually in fear lest he should be cut off from the people of God. When he had done his best any one day, he knew he had not finished; no Jew could ever talk of a finished work. The bullock was offered, but he must bring another; the lamb was offered this morning, but another must be offered this evening, another tomorrow, and another the next day. The Passover is celebrated with holy rites; it must be kept in the same manner next year. The high priest has gone within the veil once, but he must go there again; the thing is never finished, it is always beginning. He never comes any nearer to the end. "The law could not make the comer thereunto perfect."

But see *our* position: we are redeemed from this. Our law is fulfilled, for Christ is the end of the law for righteousness; our Passover is slain, for Jesus died; our righteousness is finished, for we are complete in Him; our victim is slain, our priest has gone within the veil, the blood is sprinkled; we are clean, and clean beyond any fear of defilement, "For he hath perfected forever those that were set apart." Value this precious blood, my beloved, because thus it has redeemed you from the thraldom and bondage which the law imposed upon its votaries.

II. The value of the blood lies much in its atoning efficacy.

We are told in Leviticus, that "it is the blood which maketh an atonement for the soul." God never forgave sin apart from blood under the law. This stood as a constant text—"Without shedding of blood there is no remission." Meal and honey, sweet spices and incense, would not avail without shedding of blood. There was no remission promised to future diligence or deep repentance; without shedding of blood pardon never came. The blood, and the blood alone put away sin, and permitted that man to come to God's courts to worship, because it made him one with God. The blood is the great "at-one-ment." There is no hope of pardon for the sin of any man, except through its punishment being fully endured. God must punish sin. It is not an arbitrary arrangement that sin shall be punished, but it is a part of the very constitution of moral government that sin must be punished. Never did God swerve from that, and never will He. "He will by no means clear the guilty."

Christ, therefore, came and was punished in the place and stead of all His people. Ten thousand times ten thousand are the souls for whom Jesus shed His blood. He, for the sins of all the elect, hath a complete atonement made. For every man of Adam born, who has believed or shall believe on that, or who is taken to glory before being capable of believing, Christ has made a complete atonement; and there is none other plan by which sinners can be made at one with God, except by Jesus' precious blood. I may make sacrifices; I may mortify my body; I may be baptized; I may receive sacraments; I may pray until my knees grow hard with kneeling; I may read devout words until I know them by heart; I may celebrate masses; I may worship in one language or in fifty languages; but I can never be at one with God, except by blood; and that blood, "the precious blood of Christ."

My dear friends, many of you have felt the power of Christ's redeeming blood; you are not under the law now, but under grace: you have also felt the power of the atoning blood; you know that you are reconciled unto God by the death of His Son; you feel that He is no angry God to you, that He loves you with a love unchangeable; but this is not the case with you all. O that it were! I do pray that you may know this very day the atoning power of the blood of Jesus. Creature, wouldst thou not be at one with thy Creator? Puny man, wouldst thou not have Almighty God to be thy friend? Thou canst not be at one with God except through the at-one-ment. God hath set forth Christ to be a propitiation for our sins. Oh, take the propitiation through faith in His blood, and be thou at one with God.

III. Thirdly, the precious blood of Jesus Christ has a cleansing power.

John tells us in his first Epistle, first chapter, seventh verse, "The blood of Jesus Christ his Son cleanseth us from all sin." Sin has a directly defiling effect upon the sinner, hence the need of cleansing. Suppose that God the Holy One were perfectly willing to be at one with an unholy sinner, which is supposing a case that cannot be: yet even should the pure eyes of the Most High wink at sin, still as long as we are unclean we never could feel in our own hearts anything like joy, and rest, and peace. Sin is a plague to the man who has it, as well as a hateful thing to the God who abhors it. I must be made clean, I must have mine iniquities washed away, or I never can be happy. The first mercy that is sung of in the one hundred and third Psalm is, "Who forgiveth all thine iniquities."

Now we know it is by the precious blood that sin is cleansed. Murder, adultery, theft, whatever the sin may be, there is power in the veins of Christ to take it away at once and forever. No matter how many, nor how deeply-seated our offences may be, the blood cries, "Though your sins be as scarlet, they shall be as white as snow; though they be red like crimson, they shall be as wool." It is the song of Heaven—"We have washed our robes and made them white in the blood of the Lamb." This is the experience of earth, for none was ever cleansed except in this fountain, opened for the house of David for sin and for uncleanness.

You have heard this so often that perhaps if an angel told it to you, you would not take much interest in it, except you have known experimentally the horror of uncleanness and the blessedness of being made clean. Beloved, it is a thought which ought to make our hearts leap within us, that through Jesus' blood there is not a spot left upon any believer, not a wrinkle nor any such thing. Oh precious blood, removing the Hell-stains of abundant iniquity, and permitting me to stand accepted in the beloved, notwithstanding all the many ways in which I have rebelled against my God!

IV. A fourth property of the blood of Christ is its preserving power.

You will rightly comprehend this when you remember the dreadful night of Egypt, when the destroying angel was abroad to slay God's enemies. A bitter cry went up from house to house as the firstborn of all Egypt, from Pharaoh on the throne to the firstborn of the woman behind the mill and the slave in the dungeon, fell dead in a moment. The angel sped with noiseless wing through every street of Egypt's many cities; but there were some houses which he could not enter: he sheathed his sword and breathed no malediction there. What was it which preserved the houses? The inhabitants were not better than others, their habitations were not more elegantly built, there was nothing except the bloodstain on the lintel and on the two side posts, and it is written, "When I see the blood I will pass over you."

There was nothing whatever which gained the Passover for Israel but just the sprinkling of blood. The father of the house had taken a lamb and killed it, had caught the blood in a basin, and while the lamb was roasted that it might be eaten by every inhabitant of the house, he took a bunch of hyssop, stirred the basin of blood and went outside with his children and began to strike the posts, and to strike the door, and as soon as this was done, they were all safe: no angel could touch them, the fiends of Hell themselves could not venture there.

Beloved, see, we are preserved in Christ Jesus. Did not God see the blood before you and I saw it, and was not that the reason why He spared our forfeited lives when, like barren fig trees, we brought forth no fruit for Him? When we saw the blood, let us remember it was not our seeing it, which really saved it; one sight of it gave us peace, but it was God's seeing it that saved us. "When *I* see the blood I will pass over you." And today, if my eye of faith be dim, and I can scarce see the precious blood, so as to re-joice that I am washed in it, yet God can see the blood, and as long as the undimmed eye of Jehovah looks upon the atoning sacrifice of the Lord Je-sus, He cannot smite one soul that is covered with its scarlet mantle.

Oh, how precious is this blood-red shield! My soul, cower thou down under it when the darts of Hell are flying: this is the chariot, the covering whereof is of purple; let the storm come, and the deluge rise, let even the fiery hail descend, beneath that crimson pavilion my soul must rest se-cure, for what can touch me, when I am covered with *His* precious blood?

Let me ask you to get here, right under the shelter of the Cross. Sit down now beneath the shadow of the Cross and feel,

I am safe, I am safe, O ye devils of Hell; or ye angels of God—I could challenge you all, and say, "Who shall separate me from the love of God in Christ Jesus, or who shall lay anything to my charge, seeing that Christ hath died for me."

When Heaven is on a blaze, when Earth begins to shake, when the moun-tains rock, when God divides the righteous from the wicked, happy will they be who can find a shelter beneath the blood. But there will you be, who have never trusted in its cleansing power? You will call to the rocks to hide you, and to the mountains to cover you, but all in vain. God help you now, or even the blood will not help you then.

V. Fifthly, the blood of Christ is precious because of its pleading prevalence.

Paul says in the twelfth chapter of his epistle to the Hebrews, at the twenty-fourth verse, "It speaketh better things than that of Abel." Abel's blood pleaded and prevailed; its cry was "Vengeance" and Cain was punished. Jesus' blood pleads and prevails; its cry is "Father, forgive them!" and sinners are forgiven through it. When I cannot pray as I would, how sweet to remember that the blood prays! There is no voice in my tongue, but there is always a voice in the blood. If I cannot, when I bow before my God, get farther than to say "God be merciful to me, a sinner," yet my advocate before the throne is not dumb because *I* am, and his plea has not lost its power because my faith in it may happen to be diminished.

The blood is always alike, prevalent with God. The wounds of Jesus are so many mouths to plead with God for sinners—what if I say they are so many chains with which love is lead captive, and sovereign mercy bound to bless every favored child? What if I say that the wounds of Jesus have become donors of grace through which divine love comes forth to the vilest of the vile, and doors through which our wants go up to God and plead with Him that He would be pleased to supply them? Next time you cannot pray, next time you are crying and striving and groaning up in that upper room, praise the value of the precious blood which maketh intercession before the eternal throne.

VI. Sixthly, the blood is precious where perhaps we little expect it to operate, because of its melting influence on the human heart.

> They shall look upon me whom they have pierced, and they shall mourn for him, as one that mourneth for his only son, and shall be in bitterness for him, as one that is in bitterness for his firstborn.

There is a great complaint among sinners, when they are a little awakened, that they feel their hearts so hard. The blood is a mighty melter. Alchemists of old sought after a universal solvent: the blood of Jesus is that. There is no nature so stubborn that a sight of the love of God in Christ Jesus cannot melt it, if grace shall open the blind eye to see Christ. The stone in the human heart shall melt away, when it is plunged into a bath of blood divine. Cannot you say, dear friends, that Toplady was right in his hymn:

> *Law and terrors do but harden*
> *All the while they work alone,*
> *But a sense of blood-bought pardon,*
> *Soon dissolves a heart of stone.*

Sinner, if God shall lead thee to believe this morning in Christ to save thee; if thou wilt trust thy soul in His hands to have it saved, that hard heart of thine will melt at once. You would think differently of sin, my friends, if you knew that Christ smarted for it. Oh! if you knew that out of those dear languid eyes, there looked the loving heart of Jesus upon you, I know you would say, "I hate the sin that made him mourn, and fastened him to the accursed tree." I do not think that preaching the law generally softens men's hearts. Hitting men with a hard hammer may often drive the particles of a hard heart more closely together, and make the iron yet more hard; but oh, to preach Christ's love—His great love wherewith He loved us even when we were dead in sins, and to tell to sinners that there is life in a look at the crucified One—surely this will prove that Christ was exalted on high to give repentance and remission of sins. Come for repentance, if you cannot come repenting. Come *for* a broken heart, if you cannot come *with a* broken heart. Come to be melted, if you are not melted. Come to be wounded, if you are not wounded.

VII. But then comes in a seventh property of the precious blood. The same blood that melts has a gracious power to pacify.

John Bunyan speaks of the law as coming to sweep a chamber like a maid with a broom; and when she began to sweep there was a great dust which almost choked people, and got into their eyes; but then came the gospel with its drops of water, and laid the dust, and then the broom might be used far better. Now it sometimes happens that the law of God makes such a dust in the sinner's soul, that nothing but the precious blood of Jesus Christ can make that dust lie still. The sinner is so disquieted that nothing can ever give him any relief except to know that Jesus died for him.

When I felt the burden of my sin, I do confess all the preaching I ever heard never gave me one single atom of comfort. I was told to do this and to do that, and when I had done it all, I had not advanced one inch the farther. I thought I must feel something, or pray a certain quantity; and when I had done that, the burden was quite as heavy. But the moment I saw that there was nothing whatever for me to do, that Jesus did it long, long ago, that all my sins were put on His back and that He suffered all I ought to have suffered, why then my heart had peace with God, peace by believing, peace through the precious blood.

Two soldiers were on duty in the citadel of Gibraltar. One of them had obtained peace through the precious blood of Christ, the other was in very great distress of mind. It happened to be their turn to stand, both of them, sentinel the same night; and there are many long passages in the rock, which passages are adapted to convey sounds a very great distance. The soldier in distress of mind was ready to beat his breast for grief: he felt he had rebelled against God, and could not find how he could be reconciled; when, suddenly, there came through the air what seemed to him to be a mysterious voice from Heaven saying these words, "The precious blood of Christ." In a moment he saw it all: it was that which reconciled us to God; and he rejoiced with joy unspeakable and full of glory.

Now did those words come directly from God? No. They did as far as the effect was concerned—they did come from the Holy Spirit. Who was it that had spoken those words? Curiously enough, the other sentinel at the far end of the passage was standing still and meditating, when an officer came by and it was his duty of course to give the word for the night, and with soldier-like promptitude he did give it, but not accurately, for instead of giving the proper word, he was so taken up by his meditations that he said to the officer, "The precious blood of Christ." He corrected himself in a moment, but however, he had said it, and it had passed along the passage and reached the ear for which God meant it, and the man found peace and spent his life in the fear of God, being, in after years, the means of completing one of our excellent translations of the Word of God into the Hindoo language.

Who can tell, dear friends, how much peace you may give by only telling the story of our Savior. If I only had about a dozen words to speak and knew I must die, I would say, "This is a faithful saying and worthy of all acceptation, that Christ Jesus came into the world to save sinners." The doctrine of substitution is the pith and marrow of the gospel, and if you can hold that forth, you will prove the value of the precious blood by its peace-giving power.

VIII. We can only spare a minute now upon its sanctifying influence.

The apostle tells us in the ninth chapter and the fourteenth verse that Christ sanctified the people by His own blood. Certain it is, that the same blood which justifies by taking away sin, does in its after-action act upon the new nature and lead it onward to subdue sin and to follow out the command of God. There is no motive for holiness so great as that which streams from the veins of Jesus. If you want to know why you should be obedient to God's will, my brethren, go and look upon Him who sweat, as it were, great drops of blood, and the love of Christ will constrain you, because you will thus judge, "That if one died for all, then were all dead: and that he died for all, that we which live might not henceforth live unto ourselves, but unto him that died for us and rose again."

IX. In the ninth place, another blessed property of the blood of Jesus, is its power to give entrance.

We are told that the high priest never went within the veil without blood; and surely we can never get into God's heart, nor into the secret of the Lord, which is with them that fear Him, nor into any familiar intercourse with our great Father and Friend, except by the sprinkling of the precious blood of Jesus. "We have access with boldness into this grace wherein we stand," but we never dare go a step towards God, except as we are sprinkled with this precious blood. I am persuaded some of us do not come near to God, because we forget the blood. If you try to have fellowship with God in your graces, your experiences, your believings, you will fail; but if you try to come near to God as you stand in Christ Jesus, you will have courage to come; and on the other hand, God will run to meet you when He sees you in the face of His anointed. Oh, for power to get near to God! But there is no getting near to God, except as we get near to the Cross. Praise the blood, then, for its power of giving you nearness to God.

X. Tenthly—a hint only. The blood is very precious, in the tenth place, for its confirming power.

No covenant, we are told, was ever valid, unless victims were slain and blood sprinkled; and it is the blood of Jesus which has ratified the new covenant, and made its promises sure to all the seed. Hence it is called "the blood of the everlasting covenant." The apostle changes the figure, and he says that a testament is not of force, except the testator be dead. The blood is a proof that the testator died, and now the law holds good to every legatee, because Jesus Christ has signed it with His own gore. Beloved, let us rejoice that the promises are "yea" and "amen," for no other reason than this, because Christ Jesus died and rose again. Had there been no bowing of the head upon the tree, no slumbering in the sepulcher, no rising from the tomb, then the promises had been uncertain fickle things, not "immutable things wherein it is impossible for God to lie," and consequently they could never have afforded strong consolation to those who have fled for refuge to Christ Jesus. See then the confirming nature of the blood of Jesus and count it very precious.

XI. *I have almost done; but there remains another, it is the eleventh one, and that is the invigorating power of the precious blood.*

If you want to know that, you must see it set forth as we often do when we cover the table with the white cloth and put thereon the bread and wine. What mean we by this ordinance? We mean by it, that Christ suffered for us, and that we being already washed in His precious blood and so made clean, do come to the table to drink wine as an emblem of the way in which we live and feed upon His body and upon His blood. He tells us "Except a man shall eat my flesh and drink my blood, there is no life in him." We do therefore, after a spiritual sort, drink His blood, and He says "My blood is drink indeed." Superior drink! Transcendent drink! Strengthening drink—such drink as angels never taste though they drink before the eternal throne.

Oh beloved, whenever your spirit faints, this wine shall comfort you; when your griefs are many, drink and forget your misery, and remember your sufferings no more. When you are very weak and faint, take not *a little* of this for your soul's sake, but drink *a full draught* of the wine on the lees [dregs], well refined, which was set abroach by the soldier's spike, and flowed from Christ's own heart. "Drink to the full; yea, drink abundantly O beloved," saith Christ to the spouse; and do not thou linger when He invites. You see the blood has power without to cleanse, and then it has power within to strengthen. O precious blood, how many are thy uses! May I prove them all!

XII. *Lastly, and twelfthly—twelve is the number of perfection, and we have brought out a perfect number of its uses—the blood has an overcoming power.*

It is written in the Revelation, "They overcame through the blood of the Lamb." How could they do otherwise? He that fights with the precious blood of Jesus fights with a weapon that will cut through soul and spirit, joints and marrow, a weapon that makes Hell tremble, and makes Heaven subservient, and Earth obedient to the will of the men who can wield it. The blood of Jesus! Sin dies at its presence, death ceases to be death: Hell itself would be dried up if that blood could operate there. The blood of Jesus! Heaven's gates are opened; bars of iron are pushed back. The blood of Jesus! My doubts and fears flee, my troubles and disasters disappear. The blood of Jesus! Shall I not go on conquering and to conquer so long as I can plead that! In Heaven this shall be the choice jewel which shall glitter upon the head of Jesus—that He gives to His people "Victory, victory, through the blood of the Lamb."

And now, is this blood to be had? Can it be got at? Yes, it is free, as well as full of virtue—free to every soul that believeth. Whosoever careth to come and trust in Jesus shall find the virtue of this blood in his case this very morning. Away from your own works and doings. Turn those eyes of yours to the full atonement made, to the utmost ransom paid; and if God enables thee, poor soul, this morning to say, "I take that precious blood to be my only hope," you are saved, and you may sing with the rest of us.

> *Now freed from sin, I walk at large;*
> *The Savior's blood's my full discharge,*
> *At His dear feet my soul I'll lay,*
> *A sinner saved, and homage pay.*

God grant it may be so, for His name's sake. Amen.

Mourning at the Sight of the Crucified

"And all the people that came together to that sight, beholding the things which were done, smote their breasts, and returned."—Luke 23:48.

Many in that crowd came together to behold the crucifixion of Jesus in a condition of the most furious malice. They had hounded the Savior as dogs pursue a stag, and at last, all mad with rage, they hemmed Him in for death. Others, willing enough to spend an idle hour, and to gaze upon a sensational spectacle, swelled the mob until a vast assembly congregated around the little hill upon which the three crosses were raised. There unanimously, whether of malice or of wantonness, they all joined in mockery of the Victim who hung upon the center cross. Some thrust out the tongue, some wagged their heads, others scoffed and jeered, some taunted Him in words, and others in signs, but all alike exulted over the defenseless Man who was given as a prey to their teeth.

Earth never beheld a scene in which so much unrestrained derision and expressive contempt were poured upon one man so unanimously and for so long a time. It must have been hideous to the last degree to have seen so many grinning faces and mocking eyes, and to have heard so many cruel words and scornful shouts. The spectacle was too detestable to be long endured of Heaven. Suddenly the sun, shocked at the scene, veiled his face, and for three long hours the ribald crew sat shivering in midday midnight. Meanwhile the Earth trembled beneath their feet, the rocks were rent, and the Temple, in superstitious defense of whose perpetuity they had committed the murder of the just, had its holy veil rent as though by strong invisible hands.

The news of this, and the feeling of horror produced by the darkness, and the earth-tremor, caused a revulsion of feelings; there were no more gibes and jests, no more thrustings out of the tongue and cruel mockeries, but they went their way solitary and alone to their homes, or in little silent groups, while each man, after the manner of Orientals when struck with sudden awe, smote upon his breast. Far different was the procession to the gates of Jerusalem from that march of madness which had come out therefrom. Observe the power which God hath over human minds! See how He can tame the wildest, and make the most malicious and proud to cower down at His feet when He doth but manifest Himself in the wonders of nature! How much more cowed and terrified will they be when He makes bare His arm and comes forth in the judgments of His wrath to deal with them according to their deserts!

This sudden and memorable change in so vast a multitude is the apt representative of two other remarkable mental changes. How like it is to the gracious transformation which a sight of the Cross has often worked most blessedly in the hearts of men! Many have come under the sound of the gospel resolved to scoff, but they have returned to pray. The idlest and even the basest motives have brought men under the preaching, but when Jesus has been lifted up, they have been savingly drawn to Him, and as a consequence have smitten upon their breasts in repentance, and gone their way to serve the Savior whom they once blasphemed.

Oh, the power, the melting, conquering, transforming power of that dear Cross of Christ! My brethren, we have but to abide by the preaching of it, we have but constantly to tell abroad the matchless story, and we may expect to see the most remarkable spiritual results. We need despair of no man now that Jesus has died for sinners. With such a hammer as the doctrine of the Cross, the most flinty heart will be broken; and with such a fire as the sweet love of Christ, the most mighty iceberg will be melted. We need never despair for the heathenish or superstitious races of men; if we can but find occasion to bring the doctrine of Christ crucified into contact with their natures, it will yet change them, and Christ will be their king.

We shall now draw nearer to the text, and in the first place, *analyze the general mourning around the Cross;* secondly, we shall, if God shall help us, *endeavor to join in the sorrowful chorus;* and then, ere we conclude, we shall *remind you that at the foot of the Cross our sorrow must be mingled with joy.*

I. First, then, let us analyze the general mourning which this text describes.

"All the people that came together to that sight, beholding the things which were done, smote their breasts, and returned." They all smote their breasts, but not all from the same cause. They were all afraid, not all from the same reason. The outward manifestations were alike in the whole mass, but the grades of difference in feeling were as many as the minds in which they ruled. There were many, no doubt, who were merely moved with a transient emotion. They had seen the death agonies of a remarkable Man, and the attendant wonders had persuaded them that He was something more than an ordinary being, and therefore, they were afraid. With a kind of indefinite fear, grounded upon no very intelligent reasoning, they were alarmed, because God was angry, and had closed the eye of day upon them, and made the rocks to rend; and, burdened with this indistinct fear, they went their way trembling and humbled to their several homes; but peradventure, ere the next morning light had dawned, they had forgotten it all, and the next day found them greedy for another bloody spectacle, and ready to nail another Christ to the Cross, if there had been such another to be found in the land.

Their beating of the breast was not a breaking of the heart. It was an April shower, a dewdrop of the morning, a hoar-frost that dissolved when the sun had risen. Like a shadow the emotion Crossed their minds, and like a shadow it left no trace behind. How often in the preaching of the Cross has this been the only result in tens of thousands! In this house, where so many souls have been converted, many more have shed tears which have been wiped away, and the reason of their tears has been forgotten. A handkerchief has dried up their emotions. Alas! alas! alas! that while it may be difficult to move men with the story of the Cross to weeping, it is even more difficult to make those emotions permanent.

"I have seen something wonderful this morning," said one who had listened to a faithful and earnest preacher, "I have seen a whole congregation in tears." "Alas!" said the preacher, "there is something more wonderful still, for the most of them will go their way to forget that they ever shed a tear." Ah, my hearers, shall it be always so—always so? Then, O ye impenitent, there shall come to your eyes a tear which shall drip forever, a scalding drop which no mercy shall ever wipe away; a thirst that shall never be abated; a worm that shall never die, and a fire that never shall be quenched. By the love you bear your souls, I pray you escape from the wrath to come!

Others amongst that great crowd exhibited emotion based upon more thoughtful reflection. They saw that they had shared in the murder of an innocent person. "Alas!" said they,

> . . .we see through it all now. That Man was no offender. In all that we have ever heard or seen of Him, He did good, and only good: He always healed the sick,

fed the hungry, and raised the dead. There is not a word of all His teaching that is really contrary to the law of God. He was a pure and holy Man. We have all been duped. Those priests have egged us on to put to death one whom it were a thousand mercies if we could restore to life again at once. Our race has killed its benefactor.

"Yes," saith one,

> . . .I thrust out my tongue, I found it almost impossible to restrain myself, when everybody else was laughing and mocking at His tortures; but I am afraid I have mocked at the innocent, and I tremble lest the darkness which God has sent was His reprobation of my wickedness in oppressing the innocent.

Such feelings would abide, but I can suppose that they might not bring men to sincere repentance; for while they might feel sorry that they had oppressed the innocent, yet, perceiving nothing more in Jesus than mere maltreated virtue and suffering manhood, the natural emotion might soon pass away, and the moral and spiritual result be of no great value.

How frequently have we seen in our hearers that same description of emotion! They have regretted that Christ should be put to death, they have felt like that old king of France, who said, "I wish I had been there with ten thousand of my soldiers, I would have cut their throats sooner than they should have touched Him"; but those very feelings have been evidence that they did not feel their share in the guilt as they ought to have done, and that to them the Cross of Jesus was no more a saving spectacle than the death of a common martyr. Dear hearers, beware of making the Cross to be a common-place thing with you. Look beyond the sufferings of the innocent manhood of Jesus, and see upon the tree the atoning sacrifice of Christ, or else you look to the Cross in vain.

In the motley company who all went home smiting on their breasts, let us hope that there were some who said, "Certainly this was the Son of God," and mourned to think He should have suffered for their transgressions, and been put to grief for their iniquities. Those who came to that point were saved. Blessed were the eyes that looked upon the slaughtered Lamb in such a way as that, and happy were the hearts that there and then were broken because He was bruised and put to grief for their sakes. Beloved, aspire to this. May God's grace bring you to see in Jesus Christ no other than God made flesh, hanging upon the tree in agony, to die, the just for the unjust, that we may be saved. O come and repose your trust in Him, and then smite upon your breasts at the thought that such a victim should have been necessary for your redemption; then may you cease to smite your breasts, and begin to clap your hands for very joy; for they who thus bewail a Savior may rejoice in Him, for He is theirs and they are His.

II. We shall now ask you to join in the lamentation, each man according to his sincerity of heart, beholding the Cross, and smiting upon his breast.

We will by faith put ourselves at the foot of the little knoll of Calvary: there we see in the center, between two thieves, the Son of God made flesh, nailed by His hands and feet, and dying in an anguish which words cannot portray. Look ye well, I pray you; look steadfastly and devoutly, gazing through your tears. 'Tis He who was worshiped of angels, who is now dying for the sons of men; sit down and watch the death of death's destroyer. I shall ask you first to smite your breasts, as you remember that *you see in Him your own sins.* How great He is! That thorn-covered head was once crowned with all the royalties of Heaven and earth. He who dies there is no common man. King of kings and Lord of lords is He who hangs on yonder Cross.

Then see the greatness of your sins, which required so vast a sacrifice. They must be infinite sins to require an infinite Person to lay down His life in order to their removal. Thou canst never compass or comprehend the greatness of thy Lord in His essential character and dignity, neither shalt thou ever be able to understand the blackness and heinousness of the sin which demanded His life as an atonement. Brother, smite thy breast and say, "God be merciful to me, the greatest of sinners, for I am such." Look well into the face of Jesus, and see how vile they have made Him! They have stained those cheeks with spittle, they have lashed those shoulders with a felon's scourge; they have put Him to the death which was only awarded to the meanest Roman slave; they have hung Him up between Heaven and earth, as though He were fit for neither; they have stripped Him naked and left Him not a rag to cover Him!

See here then, O believer, the shame of thy sins. What a shameful thing thy sin must have been; what a disgraceful and abominable thing, if Christ must be made such a shame for thee! O be ashamed of thyself, to think thy Lord should thus be scorned and made nothing of for thee! See how they aggravate His sorrows! It was not enough to crucify Him, they must insult Him; nor that enough, they must mock His prayers and turn His dying cries into themes for jest, while they offer Him vinegar to drink. See, beloved, how aggravated were your sins and mine! Come, my brother, let us both smite upon our breasts and say, "Oh, how our sins have piled up their guiltiness! It was not merely that we broke the law, but we sinned against light and knowledge; against rebukes and warnings. As His griefs are aggravated, even so are our sins!" Look still into His dear face, and see the lines of anguish which indicate the deeper inward sorrow which far transcends mere bodily pain and smart. God, His Father, has forsaken Him. God has made Him a curse for us.

Then what must the curse of God have been against us? What must our sins have deserved? If when sin was only imputed to Christ, and laid upon Him for awhile, His Father turned His head away and made His Son cry out, *"Lama Sabachthani!"* Oh, what an accursed thing our sin must be, and what a curse would have come upon us; what thunderbolts, what coals of fire, what indignation, and wrath from the Most High must have been our portion had not Jesus interposed! If Jehovah did not spare His Son, how little would He have spared guilty, worthless men if He had dealt with us after our sins, and rewarded us according to our iniquities!

As we still sit down and look at Jesus, we remember that His death was voluntary—He need not have died unless He had so willed: here then is another striking feature of our sin, for our sin was voluntary too. We did not sin as of compulsion, but we deliberately chose the evil way. O sinner, let both of us sit down together, and tell the Lord that we have no justification, or extenuation, or excuse to offer, we have sinned wilfully against light and knowledge, against love and mercy. Let us smite upon our breasts, as we see Jesus willingly suffer, and confess that we have willingly offended against the just and righteous laws of a most good and gracious God. I could fain keep you looking into those five wounds, and studying that marred face, and counting every purple drop that flowed from hands and feet, and side, but time would fail us. Only that one wound—let it abide with you. Smite your breast because you see in Christ your sin.

Looking again—changing, as it were, our stand-point, but still keeping our eye upon that same, dear crucified One, let us see there *the neglected and despised remedy for our sin.* If sin itself, in its first condition, as rebellion, bring no tears to our eyes, it certainly ought in its second manifestation, as ingratitude. The sin of rebellion is vile; but the sin of slighting the Savior is viler still. He that hangs on the tree, in groans and griefs unutterable, is He whom some of you have never thought of, whom you do not love, to whom you never pray, in whom you place no confidence, and whom you never serve. I will not accuse you; I will ask those dear wounds to do it, sweetly and tenderly. I will rather accuse myself; for, alas! alas! there was a time when I heard of Him as with a deaf ear; when I was told of Him, and understood the love He bore to sinners, and yet my heart was like a stone within me, and would not be moved. I stopped my ear and would not be charmed, even with such a master-fascination as the disinterested love of Jesus. I think if I had been spared to live the life of an ungodly man, for thirty, forty, or fifty years, and had been converted at last, I should never have been able to blame myself sufficiently for rejecting Jesus during all those years.

Why, even those of us who were converted in our youth, and almost in our childhood, cannot help blaming ourselves to think that so dear a Friend, who had done so much for us, was so long slighted by us. Who could have done more for us than He, since He gave Himself for our sins? Ah, how did we wrong Him while we withheld our hearts from Him! O ye sinners, how can ye keep the doors of your hearts shut against the Friend of Sinners? How can we close the door against Him who cries, "My head is wet with dew, and my locks with the drops of the night: open to me, my beloved, open to me"? I am persuaded there are some here who are His elect: you were chosen by Him from before the foundation of the world, and you shall be with Him in Heaven one day to sing His praises, and yet, at this moment, though you hear His name, you do not love Him, and, though you are told of what He did, you do not trust Him. What! shall that iron bar always fast close the gate of your heart? Shall that door still be always bolted? O Spirit of the living God, win an entrance for the blessed Christ this morning! If anything can do it, surely it must be a sight of the crucified Christ; that matchless spectacle shall make a heart of stone relent and melt, by Jesus' love subdued. O may the Holy Ghost work this gracious melting, and He shall have all the honour.

Still keeping you at the Cross foot, dear friends, every believer here may well smite upon his breast this morning as he thinks of *who it was that smarted so upon the Cross*. Who was it? It was He who loved us before ever the world was made. It was He who is this day the Bridegroom of our souls, our Best-beloved; He who has taken us into the banqueting house and waved His banner of love over us; He who has made us one with Himself, and has vowed to present us to His Father without spot. It is He, our Husband, our Ishi, who has called us His Hephzibah because His soul delighteth in us. It is He who suffereth thus for us.

Suffering does not always excite the same degree of pity. You must know something of the individual before the inner-most depths of the soul are stirred; and so it happens to us that the higher the character and the more able we are to appreciate it, the closer the relation and the more fondly we reciprocate the love, the more deeply does suffering strike the soul. You are coming to His table, some of you today, and you will partake of bread: I pray you remember that it represents the quivering flesh that was filled with pain on Calvary. You will sip of that cup: then be sure to remember that it betokens to you the blood of One who loves you better than you could be loved by mother, or by husband, or by friend. O sit you down and smite your breasts that He should grieve; that Heaven's Sun should be eclipsed; that Heaven's Lily should be spotted with blood, and Heaven's Rose should be whitened with a deadly pallor. Lament that perfection should be accused, innocence smitten, and love murdered; and that Christ, the happy and the holy, the ever blessed, who had been for ages the delight of angels, should now become the sorrowful, the acquaintance of grief, the bleeding and the dying. Smite upon your breasts, believers, and go your way!

Beloved in the Lord, if such grief as this should be kindled in you, it will be well to pursue the subject, and to reflect upon how unbelieving and how cruel we have been to Jesus since the day that we have known Him. What, doth He bleed for me and have I doubted Him? Is He the Son of God, and have I suspected His fidelity? Have I stood at the Cross foot unmoved? Have I spoken of my dying Lord in a cold, indifferent spirit? Have I ever preached Christ crucified with a dry eye and a heart unmoved? Do I bow my knee in private prayer, and are my thoughts wandering when they ought to be bound hand and foot to His dear bleeding self? Am I accustomed to turn over the pages of the Evangelists which record my Master's wondrous sacrifice, and have I never stained those pages with my tears? Have I never paused spell-bound over the sacred sentence which recorded this miracle of miracles, this marvel of marvels? Oh, shame upon thee, hard heart! Well may I smite thee. May God smite thee with the hammer of His Spirit, and break thee to shivers. O thou stony heart, thou granite soul, thou flinty spirit, well may I strike the breast which harbors thee, to think that I should be so doltish in presence of love so amazing, so divine.

Brethren, you may smite upon your breasts as you look at the Cross, and mourn that you should have done so little for your Lord. I think if anybody could have sketched my future life in the day of my conversion, and have said, "You will be dull and cold in spiritual things! and you will exhibit but little earnestness and little gratitude!" I should have said like Hazael, "Is thy servant a dog, that he should do this great thing?" I suppose I read your hearts when I say that the most of you are disappointed with your own conduct as compared with your too flattering prophecies of yourselves!

What! am I really pardoned? Am I in very deed washed in that warm stream which gushed from the riven side of Jesus, and yet am I not wholly consecrated to Christ? What! in my body do I bear the marks of the Lord Jesus, and can I live almost without a thought of Him? Am I plucked like a brand from the burning, and have I small care to win others from the wrath to come? Has Jesus stooped to win me, and do I not labor to win others for Him? Was He all in earnest about me, and am I only half in earnest about him? Dare I waste a minute, dare I trifle away an hour? Have I an evening to spend in vain gossip and idle frivolities?

O my heart, well may I smite thee, that at the sight of the death of the dear Lover of my soul, I should not be fired by the highest zeal, and be impelled by the most ardent love to a perfect consecration of every power of my nature, every affection of my spirit, every faculty of my whole man? This mournful strain might be pursued to far greater lengths. We might follow up our confessions, still smiting, still accusing, still regretting, still bewailing. We might continue upon the bass notes evermore, and yet might we not express sufficient contrition for the shameful manner in which we have treated our blessed Friend. We might say with one of our hymn writers:

> *Lord, let me weep for nought but sin,*
> *And after none but Thee;*
> *And then I would—O that I might—*
> *A constant weeper be!*

III. *Let me invite you, in the third place, to remember that at Calvary, dolorous notes are not the only suitable music.*

We admired our poet when, in the hymn which we have just sung, he appears to question with himself which would be the most fitting tune for Golgotha.

> *'It is finished'; shall we raise*
> *Songs of sorrow or of praise?*
> *Mourn to see the Savior die,*
> *Or proclaim His victory?*
>
> *If of Calvary we tell,*
> *How can songs of triumph swell?*
> *If of man redeemed from woe,*
> *How shall notes of mourning flow?*

He shows that since our sin pierced the side of Jesus, there is cause for unlimited lamentation, but since the blood which flowed from the wound has cleansed our sin, there is ground for unbounded thanksgiving; and, therefore, the poet, after having balanced the matter in a few verses, concludes with

'It is finished,' let us raise
Songs of thankfulness and praise.

After all, you and I are not in the same condition as the multitude who had surrounded Calvary; for at that time our Lord was still dead, but now He is risen indeed. There were yet three days from that Thursday evening (for there is much reason to believe that our Lord was not crucified on Friday), in which Jesus must dwell in the regions of the dead. Our Lord, therefore, so far as human eyes could see Him, was a proper object of pity and mourning, and not of thanksgiving; but now, beloved, He ever lives and gloriously reigns. No charnal house confines that blessed body. He saw no corruption; for the moment when the third day dawned, He could no longer be held with the bond of death, but He manifested Himself alive unto His disciples. He tarried in this world for forty days. Some of His time was spent with those who knew Him in the flesh; perhaps a larger part of it was passed with those saints who came out of their graves after His resurrection; but certain it is that He is gone up, as the first-fruit from the dead; He is gone up to the right hand of God, even the Father. Do not bewail those wounds, they are lustrous with supernal splendor. Do not lament His death: He lives no more to die. Do not mourn that shame and spitting:

The head that once was crowned with thorns,
Is crowned with glory now.

Look up and thank God that death hath no more dominion over Him. He ever liveth to make intercession for us, and He shall shortly come with angelic bands surrounding Him, to judge the quick and dead. The argument for joy overshadows the reason for sorrow. Like as a woman when the child is born remembereth no more her anguish, for joy that a man is born into the world, so, in the thought of the risen Savior, who has taken possession of His crown, we will forget the lamentation of the Cross, and the sorrows of the broken heart of Calvary.

Moreover, hear ye the shrill voice of the high sounding cymbals, and let your hearts rejoice within you, for in His death our Redeemer conquered all the hosts of Hell. They came against Him furiously, yea, they came against Him to eat up his flesh, but they stumbled and fell. They compassed Him about, yea, they compassed Him about like bees; but in the name of the Lord did the Champion destroy them. Against the whole multitude of sins, and all the battalions of the pit, the Savior stood, a solitary soldier fighting against innumerable bands, but He has slain them all. "Bruised is the dragon's head." Jesus has led captivity captive. He conquered when He fell; and let the notes of victory drown forever the cries of sorrow.

Moreover, brethren, let it be remembered that men have been saved. Let there stream before your gladdened eyes this morning the innumerable company of the elect. Robed in white they come in long procession; they come from distant lands, from every clime; once scarlet with sin and black with iniquity, they are all white and pure, and without spot before the throne forever; beyond temptation, beatified, and made live to Jesus. And how? It was all through Calvary. There was their sin put away; there was their everlasting righteousness brought in and consummated. Let the hosts that are before the throne, as they wave their palms, and touch their golden harps, excite you to a joy like their own, and let that celestial music hush the gentler voices which mournfully exclaim

Alas! and did my Savior bleed?
And did my Sovereign die?
Would He devote that sacred head
For such a worm as I?

Nor is that all. You yourself are saved. O brother, this will always be one of your greatest joys. That others are converted through your instrumentality is occasion for much thanksgiving, but your Savior's advice to you is, "Notwithstanding in this rejoice not, that the spirits are subject unto you; but rather rejoice, because your names are written in Heaven." You, a spirit meet to be cast away, you whose portion must have been with devils, *you* are this day forgiven, adopted, saved, on the road to Heaven. Oh! while you think that you are saved from Hell, that you are lifted up to glory, you cannot but rejoice that your sin is put away from you through the death of Jesus Christ, your Lord.

Lastly, there is one thing for which we ought always to remember Christ's death with joy, and that is; that although the crucifixion of Jesus was intended to be a blow at the honour and glory of our God—though in the death of Christ the world did, so far as it was able, put God Himself to death, and so earn for itself that hideous title, "a decidal [deity killing] world," yet never did God have such honour and glory as He obtained through the sufferings of Jesus. Oh, they thought to scorn Him, but they lifted His Name on high! They thought that God was dishonored when He was most glorified. The image of the Invisible, had they not marred it? The express image of the

Father's person, had they not defiled it? Ah, so they said! But He that sitteth in the Heavens may well laugh and have them in derision, for what did they? They did but break the alabaster box, and all the blessed drops of infinite mercy streamed forth to perfume all worlds. They did but rend the veil, and then the glory which had been hidden between the cherubim shone forth upon all lands. O nature, adoring God with thine ancient and priestly mountains, extolling him with thy trees, which clap their hands, and worshiping with thy seas, which in their fullness roar out Jehovah's praise; with all thy tempests and flames of fire, thy dragons and thy deeps, thy snow and thy hail, thou canst not glorify God as Jesus glorified Him when He became obedient unto death. O Heaven, with all thy jubilant angels, thine ever chanting cherubim and seraphim, thy thrice holy hymns, thy streets of gold and endless harmonies, thou canst not reveal the Deity as Jesus Christ revealed it on the Cross. O Hell, with all thine infinite horrors and flames unquenchable, and pains and griefs and shrieks of tortured ghosts, even thou canst not reveal the justice of God as Christ revealed it in His riven heart upon the bloody tree. O Earth and Heaven and Hell! O time and eternity, things present and things to come, visible and invisible, ye are dim mirrors of the Godhead compared with the bleeding Lamb. O heart of God, I see Thee nowhere as at Golgotha, where the Word incarnate reveals the justice and the love, the holiness and the tenderness of God in one blaze of glory. If any created mind would fain see the glory of God, he need not gaze upon the starry skies, nor soar into the Heaven of Heavens, he has but to bow at the Cross foot and watch the crimson streams which gush from Immanuel's wounds.

If you would behold the glory of God, you need not gaze between the gates of pearls, you have but to look beyond the gates of Jerusalem and see the Prince of Peace expire. If you would receive the noblest conception that ever filled the human mind of the loving-kindness and the greatness and the pity, and yet the justice and the severity and the wrath of God, you need not lift up your eyes, nor cast them down, nor look to paradise, nor gaze on Tophet [Hell] you have but to look into the heart of Christ all crushed and broken and bruised, and you have seen it all. Oh, the joy that springs from the fact that God has triumphed after all! Death is not the victor; evil is not master. There are not two rival kingdoms, one governed by the God of good, and the other by the God of evil; no, evil is bound, chained, and led captive; its sinews are cut, its head is broken; its king is bound to the dread chariot of Jehovah Jesus, and as the white horses of triumph drag the Conqueror up the everlasting hills in splendor of glory, the monster of the pit cringes at His chariot wheels. Wherefore, beloved, we close this discourse with this sentence of humble yet joyful worship,

> *Glory be unto the Father,*
> *and to the Son, and to the Holy Ghost:*
> *as it was in the beginning,*
> *is now and ever shall be, world without end. Amen.*

Christ Made a Curse for Us

"Christ hath redeemed us from the curse of the law, being made a curse for us: for it is written, 'Cursed is every one that hangeth on a tree.'"—Galatians 3:13.

The apostle Paul had been showing to the Galatians that salvation is in no degree by works. He proved this all-important truth in the verses which precede the text, by a very conclusive form of double reasoning. He showed, first, that the law could not give the blessing of salvation, for, since all had broken it, all that the law could do was to curse. He quotes the substance of the twenty-seventh chapter of Deuteronomy, "Cursed is every one that continueth not in all things which are written in the book of the law to do them"; and as no man can claim that he has continued in all things that are in the law, he pointed out the clear inference that all men under the law had incurred the curse.

He then reminds the Galatians, in the second place, that if any had ever been blessed in the olden times, the blessing came not by the law, but by their faith, and to prove this, he quotes a passage from Habakkuk 2:4, in which it is distinctly stated that the just shall live by faith: so that those who were just and righteous, did not live before God on the footing of their obedience to the law, but they were justified and made to live on the ground of their being believers. See, then, that if the law inevitably curses us all, and if the only people who are said to have been preserved in gracious life were justified not by works, but by faith, then is it certain beyond a doubt that the salvation and justification of a sinner cannot be by the works of the law, but altogether by the grace of God through faith which is in Christ Jesus.

But the apostle, no doubt feeling that now he was declaring that doctrine, he had better declare the foundation and root of it, unveils in the text before us a reason why men are not saved by their personal righteousness, but saved by their faith. He tells us that the reason is this: that men are not saved now by any personal merit, but their salvation lies in another—lies, in fact, in Christ Jesus, the representative Man, who alone can deliver us from the curse which the law brought upon us; and since works do not connect us with Christ, but faith is the uniting bond, faith becomes the way of salvation. Since faith is the hand that lays hold upon the finished work of Christ—which works could not and would not do, for works lead us to boast and to forget Christ—faith becomes the true and only way of obtaining justification and everlasting life.

In order that such faith may be nurtured in us, may God the Holy Spirit this morning lead us into the depths of the great work of Christ; may we understand more clearly the nature of His substitution, and of the suffering which it entailed upon Him. Let us see, indeed, the truth of the stanzas whose music has just died away:

> *He bore that we might never bear*
> *His Father's righteous ire.*

I. Our first contemplation, this morning, will be upon this question, what is the curse of the law here intended?

It is the curse of God. God who made the law has appended certain penal consequences to the breaking of it, and the man who violates the law, becomes at once the subject of the wrath of the Lawgiver. It is not the curse of the mere law of itself; it is a curse from the great Lawgiver whose arm is strong to defend His statutes. Hence, at the very outset of our reflections, let us be assured that the law-curse must be supremely just, and morally unavoidable. It is not possible that our God, Who delights to bless us, should inflict an atom of curse upon any one of His creatures unless the highest right shall require it; and if there be any method by which holiness and purity can be maintained without a curse, rest assured the God of love will not imprecate sorrow upon His creatures.

The curse then, if it fall, must be a necessary one, in its very essence needful for the preservation of order in the universe, and for the manifestations of the holiness of the universal Sovereign. Be assured, too, that when God curses, it is a curse of the most weighty kind. The curse causeless shall not come; but God's curses are never causeless, and they come home to offenders with overwhelming power. Sin must be punished, and when by long continuance and impenitence in evil, God is provoked to speak the malediction, I wot [know] that he whom He curses, is cursed indeed. There is something so terrible in the very idea of the omnipotent God pronouncing a curse upon a transgressor, that my blood curdles at it, and I cannot express myself very clearly or even coherently.

A father's curse, how terrible! but what is that to the malediction of the great Father of Spirits! To be cursed of men is no mean evil, but to be accursed of God is terror and dismay.

> Sorrow and anguish lie in that curse; death is involved in it and that second death which John foresaw in Patmos, and described as being cast into a lake of fire.—Rev. 20:14.

Hear ye the word of the Lord by his servant Nahum, and consider what His curse must be:

> God is jealous, and the Lord revengeth; the Lord revengeth, and is furious; the Lord will take vengeance on his adversaries, and he reserveth wrath for his enemies. . . . The mountains quake at him, and the hills melt, and the Earth is burned at his presence, yea, the world, and all that dwell herein. Who can stand before his indignation? and who can abide in the fierceness of his anger? his fury is poured out like fire, and the rocks are thrown down by him.

Remember also the prophecy of Malachi:

> "For behold, the day cometh, that shall burn as an oven; and all the proud, yea, and all that do wickedly, shall be stubble: and the day that cometh shall burn them up," saith the Lord of hosts, "that it shall leave them neither root nor branch."

Let such words, and there are many like them, sink into your hearts, that ye may fear and tremble before this just and holy Lord.

If we would look further into the meaning of the curse that arises from the breach of the law, we must remember that a curse is first of all a sign of displeasure. Now, we learn from Scripture that God is angry with the wicked every day; though towards the persons of sinners God exhibits great longsuffering, yet sin exceedingly provokes His holy mind; sin is a thing so utterly loathsome and detestable to the purity of the Most High, that no thought of evil, nor an ill word, nor an unjust action, is tolerated by Him; He observes every sin, and His holy soul, is stirred thereby. He is of purer eyes than to behold iniquity; He cannot endure it. He is a God that will certainly execute vengeance upon every evil work.

A curse implies something more than mere anger. It is suggested by burning indignation; and truly our God is not only somewhat angry with sinners, but His wrath is great towards sin. Wherever sin exists, there the fullness of the power of the divine indignation is directed; and though the effect of that wrath may be for awhile restrained through abundant long-suffering, yet God is greatly indignant with the iniquities of men. We wink at sin, yes, and even harden our hearts till we laugh at it and take pleasure in it, but oh! let us not think that God is such as we are; let us not suppose that sin can be beheld by Him and yet no indignation be felt. Ah! no, the most holy God has written warnings in His word which plainly inform us how terribly He is provoked by iniquity, as, for instance, when He saith, "Beware, ye that forget God, lest I tear you in pieces, and there be none to deliver." "Therefore saith the Lord, the Lord of hosts, the mighty One of Israel, Ah, I will ease me of mine adversaries, and avenge me of mine enemies." "For we know him that hath said, 'Vengeance belongeth unto me, I will recompense,' saith the Lord. And again, the Lord shall judge his people. It is a fearful thing to fall into the hands of the living God."

Moreover, a curse imprecates evil, and is, as it comes from God, of the nature of a threat. It is as though God should say, "By-and-by I will visit thee for this offence. Thou hast broken my law which is just and holy, and the inevitable penalty shall certainly come upon thee." Now, God has throughout His word given many such curses as these: He has threatened men over and over again. "If he turn not, he will whet his sword; he hath bent his bow, and made it ready." Sometimes the threatening is wrapped up in a plaintive lamentation. "Turn ye, turn ye from your evil ways; for why will ye die, O house of Israel?"

But still it is plain and clear that God will not suffer sin to go unpunished, and when the fullness of time shall come, and the measure shall be filled to the brim, and the weight of iniquity shall be fully reached, and the harvest shall be ripe, and the cry of wickedness shall come up mightily into the ears of the Lord God of Sabaoth, then will He come forth in robes of vengeance and overwhelm His adversaries.

But God's curse is something more than a threatening; He comes at length to blows. He uses warning words at first, but sooner or later He bares His sword for execution. The curse of God, as to its actual infliction, may be guessed at by some occasions wherein it has been seen on earth. Look at Cain, a wanderer and a vagabond upon the face of the earth! Read the curse that Jeremiah pronounced by the command of God upon Pashur; "Behold, I will make thee a terror to thyself, and to all thy friends: and they shall fall by the sword of their enemies, and thine eyes shall behold it."

Or, if you would behold the curse upon a larger scale, remember the day when the huge floodgates of earth's deepest fountains were unloosed, and the waters leaped up from their habitations like lions eager for their prey. Remember the day of vengeance when the windows of Heaven were opened, and the great deep above the firmament was confused with the deep that is beneath the firmament, and all flesh were swept away, save only the few who were hidden in the ark which God's covenant mercy had prepared—when sea-monsters whelped and stabled in the palaces of ancient kings, when millions of sinners sank to rise no more, when universal ruin flew with raven wing over a shoreless sea vomited from the mouth of death. Then was the curse of God poured out upon the earth.

Look ye yet again further down in time. Stand with Abraham at his tent door, and see towards the east the sky all red at early morning with a glare that came not from the sun; sheets of flames went up to Heaven, which were met by showers of yet more vivid fire, which preternaturally descended from the skies. Sodom and Gomorrah, having given themselves up to strange flesh, received the curse of God, and Hell was rained upon them out of Heaven until they were utterly consumed.

If you would see another form of the curse of God, remember that bright spirit who once stood as servitor in Heaven, the son of the morning, one of the chief of the angels of God. Think how he lost his lofty principality when sin entered into him! See how an archangel became an archfiend, and Satan, who is called Apollyon, fell from his lofty throne, banished forever from peace and happiness, to wander through dry places, seeking rest and finding none, to be reserved in chains of darkness unto the judgment of the last great day. Such was the curse that it withered an angel into a devil, it burned up the cities of the plain, it swept away the population of a globe.

Nor have you yet the full idea. There is a place of woe and horror, a land of darkness as darkness itself, and of the shadow of death, without any order, and where the light is darkness. There those miserable spirits who have refused repentance, and have hardened themselves against the Most High, are forever banished from their God and from all hope of peace or restoration. The curse of God is to lose God's favor; consequently, to lose the blessings which come upon that favor; to lose peace of mind, to lose hope, ultimately to lose life itself; for "the soul that sinneth, it shall die"; and that loss of life, and being cast into eternal death, is the most terrible of all, consisting as it does in everlasting separation from God and everything that makes existence truly life. A destruction lasting on forever, according to the scriptural description of it, is the fruit of the curse of the law.

Oh, heavy tidings have I to deliver this day to some of you! Hard is my task to have to testify to you thus the terrible justice of the law. But you would not understand or prize the exceeding love of Christ if you heard not the curse from which He delivers His people, therefore hear me patiently. O unhappy men, unhappy men, who are under God's curse today! You may dress yourselves in scarlet and fine linen, you may go to your feasts, and drain your full bowls of wine; you may lift high the sparkling cup, and whirl in the joyous dance, but if God's curse be on you, what madness possesses you! O sirs, if you could but see it, and understand it, this curse would darken all the windows of your mirth. Let us fly to the dear Cross of Christ, where the curse was put away, that we may never come to know in the fullness of its horror what the curse may mean.

II. A second enquiry of great importance to us this morning is this: who are under this curse?

Listen with solemn awe, O sons of men. First, especially and foremost, the Jewish nation lies under the curse, for such I gather from the connection. To them the law of God was very peculiarly given beyond all others. They heard it from Sinai, and it was to them surrounded with a golden setting of ceremonial symbol, and enforced by solemn national covenant. Moreover, there was a word in the commencement of that law which showed that in a certain sense it peculiarly belonged to Israel. "I am the Lord thy God, which brought thee out of the land of Egypt, from the house of bondage." Paul tells us that those who have sinned without law shall be punished without law; but the Jewish nation, having received the law, if they broke it, would become peculiarly liable to the curse which was threatened for such breach.

Yet further, all nations that dwell upon the face of the Earth are also subject to this curse, for this reason: that if the law was not given to all from Sinai, it has been written by the finger of God more or less legibly upon the conscience of all mankind. It needs no prophet to tell an Indian, a Laplander, a South Sea Islander, that he must not steal; his own judgment so instructs him. There is that within every man which ought to convince him that idolatry is folly, that adultery and unchastity are villainies, that theft, and murder, and covetousness, are all evil.

Now, inasmuch as all men in some degree have the law within, to that degree they are under the law; the curse of the law for transgression comes upon them. Moreover, there are some in this house this morning who are peculiarly under the curse. The apostle says, "As many as are of the works of the law are under the curse." Now, there are some of you who choose to be under the law; you deliberately choose to be judged by it. How so? Why, you are trying to reach a place in Heaven by your own good works; you are cling-ing to the idea that something you can do can save you; you have therefore elected to be under the law, and by so doing you have chosen the curse, for all that the law of works can do for you, is to leave you still accursed, because you have not fulfilled all its commands. O sirs, repent of so foolish a choice, and declare henceforth that you are willing to be saved by grace, and not at all by the works of the law. Thou art under the curse as thou now art, but I re-joice to have to tell thee that the curse has been removed through Jesus Christ our Lord. O may the Lord lead thee to see the plan of substitution and to rejoice in it.

III. Our third and main point this morning, is to answer the question, how was Christ made a curse for us?

The whole pith and marrow of the religion of Christianity lies in the doc-trine of "substitution," and I hesitate not to affirm my conviction that a very large proportion of Christians are not Christians at all, for they do not under-stand the fundamental doctrine of the Christian creed; and alas! there are preachers who do not preach, or even believe this cardinal truth. They speak of the blood of Jesus in an indistinct kind of way, and descant upon the death of Christ in a hazy style of poetry, but they do not strike this nail on the head, and lay it down that the way of salvation is by Christ's becoming a substitute for guilty man.

This shall make me the more plain and definite. Sin is an accursed thing. God, from the necessity of His holiness, must curse it; He must punish men for committing it; but the Lord's Christ, the glorious Son of the everlasting Father, became a Man, and suffered in His own proper person the curse which was due to the sons of men, that so, by a vicarious offering, God hav-ing been just in punishing sin, could extend His bounteous mercy towards those who believe in the Substitute. Now for this point. But, you enquire, how was Jesus Christ a curse?

We beg you to observe the word "made." "He was *made* a curse." Christ was no curse in Himself. In His person He was spotlessly innocent, and nothing of sin could belong personally to Him. In Him was no sin. "God made him to be sin for us," the apostle expressly adds, "who knew no sin." There must never be supposed to be any degree of blameworthi-ness or censure in the person or character of Christ as He stands as an indi-vidual. He is in that respect without spot or wrinkle, or any such thing, the immaculate Lamb of God's Passover. Nor was Christ made a curse of necessity. There was no necessity in Himself that He should ever suffer the curse; no necessity except that which His own loving suretyship created. His own intrinsic holiness kept Him from sin, and that same holiness kept Him from the curse. He was made sin *for us,* not on His own account, not with any view to Himself, but wholly because He loved us, and chose to put Himself in the place which we ought to have occupied. He was made a curse for us not, again I say, out of any personal desert, or out of any personal necessity, but because He had voluntarily undertaken to be the covenant head of His people, and to be their representative, and as their representative to bear the curse which was due to them.

Let us go farther into this truth. How was Christ made a curse? In the first place, He was made a curse because all the sins of His people were actually laid on Him. Remember the words of the apostle—it is no doctrine of mine, mark you; it is an inspired sentence, it is God's doctrine—"He made him to be sin for us;" and let me quote another passage from the prophet Isaiah, "The Lord hath laid on him the iniquity of us all;" and yet another from the same prophet, "He shall bear their iniquities." The sins of God's people were lifted from off them and imputed to Christ, and their sins were looked upon as if Christ had committed them. He was regarded as if He had been the sinner; He actually and in very deed stood in the sinner's place. Next to the imputation of sin came the curse of sin. The law, looking for sin to punish, with its quick eye detected sin laid upon Christ, and, as it must curse sin wherever it was found, it cursed the sin as it was laid on Christ.

So Christ was made a curse. Wonderful and awful words, but as they are scriptural words, we must receive them. Sin being on Christ, the curse came on Christ, and in consequence, our Lord felt an unutterable horror of soul. Surely it was that horror which made Him sweat great drops of blood when He saw and felt that God was beginning to treat Him as if He had been a sinner. The holy soul of Christ shrunk with deepest agony from the slightest contact with sin. So pure and perfect was our Lord, that never an evil thought had crossed His mind, nor had His soul been stained by the glances of evil, and yet He stood in God's sight a sinner, and therefore a solemn horror fell upon His soul; the heart refused its healthful action, and a bloody sweat bedewed His face. Then He began to be made a curse for us, nor did He cease till He had suffered all the penalty which was due on our account.

We have been accustomed in divinity to divide the penalty into two parts, the penalty of loss and the penalty of actual suffering. Christ endured both of these. It was due to sinners that they should lose God's favor and presence, and therefore Jesus cried, "My God, my God, why hast thou forsaken me?" It was due to sinners that they should lose all personal comfort; Christ was deprived of every consolation, and even the last rag of clothing was torn from Him, and He was left like Adam naked and forlorn. It was necessary that the soul should lose everything that could sustain it, and so did Christ lose every comfortable thing; He looked and there was no man to pity or help; He was made to cry, "But I am a worm, and no man; a reproach of men, and despised of the people."

As for the second part of the punishment, namely, an actual infliction of suffering, our Lord endured this also to the uttermost, as the evangelists clearly show. You have read full often the story of His bodily sufferings; take care that you never depreciate them. There was an amount of physical pain endured by our Savior which His body never could have borne unless it had been sustained and strengthened by union with His Godhead; yet the sufferings of His soul were the soul of His sufferings. That soul of His endured a torment equivalent to Hell itself. The punishment that was due to the wicked was that of Hell, and though Christ suffered not Hell, He suffered an equivalent for it; and now, can your minds conceive what that must have been?

It was an anguish never to be measured, an agony never to be comprehended. It is to God, and God alone that His griefs were fully known. Well does the Greek liturgy put it, "Thine unknown sufferings," for they must forever remain beyond guess of human imagination. See, brethren, Christ has gone thus far; He has taken the sin, taken the curse, and suffered all the penalty. The last penalty of sin was death; and therefore the Redeemer died. Behold, the mighty conqueror yields up His life upon the tree! His side is pierced; the blood and water flows forth, and His disciples lay His body in the tomb. As He was first numbered with the transgressors, He was afterwards numbered with the dead. See, beloved, here is Christ bearing the curse instead of His people. Here He is coming under the load of their sin, and God does not spare Him but smites him, as He must have smitten us, lays His full vengeance on Him, launches all His thunderbolts against Him, bids the curse wreak itself upon Him, and Christ suffers all, sustains all.

IV. And now let us conclude by considering what are the blessed consequences of Christ's having thus been made a curse for us.

The consequences are that He hath redeemed us from the curse of the law. As many as Christ died for, are forever free from the curse of the law; for when the law cometh to curse a man who believeth in Christ, he saith, "What have I to do with thee, O law? Thou sayest, 'I will curse thee,' but I reply, 'Thou hast cursed Christ instead of me. Canst thou curse twice for one offence?'" Behold how the law is silenced! God's law having received all it can demand, is not so unrighteous as to demand anything more. All that God can demand of a believing sinner, Christ has already paid, and there is no voice in earth or Heaven that can henceforth accuse a soul that believes in Jesus.

You were in debt, but a friend paid your debt; no writ can be served on you. It matters nothing that *you* did not pay it, it is paid, and you have the receipt. That is sufficient in any court of equity. So with all the penalty that was due to us, Christ has borne it. It is true I have not borne it, I have not been to Hell and suffered the full wrath of God, but Christ has suffered that wrath for me, and I am as clear as if I had myself paid the debt to God and had myself suffered His wrath.

Here is a glorious bottom to rest upon! Here is a rock upon which to lay the foundation of eternal comfort! Let a man once get to this! My Lord without the city's gate did bleed for me as my Surety, and on the Cross discharged my debt. Why, then, great God, Thy thunders I no longer fear. How canst Thou smite me now? Thou hast exhausted the quiver of Thy wrath; every arrow has been already shot forth against the person of my Lord, and I am in Him clear and clean, and absolved and delivered, even as if I had never sinned. "He hath redeemed us," saith the text.

How often I have heard certain gentry of the modern school of theology sneer at the atonement, because they charge us with the notion of its being a sort of business transaction, or what they choose to call "the mercantile view of it." I hesitate not to say that the mercantile metaphor expresses rightly God's view of redemption, for we find it so in Scripture; the atonement is a ransom—that is to say, a price paid; and in the present case the original word is more than usually expressive; it is a payment for, a price instead of. Jesus did in His sufferings perform what may be forcibly and fitly described as the pay-merit of a ransom, the giving to justice *a quid pro quo* for what was due on our behalf for our sins. Christ in His person suffered what we ought to have suffered in our persons. The sins that were ours were made His; He stood as a sinner in God's sight; though not a sinner in Himself, He was punished as a sinner, and died as a sinner upon the tree of the curse.

Then having exhausted His imputed sinnership by bearing the full penalty, He made an end of sin, and He rose again from the dead to bring in that everlasting righteousness which at this moment covers the persons of all His elect, so that they can exultingly cry, "Who shall lay anything to the charge of God's elect? It is God that justifieth. Who is he that condemneth? It is Christ that died, yea, rather, that is risen again, who is even at the right hand of God, who also maketh intercession for us."

Another blessing flows from this satisfactory substitution. It is this, that now the blessing of God, which had been hitherto arrested by the curse, is made most freely to flow. Read the verse that follows the text: "That the blessing of Abraham might come on the Gentiles through Jesus Christ; that we might receive the promise of the Spirit through faith." The blessing of Abraham was that in his seed all nations of the Earth should be blessed. Since our Lord Jesus Christ has taken away the curse due to sin, a great rock has been lifted out from the river bed of God's mercy, and the living stream comes rippling, rolling, swelling on in crystal tides, sweeping before it all human sin and sorrow, and making glad the thirsty who stoop down to drink thereat.

O my brethren, the blessings of God's grace are full and free this morning; they are as full as your necessities. Great sinners, there is great mercy for you. They are as free as your poverty could desire them to be, free as the air you breathe, or as the cooling stream that flows along the water-brook. You have but to trust Christ, and you shall live. Be you who you may, or what you may, or where you may, though at Hell's dark door you lie down to despair and die, yet the message comes to you, "God hath made Christ to be a propitiation for sin. He made him to be sin for us who knew no sin, that we might be made the righteousness of God in him."

Christ hath delivered us from the curse of the law, being made a curse for us. He that believeth, hath no curse upon him. He may have been an adulterer, a swearer, a drunkard, a murderer, but the moment he believes, God sees none of those sins in him. He sees him as an innocent man, and regards his sins as having been laid on the Redeemer, and punished in Jesus as He died on the tree. I tell thee, if thou believest in Christ this morning, my hearer, though thou be the most damnable of wretches that ever polluted the earth, yet thou shalt not have a sin remaining on thee after believing. God will look at thee as pure; even Omniscience shall not detect a sin in thee, for thy sin shall be put on the scapegoat, even Christ, and carried away into forgetfulness, so that if thy transgression be searched for, it shall not be found. If thou believest—there is the question—thou art clean; if thou wilt trust the incarnate God, thou art delivered. He that believeth is justified from all things. "Believe on the Lord

Jesus Christ, and thou shalt be saved," for "he that believeth and is baptized, shall be saved; and he that believeth not, shall be damned."

I have preached to you the gospel, God knows with what a weight upon my soul, and yet with what holy joy. This is no subject for gaudy eloquence, and for high-flying attempts at oratory; this is a matter to be put to you plainly and simply. Sinners—you must either be cursed of God, or else you must accept Christ, as bearing the curse instead of you. I do beseech you, as you love your souls, if you have any sanity left, accept this blessed and divinely appointed way of salvation. This is the truth which the apostles preached, and suffered and died to maintain; it is this for which the Reformers struggled; it is this for which the martyrs burned at Smithfield; it is the grand basis doctrine of the Reformation, and the very truth of God.

Down with your crosses and rituals, down with your pretensions to good works, and your crouchings at the feet of priests to ask absolution from them! Away with your accursed and idolatrous dependence upon yourself; Christ has finished salvation-work, altogether finished it. Hold not up your rags in competition with His fair white linen: Christ has borne the curse; bring not your pitiful penances, and your tears all full of filth to mingle with the precious fountain flowing with His blood. Lay down what is your own, and come and take what is Christ's. Put away now everything that you have thought of being or doing, by way of winning acceptance with God; humble yourselves, and take Jesus Christ to be the Alpha and Omega, the first and last, the beginning and end of your salvation.

If you do this, not only shall you be saved, but you are saved: rest, thou weary one, for thy sins are forgiven; rise, thou lame man, lame through want of faith, for thy transgression is covered; rise from the dead, thou corrupt one, rise, like Lazarus from the tomb, for Jesus calleth thee! Believe and live. The words in themselves, by the Holy Spirit, are soul-quickening. Have done with thy tears of repentance and thy vows of good living, until thou hast come to Christ; then take them up as thou wilt. Thy first lesson should be: none but Jesus, none but Jesus, none but Jesus. O come thou to Him! See, He hangs upon the Cross; His arms are open wide, and He cannot close them, for the nails hold them fast. He tarries for thee; His feet are fastened to the wood, as though He meant to tarry still. O come thou to Him! His heart has room for thee. It streams with blood and water; it was pierced for thee. That mingled stream is

> *Of sin the double cure,*
> *To cleanse thee from its guilt and power.*

An act of faith will bring thee to Jesus. Say, "Lord, I believe, help thou mine unbelief"; and if thou so doest, He cannot cast thee out, for His word is, "Him that cometh to me I will in no wise cast out." I have delivered to you the weightiest truth that ever ears heard, or that lips spoke, put it not from you. As we shall meet each other at the last tremendous day, when Heaven and Earth are on a blaze, and the trumpet shall ring and raise the dead, as we shall meet each other then, I challenge you to put this from you. If you do it, it is at your own peril, and your blood be on your own heads; but rather, accept the gospel I have delivered to you. It is Jehovah's gospel. Heaven itself speaks in the words you hear today. Accept Jesus Christ as your substitute. O do it now, this moment, and God shall have glory, but you shall have salvation. Amen.

"Bought with a Price"

"Ye are not your own: for ye are bought with a price: therefore glorify God in your body, and in your spirit, which are God's."—I Cor. 6:19, 20.

You will notice that in this chapter the apostle Paul has been dealing with sins of the flesh, with fornication and adultery. Now, it is at all times exceedingly difficult for the preacher either to speak or to write upon this subject; it demands the strictest care to keep the language guarded, so that while we are denouncing a detestable evil we do not ourselves promote it by a single expression that should be otherwise than chaste and pure. Observe how well the apostle Paul succeeds, for though he does not mask the sin, but tears the veil from it, and lets us know well what it is that he is aiming at, yet there is no sentence which we could wish to alter. Herein he is a model for all ministers, both in fidelity and prudence.

Be sure also to note that the apostle, when he is exposing sin, does not trifle with it, but like a mighty hunter before the Lord, pursues it with all his might; his hatred to it is intense; he drags it forth to the light; he bids us mark its hideous deformity; he hunts it through all its purlieus, hotfoot, as we say. He never leaves it breathing time: argument after argument he hurls like javelins upon it; he will by no means spare the filthy thing. He who above all others speaks most positively of salvation by grace, and is most clear upon the fact that salvation is not by the works of the law, is at the same time most intensely earnest for the holiness of Christians, and most zealously denounces those who would say, "Let us do evil, that good may come."

In this particular instance he sets the sin of fornication in the light of the Holy Spirit; he holds up, as it were, the seven-branched candlestick before it, and lets us see what a filthy thing it is. He tells us that the body is the Temple of the Holy Ghost, and therefore ought not to be profaned; he declares that bodily unchastity is a sacrilegious desecration of our manhood, a violation of the sacred shrine wherein the Spirit takes up its dwelling place; and then, as if this were not enough, he seizes the sin and drags it to the foot of the Cross, and there nails it hand and foot, that it may die as a criminal; for these are his words: "Ye are not your own: for ye are bought with a price:" the price being the blood of Jesus. He finds no sharper weapon, no keener instrument of destruction than this. The redemption wrought on Calvary by the death of Jesus must be the death of this sin, and of all other sins, wherever the Spirit of God uses it as his sword of execution.

Brethren and sisters, it is no slight thing to be holy. A man must not say, "I have faith," and then fall into the sins of an unbeliever; for, after all, our outer life is the test of our inner life; and if the outer life be not purified, rest assured the heart is not changed. That faith which does not bring forth the fruit of holiness is the faith of devils. The devils believe and tremble. Let us never be content with a faith which can live in Hell, but rise to that which will save us—the faith of God's elect, which purifies the soul, casting down the power of evil, and setting up the throne of Jesus Christ, the throne of holiness within the spirit.

Noticing this as being the run of the chapter, we now come to the text itself, and in order to discuss it we must take it to pieces, and I think we shall see in it at once three things very clearly. The first is *a blessed fact*, "Ye are," or as it should be rendered, "Ye were bought with a price." Then comes *a plain consequence* from that fact, a consequence of a double character, negative and positive: "Ye are not your own"; "your body and your spirit are God's." Out of that there springs inevitably *a natural conclusion*: "Therefore, glorify God in your body, and in your spirit."

I. Let us begin, then, first of all, with this blessed fact: "we are bought with a price."

Paul might, if his object were to prove that we are not our own, have said: "Ye did not make yourselves." Creation may well furnish motives for obedience to the great Lawgiver. He might also have said, "Ye do not preserve yourselves: it is God who keeps you in life; you would die if He withdrew His power." The preservation of divine providence might furnish abundant arguments for holiness. Surely He who feeds, nourishes, and upholds our life should have our service. But He prefers, for reasons known to Himself, which it would not be hard to guess, to plead the tenderer theme, redemption. He sounds that note, which if it do not thunder with that crash of power which marked the six days' labor of

Omnipotence, yet has a soft, piercing, subduing tone in it, which, like the still small voice to which Elias listened, has in it the presence of God.

The most potent plea for sanctity is not "Ye were made," or, "Ye are nourished," but "Ye are bought." This the apostle selects as a convincing proof of our duty, and as a means to make that duty our delight. And truly, beloved, it is so. If we have indeed experienced the power of redemption we fully admit that it is so. Look ye back to the day when ye were bought, when ye were bondslaves to your sins, when ye were under the just sentence of divine justice, when it was inevitable that God should punish your transgressions; remember how the Son of God became your substitute, how He bared his back to the lash that should have fallen upon you, and laid His soul beneath the sword which should have quenched its fury in your blood. You were redeemed then, redeemed from the punishment that was due to you, redeemed from the wrath of God, redeemed unto Christ to be His forever.

You will notice the text says, "Ye were bought *with a price.*" It is a common classical expression to signify that the purchase was expensive. Of course, the very expression, "Ye were bought," implies a price, but the words *"with a price"* are added, as if to show that it was not for nothing that ye were purchased. There was a something inestimably precious paid for you; and ye need scarcely that I remind you that "ye were not redeemed with corruptible things, as silver and gold"; but with the precious blood of Christ, as of a lamb without blemish and without spot."

Ah! those words slip over our tongue very glibly, but we may well chide ourselves that we can speak of redemption with dry eyes. That the blood of Christ was shed to buy our souls from death and Hell is a wonder of compassion which fills angels with amazement, and it ought to overwhelm us with adoring love whenever we think of it, glance our eye over the recording pages, or even utter the word "redemption."

What meant this purchasing us *with blood?* It signified pain. Have any of you lately been racked with pain? Have you suffered acutely? Ah! then at such times you know to some degree what the price was which the Savior paid. His bodily pains were great, hands and feet nailed to the wood, and the iron breaking through the tenderest nerves. His soul-pains were greater still, His heart was melted like wax, He was very heavy, His heart was broken with reproach, He was deserted of God, and left beneath the black thunder clouds of divine wrath, His soul was exceeding sorrowful, even unto death. It was pain that bought you. We speak of the drops of blood, but we must not confine our thoughts to the crimson life-floods which distilled from the Savior's veins; we must think of the pangs which He endured, which were the equivalent for what we ought to have suffered, what we must have suffered had we endured the punishment of our guilt forever in the flames of Hell.

But pain alone could not have redeemed us; it was by death that the Savior paid the ransom. Death is a word of horror to the ungodly. The righteous hath hope in His death; but as Christ's death was the substitute for the death of the ungodly, He was made a curse for us, and the presence of God was denied Him. His death was attended with unusual darkness; He cried, "My God, my God, why hast thou forsaken me?" O think ye earnestly on this. The Ever-living died to redeem us; the Only Begotten bowed His head in agony, and was laid in the grave that we might be saved. Ye are bought then "with a price"—a price incalculable, stupendous, infinite, and this is the plea which the apostle uses to urge upon us that we should "be holiness to the Lord." Holiness, therefore, is necessary to all the redeemed. If you cast off your responsibility to be holy, you at the same time cast away the benefit of redemption. Will you do this? As I am sure you could not renounce your salvation, and cast away your only hope, so I charge you by the living God be not so inconsistent as to say: "I am redeemed, and yet I will live as I list [choose]." As redeemed men, let the inevitable consequences follow from the fact, and be ye evidently the servants of the Lord Jesus.

Remember, too, that *this fact is the most important one in all your history.* That you were redeemed "with a price" is the greatest event in your biography. Oh, I do beseech you then, if it be so, prove it; and remember the just and righteous proof is by your not being your own, but consecrated unto God. If it be the most important thing in the world to you, that you were "bought with a price," let it exercise the most prominent influence over your entire career. Be a man, be an Englishman, but be most of all Christ's man. A citizen, a friend, a philanthropist, a patriot: all these you may be, but be most of all a saint redeemed by blood.

Recollect, again, that your being "bought with a price" *will be the most important fact in all your future existence.* What say they in Heaven when they sing? They would naturally select the noblest topic and that which most engrosses their minds, and yet in the whole range of their memory they find no theme so absorbing as this: "Thou wast slain, and hast redeemed us to God by thy blood." Redeeming love is the theme of Heaven. When you reach the upper realms your most important memory will not be that you were wealthy or poor in this life, nor the fact that you sickened and died, but that you were "bought with a price."

We do not know all that may occur in this world before the close of its history; but certainly it will be burnt up with fire and you in yonder clouds with

Christ may witness the awful conflagration. You will never forget it. There will be new Heavens and new earth, and you with Christ may see the newborn Heavens and earth, laughing in the bright sunlight of God's good pleasure; you will never forget that joyous day. And you will be caught up to dwell with Jesus forever and ever; and there will come a time when He shall deliver up the kingdom to God, even the Father and God shall be all in all. You will never forget the time of which the poet sings

> *Then the end, beneath His rod*
> *Man's last enemy shall fall.*
> *Hallelujah, Christ in God,*
> *God in Christ is all in all.*

All these divinely glorious events will impress themselves upon you, but not one of them will make an impression so lasting, so clear, so deep as this, that you were "bought with a price." High over all the mountain tops, Calvary, that was but a little mount in human estimation, shall rise; stars shall the events of history be; but this event shall be the sun in whose presence all others hide their diminished heads. "Thou wast slain," the full chorus of Heaven shall roll it forth in thundering accents of grateful zeal. "Thou wast slain, and hast redeemed us to God by thy blood"; the saints shall remember this first and foremost; and amidst the cycles of eternity this shall have the chief place in every glorified memory. What then, beloved? Shall it not have the chief place with you now? This has been *the fact* of your life hitherto, it will be the fact of your entire eternal existence: let it saturate your soul, let it penetrate your spirit, let it subdue your faculties, let it take the reins of all your powers and guide you whither it will; let the Redeemer, He whose hands were pierced for you, sway the scepter of your spirit and rule over you this day, and world without end.

If I had the power to do it, how would I seek to refresh in your souls a sense of this fact that you are "bought with a price." There, in the midnight hour, amidst the olives of Gethsemane, kneels Immanuel the Son of God; He groans, He pleads in prayer, He wrestles; see the beady drops stand on His brow, drops of sweat, but not of such sweat as pours from men when they earn the bread of life, but the sweat of Him who is procuring life itself for us. It is blood, it is crimson blood; great gouts of it are falling to the ground. O soul, thy Savior speaks to thee from out Gethsemane at this hour, and He says: "Here and thus I bought thee with a price." Come, stand and view Him in the agony of the olive garden, and understand at what a cost He procured thy deliverance. Track Him in all His path of shame and sorrow till you see

Him on the Pavement; mark how they bind His hands and fasten him to the whipping post; see, they bring the scourges and the cruel Roman whips; they tear His flesh; the ploughers make deep furrows on His blessed body, and the blood gushes forth in streams, while rivulets from His temples, where the crown of thorns has pierced them, join to swell the purple stream. From beneath the scourges He speaks to you with accents soft and low, and He says, "My child, it is here and thus I bought thee with a price."

But see Him on the Cross itself when the consummation of all has come; His hands and feet are fountains of blood; his soul is full of anguish even to heartbreak; and there, ere the soldier pierces with a spear His side, bowing down He whispers to thee and to me "It was here, and thus, I bought thee with a price." Oh, by Gethsemane, by Gabbatha, by Golgotha, by every sacred name connected with the passion of our Lord, by sponge and vinegar, and nail and spear, and everything that helped the pang and increased the anguish of His death, I conjure you, my beloved brethren, to remember that ye were "bought with a price," and "are not your own."

I push you to this; you either were, or were not, so bought; if you were, it is the grand fact of your life; if you were, it is the greatest fact that ever will occur to you! Let it operate upon you, let it dominate your entire nature, let it govern your body, your soul, your spirit, and from this day let it be said of you not only that you are a man, a man of good morals and respectable conduct, but this, above all things: that you are a man filled with love to Him who bought you, a man who lives for Christ, and knows no other passion. Would God that redemption would become the paramount influence, the lord of our soul, and dictator of our being; then were we indeed true to our obligations: short of this we are not what love and justice both demand.

II. Now, let us pass on to the second point. Here is a plain consequence arising from the blessed fact. Ye were "bought with a price." Then first it is clear as a negative, that "Ye are not your own"; and secondly, it is clear as a positive, that "your body and spirit are God's."

Take first *the negative*: if bought, you are not your own. No argument is needed for this, and indeed it is so great a boon in itself that none of us could find it in our hearts to demur to it. It is a great privilege not to be one's own. A vessel is drifting on the Atlantic hither and thither, and its end no man knoweth. It is derelict, deserted by all its crew; it is the property of no man; it is the prey of every storm, and the sport of every wind: rocks, quicksands, and shoals wait to destroy it: the ocean yearns to engulf it. It drifts onward to no man's land, and no man will mourn its shipwreck. But mark well yonder barque in the Thames which its owner surveys with pleasure. In its attempt to reach the sea, it may run ashore, or come into collision with other vessels; or in a thousand ways suffer damage; but there is no fear, it will pass through the floating forest of "the Pool"; it will thread the winding channel, and reach the Nore because its owner will secure it pilotage, skillful and apt.

How thankful you and I should be that we are not derelict today! We are not our own, not left on the wild waste of chance to be tossed to and fro by fortuitous circumstances; but there is a hand upon our helm; we have on board a pilot who owns us, and will surely steer us into the Fair Havens of eternal rest. The sheep is on the mountain side, and the winter is coming on; it may be buried in the snow; perhaps the wolf may seize it, or by-and-by, when the summer crops have been eaten, there may be little fodder for it, and it may starve; but the sheep's comfort, if it could think at all, would be this: it is not its own, it belongeth to the shepherd, who will not willingly lose his property; it bears the mark of its owner, and is the object of his care. O happy sheep of God's pasture, what a bliss it is to you that you are not your own! Does any man here think it would be a pleasure to be his own? Let me assure him that there is no ruler so tyrannical as self. He that is his own master, has a fool and a tyrant to be his lord. No man ever yet governed himself after the will of the flesh, but what he by degrees found the yoke heavy and the burden crushing. Self is a fierce dictator, a terrible oppressor; imperious lusts are cruel slave drivers.

But Christ, who says we are not our own, would have us view that truth in the light in which a loving wife would view it. She, too, is not her own. She gave herself away on a right memorable day, of which she bears the golden token on her finger. She did not weep when she surrendered herself and became her husband's; nor did they muffle the bells, or bid the organ play the "Dead March" in Saul: it was a happy day for her; she re-members it at this moment with glowing joy. She is not her own, but she has not regretted the giving herself away: she would make the same sur-render again to the self-same beloved owner, if it were to be done. That she is her husband's does not bespeak her slavery, but her happiness; she has found rest in her husband's house, and today, when the Christian con-fesses that he is not his own, he does not wish that he were. He is married to the Savior; he has given himself up, body, soul, and spirit, to the blessed Bridegroom of his heart; it was the marriage day of his true life when he became a Christian, and he looks back to it with joy and transport. Oh, it is a blissful thing not to be our own, so I shall not want arguments to prove that to which every gracious spirit gives a blissful consent.

Now, if it be true that we are not our own, and I hope it is true to many here present, then the inference from it is, "I have no right to *injure myself* in any way." My body is not my own, I have no right then, as a Christian man, to do anything with it that would defile it. The apostle is mainly arguing against sins of the flesh, and he says, "the body is not for fornication, but for the Lord; and the Lord for the body." We have no right to commit uncleanness, because our bodies are the members of Christ and not our own. He would say the same of drunkenness, gluttony, idle sleep, and even of such excessive anxiety after wealth as injures health with carking care. We have no right to profane or injure the flesh and blood which are consecrated to God; every limb of our frame belongs to God; it is His property; He has bought it "with a price." Any honest man will be more concerned about an injury done to another's property placed under his care, than if it were his own.

When the son of the prophet was hewing wood with Elisha, you remember how he said, when the axe head flew off into the water, "Alas! master, for it was borrowed." It would be bad enough to lose my own axe, but it is not my own, therefore I doubly deplore the accident. I know this would not operate upon thievish minds. There are some who, if it was another man's, and they had borrowed it, would have no further care about it: "Let the lender get it back, if he can." But we speak to honest men, and with them it is always a strong argument: your body is another's, do it no injury. As for our spirit too, that is God's, and how careful we should be of it.

I am asked sometimes to read an heretical book: well, if I believed my reading it would help its refutation, and might be an assistance to others in keeping them out of error, I might do it as a hard matter of duty, but I shall not do it unless I see some good will come from it. I am not going to drag my spirit through a ditch for the sake of having it washed afterwards, for it is not my own. It may be that good medicine would restore me if I poisoned myself with putrid meat, and I am not going to try it: I dare not experiment on a mind which no longer belongs to me. There is a mother and a child, and the child has a book to play with, and a blacklead pencil. It is making drawings and marks upon the book, and the mother takes no notice. It lays down one book and snatches another from the table, and at once the mother rises from her seat, and hurriedly takes the book away, saying: "No, my dear, you must not mark that, for it is not ours."

So with my mind, intellect, and spirit; if it belonged to me I might or might not play tomfool with it, and go to hear Socinians, Ritualists, Universalists, and such like preach, but as it is not my own, I will preserve it from such fooleries, and the pure word shall not be mingled with the errors of men. Here is the drift of the apostle's argument—I have no right to injure that which does not belong to me, and as I am not my own, I have no right to injure myself.

But, further, I have no right to let myself *lie waste*. The man who had a talent, and went and dug in the Earth and hid it, had not he a right to do so? Yes, of course, if it was his own talent, and his own napkin. If any of you have money and do not put it out to interest, if it is all your own, nobody complains. But this talent belonged to the man's master, it was only entrusted to him as a steward, and he ought to have not let it rust in the ground.

So I have no right to let my faculties run to waste since they do not belong to me. If I am a Christian I have no right to be idle. I saw the other day men using picks in the road in laying down new gas pipes; they had been resting, and just as I passed the clock struck one, and the foreman gave a signal. I think he said, *"Blow up";* and straightway each man took his pick or his shovel, and they were all at it in earnest. Close to them stood a fellow with a pipe in his mouth, who did not join in the work, but stood in a free-and-easy posture. It did not make any difference to him whether it was one o'clock or six. Why not? Because he was his own: the other men were the master's for the time being. He as an independent gentleman might do as he liked, but those who were not their own fell to labor. If any of you idle professors [Christians] can really prove that you belong to yourselves, I have nothing more to say to you, but if you profess to have a share in the redeeming sacrifice of Christ, I am ashamed of you if you do not go to work the very moment the signal is given. You have no right to waste what Jesus Christ has bought "with a price."

Further than that, if we are not our own, but "are bought with a price," we have no right to exercise any *capricious government* of ourselves. A man who is his own may say, "I shall go whither I will, and do what I will"; but if I am not my own but belong to God who has bought me, then I must submit to His government; His will must be my will, and His directions must be my law. I desire to enter a certain garden, and I ask the gardener at the gate if I may come in. "You should be very welcome, sir, indeed," says he, "if it were mine, but my master has told me not to admit strangers here, and therefore I must refuse you." Sometimes the devil would come into the garden of our souls. We tell him that our flesh might consent, but the garden is not ours, and we cannot give him space. Worldly ambition, covetousness, and so forth, might claim to walk through our soul, but we say, "No, it is not our own; we cannot, therefore, do what our old will would do, but we desire to be obedient to the will of our Father who is in Heaven." Thy will be done, my God, in me, for so should it be done where all is Thine own by purchase.

Yet, again, if we are not our own, then we have no right *to serve ourselves.* The man who is living entirely for himself, whose object is his own ease, comfort, honour, or wealth, what knows he concerning redemption by Christ? If our aims rise no higher than our personal advantages, we are false to the fact that we "are bought with a price," we are treacherous to Him in whose redemption we pretend to share.

But time would fail me if I dwelt upon this, or, indeed, at any length upon *the positive side* of this blessed fact: I will therefore only say a word or two concerning it. Our body and our spirit are God's; and, Christian, this is certainly a very high honour to you. Your body will rise again from the dead at the first resurrection, because it is not an ordinary body, it belongs to God: your spirit is distinguished from the souls of other men; it is God's spirit, and He has set His mark upon it, and honored you in so doing. You are God's because a price has been paid for you. According to some, the allusion price here is to the dowry that was paid by a husband for his wife in ancient days. According to the Rabbis, there were three ways by which a woman became the wife of a man, and one of these was by the payment of a dowry. This was always held good in Jewish law; the woman was not her own from the moment when the husband had paid to her father or natural guardian the stipulated price for her. Now, at this day, you and I rejoice that Jesus Christ has espoused us unto Himself in righteousness or ever the Earth was; we rejoice in that language which He uses by the prophet Hosea, "I will betroth thee unto me forever"; but here is our comfort, the dowry money has been paid, Christ has redeemed us unto Himself, and Christ's we are, Christ's forever and ever.

III. *And now I must close, and oh, may God give power to His word while I beg to speak upon the last point, namely, the natural conclusion, "Therefore glorify God in your body, and in your spirit."*

I am not clear that the last few words are in the original. A large number of the old manuscripts and versions, and some of the more important of them, finish the verse at the word "body"—"Therefore glorify God in your body." It was the body the apostle was speaking about, and not the spirit, and there is no necessity for the last words: still we will not further raise the question, but take them as being the inspired word of God: but still, I must make the remark, that according to the connection the force of the apostle's language falls upon the body; and perhaps it is so, because we are so apt to forget the truth, that the body is redeemed and is the Lord's, and should be made to glorify God.

The Christian man's body should glorify God by its chastity. Pure as the lily should we be from every taint of uncleanness. The body should glorify God by temperance also; in all things, in eating, drinking, sleeping, in everything that has to do with the flesh. "Whether ye eat or drink, or whatsoever ye do, do all to the glory of God," or as the apostle puts it elsewhere, "whatsoever ye do in word or deed, do all in the name of the Lord Jesus, giving thanks to God and the Father by him." The Christian man can make every meal a sacrament, and his ordinary avocations the exercise of his spiritual priesthood. The body ought to glorify God by its industry. A lazy servant is a bad Christian. A working man who is always looking for Saturday night, a man who never spends a drop of sweat except when the master is looking on, does not glorify God in his body. The best Christian is the man who is not afraid of hard work when it is due, who works not as an eye-servant or man pleaser, but in singleness of heart seeks to glorify God. Our bodies used to work hard enough for the devil; now they belong to God we will make them work for Him. Your legs used to carry you to the theater; be not too lazy to come out on a Thursday night to the house of God. Your eyes have been often open upon iniquity, keep them open during the sermon: do not drop asleep! Your ears have been sharp enough to catch the word of a lascivious song, let them be quick to observe the word of God. Those hands have often squandered your earnings in sinfulness, let them give freely to the cause of Christ. Your body was a willing horse when it was in the service of the devil, let it not be a sluggish hack now that it draws the chariot of Christ. Make the tongue speak His praises, make the mouth sing of His glory, make the whole man bow in willing subservience to the will of Him who bought it.

As for your spirit, let that glorify God too. Let your private meditations magnify God; let your songs be to Him when no one hears you but Himself, and let your public zeal, let the purity of your conversation, let the earnestness of your life, let the universal holiness of your character, glorify God with your body and with your spirit.

Beloved Christian friends, I want to say these few things and have done. Because you are God's you will be looked at more than others, therefore, glorify Him. For my part I am very glad of the lynx eyes of the worldlings. Let them watch if they will. I have heard of one who was a great caviler at Christian people, and after having annoyed a church a long time, he was about to leave, and therefore, as a parting jest with the minister, he said, "I have no doubt you will be very glad to know that I am going a hundred miles away?" "No," said the pastor, "I shall be sorry to lose you." "How? I never did you any good."

> I don't know that, for I am sure that never one of my flock put half a foot through the hedge but what you began to yelp at him, and so you have been a famous sheep dog for me.

I am glad the world observes us. It has a right to do so. If a man says, "I am God's," he sets himself up for public observation. Ye are lights in the world, and what are lights intended for but to be looked at? A city set on a hill cannot be hid.

Moreover, the world has a right to expect more from a Christian than from anybody else. He says he is "bought with a price," he says he is God's, he therefore claims more than others, and he ought to render more. If we are not holy and gracious, ungodly men are sure to say, "That is one of your believers in God; that is one of your Christians." Do not let it be so. Every soldier in a regiment ought to feel that the renown of the whole army depends upon him, and he must fight as if the winning of the battle rested upon himself. This will cause every man to be a hero. Oh, that every Christian felt as if the honour of God and the church rested upon him, for in a measure it certainly does!

May we so seek God, that when we come to die we may feel that we have lived for something; that although our hope has rested alone in what Jesus did, yet we have not made that an excuse for doing nothing ourselves. Though we shall have no good works in which to glory, yet may we bring forth fruit that shall be for the glory of our Lord. I feel I so desire to glorify God, body, soul, and spirit while I breathe, that I would even do so on Earth after I am dead. I would still urge my brethren on in our Lord's cause.

Old Zizka, the Hussite leader, when about to die, said to his soldiers:

> Our enemies have always been afraid of my name in the time of battle, and when I am dead, take my skin, and make a drum-head of it, and beat it whenever you go to battle. When the foemen hear the sound they will tremble, and you will remember that Zizka calls on his brethren to fight valiantly.

Let us so live that when we die, we live on, like Abel, who being dead yet speaketh. The only way to do this is to live in the power of the Immortal God, under the influence of his Holy Spirit: then out of our graves we shall speak to future generations.

When Doctor Payson died, he desired that his body should be placed in a coffin, and that his hearers should be invited to come and see it. Across his breast was placed a paper bearing these words, "Remember the words which I spoke unto you, being yet present with you." May our lives be such that even if we are not public speakers, yet others may remember our example, and so may hear what our lives spake while we were yet on earth. Your bodies and your spirits are God's: oh, live to God, and glorify Him in the power of His Spirit as long as you have any breath below, that so when the breath is gone, your very bones, like those of Joseph, shall be a testimony. Even in the ashes of the saints, their wonted fires live on. In their hallowed memories they rise like a phoenix from their ashes.

The Lord make us more and more practically His own, and may His Name be glorious, forever and ever. Amen, and amen.

Love's Crowning Deed

"Greater love hath no man than this, that a man lay down his life for his friends."—John 15:13.

I have lately in my ministry very much detained you in the balmy region of divine loving-kindness. Our subjects have frequently been full of love. I have, perhaps, repeated myself, and gone over the same ground again and again, but I could not help it; my own soul was in a grateful condition, and therefore out of the abundance of the heart the mouth hath spoken. Truly I have little reason to excuse myself, for the region of love to Christ is the native place of the Christian; we were first brought to know Christ and to rest in Him through His love, and there, in the warmth of His tenderness, we were born to God. Not by the terrors of justice, nor the threats of vengeance, were we reconciled, but grace drew us with cords of love.

Now, we have sometimes heard of sickly persons, that the physician has recommended them to try their native air, in hopes of restoration; so we also recommend every backsliding Christian to try the native air of Christ's love, and we charge every healthy believer to abide in it. Let the believer go back to the Cross again; there he found his hope, there he must find it again: there his love to Jesus began—we "love him because he first loved us,"—and there must his love be again inflamed.

Our subject this morning, then, is divine love, and we have chosen our highest hill in all the goodly land for you to climb; we shall take you today to love's most sacred shrine, to the Jerusalem of the holy land of love, to the Tabor of love, where it was transfigured, and put on its most beautiful garments, where it became indeed too bright for mortal eye fully to gaze upon it, too lustrous for this dim vision of ours. Let us come to Calvary where we find love stronger than death, conquering the grave for our sakes.

We shall speak, first, upon *love's crowning act:* "Greater love hath no man than this, that a man lay down his life for his friends"; but, then, since the text, grand as it is, and high, so that we cannot attain unto it, yet seems to fall short of the great argument, though it be one of the Master's own sayings, we shall speak upon *the sevenfold crown of Jesus' love;* and when we have so done, we shall have some *royal things* to say, which befit the place whereon we stand when we are gathered at the Cross-foot.

I. First, then, love's crowning deed.

There is a climax to everything, and the climax of love is to die for the beloved one. "Free grace and dying love" are the noblest themes among men, and when united they are sublimity itself. Love can do much, can do infinite things, but greater love hath no man than this, that he lay down his life for his friends. This is the *ultima thule* [ideal] of love; its sails can find no further shore, its deeds of self-denial can go no further. To lay down one's life is the most that love can do.

This is clear if we consider, first, that when a man dies for his friends, it proves *his deep sincerity.* Lip-love, proverbially, is a thing to be questioned; too often is it a counterfeit. Love which speaks can use hyperbolical expressions at its will, but when you have heard all you can hear of love's speech, you are not sure that it is love; for all are not hunters that blow the horn, all are not friends who cry up friendship. Much there is among men of a feeling which wears all the likeness of that priceless thing called love, which is more precious than the gold of Ophir, and yet for all that, as all is not gold that glitters, so it is not all love that walketh delicately and feigneth affection.

But a man is no liar when he is willing to die to prove his love. All suspicion of insincerity must then be banished. We are sure he loves who dies for love. Yea, it is not bare sincerity that we see in such a case, we see *the intensity of his affection.* A man may make us feel that he is intensely in earnest when he speaks with burning words, and he may perform many actions which may all appear to show how intense he is, and yet for all that he may but be a skillful player, understanding well the art of simulating that which he does not feel: but when a man dies for the cause he has espoused, you know that his is no superficial passion, you are sure that the core of his nature must be on fire when his love consumes his life; if he will shed his blood for the object beloved, there must be blood in the veins of his love, it is a living love.

And, again, *it proves the thorough self-abnegation of the heart* when the man risks life itself for love. Love and self-denial for the object loved go hand-in-hand. If I profess to love a certain person, and yet will neither give my silver nor my gold to relieve his wants, nor in any way deny myself comfort or ease for his sake, such love is contemptible: it wears the name, but lacks the reality of love: true love must be measured by the degree to which the person loving will be willing to subject himself to crosses and losses, to sufferings and self-denials. After all, the value of a thing in the market is what a man will give for it, and you must estimate the value of a man's love by that which he is willing to give up for it. What will he do to prove his affection? What will he suffer for the sake of benefitting his beloved? Greater love for friends hath no man than this, that he lay down his life for them.

Even Satan acknowledged the reality of the virtue which would lead a man to die, when he spake concerning Job to God: he made little of Job's losing his sheep, and his cattle, and his children, and remaining patient; but he said,

> Skin for skin; yea all that a man hath will he give for his life; but put forth now thine hand, and touch his bone and his flesh, and he will curse thee to thy face.

So if love could give up its cattle and its land, its outward treasures and possessions, it would be somewhat strong, but comparatively it would fail if it could not go further, and endure personal suffering, yea, and the laying down of life itself.

No such failure occurred in the Redeemer's love. Our Savior stripped Himself of all His glories, and by a thousand self-denials proved His love; but the most convincing evidence was given when He gave up His life for us. "Hereby perceive we the love of God," says the apostle John, "because he laid down his life for us"; as if He passed by everything else, which the Son of God had done for us, and put His finger upon His death and said, "*Hereby* we perceive the love of God towards us." It was majestic love that made the Lord Jesus lay aside "his [at]tire and rings of light," and lend their glory to the stars, strip off His azure mantle and hang it on the sky, and then come down to Earth to wear the poor, mean garments of our flesh and blood, in which to toil and labor like ourselves. But the masterpiece of love was when He would even put off the garment of His flesh, and yield Himself to the agonies superlative of death by crucifixion. He could go no further; self-abnegation had achieved its utmost; He could deny Himself no more, when He denied Himself leave to live.

Again, beloved, the reason why death for its object is the crowning deed of love is this, that *it excels all other deeds.* Jesus Christ had proved His love by dwelling among His people as their Brother, and participating in their poverty as their friend, till He could say, "Foxes have holes and the birds of the air have nests, but I, the Son of Man, have nowhere to lay my head." He had manifested His love by telling them all He knew of the Father, unveiling the secrets of eternity to simple fishermen; He showed His love by the patience with which He bore with their faults, never harshly rebuking, but only gently chiding them, and even that but seldom; He revealed His love to them by the miracles He wrought on their behalf, and the honour which He put upon them by using them in His service. Indeed, there were ten thousand princely acts of the love of Jesus Christ towards His own, but none of them can for a moment endure comparison with His dying for them—the agonizing death of the Cross surpasses all the rest. These life-actions of His love are bright as stars, and, like the stars, if you gaze upon them, they will be seen to be far greater than you dreamed, but yet they are only stars compared with this clear, blazing sun of infinite love which is to be seen in the Lord's dying for His people on the bloody tree.

Then, I must add that His death *did in effect comprehend all other acts,* for when a man lays down his life for his friend he has laid down everything else. Give up life, and you have given up wealth—where is the wealth of a dead man? Renounce life, and you have relinquished position—where is the rank of a man who lies in the sepulcher? Lay down life, and you have forsaken enjoyment—what enjoyment can there be to the denizen of the charnel-house? Giving up life, you have given up all things, hence the force of that reasoning, "He that spared not his own Son but freely delivered him up for us all, how will he not with him also freely give us all things?" The giving of the life of His dear Son was the giving of all that His Son was; and as Christ is infinite, and all in all, the delivering up of His life was the concession of all in all to us: there could be nothing more.

Beloved, I speak but too coldly upon a theme which ought to stir my soul first, and yours afterwards. Spirit of the living God, come like a quickening wind from Heaven, and let the sparks of our love glow into a mighty furnace-flame just now, even now, if it may so please thee!

Beloved, we now remark that for a man to die for his friends is evidently *the grandest of all proofs of his love in itself.* The words glide over my tongue, and drop from my lips very rapidly—"lay down his life for his friends," but do you know or feel what the words mean? To die for another! There be some who will not even give of their substance to the poor; it seems like wrenching away a limb for them to give a trifle to God's poor servants. Such people cannot guess what it must be to have love enough to die for another, any more than a blind man can imagine what colors can be like: such persons are out of court altogether. There have been loving spirits who have denied themselves comfort and ease, and even common necessaries, for the sake of their fellow men, and such as these are in a measure qualified to form an idea of what it must be to die for another; but still none of us can fully know what it means! To die for another! Conceive it! Concentrate your thoughts upon it! We start back from death, for under any light in which you may place it, human nature can never regard death as otherwise than a terrible thing.

It is no light thing to die. We speak too flippantly of death, but dying is no child's play to any man, and dying as the Savior died, in awful agonies of body and tortures of soul, it was a great thing indeed for His love to do. You may surround death if you please with luxury, you may place at the bedside all the dear assuagements of the tenderest love; you may alleviate pain by the art of the apothecary and the physician, and you may decorate the dying couch with the honour of a nation's anxious care, but death, for all that, is in itself no slight thing, and when borne for others it is the masterpiece of love.

And so, closing this point of love's crowning action, let me say that *after a man has died for another, there can be no question raised about his love.* Unbelief would be insane if it should venture to intrude itself at the Cross's foot, though, alas, it has been there, and has there proved its utter unreasonableness. If a man dies for his friend, he must love him, nobody can question that; and Jesus dying for His people must love them: who shall cast a doubt upon that fact? Shame on any of God's children that they should ever raise questions on a matter so conclusively proven! yet, as if the Lord Jesus knew that even this masterpiece of love might still be intruded upon by unbelief, He rose again from the dead, and rose with His love as fresh as ever in His heart, and went to Heaven leading captivity captive, His eyes flashing with the eternal love that brought Him down. He passed through the pearly gates, and rode in triumph up to His Great Father's throne, and though He looked upon His Father with love ineffable and eternal, He gazed upon His people too, for His heart was still theirs. Even at this hour from His throne among the seraphim, where He sits in glory, He looketh down upon His people with pitying love and con-descending grace.

> *Now, though He reigns exalted high,*
> *His love is still as great;*
> *Well He remembers Calvary,*
> *Nor lets His saints forget.*

He is all love, and altogether love. "Greater love hath no man than this, that a man lay down his life for his friends."

II. The seven crowns of Jesus' dying love are our second point.

I hope I shall have your interested attention while I show that above that highest act of human love there is a something in Christ's death for love's sake still more elevated. Men's dying for their friends—this is superlative, but Christ's dying for us is as much above man's superlative as that could be above mere commonplace. Let me show you this in seven points.

The first is this *Jesus was immortal,* hence the special character of His death. When a man lays down his life for his friend, he does not lay down what he could keep altogether; he could only have kept it for a while, even if he had lived as long as mortals can, till grey hairs are on their head, he must at last have yielded to the arrows of death. A substitutionary death for love's sake in ordinary cases would be but a slightly premature payment of that debt of nature which must be paid by all.

But such is not the case with Jesus. Jesus needed not die at all; there was no ground or reason why He should die apart from His laying down His life in the room and place and stead of His friends. Up there in the glory was the Christ of God forever with the Father, eternal and everlasting; no age passed over His brow; we may say of Him. "Thy locks are bushy and black as the raven, thou hast the dew of thy youth." He came to Earth and assumed our nature that He might be capable of death,—yet remember, though capable of death, His body need not have died; as it was it never saw corruption, because there was not in it the element of sin which necessitated death and decay. Our Lord Jesus, and none but He, could stand at the brink of the grave and say, "No man taketh my life from me, but I lay it down of myself. I have power to lay it down and I have power to take it again." We poor mortal men have only power to die, but Christ had power to live. Crown Him, then! Set a new crown upon His beloved head! Let other lovers who have died for their friends be crowned with silver, but for Jesus bring forth the golden diadem, and set it upon the head of the Immortal who never needed to have died, and yet became a mortal, yielding Himself to death's pangs without necessity, except the necessity of His mighty love.

Note, next, that in the cases of persons who have yielded up their lives for others, they may have entertained, and probably did *entertain the prospect that the supreme penalty would not have been extracted from them.* They hoped that they might yet escape. There is an old story of a pious miner, who was in the pit with an ungodly man at work. They had lighted the fuse, and were about to blast a piece of rock with the powder, and it was necessary that they should both leave the mine before the powder exploded: they both got into the bucket, but the hand above which was to wind them up was not strong enough to draw the two together, and the pious miner, leaping from the bucket, said to his friend, "You are an unconverted man, and if you die your soul will be lost. Get up in the bucket as quickly as you can; as for me, I commit my soul into the hands of God, and if I die I am saved." This lover of his neighbor's soul was spared, for he was found in perfect safety arched over by the fragments which had been blown from the rock: he escaped.

But, remember well that such a thing could not occur in the case of our dear Redeemer. He knew that if He was to give a ransom for our souls He had no loophole for escape, He must surely die. Die He or His people must, there was no other alternative. If we were to escape from the pit through Him, He must perish in the pit Himself; there was no hope for Him, there was no way by which the cup could pass from Him. Men have risked their lives for their friends bravely; perhaps had they been certain that the risk would have ended in death they would have hesitated; Jesus was certain that our salvation involved death to Him, the cup must be drained to the bottom, He must endure the mortal agony; and in all the sufferings of death extreme He must not be spared one jot or tittle; yet deliberately, for our sakes, He espoused death that He might espouse us. I say again, bring forth another diadem! Set a second crown upon that once thorn-crowned head! All hail, Immanuel! Monarch of misery, and Lord of love! Was ever love like Thine! Lift up His praises, all ye sons of song! Exalt Him, all ye heavenly ones! Aye, set His throne higher than the stars, and let Him be extolled above the angels, because with full intent He bowed His head to death. He knew that it behooved Him to suffer, it behooved that He should be made a sacrifice for sin, and yet for the joy that was set before Him He endured the Cross, despising the shame.

Note a third grand excellency in the crowning deed of Jesus' love, namely, that *He could have had no motive on that death but one of pure, unmingled love and pity.* You remember when the Russian nobleman was crossing the steppes of that vast country in the snow, the wolves followed the sledge in greedy packs, eager to devour the travelers. The horses were lashed to their utmost speed, but needed not the lash, for they fled for their lives from their howling pursuers. Whatever could stay the eager wolves for a time was thrown to them in vain. A horse was loosed: they pursued it, rent it to pieces, and still followed, like grim death. At last a devoted servant, who had long lived with his master's family, said, "There remains but one hope for you; I will throw myself to the wolves, and then you will have time to escape."

There was great love in this, but doubtless it was mingled with a habit of obedience, a sense of reverence to the head of the household, and probably emotions of gratitude for many obligations which had been received through a long course of years. I do not depreciate the sacrifice, far from it; would that there were more of such a noble spirit among the sons of men! but still you can see a wide difference between that noble sacrifice and the nobler deed of Jesus laying down His life for those who never obliged Him, never served Him, who were infinitely His inferiors, and who could have no claims upon His gratitude. If I had seen the nobleman surrender himself to the wolves to save his servant, and if that servant had in former days tried to be an assassin and had sought his life, and yet the master had given himself up for the undeserving menial, I could see some parallel, but as the case stands there is a wide distinction.

Jesus had no motive in His heart but that He loved us, loved us with all the greatness of His glorious nature, loved us, and therefore for love, pure love, and love alone, He gave Himself up to bleed and die.

> With all His sufferings full in view,
> And woes to us unknown,
> Forth to the task His spirit flew,
> 'Twas love that urged Him on.

Put the third crown upon His glorious head! Oh angels, bring forth the immortal coronet which has been stored up for ages for Him alone, and let it glitter upon that ever blessed brow!

Fourthly, remember, as I have already begun to hint, that in our Savior's case *it was not precisely, though it was, in a sense, death for His friends.*

Greater love hath no man than this towards his friends that he lay down his life for them; read the text so, and it expresses a great truth: but greater love a man may have than to lay down his life for his friends, namely, if he dies for his enemies. And herein is the greatness of Jesus' love, that though He called us "friends," the friendship was all on His side at the first. He called us friends, but our hearts called Him enemy, for we were opposed to Him. We loved not in return for His love. "We hid as it were our faces from him, he was despised, and we esteemed him not."

Oh the enmity of the human heart to Jesus! There is nothing like it. Of all enmities that have ever come from the pit that is bottomless, the enmity of the heart to the Christ of God is the strangest and most bitter of all; and yet for men polluted and depraved, for men hardened till their hearts are like the nether millstone, for men who could not return and could not reciprocate the love He felt, Jesus Christ gave Himself to die.

> Scarcely for a righteous man will one die, yet peradventure for a good (benevolent) man one could even dare to die, but God commendeth his love to us in that while we were yet sinners in due time Christ died for the ungodly.

> *O love of unexampled kind!*
> *That leaves all thought so far behind;*
> *Where length, and breadth, and depth, and height,*
> *Are lost to my astonished sight.*

Bring forth the royal diadem again, I say, and crown our loving Lord, the Lord of love; for as He is King of kings everywhere else, so is He King of kings in the region of affection.

I shall not, I hope, weary you when I now observe that there was another glorious point about Christ's dying for us, for *we had ourselves been the cause of the difficulty which required a death.* There were two brothers on board a raft once, upon which they had escaped from a foundering ship. There was not enough of food, and it was proposed to reduce the number that some at least might be able to live. So many must die. They cast lots for life and death. One of the brothers was drawn, and was doomed to be thrown into the sea. His brother interposed and said, "You have a wife and children at home; I am single, and therefore can be better spared, I will die instead of you." "Nay," said his brother, "not so; why should you? the lot has fallen upon me"; and they struggled with each other in mutual arguments of love, till at last the substitute was thrown into the sea.

Now, there was no ground of difference between those two brothers whatever; they were friends, and more than friends. They had not caused the difficulty which required the sacrifice of one of them, they could not blame one another for forcing upon them the dreadful alternative; but in our case there would never have been a need for any one to die if we had not been the offenders, the wilful offenders; and who was the offended one, whose injured honour required the death? I speak not untruthfully if I say it was the Christ that died who was Himself the offended one. Against God the sin had been committed, against the majesty of the divine Ruler; and in order to wipe the stain away from divine justice it was imperative that the penalty should be exacted and the sinful one should die.

So He who was offended took the place of the offender and died, that the debt due to His own justice might be paid. It is the case of the judge bearing the penalty which he feels compelled to pronounce upon the culprit. Like the old classic story of the father who on the judgment bench condemns his son to lose his eyes for an act of adultery, and then puts out one of his own eyes to save an eye for his son, the judge himself bore a portion of the penalty. In our case, He who vindicated the honour of His own law, and bore all the penalty, was the Christ who loved those who had offended His sovereignty, and grieved His holiness. I say again—but where are the lips that shall say it aright?—bring forth, bring forth a new diadem of more than imperial splendor, to crown the Redeemer's blessed head anew, and let all the harps of Heaven pour forth the richest music in praise of his supreme love.

Note again that there have been men who have died for others, but they have *never borne the sins of others;* they were willing to take the punishment, but not the guilt. But here, ere Christ must die, it must be written, "He was numbered with the transgressors, and he bore the sin of many." "The Lord hath laid on him the iniquity of us all." "He made him to be sin for us who knew no sin, that we might be made the righteousness of God in him." "He was made a curse for us, as it is written, 'Cursed is every one that hangeth on a tree.'" Now, far be it from our hearts to say that Christ was ever less than perfectly holy and spotless, and yet there had to be established a connection between Him and sinners by the way of substitution, which must have been hard for His perfect nature to endure. For Him to be hung up between two felons, for Him to be accused of blasphemy, for Him to be numbered with transgressors, for Him to suffer, the just for the unjust, bearing His Father's wrath as if He had been guilty, this is wonderful, and surpasses all thought! Bring forth the brightest crowns and put them on His head, while we pass on to weave a seventh chaplet for that adorable brow.

For remember, once more, the death of Christ was a proof of love superlative, because in His case *He was denied all the helps and alleviations which in other cases make death to be less than death.* I marvel not that a saint can die joyously; well may his brow be placid, and his eye be bright, for he sees his heavenly Father gazing down upon him, and glory waiting him. Well may his spirit be rapt in joy, even while the death-sweat is on his face, for the angels have come to meet him, and he sees the far off land, and the gates of pearl growing nearer every hour. But ah, to die upon a cross without a pitying eye upon you, surrounded by a scoffing multitude, and to die there appealing to God, who turns away His face, to die with this as your requiem, "My God, my God, why hast thou forsaken me!" to startle the midnight darkness with an *"Eli, Eli, lama sabachthani"* of awful anguish such as never had been heard before: this is terrible. The triumph of love in the death of Jesus rises clear above all other heroic acts of self-sacrifice! Blessed Lamb of God, our hearts love Thee, we fall at Thy feet in adoring reverence, and magnify Thee in the silence of our souls.

III. Lastly, and I must be very brief, as my time has fled, many royal things ought to be suggested to us by this royal love.

And first, dear brethren, how this thought of Christ's proving His love by His death ennobles self-denial. I do not know how you feel, but I feel utterly mean when I think of what Christ has done for me. To live a life of comparative ease and enjoyment shames me. To work to weariness seems nothing. After all, what are we doing compared with what He has done? Those who can suffer, who can lay down their lives in mission fields, and bear hardships, and poverty, and persecution for Christ—my brethren, these are to be envied, they have a portion above their brethren. It makes us feel ashamed to be at home and to possess any comforts when Jesus so denied Himself. I say the thought of the Lord's bleeding love makes us think ourselves mean to be what we are, and makes us nothing in our own sight, while it causes us to honour before God, the self-denial of others, and wish that we had the means of practicing it.

And oh, how it prompts us to heroism. When you get to the Cross you have left the realm of little men: you have reached the nursery of true chivalry. Does Christ die?—then we feel we could die too. What grand things men have done when they have lived in the love of Christ! That story of the Moravians comes to my mind, and I will repeat it, though you may often have heard it, how in the South of Africa there was, years ago, a place of lepers, into which persons afflicted with leprosy were driven. There was a tract of country surrounded by high walls, from which none could escape. There was only one gate, and he who went in never came out again. Certain Moravians looked over the wall and saw two men: one, whose arms had rotted off with leprosy, was carrying on his back another who had lost his legs, and between the two they were making holes in the ground and planting seeds.

The two Moravians thought, "They are dying of a foul disease by hundreds inside that place, we will go and preach the gospel to them." "But," they said, "if you go in, you can never come out again; there you will die of leprosy too." They went in, and they never did come out till they went home to Heaven; they died for others for the love of Jesus. Two others of these holy men went to the West Indian Islands, where there was an estate to which a man could not go to preach the gospel unless he was a slave, and these two men sold themselves for slaves, to work as others worked, that they might tell their fellow slaves the gospel. Oh, if we had that spirit of Jesus among us we should do great things. We want it back, and must have it. The church has lost everything when she has lost her old heroism; she has lost her power to conquer the world when the love of Christ no longer constrains her.

But mark how the heroic in this case is sweetly tinctured and flavored with gentleness. The chivalry of the olden times was cruel; it consisted very much in a strong fellow cased in steel going about and knocking others to pieces who did not happen to wear similar suits of steel. Now-a-days we could get a good deal of that courage back, I dare say; but we shall be best without it. We want that blessed chivalry of love in which a man feels, "I would suffer any insult from that man if I could do him good for Christ's sake, and I would be a door-mat to my Lord's temple gate, that all who come by might wipe their feet upon me, if they could honour Christ thereby." The grand heroism of being nothing for Christ's sake, or anything for the church's sake, that is the heroism of the Cross; for Christ made Himself of no reputation, and took upon Himself the form of a servant, and being found in fashion as a Man, He became obedient unto death, even the death of the Cross. O blessed Spirit, teach us to perform like heroic acts of self-abnegation for Jesus' name's sake!

And, lastly, there seems to my ears to come from the Cross, a gentle voice that saith, "Sinner, sinner, guilty sinner, I did all this for thee, what hast thou done for me?" and yet another which saith, "Return unto me! Look unto me and be ye saved, all ye ends of the earth." I wish I knew how to preach to you Christ crucified. I feel ashamed of myself that I cannot do better than I have done. I pray the Lord to set it before you in a far better way than any of my words can. But, oh, guilty sinner, there is life in a look at the Redeemer! Turn now your eyes to Him, and trust Him! Simply by trusting him, you shall find pardon, mercy, eternal life, and Heaven. Faith is a look at the Great Substitute. God help you to get that look for Jesus' sake. Amen.

The Crown of Thorns

"And when they had plaited a crown of thorns,
they put it upon his head."—Matthew 27:29.

B efore we enter the common hall of the soldiers, and gaze upon "the sacred head once wounded," it will be well to consider who and what He was who was thus cruelly put to shame. Forget not the intrinsic excellent of His person; for He is the brightness of the Father's glory, and the express image of His person; He is in Himself God over all, blessed forever, the eternal Word by Whom all things were made, and by whom all things consist. Though Heir of all things, the Prince of the kings of the earth, He was despised and rejected of men, "a man of sorrows and acquainted with grief." His head was scornfully surrounded with thorns for a crown, His body was bedecked with a faded purple robe, a poor reed was put into His hand for a scepter, and then the ribald soldiery dared to stare into His face, and worry Him with their filthy jests:

> *The soldiers also spit upon that face*
> *Which angels did desire to have the grace,*
> *And prophets once to see, but found no place.*
> *Was ever grief like Thine?*

Forget not the glory to which He had been accustomed aforetime, for ere He came to Earth He had been in the bosom of the Father, adored of cherubim and seraphim, obeyed by every angel, worshiped by every principality and power in the heavenly places; yet here He sits, treated worse than a felon, made the center of a comedy before He became the victim of a tragedy. They sat Him down in some broken chair, covered Him with an old soldier's cloak, and then insulted Him as a mimic monarch:

> *They bow their knees to Me, and cry, "Hail king":*
> *Whatever scoffs and scornfulness can bring,*
> *I am the floor, the sink, where they'd fling.*
> *Was ever grief like Mine?*

What a descent His love to us compelled Him to make! See how low He fell to lift us from our fall! Do not also fail to remember that at the very time when they were thus mocking Him, He was still the Lord of all, and could have summoned twelve legions of angels to His rescue. There was majesty in His misery; He had laid aside, it is true, the glorious pomp imperial of His Father's courts, and He was now the lowly man of Nazareth, but for all that, had He willed it, one glance of those eyes would have withered up the Roman cohorts; one word from those silent lips would have shaken Pilate's palace from roof to foundation; and had He willed it, the vacillating governor and the malicious crowd would together have gone down alive into the pit, even as Korah, Dathan, and Abiram of old.

Lo, God's own Son, Heaven's darling, and earth's prince, sits there and wears the cruel chaplet which wounds both mind and body at once: the mind with insult, and the body with piercing smart. His royal face was marred with "wounds which could not cease to bleed, trickling faint and slow," yet that "noblest brow and dearest" had once been fairer than the children of men, and was even then the countenance of Immanuel, God with us. Remember these things, and you will gaze upon Him with enlightened eyes and tender hearts, and you will be able the more fully to enter into fellowship with Him in His griefs. Remember whence He came, and it will the more astound you that He should have stooped so low. Remember what He was, and it will be the more marvelous that He should become our substitute.

And now let us press into the guard-room, and look at our Savior wearing His crown of thorns. I will not detain you long with any guesses as to what kind of thorns He wore. According to the Rabbis and the botanists there would seem to have been from twenty to twenty-five different species of thorny plants growing in Palestine; and different writers have, according to their own judgments or fancies, selected one and another of these plants as the peculiar thorns which were used upon this occasion. But why select one thorn out of many? He bore not one grief, but all; any and every thorn will suffice; the very dubiousness as to the peculiar species yields us instruction.

The soldiers may have used pliant boughs of the acacia, or shittim tree, that unrotting wood of which many of the sacred tables and vessels of the sanctuary were made; and, therefore, significantly used if such was the case. It may have been true, as the old writers generally consider, that the plant was the *spina Christi,* for it has many small and sharp spines, and its green leaves would have made a wreath such as those with which generals and emperors were crowned after a battle. But we will leave the matter; it was a crown of thorns which pierced His head, and caused Him suffering as well as shame, and that suffices us. Our inquiry now is, what do we see when our eyes behold Jesus Christ crowned with thorns? There are six things which strike me most, and as I lift the curtain I pray you watch with me, and may the Holy Spirit pour forth His divine illumination and light up the scene before our wondering souls.

I. The first thing which is seen by the most casual observer, before he looks beneath the surface, is a sorrowful spectacle.

Here is the Christ, the generous, loving, tender Christ, treated with indignity and scorn, here is the Prince of Life and Glory made an object of derision by a ribald soldiery. Behold today the lily among thorns, purity lifting up itself in the midst of opposing sin. See here the sacrifice caught in the thicket, and held fast there, as a victim in our stead to fulfil the ancient type of the ram held by the bushes, which Abraham slew instead of Isaac. Three things are to be carefully noted in this spectacle of sorrow.

Here is Christ's *lowliness and weakness triumphed over* by the lusty legionaries. When they brought Jesus into the guard-room they felt that He was entirely in their power, and that His claims to be a king were so absurd as to be only a theme for contemptuous jest. He was but meanly dressed, for He wore only the smock frock of a peasant—was He a claimant of the purple? He held His peace—was He the man to stir a nation to sedition? He was all wounds and bruises, fresh from the scourger's lash—was He the hero to inspire an army's enthusiasm and overturn old Rome? It seemed rare mirth for them, and as wild beasts sport with their victims, so did they. Many, I warrant you, were the jibes and jeers of the Roman soldiery at His expense and loud was the laughter amid their ranks. Look at His face, how meek He appears! How different from the haughty countenances of tyrants! To mock His royal claims seemed but natural to a rough soldiery. He was gentle as a child, tender as a woman; His dignity was that of calm quiet endurance, and this was not a dignity whose force these semi-barbarous men could feel, therefore did they pour contempt upon Him.

Let us remember that our Lord's weakness was undertaken for our sakes: for us He became a lamb, for us He laid aside His glory, and therefore it is the more painful for us to see that this voluntary humiliation of Himself must be made the object of so much derision and scorn, though worthy of the utmost praise. He stoops to save us, and we laugh at Him as He stoops; He leaves the throne that He may lift us up to it, but while He is graciously descending, the hoarse laughter of an ungodly world is His only reward. Ah me! was ever love treated after so unlovely a sort? Surely the cruelty it received was proportioned to the honour it deserved, so perverse are the sons of men.

> *O head so full of bruises!*
> *Brow that its lifeblood loses!*
> *Oh great humility.*
>
> *Upon His face are falling*
> *Indignities most galling;*
> *He bears them all for me.*

It was not merely that they mocked His humility, but *they mocked His claims to be a king.* "Aha," they seemed to say, "is this a king? It must be after some uncouth Jewish fashion, surely, that this poor peasant claims to wear a crown. Is this the Son of David? When will He drive Caesar and his armies into the sea, and set up a new state, and reign at Rome? This Jew, this peasant, is He to fulfill His nation's dream, and rule over all mankind?" Wonderfully did they ridicule this idea, and we do not wonder that they did, for they could not perceive His true glory.

But, beloved, my point lies here, *He was a King* in the truest and most emphatic sense. If He had not been a king, then He would, as an impostor, have deserved the scorn, but would not have keenly felt it; but being truly and really a king, every word must have stung His royal soul, and every syllable must have cut to the quick His kingly spirit. When the impostor's claims are exposed and held up to scorn, he himself must well know that he deserves all the contempt he receives, and what can he say? But if the real heir to all the estates of Heaven and Earth has His claims denied and His person mocked at, then is His heart wounded, and rebuke and reproach fill Him with many sorrows. Is it not sad that the Son of God, the blessed and only Potentate, should have been thus disgraced?

Nor was it merely mockery, but *cruelty added pain to insult.* If they had only intended to mock Him they might have plaited a crown of straw, but they meant to pain Him, and therefore they fashioned a crown of thorns. Look ye, I pray you, at His person as He suffers under their hands. They had scourged Him till probably there was no part of His body which was not bleeding beneath their blows except His head, and now that head must be made to suffer too. Alas our whole head was sick, and our whole heart faint, and so He must be made in His chastisement like to us in our transgression. There was no part of our humanity without sin, and there must be no part of His humanity without suffering. If we had escaped in some measure from iniquity, so might He have escaped from pain, but as we had worn the foul garment of transgression, and it covered us from head to foot, even so must He wear the garments of shame and derision from the crown of His head even to the sole of His foot.

> *O Love, too boundless to be shown*
> *By any but the Lord alone!*
> *O Love offended, which sustains*
> *The bold offender's curse and pains!*
> *O Love, which could no motive have,*
> *But mere benignity to save.*

II. *Removing the curtain again from this sorrowful spectacle, I see here a solemn warning which speaks softly and meltingly to us out of the spectacle of sorrow.*

Do you ask me what is that warning? It is a warning against our ever committing the same crime as the soldiers did. "The same!" say you; "why, we should never plait a crown of thorns for that dear head." I pray you never may; but there are many who have done, and are doing it. Those are guilty of this crime who, as these soldiers did, *deny His claims.* Busy are the wise men of this world at this very time all over the world, busy in gathering thorns and twisting them, that they may afflict the Lord's Anointed. Some of them cry, "Yes, he was a good man, but not the Son of God"; others even deny His superlative excellence in life and teaching; they cavil at His perfection, and imagine flaws where none exist. Never are they happier than when impugning His character. There are some who ply all their wit, and tax their utmost skill for nothing else but to discover discrepancies in the gospel narratives, or to conjure up differences between their supposed scientific discoveries and the declarations of the Word of God. Full often have they torn their own hands in weaving crowns of thorn for Him, and I fear some of them will have to lie upon a bed of thorns when they come to die, as the result of their displays of scientific research after briers with which to afflict the Lover of mankind.

Oh, that they would cease this useless and malicious trade of weaving crowns of thorns for Him who is the world's only hope, whose religion is the lone star that gilds the midnight of human sorrow, and guides mortal man to the port of peace! Even for the temporal benefits of Christianity the good Jesus should be treated with respect; He has emancipated the slave, and up-lifted the down-trodden; His gospel is the charter of liberty, the scourge of tyrants, and the death of priests. Spread it and you spread peace, freedom, order, love, and joy. He is the greatest of philanthropists, the truest friend of man. Wherefore then array yourselves against Him, ye who talk of progress and enlightenment? If men did but know Him they would crown Him with diadems of reverent love, more precious than the pearls of Ind[ia], for His reign will usher in the golden age, and even now it softens the rigor of the present, as it has removed the miseries of the past.

This crowning with thorns is wrought in another fashion by *hypocritical professions of allegiance to Him.* These soldiers put a crown on Christ's head, but they did not mean that He should be king; they put a scepter in His hand, but it was not the substantial ivory rod which signifies real power, it was only a weak and slender reed. Therein they remind us that Christ is mocked by insincere professors [Christians]. O ye who love Him not in your inmost souls, ye are those who mock Him: but you say, "Wherein have I failed to crown Him? Did I not join the church? Have I not said that I am a believer?" Oh, if your hearts are not right within you, you have only crowned Him with thorns; if you have not given Him your very soul, you have in awful mockery thrust a scepter of reed into His hand. Your very religion mocks Him. Your lying professions mock Him. Who hath required this at your hands, to tread His courts? You insult Him at His table! You insult Him on your knees! How can you say you love Him, when your hearts are not with Him? If you have never believed in Him, and repented of sin, and yielded obedience to His command, if you do not own Him in your daily life to be both Lord and King, I charge you lay down the profession which is so dishonoring to Him. If He be God, serve Him; if He be King, obey Him; if He be neither, then do not profess to be Christians. Be honest and bring no crown if you do not accept Him as King.

In a measure the same thing may be done by those who are sincere, but through want of watchfulness *walk so as to dishonor their profession.* Here, if I speak rightly, I shall compel every one of you to confess it in your spirits that you stand condemned; for every time that we act according to our sinful flesh we crown the Savior's head with thorns. Which of us has not done this? Alas, how far have we fallen short of our own ideal! We have hedged Thee about with the briers of our sin. We have been betrayed into angry tempers, so that we have spoken unadvisedly with our lips; or we have been worldly, and loved that which Thou abhorrest, or we have yielded to our passions, and indulged our evil desires.

Do I speak to any backslider whose open sin has dishonored the Cross of Christ? Surely if there be a spark of grace in you, what I am now saying must cut you to the quick, and act like salt upon a raw wound to make your very soul to smart. Do not your ears tingle as I accuse you deliberately of acts of inconsistency which have twisted a thorny crown for our dear Master's head? It is assuredly so, for you have opened the mouths of blasphemers, taught gainsayers to revile Him, grieved the generation of His people, and made many to stumble.

Dear friends, is there not room to look at home in the case of each one of us? As we do so, let us come with the sorrowful and loving penitent, and wash His dear feet with tears of repentance, because we have crowned His head with thorns.

Thus our thorn-crowned Lord and Master stands before us as a sorrowful spectacle, conveying to us a solemn warning.

III. Lifting the veil again, in the person of our tortured and insulted Lord we see triumphant endurance.

He could not be conquered. He was victorious even in the hour of deepest shame.

> *He with unflinching heart*
> *Bore all disgrace and shame,*
> *And 'mid the keenest smart*
> *Lov'd on, yea lov'd the same.*

He was bearing at that moment, first, *the substitutionary griefs* which were due to Him because He stood in our place, and from bearing them He did not turn aside. We were sinners, and the reward of sin is pain and death, therefore He bore the chastisement of our peace. He was enduring at that time what we ought to have endured, and draining the cup which justice had mingled for us. Did He start back from it? Oh, no. When first

He came to drink of that wormwood and gall in the garden He put it to His lips, and the draught seemed for an instant to stagger even His strong spirit. His soul was exceeding sorrowful, even unto death. He was like one demented, tossed to and fro with inward agony. "My Father," said He, "if it be possible, let this cup pass from me." Thrice did He utter that prayer, while every portion of His manhood was the battlefield of legions of griefs. His soul rushed out at every pore to find a vent for its swelling woes, His whole body being covered with gory sweat.

After that tremendous struggle, the strength of love mastered the weakness of manhood; He put that cup to His lips and never shrank, but He drank right on till not a dreg was left; and now the cup of wrath is empty, no trace of the terrible wine of the wrath of God can be found within it. At one tremendous draught of love the Lord forever drank destruction dry for all His people. "Who is he that condemneth? It is Christ that died, yea, rather, that hath risen again," and "there is therefore now no condemnation to them that are in Christ Jesus, who walk not after the flesh but after the Spirit." Now surely endurance had reached a very high point when He was made to endure the painful mockery which our text describes, yet He quailed not, nor removed from His settled purpose. He had undertaken, and He would go through. Look at Him, and see there a miracle of patient endurance of griefs which would have sent a world to Hell had He not borne them on our behalf.

Besides the shame and suffering due for sin, with which it pleased the Father to bruise Him, He was enduring *a superfluity of malice from the hate of men*. Why needed men have concentrated all their scorn and cruelty into His execution? Was it not enough that He must die? Did it give pleasure to their iron hearts to rack His tenderest sensibilities? Wherefore these inventions for deepening His woe? Had any of us been thus derided we should have resented it. There is not a man or woman here who could have been silent under such indignities, but Jesus sat in omnipotence of patience, possessing His soul right royally. Glorious pattern of patience, we adore Thee as we see how malice could not conquer Thine almighty love!

I venture to suggest that such was the picture of patience which our blessed Lord exhibited that it may have moved some even of the soldiery themselves. Has it ever occurred to you to ask how Matthew came to know all about that mockery? Matthew was not there. Mark also gives an account of it, but he would not have been tolerated in the guard-room. The Prætorians were far too proud and rough to tolerate Jews, much less disciples of Jesus, in their common hall.

Since there could have been nobody there except the legionaries themselves, it is well to inquire—Who told this tale? It must have been an eyewitness. May it not have been that centurion who in the same chapter is reported to have said, "Certainly this was the Son of God?" May not that scene as well as the Lord's death have led him to that conclusion?

We do not know, but this much is very evident, the story must have been told by an eyewitness, and also by one who sympathized with the sufferer, for to my ear it does not read like the description of an unconcerned spectator. I should not wonder—I would almost venture to assert—that our Lord's marred but patient visage preached such a sermon that one at least who gazed upon it felt its mysterious power, felt that such patience was more than human, and accepted the thorn-crowned Savior as henceforth his Lord and his King. This I do know, that if you and I want to conquer human hearts for Jesus we must be patient too; and if, when they ridicule and persecute us, we can but endure without repining or retaliation, we shall exercise an influence which even the most brutal will feel, and to which chosen minds will submit themselves.

IV. Drawing up the veil again, I think we have before us, in the fourth place, in the person of the triumphant sufferer, a sacred medicine.

I can only hint at the diseases which it will cure. These blood-besprinkled thorns are plants of renown, precious in heavenly surgery if they be rightly used. Take but a thorn out of this crown and use it as a lancet, and it will let out the hot blood of passion and abate the fever of pride; it is a wonderful remedy for swelling flesh and grievous boils of sin. He who sees Jesus crowned with thorns will loathe to look on self, except it be through tears of contrition. This thorn at the breast will make men sing, but not with notes of self congratulation, the notes will be those of a dove moaning for her mate. Gideon taught the men of Succoth with thorns, but the lessons were not so salutary as those which we learn from the thorns of Jesus. The sacred medicine which the good Physician brings to us in His thorny chaplet acts as a tonic, and strengthens us to endure without depression whatever shame or loss His service may bring upon us:

> *Who defeats my fiercest foes?*
> *Who consoles my saddest woes?*
> *Who revives my fainting heart,*
> *Healing all its hidden smart?*
> *Jesus crowned with thorns.*

When you begin to serve God, and for His sake endeavor to benefit your fellow mortals, do not expect any reward from men, except to be misunderstood, suspected, and abused. The best men in the world are usually the worst spoken of. An evil world cannot speak well of holy lives. The sweetest fruit is most pecked at by the birds, the most Heaven-nearing mountain is most beaten by the storms, and the loveliest character is the most assailed. Those whom you would save will not thank you for your anxiety, but blame you for your interference. If you rebuke their sins they will frequently resent your warnings, if you invite them to Jesus, they will make light of your entreaties. Are you prepared for this? If not, consider Him who endured such contradiction of sinners against Himself lest ye be weary and faint in your minds.

The thorn crown is also a remedy for discontent and affliction. When enduring bodily pain we are apt to wince and fret, but if we remember Jesus crowned with thorns, we say

> *His way was much rougher and darker than mine;*
> *Did Christ my Lord suffer, and shall I repine?*

And so our complaints grow dumb; for very shame we dare not compare our maladies with His woes. Resignation is learned at Jesus' feet, when we see our great Exempler made perfect through suffering.

The thorn crown is a cure for care. We would cheerfully wear any array which our Lord may prepare for us, but it is a great folly to plait needless thorn crowns for ourselves. Yet I have seen some who are, I hope, true believers take much trouble to trouble themselves, and labor to increase their own labors. They haste to be rich, they fret, they toil, they worry, and torment themselves to load themselves with the burden of wealth: they wound themselves to wear the thorny crown of worldly greatness. Many are the ways of making rods for our own backs. I have known mothers make thorn crowns out of their children whom they could not trust with God, they have been worn with family anxieties when they might have rejoiced in God. I have known others make thorn crowns out of silly fears, for which there were no grounds whatever; but they seemed ambitious to be fretful, eager to prick themselves with briers. O believer, say to thyself, "My Lord wore my crown of thorns for me; why should I wear it too?" He took our griefs and carried our sorrows that we might be a happy people, and be able to obey the command, "Take no thought for the morrow, for the morrow shall take thought for the things of itself." Ours is the crown of loving kindness and tender mercies, and we wear it when we cast all our care on Him who careth for us.

Who seeks for ease when he has seen the Lord Christ? If Christ wears a crown of thorns, shall we covet a crown of laurel? Even the fierce Crusader when he entered into Jerusalem, and was elected king, had sense enough to say, "I will not wear a crown of gold in the same city where my Savior wore a crown of thorns." Why should we desire, like feather-bed soldiers, to have everything arranged for our ease and pleasure? Why this reclining upon couches when Jesus hangs on a cross? Why this soft raiment when He is naked? Why these luxuries when He is barbarously entreated? Thus the thorn crown cures us at once of the vainglory of the world, and of our own selfish love of ease. The world's minstrel may cry, "Ho, boy, come hither, and crown me with rose buds!" but the voluptuary's request is not for us. For us neither delights of the flesh nor the pride of life can have charms while the Man of Sorrows is in view. For us it remains to suffer, and to labor, till the King shall bid us share His rest.

V. I must notice in the fifth place that there is before us a mystic coronation.

Bear with my many divisions. The coronation of Christ with thorns was symbolical, and had great meaning in it, for, first, it was to Him a *triumphal crown*. Christ had fought with sin from the day when He first stood foot to foot with it in the wilderness up to the time when He entered Pilate's hall, and He had conquered it. As a witness that He had gained the victory, behold sin's crown seized as a trophy! What was the crown of sin? Thorns. These sprang from the curse. "Thorns also and thistles shall it bring forth to thee," was the coronation of sin, and now Christ has taken away its crown, and put it on His own head. He has spoiled sin of its richest regalia, and He wears it Himself. Glorious champion, all hail! What if I say that the thorns constituted a mural crown? Paradise was set round with a hedge of thorns so sharp that none could enter it, but our champion leaped first upon the bristling rampart, and bore the blood-red banner of His Cross into the heart of that better new Eden, which thus He won for us never to be lost again. Jesus wears the mural chaplet which denotes that He has opened Paradise.

It was a wrestler's crown He wore, for He wrestled not with flesh and blood, but with principalities and powers, and He overthrew His foe. It was a racer's crown He wore, for He had run with the mighty and outstripped them in the race. He had well-nigh finished His course, and had but a step or two more to take to reach the goal. Here is a marvelous field for enlargement, and we must stay at once lest we go too far. It was a crown rich with glory, despite the shame which was intended by it. We see in Jesus the monarch of the realms of misery, the chief among ten thousand sufferers. Never say, "I am a great sufferer." What are our griefs compared with His? As the poet stood upon the Palatine Mount and thought of Rome's dire ruin, he exclaimed, "What are our woes and sufferings?" Even so I ask, what are our shallow griefs compared with the infinite sorrows of Immanuel? Well may we "control in our close breasts our petty misery."

VI. The last word is this. In the thorn crown I see a mighty stimulus.

A mighty stimulus to what? Why, first, to fervent love of Him. Can you see Him crowned with thorns and not be drawn to Him? Methinks, if He could come among us this morning, and we could see Him, there would be a loving press around Him to touch the hem of His garment or to kiss His feet. Savior, Thou art very precious to us. Dearest of all the names above, my Savior and my God, thou art always glorious, but in these eyes thou art never more lovely than when arrayed in shameful mockery. The Lily of the Valley, and the Rose of Sharon, both in one is He, fair in the perfection of His character, and blood-red in the greatness of His sufferings. Worship Him! Adore Him! Bless Him! And let your voices sing "Worthy the Lamb."

This sight is a stimulus, next, to repentance. Did our sins put thorns around His head? Oh, my poor fallen nature, I will scourge thee for scourging Him, and make thee feel the thorns for causing Him to endure them. What, can you see your best Beloved put to such shame, and yet hold truce or parley with the sins which pierced Him? It cannot be. Let us declare before God our soul's keen grief that we should make the Savior suffer so; then let us pray for grace to hedge our lives around with thorns that from this very day sin may not approach us.

I thought this day of how ofttimes I have seen the blackthorn growing in the hedge all bristling with a thousand prickles, but right in the center of the bush have I seen the pretty nest of a little bird. Why did the creature place its habitation there? Because the thorns become a protection to it, and shelter it from harm. As I meditated last night upon this blessed subject, I thought I would bid you build your nests within the thorns of Christ. It is a safe place for sinners. Neither Satan, sin, nor death can reach you there. Gaze on your Savior's sufferings, and you will see sin atoned for. Fly into His wounds! fly, ye timid trembling doves! there is no resting place so safe for you. Build your nests, I say again, among these thorns, and when you have done so, and trusted Jesus, and counted Him to be all in all to you, then come and crown His sacred head with other crowns.

What glory does He deserve? What is good enough for Him? If we could take all the precious things from all the treasuries of monarchs, they would not be worthy to be pebbles beneath His feet. If we could bring Him all the scepters, miters, tiaras, diadems, and all other pomp of earth, they would be altogether unworthy to be thrown in the dust before Him. Wherewith shall we crown Him? Come let us weave our praises together and set our tears for pearls, our love for gold. They will sparkle like so many diamonds in His esteem, for He loves repentance, and He loves faith. Let us make a chaplet this morning with our praises, and crown Him as the laureate of grace. This day on which He rose from the dead, let us extol Him. Oh, for grace to do it in the heart, and then in the life, and then with the tongue, that we may praise Him forever who bowed His head to shame for us.

The Agony of Gethsemane

"And being in an agony he prayed more earnestly: and his sweat was, as it were, great drops of blood falling down to the ground."—Luke 22:44.

Our Lord, after having eaten the Passover and celebrated the supper with His disciples, went with them to the Mount of Olives, and entered the garden of Gethsemane. What induced Him to select that place to be the scene of His terrible agony? Why there in preference to anywhere else would He be arrested by His enemies? May we not conceive that, as in a garden Adam's self-indulgence ruined us, so in another garden the agonies of the second Adam should restore us? Gethsemane supplies the medicine for the ills which followed upon the forbidden fruit of Eden. No flowers which bloomed upon the banks of the four-fold river were ever so precious to our race as the bitter herbs which grew hard by the black and sullen stream of Kedron.

May not our Lord also have thought of David, when on that memorable occasion he fled out of the city from his rebellious son, and it is written, "The king also himself passed over the brook Kedron," and he and his people went up bare-footed and bare-headed, weeping as they went? Behold, the greater David leaves the Temple to become desolate, and forsakes the city which had rejected His admonitions, and with a sorrowful heart crosses the foul brook, to find in solitude a solace for His woes. Our Lord Jesus, moreover, meant us to see that our sin changed everything about Him into sorrow, it turned His riches into poverty, His peace into travail, His glory into shame, and so the place of His peaceful retirement, where in hallowed devotion He had been nearest Heaven in communion with God, our sin transformed into the focus of His sorrow, the center of His woe. Where He had enjoyed most, there He must be called to suffer most.

Our Lord may also have chosen the garden, because needing every remembrance that could sustain Him in the conflict, He felt refreshed by the memory of former hours which there had passed away so quietly. He had there prayed, and gained strength and comfort. Those gnarled and twisted olives knew Him well; there was scarce a blade of grass in the garden which He had not knelt upon; He had consecrated the spot to fellowship with God. What wonder then that He preferred this favored soil? Just as a man would choose in sickness to lie in his own bed, so Jesus chose to endure His agony in His own oratory, where the recollections of former communings with His Father would come vividly before Him.

But, probably, the chief reason for His resort to Gethsemane was, that it was His well known haunt, and John tells us, "Judas also knew the place." Our Lord did not wish to conceal Himself, He did not need to be hunted down like a thief, or searched out by spies. He went boldly to the place where His enemies knew that He was accustomed to pray, for He was willing to be taken to suffering and to death. They did not drag Him off to Pilate's hall against His will, but He went with them voluntarily. When the hour was come for Him to be betrayed there was He in a place where the traitor could readily find Him, and when Judas would betray Him with a kiss His cheek was ready to receive the traitorous salutation. The blessed Savior delighted to do the will of the Lord, though it involved obedience unto death.

We have thus come to the gate of the garden of Gethsemane, let us now enter; but first let us put off our shoe from our foot, as Moses did, when he also saw the bush which burned with fire, and was not consumed. Surely we may say with Jacob, "How dreadful is this place!"

I. Meditating upon the agonizing scene in Gethsemane we are compelled to observe that our Savior there endured a grief unknown to any previous period of His life, and therefore we will commence our discourse by raising the question: what was the cause of the peculiar grief of Gethsemane?

Our Lord was the "Man of sorrows and acquainted with grief" throughout His whole life, and yet, though it may sound paradoxical, I scarcely think there existed on the face of the Earth a happier man than Jesus of Nazareth, for the griefs which He endured were counterbalanced by the peace of purity, the calm of fellowship with God, and the joy of benevolence. This last every good man knows to be very sweet, and all the sweeter in proportion to the pain which is voluntarily endured for the carrying out of its kind designs. It is always joy to do good, cost what it may.

Moreover Jesus dwelt at perfect peace with God at all times; we know that He did so, for He regarded that peace as a choice legacy which He could bequeath to His disciples, and ere He died He said to them, "Peace I leave with you, my peace I give unto you." He was meek and lowly of heart, and therefore His soul had rest; He was one of the meek who inherit the earth; one of the peacemakers who are and must be blessed. I think I mistake not when I say that our Lord was far from being an unhappy man. But in Gethsemane all seems changed, His peace is gone, His calm is turned to tempest. After supper our Lord had sung a hymn, but there was no singing in Gethsemane. Down the steep bank which led from Jerusalem to the Kedron He talked very cheerfully, saying, "I am the vine and ye are the branches," and that wondrous prayer which He prayed with His disciples after that discourse, is very full of majesty: "Father, I will that they also whom thou hast given me be with me where I am," is a very different prayer from that inside Gethsemane's walls, where He cries, "If it be possible, let this cup pass from me."

Notice that all His life long you scarcely find Him uttering an expression of grief, and yet here He says, not only by His sighs and by His bloody sweat, but in so many words, "My soul is exceeding sorrowful even unto death." In the garden the sufferer could not conceal His grief, and does not appear to have wished to do so. Backward and forward thrice He ran to His disciples, He let them see His sorrow and appealed to them for sympathy; His exclamations were very piteous, and His sighs and groans were, I doubt not, very terrible to hear. Chiefly did that sorrow reveal itself in bloody sweat, which is a very unusual phenomenon, although I suppose we must believe those writers who record instances somewhat similar. The old physician Galen gives an instance in which, through extremity of horror, an individual poured forth a discolored sweat, so nearly crimson as at any rate to appear to have been blood. Other cases are given by medical authorities. We do not, however, on any previous occasion observe anything like this in our Lord's life; it was only in the last grim struggle among the olive trees that our champion resisted unto blood, agonizing against sin. What ailed Thee, O Lord, that Thou shouldst be so sorely troubled just then?

We are clear that His deep sorrow and distress were not occasioned by any bodily pain. Our Savior had doubtless been familiar with weakness and pain, for He took our sicknesses, but He never in any previous instance complained of physical suffering. Neither at the time when He entered Gethsemane had He been grieved by any bereavement. We know why it is written "Jesus wept," it was because His friend Lazarus was dead; but here there was no funeral, nor sick bed, nor particular cause of grief in that direction. Nor was it the revived remembrance of any past reproaches which had lain dormant in His mind. Long before this "reproach had broken His heart," and He had known to the full the vexations of contumely and scorn. They had called Him a "drunken man and a wine bibber," they had charged Him with casting out devils by the prince of the devils; they could not say more, and yet He had bravely faced it all, it could not be possible that He was now sorrowful unto death for such a cause. There must have been something sharper than pain, more cutting than reproach, more terrible than bereavement, which now at this time grappled with the Savior, and made Him "exceeding sorrowful, and very heavy."

Do you suppose it was the fear of coming scorn, or the dread of crucifixion? Was it terror at the thought of death? Is not such a supposition impossible? Every man dreads death, and as man Jesus could not but shrink from it. When we were originally made we were created for immortality, and therefore to die is strange and uncongenial work to us, and the instincts of self-preservation cause us to start back from it, but surely in our Lord's case that natural cause could not have produced such specially painful results. It does not make even such poor cowards as we are sweat great drops of blood, why then should it work such terror in him? It is dishonoring to our Lord to imagine Him less brave than His own disciples, yet we have seen some of the very feeblest of His saints triumphant in the prospect of departing.

Read the stories of the martyrs, and you will frequently find them exultant in the near approach of the most cruel sufferings. The joy of the Lord has given such strength to them, that no coward thought has alarmed them for a single moment, but they have gone to the stake, or to the block, with psalms of victory upon their lips. Our Master must not be thought of as inferior to His boldest servants, it cannot be that He should tremble where they were brave. Oh, no; the noblest spirit among yon martyr-band is the Leader Himself, who in suffering and heroism surpassed them all; none could so defy the pangs of death as the Lord Jesus, who, for the joy which was set before Him, endured the Cross, despising the shame.

What is it then, think you, that so peculiarly marks off Gethsemane and the griefs thereof? We believe that now the Father put Him to grief for us. It was now that our Lord had to take a certain cup *from the Father's hand.* Not from the Jews, not from the traitor Judas, not from the sleeping disciples, not from the devil came the trial now, but it was a cup filled by one whom He knew to be His Father, but who nevertheless He understood to have appointed Him a very bitter potion, a cup not to be drunk by His body and to spend its gall upon His flesh, but a cup which specially amazed His soul and troubled His inmost heart. He shrunk from it, and therefore be ye sure that it was a draught more dreadful than physical pain, since from that He did not shrink; it was a potion more dreadful than reproach, from that He had not turned aside; more dreadful than Satanic temptation—that He had overcome: it was a something inconceivably terrible, amazingly full of dread, which came from the Father's hand. This removes all doubt as to what it was, for we read "It pleased the Lord to bruise him, he hath put him to grief: when thou shalt make his soul an offering for sin." "The Lord hath made to meet on him the iniquity of us all." He hath made Him to be sin for us though He knew no sin. This, then, is that which caused the Savior such extraordinary depression. He was now about to "taste death for every man," to bear the curse which was due to sinners, because He stood in the sinner's place and must suffer in the sinner's stead. Here is the secret of those agonies which it is not possible for me to set forth in order before you, so true is it that

> 'Tis to God, and God alone,
> That His griefs are fully known.

Yet would I exhort you to consider these griefs awhile, that you may love the sufferer. He now realized, perhaps for the first time, what it was to be a sin bearer. As God He was perfectly holy and incapable of sin, and as man He was without original taint and spotlessly pure; yet He had to bear sin, to be led forth as the scapegoat bearing the iniquity of Israel upon His head, to be taken and made a sin offering, and as a loathsome thing (for nothing was more loathsome than the sin offering) to be taken without the camp and utterly consumed with the fire of divine wrath. Do you wonder that His infinite purity started back from that? Would He have been what He was if it had not been a very solemn thing for Him to stand before God in the position of a sinner? yea, and as Luther would have said it, to be looked upon by God as if He were all the sinners in the world, and as if He had committed all the sin that ever had been committed by His people, for it was all laid on Him, and on Him must the vengeance due for it all be poured; He must be the center of all the vengeance and bear away upon Himself what ought to have fallen upon the guilty sons of men. To stand in such a position when once it was realized must have been very terrible to the Redeemer's holy soul.

Then, too, no doubt the penalty of sin began to be realized by Him in the Garden—first the sin which had put Him in the position of a suffering substitute, and then the penalty which must be borne, because He was in that position. I dread to the last degree that kind of theology which is so common nowadays, which seeks to depreciate and diminish our estimate of the sufferings of our Lord Jesus Christ. Brethren, that was no trifling suffering which made recompense to the justice of God for the sins of men. I am never afraid of exaggeration, when I speak of what my Lord endured. All Hell was distilled into that cup, of which our God and Savior Jesus Christ was made to drink. It was not eternal suffering, but since He was divine He could in a short time offer unto God a vindication of His justice which sinners in Hell could not have offered had they been left to suffer in their own persons forever. To be treated as a sinner, to be smitten as a sinner, though in Him was no sin—this it was which caused Him the agony of which our text speaks.

II. Having thus spoken of the cause of His peculiar grief, I think we shall be able to support our view of the matter, while we lead you to consider, what was the character of the grief itself?

I shall trouble you, as little as possible, with the Greek words used by the evangelists; I have studied each one of them, to try and find out the shades of their meaning, but it will suffice if I give you the results of my careful investigation. What was the grief itself? How was it described? This great sorrow assailed our Lord some four days before He suffered. If you turn to John 12:27, you find that remarkable utterance, "Now is my soul troubled." We never knew Him say that before. This was a foretaste of the great depression of spirit which was so soon to lay Him prostrate in Gethsemane. "Now is my soul troubled; and what shall I say? Father, save me from this hour; but for this cause came I unto this hour."

After that we read of Him in Matthew 26:37, that "he began to be sorrowful and very heavy." The depression had come over Him again. It was not pain, it was not a palpitation of the heart, or an aching of the brow, it was worse than these. Trouble of spirit is worse than pain of body; pain may bring trouble and be the incidental cause of sorrow, but if the mind is perfectly untroubled, how well a man can bear pain, and when the soul is exhilarated and lifted up with inward joy pain of body is almost forgotten, the soul conquering the body. On the other hand the soul's sorrow will create bodily pain, the lower nature sympathizing with the higher. Our Lord's main suffering lay in His soul—His soul-sufferings were the soul of His sufferings. "A wounded spirit who can bear?" Pain of spirit is the worst of pain, sorrow of heart is the climax of griefs. Let those who have ever known sinking spirits, despondency, and mental gloom, attest the truth of what I say!

This sorrow of heart appears to have led to a very deep depression of our Lord's spirit. In the 26th chapter of Matthew, 37th verse, you find it recorded that he was *"very heavy,"* and that expression is full of meaning—of more meaning, indeed, than it would be easy to explain. The word in the original is a very difficult one to translate. It may signify the abstraction of the mind, and its complete occupation by sorrow, to the exclusion of every thought which might have alleviated the distress. One burning thought consumed His whole soul, and burned up all that might have yielded comfort. For awhile His mind refused to dwell upon the result of His death, the consequent joy which was set before Him. His position as a sinbearer, and the desertion by His Father which was necessitated thereby, engrossed His contemplations and hurried His soul away from all else. Some have seen in the word a measure of distraction, and though I will not go far in that direction, yet it does seem as if our Savior's mind underwent perturbations and convulsions widely different from His usual calm, collected spirit. He was tossed to and fro as upon a mighty sea of trouble, which was wrought to tempest, and carried Him away in its fury. "We did esteem him stricken, smitten of God and afflicted." As the psalmist said, innumerable evils compassed Him about so that His heart failed Him. He was "very heavy." The learned Thomas Goodwin says, "The word denotes a failing, deficiency, and sinking of spirit, such as happens to men in sickness and swooning." Epaphroditus' sickness, whereby he was brought near to death, is called by the same word; so that, we see, that Christ's soul was sick and fainted. Was not His sweat produced by exhaustion? The cold, clammy sweat of dying men comes through faintness of body, but the bloody sweat of Jesus came from an utter faintness and prostration of soul. He was in an awful soul-swoon, and suffered an inward death, whose accompaniment was not watery tears from the eyes, but a weeping of blood from the entire man.

Mark tells us next, in his fourteenth chapter and thirty-third verse, that our Lord was *"sore amazed."* The Greek word does not merely import that he was astonished and surprised, but that His amazement went to an extremity of horror, such as men fall into when their hair stands on end and their flesh trembles. As the delivery of the law made Moses exceedingly fear and quake, and as David said, "My flesh trembleth because of thy judgments," so our Lord was stricken with horror at the sight of the sin which was laid upon Him and the vengeance which was due on account of it. The Savior was first "sorrowful," then depressed, and "heavy," and lastly, sore amazed and filled with amazement; for even He as a man could scarce have known what it was that He had undertaken to bear. He had looked at it calmly and quietly, and felt that whatever it was He would bear it for our sake; but when it actually came to the bearing of sin He was utterly astonished and taken aback at the dreadful position of standing in the sinner's place before God, of having His holy Father look upon Him as the sinner's representative, and of being forsaken by that Father with whom He had lived on terms of amity and delight from old eternity. It staggered His holy, tender, loving nature, and He was "sore amazed" and was "very heavy."

We are further taught that there surrounded, encompassed, and overwhelmed Him an ocean of sorrow, for the thirty-eighth verse of the twenty-sixth chapter of Matthew contains the word *perilupos,* which signifies an encompassing around with sorrows. Above Him, beneath Him, around Him, without Him, and within, all, all was anguish, neither was there one alleviation or source of consolation. His disciples could not help Him—they were all but one sleeping, and he who was awake was on the road to betray Him. His spirit cried out in the presence of the Almighty God beneath the crushing burden and unbearable load of His miseries. No griefs could have gone further than Christ's, and He Himself said, "My soul is *exceeding sorrowful,*" or surrounded with sorrow "even unto death." He did not die in the garden, but He suffered as much as if He had died.

Luke, to crown all, tells us in our text, that our Lord was *in an agony.* The expression "agony" signifies a conflict, a contest, a wrestling. With whom was the agony? With whom did He wrestle? I believe it was with Himself; the contest here intended was not with His God; no, "not as I will but as thou wilt" does not look like wrestling with God; it was not a contest with Satan, for, as we have already seen, He would not have been so sore amazed had that been the conflict, but it was a terrible combat within Himself, an agony within His own soul. Remember that He could have escaped from all this grief with one resolve of His will, and naturally the manhood in Him said, "Do not bear it!" and the purity of His heart said, "Oh do not bear it, do not stand in the place of the sinner"; and the delicate sensitiveness of His mysterious nature shrank altogether from any form of connection with sin; yet infinite love said, "Bear it, stoop beneath the load"; and so there was agony between the attributes of His nature, a battle on an awful scale in the arena of His soul. The purity which cannot bear to come into contact with sin must have been very mighty in Christ, while the love which would not let His people perish was very mighty too.

It was a struggle on a Titanic scale, as if a Hercules had met another Hercules; two tremendous forces strove and fought and agonized within the bleeding heart of Jesus. Nothing causes a man more torture than to be dragged hither and thither with contending emotions; as civil war is the worst and most cruel kind of war, so a war within a man's soul when two great passions in him struggle for the mastery, and both noble passions too, causes a trouble and distress which none but he that feels it can understand. I marvel not that our Lord's sweat was as it were great drops of blood, when such an inward pressure made Him like a cluster trodden in the wine-press.

III. Our third question shall be, what was our Lord's solace in all this?

He sought help in human companionship, and very natural it was that He should do so. God has created in our human nature a craving for sympathy. We do not amiss when we expect our brethren to watch with us in our hour of trial; but our Lord did not find that men were able to assist Him; however willing their spirit might be, their flesh was weak. What, then, did He do? He resorted to prayer, and especially to prayer to God under the character of Father. I have learned by experience that we never know the sweetness of the Fatherhood of God so much as when we are in very bitter anguish; I can understand why the Savior said "Abba, Father," it was anguish that brought Him down as a chastened child to appeal plaintively to a Father's love. In the bitterness of my soul I have cried, "If, indeed, Thou be my Father, by the bowels of Thy fatherhood have pity on Thy child"; and here Jesus pleads with His Father as we have done, and finds comfort in that pleading. Prayer was the channel of the Redeemer's comfort, earnest, intense, reverent, repeated prayer, and after each time of prayer He seems to have grown quiet, and to have gone to His disciples with a measure of restored peace of mind. The sight of their sleeping helped to bring back His griefs, and therefore He returned to pray again, and each time He was comforted, so that when He had prayed for the third time He was prepared to meet Judas and the soldiers and to go with silent patience to judgment and to death. His great comfort was prayer and submission to the divine will, for when He had laid His own will down at His Father's feet the feebleness of His flesh spoke no more complainingly, but in sweet silence, like a sheep dumb before her shearers, He contained His soul in patience and rest. Dear brothers and sisters, if any of you shall have your Gethsemane and your heavy griefs, imitate your Master by resorting to prayer, by crying to your Father, and by learning submission to His will.

I shall conclude by drawing two or three inferences from the whole subject. May the Holy Spirit instruct us.

The first is this—Learn, dear brethren, *the real humanity of our Lord Jesus Christ.* Do not think of Him as God merely, though He is assuredly divine, but feel Him to be near of kin to you, bone of your bone, flesh of your flesh. How thoroughly can He sympathize with you! He has been burdened with all your burdens and grieved with all your griefs. Are the waters very deep through which you are passing? Yet they are not deep compared with the torrents with which He was buffeted. Never a pang penetrates your spirit to which your covenant Head was a stranger. Jesus can sympathize with you in all your sorrows, for He has suffered far more than you have ever suffered, and is able therefore to succor you in your temptations. Lay hold on Jesus as your familiar friend, your brother born for adversity, and you will have obtained a consolation which will bear you through the uttermost deeps.

Next *see here the intolerable evil of sin.* You are a sinner, which Jesus never was, yet even to stand in the sinner's place was so dreadful to Him that He was sorrowful even unto death. What will sin one day be to you if you should be found guilty at the last! Oh, could we tell the horror of sin there is not one among us that would be satisfied to remain in sin for a single moment; I believe there would go up from this house of prayer this morning a weeping and a wailing such as might be heard in the very streets, if men and women here who are living in sin could really know what sin is, and what the wrath of God is that rests upon them, and what the judgments of God will be that will shortly surround them and destroy them. Oh soul, sin must be an awful thing if it so crushed our Lord. If the very imputation of it fetched bloody sweat from the pure and holy Savior, what must sin itself be? Avoid it, pass not by it, turn away from the very appearance of it, walk humbly and carefully with your God that sin may not harm you, for it is an exceeding plague, an infinite pest.

Learn next, but oh how few minutes have I in which to speak of such a lesson, *the matchless love of Jesus,* that for your sakes and mine He would not merely suffer in body, but consented even to bear the horror of being accounted a sinner, and coming under the wrath of God because of our sins although it cost Him suffering unto death and sore amazement, yet sooner than that we shall perish, the Lord smarted as our surety. Can we not cheerfully endure persecution for His sake? Can we not labor earnestly for Him? Are we so ungenerous that His cause shall know a lack while we have the means of helping it? Are we so base that His work shall flag while we have strength to carry it on? I charge you by Gethsemane, my brethren, if you have a part and lot in the passion of your Savior, love Him much who loved you so immeasurably, and spend and be spent for Him.

Again looking at Jesus in the garden, we learn the *excellence and completeness of the atonement.* How black I am, how filthy, how loathsome in the sight of God—I feel myself only fit to be cast into the lowest Hell, and I wonder that God has not long ago cast me there; but I go into Gethsemane, and I peer under those gnarled olive trees, and I see my Savior. Yes, I see Him wallowing on the ground in anguish, and hear such groans come from Him as never came from human breast before. I look upon the Earth and see it red with His blood, while His face is smeared with gory sweat, and I say to myself, "My God, my Savior, what aileth thee?" I hear Him reply, "I am suffering for thy sin," and then I take comfort, for while I fain would have spared my Lord such an anguish, now that the anguish is over I can understand how Jehovah can spare me, because He smote His Son in my stead.

Now I have hope of justification, for I bring before the justice of God and my own conscience the remembrance of my bleeding Savior, and I say,

> Canst Thou twice demand payment, first at the hand of Thy agonizing Son and then again at mine? Sinner as I am, I stand before the burning throne of the severity of God, and am not afraid of it. Canst thou scorch me, O consuming fire, when thou hast not only scorched but utterly consumed my substitute?

Nay, by faith, my soul sees justice satisfied, the law honored, the moral government of God established, and yet my once guilty soul absolved and set free. The fire of avenging justice has spent itself, and the law has exhausted its most rigorous demands upon the person of Him who was made a curse for us, that we might be made the righteousness of God in Him. Oh the sweetness of the comfort which flows from the atoning blood! Obtain that comfort, my brethren, and never leave it. Cling to your Lord's bleeding heart, and drink in abundant consolation.

Last of all, *what must be the terror of the punishment which will fall upon those men who reject the atoning blood,* and who will have to stand before God in their own proper persons to suffer for their sins. I will tell you, sir, with pain in my heart as I tell you it, what will happen to those of you who reject my Lord. Jesus Christ my Lord and Master is a sign and prophecy to you of what will happen to you. Not in a garden, but on that bed of yours where you have so often been refreshed, you will be surprised and overtaken, and the pains of death will get hold upon you. With an exceeding sorrow and remorse for your misspent life and for a rejected Savior you will be made very heavy. Then will your darling sin, your favorite lust, like another Judas, betray you with a kiss.

While yet your soul lingers on your lip you will be seized and taken off by a body of evil ones, and carried away to the bar of God, just as Jesus was taken to the judgment seat of Caiaphas. There shall be a speedy, personal, and somewhat private judgment, by which you shall be committed to prison where, in darkness and weeping, and wailing, you shall spend the night before the great assize of the judgment morning. Then shall the day break and the resurrection morning come, and as our Lord then appeared before Pilate, so will you appear before the highest tribunal, not that of Pilate, but the dread judgment seat of the Son of God, whom you have despised and rejected. Then will witnesses come against you, not false witnesses, but true, and you will stand speechless, even as Jesus said not a word before His accusers. Then will conscience and despair buffet you, until you will become such a monument of misery, such a spectacle of contempt, as to be fitly noted by another *Ecce Homo,* and men shall look at you, and say "Behold the man and the suffering which has come upon him, because he despised his God and found pleasure in sin." Then shall you be condemned. "Depart, ye cursed," shall be your sentence, even as "Let him be crucified" was the doom of Jesus. You shall be taken away by the officers of justice to your doom. To your shame, and to the confusion of your nakedness, shall you that have despised the Savior be made a spectacle of the justice of God forever. It is right it should be so, justice rightly demands it. Sin made the Savior suffer an agony, shall it not make you suffer? Moreover, in addition to your sin, you have rejected the Savior; you have said, "He shall not be my trust and confidence." Voluntarily, presumptuously, and against your own conscience you have refused eternal life; and if you die rejecting mercy what can come of it but that first your sin, and secondly your unbelief, shall condemn you to misery without limit or end. Let Gethsemane warn you, let its groans, and tears, and bloody sweat admonish you. Repent of sin, and believe in Jesus. May His Spirit enable you, for Jesus' sake. Amen.

T𝒽ree Crosses

"But God forbid that I should glory, save in the Cross of our Lord Jesus Christ, by whom the world is crucified unto me, and I unto the world."—Galatians 6:14.

Whenever we rebuke other people we should be prepared to clear ourselves of their offence. The apostle Paul had been rebuking those who wished to glory in the flesh. In denouncing false teachers and upbraiding their weak-minded followers he used sharp language, while he appealed to plain facts and maintained his ground with strong arguments; and this he did without fear of being met by a flank movement, and being charged with doing the same things himself. Very fitly, therefore, does he contrast his own determined purpose with their plausible falseness. They were for making a fair show in the flesh, but he shrunk not from the deepest shame of the Christian profession; nay, so far from shrinking, he even counted it honour to be scorned for Christ's sake, exclaiming, "God forbid that I should glory, save in the Cross of our Lord Jesus Christ."

The Galatians, and all others to whom his name was familiar, well knew how truly he spoke; for the manner of his life as well as the matter of his teaching had supplied evidence of this assertion, which none of his foemen could gainsay. There had not been in all his ministry any doctrine that he extolled more highly than this of "Christ crucified"; nor any experience that he touched on more tenderly than this "fellowship with Christ in his sufferings"; nor any rule of conduct that he counted more safe than this following in the footsteps of Him who "endured the Cross, despising the shame, and is set down at the right hand of the throne of God." His example accorded with His precept. God grant, of His grace, that there may always be with us the like transparent consistency.

The apostle in the present case warms with emotion at the thought of anybody presuming to set a carnal ordinance in front of the Cross, by wishing to glory in circumcision or any other outward institution. The idea of a ceremony claiming to be made more [important] than faith in Jesus provoked him [Paul], till his heart presently grew hot with indignation, and he thundered forth the words, "God forbid!" He never used the sacred name with lightness; but when the fire was hot within him he called God to witness that he did not, and could not, glory in anything but the Cross.

Indeed, there is to every true-hearted believer something shocking and revolting in the putting of anything before Jesus Christ, be it what it may, whether it be an idol of superstition or a toy of scepticism, whether it be the fruit of tradition or the flower of philosophy. Do you want new Scriptures to supplement the true sayings of God? Do you want a new Savior who can surpass Him whom the Father hath sealed? Do you want a new sacrifice that can save you from sins which His atoning blood could not expiate? Do you want a modern song to supersede the new song of "Worthy is the Lamb that was slain"? "O foolish Galatians!" said Paul.

The Cross was the center of his hopes; around it his affections twined; there he had found peace to his troubled conscience. God forbid that he should allow it to be trampled on. Besides, it was the theme of his ministry. "Christ crucified" had already proved the power of God to salvation to every soul who had believed the life giving message as he proclaimed it in every city. Would any of you, he asks, cast a slur on the Cross—you who have been converted—you before whose eyes Jesus Christ hath been evidently set forth crucified among you? How his eyes flash; how his lips quiver; how his heart grows hot within him; with what vehemence he protests: "God forbid that I should glory, save in the Cross of our Lord Jesus Christ." He spreads his eagle wing, and rises into eloquence at once, while still his keen eye looks fiercely upon every enemy of the Cross whom he leaves far beneath. Oftentimes in his epistles you observe this. He burns, he glows, he mounts, he soars, he is carried clean away as soon as his thoughts are in fellowship with his Lord Jesus, that meek and patient Sufferer, who offered Himself a sacrifice for our sins. When his tongue begins to speak of the glorious work which the Christ of God has done for the sons of men it finds a sudden liberty, and he becomes as "a hind let loose; he giveth goodly words."

Let us, then, in that spirit approach our text; and we notice at once three crucifixions. These are the summary of the text. "God forbid that I should glory, save in the Cross of our Lord Jesus Christ"; that is, *Christ crucified*. "By

whom," or, "by which" (read it whichever way you like), "the world is crucified unto me"; that is, *a crucified world.* "And I unto the world"; that is, *Paul
himself, or the believer, crucified with Christ.* I see, again, Calvary before me with
its three crosses—Christ in the center, and on either side of Him a crucified
person: one who dies to feel the second death, and another who dies to be
with Him in paradise. At these three crosses let us proceed to look.

I. First, then, the main part of our subject lies in Christ crucified, in whom Paul gloried.

I call your attention to the language; "God forbid that I should glory,
save in the Cross." Some popular authors and public speakers, when they
have to state a truth, count it necessary to clothe it in very delicate language.
They, perhaps, do not quite intend to conceal its point and edge; but, at any
rate, they do not want the projecting angles and bare surfaces of the truth to
be too observable, and therefore they cast a cloak around it; they are careful
to scabbard the sword of the Spirit. The apostle Paul might have done so
here, if he had chosen, but he disdains the artifice. He presents the truth "in
the worst possible form," as his opponents say—"in all its naked hideous-
ness," as the Jew would have it; for he does not say, "God forbid that I should
glory, save in the *death* of Christ"; but in the *Cross.* You do not realize, I
think—we cannot do so in these days—how the use of that word "cross"
would grate on ears refined in Galatia and elsewhere. In those days it meant
the felon's tree, the hangman's gibbet; and the apostle, therefore, does not
hesitate to put it just so: "Save in that gibbet on which my Master died." We
have become so accustomed to associate the name of "the Cross" with other
sentiments that it does not convey to us that sense of disgrace which it would
inflict upon those who heard Paul speak. A family sensitively shrinks if one of
its members has been hanged; and much the same would be the natural feeling of one who was told that his leader was crucified. Paul puts it thus baldly,
he lets it jar thus harshly, though it may prove to some a stumbling-block,
and to others foolishness; but he will not cloak it, he glories in *"the Cross!"*

On the other hand, I earnestly entreat you to observe how he seems to
contrast the glory of the person with the shame of the suffering; for it is not
simply the death of Christ, nor of Jesus, nor of Jesus Christ, nor of *the* Lord Jesus Christ, but of *"our Lord Jesus Christ."* Every word tends to set forth the excellence of His person, the majesty of His character, and the interest which all
the saints have in Him. It *was* a cross, but it was the Cross of our Lord: let us
worship Him! It was the Cross of our Lord Jesus the Savior: let us love Him!
It was the Cross of our Jesus Christ the anointed Messiah: let us reverence

Him! Let us sit at His feet and learn of Him! Each one may say, "It was the Cross of *my* Lord Jesus Christ"; but it sweetens the whole matter, and gives a largeness to it when we say, "It was the Cross of *our* Lord Jesus Christ." Oh yes, we delight to think of the contrast between the precious Christ and the painful Cross, the Son of God and the shameful gibbet. He was Immanuel, God with us; yet did He die the felon's death upon the accursed tree. Paul brings out the shame with great sharpness, and the glory with great plainness. He does not hesitate in either case, whether he would declare the sufferings of Christ or the glory which should follow.

What did he mean, however, by the Cross? Of course he cared nothing for the particular piece of wood to which those blessed hands and feet were nailed, for that was mere materialism, and has perished out of mind. He means the glorious doctrine of justification—free justification—through the atoning sacrifice of Jesus Christ. This is what he means by the Cross—the expiation for sin which our Lord Jesus Christ made by His death, and the gift of eternal life freely bestowed on all those who by grace are led to trust in Him. To Paul the Cross meant just what the brazen serpent meant to Moses. As the brazen serpent in the wilderness was the hope of the sin-bitten, and all that Moses had to do was to bid them look and live, so today the Cross of Christ—the atonement of Jesus Christ—is the hope of mankind, and our mission is continually to cry, "Look and live! Look and live!"

It is this doctrine, this gospel of Christ crucified, at which the present age, with all its vaunted culture and all its vain philosophies, sneers so broadly: it is this doctrine wherein we glory. We are not ashamed to put it very definitely: we glory in substitution, in the vicarious sacrifice of Jesus in our stead. He was "made sin for us who knew no sin, that we might be made the righteousness of God in him." "All we like sheep have gone astray; we have turned every one to his own way; and the Lord hath laid on Him the iniquity of us all." "Christ hath redeemed us from the curse of the law, being made a curse for us: for it is written, Cursed is every one that hangeth on a tree." We believe in the imputation of sin to the innocent person of our covenant Head and Representative, in the bearing of the penalty by that substituted One, and the clearing by faith of those for whom He bore the punishment of sin.

Now we glory in this. We glory in it, not as men sometimes boast in a creed which they have received by tradition from their forefathers, for we have learned this truth, each one for himself by the inward teaching of the Holy Ghost, and therefore it is very dear to us. We glory in it with no empty boast, but to the inward satisfaction of our own hearts; we prove that satisfaction by the devout consecration of our lives to make it known. We have trusted our souls to its truth. If it be a fable our hopes are forever shipwrecked, our all is embarked in that venture. We are quite prepared to run that risk, content to perish if this salvation should fail us. We live upon this faith. It is our meat and our drink. Take this away there is nothing left us in the Bible worth the having. It has become to us the head and front of our confidence, our hope, our rest, our joy. Instead of being ashamed to preach it, we wish that we could stand somewhere where all the inhabitants of the Earth should hear us, and we would thunder it out day and night. So far from being ashamed of acknowledging it, we count it to be our highest honour and our greatest delight to tell it abroad, as we have opportunity, among the sons of men.

But why do we rejoice in it? Why do we glory in it? The answer is so large that I cannot do more than glance at its manifold claims on our gratitude. In the Cross of Christ we glory, because we regard it as a matchless exhibition of the attributes of God. We see there the love of God desiring a way by which He might save mankind, aided by His wisdom, so that a plan is perfected by which the deed can be done without violation of truth and justice. In the Cross we see a strange conjunction of what once appeared to be two opposite qualities—justice and mercy. We see how God is supremely just; as just as if He had no mercy, and yet infinitely merciful in the gift of His Son. Mercy and justice in fact become counsel upon the same side, and irresistibly plead for the acquittal of the believing sinner. We can never tell which of the attributes of God shines most glorious in the sacrifice of Christ; they each one find a glorious high throne in the person and work of the Lamb of God that taketh away the sin of the world. Since it has become, as it were, the disk which reflects the character and perfections of God, it is meet that we should glory in the Cross of Christ; and none shall stay us of our boasting.

We glory in it, next, as the manifestation of the love of Jesus. He was loving inasmuch as He came to Earth at all; loving in feeding the hungry, in healing the sick, in raising the dead. He was loving in His whole life: He was embodied charity, the Prince of philanthropists, the King of kindly souls. But oh, His death!—His cruel and shameful death—bearing, as we believe He did, the wrath due to sin, subjecting Himself to the curse, though in Him was no sin—this shows the love of Christ at its highest altitude, and therefore do we glory in it, and will never be ashamed to do so.

We glory in the Cross, moreover, because it is the putting away of sin. There was no other way of making an end of sin, and making reconciliation for iniquity. To forgive the transgressions without exacting the penalty would have been contrary to all the threatenings of God. It would not have appeased the claims of justice, nor satisfied the conscience of the sinner. No peace of mind can be enjoyed without pardon, and conscience declares that no pardon can be obtained without an atonement. We should have distracted ourselves with the fear that it was only a reprieve, and not a remission, even if the most comforting promises had been given unsealed with the atoning blood. The instincts of nature have convinced men of this truth, for all the world over religion has been associated with sacrifice. Almost every kind of worship that has ever sprung up among the sons of men has had sacrifice for its most prominent feature; crime must be avenged, evil and sin cry from the ground, and a victim is sought to avert the vengeance. The heart craves for something that can calm the conscience: that craving is a relic of the ancient truth learned by man in primeval ages.

Now, Christ did make His soul an offering for sin, when His own self He bare our sins in His own body on the tree. With His expiring breath He said, "It is finished!" Oh, wondrous grace! Pardon is now freely published among the sons of men, pardon of which we see the justice and validity. As far as the east is from the west, so far hath God removed our transgressions from us by the death of Christ. This and this alone will put away sin, therefore in this Cross of Christ we glory; yea, and in it alone will we glory evermore.

It has put away our sins, blessed be God, so that this load and burden no more weigh us down! We do not speak at random now. It has breathed hope and peace and joy into our spirits. I am sure that no one knows how to glory in the Cross unless he has had an experimental acquaintance with its peace-breathing power. I speak what I do know, and testify what I have felt. The burden of my sin laid so heavy upon me that I would sooner have died than have lived. Many a day, and many a night, I felt the flames of Hell in the anguish of my heart, because I knew my guilt, but saw no way of righteous forgiveness.

Yet in a moment the load went from me, and I felt overflowing love to the Savior. I fell at His feet, awe stricken that ever he should have taken away my sin and made an end of it. That matchless deed of love won my heart to Jesus. He changed my nature and renewed my soul in that same hour. But, oh, the joy I had! Those who have sunk to the very depths of despair, and risen in a moment to the heights of peace and joy unspeakable, can tell you that they must glory in the Cross and its power to save. Why, sirs, we must believe according to our own conscience. We cannot belie that inward witness. We only wish that others had been as deeply convinced of sin, and as truly led to the Cross to feel their burden roll from off their shoulder as we have been, and then they, too, would glory in the Cross of Christ. Since then we have gone with this remedy in our hands to souls that have been near despair, and we have never found the medicine to fail.

Yet we should not glory so much in the Cross, were we not convinced that it is the greatest moral power in all the world. We glory in the Cross because it gets at men's hearts when nothing else can reach them. The story of the dying Savior's love has often impressed those whom all the moral lectures in the world could never have moved. Judged and condemned by the unanswerable reasonings of their own consciences, they have not had control enough over their passions to shake off the captivity in which they were held by the temptations that assailed them at every turn, till they have drawn near to the Cross of Jesus, and from pardon have gathered hope, and from hope have gained strength to master sin. When they have seen their sin laid on Jesus, they have loved Him, and hated the sin that made Him to suffer so grievously as their substitute. Then the Holy Ghost has come upon them, and they have resolved, with divine strength, to drive out the sin for which the Savior died; they have begun a new life, aye, and they have continued in it, sustained by that same sacred power which first constrained them, and, now they look forward to be perfected by it through the power of God.

Where are the triumphs of infidelity in rescuing men from sin? Where are the trophies of philosophy in conquering human pride? Will you bring us harlots that have been made chaste; thieves that have been reclaimed; angry men, of bear-like temper, who have become harmless as lambs, through scientific lectures? Let our amateur philanthropists, who suggest so much and do so little, produce some instances of the moral transformations that have been wrought by their sophistries. Nay; they curl their lips, and leave the lower orders to the City Missionary and the Bible Woman. It is the Cross that humbles the haughty, lifts up the fallen, refines the polluted, and gives a fresh start to those who are forlorn and desperate. Nothing else can do it. The world sinks lower and lower into the bog of its own selfishness and sin. Only this wondrous lever of the atonement, symbolized by the Cross of Christ, can lift our abject race to the place of virtue and honour which it ought to occupy.

II. The second Cross exhibits the world crucified.

The apostle says that the world was crucified to him. What does he mean by this? He regarded the world as nailed up like a felon, and hanged upon a Cross to die. Well, I suppose he means that its character was condemned. He looked out upon the world which thought so much of itself, and said, "I do not think much of thee, poor world! Thou art like a doomed malefactor." He knew that the world had crucified its Savior—crucified its God. It had gone to such a length of sin that it had hounded perfect innocence through the streets. Infinite benevolence it had scoffed at and maligned. Eternal truth it had rejected, and preferred a lie; and the Son of God, who was love incarnate, it had put to the death of the Cross.

"Now," says Paul, "I know thy character, O world! I know thee! and I hold thee in no more esteem than the wretch abhorred for his crimes, who is condemned to hang upon the gibbet and so end his detested life." This led Paul, since he condemned its character, utterly to despise its judgment. The world said, "This Paul is a fool. His gospel is foolishness and he himself is a mere babbler." "Yes," thought Paul, "a deal you know of it!" In this we unite with him. What is your judgment worth? You did not know the Son of God, poor blind world! We are sure that He was perfect, and yet you hunted Him to death. Your judgment is a poor thing, O world! You are crucified to us.

We are told to think a great deal about "public opinion," "popular belief," "the growing feeling of the age," "the sentiment of the period," and "the spirit of the age." I should like Paul to read some of our religious newspapers; and yet I could not wish the good man so distasteful a task, for I dare say he would sooner pine in the Mammertine prison than do so; but, still, I should like to see how he would look after he had read some of those expressions about the necessity of keeping ourselves abreast with the sentiment of the period. "What," he would say,

> the sentiment of the world! It is crucified to me! What can it matter what its opinion is? We are of God, little children, and the whole world lieth in the wicked one; would ye heed what the world, that is lying in the wicked one, thinks of you or of the truth of your Lord? Are you going to smooth your tongue, and soften your speech, to please the world that lieth in the wicked one?

Paul would be indignant with such a proposition. He said, "the world is crucified to me." Hence he looked upon all the world's pleasures as so much rottenness, a carcase nailed to a Cross.

Can you fancy Paul being taken to the Colosseum at Rome? I try to imagine him made to sit on one of those benches to watch a combat of gladiators. There is the emperor: there are all the great peers of Rome and the senators; and there are those cruel eyes all gazing down upon men who shed each others' blood. Can you picture how Paul would have felt if he had been forced to occupy a seat at that spectacle? It would have been martyrdom to him. He would have closed his eyes and ears against the sight of what Rome thought to be the choicest pleasure of the day. They thronged the imperial city; they poured in mighty streams into the theater each day to see poor beasts tortured, or men murdering one another: that was the world of Paul's day: and he rightly judged it to be a crucified felon. If he was compelled to see the popular pleasures of today, upon which I will say but little, would he not be well-nigh as sick of them as he would have been of the amusements of the amphitheater at Rome?

To Paul, too, all the honour of the age must have been crucified in like manner. Suppose that Paul settled his mind to think of the wretches who were reigning as emperors in his day! I use the word advisedly, for I would not speak evil of dignities; but really I speak too well of them when I call them wretches. They seem to have been inhuman monsters—"tyrants whose capricious folly violated every law of nature and decency," to whom every kind of lust was a daily habit, and who even sought out new inventions of sensuality, calling them new pleasures. As Paul thought of the iniquities of Napoli, and all the great towns to which the Romans went in their holidays—Pompeii and the like—oh, how he loathed them! And I doubt not that if the apostle were to come here now, if he knew how often rank and title are wont to sink all true dignity in shameful dissipation, and what flagrant profligacy is to be found in high quarters, he might as justly consider all the pomps and dignities and honour of the world that now is to be as little worth as a putrid carcase hanging on a tree and rotting in the sun. He says, "The world is crucified to me: it is hanging on the gallows to me, I think so little of its pleasures and of its pomps."

Alike contemptuously did Paul judge of all the treasures of the world. Paul never spent as much time as it would take to wink his eye in thinking of how much money he was worth. Having food and raiment he was therewith content. Sometimes he had scarcely that. He casually thanks the Philippians for ministering to his necessities, but he never sought to store anything, nor did he live with even half a thought of aggrandizing himself with gold and silver. "No," he said, "this will all perish with the using," and so he treated the world as a thing crucified to him. Now, Christian man, can you say as much as this—that the world, in its mercantile aspect, as well as in its motley vices and its manifold frivolities, is a crucified thing to you? Now, look what the world says.

Make money, young man, make money! Honestly if you can, but by all means make money. Look about you, for if you are not sharp you will not succeed.

Keep your own counsel, and rather play the double than be the dupe. Your character will rise with the credit you get on [the Stock] 'Change.

Now, suppose that you get the money, what is the result? The net result, as I often find it, is a paragraph in one of the newspapers to say that So-and-so Esquire's will was proved in the Probate Court under so many thousands. Then follows a grand squabble among all his relatives which shall eat him up. That is the consummation of a life of toil and care and scheming. He has lived for lucre, and he has to leave it behind. There is the end of that folly.

Oh, it is a poor thing to live for, the making of money and the hoarding of it. But still the genius of rightly getting money can be consecrated to the glory of God. You can use the wealth of this world in the service of the Master. To gain is not wrong. It is only wrong when grasping becomes the main object of life, and grudging grows into covetousness which is idolatry. To every Christian that and every other form of worldliness ought to be crucified, so that we can say, "For me to live is not myself, but it is Christ; I live that I may honour and glorify Him."

When the apostle said that the world was crucified to him, he meant just this.

I am not enslaved by any of its pursuits. I care nothing for its maxims. I am not governed by its spirit. I do not court its smiles. I do not fear its threatenings. It is not my master, nor am I its slave. The whole world cannot force Paul to lie, or to sin, but Paul will tell the world the truth, come what may.

You recollect the words of Palissy, the potter, when the king of France said to him that if he did not change his religion, and cease to be a Huguenot, he was afraid that he should have to deliver him up to his enemies. "Sire," said the potter, "I am sorry to hear you say, 'I am afraid,' for all the men in the world could not make Palissy talk like that. I am afraid of nobody, and I *must* do nothing but what is right." Oh, yes; the man that fears God and loves the Cross has a moral backbone which enables him to stand, and he snaps his fingers at the world. "Dead felon!" says he, "dead felon! Crucifier of Christ! Cosmos thou callest thyself. By comely names thou wouldst fain be greeted. Paul is nothing in thine esteem; but Paul is a match for thee, for he thinks as much of thee as thou dost of him, and no more." Hear him as he cries, "The world is crucified unto me, and I unto the world." To live to serve men is one thing, to live to bless them is another; and this we will do, God helping us, making sacrifices for their good. But to fear men, to ask their leave to think, to ask their instructions as to what we will speak, and how we shall say it—that is a baseness we cannot brook. By the grace of God, we have not so degraded ourselves, and never shall. "The world is crucified to me," says the apostle, "by the Cross of Christ."

III. Then he finishes up with the third crucifixion, which is, "I am crucified to the world."

We shall soon see the evidence of this crucifixion if we notice how they poured contempt upon him. Once Saul was a great rabbi, a man profoundly versed in Hebrew lore, a Pharisee of the Pharisees, and much admired. He was also a classic scholar and a philosophic thinker, a man of great mental powers, and fit to take the lead in learned circles. But when Paul began to preach Christ crucified—"Bah," they said, "he is an utter fool! Heed him not!" Or else they said, "Down with him! He is an apostate!" They cursed him. His name brought wrath unto the face of all Jews that mentioned it, and all intelligent Greeks likewise. "Paul? He is nobody!" He was everybody when he thought their way: he is nobody now that he thinks in God's way.

And then they put him to open shame by suspecting all his motives, and by misrepresenting all his actions. It did not matter what Paul did, they were quite certain that he was self-seeking; and he was endeavoring to make a fine thing of it for himself. When he acted so that they were forced to own that he was right, they put it in such a light that they made it out to be wrong. There were some who denied his apostleship, and said that he was never sent of God; and others questioned his ability to preach the gospel. So they crucified poor Paul one way and another to the full.

They went further still. They despised, they shunned him. His old friends forsook him. Some got out of the way, others pointed at him the finger of scorn in the streets. His persecutors showed their rancor against him, now stoning him with lynch-law, and anon with a semblance of legality dragging him before the magistrates. Paul was crucified to them. As for his teaching, they decried him as a babbler—a setter-forth of strange gods. I dare say they often sneered at the Cross of Christ which he preached as a nine days' wonder, an almost exploded doctrine, and said, "If you do but shut the mouths of such men as Paul, it will soon be forgotten." I have heard them say in modern times to lesser men, "Your old fashioned Puritanism is nearly dead, ere long it will be utterly extinct!" But we preach Christ crucified; the same old doctrine as the apostles preached, and for this by the contempt of the worldly wise we are crucified.

Now, dear Christian friends, if you keep to the Cross of Christ you must expect to have this for your portion. The world will be crucified to you, and you will be crucified to the world. You will get the cold shoulder. Old friends will become open foes. They will begin to hate you more than they loved you before. At home your foes will be the men of your own household. You will hardly be able to do anything right. When you joined in their revels you were a fine fellow; when you could drink, and sing a lascivious song, you were a jolly good fellow; but now they rate you as a fool; they scout you as a hypocrite; and slanderously blacken your character. Let their dislike be a badge of your discipleship, and say, "Now also the world is crucified to me, and I unto the world. Whatever the world says against me for Christ's sake is the maundering of a doomed malefactor, and what do I care for that? And, on the other hand, if I be rejected and despised, I am only taking what I always expected—my crucifixion—in my poor, humble way, after the manner of Christ Himself, who was despised and rejected of men."

The moral and the lesson of it all is this. Whatever comes of it, still glory in Christ. Go in for this, dear friends, that whether ye be in honour or in dishonor, in good report or in evil report, whether God multiply your substance and make you rich, or diminish it and make you poor, you will still glory in the Cross of Christ. If you have health, and strength and vigor to work for Him, or if you have to lie upon a bed of languishing and bear in patience all your heavenly Father's will, resolve that you will still glory in the Cross. Let this be the point of your glorying throughout your lives. Go down the steeps of Jordan, and go through Jordan itself, still glorying in the Cross, for in the Heaven of glory you will find that the blood-bought hosts celebrate the Cross as the trophy of their redemption.

Are you trusting in the Cross? Are you resting in Jesus? If not, may the Lord teach you this blessed privilege. There is no joy like it. There is no strength like it. There is no life like it. There is no peace like it. At the Cross we find our Heaven. While upon the Cross we gaze all heavenly, holy things abound within our hearts. If you have never been there, the Lord lead you there at this very hour; so shall you be pardoned, accepted, and blest for aye. The Lord grant that you all may be partakers of this grace for Christ's sake. Amen.

The Shame and Spitting

"I gave my back to the smiters, and my cheeks to them that plucked off the hair: I hid not my face from shame and spitting."—Isaiah 50:6.

O f whom speaketh the prophet this? Of himself or of some other? We cannot doubt but what Isaiah here wrote concerning the Lord Jesus Christ. Is not this one of the prophecies to which our Lord Himself referred in the incident recorded in the eighteenth chapter of Luke's gospel at the thirty-first verse?

> Then he took unto him the twelve, and said unto them, Behold, we go up to Jerusalem, and all things that are written by the prophets concerning the Son of man shall be accomplished. For he shall be delivered unto the Gentiles, and shall be mocked, and spitefully entreated, and spitted on: and they shall scourge him, and put him to death.

Such a remarkable prophecy of scourging and spitting as this which is now before us must surely refer to the Lord Jesus; its highest fulfilment is assuredly found in Him alone.

Of whom else, let me ask, could you conceive the prophet to have spoken if you read the whole chapter? Of whom else could he say in the same breath, "I clothe the Heavens with blackness, and I make sackcloth their covering. I gave my back to the smiters, and my cheeks to them that plucked off the hair." (Verses 3 and 6.) What a descent from the omnipotence which veils the Heavens with clouds to the gracious condescension which does not veil its own face, but permits it to be spat upon! No other could thus have spoken of Himself but He who is both God and man. He must be divine: how else could He say, "Behold, at my rebuke I dry up the sea, I make the rivers a wilderness"? (Verse 2.) And yet He must at the same time be a "Man of sorrows and acquainted with grief," for there is a strange depth of pathos in the words, "I gave my back to the smiters, and my cheeks to them that plucked off the hair: I hid not my face from shame and spitting." Whatever others may say, we believe that the speaker in this verse is Jesus of Nazareth, the King of the Jews, the Son of God and the Son of man, our Redeemer. It is the Judge of Israel whom they have smitten with a rod upon the cheek who here plaintively declares the griefs which He has undergone. We have before us the language of prophecy, but it is as accurate as though it had been written at the moment of the event. Isaiah might have been one of the Evangelists, so exactly does he describe what our Savior endured.

It was at His third trial, when He was delivered altogether to the Gentiles, that Pilate, the governor, gave Him up to the cruel process of scourging. Scourging as it was practiced in the English army was atrocious. But the lash is nothing among us compared with what it was among the Romans. I have heard that it was made of the sinews of oxen, and that in it were twisted the hucklebones of sheep, with slivers of bone, in order that every stroke might more effectually tear its way into the poor quivering flesh, which was mangled by its awful strokes. Scourging was such a punishment that it was generally regarded as worse than death itself, and indeed, many perished while enduring it, or soon afterwards. Our blessed Redeemer gave His back to the smiters, and the ploughers made deep furrows there. O spectacle of misery! How can we bear to look thereon?

Nor was that all, for Pilate's soldiers, calling all the band together, as if there were not enough for mockery unless all were mustered, put Him to derision by a mock enthronement and a mimic coronation; and when they had thus done they again buffeted and smote Him, and spat in His face. There was no kind of cruelty which their heartlessness could just then invent which they did not exercise upon His blessed person: their brutal sport had full indulgence, for their innocent victim offered neither resistance nor remonstrance. This is His own record of His patient endurance, "I gave my back to the smiters, and my cheeks to them that plucked off the hair: I hid not my face from shame and spitting."

Behold your King! I bring Him forth to you this morning in spirit and cry, "Behold the Man!" Turn hither all your eyes and hearts and look upon the despised and rejected of men! Gaze reverently and lovingly, with awe for His sufferings and love for His person. The sight demands adoration. I would remind you of that which Moses did when he saw the bush that burned and was not consumed—fit emblem of our Lord on fire with griefs and yet not destroyed; I bid you turn aside and see this great sight, but first attend to the mandate—"put off thy shoes from off thy feet, for the place whereon thou standest is holy ground." All round the Cross the soil is sacred. Our suffering Lord has consecrated every place whereon He stood, and therefore our hearts must be filled with reverence while we linger under the shadow of His passion.

May the Holy Spirit help you to see Jesus in four lights at this time. In each view He is worthy of devout attention. Let us view Him first as *the representative of God*; secondly, as *the substitute of His people*; thirdly, as *the servant of Jehovah*; and fourthly, as *the Comforter of His redeemed*.

I. First, I invite you to gaze upon your despised and rejected Lord as the representative of God.

In the person of Christ Jesus, God Himself came into the world, making a special visitation to Jerusalem and the Jewish people, but at the same time coming very near to all mankind. The Lord called to the people whom He had favored so long and whom He was intent to favor still. He says, in the second verse, "I came" and "I called." God did in very deed come down into the midst of mankind.

Be it noted, that when our Lord came into this world as the representative of God, He came with all His divine power about Him. The chapter before us says, "Is my hand shortened at all, that it cannot redeem? or have I no power to deliver? behold, at my rebuke I dry up the sea, I make the rivers a wilderness." The Son of God, when He was here, did not perform those exact miracles, because He was bent upon marvels of beneficence rather than of judgment. He did not repeat the plagues of Egypt, for He did not come to smite, but to save; but He did greater wonders and wrought miracles which ought far more powerfully to have won men's confidence in Him because they were full of goodness and mercy. He fed the hungry, He healed the sick, He raised the dead, and He cast out devils. He did equal marvels to those which were wrought in Egypt when the arm of the Lord was made bare in the eyes of all the people. It is true He did not change water into blood, but He turned water into wine. It is true He did not make their fish to stink, but by His word He caused the net to be filled even to bursting with great fishes. He did not break the whole staff of bread as He did in Egypt, but He multiplied loaves and fishes so that thousands of men and women and children were fed from His bounteous hand. He did not slay their firstborn, but He restored the dead.

I grant you that the glory of the Godhead was somewhat hidden in the person of Jesus of Nazareth, but it was still there, even as the glory was upon the face of Moses when he covered it with a veil. No essential attribute of God was absent in Christ, and every one might have been seen in Him if the people had not been wilfully blind. He did the works of His Father, and those works bare witness of Him that He was come in His Father's name. Yes, God was personally in the world when Jesus walked the blessed fields of the Holy Land, now, alas, laid under the curse for rejecting Him.

But when God thus came among men He was unacknowledged. What saith the prophet? "Wherefore when I came was there no man? when I called was there none to answer?" A few, taught by the Spirit of God, discerned Him and rejoiced; but they were so very few that we may say of the whole generation that they knew Him not. Those who had some dim idea of His excellence and majesty yet rejected Him. Herod, because he feared that He was a king, sought to slay Him. The kings of the Earth set themselves, and the rulers took counsel together, against the Lord, and against His anointed. He was emphatically and beyond all others "despised and rejected of men." Though, as I have said, the Godhead in Him was but scantily veiled, and gleams of its glory burst forth ever and anon, yet still the people would have none of it, and the cry, "Away with him, away with him, let him be crucified," was the verdict of the age upon which He descended. He called and there was none to answer; He spread out His hands all the day long unto a rebellious people who utterly rejected Him.

Yet our Lord when He came into the world was admirably adapted to be the representative of God, not only because He was God Himself, but because as man His whole nature was consecrated to the work, and in Him was neither flaw nor spot. He was untouched by any motive other than the one desire of manifesting the Father and blessing the sons of men. Oh, beloved, there was never one who had his ear so near the mouth of God as Jesus had. His Father had no need to speak to Him in dreams and visions of the night, for when all His faculties were wide awake there was nothing in them to hinder His understanding the mind of God; and therefore every morning when His Father wakened Him He spake into His ear. Jesus sat as a scholar at the Father's feet that He might learn first, and then teach. The things which He heard of the Father He made known unto men. He says that He spake not His own words but the words of Him that sent Him, and He did not His own deeds, but "my Father," said He, "that dwelleth in me, he doeth the work."

His errand, too, was all gentleness and love, for He came to speak words in season to the weary, and to comfort those that were cast down: surely such an errand should have secured Him a welcome. His course and conduct were most conciliatory, for He went among the people, and ate with publicans and sinners;

so gentle was He that He took little children in His arms, and blessed them; for this, if for nothing else, they ought to have welcomed Him right heartily and rejoiced at the sight of Him. Our text tells us how contrary was their conduct towards Him to that which He deserved: instead of being welcomed He was scourged, and instead of being honored He was scorned. Cruelty smote His back and plucked off the hair from His face, while derision jeered at Him and cast its spittle upon Him. Shame and contempt were poured upon Him, though He was God Himself. That spectacle of Christ spat upon, and scourged, represents what man virtually does to his God, what he would do to the Most High if he could. Hart well puts it:

> See how the patient Jesus stands,
> Insulted in His lowest case!
> Sinners have bound the Almighty hands,
> And spit in their Creator's face.

When our parents broke the command of their Maker, obeying the advice of the devil rather than the word of God, and preferring a poor apple to the divine favor, they did, as it were, spit into the face of God; and every sin committed since has been a repetition of the same contempt of the Eternal One. When a man will have his pleasure, even though it displeases God, he as good as declares that he despises God, prefers himself, and defies the wrath of the Most High. When a man acts contrary to the command of God he does as good as say to God,

> This is better for me to do than what Thou bidst me do. Either Thou art mistaken, in Thy prohibitions, or else Thou dost wilfully deny me the highest pleasure, and I, being a better judge of my own interests than Thou art, snatch at the pleasure which Thou dost refuse me. I judge Thee either to be unwise or unkind.

Every act of sin does despite to the sovereignty of God: it denies Him to be supreme, and refuses Him obedience. Every act of sin does dishonor to the love and wisdom of God, for it seems to say that it would have been greater love to have permitted us to do evil than to have commanded us to abstain from it. All sin is in many ways an insult to the majesty of the thrice Holy God, and He regards it as such.

Dear friends, this is especially the sin of those who have heard the gospel and yet reject the Savior, for in their case the Lord has come to them in the most gracious form, and yet they have refused Him. The Lord might well say,

> I have come to you to save you, and you will not regard me. I have come saying to you, "Look unto me and be ye saved, all the ends of the earth", and you close your eyes in unbelief. I have come saying, "Let us reason together: though your

sins be as crimson, they shall be as wool," but you will not be cleansed from your iniquity. I have come with the promise, "All manner of sin and iniquity shall be forgiven unto men." What is your reply?

In the case of many the answer is, "We prefer our own righteousness to the righteousness of God." If that is not casting spittle into the face of God I know not what is, for our righteousnesses are well described as "filthy rags," and we have the impudence to say that these are better than the righteousness of God in Christ Jesus.

Or if we do not say this when we reject the Savior, we tell Him that we do not want Him, for we do not need a Savior: this is as good as to say that God has played the fool with the life and death of His own Son. What greater derision can be cast upon God than to consider the blood of atonement to be a superfluity? He who chooses sin sooner than repentance prefers to suffer the wrath of God rather than be holy and dwell in Heaven forever. For the sake of a few paltry pleasures men forego the love of God, and are ready to run the risk of an eternity of divine wrath. They think so little of God that He is of no account with them at all. All this is in reality a scorning and despising of the Lord God, and is well set forth by the insults which were poured upon the Lord Jesus.

Woe is me that it should ever be so. My God! my God! To what a sinful race do I belong. Alas, that it should treat Thine infinite goodness so despitefully! That Thou shouldst be rejected at all, but especially that thou shouldest be rejected when dressed in robes of love and arrayed in gentleness and pity, is horrible to think upon. But there is the picture before you. God Himself set at nought, despised, rejected, put to shame, perpetually dishonored in the person of His dear Son. The sight should breed repentance in us. We should look to Him whom we have scourged, and mourn for Him. O Holy Spirit, work this tender grace in all our hearts.

II. And now, secondly, I want to set the Lord Jesus before you in another light, or rather beseech Him to shine in His own light before your eyes—as the substitute for his people.

Recollect when our Lord Jesus Christ suffered thus, it was not on His own account nor purely for the sake of His Father, but He "was wounded for our transgressions, he was bruised for our iniquities: the chastisement of our peace was upon him; and with his stripes we are healed." There has risen up a modern idea which I cannot too much reprobate, that Christ made no atonement for our sin except upon the Cross: whereas in this passage of Isaiah we are taught as plainly as possible that by His bruising and His stripes, as well as by His death, we are healed. Never divide between the life and the death of Christ. How could He have died if He had not lived? How could He suffer except while He lived? Death is not suffering, but the end of it. Guard also against the evil notion that you have nothing to do with the righteousness of Christ, for He could not have made an atonement by His blood if He had not been perfect in His life. He could not have been acceptable if He had not first been proven to be holy, harmless, and undefiled. The victim must be spotless, or it cannot be presented for sacrifice. Draw no nice lines and raise no quibbling questions, but look at your Lord as He is and bow before Him.

Understand, my dear brothers and sisters, that Jesus took upon Himself our sin, and being found bearing that sin He had to be treated as sin should be treated. Now, of all the things that ever existed sin is the most shameful thing that can be. It deserves to be scourged, it deserves to be spit upon, it deserves to be crucified; and because our Lord had taken upon Himself our sin, therefore must He be put to shame, therefore must He be scourged. If you want to see what God thinks of sin, see His only Son spat upon by the soldiers when He was made sin for us. In God's sight sin is a shameful, horrible, loathsome, abominable thing, and when Jesus takes it He must be forsaken and given up to scorn. This sight will be the more wonderful to you when you recollect who it was that was spat upon, for if you and I, being sinners, were scourged, and smitten, and despised, there would be no wonder in it; but He who took our sin was God, before whom angels bow with reverent awe, and yet, seeing the sin was upon Him, He was made subject to the most intense degree of shame. Seeing that Jesus stood in our stead, it is written of the eternal Father that "He spared not his own Son." "It pleased the Father to bruise him: he hath put him to grief"; He made His soul an offering for sin. Yes, beloved, sin is condemned in the flesh and made to appear exceeding shameful when you recollect that, even though it was only laid on our blessed Lord by imputation, yet it threw Him into the very depths of shame and woe ere it could be removed.

Reflect, also, upon the voluntariness of all this. He willingly submitted to the endurance of suffering and scorn. It is said in the text, "He *gave* his back to the smiters." They did not seize and compel Him, or, if they did, yet they could not have done it without His consent. He gave His back to the smiters. He gave His cheek to those that plucked off the hair. He did not hide His face from shame and spitting: He did not seek in any way to escape from insults. It was the voluntariness of His grief which constituted in great measure the merit of it. That Christ should stand in our stead by force were a little thing, even had it been possible; but that He should stand there of His own free will, and that being there He should willingly be treated with derision, this is grace indeed. The Son of God was willingly made a curse for us, and at His own desire was made subject to shame on our account.

I do not know how you feel in listening to me, but while I am speaking I feel as if language ought scarcely to touch such a theme as this: it is too feeble for its task. I want you to get beyond my words if you can, and for yourselves meditate upon the fact that He who covers the heavens with blackness, yet did not cover His own face, and He who binds up the universe with the girdle which holds it in one, yet was bound and blindfolded by the men He had Himself made; He whose face is as the brightness of the sun that shineth in its strength, was once spit upon. Surely we shall need faith in Heaven to believe this wondrous fact. Can it have been true, that the glorious Son of God was jeered and jested at?

I have often heard that there is no faith wanted in Heaven, but I rather judge that we shall want as much faith to believe that these things were ever done as the patriarchs had to believe that they would be done. How shall I sit down and gaze upon *Him* and think that His dear face was once profaned with spittle? When all Heaven shall lie prostrate at His feet in awful silence of adoration, will it seem possible that once He was mocked? When angels, and principalities, and powers shall all be roused to rapture of harmonious music in His praise, will it seem possible that once the most abject of men plucked out the hair? Will it not appear incredible that those sacred hands, which are "as gold rings set with the beryl," were once nailed to a gibbet, and that those cheeks which are "as a bed of spices, as sweet flowers," should have been battered and bruised? We shall be quite certain of the fact, and yet we shall never cease to wonder, that His side was gashed, and His face was spit upon? The sin of man in this instance will always amaze us. How could you commit this crime? Oh, ye sons of men, how could ye treat such an one with cruel scorn? O thou brazen thing called sin. Thou hast, indeed, as the prophet saith, "A whore's forehead"; thou hast a demon's heart, Hell burns within thee. Why couldst thou not spit upon earthly splendors? Why must Heaven be thy scorn? Or if Heaven, why not spit on angels! Was there no place for thy base deed but the Well-beloved's face? Was there no place for thy spittle but *His* face? *His* face! Woe is me! His face! Should such loveliness receive such shame as this? I could wish that man had never been created, or that, being created, he had been swept into nothingness rather than have lived to commit such horror.

Yet here is matter for our faith to rest upon. Beloved, trust yourselves in the hands of your great Substitute. Did He bear all this shame? then there must be more than enough merit and efficacy in this, which was the prelude of His precious death—and especially in His death itself—there must be merit sufficient to put away all transgression, iniquity, and sin. Our shame is ended, for He has borne it! Our punishment is removed: He has endured it all. Double for all our sins has our Redeemer paid. Return unto thy rest, O my soul, and let peace take full possession of thy weeping heart.

III. But time fails us, and therefore we will mention, next, the third light in which it is our desire to see the Savior. Beloved, we desire to see the Lord Jesus Christ as the servant of God.

He took upon Himself the form of a servant when He was made in the likeness of man. Observe how He performed this service right thoroughly, and remember we are to look upon this third picture as our copy, which is to be the guide of our life. I know that many of you are glad to call yourselves the servants of God; take not the name in vain. As Jesus was, so are you also in this world, and you are to seek to be like Him.

First, as a servant, Christ was personally prepared for service. He was thirty years and more here below, learning obedience in His Father's house, and the after years were spent in learning obedience by the things which He suffered. What a servant He was, for He never went about His own errands nor went by His own will, but He waited always upon His Father. He was in constant communication with Heaven, both by day and by night. He says, "He wakeneth morning by morning, he wakeneth mine ear to hear as the learned." The blessed Lord er ever the day broke heard that gentle voice which called Him, and at its whisper He arose before the sunrise, and there the dawning found Him, on the mountain side, waiting upon God in wrestling prayer, taking His message from the Father that He might go and deliver it to the children of men. He loved man much, but He loved His Father more, and He never came to tell out the love of God without having as man received it fresh from the divine heart. He knew that His Father heard Him always, and He lived in the spirit of conscious acceptance.

Our text assures us that this service knew no reserve in its consecration. *We* generally draw back somewhere. I am ashamed to say it, but I mourn that I have done so. Many of us could give to Christ all our health and strength, and all the money we have, very heartily and cheerfully; but when it comes to a point of reputation we feel the pinch. To be slandered, to have some filthy thing said of you; this is too much for flesh and blood. You seem to say, "I cannot be made a fool of, I cannot bear to be regarded as a mere imposter"; but a true servant of Christ must make himself of no reputation when he takes upon himself the work of his Lord. Our blessed Master was willing to be scoffed at by the lewdest and the lowest of men. The abjects jeered at Him; the reproach of them that reproached God fell upon Him. He became the song of the drunkard, and when the rough soldiery detained Him in the guard-room they heaped up their ridicule, as though He were not worthy of the name of man.

> They bow their knees to Me, and cry, 'Hail, King':
> Whatever scoffs or scornfulness can bring,
> I am the floor, the sink, where they it fling:
> Was ever grief like Mine?
>
> The soldiers also spit upon that face
> Which angels did desire to have the grace
> And prophets once to see, but found no place:
> Was ever grief like Mine?

Herod and Pilate were the very dross of men, and yet He permitted them to judge Him. Their servants were vile fellows, and yet He resigned Himself to them. If he had breathed upon them with angry breath, He might have flashed devouring fire upon them, and burned them up as stubble; but His omnipotent patience restrained His indignation, and He remained as a sheep before her shearers. He allowed His own creatures to pluck His hair and spit in His face. Such patience should be yours as servants of God. We are to be willing to be made nothing of, and even to be counted as the offscouring of all things. It is pitiful for the Christian to refuse to suffer, and to become a fighting man, crying, "We must stand up for our rights." Did you ever see Jesus in that posture? There is a propensity in us to say, "I will have it out." Yes, but you cannot picture Jesus in that attitude. I defy a painter to depict Him so: it is somebody else, and not Christ. No! He said, "I gave my back to the smiters, and my cheeks to them that plucked off the hair: I hid not my face from shame and spitting."

All this while—now follow me in this next point—there was no flinching in Him. They spat in His face, but what says He in the seventh verse. "I have set my face like a flint." If they are about to defile His face He is resolved to bear it; He girds up His loins, and makes Himself more determined. Oh, the bravery of our Master's silence! Cruelty and shame could not make Him speak. Have not your lips sometimes longed to speak out a denial and a defense? Have you not felt it wise to be quiet, but then the charge has been so excessively cruel, and it has stung you so terribly that you hungered to resent it. Base falsehoods aroused your indignation, and you felt you must speak and probably you did speak, though you tried to keep your lips as with a bridle while the wicked were before you. But our own beloved Lord in the omnipotence of His patience and love would not utter a word, but like a lamb at the slaughter He opened not His mouth. He witnessed a good confession by His matchless silence. Oh, how mighty—how gloriously mighty was His patience! We must copy it if we are to be His disciples. We, too, must set our faces like flints, to move or to sit still, according to the Father's will, to be silent or to speak, as most shall honour Him. "I have set my face like a flint," saith He, even though in another place He cries, "My heart is like wax, it is melted in the midst of my bowels."

And do you notice all the while the confidence and quiet of His spirit? He almost seems to say,

> You may spit upon Me, but you cannot find fault with Me. You may pluck My hair, but you cannot impugn My integrity; you may lash My shoulders, but you cannot impute a fault to Me. Your false witnesses dare not look Me in the face: let Me know who is Mine adversary, let him come near to Me. Behold, Adonai Jehovah will keep Me, who is he that shall condemn Me! Lo, they all shall wax old as a garment, the moth shall eat them up.

Be calm then, O true servant of God! In patience possess your soul. Serve God steadily and steadfastly though all men should belie you. Go to the bottom of the service, dive even to the very depth, and be content even to lie in Christ's grave, for you shall share in Christ's resurrection. Do not dream that the path to Heaven is up the hill of honour, it winds down into the valley of humiliation. Imagine not that you can grow great eternally by being great here. You must become less, and less, and less, even though you should be despised and rejected of men, for this is the path to everlasting glory.

IV. Lastly, I am to set Him forth in His fourth character, as the comforter of his people; but I must ask you to do this, while I just, as it were, make a charcoal sketch of the picture I would have painted.

Remember, first, our blessed Lord is well qualified to speak a word in season to him that is weary, because He Himself is lowly, and meek, and so accessible to us. When men are in low spirits they feel as if they could not take comfort from persons who are harsh and proud. The comforter must come as a sufferer; He must come in a lowly, broken spirit, if He would cheer the afflicted. You must not put on your best dress to go and visit the daughter of poverty, or go with your jewels about you to show how much better off you are than she. Sit down by the side of the downcast man and let him know that you are meek and lowly of heart. Your Master "gave his back to the smiters, and his cheek to them that plucked off the hair," and therefore He is the Comforter you want.

Remark not only His lowliness, but His sympathy. Are you full of aches and pains this morning? Jesus knows all about them, for He "gave his back to the smiters." Do you suffer from what is worse than pain, from scandal and slander? "He hid not his face from shame and spitting." Have you been ridiculed of late? Have the graceless made fun of your godliness? Jesus can sympathize with you, for you know what unholy mirth they made out of Him. In every pang that rends your heart your Lord has borne His share. Go and tell Him. Many will not understand you. You are a speckled bird, differing from all the rest, and they will all peck at you; but Jesus Christ knows this, for He was a speckled bird too. He was "holy, harmless, undefiled, and separate from sinners," but not separate from such as you. Get you to Him and He will sympathize with you.

In addition to His gentle spirit and His power to sympathize, there is this to help to comfort us—namely, His example, for He can argue thus with you, "I gave my back to the smiters. Cannot you do the like? Shall the disciple be above his master?" If I can but get on the doorstep of Heaven and sit down in the meanest place there I shall feel I have an infinitely better position than I deserve, and shall I think of my dear, blessed Lord and Master giving His face to be spit upon, and then give myself airs, and say, "I cannot bear this scorn, I cannot bear this pain!" What, does the King pass over the brook Kedron, and must there be no brook Kedron for you? Does the Master bear the Cross, and must your shoulders never be galled? Did they call the Master of the house "Beelzebub," and must they call you "Reverend Sir?" Did they laugh at Him, and scoff at Him, and must you be honored? Are you to be "gentleman" and "lady" where Christ was "that fellow?" For His birth they loaned Him a stable, and for His burial He borrowed a grave. O, friends, let pride disappear, and let us count it our highest honour to be permitted to stoop as low as ever we can.

And, then, His example further comforts us by the fact that He was calm amid it all. Oh, the deep rest of the Savior's heart! They set Him up upon that mock throne, but He did not answer with an angry word; they put a reed into His hand, but He did not change it to an iron rod, and break them like a potter's vessel, as He might have done. There was no wincing and no plead-ing for mercy. Sighs of pain were forced from Him, and He said, "I thirst," for He was not a stoic; but there was no fear of man, or timorous shrinking of heart.

The King of Martyrs well deserves to wear the martyr's crown, for right royally did He endure: there was never a patience like to His. That is your copy, brother, that is your copy, sister—you must write very carefully to write as well as that. You had need your Master held your hand; in fact, whenever children in Christ's school do write according to His copy, it is al-ways because He holds their hand by His Spirit.

Last of all, our Savior's triumph is meant to be a stimulus and encourage-ment to us. He stands before us this morning as the Comforter of His people. Consider Him that endured such contradiction of sinners against Himself lest ye be weary and faint in your minds; for though He was once abased and de-spised, yet now He sitteth at the right hand of God, and reigns over all things; and the day is coming when every knee shall bow before Him, and every tongue confess that Jesus Christ is Lord, to the glory of God the Father. They that spat upon Him will rue the day. Come hither, ye that derided Him! He has raised you from the dead, come hither and spit upon Him now! Ye that scourged Him, bring your rods, see what ye can do in this day of His glory! See, they fly before Him, they invoke the hills to shelter them, they ask the rocks to open and conceal them. Yet it is nothing but His face, that selfsame face they spat upon, which is making Earth and Heaven to flee away. Yea, all things flee before the majesty of His frown who once gave His back to the smiters, and His cheeks to them that plucked off the hair. Be like Him, then, ye who bear His name; trust Him, and live for Him, and you shall reign with Him in glory forever and ever. Amen.

The Cross Our Glory

"But God forbid that I should glory, save in the Cross of our Lord Jesus Christ, by whom the world is crucified unto me, and I unto the world."—Galatians 6:14.

Almost all men have something wherein to glory. Every bird has its own note of song. It is a poor heart that never rejoices; it is a dull packhorse that is altogether without bells. Men usually rejoice in something or other, and many men so rejoice in that which they choose that they become boastful and full of vainglory. It is very sad that men should be ruined by their glory; and yet many are so. Many glory in their shame, and more glory in that which is mere emptiness. Some glory in their physical strength, in which an ox excels them; or in their gold, which is but thick clay; or in their gifts, which are but talents with which they are entrusted. The pounds entrusted to their stewardship are thought by men to belong to themselves, and therefore they rob God of the glory of them.

O my hearers, hear ye the voice of wisdom, which crieth, "He that glorieth, let him glory only in the Lord." To live for personal glory is to be dead while we live. Be not so foolish as to perish for a bubble. Many a man has thrown his soul away for a little honour, or for the transient satisfaction of success in trifles. O men, your tendency is to glory in somewhat; your wisdom will be to find a glory worthy of an immortal mind.

The Apostle Paul had a rich choice of things in which he could have gloried. If it had been his mind to have remained among his own people, he might have been one of their most honored rabbis. He saith in his Epistle to the Philippians, in the third chapter,

> If any other man thinketh that he hath whereof he might trust in the flesh, I more: circumcised the eighth day, of the stock of Israel, of the tribe of Benjamin, an Hebrew of the Hebrews; as touching the law, a Pharisee; con-

cerning zeal, persecuting the church; touching the righteousness which is in the law, blameless.

He says that he profited in the Jews' religion above many, his equals in his own nation; and he stood high in the esteem of his fellow-professors [Christians]. But when he was converted to the faith of the Lord Jesus, he said, "What things were gain to me, those I counted loss for Christ. Yea, doubtless, and I count all things but loss for the excellency of the knowledge of Christ Jesus my Lord." As soon as he was converted he forsook all glorying in his former religion and zeal, and cried, "God forbid that I should glory in my birth, my education, my proficiency in Scripture, or my regard to orthodox ritual. God forbid that I should glory, save in the Cross of our Lord Jesus Christ."

Paul might also, if he had so chosen, have gloried in his sufferings for the Cross of Christ; for he had been a living martyr, a perpetual self-sacrifice to the cause of the Crucified. He says,

> Are they ministers of Christ? (I speak as a fool) I am more; in labors more abundant, in stripes above measure, in prisons more frequent, in deaths oft. Of the Jews five times received I forty stripes save one. Thrice was I beaten with rods, once was I stoned, thrice I suffered shipwreck, a night and a day I have been in the deep; in journeyings often, in perils of waters, in perils of robbers, in perils by mine own countrymen, in perils by the heathen, in perils in the city, in perils in the wilderness, in perils in the sea, in perils among false brethren; in weariness and painfulness, in watchings often, in hunger and thirst, in fastings often, in cold and nakedness.

He was once driven to give a summary of these sufferings to establish his apostleship; but before he did so he wrote, "Would to God ye could bear with me a little in my folly." In his heart he was saying all the while, "God forbid that I should glory, save in the Cross of our Lord Jesus Christ."

The great apostle had yet another reason for glorying, if he had chosen to do so; for he could speak of visions and revelations of the Lord. He says,

> I knew a man in Christ above fourteen years ago. . . caught up to the third Heaven. And I knew such a man. . .how that he was caught up into Paradise, and heard unspeakable words, which it is not lawful for a man to utter.

He was in danger of being exalted above measure by reason of the abundance of these revelations and hence he was humbled by a painful thorn in the flesh. Paul, when hard driven by the necessity to maintain his position in the Corinthian church, was forced to mention these things; but he liked not such glorying, he was most at ease when he said, "God forbid that I should glory, save in the Cross of our Lord Jesus Christ."

Brethren, notice that Paul does not here say that he gloried in Christ, though he did so with all his heart; but he declares that he gloried most in "the Cross of our Lord Jesus Christ," which in the eyes of men was the very lowest and most inglorious part of the history of the Lord Jesus. He could have gloried in the incarnation: angels sang of it, wise men came from the far East to behold it. Did not the newborn King awake the song from Heaven of "Glory to God in the highest?" He might have gloried in the life of Christ: was there ever such another, so benevolent and blameless? He might have gloried in the resurrection of Christ: it is the world's great hope concerning those that are asleep. He might have gloried in our Lord's ascension; for He "led captivity captive," and all His followers glory in His victory. He might have gloried in His Second Advent, and I doubt not that he did; for the Lord shall soon descend from Heaven with a shout, with the voice of the archangel and the trump of God, to be admired in all them that believe.

Yet the apostle selected beyond all these that center of the Christian system, that point which is most assailed by its foes that focus of the world's derision—the Cross; and, putting all else somewhat into the shade, he exclaims, "God forbid that I should glory, save in the Cross of our Lord Jesus Christ." Learn, then, that the highest glory of our holy religion is the Cross. The history of grace begins earlier and goes on later, but in its middle point stands the Cross. Of two eternities this is the hinge; of past decrees and future glories this is the pivot. Let us come to the Cross this morning, and think of it, till each one of us, in the power of the Spirit of God, shall say, "God forbid that I should glory, save in the Cross of our Lord Jesus Christ."

I. First, as the Lord shall help me (for who shall describe the Cross without the help of Him that did hang upon it?) what did Paul mean by the Cross?

Did he not include under this term, first, the fact of the Cross: secondly, the doctrine of the Cross: and thirdly, the Cross of the doctrine?

I think he meant, first of all, *the fact of the Cross.* Our Lord Jesus Christ did really die upon a gibbet, the death of a felon. He was literally put to death upon a tree, accursed in the esteem of men. I beg you to notice how the apostle puts it—"the Cross of our Lord Jesus Christ." In his epistles he sometimes saith "Christ," at another time "Jesus," frequently "Lord," often times "our Lord"; but here he saith "our Lord Jesus Christ." There is a sort of pomp of words in this full description, as if in contrast to the shame of the Cross. The terms are intended in some small measure to express the dignity of Him who was put to so ignominious a death. He is Christ the anointed, and Jesus the

Savior; He is the Lord, the Lord of all, and He is "our Lord Jesus Christ." He is not a Lord without subjects, for He *is* "our Lord"; nor is He a Savior without saved ones, for He is "our Lord Jesus"; nor has He the anointing for Himself alone, for all of us have a share in Him as "our Christ"; in all He is ours, and was so upon the Cross.

But next, I said that Paul gloried in *the doctrine of the Cross;* and it was so. What is that doctrine of the Cross, of which it is written that it is "to them that perish foolishness, but unto us who are saved it is the power of God and the wisdom of God?" In one word, it is the doctrine of the atonement, the doctrine that the Lord Jesus Christ was made sin for us, that Christ was once offered to bear the sins of many, and that God hath set Him forth to be the propitiation for our sins. Paul saith, "When we were yet without strength, in due time Christ died for the ungodly": and again, "Now once in the end of the world hath he appeared to put away sin by the sacrifice of himself." The doctrine of the Cross is that of sacrifice for sin: Jesus is "the Lamb of God that taketh away the sin of the world." "God so loved the world, that he gave his only-begotten Son, that whosoever believeth in him should not perish, but have everlasting life."

The doctrine is that of a full atonement made, and the utmost ransom paid. "Christ hath redeemed us from the curse of the law, being made a curse for us: for it is written, 'Cursed is every one that hangeth on a tree.'" In Christ upon the Cross we see the Just dying for the unjust, that He might bring us to God; the innocent bearing the crimes of the guilty, that they might be forgiven and accepted. That is the doctrine of the Cross, of which Paul was never ashamed.

This also is a necessary part of the doctrine: that whosoever believeth in Him is justified from all sin; that whosoever trusts in the Lord Jesus Christ is in that moment forgiven, justified, and accepted in the Beloved. "As Moses lifted up the serpent in the wilderness, even so must the Son of man be lifted up; that whosoever believeth in him should not perish, but have eternal life." Paul's doctrine was, "It is not of him that willeth nor of him that runneth, but of God that showeth mercy"; and it was His constant teaching that salvation is not of doings, nor of ceremonies, but simply and alone by believing in Jesus. We are to accept by an act of trust that righteousness which is already finished and completed by the death of our blessed Lord upon the Cross. He who does not preach atonement by the blood of Jesus does not preach the Cross; and he who does not declare justification by faith in Christ Jesus has missed the mark altogether.

But the apostle also gloried in *the Cross of the doctrine,* for the death of the Son of God upon the Cross is the *crux* of Christianity. Here is the difficulty, the stumbling block, and rock of offence. The Jew could not endure a crucified Messiah: he looked for pomp and power. Multitudinous ceremonies and diverse washings and sacrifices, were these all to be put away and nothing left but a bleeding Savior? At the mention of the Cross the philosophic Greek thought himself insulted, and vilified the preacher as a fool. In effect he said,

> You are not a man of thought and intellect; you are not abreast of the times, but are sticking in the mire of antiquated prophecies. Why not advance with the discoveries of modern thought?

The apostle, teaching a simple fact which a child might comprehend, found in it the wisdom of God. Christ upon the Cross working out the salvation of men was more to him than all the sayings of the sages. As for the Roman, he would give no heed to any glorying in a dead Jew, a crucified Jew! Crushing the world beneath his iron heel, he declared that such romancing should never win him from the gods of his fathers. Paul did not blench before the sharp and practical reply of the conquerors of the world. He trembled not before Nero in his place. Whether to Greek or Jew, Roman or barbarian, bond or free, he was not ashamed of the gospel of Christ, but gloried in the Cross. He had the Cross for his philosophy, the Cross for his tradition, the Cross for his gospel, the Cross for his glory, and nothing else.

II. But, secondly, why did Paul glory in the Cross?

He did not do so because he was in want of a theme: for, as I have shown you, he had a wide field for boasting if he had chosen to occupy it. He gloried in the Cross from solemn and deliberate choice. He had counted the cost, he had surveyed the whole range of subjects with eagle eye, and he knew what he did, and why he did it. He was master of the art of thinking. As a metaphysician, none could excel him; as a logical thinker, none could have gone beyond him. He stands almost alone in the early Christian church, as a master mind. Others may have been more poetic, or more simple, but none were more thoughtful or argumentative than he. With decision and firmness Paul sets aside everything else, and definitely declares, throughout his whole life, "I glory in the Cross." He does this exclusively, saying, "God forbid that I should glory, save in the Cross."

> *Forbid it, Lord, that I should boast,*
> *Save in the death of Christ, my God;*

> All the vain things that charm me most,
> I sacrifice them to His blood.

He would have called God to witness that he knew no ambition save that of bringing glory to the Cross of Christ. As I think of this I am ready to say, "Amen" to Paul, and bid you sing that stirring verse:

> It is the old Cross still,
> Hallelujah! hallelujah!
> Its triumphs let us tell,
> Hallelujah! hallelujah!
>
> The grace of God here shone
> Through Christ, the blessed Son,
> Who did for sin atone;
> Hallelujah for the Cross!

Why did Paul thus glory in the Cross? You may well desire to know, for there are many nowadays who do not glory in it but forsake it. Alas that it should be so! but there are ministers who ignore the atonement; they conceal the Cross, or say but little about it. You may go through service after service, and scarce hear a mention of the atoning blood; but Paul was always bringing forward the expiation for sin: Paul never tried to explain it away. Oh the numbers of books that have been written to prove that the Cross means an example of self-sacrifice; as if every martyrdom did not mean that. They cannot endure a real substitutionary sacrifice for human guilt, and an effectual purgation of sin by the death of the great substitute. Yet the Cross means that—or nothing.

I take it that this was so, first, because Paul saw in the Cross *a vindication of divine justice.* Where else can the justice of God be seen so clearly as in the death of God Himself, in the person of His dear Son? If the Lord Himself suffers on account of broken law, then is the majesty of the law honored to the full. Some time ago, a judge in America was called upon to try a prisoner who had been his companion in his early youth. It was a crime for which the penalty was a fine, more or less heavy. The judge did not diminish the fine; the case was clearly a bad one, and he fined the prisoner to the full. Some who knew the former relation to the offender thought him somewhat unkind thus to carry out the law, while others admired his impartiality. All were surprised when the judge quitted the bench and himself paid every farthing of the penalty. He had both shown his respect for the law and his goodwill to the man who had broken it; he exacted the penalty, but he paid it himself.

So God hath done in the Person of His dear Son. He has not remitted the punishment, but He has Himself endured it. His own Son, who is none other than God Himself—for there is an essential union between them—has paid the debt which was incurred by human sin. I love to think of the vindication of divine justice upon the Cross; I am never weary of it. Some cannot bear the thought; but to me it seems inevitable that sin must be punished, or else the foundations of society would be removed. If sin becomes a trifle, virtue will be a toy. Society cannot stand if laws are left without penal sanction, or if that sanction is to be a mere empty threat. Men in their own governments every now and then cry out for greater severity. When a certain offence abounds, and ordinary means fail, they demand exemplary punishment; and it is but natural that they should do so; for deep in the conscience of every man there is the conviction that sin must be punished to secure the general good. Justice must reign, even benevolence demands it. If there could have been salvation without an atonement it would have been a calamity; righteous men, and even benevolent men, might deprecate the setting aside of law in order to save the guilty from the natural result of their crimes.

For my own part I value a just salvation: an unjust salvation would never have satisfied the apprehensions and demands of my conscience. No, let God be just, if the Heavens fall; let God carry out the sentence of His law, or the universe will suspect that it was not righteous; and when such a suspicion rules the general mind, all respect for God will be gone. The Lord carries out the decree of His justice even to the bitter end, abating not a jot of its requirements. Brethren, there was an infinite efficacy in the death of such a one as our Lord Jesus Christ to vindicate the law. Though He is Man, yet is He also God; and in His passion and death He offered to the justice of God a vindication not at all inferior to the punishment of Hell. God is just indeed when Jesus dies upon the Cross rather than that God's law should be dishonored. When our August Lord Himself bore the wrath that was due for human sin, it was made evident to all that law is not to be trifled with. We glory in the Cross, for there the debt was paid, our sins on Jesus laid.

But we glory because on the Cross we have an unexampled *display of God's love*. "God commendeth his love toward us, in that, while we were yet sinners, Christ died for us." Oh to think of it, that He who was offended takes the nature of the offender, and then bears the penalty due for wanton transgression. He who is infinite, thrice holy, all glorious, forever to be worshiped, yet stoopeth to be numbered with the transgressors, and to bear the sin of many. The mythology of the gods of high Olympus contains nothing worthy to be mentioned in the same day with this wondrous deed of supreme condescension and infinite love. The ancient Shasters and Vedas have nothing of the kind. The death of Jesus Christ upon the Cross cannot be an invention of men; none of the ages have produced aught like it in the poetic dreams of any nation. If we did not hear of it so often, and think of it so little, we should be charmed with it beyond expression.

I believe again, thirdly, that Paul delighted to preach the Cross of Christ as *the removal of all guilt.* He believed that the Lord Jesus on the Cross finished transgression, made an end of sin, and brought in everlasting righteousness. He that believeth in Jesus is justified from all things from which he could not be justified by the law of Moses. Since sin was laid on Jesus, God's justice cannot lay it upon the believing sinner. The Lord will never punish twice the same offence. If He accepts a substitute for me, how can He call me to His bar and punish me for that transgression, for which my substitute endured the chastisement? Many a troubled conscience has caught at this and found deliverance from despair. Wonder not that Paul gloried in Christ, since it is written, "In the Lord shall all the seed of Israel be justified, and shall glory." This is the method of salvation which completely and eternally absolves the sinner, and makes the blackest offender white as snow.

He glories in it, again, as *a marvel of wisdom.* It seemed to him the sum of perfect wisdom and skill. He cried, "O the depths of the riches both of the wisdom and knowledge of God!" The plan of salvation by vicarious suffering is simple, but sublime. It would have been impossible for human or angelic wisdom to have invented it. Men already so hate it and fight against it that they never would have advised it. God alone out of the treasury of His infinite wisdom brought forth this matchless project of salvation for the guilty through the substitution of the innocent. The more we study it, the more we shall perceive that it is full of teaching.

It is only the superficial thinker who regards the Cross as a subject soon to be comprehended and exhausted: the most lofty intellects will here find ample room and verge enough. The profoundest minds might lose themselves in considering the splendid diversities of light which compose the pure white light of the Cross. Everything of sin and justice, of misery and mercy, of folly and wisdom, of force and tenderness, or rage and pity, on the part of man and God, may be seen here. In the Cross may be seen the concentration of eternal thought, the focus of infinite purpose, the outcome of illimitable wisdom. Of God and the Cross we may say:

> *Here I behold His inmost heart,*
> *Where grace and vengeance strangely join;*
> *Piercing His Son with sharpest smart*
> *To make the purchased pleasures mine.*

I believe that Paul gloried in the Cross, again, because it is *the door of hope*, even to the vilest of the vile. The world was very filthy in Paul's time. Roman civilization was of the most brutal and debased kind, and the masses of the people were sunken in vices that are altogether unmentionable. Paul felt that he could go into the darkest places with light in his hand when he spoke of the Cross. To tell of pardon bought with the blood of the Son of God is to carry an omnipotent message. The Cross uplifts the fallen and delivers the despairing. The Cross is the standard of victorious grace. It is the lighthouse whose cheering ray gleams across the dark waters of despair and cheers the dense midnight of our fallen race, saving from eternal shipwreck, and piloting into everlasting peace.

Again, Paul, I believe, gloried in the Cross, as I often do, because it was *the source of rest* to him and to his brethren. I make this confession, and I make it very boldly, that I never knew what rest of heart truly meant till I understood the doctrine of the substitution of our Lord Jesus Christ. Now, when I see my Lord bearing away my sins as my scapegoat, or dying for them as my sin-offering, I feel a profound peace of heart and satisfaction of spirit. The Cross is all I want for security and joy. Truly, this bed is long enough for a man to stretch himself on it. The Cross is a chariot of salvation, wherein we traverse the high road of life without fear. The pillow of atonement heals the head that aches with anguish. Beneath the shadow of the Cross I sit down with great delight, and its fruit is sweet unto my taste. I have no impatience even to haste to Heaven while resting beneath the Cross, for our hymn truly says:

> *Here it is I find my Heaven,*
> *While upon the Cross I gaze.*

Here is perfect cleansing, and hence a divine security, guarded by the justice of God; and hence a "peace of God, which passeth all understanding." To try to entice me away from the truth of substitution is labor in vain. Seduce me to preach the pretty nothings of modern thought! This child knows much better than to leave the substance for the shadow, the truth for the fancy. I see nothing that can give to my heart a fair exchange for the rest, peace, and unutterable joy which the old fashioned doctrine of the Cross now yields me. I cannot go beyond my simple faith that Jesus stood in my stead, and bore my sin, and put my sin away. This I must preach; I know nothing else. God helping me I will never go an inch beyond the Cross, for to me all else is vanity and vexation of spirit. Return unto thy rest, O my soul! Where else is there a glimpse of hope for thee but in Him who loved thee and gave Himself for thee?

I am sure Paul gloried in the Cross yet again because he saw it to be *the creator of enthusiasm*. Christianity finds its chief force in the enthusiasm which the Holy Ghost produces; and this comes from the Cross. The preaching of the Cross is the great weapon of the crusade against evil. A something lies within the truth of the Cross which sets the soul aglow; it touches the preacher's lips as with a live coal, and fires the hearers' hearts as with flame from the altar of God. We can on this gospel live, and for this gospel die. Atonement by blood, full deliverance from sin, perfect safety in Christ given to the believer, call a man to joy, to gratitude, to consecration, to decision, to patience, to holy living, to all consuming zeal. Therefore in the doctrine of the Cross we glory, neither will we be slow to speak it out with all our might.

III. My time has gone, or else I had intended to have enlarged upon the third head, of which I must now given you the mere outline. One of Paul's great reasons for glorying in the Cross was its action upon himself. What was its effect upon him?

The Cross is never without influence. Come where it may, it worketh for life or for death. "The world is crucified to me, and I unto the world." Self and the world are both crucified when Christ's Cross appears and is believed in. Beloved, what does Paul mean? Does he not mean just this—that ever since he had seen Christ he looked upon the world as a crucified, hanged up, gibbeted thing, which had no charms for him, whose frown he did not fear, whose love he did not court. The world had no more power over Paul than a criminal hanged upon a Cross. What power has a corpse on a gibbet? Such power had the world over Paul. The world despised him, and he could not go after the world if he would, and would not go after it if he could. He was dead to it, and it was dead to him: thus there was a double separation.

How does the Cross do this? To be under the dominion of this present evil world is horrible; how does the Cross help us to escape? Why, brethren, he that has ever seen the Cross looks upon the world's pomp and glory as a vain show. The pride of heraldry and the glitter of honour fade into meanness before the Crucified One. O ye great ones, what are your silks, and your furs, and your jewelry, and your gold, your stars and your garters, to one who has learned to glory in Christ crucified! The old clothes which belong to the hangman are quite as precious. The world's light is darkness when the Sun of Righteousness shines from the tree. What care we for all the kingdoms of the world and the glory thereof when once we see the thorn-crowned Lord? There is more glory about one nail of the Cross than about all the scepters of all kings. Let the knights of the Golden Fleece meet in chapter, and all the Knights of the Garter stand in their stalls, and what is all their splendor? Their glories wither before the inevitable hour of doom, while the glory of the Cross is eternal. Everything of earth grows dull and dim when seen by Cross light.

Paul also saw that the world's *wisdom* was absurd. That age talked of being wise and philosophical! Yes, and its philosophy brought it to crucify the Lord of glory. It did not know perfection, nor perceive the beauty of pure unselfishness. To slay the Messiah was the outcome of the culture of the Pharisee, to put to death the greatest teacher of all time was the ripe fruit of Sadducean thought. The cogitations of the present age have performed no greater feat than to deny the doctrine of satisfaction for sin. They have crucified our Lord afresh by their criticisms and their new theologies; and this is all the world's wisdom ever does. Its wisdom lies in scattering doubt, quenching hope, and denying certainty; and therefore the wisdom of the world to us is sheer folly. God hath poured contempt upon the wise men of this world; their foolish heart is blinded, they grope at noonday.

So, too, the apostle saw the world's *religion* to be nought. It was the world's religion that crucified Christ, the priests were at the bottom of it, the Pharisees urged it on. The church of the nation, the church of many ceremonies, the church which loved the traditions of the elders, the church of phylacteries and broad bordered garments—it was this church, which, acting by its officers, crucified the Lord. Paul therefore looked with pity upon priests and altars, and upon all the attempts of a Christless world to make up by finery of worship for the absence of the Spirit of God. Once see Christ on the Cross, and architecture and fine display become meretricious, tawdry things. The Cross calls for worship in spirit and in truth, and the world knows nothing of this.

And so it was with the world's *pursuits*. Some ran after honour, some toiled after learning, others labored for riches; but to Paul these were all trifles since he had seen Christ on the Cross. He that has seen Jesus die will never go into the toy business; he puts away childish things. A child, a pipe, a little soap, and many pretty bubbles: such is the world. The Cross alone can wean us from such play.

And so it was with the world's *pleasures* and with the world's *power*. The world, and everything that belonged to the world, had become as a corpse to Paul, and he was as a corpse to it. See where the corpse swings in chains on the gibbet. What a foul, rotten thing! We cannot endure it! Do not let it hang longer above ground to fill the air with pestilence. Let the dead be buried out of sight. The Christ that died upon the Cross now lives in our hearts. The Christ that took human guilt has taken possession of our souls, and henceforth we live only in Him, for Him, by Him. He has engrossed our affections. All our ardors burn for Him. God make it to be so with us, that we may glorify God and bless our age.

Paul concludes this epistle by saying, "From henceforth let no man trouble me: for I bear in my body the marks of the Lord Jesus." He was a slave, branded with his Master's name. That stamp could never be got out, for it was burned into his heart. Even thus, I trust, the doctrine of the atonement is our settled belief, and faith in it is part of our life. We are rooted and grounded in the unchanging verities. Do not try to convert me to your new views; I am past it. Give me over. You waste your breath. It is done: on this point the wax takes no further impress. I have taken up my standing, and will never quit it. A crucified Christ has taken such possession of my entire nature, spirit, soul, and body, that I am henceforth beyond the reach of opposing arguments.

Brethren, sisters, will you enlist under the conquering banner of the Cross? Once rolled in the dust and stained in blood, it now leads on the armies of the Lord to victory! Oh that all ministers would preach the true doctrine of the Cross! Oh that all Christian people would live under the influence of it, and we should then see brighter days than these! Unto the Crucified be glory forever and ever. Amen.

Cries from the Cross

The First Cry from the Cross

"Then said Jesus, 'Father, forgive them;
for they know not what they do.'"—Luke 23:34.

Our Lord was at that moment enduring the first pains of crucifixion; the executioners had just then driven the nails through His hands and feet. He must have been, moreover, greatly depressed, and brought into a condition of extreme weakness by the agony of the night in Gethsemane, and by the scourgings and cruel mockings which He had endured all through the morning, from Caiaphas, Pilate, Herod, and the Praetorian guards. Yet neither the weakness of the past, nor the pain of the present, could prevent Him from continuing in prayer. The Lamb of God was silent to men, but He was not silent to God. Dumb as a sheep before her shearers, He had not a word to say in His own defense to man, but He continues in His heart crying unto His Father, and no pain and no weakness can silence His holy supplications. Beloved, what an example our Lord herein presents to us! Let us continue in prayer so long as our heart beats; let no excess of suffering drive us away from the throne of grace, but rather let it drive us closer to it.

> Long as they live should Christians pray,
> For only while they pray they live.

To cease from prayer is to renounce the consolations which our case requires. Under all distractions of spirit, and overwhelmings of heart, great God, help us still to pray, and never from the mercy-seat may our footsteps be driven by despair. Our blessed Redeemer persevered in prayer even when the cruel iron rent His tender nerves, and blow after blow of the hammer jarred His whole frame with anguish; and this perseverance may be accounted for by the fact that He was so in the habit of prayer that He could not cease from it; He had acquired a mighty velocity of intercession which forbade Him to pause. Those long nights upon the cold mountain side, those many days which had been spent in solitude, those perpetual ejaculations which He was wont to dart up to Heaven, all these had formed in Him a habit so powerful, that the severest torments could not stay its force. Yet it was more than habit. Our Lord was baptized in the spirit of prayer; He lived in it; it lived in Him, it had come to be an element of His nature. He was like that precious spice, which, being bruised, doth not cease to give forth its perfume, but rather yieldeth it all the more abundantly because of the blows of the pestle, its fragrance being no outward and superficial quality, but an inward virtue essential to its nature, which the pounding in the mortar did but fetch from it, causing it to reveal its secret soul of sweetness. So Jesus prays, even as a bundle of myrrh gives forth its smell, or as birds sing because they cannot do otherwise. Prayer enwrapped His very soul as with a garment, and His heart went forth in such array. I repeat it, let this be our example—never, under any circumstances, however severe the trial, or depressing the difficulty, let us cease from prayer.

Observe, further, that our Lord, in the prayer before us, remains in the vigor of faith as to His Sonship. The extreme trial to which He now submitted himself could not prevent His holding fast His Sonship. His prayer begins, "Father." It was not without meaning that He taught us when we pray to say, "Our Father," for our prevalence in prayer will much depend upon our confidence in our relationship to God. Under great losses and crosses, one is apt to think that God is not dealing with us as a father with a child, but rather as a severe judge with a condemned criminal; but the cry of Christ, when He is brought to an extremity which we shall never reach, betrays no faltering in the spirit of sonship. In Gethsemane, when the bloody sweat fell fast upon the ground, His bitterest cry commenced with, *"My Father,"* asking that if it were possible the cup of gall might pass from him; He pleaded with the Lord as His Father, even as He over and over again had called Him on that dark and doleful night. Here, again, in this, the first of His seven expiring cries, it is "Father." O that the Spirit that makes us cry, "Abba, Father," may never cease His operations! May we never be brought into spiritual bondage by the suggestion, "If thou be the Son of God"; or if the tempter should so assail us, may we triumph as Jesus did in the hungry wilderness. May the Spirit which crieth, "Abba, Father," repel each unbelieving fear. When we are chastened, as we must be (for what son is there whom his father chasteneth not?) may we be in loving subjection to the Father of our spirits, and live; but never may we become captives to the spirit of bondage, so as to doubt the love of our gracious Father, or our share in His adoption.

More remarkable, however, is the fact that our Lord's prayer to His Father was not for himself. He continued on the cross to pray for himself, it is true, and His lamentable cry, "My God, my God, why hast thou forsaken me?" shows the personality of His prayer; but the first of the seven great cries on the cross has scarcely even an indirect reference to himself. It is, "Father, forgive *them.*" The petition is altogether for others, and though there is an allusion to the cruelties which they were exercising upon himself, yet it is remote; and you will observe, He does not say, "I forgive them"—that is taken for granted—he seems to lose sight of the fact that they were doing any wrong to himself, it is the wrong which they were doing to the Father that is on His mind, the insult which they are paying to the Father, in the person of the Son; He thinks not of himself at all. The cry, "Father, forgive them," is altogether unselfish. He himself is, in the prayer, as though He were not; so complete is His self-annihilation, that He loses sight of himself and His woes. My brethren, if there had ever been a time in the life of the Son of man when He might have rigidly confined His prayer to himself, without any one caviling thereat, surely it was when He was beginning His death throes. We could not marvel, if any man here were fastened to the stake, or fixed to a cross, if his first, and even his last and all his prayers, were for support under so arduous a trial. But see, the Lord Jesus began His prayer by pleading for others. See ye not what a great heart is here revealed! What a soul of compassion was in the Crucified! How Godlike, how divine! Was there ever such a one before him, who, even in the very pangs of death, offers as His first prayer an intercession for others? Let this unselfish spirit be in you also, my brethren. Look not every man upon his own things, but every man also on the things of others. Love your neighbors as yourselves, and as Christ has set before you this paragon of unselfishness, seek to follow him, treading in His steps.

There is, however, a crowning jewel in this diadem of glorious love. The Sun of Righteousness sets upon Calvary in a wondrous splendor; but amongst the bright colors which glorify His departure, there is this one—the prayer was not alone for others, but it was for His cruelest enemies. His enemies, did I say? There is more than that to be considered. It was not a prayer for enemies who had done Him an ill deed years before, but for those who were there and then murdering him. Not in cold blood did the Savior pray, after He had forgotten the injury, and could the more easily forgive it, but while the first red drops of blood were spurting on the hands which drove the nails; while yet the hammer was bestained with crimson gore, His blessed mouth poured out the fresh warm prayer, "Father, forgive them, for they know not what they do." Not that that prayer was confined to His immediate executioners. I believe that it was a far-reaching prayer, which included Scribes and Pharisees, Pilate and Herod, Jews and Gentiles—yea, the whole human race in a certain sense, since we were all concerned in that murder; but certainly the immediate persons, upon whom that prayer was poured like precious nard, were those who there and then were committing the brutal act of fastening Him to the accursed tree. How sublime is this prayer if viewed in such a light! It stands alone upon a mount of solitary glory. No other had been prayed like it before. It is true, Abraham, and Moses, and the prophets had prayed for the wicked; but not for wicked men who had pierced their hands and feet. It is true, that Christians have since that day offered the same prayer, even as Stephen cried, "Lay not this sin to their charge;" and many a martyr has made his last words at the stake words of pitying intercession for his persecutors; but you know where they learnt this: let me ask you where did *he* learn it? Was not Jesus the divine original? He learnt it nowhere; it leaped up from His own Godlike nature. A compassion peculiar to himself dictated this originality of prayer; the inward royalty of His love suggested to Him so memorable an intercession, which may serve us for a pattern, but of which no pattern had existed before. I feel as though I could better kneel before my Lord's cross at this moment than stand in this pulpit to talk to you. I want to adore him, I worship Him in heart for that prayer; if I knew nothing else of Him but this one prayer, I must adore Him, for that one matchless plea for mercy convinces me most overwhelmingly of the deity of Him who offered it, and fills my heart with reverent affection.

Thus have I introduced to you our Lord's first vocal prayer upon the cross. I shall now, if we are helped by God's Holy Spirit, make some use of it. First, we shall view it as *illustrative of our Savior's intercession*; secondly, we shall regard the text as *instructive of the church's work*; thirdly, we shall consider it as *suggestive to the unconverted*.

I. First, my dear brethren, let as look at this very wonderful text as illustrative of our Lord's intercession.

He prayed for His enemies then, He is praying for His enemies now; the past on the cross was an earnest of the present on the throne. He is in a higher place, and in a nobler condition, but His occupation is the same; He continues still before the eternal throne to present pleas on the behalf of guilty men, crying. "Father, O forgive them." All His intercession is in a measure like the intercession on Calvary, and Calvary's cries may help us to guess the character of the whole of His intercession above.

The first point in which we may see the character of His intercession is this—it is *most gracious*. Those for whom our Lord prayed, according to the text, did not deserve His prayer. They had done nothing which could call forth from Him a benediction as a reward for their endeavors in His service; on the contrary, they were most undeserving persons, who had conspired to put Him to death. They had crucified him, crucified Him wantonly and malignantly; they were even then taking away His innocent life. His clients were persons who, so far from being meritorious, were utterly undeserving of a single good wish from the Savior's heart. They certainly never asked Him to pray for them—it was the last thought in their minds to say, "Intercede for us, thou dying King! Offer petitions on our behalf, thou Son of God!" I will venture to believe the prayer itself, when they heard it, was either disregarded, and passed over with contemptuous indifference, or perhaps it was caught at as a theme for jest. I admit that it seems to be too severe upon humanity to suppose it possible that such a prayer could have been the theme for laughter, and yet there were other things enacted around the cross which were quite as brutal, and I can imagine that this also might have happened. Yet our Savior prayed for persons who did not deserve the prayer, but, on the contrary, merited a curse— persons who did not ask for the prayer, and even scoffed at it when they heard it. Even so in Heaven there stands the great High Priest, who pleads for guilty men—for *guilty* men, my hearers. There are none on Earth that deserve His intercession. He pleads for none on the supposition that they do deserve it. He stands there to plead as the just One on the behalf of the unjust. Not if any man be righteous, but "if any man sin, we have an advocate with the Father." Remember, too, that our great Intercessor pleads for such as never asked Him to plead for them. His elect, while yet dead in trespasses and sins, are the objects of His compassionate intercessions, and while they even *scoff* at His gospel, His heart of love is entreating the favor of Heaven on their behalf. See, then, beloved, if such be the truth, how sure you are to speed with God who earnestly ask the Lord Jesus Christ to plead for you. Some of you, with many tears and much earnestness, have been beseeching the Savior to be your advocate? Will He refuse you? Stands it to reason that He can? He pleads for those that reject His pleadings, much more for you who prize them beyond gold. Remember, my dear hearer, if there be nothing good in you, and if there be everything conceivable that is malignant and bad, yet none of these things can be any barrier to prevent

Christ's exercising the office of Intercessor for you. Even for you He will plead. Come, put your case into His hands; for you He will find pleas which you cannot discover for yourselves, and He will put the case to God for you as for His murderers, "Father, forgive them."

A second quality of His intercession is this—its *careful spirit*. You notice in the prayer, "Father, forgive them, for they know not what they do." Our Savior did, as it were, look His enemies through and through to find something in them that He could urge in their favor; but He could see nothing until His wisely affectionate eye lit upon their ignorance: "they know not what they do." How carefully He surveyed the circumstances, and the characters of those for whom He importuned. Just so it is with Him in Heaven. Christ is no careless advocate for His people. He knows your precise condition at this moment, and the exact state of your heart with regard to the temptation through which you are passing; more than that, He foresees the temptation which is awaiting you, and in His intercessions He takes note of the future event which His prescient eye beholds. "Satan has desired to have thee, that He may sift thee as wheat; but I have prayed for thee that thy faith fail not." Oh, the condescending tenderness of our great High Priest! He knows us better than we know ourselves. He understands every secret grief and groaning. You need not trouble your self about the wording of your prayer, He will put the wording right. And even the understanding as to the exact petition, if you should fail in it, He cannot, for as He knoweth what is the mind of God, so He knoweth what is your mind also. He can spy out some reason for mercy in you which you cannot detect in yourselves, and when it is so dark and cloudy with your soul that you cannot discern a foothold for a plea that you may urge with Heaven, the Lord Jesus has the pleas ready framed, and petitions ready drawn up, and He can present them acceptable before the mercy-seat. His intercession, then, you will observe is very gracious, and in the next place it is very thoughtful.

We must next note its *earnestness*. No one doubts who reads these words, "Father, forgive them, for they know not what they do," that they were Heaven-piercing in their fervor. Brethren, you are certain, even without a thought, that Christ was terribly in earnest in that prayer. But there is an argument to prove that. Earnest people are usually witty, and quick of understanding, to discover anything which may serve their turn. If you are pleading for life, and an argument for your being spared be asked of you, I will warrant you that you will think of one when no one else might. Now, Jesus was so in earnest for the salvation of His enemies, that He struck upon an argument for mercy which a less anxious spirit would not have thought of: "They know not what they do." Why, sirs, that was in strictest justice but a scant reason for mercy; and indeed, ignorance, if it be willful, does not extenuate sin, and yet the ignorance of many who surrounded the cross was a willful ignorance. They might have known that He was the Lord of glory. Was not Moses plain enough? Had not Esaias been very bold in his speech? Were not the signs and tokens such that one might as well doubt which is the sun in the firmament as the claims of Jesus to be the Messiah? Yet, for all that, the Savior, with marvelous earnestness and consequent dexterity, turns what might not have been a plea into a plea, and puts it thus: "Father, forgive them, *for* they know not what they do." Oh, how mighty are His pleas in Heaven, then, in their earnestness! Do not suppose that He is less quick of understanding there, or less intense in the vehemence of His entreaties. No, my brethren, the heart of Christ still labors with the eternal God. He is no slumbering intercessor, but, for Zion's sake, He doth not hold His peace, and for Jerusalem's sake, He doth not cease, nor will he, till her righteousness go forth as brightness, and her salvation as a lamp that burneth.

It is interesting to note, in the fourth place, that the prayer here offered helps us to judge of His intercession in Heaven as to its *continuance,* perseverance, and perpetuity. As I remarked before, if our Savior might have paused from intercessory prayer, it was surely when they fastened Him to the tree; when they were guilty of direct acts of deadly violence to His divine person, He might then have ceased to present petitions on their behalf. But sin cannot tie the tongue of our interceding Friend. Oh, what comfort is here! You have sinned, believer, you have grieved His Spirit, but you have not stopped that potent tongue which pleads for you. You have been unfruitful, perhaps, my brother, and like the barren tree, you deserve to be cut down; but your want of fruitfulness has not withdrawn the Intercessor from His place. He interposes at this moment, crying, "Spare it yet another year." Sinner, you have provoked God by long rejecting His mercy and going from bad to worse, but neither blasphemy nor unrighteousness, nor infidelity, shall stay the Christ of God from urging the suit of the very chief of sinners. He lives, and while He lives He pleads; and while there is a sinner upon Earth to be saved, there shall be an intercessor in Heaven to plead for him. These are but fragments of thought, but they will help you, I hope, to realize the intercession of our great High Priest.

Think yet again, this prayer of our Lord on Earth is like His prayer in Heaven, because of its *wisdom*. He seeks the best thing, and that which His clients most need, "Father, *forgive* them." That was the great point in hand; they wanted most of all there and then forgiveness from God. He does not say, "Father, enlighten them, for they know not what they do," for mere enlightenment would but have created torture of conscience and hastened on their Hell; but He crieth, "Father, forgive;" and while He used His voice, the precious drops of blood which were then distilling from the nail wounds were pleading too, and God heard, and doubtless did forgive. The first mercy which is needful to guilty sinners is forgiven sin. Christ wisely prays for the boon most wanted. It is so in Heaven; He pleads wisely and prudently. Let Him alone, He knows what to ask for at the divine hand. Go you to the mercy-seat, and pour out your desires as best you can, but when you have done so always put it thus, "O my Lord Jesus, answer no desire of mine if it be not according to thy judgment; and if in aught that I have asked I have failed to seek for what I want, amend my pleading, for thou art infinitely wiser than I." Oh, it is sweet to have a friend at court to perfect our petitions for us before they come unto the great King. I believe that there is never presented to God anything but a perfect prayer now; I mean, that before the great Father of us all, no prayer of His people ever comes up imperfect; there is nothing left out, and there is nothing to be erased; and this, not because their prayers were originally perfect in themselves; but because the Mediator makes them perfect through His infinite wisdom, and they come up before the mercy-seat molded according to the mind of God himself, and He is sure to grant such prayers.

Once more, this memorable prayer of our crucified Lord was like to His universal intercession in the matter of its *prevalence*. Those for whom He prayed were many of them forgiven. Do you remember that He said to His disciples when He bade them preach, "beginning at Jerusalem," and on that day when Peter stood up with the eleven, and charged the people that, with wicked hands they had crucified and slain the Savior, three thousand of these persons who were thus justly accused of His crucifixion became believers in him, and were baptized in His name. That was an answer to Jesus' prayer. The priests were at the bottom of our Lord's murder, they were the most guilty; but it is said, "a great company also of the priests believed." Here was another answer to the prayer. Since all men had their share representatively, Gentiles as well as Jews, in the death of Jesus, the gospel was soon preached to the Jews, and within a short time it was preached to the Gentiles also. Was not this prayer, "Father, forgive them," like a stone cast into a lake, forming at first a narrow circle, and then a wider ring, and soon a larger sphere, until the whole lake is covered with circling waves? Such a prayer as this, cast into the whole world, first created a little ring of Jewish converts and of priests, and then a wider circle of such as were beneath the Roman sway; and today its circumference is wide as the globe itself, so that tens of thousands are saved through the prevalence of this one intercession: "Father, forgive them." It is certainly so with Him in Heaven, He never pleads in vain. With bleeding hands, He yet won the day; with feet fastened to the wood, He was yet victorious; forsaken of God and despised of the people, He was yet triumphant in His pleas; how much more so now the tiara is about His brow, His hand grasps the universal scepter, and His feet are shod with silver sandals, and He is crowned King of kings, and Lord of lords! If tears and cries out of weakness were omnipotent, even more mighty if possible must be that sacred authority which as the risen Priest He claims when He stands before the Father's throne to mention the covenant which the Father made with him. O ye trembling believers, trust Him with your concerns! Come hither, ye guilty, and ask Him to plead for you. O you that cannot pray, come, ask Him to intercede for you. Broken hearts and weary heads, and disconsolate bosoms, come ye to Him who into the golden censer will put His merits, and then place your prayers with them, so that they shall come up as the smoke of perfume, even as a fragrant cloud into the nostrils of the Lord God of hosts, who will smell a sweet savior, and accept you and your prayers in the Beloved. We have now opened up more than enough sea-room for your meditations at home this afternoon, and, therefore we leave this first point. We have had an illustration in the prayer of Christ on the cross of what His prayers always are in Heaven.

II. Secondly, the text is instructive of the church's work.

As Christ was, so His church is to be in this world. Christ came into this world not to be ministered unto, but to minister, not to be honored, but to save others. His church, when she understands her work, will perceive that she is not here to gather to herself wealth or honor, or to seek any temporal aggrandizement and position; she is here unselfishly to live, and if need be, unselfishly to die for the deliverance of the lost sheep, the salvation of lost men. Brethren, Christ's prayer on the cross I told you was altogether an unselfish one. He does not remember himself in it. Such ought to be the church's life-prayer, the church's active interposition on the behalf of sinners. She ought to live never for her ministers or for herself, but ever for the lost sons of men. Imagine you that churches are formed to maintain ministers? Do you conceive that the church exists in this land merely that so much salary may be given to bishops, and deans, and prebends, and curates, and I know not what? My brethren, it were well if the whole thing were abolished if that were its only aim. The aim of the church is not to provide outdoor relief for the younger sons of the nobility; when they have not brains enough to win anyhow else their livelihood, they are stuck into family livings. Churches are not made that men of ready speech may stand up on Sundays and talk, and so win daily bread from their admirers. Nay, there is another end and aim from this. These places of worship are not built that you may sit here comfortably, and hear something that shall make you pass away your Sundays with pleasure. A church in London which does not exist to do good in the slums, and dens, and kennels of the city, is a church that has no reason to justify its longer existing. A church that does not exist to reclaim heathenism, to fight with evil, to destroy error, to put down falsehood, a church that does not exist to take the side of the poor, to denounce injustice and to hold up righteousness, is a church that has no right to be. Not for thyself, O church, dost thou exist, any more than Christ existed for himself. His glory was that He laid aside His glory, and the glory of the church is when she lays aside her respectability and her dignity, and counts it to be her glory to gather together the outcasts, and her highest honor to seek amid the foulest mire the priceless jewels for which Jesus shed His blood. To rescue souls from Hell and lead to God, to hope, to Heaven, this is her heavenly occupation. O that the church would always feel this! Let her have her bishops and her preachers, and let them be supported, and let everything be done for Christ's sake decently and in order, but let the end be looked to, namely, the conversion of the wandering, the teaching of the ignorant, the help of the poor, the maintenance of the right, the putting down of the wrong, and the upholding at all hazards of the crown and kingdom of our Lord Jesus Christ.

Now the prayer of Christ had *a great spirituality of aim.* You notice that nothing is sought for these people but that which concerns their souls, "Father, *forgive* them." And I believe the church will do well when she recollects that she wrestles not with flesh and blood, nor with principalities and powers, but with spiritual wickedness, and that what she has to dispense is not the law and order by which magistrates may be upheld, or tyrannies pulled down, but the spiritual government by which hearts are conquered to Christ, and judgments are brought into subjection to His truth. I believe that the more the church of God strains after, before God, the forgiveness of sinners, and the more she seeks in her life prayer to teach sinners what sin is, and what the blood of Christ is, and what the Hell that must follow if sin be not washed out, and what the Heaven is which will be ensured to all those who are cleansed from sin, the more she keeps to this the better. Press forward as one man, my brethren, to secure the root of the matter in the forgiveness of sinners. As to all the evils that afflict humanity, by all means take your share in battling with them; let temperance be maintained, let education be supported; let reforms, political and ecclesiastical, be pushed forward as far as you have the time and effort to spare, but the first business of every Christian man and woman is with the hearts and consciences of men as they stand before the everlasting God. O let nothing turn you aside from your divine errand of mercy to undying souls. This is your one business. Tell to sinners that sin will damn them, that Christ alone can take away sin, and make this the one passion of your souls,

> Father, forgive them, forgive them! Let them know how to be forgiven. Let them be actually forgiven, and let me never rest except as I am the means of bringing sinners to be forgiven, even the guiltiest of them.

Our Savior's prayer teaches the church that while her spirit should be unselfish, and her aim should be spiritual, *the range of her mission is* to be unlimited. Christ prayed for the wicked—what if I say the most wicked of the wicked—that ribald crew that had surrounded His cross! He prayed for the ignorant. Doth He not say, "They know not what they do"? He prayed for His persecutors; the very persons who were most at enmity with him, lay nearest to His heart. Church of God, your mission is not to the respectable few who will gather about your ministers to listen respectfully to their words; your mission is not to the elite and the eclectic, the intelligent who will criticize your words and pass judgment upon every syllable of your teaching; your mission is not to those who treat you kindly, generously, affectionately, not to these I mean alone, though certainly to these as among the rest. But your great errand is to the harlot, to the thief, to the swearer and the drunkard, to the most depraved and debauched. If no one else cares for these, the church always must, and if there be any who are first in her prayers it should be these who alas! are generally last in our thoughts. The ignorant we ought diligently to consider. It is not enough for the preacher that he preaches so that those instructed from their youth up can understand him; he must think of those to whom the commonest phrases of theological truth are as meaningless as the jargon of an unknown tongue; he must preach so as to reach the meanest comprehension; and if the ignorant many come not to hear him, he must use such means as best he may to induce them, nay, compel them to hear the good news. The gospel is meant also for those who persecute religion; it aims its arrows of love against the hearts of its foes. If there be any whom we should first seek to bring to Jesus, it should be just these who are the farthest off and most opposed to the gospel of Christ. "Father, *forgive them;* if thou dost pardon none besides, yet be pleased to forgive *them.*"

So, too, the church should be *earnest as* Christ was; and if she be so, she will be quick to notice any ground of hope in those she deals with, quick to observe any plea that she may use with God for their salvation.

She must be *hopeful* too, and surely no church ever had a more hopeful sphere than the church of this present age. If ignorance be a plea with God, look on the heathen at this day—millions of them never heard Messiah's name. Forgive them, great God, indeed they know not what they do. If ignorance be some ground for hope, there is hope enough in this great city of London, for have we not around us hundreds of thousands to whom the simplest truths of the gospel would be the greatest novelties? Brethren, it is sad to think that this country should still lie under such a pall of ignorance, but the sting of so dread a fact is blunted with hope when we read the Savior's prayer aright—it helps us to hope while we cry, "Forgive them, for they know not what they do."

It is the church's business to seek after the most fallen and the most ignorant, and to seek them perseveringly. She should never stay her hand from doing good. If the Lord be coming tomorrow, it is no reason why you Christian people should subside into mere talkers and readers, meeting together for mutual comfort, and forgetting the myriads of perishing souls. If it be true that this world is going to pieces in a fortnight, and that Louis Napoleon is the Apocalyptic beast, or if it be not true, I care not a fig, it makes no difference to my duty, and does not change my service. Let my Lord come when He will, while I labor for Him, I am ready for His appearing. The business of the church is still to watch for the salvation of souls. If she stood gazing, as modern prophets would have her; if she gave up her mission to indulge in speculative interpretations, she might well be afraid of her Lord's coming; but if she goes about her work, and with incessant toil searches out her Lord's precious jewels, she shall not be ashamed when her Bridegroom cometh.

My time has been much too short for so vast a subject as I have under-taken, but I wish I could speak words that were as loud as thunder, with a sense and earnestness as mighty as the lightning. I would fain excite every Christian here, and kindle in him a right idea of what his work is as a part of Christ's church. My brethren, you must not live to yourselves; the ac-cumulation of money, the bringing up of your children, the building of houses, the earning of your daily bread, all this you may do; but there must be a greater object than this if you are to be Christlike, as you should be, since you are bought with Jesus' blood. Begin to live for others, make it apparent unto all men that you are not yourselves the end-all and be-all of your own existence, but that you are spending and being spent, that through the good you do to men, God may be glorified, and Christ may see in you His own image and be satisfied.

III. Time fails me, but the last point was to be a word suggestive to the unconverted.

Listen attentively to these sentences. I will make them as terse and con-densed as possible. Some of you here are not saved. Now, some of you have been very ignorant, and when you sinned you did not know what you did. You knew you were sinners, you knew that, but you did not know the far-reaching guilt of sin. You have not been attending the house of prayer long, you have not read your Bible, you have not Christian parents. Now you are beginning to be anxious about your souls. Remember your ignorance does not excuse you, or else Christ would not say, "Forgive them;" they must be forgiven, even those that know not what they do, hence they are individu-ally guilty; but still that ignorance of yours gives you just a little gleam of hope. The times of your ignorance God winked at, but now commandeth all men everywhere to repent. Bring forth, therefore, fruits meet for repen-tance. The God whom you have ignorantly forgotten is willing to pardon and ready to forgive. The gospel is just this: trust Jesus Christ who died for the guilty, and you shall be saved. O may God help you to do so this very morning, and you will become new men and new women, a change will take place you equal to a new birth; you will be new creatures in Christ Jesus.

But ah! my friends, there are some here for whom even Christ himself could not pray this prayer, in the widest sense at any rate, "Father, forgive them; for they know not what they do," for you have known what you did, and every ser-mon you hear, and especially every impression that is made upon your under-standing and conscience by the gospel, adds to your responsibility, and takes away from you the excuse of not knowing what you do. Ah! sirs, you know that there is the world and Christ, and that you cannot have both. You know that there is sin and God, and that you cannot serve both. You know that there are the pleasures of evil and the pleasures of Heaven, and that you cannot have both. Oh! in the light which God has given you, may His Spirit also come and help you to choose that which true wisdom would make you choose. Decide today for God, for Christ, for Heaven. The Lord decide you for His name's sake. Amen.

Christ's Plea for Ignorant Sinners

"Then said Jesus, 'Father, forgive them; for they know not what they do.'"—Luke 23:34.

What tenderness we have here; what self-forgetfulness; what almighty love! Jesus did not say to those who crucified him, "Begone!" One such word, and they must have all fled. When they came to take Him in the garden, they went backward, and fell to the ground, when He spoke but a short sentence; and now that He is on the cross, a single syllable would have made the whole company fall to the ground, or flee away in fright.

Jesus says not a word in His own defense. When He prayed to His Father, He might justly have said, "Father, note what they do to thy beloved Son. Judge them for the wrong they do to Him who loves them, and who has done all He can for them." But there is no prayer against them in the words that Jesus utters. It was written of old, by the prophet Isaiah, "He made intercession for the transgressors;" and here it is fulfilled. He pleads for His murderers, "Father, forgive them."

He does not utter a single word of upbraiding. He does not say, "Why do ye this? Why pierce the hands that fed you? Why nail the feet that followed after you in mercy? Why mock the Man who loved to bless you?" No; not a word even of gentle upbraiding, much less of anything like a curse. "Father, forgive them." You notice, Jesus does not say, "I forgive them," but you may read that between the lines. He says that all the more because He does not say it in words. But He has laid aside His majesty, and is fastened to the cross; and therefore He takes the humble position of a suppliant, rather than the more lofty place of one who had power to forgive. How often, when men say, "I forgive you," is there a kind of selfishness about it! At any rate, self is asserted in the very act of forgiving.

Jesus takes the place of a pleader, a pleader for those who were committing murder upon himself. Blessed be His name!

This word of the cross we shall use tonight, and we shall see if we cannot gather something from it for our instruction; for, though we were not there, and we did not actually put Jesus to death, yet we really caused His death, and we, too, crucified the Lord of glory; and His prayer for us was, "Father, forgive them; for they know not what they do."

I am not going to handle this text so much by way of exposition, as by way of experience. I believe there are many here, to whom these words will be very appropriate. This will be our line of thought. First, *we were in measure ignorant;* secondly, *we confess that this ignorance is no excuse;* thirdly, *we bless our Lord for pleading for us;* and fourthly, *we now rejoice in the pardon we have obtained.* May the Holy Spirit graciously help us in our meditation!

I. Looking back upon our past experience, let me say, first, that we were in measure ignorant.

We who have been forgiven, we who have been washed in the blood of the Lamb, we once sinned, in a great measure, through ignorance. Jesus says, "They know not what they do." Now, I shall appeal to you, brothers and sisters, when you lived under the dominion of Satan, and served yourselves and sin, was there not a measure of ignorance in it? You can truly say, as we said in the hymn we sang just now—

"*Alas! I knew not what I did.*"

It is true, first, that we were ignorant of *the awful meaning of sin.* We began to sin as children; we knew that it was wrong, but we did not know all that sin meant. We went on to sin as young men; peradventure we plunged into much wickedness. We knew it was wrong; but we did not see the end from the beginning. It did not appear to us as rebellion against God. We did not think that we were presumptuously defying God, setting at naught His wisdom, defying His power, deriding His love, spurning His holiness; yet we were doing all that. There is an abysmal depth in sin. You cannot see to the bottom of it. When we rolled sin under our tongue as a sweet morsel, we did not know all the terrible ingredients compounded in that deadly bittersweet. We were in a measure ignorant of the tremendous crime we committed when we dared to live in rebellion against God. So far, I think, you go with me.

We did not know, at that time, *God's great love to us.* I did not know that He had chosen me from before the foundation of the world; I never dreamed of that. I did not know that Christ stood for me as my Substitute, to redeem me from among men. I did not know that He had espoused me unto himself in righteousness and in faithfulness, to be one with Him forever. You, dear friends, who now know the love of Christ, did not understand it then. You did not know that you were sinning against eternal love, against infinite compassion, against a distinguishing love such as God had fixed on you from eternity. So far, we knew not what we did.

I think, too, that we did not know all that we were doing in *our rejection of Christ, and putting Him to grief.* He came to us in our youth; and impressed by a sermon we began to tremble, and to seek His face; but we were decoyed back to the world, and we refused Christ. Our mother's tears, our father's prayers, our teacher's admonitions, often moved us; but we were very stubborn, and we rejected Christ. We did not know that, in that rejection, we were virtually putting Him away and crucifying him. We were denying His Godhead, or else we should have worshiped him. We were denying His love, or else we should have yielded to him. We were practically, in every act of sin, taking the hammer and the nails, and fastening Christ to the cross, but we did not know it. Perhaps, if we had known it, we should not have crucified the Lord of glory. We did know we were doing wrong; but we did not know all the wrong that we were doing.

Nor did we know fully *the meaning of our delays.* We hesitated: we were on the verge of conversion; we went back, and turned again to our old follies. We were hardened, Christless, prayerless still; and each one of us said, "Oh, I am only waiting a little while till I have fulfilled my present engagements, till I am a little older, till I have seen a little more of the world!" The fact is, we were refusing Christ, and choosing the pleasures of sin instead of him; and every hour of delay was an hour of crucifying Christ, grieving His Spirit, and choosing this harlot world in the place of the lovely and ever-blessed Christ. We did not know that.

I think we may add one thing more. *We did not know the meaning of our self-righteousness.* We used to think, some of us, that we had a righteousness of our own. We had been to church regularly, or we had been to the meeting-house whenever it was open. We were christened; we were confirmed; or, peradventure, we rejoiced that we never had either of those things done to us. Thus, we put our confidence in ceremonies, or the absence of ceremonies. We said our prayers; we read a chapter in the Bible night and morning; we did—oh I do not know what we did not do! But there we rested: we were righteous in our own esteem. We had not any particular sin to confess, nor any reason to lie in the dust before the throne of God's majesty. We were about as good as we could be; and we did not know that we were even then perpetrating the highest insult upon Christ; for, if we were not sinners, why did Christ die; and, if we had a righteousness of our own which was good enough, why did Christ come here to work out a righteousness for us? We made out Christ to be a superfluity, by considering that we were good enough without resting in His atoning sacrifice. Ah, we did not think we were doing that! We thought we were pleasing God by our religiousness, by our outward performances, by our ecclesiastical correctness; but all the while we were setting up anti-Christ in the place of Christ. We were making out that Christ was not wanted; we were robbing Him of His office and glory! Alas! Christ could say of us, with regard to all these things, "They know not what they do." I want you to look quietly at the time past wherein you served sin, and just see whether there was not a darkness upon your mind, a blindness in your spirit, so that you did not know what you did.

II. *Well now, secondly, we confess that this ignorance is no excuse.*

Our Lord might urge it as a plea; but we never could. We did not know what we did, and so we were not guilty to the fullest possible extent; but we were guilty enough, therefore let us own it.

For first, remember, *the law never allows this as a plea.* In our own English law, a man is supposed to know what the law is. If he breaks it, it is no excuse to plead that he did not know it. It may be regarded by a judge as some extenuation; but the law allows nothing of the kind. God gives us the law, and we are bound to keep it. If I erred through not knowing the law, still it was a sin. Under the Mosaic law, there were sins of ignorance, and for these there were special offerings. The ignorance did not blot out the sin. That is clear in my text; for, if ignorance rendered an action no longer sinful, then why should Christ say, "Father, forgive them"? But He does; He asks for mercy for what is sin, even though the ignorance in some measure be supposed to mitigate the criminality of it.

But, dear friends, *we might have known.* If we did not know, it was because we would not know. There was the preaching of the Word; but we did not care to hear it. There was this blessed Book; but we did not care to read it. If you and I had sat down, and looked at our conduct by the light of Holy Scripture, we might have known much more of the evil of sin, and much more of the love of Christ, and much more of the ingratitude which is possible in refusing Christ, and not coming to him.

In addition to that, *we did not think.* "Oh, but," you say, "young people never do think!" But young people should think. If there is anybody who need not think, it is the old man, whose day is nearly over. If he does think, he has but a very short time in which to improve; but the young have all their life before them. If I were a carpenter, and had to make a box, I should not think about it after I had made the box; I should think, before I began to cut my timber, what sort of box it was to be. In every action, a man thinks before he begins, or else he is a fool. A young man ought to think more than anybody else, for now he is, as it were, making his box. He is beginning his life-plan; he should be the most thoughtful of all men. Many of us, who are now Christ's people, would have known much more about our Lord if we had given Him more careful consideration in our earlier days. A man will consider about taking a wife, he will consider about taking a business, he will consider about buying a horse or a cow; but he will not consider about the claims of Christ, and the claims of the Most High God; and this renders his ignorance willful, and inexcusable.

Beside that, dear friends, although we have confessed to ignorance, *in many sins we did know a great deal.* Come, let me quicken your memories. There were times when you knew that such an action was wrong, when you started back from it. You looked at the gain it would bring you, and you sold your soul for that price, and deliberately did what you were well aware was wrong. Are there not some here, saved by Christ, who must confess that, at times, they did violence to their conscience? They did despite to the Spirit of God, quenched the light of Heaven, drove the Spirit away from them, distinctly knowing what they were doing. Let us bow before God in the silence of our hearts, and own to all this. We hear the Master say, "Father, forgive them; for they know not what they do." Let us add our own tears as we say,

> And forgive us, also, because in some things we did know; in all things we might have known; but we were ignorant for want of thought, which thought was a solemn duty which we ought to have rendered to God.

One thing more I will say on this head. When a man is ignorant and does not know what he ought to do, what should he do? Well he should do nothing till he does know. But here is the mischief of it, that *when we did not know, yet we chose to do the wrong thing.* If we did not know, why did we not choose the right thing? But, being in the dark, we never turned to the right; but always blundered to the left, from sin to sin. Does not this show us how depraved our hearts are? Though we are seeking to be right, when we are let alone, we go wrong of ourselves. Leave a child alone;

leave a man alone; leave a tribe alone without teaching and instruction; what comes of it? Why, the same as when you leave a field alone. It never, by any chance, produces wheat or barley. Leave it alone, and there are rank weeds, and thorns, and briars, showing that the natural set of the soil is towards producing that which is worthless. O friends, confess the innate evil of your hearts as well as the evil of your lives, in that when you did not know, yet, having a perverse instinct, you chose, the evil, and refused the good; and, when you did not know enough of Christ, and did not think enough of Him to know whether you ought to have Him or not, you would not come unto Him that you might have life. You needed light; but you shut your eyes to the sun. You were thirsty; but you would not drink of the living spring and so your ignorance, though it was there, was a criminal ignorance which you must confess before the Lord. Oh, come ye to the cross, ye who have been there before, and have lost your burden there. Come and confess your guilt over again; and clasp that cross afresh and look to Him who bled upon it, and praise His dear name that He once prayed for you, "Father, forgive them; for they know not what they do."

Now, I am going a step further. We were in a measure ignorant; but we confess that that measurable ignorance was no excuse.

III. Now, thirdly, we bless our Lord for pleading for us.

Do you notice when it was that Jesus pleaded? It was, *while they were crucifying Him.* They had just driven in the nails, they had lifted up the cross, and dashed it down into its socket, and dislocated all His bones, so that He could say, "I am poured out like water, and all my bones are out of joint." Ah, dear friends, it was then that, instead a cry or a groan, this dear Son of God said, "Father, forgive them for they know not what they do." They did not ask forgiveness for themselves; Jesus asked forgiveness for them. Their hands were imbrued in His blood; and it was then, even then, that He prayed them. Let us think of the great love wherewith He loved us, eve while we were yet sinners, when we rioted in sin, when we drank down as the ox drinketh down water. Even then He prayed for you, "While we were yet without strength, in due time Christ died for the ungodly." Bless His name tonight. He prayed for you when you did not pray for yourself. He prayed for you when you were crucifying him.

Then think of His plea, He *pleads His Sonship.* He says, "Father forgive them." He was the Son of God, and He puts His divine Sonship into the scale on our behalf. He seems to say, "Father, as I am thy Son, grant me this request, and pardon these rebels. Father, forgive them." The filial rights of Christ were very great. He was the Son of God, not as we are, by adoption, but by nature; by eternal filiation, He was the Son of the Highest, "Light of light, very God of very God," the second Person in the Divine Trinity; and He puts that Sonship here before God, and says, "Father, Father, forgive them." Oh, the power of that word from the Son's lip when He is wounded, when He is in agony, when He is dying! He says, "Father, Father, grant my one request; O Father, forgive them; for they know not what they do"; and the great Father bows His awful head, in token that the petition is granted.

Then notice, that Jesus here, silently, but really *pleads His sufferings.* The attitude of Christ when He prayed this prayer is very noteworthy. His hands were stretched upon the transverse beam; His feet were fastened to the upright tree; and there He pleaded. Silently His hands and feet were pleading, and His agonized body from every sinew and muscle pleaded with God. His sacrifice was presented there before the Father's face; not yet complete, but in His will complete; and so it is His cross that takes up the plea, "Father, forgive them." O blessed Christ! It is thus that we have been forgiven, for His Sonship and His cross have pleaded with God, and have prevailed on our behalf.

I love this prayer, also, because of the *indistinctness of* it. It is "Father, forgive them." He does not say, "Father, forgive the soldiers who have nailed me here." He includes them. Neither does He say, "Father, forgive the people who are beholding me." He means them. Neither does He say, "Father, forgive sinners in ages to come who will sin against me." But He means them. Jesus does not mention them by any accusing name: "Father, forgive my enemies. Father, forgive my murderers." No, there is no word of accusation upon those dear lips. "Father, forgive them." Now into that pronoun "them" I feel that I can crawl. Can you get in there? Oh, by a humble faith, appropriate the cross of Christ by trusting in it; and get into that big little word "them"! It seems like a chariot of mercy that has come down to earth, into which a man may step, and it shall bear Him up to Heaven. "Father, forgive them."

Notice, also, what it was that Jesus asked for; to omit that, would be to leave out the very essence of His prayer. *He asked for full absolution for His enemies:*

Father, forgive them. Do not punish them; forgive them. Do not remember their sin; forgive it, blot it out; throw it into the depths of the sea. Remember it not, my Father. Mention it not against them any more forever. Father, forgive them.

Oh, blessed prayer, for the forgiveness of God is broad and deep! When man forgives, he leaves the remembrance of the wrong behind; but when God pardons, He says, "I will forgive their iniquity, and I will remember their sin no more." It is this that Christ asked for you and me long before we had any repentance, or any faith; and in answer to that prayer, we were brought to feel our sin, we were brought to confess it, and to believe in him; and now, glory be to His name, we can bless Him for having pleaded for us, and obtained the forgiveness of all our sins.

IV. *I come now to my last remark, which is this: we now rejoice in the pardon we have obtained.*

Have you obtained pardon? Is this your song?

> *Now, oh joy! my sins are pardon'd,*
> *Now I can, and do believe.*

I have a letter in my pocket, from a man of education and standing, who has been an agnostic; he says that he was a sarcastic agnostic, and he writes praising God, and invoking every blessing upon my head for bringing Him to the Savior's feet. He says, "I was without happiness for this life, and without hope for the next." I believe that that is a truthful description of many an unbeliever. What hope is there for the world to come, apart from the cross of Christ? The best hope such a man has is that he may die the death of a dog, and there may be an end of him. What is the hope of the Romanist when he comes to die? I feel so sorry for many devout and earnest friends, for I do not know what their hope is. They do not hope to go to Heaven yet, at any rate; some purgatorial pains must be endured first. Ah, this is a poor, poor faith to die on, to have such a hope as that to trouble your last thoughts. I do not know of any religion but that of Christ Jesus which tells us of sin pardoned, absolutely pardoned. Now, listen. Our teaching is not that, when you come to die, you may, perhaps, find out that it is all right, but, "Beloved, now are we the sons of God." "He that believeth on the Son hath everlasting life." He has it now, and he knows it, and he rejoices in it. So I come back to the last head of my discourse, we rejoice in the pardon Christ has obtained for us. We are pardoned. I hope that the larger portion of this audience can say, "By the grace of God, we know that we are washed in the blood of the Lamb."

Pardon has come to us through Christ's plea. Our hope lies in the plea of Christ, and specially in His death. If Jesus paid my debt, and He did if I am a believer in him, then I am out of debt. If Jesus bore the penalty of my sin, and He did if I am a believer, then there is no penalty for me to pay, for we can say to him,

> *Complete atonement thou hast made,*
> *And to the utmost farthing paid*
> *Whate'er thy people owed:*
> *Nor can His wrath on me take place,*
> *If sheltered in thy righteousness,*
> *And sprinkled with thy blood.*
>
> *If thou hast my discharge procured,*
> *And freely in my room endured*
> *The whole of wrath divine:*
> *Payment God cannot twice demand,*
> *First at my bleeding Surety's hand,*
> *And then again at mine.*

If Christ has borne my punishment, I shall never bear it. Oh, what joy there is in this blessed assurance! Your hope that you are pardoned lies in this, that Jesus died. Those dear wounds of His bleed life for you.

We praise Him for our pardon because *we do know now what we did.* Oh, brethren, I know not how much we ought to love Christ, because we sinned against Him so grievously! Now we know that sin is "exceeding sinful." Now we know that sin crucified Christ. Now we know that we stabbed our heavenly Lover to His heart. We slew, with ignominious death, our best and dearest Friend and Benefactor. We know that now; and we could almost weep tears of blood to think that we ever treated Him as we did. But it is all forgiven, all gone. Oh, let us bless that dear Son of God, who has put away even such sins as ours! We feel them more now than ever before. We know they are forgiven, and our grief is because of the pain that the purchase of our forgiveness cost our Savior. We never knew what our sins really were till we saw Him in a bloody sweat. We never knew the crimson hue of our sins till we read our pardon written in crimson lines with His precious blood. Now, we see our sin, and yet we do not see it; for God has pardoned it, blotted it out, cast it behind His back forever.

Henceforth *ignorance*, such as we have described, *shall be hateful to us.* Ignorance of Christ and eternal things shall be hateful to us. If, through ignorance, we have sinned, we will have done with that ignorance. We will be students of His Word. We will study that masterpiece of all the sciences, the knowledge of Christ crucified. We will ask the Holy Ghost to drive far from us the ignorance that gendereth sin. God grant that we may not fall into sins of ignorance any more; but may we be able to say, "I know whom I have believed; and henceforth I will seek more knowledge, till I comprehend, with all saints, what are the heights, and depths, and lengths, and breadths of the love of Christ, and know the love of God, which passeth knowledge!"

I put in a practical word here. If you rejoice that you are pardoned, *show your gratitude by your imitation of Christ*. There was never before such a plea as this, "Father, forgive them; for they know not what they do." Plead like that for others. Has anybody been injuring you? Are there persons who slander you? Pray tonight, "Father, forgive them; for they know not what they do." Let us always render good for evil, blessing for cursing; and when we are called to suffer through the wrong-doing of others, let us believe that they would not act as they do if it were not because of their ignorance. Let us pray for them; and make their very ignorance the plea for their forgiveness: "Father, forgive them; for they know not what they do."

I want you also to think of the millions of London just now. See those miles of streets, pouring out their children this evening; but look at those public-houses with the crowds streaming in and out. Go down our streets by moonlight. See what I almost blush to tell. Follow men and women, too, to their homes, and be this your prayer: "Father, forgive them; for they know not what they do." That silver bell—keep it always ringing. What did I say? That silver bell? Nay, it is the *golden* bell upon the priest's garments. Wear it on your garments, ye priests of God, and let it always ring out its golden note, "Father, forgive them; for they know not what they do." If I can set all God's saints imitating Christ with such a prayer as this, I shall not have spoken in vain.

Brethren, I see *reason for hope in the very ignorance that surrounds us*. I see hope for this poor city of ours, hope for this poor country, hope for Africa, China, and India. "They know not what they do." Here is a strong argument in their favor, for they are more ignorant than we were. They know less of the evil of sin, and less of the hope of eternal life, than we do. Send up this petition, ye people of God! Heap your prayers together with cumulative power, send up this fiery shaft of prayer, straight to the heart of God, while Jesus from His throne shall add His prevalent intercession, "Father, forgive them; for they know not what they do."

If there be any unconverted people here, and I know that there are some, we will mention them in our private devotion, as well as in the public assembly; and we will pray for them in words like these, "Father, forgive them; for they know not what they do." May God bless you all, for Jesus Christ's sake! Amen.

The Believing Thief

*"And he said unto Jesus, 'Lord, remember me when thou comest
into thy kingdom.' And Jesus said unto him, 'Verily I say unto thee,
today shalt thou be with me in paradise.'"—Luke 23:42, 43.*

Some time ago I preached upon the whole story of the dying thief. I do
not propose to do the same today, but only to look at it from one particular point of view. The story of the salvation of the dying thief is a
standing instance of the power of Christ to save, and of his abundant willingness to receive all that come to him, in whatever plight they may be. I
cannot regard this act of grace as a solitary instance, any more than the salvation of Zacchæus, the restoration of Peter, or the call of Saul, the perse-
cutor. Every conversion is, in a sense, singular: no two are exactly alike,
and yet any one conversion is a type of others. The case of the dying thief
is much more similar to our conversion than it is dissimilar; in point of
fact, his case may be regarded as typical, rather than as an extraordinary
incident. So I shall use it at this time. May the Holy Spirit speak through it
to the encouragement of those who are ready to despair!

Remember, beloved friends, that our Lord Jesus, at the time He saved
this malefactor, was at His lowest. His glory had been ebbing out in Gethsemane, and before Caiaphas and Herod, and Pilate; but it had now reached
the utmost low-water mark. Stripped of His garments, and nailed to the
cross, our Lord was mocked by a ribald crowd, and was dying in agony: then
was He "numbered with the transgressors," and made as the offscouring of
all things. Yet, while in that condition, He achieved this marvelous deed of
grace. Behold the wonder wrought by the Savior when emptied of all His
glory, and hanged up a spectacle of shame upon the brink of death! How certain is it that He can do wonders of mercy now, seeing that great He has

returned unto His glory, and sitteth upon the throne of light! "He is able to save them to the uttermost that come unto God by him, seeing He ever liveth to make intercession for them." If a dying Savior saved the thief, my argument is, that He can do even more now that He liveth and reigneth. All power is given unto Him in Heaven and in earth; can anything at this present time surpass the power of His grace?

It is not only the weakness of our Lord which makes the salvation of the penitent thief memorable; it is the fact that the dying malefactor saw it before his very eyes. Can you put yourself into his place, and suppose yourself to be looking upon one who hangs in agony upon a cross? Could you readily believe Him to be the Lord of glory, who would soon come to His kingdom? That was no mean faith which, at such a moment, could believe in Jesus as Lord and King. If the apostle Paul were here, and wanted to add a New Testament chapter to the eleventh of Hebrews, he might certainly commence his instances of remarkable faith with this thief, who believed in a crucified, derided, and dying Christ, and cried to Him as to one whose kingdom would surely come. The thief's faith was the more remarkable because he was himself in great pain, and bound to die. It is not easy to exercise confidence when you are tortured with deadly anguish. Our own rest of mind has at times been greatly hindered by pain of body. When we are the subjects of acute suffering it is not easy to exhibit that faith which we fancy we possess at other times. This man, suffering as he did, and seeing the Savior in so sad a state, nevertheless believed unto life eternal. Herein was such faith as is seldom seen.

Recollect, also, that He who, at such a time, could save such a man, and give him so great a faith, and so perfectly and speedily prepare him for eternal bliss. Behold the power of that divine Spirit who could produce such faith on soil so unlikely, and in a climate so unpropitious.

Let us enter at once into the center of our sermon. First, *note the man who was our Lord's last companion on earth;* secondly, *note that this same man was our Lord's first companion at the gate of paradise;* and then, thirdly, let us *note the sermon which our Lord preaches to us from this act of grace.* Oh, for a blessing from the Holy Spirit all the sermon through!

I. Carefully note that the crucified thief was our Lord's last companion on Earth.

What sorry company our Lord selected when He was here! He did not consort with the religious Pharisees or the philosophic Sadducees, but He was known as "the friend of publicans and sinners." How I rejoice at this! It gives me assurance that He will not refuse to associate with *me*. When the Lord Jesus made a friend of me, He certainly did not make a choice which brought Him credit. Do you think He gained any honor when He made a friend of you? Has He ever gained anything by us? No, my brethren; if Jesus had not stooped very low, He would not have come to me; and if He did not seek the most unworthy, He might not have come to you. You feel it so, and you are thankful that He came "not to call the righteous, but sinners to repentance." As the great physician, our Lord was much with the sick: He went where there was room for Him to exercise His healing art. The whole have no need of a physician: they cannot appreciate him, nor afford scope for His skill; and therefore He did not frequent their abodes. Yes, after all, our Lord did make a good choice when He saved you and me; for in us He has found abundant room for His mercy and grace. There has been elbow room for His love to work within the awful emptinesses of our necessities and sins; and therein He has done great things for us, whereof we are glad.

Lest any here should be despairing, and say, "He will never deign to look on me," I want you to notice that *the last companion of Christ on Earth was a sinner, and no ordinary sinner*. He had broken even the laws of man, for he was a robber. One calls him "a brigand"; and I suppose it is likely to have been the case. The brigands of those days mixed murder with their robberies: he was probably a freebooter in arms against the Roman government, making this a pretext for plundering as he had opportunity. At last he was arrested, and was condemned by a Roman tribunal, which, on the whole, was usually just, and in this case was certainly just; for he himself confesses the justice of his condemnation. The malefactor who believed upon the cross was a convict, who had lain in the condemned cell, and was then undergoing execution for his crimes. A convicted felon was the person with whom our Lord last consorted upon earth. What a lover of the souls of guilty men is he! What a stoop He makes to the very lowest of mankind! To this most unworthy of men the Lord of glory, ere He quitted life, spoke with matchless grace. He spoke to him such wondrous words as never can be excelled if you search the Scriptures through: "Today shalt thou be with me in paradise." I do not suppose that anywhere in this Tabernacle [Spurgeon's 6000-seat church] there will be found a man who has been convicted before the law, or who is even chargeable with a crime against common honesty; but if there should be such a person among my hearers, I would invite him to find pardon and change of heart through our Lord Jesus Christ. You may come to him, whoever you may be; for this man did. Here is a specimen of one who had gone to the extreme of guilt, and who acknowledged that he had done so; he made no excuse, and sought no cloak for his sin; he was in the hands of justice, confronted with the death-doom, and yet he believed in Jesus, and breathed a humble prayer to him, and he was saved upon the spot. As is the sample, such is the bulk. Jesus saves others of like kind. Let me, therefore, put it very plainly here, that none may mistake me. None of you are excluded from the infinite mercy of Christ, however great your iniquity: if you believe in Jesus, He will save *you*.

This man was not only a sinner; *he was a sinner newly awakened*. I do not suppose that he had seriously thought of the Lord Jesus before. According to the other Evangelists, he appears to have joined with his fellow thief in scoffing at Jesus: if he did not actually himself use opprobrious words, he was so far consenting thereunto, that the Evangelist did him no injustice when he said, "The thieves also, which were crucified with him, cast the same in His teeth." Yet, now, on a sudden, he wakes up to the conviction that the man who is dying at his side is something more than a man. He reads the title over His head, and believes it to be true—"This is Jesus the King of the Jews." Thus believing, he makes his appeal to the Messiah, whom he had so newly found, and commits himself to His hands. My hearer, do you see this truth, that the moment a man knows Jesus to be the Christ of God he may at once put his trust in Him and be saved? A certain preacher, whose gospel was very doubtful, said, "Do you, who have been living in sin for fifty years, believe that you can in a moment be made clean through the blood of Jesus? "I answer, "Yes, we do believe that in one moment, through the precious blood of Jesus, the blackest soul can be made white. We do believe that in a single instant the sins of sixty or seventy years can be absolutely forgiven, and that the old nature, which has gone on growing worse and worse, can receive its death-wound in a moment of time, while the life eternal may be implanted in the soul at once." It was so with this man. He had reached the end of his tether, but all of a sudden he woke up to the assured conviction that the Messiah was at his side, and, believing, he looked to Him and lived.

So now, my brothers, if you have never in your life before been the subject of any religious conviction, if you have lived up till now an utterly ungodly life, yet if now you will believe that God's dear Son has come into the world to save men from sin, and will unfeignedly confess your sin and trust in him, you shall be immediately saved. Aye, while I speak the word, the deed of grace may be accomplished by that glorious One who has gone up into the Heaven with omnipotent power to save.

I desire to put this case very plainly: *this man, who was the last companion of Christ upon earth, was a sinner in misery.* His sins had found him out: he was now enduring the reward of his deeds. I constantly meet with persons in this condition: they have lived a life of wantonness, excess, and carelessness, and they begin to feel the fire-flakes of the tempest of wrath falling upon their flesh; they dwell in an earthly Hell, a prelude of eternal woe. Remorse, like an asp, has stung them, and set their blood on fire: they cannot rest, they are troubled day and night. "Be sure your sin will find you out." It has found them out, and arrested them, and they feel the strong grip of conviction. This man was in that horrible condition: what is more, he was *in extremis.* He could not live long: the crucifixion was sure to be fatal; in a short time his legs would be broken, to end his wretched existence. He, poor soul, had but a short time to live—only the space between noon and sundown; but it was long enough for the Savior, who is mighty to save. Some are very much afraid that people will put off coming to Christ, if we state this. I cannot help what wicked men do with truth, but I shall state it all the same. If you are now within an hour of death, believe in the Lord Jesus Christ, and you shall be saved. If you never reach your homes again, but drop dead on the road, if you will now believe in the Lord Jesus, you shall be saved: saved now, on the spot. Looking and trusting to Jesus, He will give you a new heart and a right spirit, and blot out your sins. This is the glory of Christ's grace. How I wish I could extol it in proper language! He was last seen on Earth before His death in company with a convicted felon, to whom He spoke most lovingly. Come, O ye guilty, and He will receive you graciously!

Once more, *this man whom Christ saved at last was a man who could do no good works.* If salvation had been by good works, he could not have been saved; for he was fastened hand and foot to the tree of doom. It was all over with him as to any act or deed of righteousness. He could say a good word or two, but that was all; he could perform no acts; and if his salvation had depended on an active life of usefulness, certainly he never could have been saved.

He was a sinner also, who could not exhibit a long-enduring repentance for sin, for he had so short a time to live. He could not have experienced bitter convictions, lasting over months and years, for his time was as measured by moments, and he was on the borders of the grave. His end was very near, and yet the Savior could save him, and did save him so perfectly, that the sun went not down till he was in paradise with Christ.

This sinner, whom I have painted to you in colors none too black, was *one who believed in Jesus, and confessed his faith.* He did trust the Lord. Jesus was a man, and he called Him so but he knew that He was also Lord, and he called Him so, and said, "Lord, remember me." He had such confidence in Jesus, that, if He would but only think of him, if He would only remember him when He came into His kingdom, that would be all that he would ask of him. Alas, my dear hearers! the trouble about some of you is that you know all about my Lord, and yet you do not trust him. Trust is the saving act. Years ago you were on the verge of really trusting Jesus, but you are just as far off from it now as you were then. This man did not hesitate: he grasped the one hope for himself. He did not keep his persuasion of our Lord's Messiahship in his mind as a dry, dead belief, but he turned it into trust and prayer, "Lord, remember me when thou comest into thy kingdom." Oh, that in His infinite mercy many of you would trust my Lord this morning! You shall be saved, I am sure you shall: if you are not saved when you trust, I must myself also renounce all hope. This is all that we have done: we looked, and we lived, and we continue to live because we look to the living Savior. Oh, that this morning, feeling your sin, you would look to Jesus, trusting him, and confessing that trust! Owning that He is Lord to the glory of God the Father, you must and shall be saved.

In consequence of having this faith which saved him, *this poor man breathed the humble but fitting prayer,* "Lord, remember me." This does not seem to ask much; but as he understood it, it meant all that an anxious heart could desire. As he thought of the kingdom, he had such clear ideas of the glory of the Savior, that he felt that if the Lord would think of him, his eternal state would be safe. Joseph, in prison, asked the chief butler to remember him when he was restored to power; but he forgot him. Our Joseph never forgets a sinner who cried to Him in the low dungeon; in His kingdom He remembers the moanings and groanings of poor sinners who are burdened with a sense of sin. Can you not pray this morning, and thus secure a place in the memory of the Lord Jesus?

Thus I have tried to describe the man; and, after having done my best, I shall fail of my object unless I make you see that whatever this thief was, he is a picture of what you are. Especially if you have been a great offender, and if you have been living long without caring for eternal things, you are like that malefactor; and yet you, even you, may do as that thief did; you may believe that Jesus is the Christ, and commit your souls into His hands, and He will save you as surely as He saved the condemned brigand. Jesus graciously says, "Him that cometh to me I will in no wise cast out." This means that if *you* come and trust him, whoever you may be, He will for no reason, and on no ground, and under no circumstances, ever cast you out. Do you catch that thought? Do you feel that it belongs to you, and that if *you* come to him, *you* shall find eternal life? I rejoice if you so far perceive the truth.

Few persons have so much intercourse with desponding and despairing souls as I have. Poor cast down ones write to me continually. I scarce know why. I have no special gift of consolation, but I gladly lay myself out to comfort the distressed, and they seem to know it. What joy I have when I see a despairing one find peace! I have had this joy several times during the week just ended. How much I desire that any of you who are breaking your hearts because you cannot find forgiveness would come to my Lord, and trust him, and enter into rest! Has He not said, "Come unto me, all ye that labor and are heavy laden, and I will give you rest"? Come and try him, and that rest shall be yours.

II. In the second place, note, that this man was our Lord's companion at the gate of Paradise.

I am not going into any speculations as to where our Lord went when He quitted the body which hung on the cross. It would seem, from some Scriptures, that He descended into the lower parts of the earth, that He might fill all things. But He very rapidly traversed the regions of the dead. Remember that He died, perhaps an hour or two before the thief, and during that time the eternal glory flamed through the underworld, and was flashing through the gates of paradise just when the pardoned thief was entering the eternal world. Who is this that entereth the pearl-gate at the same moment as the King of glory? Who is this favored companion of the Redeemer? Is it some honored martyr? Is it a faithful apostle? Is it a patriarch, like Abraham; or a prince, like David? It is none of these. Behold, and be amazed at sovereign grace. He that goeth in at the gate of paradise, with the King of glory, is a thief, who was saved in the article of death. He is saved in no inferior way, and received into bliss in no secondary style. Verily, there are last which shall be first!

Here I would have you notice *the condescension of our Lord's choice*. The comrade of the Lord of glory, for whom the cherub turns aside his sword of fire, is no great one, but a newly-converted malefactor. And why? I think the Savior took him with Him as a specimen of what He meant to do. He seemed to say to all the heavenly powers, "I bring a sinner with me; he is a sample of the rest." Have you never heard of him who dreamed that he stood without the gate of Heaven, and while there he heard sweet music from a band of venerable persons who were on their way to glory? They entered the celestial portals, and there were great rejoicing and shouts. Enquiring "What are these?" he was told that they were the goodly fellowship of the prophets. He sighed, and said, "Alas! I am not one of those." He waited a while, and another band of shining ones drew nigh, who also entered Heaven with hallelujahs, and when *he* enquired, "Who are these, and whence came they?" the answer was, "These are the glorious company of the apostles." Again he sighed, and said, "I cannot enter with them." Then came another body of men white-robed, and bearing palms in their hands, who marched amid great acclamation into the golden city. These he learned were the noble army of martyrs; and again he wept, and said, "I cannot enter with these." In the end he heard the voices of much people, and saw a greater multitude advancing, among whom he perceived Rahab and Mary Magdalene, David and Peter, Manasseh and Saul of Tarsus, and he espied especially the thief, who died at the right hand of Jesus. These all entered in—a strange company. Then he eagerly enquired, "Who are these?" and they answered, "This is the host of sinners saved by grace." Then was he exceeding glad, and said, "I can go with these." Yet, he thought there would be no shouting at the approach of this company, and that they would enter Heaven without song; instead of which, there seemed to rise a seven-fold hallelujah of praise unto the Lord of love; for there is joy in the presence of the angels of God over sinners that repent.

I invite any poor soul here that can neither aspire to serve Christ, nor to suffer for Him as yet, nevertheless to come in with other believing sinners, in the company of Jesus, who now sets before us an open door.

While we are handling this text, note well *the blessedness of the place* to which the Lord called this penitent. Jesus said, "Today shalt thou be with me in paradise." Paradise means a garden, a garden filled with delights. The garden of Eden is the type of Heaven. We know that paradise means Heaven, for the apostle speaks of such a man caught up into paradise, and anon he calls it the third Heaven. Our Savior took this dying thief into the paradise of infinite delight, and this is where He will take all of us sinners who believe in him. If we are trusting him, we shall ultimately be with Him in paradise.

The next word is better still. Note *the glory of the society* to which this sinner is introduced: "Today shalt thou be with *me* in paradise." If the Lord said, "Today shalt thou be *with me*," we should not need Him to add another word; for where He is, is Heaven to us. He added the word "paradise," because else none could have guessed where He was going. Think of it, you uncomely soul; you are to dwell with the altogether-lovely One forever. You poor and needy ones, you are to be with Him in His glory, in His bliss, in His perfection. Where He is, and as He is, you shall be. The Lord looks into those weeping eyes of yours this morning, and He says, "Poor sinner, thou shalt one day be with me." I think I hear you say, "Lord, that is bliss too great for such a sinner as I am"; but He replies—"I have loved thee with an everlasting love: therefore with lovingkindness will I draw thee, till thou shalt be with me where I am."

The stress of the text lies in *the speediness of all this*. "Verily I say unto thee, *today* shalt thou be with me in paradise." "Today." Thou shalt not lie in purgatory for ages, nor sleep in limbo for so many years; but thou shalt be ready for bliss at once, and at once thou shalt enjoy it. The sinner was hard by the gates of Hell, but almighty mercy lifted him up, and the Lord said, "*Today* shalt thou be with me in paradise." What a change from the cross to the crown, from the anguish of Calvary to the glory of the New Jerusalem! In those few hours the beggar was lifted from the dunghill and set among princes. "Today shalt thou be with me in paradise." Can you measure the change from that sinner, loathsome in his iniquity, when the sun was high at noon, to that same sinner, clothed in pure white, and accepted in the Beloved, in the paradise of God, when the sun went down? O glorious Savior, what marvels thou canst work! How rapidly canst thou work them!

Please notice, also, *the majesty of the Lord's grace* in this text. The Savior said to him, "Verily *I say* unto thee, today shalt thou be with me in paradise." Our Lord gives His own will as the reason for saving this man. "I say." He says it, who claims the right thus to speak. It is He who will have mercy on whom He will have mercy, and will have compassion on whom He will have compassion. He speaks royally, "Verily I say unto thee." Are they not imperial words? The Lord is a King in whose word there is power. What He says none can gainsay. He that hath the keys of Hell and of death saith, "I say unto thee, today shalt thou be with me in paradise." Who shall prevent the fulfillment of His word?

Notice *the certainty of it*. He says, "Verily." Our blessed Lord on the cross returned to His old majestic manner, as He painfully turned His head, and looked on His convert. He was wont to begin His preaching with, "Verily, verily, I say unto you"; and now that He is dying He uses His favorite manner, and says, "Verily." Our Lord took no oath; His strongest asseveration was, "Verily, verily." To give the penitent the plainest assurance, He says,

"Verily I say unto thee, today shalt thou be with me in paradise." In this he had an absolutely indisputable assurance that though he must die, yet he would live and find himself in paradise with his Lord.

I have thus shown you that our Lord passed within the pearly gate in company with one to whom he had pledged Himself. Why should not you and I pass through that pearl-gate in due time, clothed in His merit, washed in His blood, resting on His power? One of these days angels will say of you, and of me, "Who is this that cometh up from the wilderness, leaning upon her beloved?" The shining ones will be amazed to see some of us coming. If you have lived a life of sin until now, and yet shall repent and enter Heaven, what an amazement there will be in every golden street to think that you have come there! In the early Christian church Marcus Caius Victorinus was converted; but he had reached so great an age, and had been so gross a sinner, that the pastor and church doubted him. He gave, however, clear proof of having undergone the divine change, and then there were great acclamations, and many shouts of "Victorinus has become a Christian!" Oh, that some of you big sinners might be saved! How gladly would we rejoice over you! Why not? Would it not glorify God? The salvation of this convicted highwayman has made our Lord illustrious for mercy even unto this day; would not your case do the same? Would not saints cry, "Hallelujah! hallelujah!" if they heard that some of you had been turned from darkness to marvelous light? Why should it not be? Believe in Jesus, and it is so.

III. *Now I come to my third and most practical point: note the Lord's sermon to us from all this.*

The devil wants to preach this morning a bit. Yes, Satan asks to come to the front and preach to you; but he cannot be allowed. Avaunt, thou deceiver! Yet I should not wonder if he gets at certain of you when the sermon is over, and whispers, "You see you can be saved at the very last. Put off repentance and faith; you may be forgiven on your death-bed." Sirs, you know who it is that would ruin you by this suggestion. Abhor his deceitful teaching. Do not be ungrateful because God is kind. Do not provoke the Lord because He is patient. Such conduct would be unworthy and ungrateful. Do not run an awful risk because one escaped the tremendous peril. The Lord will accept all who repent; but how do you know that you will repent? It is true that one thief was saved—but the other thief was lost. One is saved, and we may not despair; the other is lost, and we may not presume. Dear friends, I trust you are not made of such diabolical stuff as to fetch from the mercy of God an argument for continuing in sin. If you do, I can only say of you, your damnation will be just; you will have brought it upon yourselves.

Consider now the teaching of our Lord; see *the glory of Christ in salvation*. He is ready to save at the last moment. He was just passing away; His foot was on the doorstep of the Father's house. Up comes this poor sinner the last thing at night, at the eleventh hour, and the Savior smiles and declares that He will not enter except with this belated wanderer. At the very gate He declares that this seeking soul shall enter with him. There was plenty of time for him to have come before: you know how apt we are to say, "You have waited to the last moment. I am just going off, and I cannot attend to you now." Our Lord had His dying pangs upon him, and yet He attends to the perishing criminal, and permits him to pass through the heavenly portal in His company. Jesus easily saves the sinners for whom He painfully died. Jesus loves to rescue sinners from going down into the pit. You will be very happy if you are saved, but you will not be one half so happy as He will be when He saves you. See how gentle He is!

> His hand no thunder bears,
> No terror clothes His brow;
> No bolts to drive our guilty souls
> To fiercer flames below."

He comes to us full of tenderness, with tears in His eyes, mercy in His hands, and love in His heart. Believe Him to be a great Savior of great sinners. I have heard of one who had received great mercy who went about saying, "He is a great forgiver"; and I would have you say the same. You shall find your transgressions put away, and your sins pardoned once for all, if you now trust him.

The next doctrine Christ preaches from this wonderful story is *faith in its permitted attachment*. This man believed that Jesus was the Christ. The next thing he did was to appropriate that Christ. He said, "Lord, remember me." Jesus might have said, "What have I to do with you, and what have you to do with me? What has a thief to do with the perfect One?" Many of you, good people, try to get as far away as you can from the erring and fallen. They might infect your innocence! Society claims that we should not be familiar with people who have offended against its laws. We must not be seen associating with them, for it might discredit us. Infamous bosh! Can anything discredit sinners such as we are by nature and by practice? If we know ourselves before God, are we not degraded enough in and of ourselves? Is there anybody, after all, in the world, who is worse than we are when we see ourselves in the faithful glass of the Word? As soon as ever a man believes that Jesus is the Christ, let him hook himself on to him. The moment you believe Jesus to be the Savior, seize upon Him as your Savior. If I remember rightly, Augustine called this man, *"Latro laudabilis et mirabilis,"* a thief to be praised and wondered at, who dared, as it were, to seize the Savior for his own. In this he is to be imitated. Take the Lord to be yours, and you have him. Jesus is the common property of all sinners who make bold to take him. Every sinner who has the will to do so may take the Lord home with him. He came into the world to save the sinful. Take Him by force, as robbers take their prey; for the kingdom of Heaven suffereth the violence of daring faith. Get him, and He will never get himself away from you. If you trust him, He must save you.

Next, notice the doctrine of *faith in its immediate power.*

> The moment a sinner believes,
> And trusts in his crucified God,
> His pardon at once he receives,
> Redemption in full through His blood.

"Today shalt thou be with me in paradise." He has no sooner believed than Christ gives him the seal of his believing in the full assurance that he shall be with Him forever in His glory. O dear hearts, if you believe this morning, you shall be saved this morning! God grant that you, by His rich grace, may be brought into salvation here, on the spot, and at once!

The next thing is, *the nearness of eternal things.* Think of that a minute. Heaven and Hell are not places far away. You may be in Heaven before the clock ticks again, it is so near. Could we but rend that veil which parts us from the unseen! It is all there, and all near. "Today," said the Lord; within three or four hours at the longest, "shalt thou be with me in paradise;" so near is it. A statesman has given us the expression of being "within measurable distance." We are all within measurable distance of Heaven or Hell; if there be any difficulty in measuring the distance, it lies in its brevity rather than in its length.

> One gentle sigh the fetter breaks,
> We scarce can say, "He's gone,"
> Before the ransomed spirit takes
> Its mansion near the throne.

Oh, that we, instead of trifling about such things, because they seem so far away, would solemnly realize them, since they are so very near! This very day, before the sun goes down, some hearer, now sitting in this place, may see, in His own spirit, the realities of Heaven or Hell. It has frequently happened, in this large congregation, that some one of our audience has died ere the next Sabbath has come round: it may happen this week. Think of that, and let eternal things impress you all the more because they lie so near.

Furthermore, know that *if you have believed in Jesus you are prepared for Heaven.* It may be that you will have to live on Earth twenty, or thirty, or forty years to glorify Christ; and, if so, be thankful for the privilege; but if you do not live another hour, your instantaneous death would not alter the fact that he that believeth in the Son of God is meet for Heaven. Surely, if anything beyond faith is needed to make us fit to enter paradise, the thief would have been kept a little longer here; but no, he is, in the morning, in the state of nature, at noon he enters the state of grace, and by sunset he is in the state of glory. The question never is whether a death-bed repentance is accepted if it be sincere: the question is—is it sincere? If it be so, if the man dies five minutes after his first act of faith, he is as safe as if he had served the Lord for fifty years. If your faith is true, if you die one moment after you have believed in Christ, you will be admitted into paradise, even if you shall have enjoyed no time in which to produce good works and other evidences of grace. He that reads the heart will read your faith written on its fleshy tablets, and He will accept you through Jesus Christ, even though no act of grace has been visible to the eye of man.

I conclude by again saying that *this is not an exceptional case.* I began with that, and I want to finish with it, because so many demi-semi-gospelers are so terribly afraid of preaching free grace too fully. I read somewhere, and I think it is true, that some ministers preach the gospel in the same way as donkeys eat thistles, namely, very, very cautiously. On the contrary, I will preach it boldly. I have not the slightest alarm about the matter. If any of you misuse free-grace teaching, I cannot help it. He that will be damned can as well ruin himself by perverting the gospel as by anything else. I cannot help what base hearts may invent; but mine it is to set forth the gospel in all its fullness of grace, and I will do it. If the thief was an exceptional case—and our Lord does not usually act in such a way—there would have been a hint given of so important a fact. A hedge would have been set about this exception to all rules. Would not the Savior have whispered quietly to the dying man, "You are the only one I am going to treat in this way"? Whenever I have to do an exceptional favor to a person, I have to say, "Do not mention this, or I shall have so many besieging me." If the Savior had meant this to be a solitary case, He would have faintly said to him, "Do not let anybody know; but you shall today be in the kingdom with me." No, our Lord spoke openly, and those about Him heard what He said. Moreover, the inspired penman has recorded it. If it had been an exceptional case, it would not have been written in the Word of God. Men will not publish their actions in the newspapers if they feel that the record might lead others to expect from them what they cannot give. The Savior had this wonder of grace reported in the daily news of the gospel, because He means to repeat the marvel every day. The bulk shall be equal to the sample, and therefore He sets the sample before you all. He is able to save to the uttermost, for He saved the dying thief. The case would not have been put there to encourage hopes which He cannot fulfill. Whatsoever things were written aforetime were written for our learning, and not for our disappointing. I pray you, therefore, if any of you have not yet trusted in my Lord Jesus, come and trust in Him now. Trust Him wholly; trust Him only; trust Him at once. Then will you sing with me:

> *The dying thief rejoiced to see*
> *That fountain in his day,*
> *And there have I, though vile as he,*
> *washed all my sins away.*

Lama Sabachthani?

"And about the ninth hour Jesus cried with a loud voice, saying,
'Eli, Eli, lama sabachthani?' that is to say, 'My God, my God,
why hast thou forsaken me?'"—Matthew 27:46.

There was darkness over all the land unto the ninth hour": this cry came out of that darkness. Expect not to see through its every word, as though it came from on high as a beam from the unclouded Sun of Righteousness. There is light in it, bright, flashing light; but there is a center of impenetrable gloom, where the soul is ready to faint because of the terrible darkness.

Our Lord was then in the darkest part of His way. He had trodden the winepress now for hours, and the work was almost finished. He had reached the culminating point of His anguish. This is His dolorous lament from the lowest pit of misery—"My God, my God, why hast thou forsaken me?" I do not think that the records of time, or even of eternity, contain a sentence more full of anguish. Here the wormwood and the gall, and all the other bitternesses, are outdone. Here you may look as into a vast abyss; and though you strain your eyes, and gaze till sight fails you, yet you perceive no bottom; it is measureless, unfathomable, inconceivable. This anguish of the Savior on your behalf and mine is no more to be measured and weighed than the sin which needed it, or the love which endured it. We will adore where we cannot comprehend.

I have chosen this subject that it may help the children of God to understand a little of their infinite obligations to their redeeming Lord. You shall measure the height of His love, if it be ever measured, by the depth of His grief, if that can ever be known. See with what a price He hath redeemed us from the curse of the law! As you see this, say to yourselves:

"What manner of people ought we to be! What measure of love ought we to return to one who bore the utmost penalty, that we might be delivered from the wrath to come?" I do not profess that I can dive into this deep: I will only venture to the edge of the precipice, and bid you look down, and pray the Spirit of God to concentrate your mind upon this lamentation of our dying Lord, as it rises up through the thick darkness—"My God, my God, why hast thou forsaken me?"

Our first subject of thought will be *the fact;* or, what He suffered—God had forsaken him. Secondly, we will note, *the inquiry;* or, why He suffered: this word "why" is the edge of the text. "Why hast thou forsaken me?" Then, thirdly, we will consider *the answer;* or, what came of His suffering. The answer flowed softly into the soul of the Lord Jesus without the need of words, for he ceased from His anguish with the triumphant shout of, "It is finished." His work was finished, and His bearing of desertion was a chief part of the work He had undertaken for our sake.

I. By the help of the Holy Spirit, let us first dwell upon "the fact," or, what our Lord suffered.

God had forsaken him. Grief of mind is harder to bear than pain of body. You can pluck up courage and endure the pang of sickness and pain, so long as the spirit is hale and brave; but if the soul itself be touched, and the mind becomes diseased with anguish, then every pain is increased in severity, and there is nothing with which to sustain it. Spiritual sorrows are the worst of mental miseries. A man may bear great depression of spirit about worldly matters, if he feels that he has his God to go to. He is cast down, but not in despair. Like David, he dialogues with himself, and he enquires, "Why art thou cast down, O my soul? and why art thou disquieted in me? Hope thou in God: for I shall yet praise him." But if the Lord be once withdrawn, if the comfortable light of His presence be shadowed even for an hour, there is a torment within the breast, which I can only liken to the prelude of Hell. This is the greatest of all weights that can press upon the heart. This made the Psalmist plead, "Hide not thy face from me; put not thy servant away in anger." We can bear a bleeding body, and even a wounded spirit; but a soul conscious of desertion by God is beyond conception unendurable. When He holdeth back the face of His throne, and spreadeth His cloud upon it, who can endure the darkness?

This voice out of "the belly of Hell" marks the lowest depth of the Savior's grief. *The desertion was real.* Though under some aspects our Lord could say, "The Father is with me"; yet was it solemnly true that God did forsake him. It was not a failure of faith on His part which led Him to imagine what was not actual fact. Our faith fails us, and then we think that God has forsaken us; but our Lord's faith did not for a moment falter, for He says twice, "My God, my God." Oh, the mighty double grip of His unhesitating faith! He seems to say, "Even if thou hast forsaken me, I have not forsaken thee." Faith triumphs, and there is no sign of any faintness of heart towards the living God. Yet, strong as is His faith, He feels that God has withdrawn His comfortable fellowship, and He shivers under the terrible deprivation.

It was no fancy, or delirium of mind, caused by His weakness of body, the heat of the fever, the depression of His spirit, or the near approach of death. He was clear of mind even to this last. He bore up under pain, loss of blood, scorn, thirst, and desolation; making no complaint of the cross, the nails, and the scoffing. We read not in the Gospels of anything more than the natural cry of weakness, "I thirst." All the tortures of His body He endured in silence; but when it came to being forsaken of God, then His great heart burst out into its *"Lama sabachthani?"* His one moan is concerning His God. It is not, "Why has Peter forsaken me? Why has Judas betrayed me?" These were sharp griefs, but this is the sharpest. This stroke has cut Him to the quick: "My God, my God, why hast *thou* forsaken me?" It was no phantom of the gloom; it was a real absence which He mourned.

This was *a very remarkable desertion.* It is not the way of God to leave either His sons or His servants. His saints, when they come to die, in their great weakness and pain, find Him near. They are made to sing because of the presence of God: "Yea, though I walk through the valley of the shadow of death, I will fear no evil: for thou art with me." Dying saints have clear visions of the living God. Our observation has taught us that if the Lord be away at other times, He is never absent from His people in the article of death, or in the furnace of *affliction.* Concerning the three holy children, we do not read that the Lord was ever visibly with them till they walked the fires of Nebuchadnezzar's furnace; but there and then the Lord met with them. Yes, beloved, it is God's use and wont to keep company with His afflicted people; and yet He forsook His Son in the hour of His tribulation! How usual it is to see the Lord with His faithful witnesses when resisting even unto blood! Read *[Foxe's] Book of Martyrs,* and I care not whether you study the former or the later persecutions, you will find them all lit up with the evident presence of the Lord with His witnesses. Did the Lord ever fail to support a martyr at the stake? Did He ever forsake one of His testifiers upon the scaffold? The testimony of the church has always been, that while the Lord has permitted His saints to suffer in body He has so divinely sustained their spirits that they have been more than conquerors, and have treated their sufferings as light afflictions. The fire has not been "a bed of roses," but it has been a chariot of victory. The sword is sharp, and death is bitter; but the love of Christ is sweet, and to die for Him has been turned into glory. No, it is not God's way to forsake His champions, nor to leave even the least of His children in the trial hour.

As to our Lord, this forsaking was *singular*. Did His Father ever leave Him before? Will you read the four Evangelists through and find any previous instance in which He complains of His Father for having forsaken him? No. He said, "I know that thou hearest me always." He lived in constant touch with God. His fellowship with the Father was always near and dear and clear; but now, for the first time, He cries, "why hast thou forsaken me?" It was very remarkable. It was a riddle only to be solved by the fact that He loved us and gave himself for us, and in the execution of His loving purpose came even unto this sorrow, of mourning the absence of His God.

This forsaking was *very terrible*. Who can fully tell what it is to be forsaken of God? We can only form a guess by what we have ourselves felt under temporary and partial desertion. God has never left us, altogether; for He has expressly said, "I will never leave thee nor forsake thee"; yet we have sometimes felt as if He had cast us off. We have cried, "Oh, that I knew where I might find him!" The clear shinings of His love have been withdrawn. Thus we are able to form some little idea of how the Savior felt when His God had forsaken him. The mind of Jesus was left to dwell upon one dark subject, and no cheering theme consoled him. It was the hour in which He was made to stand before God as consciously the sin-bearer, according to that ancient prophecy, "He shall bear their iniquities." Then was it true, "He hath made Him to be sin for us." Peter puts it, "He His own self bare our sins in His own body on the tree." Sin, sin, sin was everywhere around and about Christ. He had no sin of His own; but the Lord had "laid on Him the iniquity of us all." He had no strength given Him from on high, no secret oil and wine poured into His wounds; but He was made to appear in the lone character of the Lamb of God, which taketh away the sin of the world; and therefore He must feel the weight of sin, and the turning away of that sacred face which cannot look thereon.

His Father, at that time, gave Him no open acknowledgment. On certain other occasions a voice had been heard, saying, "This is my beloved Son, in whom I am well pleased"; but now, when such a testimony seemed most of all required, the oracle was dumb. He was hung up as an accursed thing upon the cross; for He was "made a curse for us, as it is written, 'Cursed is every one that hangeth on a tree'"; and the Lord his God did not own him before men. If it had pleased the Father, he might have sent him twelve legions of angels; but not an angel came after the Christ had quitted Gethsemane. His despisers might spit in his face, but no swift seraph came to avenge the indignity. They might bind him, and scourge him, but none of all the heavenly host would interpose to screen his shoulders from the lash. They might fasten him to the tree with nails, and lift him up, and scoff at him; but no cohort of ministering spirits hastened to drive back the rabble, and release the Prince of life. No, he appeared to be forsaken, "smitten of God and afflicted," delivered into the hands of cruel men, whose wicked hands worked him misery without stint. Well might he ask, "My God, my God, why hast thou forsaken me?"

But this was not all. His Father now dried up that sacred stream of peaceful communion and loving fellowship which had flowed hitherto throughout His whole earthly life. He said himself, as you remember, "Ye shall be scattered, every man to His own, and shall leave me alone: and yet I am not alone, because the Father is with me." Here was His constant comfort: but all comfort from this source was to be withdrawn. The divine Spirit did not minister to His human spirit. No communications with His Father's love poured into His heart. It was not possible that the Judge should smile upon one who represented the prisoner at the bar. Our Lord's faith did not fail him, as I have already shown you, for He said, "My God, my God": yet no sensible supports were given to His heart, and no comforts were poured into His mind. One writer declares that Jesus did not taste of divine wrath, but only suffered a withdrawal of divine fellowship. What is the difference? Whether God withdraw heat or create cold is all one. He was not smiled upon, nor allowed to feel that He was near to God; and this, to His tender spirit, was grief of the keenest order. A certain saint once said that in his sorrow he had from God "necessaries, but not suavities"—that which was meet, but not that which was sweet. Our Lord suffered to the extreme point of deprivation. He had not the light which makes existence to be life, and life to be a boon. You that know, in your degree, what it is to lose the conscious presence and love of God, you can faintly guess what the sorrow of the Savior was, now that He felt He had been forsaken of His God. "If the foundations be removed, what can the righteous do?" To our Lord, the Father's love was the foundation of everything; and when that was gone, all was gone. Nothing remained, within, without, above, when His own God, the God of His entire confidence, turned from Him. Yes, God in very deed forsook our Savior.

To be forsaken of God was *much more a source of anguish to Jesus than it would be to us.* "Oh," say you, "how is that?" I answer, because He was perfectly holy. A rupture between a perfectly holy being and the thrice holy God must be in the highest degree strange, abnormal, perplexing, and painful. If any man here, who is not at peace with God, could only know his true condition, he would swoon with fright. If you unforgiven ones only knew where you are, and what you are at this moment in the sight of God, you would never smile again till you were reconciled to Him. Alas! we are insensible, hardened by the deceitfulness of sin, and therefore we do not feel our true condition. His perfect holiness made it to our Lord a dreadful calamity to be forsaken of the thrice holy God.

Remember, also, that our blessed Lord had lived in unbroken fellowship with God, and to be forsaken was a new grief to him. He had never known what the dark was till then: His life had been lived in the light of God. Think, dear child of God, if you had always dwelt in full communion with God, your days would have been as the days of Heaven upon Earth; and how cold it would strike to your heart to find yourself in the darkness of desertion. If you can conceive such a thing as happening to a perfect man, you can see why to our Well-beloved it was a special trial. Remember, He had enjoyed fellowship with God more richly, as well as more constantly, than any of us. His fellowship with the Father was of the highest, deepest, fullest order; and what must the loss of it have been? We lose but drops when we lose our joyful experience of heavenly fellowship; and yet the loss is killing: but to our Lord Jesus Christ the sea was dried up—I mean His sea of fellowship with the infinite God.

Do not forget that He was such a One that to Him to be without God must have been an overwhelming calamity. In every part He was perfect, and in every part fitted for communion with God to a supreme degree. A sinful man has an awful need of God, but he does not know it; and therefore he does not feel that hunger and thirst after God which would come upon a perfect man, could he be deprived of God. The very perfection of his nature renders it inevitable that the holy man must either be in communion with God, or be desolate. Imagine a stray angel! a seraph who has lost his God! Conceive him to be perfect in holiness, and yet to have fallen into a condition in which he cannot find his God! I cannot picture him; perhaps a Milton might have done so. He is sinless and trustful, and yet he has an overpowering feeling that God is absent from him. He has drifted into the nowhere—the unimaginable region behind the back of God. I think I hear the wailing of the cherub: "My God, my God, my God, where art thou?" What a sorrow for one of the sons of the morning! But here we have the lament of a Being far more capable of fellowship with the Godhead. In proportion as He is more fitted to receive the love of the great Father, in that proportion is His pining after it the more intense. As a Son, He is more able to commune with God than ever a servant-angel could be; and now that He is forsaken of God, the void within is the greater, and the anguish more bitter.

Our Lord's heart, and all His nature were, morally and spiritually, so delicately formed, so sensitive, so tender, that to be without God, was to Him a grief which could not be weighed. I see Him in the text bearing desertion, and yet I perceive that He cannot bear it. I know not how to express my meaning except by such a paradox. He cannot endure to be without God. He had surrendered himself to be left of God, as the representative of sinners must be, but His pure and holy nature, after three hours of silence, finds the position unendurable to love and purity; and breaking forth from it, now that the hour was over, He exclaims, "Why hast thou forsaken me?" He quarrels not with the suffering, but He cannot abide in the position which caused it. He seems as if He must end the ordeal, not because of the pain, but because of the moral shock. We have here the repetition after His passion of that loathing which He felt before it, when He cried, "If it be possible let this cup pass from me: nevertheless not as I will, but as thou wilt." "My God, my God, why hast thou forsaken me?" is the holiness of Christ amazed at the position of substitute for guilty men.

There, friends; I have done my best, but I seem to myself to have been prattling like a little child, talking about something infinitely above me. So I leave the solemn fact, that our Lord Jesus was on the tree forsaken of His God.

II. This brings us to consider the inquiry, or, why He suffered.

Note carefully this cry—"My God, my God, why hast thou forsaken me?" It is pure anguish, undiluted agony, which crieth like this but it is the agony of a godly soul; for only a man of that order would have used such an expression. Let us learn from it useful lessons. This cry is taken from "the Book." Does it not show our Lord's love of the sacred volume, that when He felt His sharpest grief, He turned to the Scripture to find a fit utterance for it? Here we have the opening sentence of the twenty-second Psalm. Oh, that we may so love the inspired Word that we may not only sing to its score, but even weep to its music!

Note, again, that our Lord's lament is an address to God. The godly, in their anguish, turn to the hand which smites them. The Savior's outcry is not *against* God, but *to* God. "My God, my God": He makes a double effort to draw near. True Sonship is here. The child in the dark is crying after His Father—"My God, my God." Both the Bible and prayer were dear to Jesus in His agony.

Still, observe, it is a faith-cry; for though it asks, "Why hast thou forsaken me?" yet it first says, twice over, "My God, my God." The grip of appropriation is in the word "my"; but the reverence of humility is in the word "God." It is—

"*My God, my God,*" thou art ever God to me, and I a poor creature. I do not quarrel with thee. Thy rights are unquestioned, for thou art *my God*. Thou canst do as thou wilt, and I yield to thy sacred sovereignty. I kiss the hand that smite me, and with all my heart I cry, "My God, my God."

When you are delirious with pain, think of your Bible still: when your mind wanders, let it roam towards the mercy seat; and when your heart and your flesh fail, still live by faith, and still cry, "My God, my God."

Let us come close to the inquiry. It looked to me, at first sight, like *a question as of one distraught*, driven from the balance of His mind—not unreasonable, but too much reasoning, and therefore tossed about. "Why hast thou forsaken me?" Did not Jesus know? Did He not know why He was forsaken? He knew it most distinctly, and yet His manhood, while it was being crushed, pounded, dissolved, seemed as though it could not understand the reason for so great a grief. He must be forsaken; but could there be a sufficient cause for so sickening a sorrow? The cup must be bitter; but why this most nauseous of ingredients? I tremble lest I say what I ought not to say. I have said it, and I think there is truth—the Man of Sorrows was overborne with horror. At that moment the finite soul of the man Christ Jesus came into awful contact with the infinite justice of God. The one Mediator between God and man, the man Christ Jesus, beheld the holiness of God in arms against the sin of man, whose nature He had espoused. God was for Him and with Him in a certain unquestionable sense; but for the time, so far as His feeling went, God was against him, and necessarily withdrawn from him. It is not surprising that the holy soul of Christ should shudder at finding itself brought into painful contact with the infinite justice of God, even though its design was only to vindicate that justice, and glorify the Law-giver. Our Lord could now say, "All thy waves and thy billows are gone over me"; and therefore He uses language which is all too hot with anguish to be dissected by the cold hand of a logical criticism. Grief has small regard for the laws of the grammarian. Even the holiest, when in extreme agony, though they cannot speak otherwise than according to purity and truth, yet use a language of their own, which only the ear of sympathy can fully receive. I see not all that is here, but what I can see I am not able to put in words for you.

I think I see, in the expression, submission and resolve. Our Lord does not draw back. There is a forward movement in the question: they who quit a business ask no more questions about it. He does not ask that the forsaking may end prematurely, He would only understand anew its meaning. He does not shrink, but rather dedicates himself anew to God by the words, "My God, my God," and by seeking to review the ground and reason of that anguish, which He is resolute to bear even to the bitter end. He would fain feel anew the motive which has sustained him, and must sustain Him to the end. The cry sounds to me like deep submission and strong resolve, pleading with God.

Do you not think that *the amazement of our Lord, when He was "made sin for us"* (2 Cor. 5:21), led Him thus to cry out? For such a sacred and pure being to be made a sin-offering was an amazing experience. Sin was laid on him, and He was treated as if He had been guilty, though He had personally never sinned; and now the infinite horror of rebellion against the most holy God fills His holy soul, the unrighteousness of sin breaks His heart, and He starts back from it, crying, "My God, my God, why hast thou forsaken *me?*" Why must I bear the dread result of conduct I so much abhor?

Do you not see, moreover, *there was here a glance at His eternal purpose, and at His secret source of joy?* That "why" is the silver lining of the dark cloud, and our Lord looked wishfully at it. He knew that the desertion was needful in order that He might save the guilty, and He had an eye to that salvation as His comfort. He is not forsaken needlessly, nor without a worthy design. The design is in itself so dear to His heart that He yields to the passing evil, even though that evil be like death to him. He looks at that "why," and through that narrow window the light of Heaven comes streaming into His darkened life.

My God, my God, why hast thou forsaken me?" Surely our Lord dwelt on that "why," *that we might also turn our eyes that way. He* would have us see the why and the wherefore of His grief. He would have us mark the gracious motive for its endurance. Think much of all your Lord suffered, but do not overlook the reason of it. If you cannot always understand how this or that grief worked toward the great end of the whole passion, yet believe that it has its share in the grand "why." Make a life-study of that bitter but blessed question, "Why hast thou forsaken me?" Thus the Savior raises an inquiry not so much for himself as for us; and not so much because of any despair within His heart as because of a hope and a joy set before him, which were wells of comfort to Him in His wilderness of woe.

Bethink you, for a moment, that the Lord God, in the broadest and most unreserved sense, could never, in very deed, have forsaken His most obedient Son. He was ever with Him in the grand design of salvation. Towards the Lord Jesus, personally, God himself, personally, must ever have stood on terms of infinite love. Truly the Only Begotten was never more lovely to the Father than when He was obedient unto death, even the death of the cross! But we must look upon God here as the Judge of all the earth, and we must look upon the Lord Jesus also in His official capacity, as the Surety of the covenant, and the Sacrifice for sin. The great Judge of all cannot smile upon Him who has become the substitute for the guilty. Sin is loathed of God; and if, in order to its removal, His own Son is made to bear it, yet, as sin, it is still loathsome, and He who bears it cannot be in happy communion with God. This was the dread necessity of expiation; but in the essence of things the love of the great Father to His Son never ceased, nor ever knew a diminution. Restrained in its flow it must be, but lessened at its fountain-head it could not be. Therefore, wonder not at the question, "Why hast thou forsaken me?"

III. Hoping to be guided by the Holy Spirit, I am coming to the answer, concerning which I can only use the few minutes which remain to me.

"My God, my God, why hast thou forsaken me?" What is the outcome of this suffering? What was the reason for it? Our Savior could answer His own question. If for a moment His manhood was perplexed, yet His mind soon came to clear apprehension; for He said, "It is finished"; and, as I have already said, He then referred to the work which in His lonely agony He had been performing. Why, then, did God forsake His Son? I cannot conceive any other answer than this—*he stood in our stead*. There was no reason in Christ why the Father should forsake him: He was perfect, and His life was without spot. God never acts without reason; and since there were no reasons in the character and person of the Lord Jesus why His Father should forsake him, we must look elsewhere. I do not know how others answer the question. I can only answer it in this one way.

> *Yet all the griefs He felt were ours,*
> *Ours were the woes He bore;*

Pangs, not His own, His spotless soul
With bitter anguish tore.

We held Him as condemn'd of Heaven,
An outcast from His God;
While for our sins He groaned, He bled,
Beneath His Father's rod.

He bore the sinner's sin, and He had to be treated, therefore, as though He were a sinner, though sinner He could never be. With His own full consent He suffered as though He had committed the transgressions which were laid on him. Our sin, and His taking it upon himself, is the answer to the question, "Why hast thou forsaken me?"

In this case we now see that *His obedience was perfect.* He came into the world to obey the Father, and He rendered that obedience to the very uttermost. The spirit of obedience could go no farther than for one who feels forsaken of God still to cling to Him in solemn, avowed allegiance, still declaring before a mocking multitude His confidence in the afflicting God. It is noble to cry, "My God, my God," when one is asking, "Why hast thou forsaken me?" How much farther can obedience go? I see nothing beyond it. The soldier at the gate of Pompeii remaining at his post as sentry when the shower of burning ashes is falling, was not more true to his trust than he who adheres to a forsaking God with loyalty of hope.

Our Lord's suffering in this particular form was appropriate and necessary. It would not have sufficed for our Lord merely to have been pained in body, nor even to have been grieved in mind in other ways: He must suffer in this particular way. He must feel forsaken of God, because this is the necessary consequence of sin. For a man to be forsaken of God is the penalty which naturally and inevitably follows upon his breaking his relation with God. What is death? What was the death that was threatened to Adam? "In the day that thou eatest thereof thou shalt surely die." Is death annihilation? Was Adam annihilated that day? Assuredly not: he lived many a year afterwards. But in the day in which he ate of the forbidden fruit he died, by being separated from God. The separation of the soul from God is spiritual death; just as the separation of the soul from the body is natural death. The sacrifice for sin must be put in the place of separation, and must bow to the penalty of death. By this placing of the Great Sacrifice under forsaking and death, it would be seen by all creatures throughout the universe that God could not have fellowship with sin. If even the Holy One, who stood the Just for the unjust, found God forsaking him, what must the doom of the actual sinner be! Sin is evidently always, in every case, a dividing influence, putting even the Christ himself, as a sin-bearer, in the place of distance.

This was necessary for another reason: there could have been no laying on of suffering for sin without the forsaking of the vicarious Sacrifice by the Lord God. So long as the smile of God rests on the man the law is not afflicting him. The approving look of the great Judge cannot fall upon a man who is viewed as standing in the place of the guilty. Christ not only suffered *from* sin, but *for* sin. If God will cheer and sustain him, He is not suffering for sin. The Judge is not inflicting suffering for sin if He is manifestly succoring the smitten one. There could have been no vicarious suffering on the part of Christ for human guilt, if He had continued consciously to enjoy the full sunshine of the Father's presence. It was essential to being a victim in our place that He should cry, "My God, my God, why hast thou forsaken me?"

Beloved, see how marvelously, in the person of Christ, the Lord our God has vindicated His law! If to make His law glorious, He had said, "These multitudes of men have broken my law, and therefore they shall perish," the law would have been terribly magnified. But, instead thereof, He says,

> Here is my Only Begotten Son, my other self; He takes on himself the nature of these rebellious creatures, and He consents that I should lay on Him the load of their iniquity, and visit in His person the offences which might have been punished in the persons of all these multitudes of men: and I will have it so.

When Jesus bows His head to the stroke of the law, when He submissively consents that His Father shall turn away His face from him, then myriads of worlds are astonished at the perfect holiness and stern justice of the Lawgiver. There are, probably, worlds innumerable throughout the boundless creation of God, and all these will see, in the death of God's dear Son, a declaration of His determination never to allow sin to be trifled with. If His own Son is brought before him, bearing the sin of others upon him, He will hide His face from him, as well as from the actually guilty. In God infinite love shines over all, but it does not eclipse His absolute justice any more than His justice is permitted to destroy His love. God hath all perfections in perfection, and in Christ Jesus we see the reflection of them. Beloved, this is a wonderful theme! Oh, that I had a tongue worthy of this subject! but who could ever reach the height of this great argument?

Once more, when inquiring, "Why did Jesus suffer to be forsaken of the Father?" We see the fact that *the Captain of our salvation was thus made perfect through suffering.* Every part of the road has been traversed by our Lord's own feet. Suppose, beloved, the Lord Jesus had never been thus forsaken, then one of His disciples might have been called to that sharp endurance, and the Lord Jesus could not have sympathized with him in it. He would turn to his Leader and Captain, and say to him, "Didst thou, my Lord, ever feel this darkness?" Then the Lord Jesus would answer, "No. This is a descent such as I never made." What a dreadful lack would the tried one have felt! For the servant to bear a grief his Master never knew would be sad indeed.

There would have been a wound for which there was no ointment, a pain for which there was no balm. But it is not so now. "In all their affliction He was afflicted." "He was in all points tempted like as we are, yet without sin." Wherein we greatly rejoice at this time, and so often as we are cast down. Underneath us is the deep experience of our forsaken Lord.

I have done when I have said three things. The first is, you and I that are believers in the Lord Jesus Christ, and are resting in Him alone for salvation, *let us lean hard,* let us bear with all our weight on our Lord. He will bear the full weight of all our sin and care. As to my sin, I hear its harsh accusing no more when I hear Jesus cry, "Why hast thou forsaken me?" I know that I deserve the deepest Hell at the hand of God's vengeance; but I am not afraid. He will never forsake *me,* for He forsook His Son on my behalf. I shall not suffer for my sin, for Jesus has suffered to the full in my stead; yea, suffered so far as to cry, "My God, my God, why hast thou forsaken me?" Behind this brazen wall of substitution a sinner is safe. These "munitions of rock" guard all believers, and they may rest secure. The rock is cleft for me; I hide in its rifts, and no harm can reach me. You have a full atonement, a great sacrifice, a glorious vindication of the law; wherefore rest at peace, all you that put your trust in Jesus.

Next, if ever in our lives henceforth we should think that God hath deserted us, *let us learn from our Lord's example how to behave ourselves.* If God hath left thee, do not shut up thy Bible; nay, open it, as thy Lord did, and find a text that will suit thee. If God hath left thee, or thou thinkest so, do not give up prayer; nay, pray as thy Lord did, and be more earnest than ever. If thou thinkest God has forsaken thee, do not give up thy faith in Him; but, like thy Lord, cry thou, "My God, my God," again and again. If thou hast had one anchor before, cast out two anchors now, and double the hold of thy faith. If thou canst not call Jehovah "Father," as was Christ's wont, yet call Him thy "God." Let the personal pronouns take their hold—"My God, my God." Let nothing drive thee from thy faith. Still hold on Jesus, sink or swim. As for me, if ever I am lost, it shall be at the foot of the cross. To this pass have I come, that if I never see the face of

God with acceptance, yet I will believe that He will be faithful to His Son, and true to the covenant sealed by oaths and blood. He that believeth in Jesus hath everlasting life: there I cling, like the limpet to the rock. There is but one gate of Heaven, and even if I may not enter it, I will cling to the posts of its door. What am I saying? I shall enter in; for that gate was never shut against a soul that accepted Jesus; and Jesus saith, "Him that cometh to me I will in no wise cast out."

The last of the three points is this, *let us abhor the sin which brought such agony upon our beloved Lord.* What an accursed thing is sin, which crucified the Lord Jesus! Do you laugh at it? Will you go and spend an evening to see a mimic performance of it? Do you roll sin under your tongue as a sweet morsel, and then come to God's house, on the Lord's-day morning, and think to worship him? Worship him! Worship him, with sin indulged in your breast. Worship him, with sin loved and pampered in your life! O sirs, if I had a dear brother who had been murdered, what would you think of me if I valued the knife which had been crimsoned with His blood?—if I made a friend of the murderer, and daily consorted with the assassin, who drove the dagger into my brother's heart? Surely I, too, must be an accomplice in the crime! Sin murdered Christ; will you be a friend to it? Sin pierced the heart of the Incarnate God: can you love it? Oh, that there was an abyss as deep as Christ's misery, that I might at once hurl this dagger of sin into its depths whence it might never be brought to light again! Begone, O sin! Thou art banished from the heart where Jesus reigns! Begone, for thou hast crucified my Lord, and made Him cry, "Why hast thou forsaken me?" O my hearers, if you did but know yourselves, and know the love of Christ, you would each one vow that you would harbor sin no longer. You would be indignant at sin, and cry,

> The dearest idol I have known,
> Whate'er that idol be,
> Lord, I will tear it from its throne,
> And worship only thee.

May that be the issue of my morning's discourse, and then I shall be well content. The Lord bless you! May the Christ who suffered for you, bless you, and out of His darkness may your light arise! Amen.

The Shortest of the Seven Cries

"After this, Jesus knowing that all things were now accomplished, that the scripture might be fulfilled, saith, 'I thirst.'"—John 19:28.

It was most fitting that every word of our Lord upon the cross should be gathered up and preserved. As not a bone of Him shall be broken, so not a word shall be lost. The Holy Spirit took special care that each of the sacred utterances should be fittingly recorded. There were, as you know, seven of those last words, and seven is the number of perfection and fullness; the number which blends the three of the infinite God with the four of complete creation. Our Lord in His death-cries, as in all else, was perfection itself. There is a fullness of meaning in each utterance which no man shall be able fully to bring forth, and when combined they make up a vast deep of thought, which no human line can fathom. Here as everywhere else, we are constrained to say of our Lord, "Never man spake like this man." Amid all the anguish of His spirit His last words prove Him to have remained fully self-possessed, true to His forgiving nature, true to His kingly office, true to His filial relationship, true to His God, true to His love of the written Word, true to His glorious work, and true to His faith in His Father.

As these seven sayings were so faithfully recorded, we do not wonder that they have frequently been the subject of devout meditation. Fathers and confessors, preachers and divines have delighted to dwell upon every syllable of these matchless cries. These solemn sentences have shone like the seven golden candlesticks or the seven stars of the Apocalypse, and have lighted multitudes of men to Him who spake them. Thoughtful men have drawn a wealth of meaning from them, and in so doing have arranged them into different groups, and placed them under several heads. I cannot give you more than a mere taste of this rich subject, but I have been most struck with two ways of regarding our Lord's last words. First, they teach and confirm many of the doctrines of our holy faith. *"Father, forgive them; for they know not what they do"* is the first. Here is the forgiveness of sin—free forgiveness in answer to the Savior's plea. *"Today shall thou be with me in paradise."* Here is the safety of the believer in the hour of his departure, and his instant admission into the presence of his Lord. It is a blow at the fable of purgatory which strikes it to the heart. *"Woman, behold thy son!"* This very plainly sets forth the true and proper humanity of Christ, who to the end recognized His human relationship to Mary, of whom He was born. Yet His language teaches us not to worship *her,* for He calls her "woman," but to honor Him who in His direst agony thought of her needs and griefs, as He also thinks of all His people, for these are His mother and sister and brother. *"Eloi, Eloi, lama sabachthani?"* is the fourth cry, and it illustrates the penalty endured by our Substitute when He bore our sins, and so was forsaken of His God. The sharpness of that sentence no exposition can fully disclose to us: it is keen as the very edge and point of the sword which pierced His heart. *"I thirst"* is the fifth cry, and its utterance teaches us the truth of Scripture, for all things were accomplished, that the Scripture might be fulfilled, and therefore our Lord said, "I thirst." Holy Scripture remains the basis of our faith, established by every word and act of our Redeemer. The last word but one is, *"It is finished."* There is the complete justification of the believer, since the work by which he is accepted is fully accomplished. The last of His last words is also taken from the Scriptures, and shows where His mind was feeding. He cried, ere He bowed the head which He had held erect amid all His conflict, as one who never yielded, *"Father, into thy hands I commend my spirit."* In that cry there is reconciliation to God. He who stood in our stead has finished all His work, and now His spirit comes back to the Father, and He brings us with him. Every word, therefore, you see, teaches us some grand fundamental doctrine of our blessed faith. "He that hath ears to hear, let him hear."

A second mode of treating these seven cries is to view them as setting forth the person and offices of our Lord who uttered them. *"Father, forgive them; for they know not what they do"* —here we see the Mediator interceding: Jesus standing before the Father pleading for the guilty. *"Verily I say unto thee, today shalt thou be with me in paradise"*—this is the Lord Jesus in kingly power, opening with the key of David a door which none can shut, admitting into the gates of Heaven the poor soul who had confessed Him on the tree. Hail, everlasting King in Heaven, thou dost admit to thy paradise whomsoever thou wilt! Nor dost thou set a time for waiting, but instantly thou dost set wide the gate of pearl; thou hast all power in Heaven as well as upon earth. Then came, *"Woman, behold thy son!"* wherein we see the Son of man in the gentleness of a son caring for His bereaved mother. In the former cry, as He opened Paradise, you saw the Son of God; now you see Him who was verily and truly born of a woman, made under the law; and under the law you see Him still, for He honors His mother and cares for her in the last article of death. Then comes the *"My God, my God, why hast thou forsaken me?"* Here we behold His human *soul* in anguish, His inmost heart overwhelmed by the withdrawing of Jehovah's face, and made to cry out as if in perplexity and amazement. *"I thirst,"* is His human *body* tormented by grievous pain. Here you see how the mortal flesh had to share in the agony of the inward spirit. *"It is finished"* is the last word but one, and there you see the perfected Savior, the Captain of our salvation, who has completed the undertaking upon which He had entered, finished transgression, made an end of sin, and brought in everlasting righteousness. The last expiring word in which He *commended His spirit to His Father,* is the note of acceptance for himself and for us all. As He commends His spirit into the Father's hand, so does He bring all believers nigh to God, and henceforth we are in the hand of the Father, who is greater than all, and none shall pluck us thence. Is not this a fertile field of thought? May the Holy Spirit often lead us to glean therein.

There are many other ways in which these words might be read, and they would be found to be all full of instruction. Like the steps of a ladder or the links of a golden chain, there is a mutual dependence and interlinking of each of the cries, so that one leads to another and that to a third. Separately or in connection, our Master's words overflow with instruction to thoughtful minds: but of all save one I must say, "Of which we cannot now speak particularly."

Our text is the shortest of all the words of Calvary; it stands as two words in our language—"I thirst," but in the Greek it is only one. I cannot say that it is short and sweet, for, alas, it was bitterness itself to our Lord Jesus; and yet out of its bitterness I trust there will come great sweetness to us. Though bitter to Him in the speaking it will be sweet to us in the hearing—so sweet that all the bitterness of our trials shall be forgotten as we remember the vinegar and gall of which He drank.

We shall by the assistance of the Holy Spirit try to regard these words of our Savior in a five-fold light.

I. First, we shall look upon them as the ensign of His true humanity.

Jesus said, "I thirst," and this is the complaint of a man. Our Lord is the Maker of the ocean and the waters that are above the firmament: it is His hand that stays or opens the bottles of Heaven, and sendeth rain upon the evil and upon the good. "The sea is his, and He made it," and all fountains and springs are of His digging. He poureth out the streams that run among the hills, the torrents which rush adown the mountains, and the flowing rivers which enrich the plains. One would have said, "If He were thirsty He would not tell us, for all the clouds and rains would be glad to refresh His brow, and the brooks and streams would joyously flow at His feet." And yet, though He was Lord of all He had so fully taken upon himself the form of a servant and was so perfectly made in the likeness of sinful flesh, that He cried with fainting voice, "I thirst." How truly man He is; He is, indeed, "bone of our bone and flesh of our flesh," for He bears our infirmities. I invite you to meditate upon the true humanity of our Lord very reverently, and very lovingly. Jesus was proved to be really man, because He suffered the pains which belong to manhood. Angels cannot suffer thirst. A phantom, as some have called him, could not suffer in this fashion: but Jesus really suffered, not only the more refined pains of delicate and sensitive minds, but the rougher and commoner pangs of flesh and blood. Thirst is a commonplace misery, such as may happen to peasants or beggars; it is a real pain, and not a thing of a fancy or a nightmare of dreamland. Thirst is no royal grief, but an evil of universal manhood; Jesus is brother to the poorest and most humble of our race. Our Lord, however, endured thirst to an extreme degree, for it was the thirst of death which was upon him, and more, it was the thirst of one whose death was not a common one, "for He tasted death for every man." That thirst was caused, perhaps, in part by the loss of blood, and by the fever created by the irritation caused by His four grievous wounds. The nails were fastened in the most sensitive parts of the body, and the wounds were widened as the weight of His body dragged the nails through His blessed flesh, and tore His tender nerves. The extreme tension produced a burning feverishness. It was pain that dried His mouth and made it like an oven, till He declared, in the language of the twenty-second psalm, "My tongue cleaveth to my jaws." It was a thirst such as none of us have ever known, for not yet has the death dew condensed upon our brows. We shall perhaps know it in our measure in our dying hour, but not yet, nor ever so terribly as He did. Our Lord felt that grievous drought of dissolution by which all moisture seems dried up, and the flesh returns to the dust of death: this those know who have commenced to tread the valley of the shadow of death. Jesus, being a man, escaped none of the ills which are allotted to man in death. He is indeed Immanuel, God with us everywhere.

Believing this, let us tenderly feel how very near akin to us our Lord Jesus has become. You have been ill, and you have been parched with fever as He was, and then you too have gasped out "I thirst." Your path runs hard by that of your Master. He said, "I thirst," in order that someone might bring Him drink, even as you have wished to have a cooling draught handed to you when you could not help yourself. Can you help feeling how very near Jesus is to us when His lips must be moistened with a sponge, and He must be so dependent upon others as to ask drink from their hand? Next time your fevered lips murmur "I am very thirsty," you may say to yourself, "Those are sacred words, for my Lord spake in that fashion." The words, "I thirst," are a common voice in death chambers. We can never forget the painful scenes of which we have been witness, when we have watched the dissolving of the human frame. Some of those whom we loved very dearly we have seen quite unable to help themselves; the death sweat has been upon them, and this has been one of the marks of their approaching dissolution, that they have been parched with thirst, and could only mutter between their half-closed lips, "Give me to drink." Ah, beloved, our Lord was so truly man that all our griefs remind us of him: the next time we are thirsty we may gaze upon him; and whenever we see a friend faint and thirsting while dying we may behold our Lord dimly, but truly, mirrored in His members. How near akin the thirsty Savior is to us; let us love Him more and more.

How great the love which led Him to such a condescension as this! Do not let us forget the infinite distance between the Lord of glory on His throne and the Crucified dried up with thirst. A river of the water of life, pure as crystal, proceedeth today out of the throne of God and of the Lamb, and yet once He condescended to say, "I thirst." He is Lord of fountains and all deeps, but not a cup of cold water was placed to His lips. Oh, if He had at any time said, "I thirst," before His angelic guards, they would surely have emulated the courage of the men of David when they cut their way to the well of Bethlehem that was within the gate, and drew water in jeopardy of their lives. Who among us would not willingly pour out his soul unto death if he might but give refreshment to the Lord? And yet He placed himself for our sakes into a position of shame and suffering where none would wait upon him, but when He cried, "I thirst," they gave Him vinegar to drink. Glorious stoop of our exalted Head! O Lord Jesus, we love thee and we worship thee! We would fain lift thy name on high in grateful remembrance of the depths to which thou didst descend!

While thus we admire His condescension let our thoughts also turn with delight to His sure sympathy: for if Jesus said, "I thirst," then He knows all our frailties and woes. The next time we are in pain or are suffering depression of spirit we will remember that our Lord understands it all, for He has had practical, personal experience of it. Neither in torture of body nor in sadness of heart are we deserted by our Lord; His line is parallel with ours. The arrow which has lately pierced thee, my brother, was first stained with His blood. The cup of which thou art made to drink, though it be very bitter, bears the mark of His lips about its brim. He hath traversed the mournful way before thee, and every footprint thou leavest in the sodden soil is stamped side by side with His footmarks. Let the sympathy of Christ, then, be fully believed in and deeply appreciated, since He said, "I thirst."

Henceforth, also, let us cultivate the spirit of resignation, for we may well rejoice to carry a cross which His shoulders have borne before us. Beloved, if our Master said, "I thirst," do we expect every day to drink of streams from Lebanon? He was innocent, and yet He thirsted; shall we marvel if guilty ones are now and then chastened? If He was so poor that His garments were stripped from him, and He was hung up upon the tree, penniless and friendless, hungering and thirsting, will you henceforth groan and murmur because you bear the yoke of poverty and want? There is bread upon your table today, and there will be at least a cup of cold water to refresh you. You are not, therefore, so poor as He. Complain not, then. Shall the servant be above his Master, or the disciple above his Lord? Let patience have her perfect work. You do suffer. Perhaps, dear sister, you carry about with you a gnawing disease which eats at your heart, but Jesus took our sicknesses, and His cup was more bitter than yours. In your chamber let the gasp of your Lord as He said, "I thirst," go through your ears, and as you hear it let it touch your heart and cause you to gird up yourself and say, "Doth He say, 'I thirst'? Then I will thirst with Him and not complain, I will suffer with Him and not murmur." The Redeemer's cry of "I thirst" is a solemn lesson of patience to His afflicted.

Once again, as we think of this "I thirst," which proves our Lord's humanity, let us resolve to shun no denials, but rather court them that we may be conformed to His image. May we not be half ashamed of our pleasures when He says, "I thirst"? May we not despise our loaded table while He is so neglected? Shall it ever be a hardship to be denied the satisfying draught when He said, I thirst." Shall carnal appetites be indulged and bodies pampered when Jesus cried "I thirst"? What if the bread be dry, what if the medicine be nauseous; yet for His thirst there was no relief but gall and vinegar, and dare we complain? For His sake we may rejoice in self-denials, and accept Christ and a crust as all we desire between here and Heaven. A Christian living to indulge the base appetites of a brute beast, to eat and to drink almost to gluttony and drunkenness, is utterly unworthy of the name. The conquest of the appetites, the entire subjugation of the flesh, must be achieved, for before our great Exemplar said, "It is finished," wherein methinks He reached the greatest height of all, He stood as only upon the next lower step to that elevation, and said, "I thirst." The power to suffer for another, the capacity to be self-denying even to an extreme to accomplish some great work for God—this is a thing to be sought after, and must be gained before our work is done, and in this Jesus is before us our example and our strength.

Thus have I tried to spy out a measure of teaching, by using that one glass for the soul's eye, through which we look upon "I thirst" as the ensign of His true humanity.

II. Secondly, we shall regard these words, "I thirst," as the token of His suffering substitution.

The great Surety says, "I thirst," because He is placed in the sinner's stead, and He must therefore undergo the penalty of sin for the ungodly. "My God, my God, why hast thou forsaken me?" points to the anguish of His soul; "I thirst" expresses in part the torture of His body; and they were both needful, because it is written of the God of justice that He is "able to destroy both soul and body in Hell," and the pangs that are due to law are of both kinds, touching both heart and flesh. See, brethren, where sin begins, and mark that there it ends. It began with the mouth of appetite, when it was sinfully gratified, and it ends when a kindred appetite is graciously denied. Our first parents plucked forbidden fruit, and by eating slew the race. Appetite was the door of sin, and therefore in that point our Lord was put to pain. With "I thirst" the evil is destroyed and receives its expiation. I saw the other day the emblem of a serpent with its tail in its mouth, and if I carry it a little beyond the artist's intention, the symbol may set forth appetite swallowing up itself. A carnal appetite of the body, the satisfaction of the desire for food, first brought us down under the first Adam, and now the pang of thirst, the denial of what the body craved for, restores us to our place.

Nor is this all. We know from experience that the present effect of sin in every man who indulges in it is thirst of soul. The mind of man is like the daughters of the horseleech, which cry forever "Give, give." Metaphorically understood, thirst is dissatisfaction, the craving of the mind for something which it has not, but which it pines for. Our Lord says, "If any man thirst, let Him come unto me and drink," that thirst being the result of sin in every ungodly man at this moment. Now Christ standing in the stead of the ungodly, suffers thirst as a type of His enduring the result of sin. More solemn still is the reflection that according to our Lord's own teaching, thirst will also be the eternal result of sin, for He says, concerning the rich glutton, "In Hell he lift up his eyes, being in torment," and his prayer, which was denied him, was, "Father Abraham, send Lazarus, that he may dip the tip of his finger in water and cool my tongue, for I am tormented in this flame." Now recollect, if Jesus had not thirsted, every one of us would have thirsted forever afar off from God, with an impassable gulf between us and Heaven. Our sinful tongues, blistered by the fever of passion, must have burned forever had not His tongue been tormented with thirst in our stead. I suppose that the "I thirst" was uttered softly, so that perhaps only one and another who stood near the cross heard it at all; in contrast with the louder cry of *"Lama sabachthani"* and the triumphant shout of "It is finished": but that soft, expiring sigh, "I thirst," has ended for us the thirst which else, insatiably fierce, had preyed upon us throughout eternity. Oh, wondrous substitution of the just for the unjust, of God for man, of the perfect Christ for us guilty, Hell-deserving rebels. Let us magnify and bless our Redeemer's name.

It seems to me very wonderful that this "I thirst" should be, as it were, the clearance of it all. He had no sooner said "I thirst," and sipped the vinegar, than He shouted, "It is finished"; and all was over: the battle was fought and the victory won forever, and our great Deliverer's thirst was the sign of His having smitten the last foe. The flood of His grief had passed the high-water mark, and began to be assuaged. The "I thirst" was the bearing of the last pang; what if I say it was the expression of the fact that His pangs had at last begun to cease, and their fury had spent itself, and left Him able to note His lesser pains? The excitement of a great struggle makes men forget thirst and faintness; it is only when all is over that they come back to themselves and note the spending of their strength. The great agony of being forsaken by God was over, and He felt faint when the strain was withdrawn. I like to think of our Lord's saying, "It is finished," directly after He had exclaimed, "I thirst"; for these two voices come so naturally together. Our glorious Samson had been fighting our foes; heaps upon heaps He had slain His thousands, and now like Samson He was sore athirst. He sipped of the vinegar, and He was refreshed, and no sooner has He thrown off the thirst than He shouted like a conqueror, "It is finished," and quitted the field, covered with renown. Let us exult as we see our Substitute going through with His work even to the bitter end, and then with a *"Consummatum est"* returning to His Father, God. O souls, burdened with sin, rest ye here, and resting live.

III. We will now take the text in a third way, and may the Spirit of God instruct us once again. The utterance of "I thirst" brought out a type of man's treatment of his Lord.

It was a confirmation of the Scripture testimony with regard to man's natural enmity to God. According to modern thought, man is a very fine and noble creature, struggling to become better. He is greatly to be commended and admired, for his sin is said to be a seeking after God, and his superstition is a struggling after light. Great and worshipful being that he is, truth is to be altered for him, the gospel is to be modulated to suit the tone of his various generations, and all the arrangements of the universe are to be rendered subservient to his interests. Justice must fly the field lest it be severe to so deserving a being; as for punishment, it must not be whispered to his ears polite. In fact, the tendency is to exalt man above God and give him the highest place. But such is not the truthful estimate of man according to the Scriptures: there man is a fallen creature, with a carnal mind which cannot be reconciled to God; a worse than brutish creature, rendering evil for good, and treating his God with vile ingratitude. Alas, man is the slave and the dupe of Satan, and a black-hearted traitor to his God. Did not the prophecies say that man would give to his incarnate God gall to eat and vinegar to drink? It is done. He came to save, and man denied Him hospitality: at the first there was no room for Him at the inn, and at the last there was not one cool cup of water for Him to drink; but when He thirsted they gave Him vinegar to drink. This is man's treatment of his Savior. Universal manhood, left to itself, rejects, crucifies, and mocks the Christ of God. This was the act too, of man at his best, when he is moved to pity; for it seems clear that he who lifted up the wet sponge to the Redeemer's lips, did it in compassion. I think that Roman soldier meant well, at least well for a rough warrior with his little light and knowledge. He ran and filled a sponge with vinegar: it was the best way he knew of putting a few drops of moisture to the lips of one who was suffering so much; but though he felt a degree of pity, it was such as one might show to a dog; he felt no reverence, but mocked as he relieved. We read, "The soldiers also mocked Him, offering Him vinegar." When our Lord cried, "Eloi, Eloi," and afterwards said, "I thirst," the persons around the cross said, "Let be, let us see whether Elias will come to save Him," mocking Him; and, according to Mark, he who gave the vinegar uttered much the same words. He pitied the sufferer, but he thought so little of Him that he joined in the voice of scorn. Even when man compassionates the sufferings of Christ, and man would have ceased to be human if he did not, still he scorns Him; the very cup which man gives to Jesus is at once scorn and pity, for "the tender mercies of the wicked are cruel." See how man at his best mingles admiration of the Savior's person with scorn of His claims; writing books to hold Him up as an example and at the same moment rejecting His deity; admitting that He was a wonderful man, but denying His most sacred mission; extolling His ethical teaching and then trampling on His blood: thus giving Him drink, but that drink vinegar. O my hearers, beware of praising Jesus and denying His atoning sacrifice. Beware of rendering Him homage and dishonoring His name at the same time.

Alas, my brethren, I cannot say much on the score of man's cruelty to our Lord without touching myself and you. Have *we* not often given Him vinegar to drink? Did we not do so years ago before we knew Him? We used to melt when we heard about His sufferings, but we did not turn from our sins. We gave Him our tears and then grieved Him with our sins. We thought sometimes that we loved Him as we heard the story of His death, but we did not change our lives for His sake, nor put our trust in Him, and so we gave Him vinegar to drink. Nor does the grief end here, for have not the best works we have ever done, and the best feelings we have ever felt, and the best prayers we have ever offered, been tart and sour with sin? Can they be compared to generous wine? are they not more like sharp vinegar? I wonder He has ever received them, as one marvels why He received this vinegar; and yet He has received them, and smiled upon us for presenting them. He knew once how to turn water into wine, and in matchless love He has often turned our sour drink-offerings into something sweet to Himself, though in themselves, methinks, they have been the juice of sour grapes, sharp enough to set His teeth on edge. We may therefore come before Him, with all the rest of our race, when God subdues them to repentance by His love, and look on Him whom we have pierced, and mourn for Him as one that is in bitterness for His firstborn. We may well remember our faults this day,

> We, whose proneness to forget
> Thy dear love, on Olivet
> Bathed thy brow with bloody sweat;
>
> We, whose sins, with awful power,
> Like a cloud did o'er thee lower,
> In that God-excluding hour;
>
> We, who still, in thought and deed,
> Often hold the bitter reed
> To thee, in thy time of need.

I have touched that point very lightly because I want a little more time to dwell upon a fourth view of this scene. May the Holy Ghost help us to hear a fourth tuning of the dolorous music, "I thirst."

IV. I think, beloved friends, that the cry of "I thirst" was the mystical expression of the desire of His heart: "I thirst."

I cannot think that natural thirst was all He felt. He thirsted for water doubtless, but His soul was thirsty in a higher sense; indeed, He seems only to have spoken that the Scriptures might be fulfilled as to the offering Him vinegar. Always was He in harmony with himself, and His body was always expressive of His soul's cravings as well as of its own longings. "I thirst" meant that His heart was thirsting to save men. This thirst had been on Him from the earliest of His earthly days. "Wist ye not," said he, while yet a boy, "that I must be about my Father's business?" Did He not tell His disciples, "I have a baptism to be baptized with, and how am I straitened till it be accomplished?" He thirsted to pluck us from between the jaws of Hell, to pay our redemption price, and set us free from the eternal condemnation which hung over us; and when on the cross the work was almost done His thirst was not assuaged, and could not be till He could say, "It is finished." It is almost done, thou Christ of God; thou hast almost saved thy people; there remaineth but one thing more, that thou shouldst actually die, and hence thy strong desire to come to the end and complete thy labor. Thou wast still straitened till the last pang was felt and the last word spoken to complete the full redemption, and hence thy cry, "I thirst."

Beloved, there is now upon our Master, and there always has been, a thirst after the love of His people. Do you not remember how that thirst of His was strong in the old days of the prophet? Call to mind His complaint in the fifth chapter of Isaiah,

> Now will I sing to my well-beloved a song of my beloved touching His vineyard. My well-beloved hath a vineyard in a very fruitful hill: and He fenced it, and gathered out the stones thereof, and planted it with the choicest vine, and built a tower in the midst of it, and also made a winepress therein.

What was He looking for from His vineyard and its winepress? What but for the juice of the vine that He might be refreshed? "And He looked that it should bring forth grapes, and it brought forth wild grapes,"—vinegar, and not wine; sourness, and not sweetness. So He was thirsting then. According to the sacred canticle of love, in the fifth chapter of the Song of Songs, we learn that when He drank in those olden times it was in the garden of His church that He was refreshed. What doth He say? "I am come into my garden, my sister, my spouse: I have gathered my myrrh with my spice; I have eaten my honeycomb with my honey; I have drunk my wine with my milk; eat, O friends; drink, yea, drink abundantly, O beloved." In the same song He speaks of His church, and says, "The roof of thy mouth is as the best wine for my beloved, that goeth down sweetly, causing the lips of those that are asleep to speak." And yet again in the eighth chapter the bride saith, "I would cause thee to drink of spiced wine of the juice of my pomegranate." Yes, He loves to be with His people; they are the garden where He walks for refreshment, and their love, their graces, are the milk and wine of which He delights to drink. Christ was always thirsty to save men, and to be loved of men; and we see a type of His life-long desire when, being weary, He sat thus on the well and said to the woman of Samaria, "Give me to drink." There was a deeper meaning in His words than she dreamed of, as a verse further down fully proves, when He said to His disciples, "I have meat to eat that ye know not of." He derived spiritual refreshment from the winning of that woman's heart to Himself.

And now, brethren, our blessed Lord has at this time a thirst for communion with each one of you who are His people, not because you can do Him good, but because He can do you good. He thirsts to bless you and to receive your grateful love in return; He thirsts to see you looking with believing eye to His fullness, and holding out your emptiness that He may supply it. He saith, "Behold, I stand at the door and knock." What knocks He for? It is that He may eat and drink with you, for He promises that if we open to Him He will enter in and sup with us and we with Him. He is thirsty still, you see, for our poor love, and surely we cannot deny it to Him. Come let us pour out full flagons, until His joy is fulfilled in us. And what makes Him love us so? Ah, that I cannot tell, except His own great love. He *must* love; it is His nature. He must love His chosen whom He has once begun to love, for He is the same yesterday, today, and forever. His great love makes Him thirst to have us much nearer than we are; He will never be satisfied till all His redeemed are beyond gunshot of the enemy. I will give you one of His thirsty prayers—"Father, I will that they also whom thou hast given me be with me where I am, that they may behold my glory." He wants you, brother, He wants you, dear sister, He longs to have you wholly to Himself. Come to Him in prayer, come to Him in fellowship, come to Him by perfect consecration, come to Him by surrendering your whole being to the sweet mysterious influences of His Spirit. Sit at His feet with Mary, lean on His breast with John; yea, come with the spouse in the song and say, "Let Him kiss me with the kisses of His mouth, for His love is better than wine." He calls for that: will you not give it to him? Are you so frozen at heart that not a cup of cold water can be melted for Jesus? Are you lukewarm? O brother, if He says, "I thirst" and you bring Him a lukewarm heart, that is worse than vinegar, for He has said, "I will spew thee out of my mouth." He can receive vinegar, but not lukewarm love. Come, bring Him your warm heart, and let Him drink from that purified chalice as much as He wills. Let all your love be His. I know He loves to receive from you, because He delights even in a cup of cold water that you give to one of His disciples; how much more will He delight in the giving of your whole self to Him? Therefore while He thirsts give Him to drink this day.

V. Lastly, the cry of "I thirst" is to us the pattern of our death with Him.

Know ye not, beloved—for I speak to those who know the Lord—that ye are crucified together with Christ? Well, then, what means this cry, "I thirst," but this, that we should thirst too? We do not thirst after the old manner wherein we were bitterly afflicted, for He hath said, "He that drinketh of this water shall never thirst," but now we covet a new thirst, a refined and heavenly appetite, a craving for our Lord. O thou blessed Master, if we are indeed nailed up to the tree with thee, give us to thirst after thee with a thirst which only the cup of "the new covenant in thy blood" can ever satisfy. Certain philosophers have said that they love the pursuit of truth even better than the knowledge of truth. I differ from them greatly, but I will say this, that next to the actual enjoyment of my Lord's presence I love to hunger and to thirst after Him. Rutherford used words somewhat to this effect,

> I thirst for my Lord and this is joy; a joy which no man taketh from me. Even if I may not come at Him, yet shall I be full of consolation, for it is Heaven to thirst after Him, and surely He will never deny a poor soul liberty to admire Him, and adore Him, and thirst after Him.

As for myself, I would grow more and more insatiable after my divine Lord, and when I have much of Him I would still cry for more; and then for more, and still for more. My heart shall not be content till He is all in all to me, and I am altogether lost in Him. O to be enlarged in soul so as to take deeper draughts of His sweet love, for our heart cannot have enough. One would wish to be as the spouse, who, when she had already been feasting in the banqueting-house, and had found his fruit sweet to her taste, so that she was overjoyed, yet cried out, "Stay me with flagons, comfort me with apples, for I am sick of love." She craved full flagons of love though she was already overpowered by it. This is a kind of sweet whereof if a man hath much he must have more, and when he hath more he is under a still greater necessity to receive more, and so on, his appetite forever growing by that which it feeds upon, till he is filled with all the fullness of God. "I thirst,"—aye, this is my soul's word with her Lord. Borrowed from his lips it well suiteth my mouth.

> *I thirst, but not as once I did,*
> *The vain delights of Earth to share;*
> *Thy wounds, Emmanuel, all forbid*
> *That I should seek my pleasures there.*
>
> *Dear fountain of delight unknown!*
> *No longer sink below the brim;*
> *But overflow, and pour me down*
> *A living and life-giving stream.*

Jesus thirsted, then let us thirst in this dry and thirsty land where no water is. Even as the hart panteth after the water brooks, our souls would thirst after thee, O God.

Beloved, let us thirst for the souls of our fellow-men. I have already told you that such was our Lord's mystical desire; let it be ours also. Brother, thirst to have your children saved. Brother, thirst I pray you to have your workpeople saved. Sister, thirst for the salvation of your class, thirst for the redemption of your family, thirst for the conversion of your husband. We ought all to have a longing for conversions. Is it so with each one of you? If not, bestir yourselves at once. Fix your hearts upon some unsaved one, and thirst until he is saved. It is the way whereby many shall be brought to Christ, when this blessed soul-thirst of true Christian charity shall be upon those who are themselves saved. Remember how Paul said, "I say the truth in Christ, I lie not, my conscience also bearing me witness in the Holy Ghost, that I have great heaviness and continual sorrow in my heart. For I could wish that myself were accursed from Christ for my brethren, my kinsmen according to the flesh." He would have sacrificed himself to save his countrymen, so heartily did he desire their eternal welfare. Let this mind be in you also.

As for yourselves, thirst after perfection. Hunger and thirst after righteousness, for you shall be filled. Hate sin, and heartily loathe it; but thirst to be holy as God is holy, thirst to be like Christ, thirst to bring glory to His sacred name by complete conformity to His will.

May the Holy Ghost work in you the complete pattern of Christ crucified, and to Him shall be praise forever and ever. Amen.

Christ's Dying Word for His Church

"It is finished."—John 19:30.

In the original Greek of John's Gospel, there is only one word for this utterance of our Lord. To translate it into English, we have to use three words; but when it was spoken, it was only one—an ocean of meaning in a drop of language, a mere drop, for that is all that we can call one word. "It is finished." Yet it would need all the other words that ever were spoken, or ever can be spoken, to explain this one word. It is altogether immeasurable. It is high; I cannot attain to it. It is deep; I cannot fathom it. "Finished." I can half imagine the tone in which our Lord uttered this word, with a holy glorying, a sense of relief, the bursting out of a heart that had long been shut up within walls of anguish. "Finished." It was a Conqueror's cry; it was uttered with a loud voice. There is nothing of anguish about it, there is no wailing in it. It is the cry of One who has completed a tremendous labor, and is about to die; and ere He utters His death-prayer, "Father, into thy hands I commend my spirit," He shouts His life's last hymn in that one word, "Finished."

May God the Holy Spirit help me to handle aright this text that is at once so small and yet so great! There are four ways in which I wish to look at it with you. First, I will speak of this dying saying of our Lord *to His glory;* secondly, I will use the text *to the Church's comfort;* thirdly, I will try to handle the subject *to every believer's joy;* and fourthly, I will seek to show how our Lord's words ought to lead *to our own arousement.*

I. First, then, I will endeavor to speak of this dying saying of Christ to his glory. Let us begin with that.

Jesus said, "It is finished." Let us glory in Him that it is finished. You and I may well do this when we recollect how very few things we have finished.

We begin many things; and, sometimes, we begin well. We commence running like champions who must win the race; but soon we slacken our pace, and we fall exhausted on the course. The race commenced is never completed. In fact, I am afraid that we have never finished anything perfectly. You know what we say of some pieces of work, "Well, the man has done it; but there is no 'finish' about it." No, and you must begin with "finish," and go on with "finish," if you are at last able to say broadly as the Savior said without any qualification, "It is finished."

What was it that was finished? His life-work and His atoning sacrifice on our behalf. He had interposed between our souls and divine justice, and He had stood in our stead, to obey and suffer on our behalf. He began this work early in life, even while He was a child. He persevered in holy obedience three and thirty years. That obedience cost Him many a pang and groan. Now it is about to cost Him His life; and as He gives away His life to finish the work of obedience to the Father, and of redemption for us, He says, "It is finished." It was a wonderful work even to contemplate; only infinite love would have thought of devising such a plan. It was a wonderful work to carry on for so long; only boundless patience would have continued at it; and now that it requires the offering of himself, and the yielding up of His earthly life, only a Divine Savior, very God of very God, would or could have consummated it by the surrender of His breath. What a work it was! Yet it was finished; while you and I have lots of little things lying about that we have never finished. We have begun to do something for Jesus that would bring Him a little honor and glory; but we have never finished it. We did mean to glorify Christ; have not some of you intended, oh! so much? Yet it has never come to anything; but Christ's work, which cost Him heart and soul, body and spirit, cost Him everything, even to His death on the cross, He pushed through all that till it was accomplished, and He could say, "It is finished."

To whom did our Savior say, "It is finished"? He said it to all whom it might concern; but it seems to me that He chiefly said it to His Father, for, immediately after, apparently in a lower tone of voice, He said, "Father, into thy hands I commend my spirit." Beloved, it is one thing for me to say to you, "I have finished my work,"—possibly, if I were dying, you might say that I had finished my work; but for the Savior to say that to God, to hang in the presence of Him whose eyes are as a flame of fire, the great Reader and Searcher of all hearts, for Jesus to look the dread Father in the face, and say, as He bowed His head, "Father, it is finished; I have finished the work which thou gavest me to do,"—oh, who but He could venture to make such a declaration as that? We can find a thousand flaws in our best works; and when we lie dying, we shall still have to lament our shortcomings and excesses; but there is nothing of imperfection about Him who stood as Substitute for us; and unto the Father himself He can say, concerning all His work, "It is finished." Wherefore, glorify Him tonight. Oh, glorify Him in your hearts tonight that, even in the presence of the Great Judge of all, your Surety and your Substitute is able to claim perfection for all His service!

Just think also, for a minute or two, now that you have remembered what Jesus finished, and to whom He said that He had finished it, *how truly He had finished it*. From the beginning to the end of Christ's life there is nothing omitted, no single act of service ever left undone; neither is there any action of His slurred over, or performed in a careless manner. "It is finished," refers as much to His childhood as to His death. The whole of the service that He was to render to God, when He came here in human form, was finished in every single part and portion of it. I take up a piece of a cabinet-maker's work; and it bears a good appearance. I open the lid, and am satisfied with the workmanship; but there is something about the hinge that is not properly finished. Or, perhaps, if I turn it over, and look at the bottom of the box, I shall see that there is a piece that has been scamped, or that one part has not been well planed or properly polished. But if you examine the Master's work right through, if you begin at Bethlehem and go on to Golgotha, and look minutely at every portion of it, the private as well as the public, the silent as well as the spoken part, you will find that it is finished, completed, perfected. We may say of it that, among all works, there is none like it; a multitude of perfections joined together to make up one absolute perfection. Wherefore, let us glorify the name of our blessed Lord. Crown him; crown him; for He hath done His work well. Come, ye saints, speak much to His honor, and in your hearts keep on singing to the praise of Him who did so thoroughly, so perfectly, all the work which His Father gave Him to do.

In the first place, then, we use our Lord's words to His glory. Much might be said upon such a theme; but time will not permit it now.

II. Secondly, we will use the text to the Church's comfort.

I am persuaded that it was so intended to be used, for none of the words of our Lord on the cross are addressed to His Church but this one. I cannot believe that, when He was dying, He left His people, for whom He died, without a word. "Father, forgive them; for they know not what they do," is for sinners, not for saints. "I thirst," is for Himself; and so is that bitter cry,

"My God, my God, why hast thou forsaken me?" "Woman, behold thy son!" is for Mary. "Today shalt thou be with me in paradise," is for the penitent thief. "Into thy hands I commend my spirit," is for the Father. Jesus must have had something to say, in the hour of death, for His Church; and, surely, this is His dying word for her. He tells her, shouting it in her ear that has become dull and heavy with despair, "It is finished." "It is finished, O my redeemed one, my bride, my well-beloved, for whom I came to lay down my life; it is finished, the work is done!"

> *Love's redeeming work is done;*
> *Fought the fight, the battle won.*

"Christ loved the church, and gave Himself for it." John, in the Revelation, speaks of the Redeemer's work as already accomplished, and therefore he sings,

> Unto Him that loved us, and washed us from our sins in His own blood, and
> hath made us kings and priests unto God and His Father; to Him be glory and
> dominion forever and ever. Amen.

This truth is full of comfort to the people of God.

And, first, as it concerns Christ, do you not feel greatly comforted to think that He is to be humiliated no longer? *His suffering and shame are finished.* I often sing, with sacred exultation and pleasure, those lines of Dr. Watts,

> *No more the bloody spear,*
> *The cross and nails no more,*
> *For Hell itself shakes at His name,*
> *And all the heavens adore.*
>
> *There His full glories shine*
> *With uncreated rays,*
> *And bless His saints' and angels' eyes*
> *To everlasting days.*

I like also that expression in another of our hymns—

> *Now both the Surety and sinner are free.*

Not only are they free for whom Christ became a Surety, but He Himself is forever free from all the obligations and consequences of His suretyship. Men will never spit in His face again; the Roman soldiers will never scourge Him again. Judas, where art thou? Behold the Christ sitting upon His great white throne, the glorious King who was once the Man of sorrows! Now Judas, come, and betray Him with a kiss! What, man, dare you not do it? Come

Pilate, and wash your hands in pretended innocency, and say now that you are guiltless of His blood! Come, ye Scribes and Pharisees, and accuse Him; and oh, ye Jewish mob and Gentile rabble, newly-risen from the grave, shout now, "Away with him! Crucify him!" But see! they flee from Him; they cry to the mountains and rocks, "Fall on us, and hide us from the face of Him that sitteth on the throne!" Yet that is the face that was more marred than any man's, the face of Him whom they once despised and rejected. Are you not glad to think that they cannot despise Him now, that they cannot ill-treat Him now?

> 'Tis past—that agonizing hour
> Of torture and of shame;

and Jesus says of it, "It is finished."

We derive further comfort and joy as we think that, not only are Christ's pangs and sufferings finished, but His *Father's will and word have had a perfect completion*. Certain things were written that were to be done; and these are done. Whatsoever the Father required has been rendered. "It is finished." My Father will never say to me, "I cannot save thee by the death of my Son, for I am dissatisfied with His work." Oh, no, beloved; God is well pleased with Christ, and with us in Him! There is nothing which was arranged in the eternal mind to be done, yea, not a jot or tittle, but what Christ has done it all. As His eye, that eye that often wept for us, reads down the ancient writing, Christ is able to say, "I have finished the work which my Father gave me to do. Wherefore, be comforted, O my people, for my Father is well pleased with me, and well pleased with you in me!" I like, when I am in prayer, sometimes to say to the great Father,

> Father, look on thy Son. Is He not all loveliness? Are there not in Him unutterable beauties? Dost thou not delight in Him? If thou hast looked on me, and grown sick of me, as well thou mayest, now refresh thyself by looking on thy Well-beloved, delight thyself in Him;

> Him, and then the sinner see,
> Look through Jesus' wounds on me.

The perfect satisfaction of the Father with Christ's work for His people, so that Christ could say, "It is finished," is a ground of solid comfort to His Church evermore.

Dear friends, once more, take comfort from this "It is finished," for *the redemption of Christ's Church is perfected*. There is not another penny to be paid for her full release. There is no mortgage upon Christ's inheritance. Those whom He bought with blood are forever clear of all charges, paid for to the utmost. There was a handwriting of ordinances against us; but Christ hath taken it away, He hath nailed it to His cross. "It is finished," finished forever. All those overwhelming debts, which would have sunk us to the lowest hell, have been discharged; and they who believe in Christ may appear with boldness even before the throne of God itself. "It is finished." What comfort there is in this glorious truth!

> Lamb of God! thy death hath given
> Pardon, peace, and hope of Heaven:
> 'It is finished ' let us raise
> Songs of thankfulness and praise!

And I think that we may say to the Church of God that, when Jesus said, "It is finished," *her ultimate triumph was secured.* "Finished!" By that one word He declared that He had broken the head of the old dragon. By His death, Jesus has routed the hosts of darkness, and crushed the rising hopes of Hell. We have a stern battle yet to fight; nobody can tell what may await the Church of God in years to come, it would be idle for us to attempt to prophesy; but it looks as if there were to be sterner times and darker days than we have ever yet known; but what of that? Our Lord has defeated the foe; and we have to fight with one who is already vanquished. The old serpent has been crushed, His head is bruised, and we have now to trample on him. We have this sure word of promise to encourage us, "The God of peace shall bruise Satan under your feet shortly." Surely, "It is finished," sounds like the trumpet of victory; let us have faith to claim that victory through the blood of the Lamb, and let every Christian here, let the whole Church of God, as one mighty army, take comfort from this dying word of the now risen and ever-living Savior, "It is finished." His Church may rest perfectly satisfied that His work for her is fully accomplished.

III. *Now, thirdly, I want to use this expression, "It is finished," to every believer's joy.*

When our Lord said, "It is finished," there was something to make every believer in Him glad. What did that utterance mean? You and I have believed in Jesus of Nazareth; we believe Him to be the Messiah, sent of God. Now, if you will turn to the Old Testament, you will find that the marks of the Messiah are very many, and very complicated; and if you will then turn to the life and death of Christ, you will see in Him *every mark of the Messiah plainly exhibited.* Until He had said, "It is finished," and until He had actually died, there was some doubt that there might be some one prophecy unfulfilled; but now that He hangs upon the cross, every mark, and every sign, and every token of His Messiahship have been fulfilled, and He says. "It is finished." The life and death of Christ and the types of the Old Testament fit each other like hand and glove. It would be quite impossible for any person to write the life of a man, by way of fiction, and then in another book to write out a series of types, personal and sacrificial, and to make the character of the man fit all the types; even if he had permission to make both books, he could not do it. If he were allowed to make both the lock and the key, he could not do it; but here we have the lock made beforehand. In all the books of the Old Testament, from the prophecy in the Garden of Eden right away down to Malachi, the last of the prophets, there were certain marks and tokens of the Christ. All these were so very singular that it did not appear as if they could all meet in one person; but they did all meet in One, every one of them, whether it concerned some minute point or some prominent characteristic. When the Lord Jesus Christ had ended His life, He could say, "It is finished; my life has tallied with all that was said of it from the first word of prophecy even to the last." Now, that ought greatly to encourage your faith. You are not following cunningly-devised fables; but you are following One who must be the Messiah of God, since He so exactly fits all the prophecies and all the types that were given before concerning Him.

"It is finished." Let every believer be comforted in another respect, that *every honor which the law of God could require has been rendered to it.* You and I have broken that law, and all the race of mankind has broken it, too. We have tried to thrust God from His throne; we have dishonored His law; we have broken His commandments willfully and wickedly; but there has come One who is Himself God, the Law-giver, and He has taken human nature, and in that nature He has kept the law perfectly; and inasmuch as the law had been broken by man, He has in the nature of man borne the sentence due for all man's transgressions. The Godhead, being linked with the manhood, gave supreme virtue to all that the manhood suffered; and Christ, in life and in death, has magnified the law, and made it honorable; and God's law at this day is raised to even greater honor than it had before man broke it. The death of the Son of God, the sacrifice of the Lord Jesus Christ, has vindicated the great moral principle of God's government, and made His throne to stand out gloriously before the eyes of men and angels forever and ever. If Hell were filled with men, it would not be such a vindication of divine justice as when God spared not His own Son, but delivered Him up for us all, and made Him to die, the Just for the unjust, to bring us to God. Now let every believer rejoice in the great fact that, by the death of Christ, the law of God is abundantly honored. You can be saved without impugning the holiness of God; you are saved without putting any stain upon the divine statute-book. The law is kept, and mercy triumphs, too.

And, beloved, here is included, of necessity, another comforting truth. Christ might well say, "It is finished," for *every solace conscience can need is now given.* When your conscience is disturbed and troubled, if it knows that God is perfectly honored, and His law vindicated, then it becomes easy. Men are always starting some new theory of the atonement; and one has said lately that the atonement was simply meant as an easement to the conscience of men. It is not so, my brethren; there would be no easing of the conscience by anything that was meant for that alone. Conscience can only be satisfied if God is satisfied. Until I see how the law is vindicated, my troubled conscience can never find rest. Dear heart, are thine eyes red with weeping? Yet look thou to Him who hangs upon the tree. Is thy heart heavy even to despair? Look to Him who hangs upon the tree, and believe in Him. Take Him to be thy soul's atoning Lamb, suffering in thy stead. Accept of Him as thy Representative, dying thy death that thou mayest live His life, bearing thy sin that thou mayest be made the righteousness of God in Him. This is the best *quietus* in the world for every fear that conscience can raise; let every believer know that it is so.

Once more, there is joy to every believer when he remembers that, as Christ said, "It is finished," *every guarantee was given of the eternal salvation of all the redeemed.* It appears to me that, if Christ finished the work *for* us, He will finish the work *in* us. If He has undertaken so supreme a labor as the redemption of our souls by blood, and that is finished, then the great but yet minor labor of renewing our natures, and transforming us even unto perfection, shall be finished, too. If, when we were sinners, Christ loved us so as to die for us, now that He has redeemed us, and has already reconciled us to himself, and made us His friends and His disciples, will He not finish the work that is necessary to make us fit to stand among the golden lamps of Heaven, and to sing His praises in the country where nothing that defileth can ever enter?

> *The work which His goodness began,*
> *The arm of His strength will complete;*
> *His promise is yea and Amen,*
> *And never was forfeited yet:*
> *Things future, nor things that are now,*
> *Not all things below nor above,*
> *Can make Him His purpose forego,*
> *Or sever my soul from His love.*

I believe it, my brethren. He who has said, "It is finished," will never leave anything undone. It shall never be said of Him, "This Man began, but was not able to finish." If He has bought me with His blood, and called me by His grace, and I am resting on His promise and power, I shall be with Him where He is, and I shall behold His glory, as surely as He is Christ the Lord, and I am a believer in Him. What comfort this truth brings to every child of God!

Are there any of you here who are trying to do something to make a righteousness of your own? How dare you attempt such a work, when Jesus says, "It is finished"? Are you trying to put a few of your own merits together, a few odds and ends, fig-leaves and filthy rags of your own righteousness? Jesus says, "It is finished." Why do you want to add anything of your own to what He has completed? Do you say that you are not fit to be saved? What! have you to bring some of your fitness to eke out Christ's work? "Oh!" say you, "I hope to come to Christ one of these days when I get better." What! What! What! What! Are you to make yourself better, and then is Christ to do the rest of the work? You remind me of the railways to our country towns; you know that, often, the station is half-a-mile or a mile out of the town, so that you cannot get to the station without having an omnibus to take you there. But my Lord Jesus Christ comes right to the town of Mansoul. His railway runs close to your feet, and there is the carriage-door wide open; step in. You have not even to go over a bridge, or under a subway; there stands the carriage just before you. This royal railroad carries souls all the way from Hell's dark door, where they lie in sin, up to Heaven's great gate of pearl, where they dwell in perfect righteousness forever. Cast yourself on Christ; take Him to be everything you need, for He says of the whole work of salvation, "It is finished."

I recollect the saying of a Scotswoman, who had applied to be admitted to the communion of the kirk [church]. Being thought to be very ignorant, and little instructed in the things of God, she was put back by the elders. The minister also had seen her, and thought that, at least for a while, she should wait. I wish I could speak Scotch, so as to give you her answer, but I am afraid that I should make a mistake if I tried it. It is a fine language, doubtless, for those who can speak it. She said something like this, "Aweel, sir; aweel, sir, but I ken [know] ae thing. As the lintbell opens to the sun, so my heart opens to the name of Jesus." You have, perhaps, seen the flax-flower shut itself up when the sun has gone; and, if so, you know that, whenever the sun has come back, the flower opens itself at once. "So," said the poor woman, "I ken one thing, that as the flower opens to the sun, so my heart opens to the name of Jesus." Do you know that, friends? Do you ken that one thing? Then I do not care if you do not ken much else; if that one thing is known by you, and if it be really so, you may be far from perfect in your own estimation, but you are a saved soul.

One said to me, when she came to join the church, and I asked her whether she was perfect, "Perfect? Oh, dear no, sir! I wish that I could be." "Ah, yes!" I replied, "that would just please you, would it not?" "Yes; it would indeed," she answered. "Well, then," I said,

> that shows that your heart is perfect, and that you love perfect things; you are pining after perfection; there is a something in you, an "I" in you, that sinneth not, but that seeketh after that which is holy; and yet you do that which you would not, and you groan because you do, and the apostle is like you when He says, "It is no more I, the real I, that do it, but sin that dwelleth in me."

May the Lord put that "I" into many of you tonight, that "I" which will hate sin, that "I" which will find its Heaven in being perfectly free from sin, that "I" which will delight itself in the Almighty, that "I" which will sun itself in the smile of Christ, that "I" which will strike down every evil within as soon as ever it shows its head! So will you sing that familiar prayer of Toplady's that we have often sung,

> Let the water and the blood,
> From thy riven side which flow'd,
> Be of sin the double cure,
> Cleanse me from its guilt and power!

IV. *I close by saying, in the fourth place, that we shall use this text, "It is finished," to our own arousement.*

Somebody once wickedly said, "Well, if Christ has finished it, there is nothing for me to do now but to fold my hands, and go to sleep." That is the speech of a devil, not of a Christian! There is no grace in the heart when the mouth can talk like that. On the contrary, the true child of God says, "Has Christ finished His work for me? Then tell me what work I can do for Him." You remember the two questions of Saul of Tarsus. The first enquiry, after He had been struck down, was, "Who art thou, Lord?" And the next was, "Lord, what wilt thou have me to do?" If Christ has finished the work for you which you could not do, now go and finish the work for Him which you are privileged and permitted to do. Seek to:

> Rescue the perishing,
> Care for the dying,

Snatch them in pity from sin and the grave;
Weep o'er the erring one,
Lift up the fallen,
Tell them of Jesus, the Mighty to save

My inference from this saying of Christ, "It is finished," is this—Has He finished His work for me? Then I must get to work for Him, and I *must persevere until I finish my work, too;* not to save myself, for that is all done, but because I am saved. Now I must work for Him with all my might; and if there come discouragements, if there come sufferings, if there comes a sense of weakness and exhaustion, yet let me not give way to it; but, inasmuch as He pressed on till He could say, "It is finished," let me press on till I, too, shall be able to say, "I have finished the work which thou gavest me to do." You know how men who go fishing look out for the fish. I have heard of a man going to Keston Ponds on Saturday fishing, and stopping all day Sunday, Monday, Tuesday, Wednesday. There was another man fishing there, and the other man had only been there two days. He said, "I have been here two days, and I have only had one bite." "Why!" replied the other, "I have been here ever since last Saturday, and I have not had a bite yet; but I mean to keep on." "Well," answered the other, "I cannot keep on without catching anything." "Oh!" said number one, "but I have such a longing to catch some fish that I shall stop here till I do." I believe that fellow would catch some fish ultimately, if there were any to be caught; he is the kind of fisherman to do it, and we want to have men who feel that they must win souls for Christ, and that they will persevere till they do. It must be so with us, brethren and sisters; we cannot let men go down to Hell if there is any way of saving them.

The next inference is, that *we can finish our work, for Christ finished His.* You can put a lot of "finish" into your work, and you can hold on to the end, and complete the work by divine grace; and that grace is waiting for you, that grace is promised to you. Seek it, find it, get it. Do not act as some do, ah, even some who are before me now! They served God once, and then they ran away from Him. They have come back again; God bless them, and help them to be more useful! But future earnest service will never make up for that sad gap in their earlier career. It is best to keep on, and on, and on, from the commencement to the close; the Lord help us to persevere to the end, till we can truly say of our life-work, "It is finished!"

One word of caution I must give you. *Let us not think that our work is finished till we die.* "Well," says one, "I was just going to say of my work, 'It is finished.'" Were you? Were you? I remember that, when John Newton wrote a book about grace in the blade, and grace in the ear, and grace in the full corn in the ear, a very talkative body said to him, "I have been reading your valuable book, Mr. Newton; it is a splendid work; and when I came to that part, 'The full corn in the ear,' I thought how wonderfully you had described me." "Oh!" replied Mr. Newton, "but you could not have read the book rightly, for it is one of the marks of the full corn in the ear that it hangs its head very low." So it is; and when a man, in a careless, boastful spirit, says of his work, "It is finished," I am inclined to ask, "Brother, was it ever begun? If your work for Christ is finished, I should think that you never realized what it ought to be." As long as there is breath in our bodies, let us serve Christ; as long as we can think, as long as we can speak, as long as we can work, let us serve Him, let us even serve Him with our last gasp; and, if it be possible, let us try to set some work going that will glorify Him when we are dead and gone. Let us scatter some seed that may spring up when we are sleeping beneath the hillock in the cemetery. Ah, beloved, we shall never have finished our work for Christ until we bow our heads, and give up the ghost! The oldest friend here has a little something to do for the Master. Someone said to me, the other day, "I cannot think why old Mrs. So-and-so is spared; she is quite a burden to her friends." "Ah!" I replied, "she has something yet to do for her Lord, she has another word to speak for Him." Sister, look up your work, and get it done; and you, brother, see what remains of your life-work yet incomplete. Wind off the ends, get all the little corners finished. Who knows how long it may be before you and I may have to give in our account? Some are called away very suddenly; they are apparently in good health one day, and they are gone the next. I should not like to leave a half-finished life behind me. The Lord Jesus Christ said, "It is finished," and your heart should say, "Lord, and I will finish, too; not to mix my work with thine, but because thou hast finished thine, I will finish mine."

Now may the Lord give us the joy of His presence at His table! May the bread and wine speak to you much better than I can! May every heir of Heaven see Christ tonight, and rejoice in His finished work, for His dear name's sake! Amen.

It Is Finished!

"When Jesus therefore had received the vinegar, he said, 'It is finished':
and He bowed his head, and gave up the ghost."—John 19:30.

My brethren, I would have you attentively observe the singular clearness, power, and quickness of the Savior's mind in the last agonies
of death. When pains and groans attend the last hour, they frequently
have the effect of discomposing the mind, so that it is not possible for the
dying man to collect his thoughts, or having collected them, to utter them
so that they can be understood by others. In no case could we expect a remarkable exercise of memory, or a profound judgment upon deep subjects from an expiring man. But the Redeemer's last acts were full of
wisdom and prudence, although His sufferings were beyond all measure
excruciating. Remark how clearly He perceived the significance of every
type! How plainly He could read with dying eye those divine symbols
which the eyes of angels could only desire to look into! He saw the secrets
which have bewildered sages and astonished seers, all fulfilled in His own
body. Nor must we fail to observe the power and comprehensiveness by
which He grasped the chain which binds the shadowy past with the sun-lit
present. We must not forget the brilliance of that intelligence which
threaded all the ceremonies and sacrifices on one string of thought, beheld all the prophecies as one great revelation, and all the promises as the
heralds of one person, and then said of the whole, "'It is finished,' finished
in me." What quickness of mind was that which enabled Him to traverse
all the centuries of prophecy; to penetrate the eternity of the covenant,
and then to anticipate the eternal glories! And all this when He is mocked
by multitudes of enemies, and when His hands and feet are nailed to the
cross! What force of mind must the Savior have possessed, to soar above

those Alps of Agony, which touched the very clouds. In what a singular mental condition must He have been during the period of His crucifixion, to be able to review the whole roll of inspiration! Now, this remark may not seem to be of any great value, but I think its value lies in certain inferences that may be drawn from it. We have sometimes heard it said, "How could Christ, in so short a time, bear suffering which should be equivalent to the torments—the eternal torments of Hell?" Our reply is, we are not capable of judging what the Son of God might do even in a moment, much less what He might do and what He might suffer in His life and in His death. It has been frequently affirmed by persons who have been rescued from drowning, that the mind of a drowning man is singularly active. One who, after being some time in the water, was at last painfully restored, said that the whole of his history seemed to come before his mind while he was sinking, and that if any one had asked him how long he had been in the water, he should have said twenty years, whereas he had only been there for a moment or two. The wild romance of Mahomet's journey upon Alborak is not an unfitting illustration. He affirmed that when the angel came in vision to take him on his celebrated journey to Jerusalem, he went through all the seven heavens, and saw all the wonders thereof, and yet he was gone so short a time, that though the angel's wing had touched a basin of water when they started, they returned soon enough to prevent the water from being spilt. The long dream of the epileptic impostor may really have occupied but a second of time. The intellect of mortal man is such that, if God wills it, when it is in certain states, it can think out centuries of thought at once; it can go through in one instant what we should have supposed would have taken years upon years of time for it to know or feel. We think, therefore, that from the Savior's singular clearness and quickness of intellect upon the cross, it is very possible that He did in the space of two or three hours endure not only the agony which might have been contained in centuries, but even an equivalent for that which might be comprehended in everlasting punishment. At any rate, it is not for us to say that it could not be so. When the Deity is arrayed in manhood, then manhood becomes omnipotent to suffer; and just as the feet of Christ were once almighty to tread the seas, so now was His whole body become almighty to dive into the great waters, to endure an immersion in "unknown agonies." Do not, I pray you, let us attempt to measure Christ's sufferings by the finite line of your own ignorant reason, but let us know and believe that what He endured there was accepted by God as an equivalent for all our pains, and therefore it could not have been a trifle, but must have been all that Hart conceived it to be, when he says He bore

> *All that incarnate God could bear,*
> *With strength enough, but none to spare.*

My discourse will, I have no doubt, more fully illustrate the remark with which I have commenced; let us proceed to it at once. First, *let us hear the text and understand it;* then *let us hear it and wonder at it;* and then, thirdly, *let us hear it and proclaim it.*

I. Let us hear the text and understand it.

The Son of God has been made man. He has lived a life of perfect virtue and of total self-denial. He has been all that life long despised and rejected of men, a man of sorrows and acquainted with grief. His enemies have been legion; His friends have been few, and those few faithless. He is at last delivered over into the hands of them that hate him. He is arrested while in the act of prayer; He is arraigned before both the spiritual and temporal courts. He is robed in mockery, and then unrobed in shame. He is set upon His throne in scorn, and then tied to the pillar in cruelty. He is declared innocent, and yet He is delivered up by the judge who ought to have preserved Him from His persecutors. He is dragged through the streets of that Jerusalem which had killed the prophets, and would now crimson itself with the blood of the prophets' Master. He is brought to the cross; He is nailed fast to the cruel wood. The sun burns Him. His cruel wounds increase the fever. God forsakes Him. "My God, my God, why hast thou forsaken me?" contains the concentrated anguish of the world. While He hangs there in mortal conflict with sin and Satan, His heart is broken, His limbs are dislocated. Heaven fails Him, for the sun is veiled in darkness. Earth forsakes Him, for "his disciples forsook Him and fled." He looks everywhere, and there is none to help; He casts His eye around, and there is no man that can share His toil. He treads the winepress alone; and of the people there is none with Him. On, on, He goes, steadily determined to drink the last dreg of that cup which must not pass from Him if His Father's will be done. At last He cries—"It is finished," and He gives up the ghost. Hear it, Christians, hear this shout of triumph as it rings today with all the freshness and force which it had eighteen hundred years ago! Hear it from the Sacred Word, and from the Savior's lips, and may the Spirit of God open your ears that you may hear as the learned, and understand what you hear!

1. What meant the Savior, then, by this—"It is finished"? He meant, first of all, *that all the types, promises, and prophecies were now fully accomplished in him.* Those who are acquainted with the original will find that the words—"It is finished," occur twice within three verses. In the 28th verse, we have the word in the Greek; it is translated in our version "accomplished," but there it stands—"After this, Jesus knowing that all things were now *finished*, that the Scripture might be fulfilled, saith, 'I thirst.'" And then He afterwards said, "It is finished." This leads us to see His meaning very clearly, that all the Scripture was now fulfilled, that when He said, "It is finished," the whole book, from the first to the last, in both the law and the prophets, was finished in him. There is not a single jewel of promise, from that first emerald which fell on the threshold of Eden, to that last sapphire-stone of Malachi, which was not set in the breast-plate of the true High Priest. Nay, there is not a type, from the red heifer downward to the turtle-dove, from the hyssop upwards to Solomon's temple itself, which was not fulfilled in him; and not a prophecy, whether spoken on Chebar's bank, or on the shores of Jordan; not a dream of wise men, whether they had received it in Babylon, or in Samaria, or in Judea, which was not now fully wrought out in Christ Jesus. And, brethren, what a wonderful thing it is, that a mass of promises, and prophecies, and types, apparently so heterogeneous, should all be accomplished in one person! Take away Christ for one moment, and I will give the Old Testament to any wise man living, and say to him,

> Take this; this is a problem; go home and construct in your imagination an ideal character who shall exactly fit all that which is herein foreshadowed; remember, He must be a prophet like unto Moses, and yet a champion like to Joshua; He must be an Aaron and a Melchisedek; He must be both David and Solomon, Noah and Jonah, Judah and Joseph. Nay, He must not only be the lamb that was slain, and the scapegoat that was not slain, the turtle-dove that was dipped in blood, and the priest who slew the bird, but He must be the altar, the tabernacle, the mercy-seat, and the shewbread.

Nay, to puzzle this wise man further, we remind Him of prophecies so apparently contradictory, that one would think they never could meet in one man. Such as these, "All kings shall fall down before him, and all nations shall serve Him;" and yet, "He is despised and rejected of men." He must begin by showing a man born of a virgin mother—"A virgin shall conceive and bear a son." He must be a man without spot or blemish, but yet one upon whom the Lord doth cause to meet the iniquities of us all. He must be a glorious one, a Son of David, but yet a root out of a dry ground. Now, I say it boldly, if all the

greatest intellects of all the ages could set themselves to work out this problem, to invent another key to the types and prophecies, they could not do it. I
see you, ye wise men, ye are poring over these hieroglyphs; one suggests one
key, and it opens two or three of the figures, but you cannot proceed, for the
next one puts you at a nonplus. Another learned man suggests another clue,
but that fails most where it is most needed, and another, and another, and
thus these wondrous hieroglyphs traced of old by Moses in the wilderness,
must be left unexplained, till one comes forward and proclaims, "The cross of
Christ and the Son of God incarnate," then the whole is clear, *so* that he that
runs may read, and a child may understand. Blessed Savior! In thee we see everything fulfilled, which God spoke of old by the prophets; in thee we discover everything carried out in substance, which God had set forth us in the
dim mist of sacrificial smoke. Glory be unto thy name! "It is finished"—everything is summed up in thee.

2. But the words have richer meaning. Not only were all types, and prophecies, and promises thus finished in Christ, but *all the typical sacrifices of the old Jewish law, were now abolished as well as explained.* They were finished—finished in
Him. Will you imagine for a minute the saints in Heaven looking down upon
what was done on earth—Abel and his friends who had long ago before the
flood been sitting in the glories above. They watch while God lights star after star
in Heaven. Promise after promise flashes light upon the thick darkness of earth.
They see Abraham come, and they look down and wonder while they see God
revealing Christ to Abraham in the person of Isaac. They gaze just as the angels
do, desiring to look into the mystery. From the times of Noah, Abraham, Isaac,
and Jacob, they see altars smoking, recognitions of the fact that man is guilty, and
the spirits before the throne say, "Lord, when will sacrifices finish?—when will
blood no more be shed?" The offering of bloody sacrifices soon increases. It is
now carried on by men ordained for the purpose. Aaron and the high priests, and
the Levites, every morning and every evening offer a lamb, while great sacrifices
are offered on special occasions. Bullocks groan, rams bleed, the necks of doves
are wrung, and all the while the saints are crying, "O Lord, how long?—when
shall the sacrifice cease?" Year after year the high priest goes within the veil and
sprinkles the mercy-seat with blood; the next year sees him do the like, and the
next, and again, and again, and again. David offers hecatombs [slaughters hundreds in sacrifice], Solomon slaughters tens of thousands, Hezekiah offers rivers
of oil, Josiah gives thousands of the fat of fed beasts, and the spirits of the just say,

Will it never be complete?—Will the sacrifice never be finished?—Must
there always be a remembrance of sin?—Will not the last High Priest soon

come?—Will not the order and line of Aaron soon lay aside its labor, because the whole is finished?

Not yet, not yet, ye spirits of the just, for after the captivity the slaughter of victims still remains. But lo, He comes! Gaze more intently than before—He comes who is to close the line of priests! Lo! there He stands, clothed—not now with linen ephod, not with ringing bells, nor with sparkling jewels on His breastplate—but arrayed in human flesh He stands, His cross His altar, His body and His soul the victim, himself the priest, and lo! before His God He offers up His own soul within the veil of thick darkness which hath covered Him from the sight of men. Presenting His own blood, He enters within the veil, sprinkles it there, and coming forth from the midst of the darkness, He looks down on the astonished earth, and upward to expectant Heaven, and cries, *"It is* finished! *it is* finished!"—that for which ye looked so long, is fully achieved and perfected forever.

3. The Savior meant, we doubt not, that in this moment His *perfect obedience was finished*. It was necessary, in order that man might be saved, that the law of God should be kept, for no man can see God's face except he be perfect in righteousness. Christ undertook to keep God's law for His people, to obey its every mandate, and preserve its every statute intact. Throughout the first years of His life He privately obeyed, honoring His father and His mother; during the next three years He publicly obeyed God, spending and being spent in His service, till if you would know what a man would be whose life was wholly conformed to the law of God, you may see Him in Christ.

> *My dear Redeemer and my Lord,*
> *I read my duty in thy word,*
> *But in thy life the law appears*
> *Drawn out in living characters*

It needed nothing to complete the perfect virtue of life but the entire obedience of death. He who would serve God must be willing not only to give all his soul and his strength while he lives, but he must stand prepared to resign life when it shall be for God's glory. Our perfect substitute put the last stroke upon His work by dying, and therefore He claims to be absolved from further debt, for "it is finished." Yes, glorious Lamb of God, it is finished! Thou hast been tempted in all points like as we are, yet hast thou sinned in none! It *was* finished, for the last arrow out of Satan's quiver had been shot at thee; the last blasphemous insinuation, the last wicked temptation had spent its fury on thee; the Prince of this world had surveyed thee from head to foot, within and without, but he had found nothing in thee. Now thy trial is over, thou hast finished the work which thy Father gave thee to do, and so finished it that Hell itself cannot accuse thee of a flaw. And now, looking upon thine entire obedience, thou sayest, "It is finished," and we thy people believe most joyously that it is even so. Brothers and sisters, this is more than you or I could have said if Adam had never fallen. If we had been in the garden of Eden today, we could never have boasted a finished righteousness, since a creature can never finish its obedience. As long as a creature lives it is bound to obey, and as long as a free agent exists on Earth it would be in danger of violating the vow of its obedience. If Adam had been in Paradise from the first day until now, he might fall tomorrow. Left to himself there would be no reason why that king of nature should not yet be uncrowned. But Christ the Creator, who finished creation, has perfected redemption. God can ask no more. The law has received all it claims; the largest extent of justice cannot demand another hour's obedience. It is done; it is complete; the last throw of the shuttle is over, and the robe is woven from the top throughout. Let us rejoice, then, in this that the Master meant by His dying cry that His perfect righteousness wherewith He covers us, was finished.

4. But next, the Savior meant *that the satisfaction which He rendered to the justice of God was finished.* The debt was now, to the last farthing, all discharged. The atonement and propitiation were made once for all, and forever, by the one offering made in Jesus' body on the tree. There was the cup; Hell was in it; the Savior drank it—not a sip and then a pause; not a draught and then a ceasing; but He drained it till there is not a dreg left for any of His people. The great ten-thonged whip of the law was worn out upon His back; there is no lash left with which to smite one for whom Jesus died. The great cannonade of God's justice has exhausted all its ammunition; there is nothing left to be hurled against a child of God. Sheathed is thy sword, O Justice! Silenced is thy thunder, O Law! There remaineth nothing now of all the griefs, and pains, and agonies which chosen sinners ought to have suffered for their sins, for Christ has endured all for His own beloved, and "it is finished." Brethren, it *is more than the damned in Hell can ever say.* If you and I had been constrained to make satisfaction to God's justice by being sent to Hell we never could have said, "It is finished." Christ has paid the debt which all the torments of eternity could not have paid. Lost souls, ye suffer today as ye have suffered for ages past, but God's justice is not satisfied; His law is not fully magnified. And when time shall fail, and eternity shall have been flying on, still forever, forever, the uttermost farthing never having been paid, the chastisement for sin must fall upon unpardoned sinners. But Christ has done

what all the flames of the pit could not do in all eternity; He has magnified the law and made it honorable, and now from the cross He cries—"It is finished."

5. Once again: when He said, "It is finished," *Jesus had totally destroyed the power of Satan, of sin, and of death.* The champion had entered the lists to do battle for our soul's redemption, against all our foes. He met Sin. Horrible, terrible, all but omnipotent Sin nailed Him to the cross; but in that deed, Christ nailed Sin also to the tree. There they both did hang together—Sin, and Sin's destroyer. Sin destroyed Christ, and by that destruction Christ destroyed Sin. Next came the second enemy, Satan. He assaulted Christ with all his hosts. Calling up his myrmidons from every corner and quarter of the universe, he said, "Awake, arise, or be forever fallen! Here is our great enemy who has sworn to bruise my head; now let us bruise His heel!" They shot their hellish darts into His heart; they poured their boiling cauldrons on His brain; they emptied their venom into His veins; they spat their insinuations into His face; they hissed their devilish fears into His ear. He stood alone, the lion of the tribe of Judah, hounded by all the dogs of Hell. Our champion quailed not, but used His holy weapons, striking right and left with all the power of God-supported manhood. On came the hosts; volley after volley was discharged against Him. No mimic thunders were these, but such as might shake the very gates of Hell. The conqueror steadily advanced, overturning their ranks, dashing in pieces His enemies, breaking the bow and cutting the spear in sunder, and burning the chariots in the fire, while He cried, "In the name of God will I destroy ye!" At last, foot to foot, He met the champion of Hell, and now our David fought with Goliath. Not long was the struggle; thick was the darkness which gathered round them both; but He who is the Son of God as well as the Son of Mary, knew how to smite the fiend, and He did smite him with divine fury, till, having despoiled him of his armor, having quenched his fiery darts, and broken his head, He cried, "It is finished," and sent the fiend, bleeding and howling, down to Hell. We can imagine him pursued by the eternal Savior, who exclaims:

> *Traitor!*
> *My bolt shalt find and pierce thee through,*
> *Though under Hell's profoundest wave*
> *Thou div'st, to seek a shelt'ring grave.*

His thunderbolt o'ertook the fiend, and grasping him with both His hands, the Savior drew around him the great chain. The angels brought the royal chariot from on high, to whose wheels the captive fiend was bound. Lash the coursers up the everlasting hills! Spirits made perfect come forth to meet

Him. Hymn the conqueror who drags death and Hell behind him, and leads captivity captive! "Lift up your heads, O ye gates, and be ye lifted up, ye everlasting doors, that the King of glory may come in!" But stay; ere He enters, let Him be rid of this His burden. Lo! He takes the fiend, and hurls him down through illimitable night, broken, bruised, with his power destroyed, bereft of his crown, to lie forever howling in the pit of Hell. Thus, when the Savior cried, "It is finished," He had defeated Sin and Satan; nor less had He vanquished Death. Death had come against Him, as Christmas Evans puts it, with his fiery dart, which he struck right through the Savior, till the point fixed in the cross, and when he tried to pull it out again, he left the sting behind. What could he do more? He was disarmed. Then Christ set some of his prisoners free; for many of the saints arose and were seen of many: then He said to him, "Death, I take from thee thy keys; thou must live for a little while to be the warder of those beds in which my saints shall sleep, but give me thy keys." And lo! the Savior stands today with the keys of death hanging at His girdle, and He waits until the hour shall come of which no man knoweth; when the trump of the archangel shall ring like the silver trumpets of Jubilee, and then He shall say, "Let my captives go free." Then shall the tombs be opened in virtue of Christ's death, and the very bodies of the saints shall live again in an eternity of glory.

> "It is finish'd!"
> Hear the dying Savior cry.

II. Secondly, *let us hear and wonder. Let us perceive what mighty things were effected and secured by these words, "It is finished."*

Thus He *ratified the covenant.* That covenant was signed and sealed before, and in all things it was ordered well, but when Christ said, "It is finished," then the covenant was made doubly sure; when the blood of Christ's heart bespattered the divine roll, then it could never be reversed, nor could one of its ordinances be broken, nor one of its stipulations fail. You know the covenant was on this wise. God covenants on His part that He would give Christ to see of the travail of His soul; that all who were given to Him should have new hearts and right spirits; that they should be washed from sin, and should enter into life through Him. Christ's side of the covenant was this—"Father, I will do thy will; I will pay the ransom to the last jot and tittle; I will give thee perfect obedience and complete satisfaction." Now if this second part of the covenant had never been fulfilled, the first part would have been invalid, but when Jesus said, "It is finished," then there was nothing left to be performed on His part, and now the covenant is all on one side. It is God's "I will," and "They shall." "A new heart will I give you, and a right spirit will I put within you." "I will sprinkle clean water upon you and ye shall be clean." "From all your iniquities will I cleanse you." "I will lead you by a way that ye know not." "I will surely bring them in." The covenant that day was ratified. When Christ said, "It is finished," His *Father was honored, and divine justice was fully displayed*. The Father always did love his people. Do not think that Christ died to make God the Father loving. He always had loved them from before the foundation of the world, but—"It is finished," took away the barriers which were in the Father's way. He would, as a God of love, and now He could, as a God of justice, bless poor sinners. From that day the Father is well pleased to receive sinners to His bosom. When Christ said—"It is finished," *He Himself was glorified*. Then on His head descended the all-glorious crown. Then did the Father give to Him honors, which He had not before. He had honor as God, but as man He was despised and rejected; now as God and man Christ was made to sit down forever on His Father's throne, crowned with honor and majesty. Then, too, by "It is finished," the Spirit was procured for us.

> 'Tis by the merit of His death
> Who hung upon the tree
> The Spirit is sent down to breathe
> On such dry bones as we.

Then the Spirit which Christ had aforetime promised, perceived a new and living way by which He could come to dwell in the hearts of men, and men might come up to dwell with Him above. That day too, when Christ said—"It is finished," *the words had effect on Heaven*. Then the walls of chrysolite stood fast; then the jasper-light of the pearly-gated city shone like the light of seven days. Before, the saints had been saved as it were on credit. They had entered Heaven, God having faith in His Son Jesus. Had not Christ finished His work, surely they must have left their shining spheres, and suffered in their own persons for their own sins. I might represent Heaven, if my imagination might be allowed a moment, as being ready to totter if Christ had not finished His work; its stones would have been unloosed; massive and stupendous though its bastions are, yet had they fallen as earthly cities reel under the throes of earthquake. But Christ said, "It is finished," and oath, and covenant, and blood set fast the dwelling place of the redeemed, made their mansions safely and eternally their own, and bade their feet stand immovably upon the rock. Nay, more, that word "It is finished!" took effect in the gloomy caverns and depths of *hell*. Then Satan bit his iron bands in rage, howling,

I am defeated by the very man whom I thought to overcome; my hopes are blasted; never shall an elect one come into my prison-house, never a blood-bought one be found in my abode.

Lost souls mourned that day, for they said—"'It is finished!' and if Christ Himself, the Substitute, could not be permitted to go free till He had finished all His punishment, then we shall never be free." It was their double death-knell, for they said, "Alas for us! Justice, which would not suffer the Savior to escape, will never suffer us to be at liberty. It is finished with Him, and therefore it shall never be finished for us." That day, too, the Earth had a gleam of sunlight cast over her which she had never known before. Then her hilltops began to glisten with the rising of the sun, and though her valleys still are clothed with darkness, and men wander hither and thither, and grope in the noonday as in the night, yet that sun is rising, climbing still its heavenly steeps, never to set, and soon shall its rays penetrate through the thick mists and clouds, and every eye shall see Him, and every heart be made glad with His light. The words "It is finished!" consolidated Heaven, shook Hell, comforted Earth, delighted the Father, glorified the Son, brought down the Spirit, and confirmed the everlasting covenant to all the chosen seed.

III. And now I come to my last point, very briefly. "It is finished!" let us publish it.

Children of God, ye who by faith received Christ as your all in all, tell it every day of your lives that "it is finished." Go and tell it to those who are torturing themselves, thinking through obedience and mortification to offer satisfaction. Yonder Hindu is about to throw himself down upon the spikes. Stay, poor man! wherefore wouldst thou bleed, for "it is finished?" Yonder Fakir is holding his hand erect till the nails grow through the flesh, torturing himself with fastings and with self-denials. Cease, cease, poor wretch, from all these pains, for "it is finished!" In all parts of the Earth there are those who think that the misery of the body and the soul may be an atonement for sin. Rush to them, stay them in their madness and say to them, "Wherefore do ye this? 'It is finished.'" All the pains that God asks, Christ has suffered; all the satisfaction by way of agony in the flesh that the law demandeth, Christ hath already endured. "It is finished!" And when ye have done this, go ye next to the benighted votaries of Rome, when ye see the priests with their backs to the people, offering every day the pretended sacrifice of the mass, and lifting up the host on high—a sacrifice, they say—"an unbloody sacrifice for the quick and the dead,"—cry, "Cease, false priest, cease! for 'it is finished!'

Cease, false worshiper, cease to bow, for 'it is finished!'" God neither asks nor accepts any other sacrifice than that which Christ offered once for all upon the cross. Go ye next to the foolish among your own countrymen who call themselves Protestants, but who are Papists after all, who think by their gifts and their gold, by their prayers and their vows, by their church-goings and their chapel-goings, by their baptisms and their confirmations, to make themselves fit for God; and say to them,

> Stop, "it is finished"; God needs not this of you. He has received enough; why will ye pin your rags to the fine linen of Christ's righteousness? Why will you add your counterfeit farthing to the costly ransom which Christ has paid in to the treasure-house of God? Cease from your pains, your doings, your performances, for "it is finished"; Christ has done it all.

This one text is enough to blow the Vatican to the four winds. Lay but this beneath Popery, and like a train of gunpowder beneath a rock, it shall blast it into the air. This is a thunderclap against all human righteousness. Only let this come like a two-edged sword, and your good works and your fine performances are soon cast away. "It is finished." Why improve on what is finished? Why add to that which is complete? The Bible is finished, he that adds to it shall have his name taken out of the Book of Life, and out of the holy city: Christ's atonement is finished, and he that adds to that must expect the selfsame doom. And when ye shall have told it thus to the ears of men of every nation and of every tribe, tell it to all poor despairing souls. Ye find them on their knees, crying, "O God, what can I do to make recompense for my offences?" Tell them, "It is finished"; the recompense is made already. "O God!" they say, "how can I ever get a righteousness in which thou canst accept such a worm as I am?" Tell them, "It is finished"; their righteousness is wrought out already; they have no need to trouble themselves about adding to it, if "it is finished." Go to the poor despairing wretch, who has given himself up, not for death merely, but for damnation—he who says, "I cannot escape from sin, and I cannot be saved from its punishment." Say to him, "Sinner, the way of salvation is finished once for all." And if ye meet some professed Christians in doubts and fears, tell them, "It is finished." Why, we have hundreds and thousands that really are converted, who do not know that "it is finished." They never know that they are safe. They do not know that "it is finished." They think they have faith today, but perhaps they may become unbelieving tomorrow. They do not know that "it is finished." They hope God will accept them, if they do some things, forgetting that the way of acceptance is finished.

God as much accepts a sinner who only believed in Christ five minutes ago, as He will a saint who has known and loved Him eighty years, for He does not accept men because of anything they do or feel, but simply and only for what Christ did, and that is finished. Oh! poor hearts! some of you do love the Savior in a measure, but blindly. You are thinking that you must be this, and attain to that, and then you may be assured that you are saved. Oh! you may be assured of it today—if you believe in Christ you are saved. "But I feel imperfections." Yes, but what of that? God does not regard your imperfections, but He covers them with Christ's righteousness. He sees them to remove them, but not to lay them to thy charge. "Aye, but I cannot be what I would be." But what if thou canst not? Yet God does not look at thee, as what thou art in thyself, but as what thou art in Christ.

Come with me, poor soul, and thou and I will stand together this morning, while the tempest gathers, for we are not afraid. How sharp that lightning flash! but yet we tremble not. How terrible that peal of thunder! and yet we are not alarmed, and why? Is there anything in us why we should escape? No, but we are standing beneath the Cross—that precious Cross, which like some noble lightning-conductor in the storm, takes itself all the death from the lightning, and all the fury from the tempest. We are safe. Loud mayest thou roar, O thundering law, and terribly mayest thou flash, O avenging justice! We can look up with calm delight to all the tumult of the elements, for we are safe beneath the Cross.

Come with me again. There is a royal banquet spread; the King Himself sits at the table, and angels are the servitors. Let us enter. And we do enter, and we sit down and eat and drink; but how dare we do this? Our righteousness are as filthy rags—how could we venture to come here? Oh, because the filthy rags are not ours any longer. We have renounced our own righteousness, and therefore we have renounced the filthy rags, and now today we wear the royal garments of the Savior, and are from head to foot arrayed in white, without spot or wrinkle or any such thing; standing in the clear sunlight—black, but comely; loathsome in ourselves, but glorious in Him; condemned in Adam, but accepted in the Beloved. We are neither afraid nor ashamed to be with the angels of God, to talk with the glorified; nay, nor even alarmed to speak with God Himself and call Him our friend.

And now last of all, I publish this to sinners. I know not where thou art this morning, but may God find thee out; thou who hast been a drunkard, swearer, thief; thou who hast been a blackguard of the blackest kind; thou who hast dived into the very kennel, and rolled thyself in the mire—if to-day thou feelest that sin is hateful to thee, believe in Him who has said, "It is finished." Let me link thy hand in mine; let us come together, both of us, and say, "ere are two poor naked souls, good Lord; we cannot clothe ourselves;" and He will give us a robe, for "it is finished." "But, Lord, is it long enough for such sinners, and broad enough for such offenders?" "Yes," saith He, "it is finished." "But we need washing, Lord! Is there anything that can take away black spots so hideous as ours?" "Yes," saith He, "here is the bath of blood." "But must we not add our tears to it?" "No," says He, "no, it is finished, there is enough." "And now, Lord, thou hast washed us, and thou hast clothed us, but we would be still completely clean within, so that we may never sin any more; Lord, is there a way by which this can be done?" "Yes," saith He, "there is the bath of water which floweth from the wounded side of Christ." "And, Lord, is there enough there to wash away my guiltiness as well as my guilt?" "Aye," saith He, "it is finished. Jesus Christ is made unto you sanctification as well as redemption." Child of God, wilt thou have Christ's finished righteousness this morning, and wilt thou rejoice in it more than ever thou hast done before? And oh! poor sinner, wilt thou have Christ or no? "Ah," saith one, "I am willing enough, but I am not worthy." He does not want any worthiness. All He asks is willingness, for you know how He puts it, "Whoever will, let him come." If He has given you willingness, you may believe in Christ's finished work this morning. "Ah!" say you, "but you cannot mean *me.*" But I do, for it says, "Ho, *everyone that thirsteth.*" Do you thirst for Christ? Do you wish to be saved by him? "*Everyone* that thirsteth,"—not only that young woman yonder, not simply that grey-headed old rebel yonder who has long despised the Savior, but this mass below, and you in these double tiers of gallery—"Everyone that thirsteth, come ye to the waters, and he that hath no money come." O that I could "compel" you to come! Great God, do thou make the sinner willing to be saved, for he wills to be damned, and will not come unless thou change his will! Eternal Spirit, source of light, and life, and grace, come down and bring the strangers home! "It is finished." Sinner, there is nothing for God to do. "It is finished"; there is nothing for you to do. "It is finished"; Christ need not bleed. "It is finished"; you need not weep. "It is finished"; God the Holy Spirit need not tarry because of your unworthiness, nor need you tarry because of your helplessness. "It is finished"; every stumbling block is rolled out of the road; every gate is opened; the bars of brass are broken, the gates of iron are burst asunder. "It is finished"; come and welcome, come and welcome! The table is laid; the fatlings are killed; the oxen are ready. Lo! here stands the messenger! Come from the highways and from the hedges; come from the dens and from the kens of London; come, ye vilest of the vile; ye who hate yourselves today, come! Jesus bids you; oh! will you tarry? Oh! Spirit of God, do thou repeat the invitation, and make it an effectual call to many a heart, for Jesus' sake! Amen.

The Last Words of Christ on the Cross

"And when Jesus had cried with a loud voice, he said, 'Father, into thy hands I commend my spirit': and having said thus, he gave up the ghost."—Luke 23:46.

"Into thine hand I commit my spirit: thou hast redeemed me, O Lord God of truth."—Psalm 31:5.

"And they stoned Stephen, calling upon God, and saying, 'Lord Jesus, receive my Spirit.'"—Acts 7:59.

This morning, dear friends, I spoke upon the first recorded words of our Lord Jesus when He said to His mother and to Joseph, "How is it that ye sought me? wist ye not that I must be about my Father's business?" Now, by the help of the blessed Spirit, we will consider the last words of our Lord Jesus before He gave up the ghost, and with them we will examine two other passages in which similar expressions are used.

The words, "Father, into thy hands I commend my spirit," if we judge them to be the last which our Savior uttered before His death, ought to be coupled with those other words, "It is finished," which some have thought were actually the last He used. I think it was not so; but, anyhow, these utterances must have followed each other very quickly, and we may blend them together, and then we shall see how very similar they are to His first words as we explained them this morning. There is the cry, "It is finished," which you may read in connection with our Authorized Version: "Wist ye not that I must be about my Father's business?" That business was all finished; He had been about it all His life, and now that He had come to the end of His days, there was nothing left undone, and He could say to His Father, "I have finished the work which thou gavest me to do." Then if you take the other utterance of our Lord on the cross, "Father, into thy hands I commend my spirit," see how well it agrees with the other reading of our morning text, "Wist ye not that I must be in my Father's house?" Jesus is putting himself into the Father's hands because He had always desired to be there—in the Father's house with the Father; and now He is committing His spirit, as a sacred trust, into the Father's hands that He may depart to be with the Father, to abide in His house, and go no more out forever.

Christ's life is all of a piece, just as the alpha and the omega are letters of the same alphabet. You do not find Him one thing at the first, another thing afterwards, and a third thing still later; but He is "Jesus Christ; the same yesterday, and today, and forever." There is a wondrous similarity about everything that Christ said and did. You never need write the name "Jesus" under any one of His sayings, as you have to put the names of human writers under their sayings, for there is no mistaking any sentence that He has uttered.

If there is anything recorded as having been done by Christ, a believing child can judge whether it is authentic or not. Those miserable false gospels that were brought out did very little if any mischief, because nobody, with any true spiritual discernment, was ever duped into believing them to be genuine. It is possible to manufacture a spurious coin which will, for a time, pass for a good one; but it is not possible to make even a passable imitation of what Jesus Christ has said and done. Everything about Christ is like Himself; there is a Christlikeness about it which cannot be mistaken. This morning, for instance, when I preached about the Holy Child Jesus, I am sure you must have felt that there was never such another child as He was; and in His death He was as unique as in His birth, and childhood, and life. There was never another who died as He did, and there was never another who lived altogether as He did. Our Lord Jesus Christ stands by Himself; some of us try to imitate him, but how feebly do we follow in His steps! The Christ of God still standeth by Himself, and there is no possible rival to Him.

I have already intimated to you that I am going to have three texts for my sermon; but when I have spoken upon all three of them, you will see that they are so much alike that I might have been content with one of them.

I. I invite you first to consider our Savior's words just before His death: "Father, into thy hands I commend my spirit."

Here observe, first, *how Christ lives and passes away in the atmosphere of the Lord of God.* Christ was a grand original thinker, and He might always have given us words of His own. He never lacked suitable language, for "never man spake like this Man." Yet you must have noticed how continually He quoted Scripture; the great majority of His expressions may be traced to the Old Testament. Even where they are not exact quotations, His words drop into Scriptural shape and form. You can see that the Bible has been His one Book. He is evidently familiar with it from the first page to the last, and not with its letter only, but with the innermost soul of its most secret sense; and, therefore, when dying, it seemed but natural for Him to use a passage from a Psalm of David as His expiring words. In His death, He was not driven beyond the power of quiet thought, He was not unconscious, He did not die of weakness, He was strong even while He was dying. It is true that He said "I thirst"; but, after He had been a little refreshed, He cried with a loud voice, as only a strong man could, "It is finished." And now, ere He bows His head in the silence of death, He utters His final words, "Father, into thy hands I commend my spirit." Our Lord might, I say again, have made an original speech as His dying declaration; His mind was clear, and calm, and undisturbed; in fact, He was perfectly happy, for He had said, "It is finished." So His sufferings were over, and He was already beginning to enjoy a taste of the sweets of victory; yet, with all that clearness of mind, and freshness of intellect, and fluency of words that might have been possible to Him, He did not invent a new sentence, but He went to the Book of Psalms, and took from the Holy Spirit this expression, "Into thy hands I commit my spirit."

How instructive to us is this great truth that the Incarnate Word lived on the Inspired Word! It was food to Him, as it is to us; and, brothers and sisters, if Christ thus lived upon the Word of God, should not you and I do the same? He, in some respects, did not need this Book as much as we do. The Spirit of God rested upon Him without measure, yet He loved the Scripture, and He went to it, and studied it, and used its expressions continually. Oh, that you and I might get into the very heart of the Word of God, and *get that* Word into ourselves! As I have seen the silkworm eat into the leaf, and consume it, so ought we to do with the Word of the Lord—not crawl over its surface, but eat right into it till we have taken it into our inmost parts. It is idle merely to let the eye glance over the words, or to recollect the poetical expressions, or the historic facts; but it is blessed to eat into the very soul of the Bible until, at last, you come to talk in Scriptural language, and your very style is fashioned upon Scripture models, and, what is better still, your spirit is flavored with the words of the Lord. I would quote John Bunyan as an instance of what I mean. Read anything of his, and you will see that it is almost like reading the Bible itself. He had studied our Authorized Version, which will never be bettered, as I judge, till Christ shall come; he had read it till his very soul was saturated with Scripture; and, though his writings are charmingly full of poetry, yet he cannot give us his *Pilgrim's Progress*—that sweetest of all prose poems—without continually making us feel and say, "Why, this man is a living Bible!" Prick him anywhere; his blood is Bibline, the very essence of the Bible flows from him. He cannot speak without quoting a text, for his very soul is full of the Word of God. I commend his example to you, beloved, and, still more, the example of our Lord Jesus. If the Spirit of God be in you, He will make you love the Word of God; and, if any of you imagine that the Spirit of God will lead you to dispense with the Bible, you are under the influence of another spirit which is not the Spirit of God at all. I trust that the Holy Spirit will endear to you every page of this Divine Record, so that you will feed upon it yourselves, and afterwards speak it out to others. I think it is well worthy of your constant remembrance that, even in death, our blessed Master showed the ruling passion of His spirit, so that His last words were a quotation from Scripture.

Now notice, secondly, that *our Lord, in the moment of His death, recognized a personal God:* "Father, into thy hands I commend my spirit." God is to some men an unknown God. "There may be a God," so they say, but they get no nearer the truth than that. "All things are God," says another. "We cannot be sure that there is a God," say others, "and therefore it is no use our pretending to believe in him, and so to be, possibly, influenced by a supposition." Some people say, "Oh, certainly, there is a God, but He is very far off! He does not come near to us, and we cannot imagine that He will interfere in our affairs." Ah! but our blessed Lord Jesus Christ believed in no such impersonal, pantheistic, dreamy, far-off God; but in One to whom He said, "Father, into thy hands I commend my spirit." His language shows that He realized the personality of God as much as I should recognize the personality of a banker if I said to him, "Sir, I commit that money into your hands." I know that I should not say such a thing as that to a mere dummy, or to an abstract something or nothing; but to a living man I should say it, and I should say it only to a living man. So, beloved, men do not commit their souls into the keeping of impalpable nothings; they do not, in death, smile as they resign themselves to the infinite unknown, the cloudy Father of everything, who may himself be nothing or everything. No, no; we only trust what we know; and so Jesus knew the Father, and knew Him to be a real Person having hands, into those hands He commended His departing spirit. I am not now speaking materially, mark you, as though God had hands like ours; but

He is an actual Being, who has powers of action, who is able to deal with men as He pleases, and who is willing to take possession of their spirits, and to protect them forever and ever. Jesus speaks like one who believed that; and I pray that, both in life and in death, you and I may ever deal with God in the same way. We have far too much fiction in religion, and a religion of fiction will bring only fictitious comfort in the dying hour. Come to solid facts, man. Is God as real to thee as thou art to thyself? Come now; dost thou speak with Him "as a man speaketh unto his friend?" Canst thou trust Him, and rely upon Him as thou dost trust and rely upon the partner of thy bosom? If thy God be unreal, thy religion is unreal. If thy God be a dream, thy hope will be a dream; and woe be unto thee when thou shalt wake up out of it! It was not so that Jesus trusted. "Father," said He, "into thy hands I commend my spirit."

But, thirdly, here is a better point still. Observe *how Jesus Christ here brings out the Fatherhood of God.* The Psalm from which He quoted did not say, "Father." David did not get as far as that in words, though in spirit he often did; but Jesus had the right to alter the Psalmist's words. He can improve on Scripture, though you and I cannot. He did not say, "O God, into thine hand I commit my spirit; but He said, "Father." Oh, that sweet word! That was the gem of our thought, this morning, that Jesus said, "Wist ye not that I must be at my Father's—that I must be in my Father's house?" Oh, yes! the Holy Child knew that He was specially, and in a peculiar sense, the Son of the Highest; and therefore He said, "My Father"; and, in dying, His expiring heart was buoyed up and comforted with the thought that God was His Father. It was because He said that God was His Father that they put Him to death, yet He still stood to it even in His dying hour, and said, "Father, into thy hands I commend my spirit."

What a blessed thing it is for us also, my brethren, to die conscious that we are sons of God! Oh, how sweet, in life and in death, to feel in our soul the spirit of adoption whereby we cry, "Abba, Father!" In such a case as that,

> *It is not death to die.*

Quoting the Savior's words, "It is finished," and relying upon His Father and our Father, we may go even into the jaws of death without the "quivering lips" of which we sang just now. Joyful, with all the strength we have, our lips may confidently sing, challenging death and the grave to silence our ever-rising and swelling music. O my Father, my Father, if I am in thy hands, I may die without fear!

There is another thought, however, which is perhaps the chief one of all. From this passage, we learn that *our Divine Lord cheerfully rendered up His soul* to His Father when the time had come for Him to die: "Father, into thy hands I commend my spirit." None of us can, with strict propriety, use these words. When we come to die, we may perhaps utter them, and God will accept them; these were the very death-words of Polycarp, and Bernard, and Luther, and Melancthon, and Jerome of Prague, and John Huss, and an almost endless list of saints: "Into thy hands I commit my spirit." The Old Testament rendering of the passage, or else our Lord's version of it, has been turned into a Latin prayer, and commonly used among Romanists almost as a charm; they have repeated the Latin words when dying, or, if they were unable to do so, the priest repeated the words for them, attaching a sort of magical power to that particular formula. But, in the sense in which our Savior uttered these words, we cannot any of us fully use them. We can commit or commend our spirit to God; but yet, brethren, remember that, unless the Lord comes first, we must die; and dying is not an act on our part. We have to be passive in the process, because it is no longer in our power to retain our life. I suppose that, if a man could have such control of his life, it might be questionable when he should surrender it, because suicide is a crime, and no man can be required to kill himself. God does not demand such action as that at any man's hand; and, in a certain sense, that is what would happen whenever a man yielded himself to death. But there was no necessity for our blessed Lord and Master to die except the necessity which He had taken upon Himself in becoming the Substitute for His people. There was not any necessity for His death even at the last moment upon the cross, for, as I have reminded you, He cried with a loud voice when natural weakness would have compelled Him to whisper or to sigh. But His life was strong within Him; if He had willed to do so, He could have unloosed the nails, and come down into the midst of the crowd that stood mocking Him. He died of His own free will, "the Just for the unjust, that He might bring us to God." A man may righteously surrender His life for the good of His country, and for the safety of others. There have frequently been opportunities for men to do this, and there have been brave fellows who have worthily done it; but, then, all those men would have had to die at some time or other. They were only slightly anticipating the payment of the debt of nature; but, in our Lord's case, He was rendering up to the Father the spirit which He might have kept if He had chosen to do so. "No man taketh it from me," said He concerning His life; "I lay it down of myself"; and there is here a cheerful willingness to yield up His spirit into His Father's hands. It is rather remarkable that none of the Evangelists describe our Lord as dying. He did die, but they all speak of Him as giving up the ghost—

surrendering to God His spirit. You and I passively die; but He actively yielded up His spirit to His Father. In His case, death was an act; and He performed that act from the glorious motive of redeeming us from death and Hell; so, in this sense, Christ stands alone in His death. But, oh, dear brothers and sisters, if we cannot render up our spirit as He did, yet, when our life is taken from us, let us be perfectly ready to give it up. May God bring us into such a state of mind and heart that there shall be no struggling to keep our life, but a sweet willingness to let it be just as God would have it—a yielding up of everything to His hands, feeling sure that, in the world of spirits, our soul shall be quite safe in the Father's hand, and that, until the resurrection day, the life-germ of the body will be securely in His keeping, and certain that, when the trumpet shall sound, spirit, soul, and body—that trinity of our manhood—shall be reunited in the absolute perfection of our being to behold the King in his beauty in the land that is very far off. When God calls us to die, it will be a sweet way of dying if we can, like our Lord, pass away with a text of Scripture upon our lips, with a personal God ready to receive us, with that God recognized distinctly as our Father, and so die joyously, resigning our will entirely to the sweet will of the ever-blessed One, and saying, "It is the Lord," "my Father," "let Him do as seemeth Him good."

II. *My second text is in the 31st Psalm, at the 5th verse; and it is evidently the passage which our Savior had in His mind just then: "Into thine hand I commit my spirit: thou hast redeemed me, O Lord God of truth."*

It seems to me that these are words to be used in life, for this Psalm is not so much concerning the believer's death as concerning His life.

Is it not very singular, dear friends, that the words which Jesus uttered on the cross you may still continue to use? You may catch up their echo, and not only when you come to die, but tonight, tomorrow morning, and as long as you are here, you may still repeat the text the Master quoted, and say, "Into thine hand I commit my spirit."

That is to say, first, *let us cheerfully entrust our souls to God, and* feel that they are quite safe in His hands. Our spirit is the noblest part of our being; our body is only the husk, our spirit is the living kernel, so let us put it into God's keeping. Some of you have never, yet done that, so I invite you to do it now. It is the act of faith which saves the soul, that act which a man performs when He says, "I trust myself to God as He reveals himself in Christ Jesus; I cannot keep myself, but He can keep me; by the precious blood of Christ He can cleanse me; so I just take my spirit, and give it over into the great Father's hand." You never really live till you do that; all that comes before that act of full surrender is death; but when you have once trusted Christ, then you have truly begun to live. And every day, as long as you live, take care that you repeat this process, and cheerfully leave yourselves in God's hands without any reserve; that is to say, give yourself up to God—your body, to be healthy or to be sick, to be long-lived or to be suddenly cut off—your soul and spirit, give them also up to God, to be made happy or to be made sad, just as He pleases. Give your whole self up to Him, and say to Him,

> My Father, make me rich or make me poor, give me eyesight or make me blind, let me have all my senses or take them away, make me famous or leave me to be obscure; I just give myself up to thee; into thine hand I commit my spirit. I will no longer exercise my own choice, but thou shalt choose my inheritance for me. My times are in thy hands.

Now, dear children of God, are you always doing this? Have you ever done it? I am afraid that there are some, even among Christ's professing followers, who kick against God's will; and even when they say to God, "Thy will be done," they spoil it by adding, in their own mind, "and my will, too." They pray, "Lord, make my will thy will," instead of saying, "Make thy will my will." Let us each one pray this prayer every day, "Into thine hand I commit my spirit." I like, at family prayer, to put myself and all that I have into God's hands in the morning, and then, at night, just to look between His hands, and see how safe I have been, and then to say to Him, "Lord, shut me up again tonight; take care of me all through the night-watches. 'Into thine hand I commit my spirit.'"

Notice, dear friends, that our second text has these words at the end of it: *"Thou hast redeemed me, O Lord God of truth."* Is not that a good reason for giving yourself up entirely to God? Christ has redeemed you, and therefore you belong to Him. If I am a redeemed man, and I ask God to take care of me, I am but asking the King to take care of one of His own jewels—a jewel that cost Him the blood of His heart.

And I may still more specially expect that He will do so, because of the title which is here given to Him: "Thou hast redeemed me, O *Lord God of truth.*" Would He be the God of truth if He began with redemption, and ended with destruction—if He began by giving His Son to die for us, and then kept back other mercies which we daily need to bring us to Heaven? No; the gift of His Son is the pledge that He will save His people from their sins, and bring them home to glory; and He will do it. So, every day, go to Him with this declaration, "Into thine hand I commit my spirit." Nay, not only every day, but all through the day. Does a horse run away with you? Then you cannot do better than say, "Father, into thine hand I commit my spirit." And if the horse does not run away with you, you cannot do better than say the same words. Have you to go into a house where there is fever; I mean, is it your duty to go there? Then go saying, "Father, into thine hand I commit my spirit." I would advise you to do this every time you walk down the street, or even while you sit in your own house. Dr. Gill, my famous predecessor, spent very much time in his study; and, one day, somebody said to him, "Well, at any rate, the studious man is safe from most of the accidents of life." It so happened that, one morning, when the good man left his familiar armchair for a little while, there came a gale of wind that blew down a stack of chimneys, which crashed through the roof, and fell right into the place where he would have been sitting if the providence of God had not just then drawn him away; and he said, "I see that we need divine providence to care for us in our studies just as much as in the streets." "Father, into thy hands I commit my spirit." I have often noticed that, if any of our friends get into accidents and troubles, it is usually when they are away for a holiday; it is a curious thing, but I have often remarked it. They go out for their health, and come home ill; they leave us with all their limbs whole, and return to us crippled; therefore, we must pray God to take special care of friends in the country or by the sea, and we must commit ourselves to His hands wherever we may be. If we had to go into a lazar-house, we should certainly ask God to protect us from the deadly leprosy; but we ought equally to seek the Lord's protection while dwelling in the healthiest place or in our own homes.

David said to the Lord, "Into thine hand I commit my spirit"; but let me beg you to add that word which our Lord inserted, *"Father."* David is often a good guide for us, but David's Lord is far better; and if we follow Him, we shall improve upon David. So, let us each say, *"Father, Father, into thine hand I commit my spirit."* That is a sweet way of living every day, committing everything to our Heavenly Father's hand, for that hand can do His child no unkindness. "Father, I might not be able to trust thine angels, but I can trust thee." The psalmist does not say, "Into the hand of providence I commit my spirit." Do you notice how men try to get rid of God by saying, "Providence did this," and "Providence did that," and "Providence did the other"? If you ask them, "What is providence?"—they will probably reply, "Well, providence is—providence." That is all they can say. There is many a man who talks very confidently about reverencing nature, obeying the laws of nature, noting the powers of nature, and so on. Step up to that eloquent lecturer, and say to him, "Will you kindly explain to me what nature is?" He answers, "Why, nature—well, it is—nature." Just so, sir; but, then, what *is* nature? And He says, "Well—well—it is nature"; and that is all you will get out of him. Now, I believe in nature, and I believe in providence; but, at the back of everything, I believe in God, and in the God who has hands—not in an idol that has no hands, and can do nothing—but in the God to whom I can say, "'Father, into thine hand I commit my spirit.' I rejoice that I am able to put myself there, for I feel absolutely safe in trusting myself to thy keeping." So live, beloved, and you shall live safely, and happily; and you shall have hope in your life, and hope in your death.

III. My third text will not detain us many minutes; it is intended to explain to us the use of our Savior's dying words for ourselves.

Turn to the account of the death of Stephen, in the 7th chapter of Acts, at the 59th verse, and you will see there how far a man of God may dare to go in his last moments in quoting from David and from the Lord Jesus Christ: "And they stoned Stephen, calling upon God, and saying, 'Lord Jesus, receive my spirit.'" So here is a text for us to use when we come to die: "Lord Jesus, receive my spirit." I have explained to you that, strictly, we can hardly talk of yielding up our spirit, but we may speak of Christ receiving it, and say, with Stephen, "Lord Jesus, receive my spirit."

What does this prayer mean? I must just hurriedly give you two or three thoughts concerning it, and so close my discourse. I think this prayer means that, if *we can die as Stephen did, we shall die with a certainty of immortality.* Stephen prayed, "Lord Jesus, receive my spirit." He did not say, "I am afraid my poor spirit is going to die." No; the spirit is something which still exists after death, something which Christ can receive, and therefore Stephen asks Him to receive it. You and I are not going upstairs to die as if we were only like cats and dogs; we go up there to die like immortal beings who fall asleep on earth, and open our eyes in Heaven. Then, at the sound of the archangel's trumpet, our very body is to rise to dwell again with our spirit; we have not any question about this matter. I think I have told you what an infidel once said to a Christian man, "Some of you Christians have great fear in dying because you believe that there is another state to follow this one. I have not the slightest fear, for I believe that I shall be annihilated, and therefore all fear of death is gone from me."

"Yes," said the Christian man, "and in that respect you seem to me to be on equal terms with that bullock grazing over there, which, like yourself, is free from any fear of death. Pray, sir, let me ask you a simple question. Have you any hope?" "Hope, sir? Hope, sir? No, I have no hope; of course, I have no hope, sir." "Ah, then!" replied the other, "despite the fears that sometimes come over feeble believers, they have a hope which they would not and could not give up." And that hope is, that our spirit—even that spirit which we commit into Jesus Christ's hands—shall be "forever with the Lord."

The next thought is that, *to a man who can die as Stephen did, there is a certainty that Christ is near*—so near that the man speaks to him, and says, "Lord Jesus, receive my spirit." In Stephen's case, the Lord Jesus was so near that the martyr could see Him, for he said, "Behold, I see the Heavens opened, and the Son of man standing on the right hand of God." Many dying saints have borne a similar testimony; it is no strange thing for us to hear them say, before they died, that they could see within the pearly gates; and they have told us this with such evident truthfulness, and with such rapture, or sometimes so calmly, in such a businesslike tone of voice, that we were sure that they were neither deceived nor speaking falsehood. They spake what they knew to be true, for Jesus was there with them. Yes, beloved, before you can call your children about your death-bed, Jesus will be there already, and into His hands you may commit your spirit.

Moreover, *there is a certainty that we are quite safe in His hands*. Wherever else we are insecure, if we ask Him to receive our spirit, and He receives it, who can hurt us? Who can pluck us out of His hands? Rouse ye, death and Hell! Come forth, all ye powers of darkness! What can you do when once a spirit is in the hands of the omnipotent Redeemer? We must be safe there.

Then there is the other certainty, *that He is quite willing to take us into His hands*. Let us put ourselves into His hands now; and then we need not be ashamed to repeat the operation every day, and we may be sure that we shall not be rejected at the last. I have often told you of the good old woman, who was dying, and to whom someone said, "Are you not afraid to die?" "Oh, no," she replied, "there is nothing at all to fear. I have dipped my foot in the river of death every morning before I have had my breakfast, and I am not afraid to die now." You remember that dear saint, who died in the night, and who had left written on a piece of paper by her bedside these lines which, ere she fell asleep, she felt strong enough to pencil down,

> *Since Jesus is mine, I'll not fear undressing,*
> *But gladly put off these garments of clay;*
> *To die in the Lord, is a covenant blessing,*
> *Since Jesus to glory thro' death led the way.*

It was well that she could say it, and may we be able to say the same whenever the Master calls us to go up higher! I want, dear friends, that we should all of us have as much willingness to depart as if it were a matter of will with us. Blessed be God, it is not left to our choice, it is not left to our will, when we shall die. God has appointed that day, and ten thousand devils cannot consign us to the grave before our time. We shall not die till God decrees it.

> *Plagues and deaths around me fly,*
> *Till He please I cannot die;*
> *Not a single shaft can hit*
> *Till the God of love sees fit.*

But let us be just as willing to depart as if it were really a matter of choice; for, wisely, carefully, coolly, consider that, if it were left to us, we should none of us be wise if we did not choose to go. Apart from the coming of our Lord, the most miserable thing that I know of would be a suspicion that we might not die. Do you know what quaint old Rowland Hill used to say when he found himself getting very old? He said, "Surely they must be forgetting me up there;" and every now and then, when some dear old saint was dying, he would say, "When you get to Heaven, give my love to John Berridge, and John Bunyan, and ever so many more of the good Johns, and tell them I hope they will see poor old Rawly up there before long." Well, there was common sense in that wishing to get home, longing to be with God. To be with Christ is far better than to be here.

Sobriety itself would make us choose to die; well, then, do not let us run back, and become utterly unwilling, and struggle and strive and fret and fume over it. When I hear of believers who do not like to talk about death, I am afraid concerning them. It is greatly wise to be familiar with our resting place. When I went recently, to the cemetery at Norwood, to lay the body of our dear brother Perkins there for a little while, I felt that it was a healthy thing for me to stand at the grave's brink, and to walk amid that forest of memorials of the dead, for this is where I, too, must go. Ye living men, come and view the ground where you must shortly lie; and, as it must be so, let us who are believers welcome it.

But what if you are not believers? Ah! that is another matter altogether. If you have not believed in Christ, you may well be afraid even to rest on the seat where you are sitting. I wonder that the Earth itself does not say, "O God, I will not hold this wretched sinner up any longer! Let me open my mouth, and swallow him!" All nature must hate the man who hates God. Surely, all things must loathe to minister to the life of a man who does not live unto God. Oh that you would seek the Lord, and trust Christ, and find eternal life! If you have done so, do not be afraid to go forth to live, or to die, just as God pleases. Amen.

Our Lord's Last Cry from the Cross

"And when Jesus had cried with a loud voice, he said, 'Father, into thy hands I commend my spirit': and having said thus, he gave up the ghost."—Luke 23:46.

These were the dying words of our Lord Jesus Christ, "Father, into thy hands I commend my spirit." It may be instructive if I remind you that the words of Christ upon the cross were seven. Calling each of His cries, or utterances, by the title of a word, we speak of the seven last words of the Lord Jesus Christ. Let me rehearse them in your hearing. The first, when they nailed Him to the cross, was, "Father, forgive them; for they know not what they do." Luke has preserved that word. Later, when one of the two thieves said to Jesus, "Lord, remember me when thou comest into thy kingdom," Jesus said to him, "Verily I say unto thee, today shalt thou be with me in paradise." This also Luke has carefully preserved. Farther on, our Lord, in His great agony, saw His mother, with breaking heart, standing by the cross, and looking up to Him with unutterable love and grief, and He said to her, "Woman, behold thy son!" and to the beloved disciple, "Behold thy mother!" and thus He provided a home for her when He Himself should be gone away. This utterance has only been preserved by John.

The fourth and central word of the seven was, *"Eloi, Eloi, lama sabachthani?"* which is, being interpreted, "My God, my God, why hast thou forsaken me?" This was the culmination of His grief, the central point of all His agony. That most awful word that ever fell from the lips of man, expressing the quintessence of exceeding agony, is well put forth, as though it had need of three words before it, and three words after it, as its bodyguard. It tells of a good man, a son of God, *the* Son of God, forsaken of His God. That central word of the seven is found in Matthew and in

Mark, but not in Luke or John; but the fifth word has been preserved by John; that is, "I thirst," the shortest, but not quite the sharpest of all the Master's words, though under a bodily aspect, perhaps the sharpest of them all. John has also treasured up another very precious saying of Jesus Christ on the cross, that is the wondrous word, "It is finished." This was the last word but one, "It is finished," the gathering up of all His lifework, for He had left nothing undone, no thread was left a-raveling, the whole fabric of redemption had been woven, like His garment, from the top throughout, and it was finished to perfection. After He had said, "It is finished," He uttered the last word of all, "Father, into thy hands I commend my spirit," which I have taken for a text tonight; but to which I will not come immediately.

There has been a great deal said about these seven cries from the cross by diverse writers; and though I have read what many of them have written, I cannot add anything to what they have said, since they have delighted to dwell upon these seven last cries; and here the most ancient writers, of what would be called the Romish school, are not to be excelled, even by Protestants, in their intense devotion to every letter of our Savior's dying words; and they sometimes strike out new meanings, richer and more rare than any that have occurred to the far cooler minds of modern critics, who are as a rule greatly blessed with moles' eyes, able to see where there is nothing to be seen, but never able to see when there is anything worth seeing. Modern criticism, like modern theology, if it were put in the Garden of Eden, would not see a flower. It is like the sirocco that blasts and burns, it is without either dew or unction; in fact, it is the very opposite of these precious things, and proves itself to be unblest of God, and unblessing to men.

Now concerning these seven cries from the cross, many authors have drawn from them lessons concerning *seven duties*. Listen. When our Lord said, "Father, forgive them," in effect, He said to us, "Forgive your enemies." Even when they despitefully use you, and put you to terrible pain, be ready to pardon them. Be like the sandalwood tree, which perfumes the axe that fells it. Be all gentleness, and kindness, and love; and be this your prayer, "Father, forgive them."

The next duty is taken from the second cry, namely, that of penitence and faith in Christ, for He said to the dying thief, "Today shalt thou be with me in paradise." Have you, like him, confessed your sin? Have you his faith, and his prayerfulness? Then you shall be accepted even as he was. Learn, then, from the second cry, the duty of penitence and faith.

When our Lord, in the third cry, said to His mother, "Woman, behold thy son!" he taught us the duty of filial love. No Christian must ever be short of love to his mother, his father, or to any of those who are endeared to him by relationships which God has appointed for us to observe. Oh, by the dying love of Christ to His mother, let no man here unman himself by forgetting his mother! She bore you; bear her in her old age, and lovingly cherish her even to the last.

Jesus Christ's fourth cry teaches us the duty of clinging to God, and trusting in God: "My God, my God." See how, with both hands, He takes hold of Him: "My God, my God, why hast thou forsaken me?" He cannot bear to be left of God; all else causes Him but little pain compared with the anguish of being forsaken of His God. So learn to cling to God, to grip Him with a double-handed faith; and if thou dost even think that He has forsaken thee, cry after Him, and say, "Show me wherefore thou contendest with me, for I cannot bear to be without thee."

The fifth cry, "I thirst," teaches us to set a high value upon the fulfillment of God's Word. "After this, Jesus knowing that all things were now accomplished, that the scripture might be fulfilled, saith, 'I thirst.'" Take thou good heed, in all thy grief and weakness, still to preserve the Word of thy God, and to obey the precept, learn the doctrine, and delight in the promise. As thy Lord, in His great anguish said, "I thirst," because it was written that so He would speak, do thou have regard unto the Word of the Lord even in little things.

That sixth cry, "It is finished," teaches us perfect obedience. Go through with thy keeping of God's commandment; leave out no command, keep on obeying till thou canst say, "It is finished." Work thou likewise, obey thy Master, suffer or serve according to His will, but rest not till thou canst say with thy Lord, "It is finished. I have finished the work which thou gavest me to do."

And that last word, "Father, into thy hands I commend my spirit," teaches us resignation. Yield all things, yield up even thy spirit to God at His bidding. Stand still, and make a full surrender to the Lord, and let this be thy watchword from the first even to the last, "Into thy hands, my Father, I commend my spirit."

I think that this study of Christ's last words should interest you; therefore let me linger a little longer upon it. Those seven cries from the cross also teach us something about *the attributes and offices of our Master*. They are seven windows of agate, and gates of carbuncle, through which you may see Him, and approach Him.

First, would you see Him as Intercessor? Then He cries, "Father, forgive them; for they know not what they do." Would you look at Him as King? Then hear His second word, "Verily I say unto thee, today shalt thou be with me in paradise." Would you mark Him as a tender Guardian? Hear Him say to Mary, "Woman, behold thy son!" and to John, "Behold thy mother!" Would you peer into the dark abyss of the agonies of His soul? Hear Him cry, "My God, my God, why hast thou forsaken me?" Would you understand the reality and the intensity of His bodily sufferings? Then hear Him say, "I thirst," for there is something exquisite in the torture of thirst when brought on by the fever of bleeding wounds. Men on the battlefield, who have lost much blood, are devoured with thirst, and tell you that it is the worst pang of all. "I thirst," says Jesus. See the Sufferer in the body, and understand how He can sympathize with you who suffer, since He suffered so much on the cross. Would you see Him as the Finisher of your salvation? Then hear His cry, *"Consurnmatum est"*—"It is finished." Oh, glorious note! Here you see the blessed Finisher of your faith. And would you then take one more gaze, and understand how voluntary was His suffering? Then hear Him say, not as one who is robbed of life, but as one who takes His soul, and hands it over to the keeping of another, "Father, into thy hands I commend my spirit."

Is there not much to be learnt from these cries from the cross? Surely these seven notes make a wondrous scale of music if we do but know how to listen to them. Let me run up the scale again. Here, first, you have Christ's fellowship with men: "Father, forgive them." He stands side by side with sinners, and tries to make an apology for them: "They know not what they do." Here is, next, His kingly power. He sets open Heaven's gate to the dying thief, and bids Him enter. "Today shalt thou be with me in paradise." Thirdly, behold His human relationship. How near of kin He is to us! "Woman, behold thy son!" Remember how He says, "Whosoever shall do the will of my Father who is in Heaven, the same is my brother, and sister, and mother." He is bone of our bone, and flesh of our flesh. He belongs to the human family. He is more of a man than any man. As surely as He is very God of very God, He is also very man of very man, taking into Himself the nature, not of the Jew only, but of the Gentile, too. Belonging to His own nationality, but rising above all, He is the Man of men, the Son of man.

See, next, His taking our sin. You say, "Which note is that?" Well, they are all to that effect; but this one chiefly, "My God, my God, why hast thou forsaken me?" It was because He bore our sins in His own body on the tree that He was forsaken of God. "He hath made Him to be sin for us who knew no sin," and hence the bitter cry, *"Eloi, Eloi, lama sabachthani?"* Behold Him, in that fifth cry, "I thirst," taking not only our sin, but also our infirmity, and all the suffering of our bodily nature. Then, if you would see His fullness as well as His weakness, if you would see His all-sufficiency as well as His sorrow, hear Him cry, "It is finished." What a wonderful fullness there is in that note! Redemption is all accomplished; it is all complete; it is all perfect. There is nothing left, not a drop of bitterness in the cup of gall: Jesus has drained it dry. There is not a farthing to be added to the ransom price; Jesus has paid it all. Behold His fullness in the cry, "It is finished." And then, if you would see how He has reconciled us to Himself, behold Him, the Man who was made a curse for us, returning with a blessing to His Father, and taking us with Him, as He draws us all up by that last dear word, "Father, into thy hands I commend my spirit."

Now both the Surety and sinner are free.

Christ goes back to the Father, for "It is finished," and you and I come to the Father through His perfect work.

I have only practiced two or three tunes that can be played upon this harp, but it is a wonderful instrument. If it be not a harp of ten strings, it is, at any rate, an instrument of seven strings, and neither time nor eternity shall ever be able to fetch all the music out of them. Those seven dying words of the ever living Christ will make melody for us in glory through all the ages of eternity.

I shall now ask your attention for a little time to the text itself: "Father, into thy hands I commend my spirit."

Do you see our Lord? He is dying; and as yet, His face is toward man. His last word to man is the cry, "It is finished." Hear, all ye sons of men, He speaks to you, "It is finished." Could you have a choicer word with which He should say "Adieu" to you in the hour of death? He tells you not to fear that His work is imperfect, not to tremble lest it should prove insufficient. He speaks to you, and declares with His dying utterance, "It is finished." Now He has done with you, and He turns His face the other way. His day's work is done, His more than Herculean toil is accomplished, and the great Champion is going back to His Father's throne, and He speaks; but not to you. His last word is addressed to His Father, "Father, into thy hands I commend my spirit." These are His first words in going home to His Father, as "It is finished," is His last word as, for a while, He quits our company. Think of these words, and may they be your first words, too, when you return to your Father! May you speak thus to your Divine Father in the hour of death! The words were much hackneyed in Romish times; but they are not spoilt even for that. They used to be said in the Latin by dying men, *"In manus tuas, Domine, commendo spiritum meum."* Every dying man used to try to say those words in Latin; and if He did not, somebody tried to say them for him. They were made into a kind of spell of witchcraft; and so they lost that sweetness to our ears in the Latin; but in the English they shall always stand as the very essence of music for a dying saint, "Father, into thy hands I commend my spirit."

It is very noteworthy that the last words that our Lord used were quoted from the Scriptures. This sentence is taken, as I daresay most of you know, from the thirty-first Psalm, and the fifth verse. Let me read it to you. What a proof it is of how full Christ was of the Bible! He was not one of those who think little of the Word of God. He was saturated with it. He was as full of Scripture as the fleece of Gideon was full of dew. He could not speak even in His death without uttering Scripture. This is how David put it, "Into thine hand I commit my spirit: thou hast redeemed me, O Lord God of truth." Now, beloved, the Savior altered this passage, or else it would not quite have suited him. Do you see, first, He was obliged, in order to fit it to His own case, to add something to it? What did He add to it? Why, that word, "Father." David said, "Into thine hand I commit my spirit"; but Jesus says, *"Father,* into thy hands I commend my spirit." Blessed advance! He knew more than David did, for He was more the Son of God than David could be. He was *the* Son of God in a very high and special sense by eternal filiations; and so He begins the prayer with, "Father." But then He takes something from it. It was needful that He should do so, for David said, "Into thine hand I commit my spirit: thou hast redeemed me." Our blessed Master was not redeemed, for He was the Redeemer; and He could have said, "Into thine hand I commit my spirit, for I have redeemed my people"; but that He did not choose to say. He simply took that part which suited himself, and used it as His own, "Father, into thy hands I commend my spirit." Oh, my brethren, you will not do better, after all, than to quote Scripture, especially in prayer. There are no prayers so good as those that are full of the Word of God. May all our speech be flavored with texts! I wish that it were more so. They laughed at our Puritan forefathers because the very names of their children were fetched out of passages of Scripture; but I, for my part, had much rather be laughed at for talking much of Scripture than for talking much of trashy novels—novels with which (I am ashamed to say it) many a sermon nowadays is larded, aye, larded with novels that are not fit for decent men to read, and which are coated over till one hardly knows whether he is hearing about a historical event, or only a piece of fiction—from which abomination, good Lord, deliver us!

So, then, you see how well the Savior used Scripture, and how, from His first battle with the devil in the wilderness till His last struggle with death on the cross, His weapon was ever, "It is written."

Now, I am coming to the text itself, and I am going to preach from it for only a very short time. In doing so, firstly, *let us learn the doctrine* of this last cry from the cross; secondly, *let us practice the duty;* and thirdly, *let us enjoy the privilege.*

I. First, let us learn the doctrine of Our Lord's last cry from the cross.

What is the doctrine of this last word of our Lord Jesus Christ? *God is His Father, and God is our Father.* He who Himself said, "Father," did not say for Himself, "Our Father," for the Father is Christ's Father in a higher sense than He is ours; but yet He is not more truly the Father of Christ than He is our Father if we have believed in Jesus. "Ye are all the children of God by faith in Christ Jesus." Jesus said to Mary Magdalene, "I ascend unto my Father, and your Father; and to my God, and your God." Believe the doctrine of the Fatherhood of God to His people. As I have warned you before, abhor the doctrine of the universal fatherhood of God, for it is a lie, and a deep deception. It stabs at the heart, first, of the doctrine of the adoption, which is taught in Scripture, for how can God adopt men if they are all His children already? In the second place, it stabs at the heart of the doctrine of regeneration, which is certainly taught in the Word of God. Now it is by regeneration and faith that we become the children of God, but how can that be if we are the children of God already? "As many as received Him, to them gave He power to become the sons of God, even to them that believe on His name: which were born, not of blood, nor of the will of the flesh, nor of the will of man, but of God." How can God give to men the power to become His sons if they have it already? Believe not that lie of the devil, but believe this truth of God, that Christ and all who are by living faith in Christ may rejoice in the Fatherhood of God.

Next learn this doctrine, that *in this fact lies our chief comfort.* In our hour of trouble, in our time of warfare, let us say, "Father." You notice that the first cry from the cross is like the last; the highest note is like the lowest. Jesus begins with, "Father, forgive them," and He finishes with, "Father, into thy hands I commend my spirit." To help you in a stern duty like forgiveness, cry, "Father." To help you in sore suffering and death, cry, "Father." Your main strength lies in your being truly a child of God.

Learn the next doctrine, that *dying is going home to our Father*. I said to an old friend, not long ago, "Old Mr. So-and-so has gone home." I meant that he was dead. He said, "Yes, where else should he go?" I thought that was a wise question. Where else should we go? When we grow grey, and our day's work is done, where should we go but home? So, when Christ has said, "It is finished," His next word, of course, is "Father." He has finished His earthly course, and now He will go home to Heaven. Just as a child runs to its mother's bosom when it is tired, and wants to fall asleep, so Christ says, "Father," ere He falls asleep in death.

Learn another doctrine, that if God is our Father, and we regard ourselves as going home when we die, because we go to Him, then He *will receive us*. There is no hint that we can commit our spirit to God, and yet that God will not have us. Remember how Stephen, beneath a shower of stones, cried, "Lord Jesus, receive my spirit." Let us, however we may die, make this our last emotion if not our last expression, "Father, receive my spirit." Shall not our heavenly Father receive His children? If ye, being evil, receive your children at nightfall, when they come home to sleep, shall not your Father, who is in Heaven, receive you when your day's work is done? That is the doctrine we are to learn from this last cry from the cross, the Fatherhood of God and all that comes of it to believers.

II. Secondly, let us practice the duty.

That duty seems to me to be, first, *resignation*. Whenever anything distresses and alarms you, resign yourself to God. Say, "Father, into thy hands I commend my spirit." Sing with Faber—

> *I bow me to thy will, O God,*
> *And all thy ways adore;*
> *And every day I live I'll seek*
> *To please thee more and more.*

Learn, next, the duty of *prayer*. When thou art in the very anguish of pain, when thou art surrounded by bitter griefs of mind as well as of body, still pray. Drop not the "Our Father." Let not your cries be addressed to the air; let not your moans be to your physician, or your nurse; but cry,

"Father." Does not a child so cry when it has lost its way? If it be in the dark at night, and it starts up in a lone room, does it not cry out, "Father"; and is not a father's heart touched by that cry? Is there anybody here who has never cried to God? Is there one here who has never said "Father?" Then, my Father, put thy love into their hearts, and make them tonight say, "I will arise, and go to my Father." You shall truly be known to be the sons of God if that cry is in your heart and on your lips.

The next duty is *the committal of ourselves to God by faith*. Give yourselves up to God, trust yourselves with God. Every morning, when you get up, take yourself, and put yourself into God's custody; lock yourself up, as it were, in the casket of divine protection; and every night, when you have unlocked the box, ere you fall asleep, lock it again, and give the key into the hand of Him who is able to keep you when the image of death is on your face. Before you sleep, commit yourself to God; I mean, do that when there is nothing to frighten you, when everything is going smoothly, when the wind blows softly from the south, and the barque is speeding towards its desired haven, still make not thyself quiet with thine own quieting. He who carves for himself will cut his fingers, and get an empty plate. He who leaves God to carve for him shall often have fat things full of marrow placed before him. If thou canst trust, God will reward thy trusting in a way that thou knowest not as yet.

And then practice one other duty, that of *the personal and continual realization of God's presence*.

> Father, into thy hands I commend my spirit. Thou art here; I know that thou art. I realize that thou art here in the time of sorrow, and of danger; and I put myself into thy hands. Just as I would give myself to the protection of a policeman, or a soldier, if anyone attacked me, so do I commit myself to thee, thou unseen Guardian of the night, thou unwearied Keeper of the day. Thou shalt cover my head in the day of battle. Beneath thy wings will I trust, as a chick hides beneath the hen.

See, then, your duty. It is to resign yourself to God, pray to God, commit yourself to God, and rest in a sense of the presence of God. May the Spirit of God help you in the practice of such priceless duties as these!

III. *Now, lastly, let us enjoy the privilege.*

First, let us enjoy the high privilege of *resting in God in all times of danger and pain*. The doctor has just told you that you will have to undergo an operation. Say, "Father, into thy hands I commend my spirit." There is every probability that that weakness of yours, or that disease of yours, will increase upon you, and that by-and-by you will have to take to your bed, and lie there perhaps for many a day. Then say, "Father, into thy hands I commend my spirit." Do not fret; for that will not help you. Do not fear the future; for that will not aid you. Give yourself up (it is your privilege to do so) to the keeping of those dear hands that were pierced for you, to the love of that dear heart which was set abroach with the spear to purchase your redemption. It is wonderful what rest of spirit God can give to a man or a woman in the very worst condition. Oh, how some of the martyrs have sung at the stake! How they have rejoiced when on the rack! Bonner's coal-hole, across the water there, at Fulham, where he shut up the martyrs, was a wretched place to lie in on a cold winter's night; but they said, "They did rouse them in the straw, as they lay in the coal-hole; with the sweetest singing out of Heaven, and when Bonner said, 'Fie on them that they should make such a noise!' they told him that he, too, would make such a noise if he was as happy as they were." When you have commended your spirit to God, then you have sweet rest in time of danger and pain.

The next privilege is that of *a brave confidence, in the time of death, or in the fear of death*. I was led to think over this text by using it a great many times last Thursday night. Perhaps none of you will ever forget last Thursday night. I do not think that I ever shall, if I live to be as old as Methuselah. From this place till I reached my home, it seemed one continued sheet of fire; and the further I went, the more vivid became the lightning flashes; but when I came at last to turn up Leigham Court Road, then the lightning seemed to come in very bars from the sky; and at last, as I reached the top of the hill, and a crash came of the most startling kind, down poured a torrent of hail, hailstones that I will not attempt to describe, for you might think that I exaggerated, and then I felt, and my friend with me, that we could hardly expect to reach home alive. We were there at the very center and summit of the storm. All around us, on every side, and all within us, as it were, seemed nothing but the electric fluid; and God's right arm seemed bared for war. I felt then, "Well, now I am very likely going home," and I commended my spirit to God; and from that moment, though I cannot say that I took much pleasure in the peals of thunder, and the flashes of lightning, yet I felt quite as calm as I do here at this present moment; perhaps a little more calm than I do in the presence of so many people; happy at the thought that, within a single moment, I might understand more than all I could ever learn on earth, and see in an instant more than I could hope to see if I lived here for a century. I could only say to my friend, "Let us commit ourselves to God; we know that we are doing our

duty in going on as we are going, and all is well with us." So we could only rejoice together in the prospect of being soon with God. We were not taken
home in the chariot of fire; we are still spared a little longer to go on with
life's work; but I realize the sweetness of being able to have done with it all, to
have no wish, no will, no word, scarcely a prayer, but just to take one's heart
up, and hand it over to the great Keeper, saying, "Father, take care of me. So
let me live, so let me die. I have henceforth no desire about anything; let it be
as *thou* pleasest. Into thy hands I commend my spirit."

This privilege is not only that of having rest in danger, and confidence in
the prospect of death; it is also full of *consummate joy*. Beloved, if we know
how to commit ourselves into the hands of God, what a place it is for us to be
in! What a place to be in—in the hands of God! There are the myriads of stars;
there is the universe itself; God's hand upholds its everlasting pillars, and
they do not fall. If we get into the hands of God, we get where all things rest,
and we get home and happiness. We have got out of the nothingness of the
creature into the all-sufficiency of the Creator. Oh, get you there; hasten to
get you there, beloved friends, and live henceforth in the hands of God!

"It is finished." You have not finished; but Christ has. It is all done. What
you have to do will only be to work out what He has already finished for you,
and show it to the sons of men in your lives. And because it is all finished,
therefore say,

> Now, Father, I return to thee. My life henceforth shall be to be in thee. My joy
> shall be to shrink to nothing in the presence of the All-in-all, to die into the eter-
> nal life, to sink my *ego* into Jehovah, to let my manhood, my creaturehood live
> only for its Creator, and manifest only the Creator's glory.

O beloved, begin tomorrow morning and end tonight with, "Father, into thy
hands I commend my spirit." The Lord be with you all! Oh, if you have never
prayed, God help you to begin to pray now, for Jesus' sake! Amen.

The Miracles of Our Lord's Death

"Jesus, when He had cried again with a loud voice, yielded up the ghost. And, behold, the veil of the temple was rent in twain from the top to the bottom; and the Earth did quake, and the rocks rent; and the graves were opened; and many bodies of the saints which slept arose, and came out of the graves after His resurrection, and went into the holy city, and appeared unto many."—Matthew 27:50-53.

Our Lord's death is a marvel set in a surrounding of marvels. It reminds one of a Kohinoor surrounded with a circle of gems. As the sun, in the midst of the planets which surround it, far outshines them all, so the death of Christ is more wonderful than the miracles which happened at the time. Yet, after having seen the sun, we take a pleasure in studying the planets, and so, after believing in the unique death of Christ, and putting our trust in Him as the Crucified One, we find it a great pleasure to examine in detail those four planetary wonders mentioned in the text, which circle round the great sun of the death of our Lord himself.

Here they are: *the veil of the temple was rent in twain; the Earth did quake; the rocks rent; the graves were opened.*

I. To begin with the first of these wonders. *I cannot, tonight, enlarge. I have not the strength. I wish merely to suggest thoughts.*

Consider *the rent veil*, or *mysteries laid open*. By the death of Christ the veil of the temple was rent in twain from the top to the bottom, and the mysteries which had been concealed in the most holy place throughout many generations were laid open to the gaze of all believers. Beginning, as it were, at the top in the Deity of Christ, down to the lowest part of Christ's manhood, the veil was rent, and everything was discovered to every spiritual eye.

1. *This was the first miracle of Christ after death.* The first miracle of Christ in life was significant, and taught us much. He turned the water into wine, as if to show that He raised all common life to a higher grade, and put into all truth a power and a sweetness, which could not have been there apart from Him. But this first miracle of His after death stands above the first miracle of His life, because, if you will remember, that miracle was wrought in His presence. He was there, and turned the water into wine. But Jesus, as man, was not in the temple. That miracle was wrought in His absence, and it enhances its wonder. They are both equally miraculous, but there is a touch that is more striking about this second miracle—that He was not there to speak and make the veil rend in twain. His soul had gone from His body, and neither His body nor His soul was in that secret place of the tabernacles of the Most High; and yet, at a distance, His will sufficed to rend that thick veil of fine twined linen and cunning work.

The miracle of turning water into wine was wrought in a private house, amidst the family and such disciples as were friends of the family; but this marvel was wrought in the temple of God. There is a singular sacredness about it, because it was a deed of wonder done in that most awful and mysterious place, which was the center of hallowed worship, and the abode of God. See! He dies, and at the very door of God's high sanctuary He rends the veil in twain. There is a solemnity about this miracle, as wrought before Jehovah, which I can hardly convey in speech, but which you will feel in your own souls.

Do not forget also that this was done by the Savior after His death, and this sets the miracle in a very remarkable light. He rends the veil at the very instant of death. Jesus yielded up the ghost, and, behold, the veil of the temple was rent in twain. For thirty years He seems to have prepared himself for the first miracle of His life; He works His first miracle after death in the moment of expiring. As His soul departed from His body our blessed Lord at that same moment laid hold upon the great veil of His Father's symbolical house, and rent it in twain.

2. This first miracle after death stands in such a place that we cannot pass it by without grave thought. *It was very significant, as standing at the head of what I may call a new dispensation.* The miracle of turning water into wine begins His public life, and sets the key of it. This begins His work after death, and marks the tone of it. What does it mean?

Does it not mean that *the death of Christ is the revelation and explanation of secrets?* Vanish all the types and shadows of the ceremonial law—vanish because they are fulfilled and explained in the death of Christ. The death of the Lord Jesus is the key of all true philosophy: God made flesh, dying for man—if that does not explain a mystery, it cannot be explained. If with this thread in your hand you cannot follow the labyrinth of human affairs, and learn the great purpose of God, then you cannot follow it at all. The death of Christ is the great veil-render, the great revealer of secrets.

It is also the great opener of entrances. There was no way into the holy place till Jesus, dying, rent the veil; the way into the most holy of all was not made manifest till He died. If you desire to approach God, the death of Christ is the way to Him. If you want the nearest access and the closest communion that a creature can have with his God, behold, the sacrifice of Christ reveals the way to you. Jesus not only says, "I am the way," but, rending the veil, He makes the way. The veil of His flesh being rent, the way to God is made most clear to every believing soul.

Moreover, *the cross is the clearing of all obstacles.* Christ by death rent the veil. Then between His people and Heaven there remains no obstruction, or if there be any—if your fears invent an obstruction, the Christ who rent the veil continues still to rend it. He breaks the gates of brass, and cuts the bars of iron in sunder. Behold, in His death "the breaker is come up before them, and the Lord on the head of them." He has broken up and cleared the way, and all His chosen people may follow Him up to the glorious throne of God.

This is significant of the spirit of the dispensation under which we now live. Obstacles are cleared; difficulties are solved; Heaven is opened to all believers.

3. It was a miracle worthy of Christ. Stop a minute and adore your dying Lord. Does He with such a miracle signalize His death? Does it not prove His *immortality?* It is true He has bowed His head in death. Obedient to His Father's will, when He knows that the time has come for Him to die, He bows His head in willing acquiescence; but at that moment when you call Him dead, He rends the veil of the temple. Is there not immortality in Him though He died?

And see what *power* He possessed. His hands are nailed; His side is about to be pierced. As He hangs there He cannot protect Himself from the insults of the soldiery, but in His utmost weakness He is so strong that He rends the heavy veil of the temple from the top to the bottom.

Behold His *wisdom,* for in this moment, viewing the deed spiritually, He opens up to us all wisdom, and lays bare the secrets of God. The veil which

Moses put upon his face, Christ takes away in the moment of His death. The true Wisdom in His dying preaches His grandest sermon by tearing away that which hid the supremest truth from the gaze of all believing eyes.

Beloved, if Jesus does this for us in His death, surely, we shall be saved by His life. Jesus who died is yet alive, and we trust in Him to lead us into "the holy places made without hands."

Before I pass on to the second wonder, I invite everyone here, who as yet does not know the Savior, seriously to think upon the miracles which attended His death, and judge what sort of man He was who, for our sins, thus laid down His life. He was not suffered by the Father to die without a miracle to show that He had made a way for sinners to draw near to God.

II. Pass on now to the second wonder—"the Earth did quake."

The immovable was stirred by the death of Christ. Christ did not touch the Earth: He was uplifted from it on the tree. He was dying, but in the laying aside of His power, in the act of death, He made the Earth beneath him, which we call "the solid globe," itself to quake. What did it teach?

Did it not mean, first, *the physical universe fore-feeling the last terrible shake of its doom?* The day will come when the Christ will appear upon the earth, and in due time all things that are shall be rolled up, like garments worn out, and put away. Once more will He speak and then will He shake not only the Earth, but also Heaven. The things which cannot be shaken will remain, but this Earth is not one of them: it will be shaken out of its place. "The Earth also and the works that are therein shall be burned up." Nothing shall stand before Him. He alone is. These other things do but seem to be; and before the terror of His face all men shall tremble, and Heaven and Earth shall flee away. So, when He died, Earth seemed to anticipate its doom, and quaked in His presence. How will it quake when He that lives again shall come with all the glory of God! How will you quake, my hearer, if you should wake up in the next world without a Savior! How will you tremble in that day when He shall come to judge the world in righteousness, and you shall have to face the Savior whom you have despised! Think of it, I pray you.

Did not that miracle also mean this?—that *the spiritual world is to be moved by the cross of Christ.* He dies upon the cross and shakes the material world, as a prediction that that death of His would shake the world that lieth in the wicked one, and cause convulsions in the moral kingdom. Brothers, think of it. We say of ourselves, "How shall we ever move the world?" The apostles did not ask that question. They had confidence in the gospel which they preached. Those who heard them saw that confidence; and when they opened their mouths they said, "The men that have turned the world upside down have come hither unto us." The apostles believed in shaking the world with the simple preaching of the gospel. I entreat you to believe the same. It is a vast city this—this London. How can we ever affect it? China, Hindustan, Africa—these are immense regions. Will the cross of Christ tell upon them? Yes, my brethren, for it shook the earth, and it will yet shake the great masses of mankind. If we have but faith in it, and perseverance to keep on with the preaching of the Word, it is but a matter of time when the name of Jesus shall be known of all men, and when every knee shall bow to Him, and every tongue confess that He is Christ, to the glory of God the Father. The Earth did quake beneath the cross; and it shall again. The Lord God be praised for it.

That old world—how many years it had existed I cannot tell. The age of the world, from that beginning which is mentioned in the first verse of the Book of Genesis, we are not able to compute. However old it was, it had to shake when the Redeemer died. This carries us over another of our difficulties. The system of evil we have to deal with is so long-established, hoary, and reverent with antiquity, that we say to ourselves, "We cannot do much against old prejudices." But it was the old, old Earth that quivered and quaked beneath the dying Christ, and it shall do so again. Magnificent systems, sustained by philosophy and poetry, will yet yield before what is called the comparatively new doctrine of the cross. Assuredly it is not new, but older than the Earth itself. It is God's own gospel, everlasting and eternal. It will shake down the antique and the venerable, as surely as the Lord liveth; and I see the prophecy of this in the quaking of the Earth beneath the cross.

It does seem impossible, does it not, that the mere preaching of Christ can do this? And hence certain men must link to the preaching of Christ all the aids of music and architecture, and I know not what beside, till the cross of Christ is overlaid with human inventions, crushed and buried beneath the wisdom of man. But what was it that made the Earth quake? Simply our Lord's death, and no addition of human power or wisdom. It seemed a very inadequate means to produce so great a result; but it was sufficient, for the "weakness of God is stronger than men, and the foolishness of God is wiser than men"; and Christ, in His very death, suffices to make the Earth quake beneath His cross. Come, let us be well content in the battle in which we are engaged, to use no weapon but the gospel, no battle-axe but the cross. Could we but believe it the old, old story is the only story that is needed to be told to reconcile man to God. Jesus died in the sinner's stead, the just for the unjust, a magnificent display of God's grace and justice in one single act. Could we but keep to this only, we should see the victory coming speedily to our conquering Lord.

I leave that second miracle; wherein you see the immovable stirred in the quaking of the earth.

III. Only a hint or two upon the third miracle—the rocks rent.

I have been informed that, to this very day, there are at Jerusalem certain marks of rock-rending of the most unusual kind. Travelers have said that they are not such as are usually produced by earthquake, or any other cause. Upon that I will say but little; but it is a wonderful thing that, as Jesus died, as His soul was rent from His body, as the veil of the temple was rent in two, so the earth, the rocky part of it, the most solid structure of all, was rent in gulfs and chasms in a single moment. What does this miracle show us but this—*the insensible startled?* What! Could rocks feel? Yet they rent at the sight of Christ's death. Men's hearts did not respond to the agonizing cries of the dying Redeemer, but the rocks responded: the rocks were rent. He did not die for rocks; yet rocks were more tender than the hearts of men, for whom He shed His blood.

> *Of reason all things show some sign,*
> *But this unfeeling heart of mine,*

said the poet; and he spoke the truth. Rocks could rend, but yet some men's hearts are not rent by the sight of the cross. However, beloved, here is the point that I seem to see here—that obstinacy and *obduracy will be conquered* by the death of Christ. You may preach to a man about death, and he will not tremble at its certainty or solemnity; yet try him with it. You may preach to a man about Hell, but he will harden his heart, like Pharaoh, against the judgment of the Lord; yet try him with it. All things that can move man should be used. But that which does affect the most obdurate and obstinate is the great love of God, so strangely seen in the death of the Lord Jesus Christ. I will not stay to show you how it is, but I will remind you that it is so. It was this which, in the case of many of us, brought tears of repentance to our eyes, and led us to submit to the will of God. I know that it was so with me. I looked at a thousand things, and I did not relent; but when

> *I saw One hanging on a tree*
> *In agonies and blood,*

and dying there for me, then did I smite upon my breast, and I was in bitterness for him, as one that is in bitterness for His first-born. I am sure your own hearts confess that the great rock-render is the dying Savior.

Well, now, as it is with you, so shall you find it with other men. When you have done your best, and have not succeeded, bring out this last hammer—the cross of Christ. I have often seen on pieces of cannon, in Latin words, this inscription, "The last argument of kings." That is to say, cannons are the last argument of kings. But the cross is the last argument of God. If a dying Savior does not convert you, what will? If His bleeding wounds do not attract you to God, what will? If Jesus bears our sin in His own body on the tree, and puts it away, and if this does not bring you to God, with confession of your sin, and hatred of it, then there remains nothing more for you. "How shall we escape if we neglect so great salvation?" The cross is the rock-render. Brothers and sisters, go on teaching the love of the dying Son of God. Go on preaching Christ. You will tunnel the Alps of pride and the granite hills of prejudice with this. You shall find an entrance for Christ into the inmost hearts of men, though they be hard as adamant; and this will be by the preaching of the cross in the power of the Spirit.

IV. But now I close with the last miracle. These wonders accumulate, and they depend upon each other. The quaking Earth produced, no doubt, the rending of the rocks; and the rending of the rocks aided in the fourth wonder. "The graves were opened."

The graves opened, and *the dead revived*. That is our fourth head. It is the great consequence of the death of Christ. The graves were opened. Man is the only animal that cares about a sepulcher. Some persons fret about how they shall be buried. That is the last concern that ever would cross my mind. I feel persuaded that people will bury me out of hatred, or out of love, and especially out of love to themselves. We need not trouble about that. But man has often shown his pride by his tomb. That is a strange thing. To garland the gallows is a novelty, I think, not yet perpetrated; but to pile marble and choice statuary upon a tomb—what is it but to adorn a gibbet, or to show man's great grandeur where his littleness is alone apparent. Dust, ashes, rottenness, putridity, and then a statue, and all manner of fine things, to make you think that the creature that goes back to dust is, after all, a great one. Now, when Jesus died, *sepulchers were laid bare, and the dead were exposed:* what does this mean?

I think we have in this last miracle "the history of a man." There he lies dead—corrupt, dead in trespasses and sins. But what a beautiful sepulcher he lies in! He is a church-goer; he is a dissenter—whichever you please of the two; he is a very moral person; he is a gentleman; he is a citizen; he is Master of his Company; he will be Lord Mayor one day; he is so good—oh, he is so good! yet he has no grace in his heart, no Christ in his faith, no love to God. You see what a sepulcher he lies in—a dead soul in a gilded tomb. By His Cross our Lord splits this sepulcher and destroys it. What are our merits worth in the presence of the cross? The death of Christ is the death of self-righteousness. Jesus' death is a superfluity if we can save ourselves. If we are so good that we do not want the Savior, why, then, did Jesus bleed His life away upon the tree? The cross breaks up the sepulchers of hypocrisy, formalism, and self-righteousness in which the spiritually dead are hidden away.

What next? *It opens the graves.* The Earth springs apart. There lies the dead man: he is revealed to the light. The cross of Christ does that! The man is not yet made alive by grace, but he is discovered to himself. He knows that he lies in the grave of his sin. He has sufficient of the power of God upon him to make him lie, not like a corpse covered up with marble, but like a corpse from which the grave-digger has flung away the sods, and left it naked to the light of day. Oh, it is a grand thing when the cross thus opens the graves! You cannot convince men of sin except by the preaching of a crucified Savior. The lance with which we reach the hearts of men is that same lance which pierced the Savior's heart. We have to use the crucifixion as the means of crucifying self-righteousness, and making the man confess that he is dead in sin.

After the sepulchers had been broken up, and the graves had been opened, what followed next? *Life was imparted.* "Many of the bodies of the saints which slept arose." They had turned to dust; but when you have a miracle you may as well have a great one. I wonder that people, when they can believe one miracle, make any difficulty of another. Once introduce Omnipotence, and difficulties have ceased. So in this miracle. The bodies came together on a sudden, and there they were, complete and ready for the rising. What a wonderful thing is the implantation of life! I will not speak of it in a dead man, but I would speak of it in a dead *heart*. O God, send thy life into some dead heart at this moment while I speak! That which brings life into dead souls is the death of Jesus. While we behold the atonement, and view our Lord bleeding in our stead, the divine Spirit works upon the man, and life is breathed into him. He takes away the heart of stone, and gives a heart of flesh that palpitates with a new life. This is the wondrous work of the cross: it is *by* the death of our Lord that regeneration comes to men. There were no new births if it were not for that one death. If Jesus had not died, we had remained dead. If He had not bowed His head, none of us could have lifted up our heads. If He had not there on the cross passed from among the living, we must have remained among the dead forever and forever.

Now pass on, and you will see that those persons who received life, in due time *quitted their graves*. It is written that they came out of their graves. Of course they did. What living men would wish to stay in their graves? And you, my dear hearers, if the Lord quickens you, will not stay in your graves. If you have been accustomed to strong drink, or to any other besetting sin, you will quit it; you will not feel any attachment to your sepulcher. If you have lived in ungodly company, and found amusement in questionable places, you will not stop in your graves. We shall not have need to come after you to lead you away from your old associations. You will be eager to get out of them. If any person here should be buried alive, and if he should be discovered in his coffin before he had breathed his last, I am sure that, if the sod were lifted, and the lid were taken off, he would not need prayerful entreaties to come out of his grave. Far from it. Life loves not the prison of death. So may God grant that the dying Savior may fetch you out of the graves in which you are still living; and, if He now quickens you, I am sure that the death of our Lord will make you reckon that if one died for all, then all died, and that He died for all, that they which live should not live henceforth unto themselves, but unto Him that died for them and rose again.

Which way did these people go after they had come out of their graves? We are told that *"they went into the holy city."* Exactly so. And he that has felt the power of the cross may well make the best of his way to holiness. He will long to join himself with God's people; he will wish to go up to God's house, and to have fellowship with the thrice-holy God. I should not expect that quickened ones would go anywhere else. Every creature goes to its own company, the beast to its lair, and the bird to its nest; and the restored and regenerated man makes his way to the holy city. Does not the cross draw us to the church of God? I would not wish one to join the church from any motive that is not fetched from the five wounds and bleeding side of Jesus. We give ourselves first to Christ, and then to His people for His dear sake. It is the cross that does it:

> *Jesus dead upon the tree*
> *Achieves this wondrous victory.*

We are told—to close this marvelous story—that they went into the Holy City *"and appeared unto many."* That is, some of them who had been raised from the dead, I do not doubt, appeared unto their wives. What rapture as they saw again the beloved husband! It may be that some of them appeared to father and mother; and I doubt not that many a quickened mother or father would make the first appearance to their children. What does this teach us, but that, if the Lord's grace should raise us from the dead, we must take care to show it? Let us appear unto many. Let the life that God has given us be manifest. Let us not hide it, but let us go to our former friends and make our epiphanies as Christ made His. For His glory's sake let us have our manifestation and appearance unto others. Glory be to the dying Savior! All praise to the great Sacrifice!

Oh, that these poor, feeble words of mine would excite some interest in you about my dying Master! Be ready to die for Him. And you that do not know Him—think of this great mystery—that God should take your nature and become a man and die, that you might not die, and bear your sin that you should be free from it. Come and trust my Lord tonight, I pray you. While the people of God gather at the table to the breaking of bread, let your spirits hasten, not to the table and the sacrament, but to Christ Himself and His sacrifice. Amen.

The Messages of Our Lord's Love

"Go your way, tell his disciples and Peter that he goeth before you into Galilee: there shall ye see him, as he said unto you."—Mark 16:7.

See, brethren! Jesus delights to meet His people. He is no sooner risen from the dead than He sends a message by an angel to say that He will meet His disciples. His delight is in them. He loves them with a very tender love, and He is happiest when He is in their midst. Do not think that you will have to entreat and persuade your Lord to come to you; He delights in near and dear fellowship. The heavenly Bridegroom finds solace in your company, if you be indeed espoused to Him. Oh, that you were more anxious to be with Him!

Our Lord knows that, to His true people, the greatest joy they ever have is for Him to meet them. The disciples were at their saddest. Their Lord, as they thought, was dead. They had just passed the dreariest Sabbath of their lives, for He was in the tomb; and now, to comfort them, He sends no message but this—that He will meet them. He knew that there would be magic in that news to cheer their aching hearts. *He would meet them:* that would be all-sufficient consolation: "Go into Galilee; there shall ye see Him."

If all the sorrows of God's people could be poured out in one vast pile, what a mountain they would make! How varied our distresses! How diverse our depressions! But, beloved, if Jesus will meet us, all the sadness will fly away, and all the sorrow will grow light. Only give us His company, and we have all things. You know what I mean, many of you. Our Lord has made our hearts to leap for joy in sorrowful times. When we have been filled with physical pain, His company has made us forget the body's weakness; and when we have newly come from the grave, and our heart has been ready to break through bereavement, the sight of the Savior has sweetened our bitter cup. In His presence we have felt resigned to the great Father's will, and content to say, "It is the Lord: let Him do what seemeth Him good." Until the day break, and the shadows flee away forever, we want nothing but our Well-beloved's company. "Abide with me! Abide with me!"—this is our one prayer; and if we have that fulfilled, all other desires may wait their turn.

My subject is chosen with a view to our coming, as we always do on the first day of the week, to this table of communion. I want every child of God here to seek after, nay, to gain, full fellowship with Christ. I long to enjoy it myself, that I may preach a Savior in whose presence I live. I long for you to enjoy it, that you may hear, not my voice, but His voice, which is sweeter than the music of angels' harps. Oh, that those who do not know our Lord may now be set a-hungering after His surpassing sweetness! He is willing to come to you. A prayer will find Him; a tear will draw Him; a look of faith will hold Him fast. Cast yourself on Jesus, and His open arms will joyously receive you.

But now to the text. I shall take it just as it stands, and make five observations upon it.

I. *The first is: Jesus, that He may meet His people, issues invitations, and the invitations are very gracious—"Go, tell His disciples and Peter."*

"*Tell His disciples.*" The invitation is most gracious as directed to them, for "they all forsook Him, and fled." On that night, that doleful night, when He most needed company, they slept; and when He woke, and was taken off to the hall of Caiaphas, they fled—yes, every one of them; there was not a steadfast spirit among them. They all fled. "Shame on them!" say you? Yes, but Jesus was not ashamed of them; for in one of the first speeches of His glorious life on Earth He specially mentions them. "Tell my disciples": not picking and choosing, here and there, a heart more faithful than the rest, but mentioning the whole coward company, He says, "Tell my disciples." Brethren, disciples of Christ, Jesus would meet us now; let us hasten to His presence. Not one among us dares plume himself upon his fidelity; we have all at times played the coward. We may each one of us hide our faces when we think of our Lord's most faithful love to us. We have never acted towards Him according to His deserts. If He had banished us: if He had said, "I will no more acknowledge this dastard company," we could not have wondered, but He invites us all, all who are His disciples—invites us to Himself. Will you stay away? Will any of you be satisfied without beholding that dear countenance, more marred than that of any man, and yet more lovely than the face of angels? Come ye, all who follow Him, for He bids you come. Hear the address of the message—"Tell my disciples."

But the bounty and beauty of His grace lay in this—that one had been worse than the rest, and, therefore, for Him there is a special finger to beckon him, a special word to call him: "Tell my disciples *and Peter.*" He that denied his Lord, he that cursed as he denied, he who, after boisterous self-confidence, trembled at the jest of a maid, is he to be called? Yes, "Tell my disciples *and Peter.*" If any of you have behaved worse to your Master than others, you are peculiarly called to come to Him now. You have grieved Him, and you have been grieving because you have grieved Him. You have been brought to repentance after having slidden away from Him, and now He seals your pardon by inviting you to Himself. He bids you not to stand in the background, but to come in with the rest and commune with Him.

Peter, where art thou? The crowing of the cock is still in thine ear, and the tear is still in thine eye, yet come and welcome, for thou lovest Him. He knows thou dost. Thou art grieved that a doubt should be put upon thy love. Come, He has forgiven thee; He has given thee tokens of it in thy broken heart and tearful eye. Come, Peter! Come thou, if nobody else should come. Jesus Christ invites thee by name before any other. In this place may be believers who have acted strangely, and have even forsaken the Lord, and they are now bemoaning themselves. Go on with your holy sorrow, but come to your Lord. Be not content till you have seen Him, till you have laid hold upon Him by a fresh grip of faith, and till you can say, "My beloved is mine, and I am His."

Most tender, then, are the invitations which Jesus issues. Part of the tenderness now lies in *the lips which deliver the message* on the Lord's behalf. The women came, and said—"Jesus has said to us, by an angel, He will go before us into Galilee, and there shall ye see Him." I am always thankful that God has committed the ministry of the Word, not to angels, but to us poor men. As I told you a little while ago, you may grow tired of me and my stammerings; but yet they are more suitable for you than nobler strains might be. I have no doubt that if you had an angel to preach to you, there would be a very great crowd, and for a time you would say, "It is wonderful"; but it would be so cold from lack of human sympathy, that you would soon weary of the lofty style. An angel would try to be kind, as became his heavenly nature, but he would not be *kin,* and you must necessarily miss the kindness which comes of kinship. I speak to you as bone of your bone, and flesh of your flesh: I speak to you, teacher, for I am a teacher. I speak to you, disciple, for I am a disciple, and I dare not think myself greater than the least of you. Let us come hand in hand to our dear Savior, and all together let us pray Him to manifest Himself to us as He doth not unto the world. This, then, is my first point—His invitations are gracious.

II. Secondly, we see in our text that Jesus keeps His tryst.

"I will go before you into Galilee." If you turn to Mark 14:27, 28, you will see that He told them before He died,

> All ye shall be offended because of me this night: for it is written, I will smite the shepherd, and the sheep shall be scattered. But after that I am risen, I will go before you into Galilee.

He will be where He says He will be. Jesus never breaks a promise. It is a great vexation, especially to us who are very busy, when somebody says, "Will you meet me at such and such a place?" "Yes; at what hour?" The hour is appointed. We are there. Thank God, we never were a half minute behind time when it was possible to be punctual; but punctuality is a lesson which very few persons as yet have learned. We wait, and wait wearily, and perhaps we leave the place to let our dilatory friends know that if they are in eternity we are in time, and cannot afford to lose any of it. Many people make an engagement and break it, as if it were just nothing at all to be guilty of a practical lie. It is not so with Jesus: He says, "I will go before you into Galilee"; and into Galilee He will go. When He promises to meet His people He will meet with them without fail, and without delay.

Let us dwell on this appointment for a minute. Why did our Lord say that He would go to Galilee? Was it because *it was His old haunt,* and being risen from the dead, He desired to go back to the spot where He had been accustomed to be—to the lake, and to the hillside? Surely there is something in that. It was *their* old haunt, too: they were fishermen on that lake, and He would take them back to the place where a thousand memories would be awakened by their voices, like echoes which lie asleep among the hills. Besides it would provide witnesses to His identity, for the Galileans knew Him well: since there He had been brought up. He would go where He was known, and show himself in His former places of resort.

Perhaps, too, it was because *the place was despised.* He has risen, and He will go to Galilee. He is not ashamed to be called the Galilean and the Nazarene. The risen One does not go to the halls of princes, but to the villages of peasants and fishermen. There was no pride in Jesus: not even the smell of that fire had passed upon Him. He was ever meek and lowly in heart.

Did He not also go to Galilee, because *it was some little distance* from Jerusalem, that those who would meet Him might take a little trouble? Our Beloved would be sought after. A journey after Him will endear His society. He will not meet you at Jerusalem, perhaps—at least, not the whole company of you; but He will show himself by the sea in distant Galilee.

Do you think He went to Galilee because *it was "Galilee of the Gentiles,"* that He might get as near to us Gentiles as His mission allowed? He was sent as a preacher only to the lost sheep of the house of Israel; but He traveled to the very edge of His diocese to get as near to the Gentiles (I mean to ourselves) as He could. Oh, happy word for us aliens!—"I will go before you into Galilee." So He said; and when He left the tomb, He kept His word.

Now, beloved, we have His word for it, that He will come and meet us where we are met together. "Where two or three are gathered together in my name, there am I in the midst of them"; and does He not keep His word? How many times in our assemblies, great and small, have we said, "The Lord was there!" How frequently have we forgotten preacher and fellow-worshipers, feeling ourselves in the presence of a greater than mortal man! Our eyes of faith have seen the King in His beauty, revealing His love to us. Oh, yes! He keeps His tryst. He comes to His people, and He never disappoints them. I think this is particularly true of the table of communion. How often He has met us there! I am compelled to repeat my personal testimony. I have never omitted being at the Lord's table on any Sabbath of my life for many years past, except when I have been ill, or unable to attend; and I am therefore able to answer the question—Does not frequency diminish the solemnity of the ordinance? I have not found it so; but the rather it grows upon me. That broken bread, that poured out wine, the emblems of His flesh and blood—these bring Him very near. It seems as if sense lent aid to faith; and through these two windows of agates, and gates of carbuncles, we come very near to our Lord. What have we here but Himself, under instructive emblems? What do we here but remember Him? What is our business here but to show His death until He come? And so, though we may not have seen Him in converse by the way, for our eyes have been holden, yet we have seen Him in the breaking of bread. May it be always so! May we prove that Jesus keeps His pledge. He will be with us even now. Suppose Jesus had said that He would come into this place tonight in literal flesh and blood, you would be all sitting in expectation, and saying to each other, "When will He come?" The preacher would be waiting to drop back, or fall upon his knees in adoration, while his Master stood in the front. You will not see Him *so* ; but may your faith, which is much better than eyesight, realize Him as the present Christ, near to each one of you. If He were here in the flesh, He might stand *here,* and then He might be near to me, but far off from my friends yonder; but coming in spirit He can be equally near to us all, and speak to each one of us personally, as though each one were the only person present.

III. *My third observation is, Jesus is always first at every appointed meeting.*

So runs the text: *"He goeth before you* into Galilee." Remember that promise, "Where two or three are gathered together in my name, there *am* I"—not "there will I be." Jesus is there before His disciples reach the place. The first to reach the house is He who is first in the house. We come to Him: it is not that we meet, and then He comes to us; but He goes before us, and we gather to Him.

Does it not teach us that He *is the shepherd?* He said, "Smite the shepherd, and the sheep shall be scattered; but after I am risen, I will go before you into Galilee." He would take up the shepherd's place again, and go before the flock, and the sheep would take up the position of the flock again, no longer scattered, but following at the Shepherd's heel. Great Master, come tonight; call thy sheep to thyself! Speak to us, look upon us, and we will arise, and follow thee.

Is He not first, next, because He *is the center?* We gather to Him. You must choose a center before you can mark the circumference. When Israel traveled through the wilderness, the first place to pitch upon for an encampment was the place where the tabernacle and the ark should rest, and then the tents were set around it. Jesus is our center; He must therefore be first, and we rejoice to hear Him say, "I will go before you into Galilee." He will take the first place, and we will cluster about Him as bees around their queen. Do you always gather to the name of Christ, beloved? If you gather to the name of any minister, or any sect, you gather amiss. Our gatherings must be unto the Lord Jesus: He must be the center, and He alone; let us take care of that.

Next, He goes before us naturally, because He *is the host.* If there is to be a feast, the first person to be there is the one who provides it—the master or mistress who sits at the head of the table. It would never do for the guests to be there first, and then for the master to come hurrying home, crying, "Excuse me: I quite forgot that you were to be here at six o'clock!" Oh no, the host must be first! When Jesus bids us come to Him, and says He will sup with us, and we with Him, He will be sure to be first, so as to prepare the feast. He goes before us into Galilee.

But surely, the reason why He is first is this—that He *is more ready for us than we are for Him*. It takes us time to get ready for communion, to dress our souls, and collect our thoughts. Are you all ready for the Lord's Supper tonight? Some of you, perhaps, have come carelessly here, and yet you are members of the church, and mean to stay to the Supper. Beloved, try to come with a prepared heart, for the communion will be to you very much what you make it; and if your thoughts and desires are not right, what can the outward emblems be to you? On our Lord's part all things are ready, and He waits to receive you, and to bless you. Therefore He is first at the appointed meeting place.

I may also add that He *is much more eager to have fellowship with you than you are to have fellowship with him.* It is a strange thing that it should be so, but so it is. He, the great lover of our souls, burns with a passionate desire to press His people to His heart; and we, the objects of such a matchless love, start back, and reward the ardor of His affection with lukewarmness. It must not be so on this occasion. I have said to my Lord, "Let me either feast upon thee or hunger after thee." I pray that you may have such a burning thirst for Jesus at this hour that you *must* drink of His cup or pine with thirst for Him.

IV. The fourth observation is this: the Lord Jesus reveals Himself to His people.

How does the text run? "He goeth before you into Galilee. *There shall ye see Him.*" The main object is to *see Him*. He will go to Galilee on purpose that He may reveal Himself to them. My dear brethren, this is what they needed beyond all else. Their sorrow was because they thought Him dead; their joy would be because they saw Him alive. Their griefs were multiform, but this one consolation would end them all. If they could but see Jesus, they would look their fears away. What have you come here for tonight, children of God? I trust that you can answer, "Sir, we would see Jesus." If our Master will come, and we shall feel His presence, it will not matter how feebly I speak, or how poor the service may be in itself; you will say, "It was good to be there, for the Lord drew near to us in all the glory of His love." *His presence is what you want.*

And *this is what He readily gives.* Jesus is very familiar with His people. Some worship a Savior who sits enthroned above in the stately dignity of indifference; but our Lord is not so. Though reigning in Heaven, He is still conversant with His people below. He is a brother born for adversity.

Spiritually He communes with us. Do you know what the company of Christ is? Are you altogether taken up with doctrines about Him, or with ceremonies that concern Him? If so, yours is a poor life; but the joy of the inner life is to know, and to speak with, and to dwell with the Lord Jesus. Do you understand this? I charge you, be not satisfied till you come to personal and intimate intercourse with your Lord. Short of this, you are short of the privilege which He sees you need, for this is His great promise, "There shall ye see me."

What is more, this sight of Him *is what our Lord effectually bestows.* Jesus not only exhibits Himself, but He opens our eyes, that we may enjoy the sight. "There *shall* ye see me." He may be manifest, and yet blind eyes will not see Him. Blessed Master, come and take the scales away and make our hearts capable of spiritual perception! It is not everybody that can see God, and yet God is everywhere. The eye must first be cleansed. Jesus says, "There shall ye see me"; and He knows how to open our eyes, so that we do see Him. Our Lord can make this to be the absorbing occupation of His people. "He goeth before you into Galilee"—and what then? "There shall ye see Him." Why, they went fishing, did they not? Yes, but they were called off from that. "There shall ye see Him." They took a great haul of fish, did they not? Yes, yes, yes; but that was a mere incident: the grand fact was, that they *saw Him.* I pray the Lord to make the one occupation of our lives the seeing of *Him.* May all the lower lights grow dim. Where are the stars at midday? They are all in their places, but you only see the sun. Where are a thousand things when Christ appears? They are all where they should be, but you only see *Him.* May the Lord cause all other loves to vanish, and Himself alone to fill our hearts, so that it may be true of us, "There shall ye see Him"!

I have thus far proceeded, crying to the Holy Ghost for help, and now comes the fifth observation, with which we close.

V. Our Lord remembers His own promises.

It was before He died that He said He would go before them into Galilee, and now that He has risen from the dead, He says, by the mouth of His angel, "There shall ye see him, *as He said unto you."* The rule of Christ's action is His own word. What He has said He will perform. You and I forget His promises, but He never does. "As He said unto you" is the remembrance of all that He has spoken. Why does our Lord remember and repeat what He has so graciously spoken?

He does so because He *spoke with foresight,* and forethought, and care. We make promises and forget them because we did not consider well the matter before we spoke; but if we have thought, calculated, weighed, estimated, and come to a deliberate resolve before we speak, then we earnestly remember what we resolved upon. No promise of our Lord Jesus has been spoken in haste, to be repented of afterwards. Infinite wisdom directs infinite love; and when infinite love takes the pen to write a promise, infallible wisdom dictates every syllable.

Jesus does not forget, because He *spoke the promise with His whole heart.* It is not every tongue that represents a heart at all; but even though true people, we say many things which we mean, but there is no depth of feeling, no potent emotion, no stirring of the heart's center. Our Lord, when He said, "Ye shall be scattered; but after that I am risen, I will go before you into Galilee," spoke with a heavy heart, with many a melting sigh; and His whole soul went with the promise which closed the mournful scene. He has purchased what He promised, purchased it with His blood, and therefore He speaks most solemnly, and with His whole heart. There is no trifling on Christ's part with one to whom He makes a promise, and therefore He never forgets.

And, once more, His *honor is bound up with every promise.* If He had said that He would go to Galilee, and He had not gone, His disciples would have felt that He had made a mistake, or that He had failed. Brethren, if Christ's promise were to fail, what should we think of it? But He will never jeopardize His faithfulness and veracity.

> As well might He His being quit,
> As break His promise or forget.

Let the words of man be blown away like the chaff; but the words of Jesus must stand, for He will not tarnish His truth, which is one of the choicest of His crown-jewels.

I want you to turn over this thought in your quietude. Jesus remembers all that He has spoken; let not our hearts forget. Go to Him with His covenant bonds and gracious promises: He will recognize His own signature. He will honor His own promises to the utmost, and none that trust in Him shall complain of His having exaggerated.

I have done when I have said just this. I am very anxious that at this time we should come into real fellowship with Christ, at the table. Jesus, thou hast made us hunger after thee; wilt thou not feed us? Thou hast made us thirst after thee; wilt thou not supply that thirst? Do you think that our Beloved means to tantalize us? Our hunger is such that it would break through stone walls; shall we find

His heart hard as a stone wall? No; He will clear the way, and we on our part will burst through all obstacles to come to Him. "But," says one, "how can I come to him, poor, unknown, unworthy one that I am?" Such were the disciples at the lake. They were fishermen; and when He came to them, they had been toiling all night. Are you working for Him? Then He will come to you. Expect Him now. "Ah!" says one, "I have been working without success"—you are a poor minister whose congregation is falling off, whose church is not increased by conversions—you have toiled all the night, and taken nothing. Or you are a Sunday-school teacher, who cannot see her girls converted; or a brother who mourns that his boys are not coming to Christ. Well, I see who you are; you are just the sort of people that Jesus came to, for they had toiled all night in vain. Are you hungry? Jesus cries, "Children, have you any meat?" He comes to you and enquires about your hunger; while on the shore He has a fire of coals, and fish laid thereon, and bread. "Come and dine," says He. The table is spread. Come to Himself! He is your food, your hope, your joy, your Heaven. Come to Him; give Him no rest till He reveals Himself to you, and you know of a surety that it is your Lord who embraces you. So may He do, to each of us just now, for His sweet love's sake! Amen.

The Evidence of Our Lord's Wounds

*"Then saith he to Thomas, 'Reach hither thy finger, and behold
my hands; and reach hither thy hand, and thrust it into my side:
and be not faithless, but believing.'"—John 20:27.*

A mong us at this day we have many persons who are like Thomas—du-
bious, demanding signs and tokens, suspicious, and ofttimes sad. I am
not sure that there is not a slight touch of Thomas in most of us. There are
times and seasons when the strong man fails, and when the firm believer has
to pause a while, and say, "Is it so?" It may be that our meditation upon the
text before us may be of service to those who are touched with the malady
which afflicted Thomas.

Notice, before we proceed to our subject in full, that *Thomas asked of our
Lord what He ought not to have asked.* He wanted to put our risen Lord to tests
which were scarcely reverent to His sacred person. Admire His Master's patience with him. He does not say, "If he does not choose to believe he may
continue to suffer for his unbelief." But no; He fixes His eye upon the
doubter, and addresses Himself specially to him; yet not in words of reproach
or anger. Jesus could bear with Thomas, though Thomas had been a long
time with Him, and had not known Him. To put his finger into the print of
the nails, and thrust his hand into His side, was much more than any disciple
had a right to ask of his divine Master; and yet see the condescension of Jesus!
Rather than Thomas should suffer from unbelief, Christ will let him take
great liberties. Our Lord does not always act towards us according to His
own dignity, but according to our necessity; and if we really are so weak that
nothing will do but thrusting a hand into His side, He will let us do it. Nor do
I wonder at this: if, for our sakes, He suffered a spear to be thrust there, He
may well permit a hand to follow.

Observe that *Thomas was at once convinced*. He said: "My Lord, and my God." This shows our Master's wisdom, that He indulged him with such familiarity, because He knew that, though the demand was presumptuous, yet the act would work for his good. Our Lord sometimes wisely refuses—saying, "Touch me not; for I am not yet ascended"; but at other times, He wisely grants, because, though it be too much for us to ask, yet He thinks it wise to give.

The subject for our present meditation is just this: *the cure of doubts*. Thomas was permitted to put his finger into the print of the nails for the curing of his doubts. Perhaps you and I wish that we could do something like it. Oh, if our Lord Jesus would appear to me for once, and I might thrust my hand into His side; or, if I might for once see Him, or speak with Him, how confirmed should I be! No doubt that thought has arisen in the minds of many. We shall not have such proofs, my brethren, but we shall have something near akin to them, which will answer the same purpose.

I. *The first head of my discourse shall be this: crave no signs. If such signs be possible, crave them not. If there be dreams, visions, voices, ask not for them.*

Crave not wonders, first, because *it is dishonoring to the sacred Word to ask for them*. You believe this Bible to be an inspired volume—the Book of God. The apostle Peter calls it "A more sure word of prophecy; whereunto ye do well that ye take heed." Are you not satisfied with that? When a person, in whose veracity you have the utmost confidence, bears testimony to this or that, if you straightway reply, "I would be glad of further evidence," you are slighting your friend, and casting unjust suspicion upon him. Will you cast suspicion upon the Holy Ghost, who, by this word, bears witness unto Christ? Oh, no! let us be content with His witness. Let us not wish to see, but remain satisfied to believe. If there be difficulties in believing, is it not natural there should be, when he that believes is finite, and the things to be believed are, in themselves, infinite? Let us accept the difficulties as being in themselves, in some measure, proofs of the correctness of our position, as inevitable attendants of heavenly mysteries, when they are looked at by such poor minds as ours. Let us believe the Word, and crave no signs.

Crave no signs, because *it is unreasonable that we should desire more than we have already*. The testimony of the Lord Jesus Christ, contained in the Word, should alone suffice us. Beside that, we have the testimony of saints and martyrs, who have gone before us, dying triumphant in the faith. We have the testimony of many still among us, who tell us that these things are so. In part, we have the testimony of our own conscience, of our own conversion, of our own after-experience, and this is convincing testimony. Let us be satisfied with it. Thomas ought to have been content with the testimony of Mary Magdalene, and the other disciples, but he was not. We ought to trust our brethren's word. Let us not be unreasonable in craving after proofs when already proofs are afforded us without stint.

Crave no signs, because *it may be you will be presumptuous in so doing*. Who are you, to set God a sign? What is it He is to do before you will believe in Him? Suppose He does not choose to do it, are you therefore arrogantly to say, "I refuse to believe unless the Lord will do my bidding"? Do you imagine that any angel would demean himself to pay attention to you, who set yourself up to make demands of the Most High? Assuredly not. It is presumption which dares to ask of God anything more than the testimony of Himself which He chooses to grant us in His Word.

It is, moreover, damaging to ourselves to crave signs. Jesus says, "Blessed are they that have not seen, and yet have believed." Thomas had his sign, and he believed; and so far, so good, but he missed a blessing peculiar to those who have not seen, and yet have believed. Do not, therefore, rob yourselves of the special favor which lights on those who, with no evidence but the witness of the Spirit of God, are prepared at once to believe in the Lord Jesus unto eternal life.

Again, crave no signs, for *this craving is highly perilous*. Translated according to many, and I think translated correctly, our Savior said, "Reach hither thy finger, and put it into the print of the nails; and *become* not faithless, but believing," intending to indicate that Thomas, by degrees, would become faithless. His faith had grown to be so little that, if he continued insisting upon this and that, as a sign or evidence, that faith of his would get down to the very lowest; yea, he would have no faith left. "Become not faithless, but believing." Dear friends, if you began to seek signs, and if you were to see them, do you know what would happen? Why, you would want more; and when you had these, you would demand still more. Those who live by their feelings judge of the truth of God by their own condition. When they have happy feelings, then they believe; but if their spirits sink, if the weather happens to be a little damp, or if their constitution happens to be a little disordered, down go their spirits, and, straightaway, down goes their faith. He that lives by a faith which does not rest on feeling, but is built upon the Word of the Lord, will remain fixed and steadfast as the mount of God; but he that craves for this thing and that thing, as a token for good at the hand of the

Lord, stands in danger of perishing from want of faith. He shall not perish, if he has even a grain of living faith, for God will deliver him from the temptation; but the temptation is a very trying one to faith.

Crave, therefore, no sign. If you read a story of a person who saw a vision, or if you hear another declare that a voice spake to him—believe those things, or not, as you like; but do not desire them for yourself. These wonders may, or may not, be freaks of the imagination: I will not judge; but we must not rely upon them, for we are not to walk by sight, but by faith. Rely not upon anything that can be seen of the eyes, or heard of the ears; but simply trust Him whom we know to be the Christ of God, the Rock of our salvation.

II. Secondly, when you want comfort, crave no sign, but turn to the wounds of your Lord.

You see what Thomas did. He wanted faith, and he looked for it to Jesus wounded. He says nothing about Christ's head crowned with glory. He does not say that he must see him "girt about the paps with a golden girdle." Thomas, even in his unbelief, is wise; he turns to his Lord's wounds for comfort. Whenever your unbelief prevails, follow in this respect the conduct of Thomas, and turn your eyes straightway to the wounds of Jesus. These are the founts of never-failing consolation, from which, if a man doth once drink, he shall forget his misery, and remember his sorrow no more. Turn to the Lord's wounds; and if you do, what will you see?

First, you will see *the tokens of your Master's love.* O Lord Jesus, what are these wounds in thy side, and in thy hands? He answers,

> These I endured when suffering for thee. How can I forget thee? I have graven thee upon the palms of my hands. How can I ever fail to remember thee? On my very heart the spear has written thy name.

Look at Jesus, dead, buried, risen, and then say, "He loved me, and gave Himself for me!" There is no restorative for a sinking faith like a sight of the wounded Savior. Look, soul, and live by the proofs of His death! Come and put thy finger, by faith, into the print of the nails, and these wounds shall heal thee of unbelief. The wounds of our Lord are the tokens of His love.

They are, again, *the seals of His death,* especially that wound in His side. He must have died; for "one of the soldiers, with a spear, pierced His side, and forthwith came there out blood and water. And he that saw it bare witness." The Son of God did assuredly die. God, who made the Heavens and the earth, took to Himself our nature, and in one wondrous person He was both God and man; and lo! this wondrous Son of God bore sufferings unutterable, and consummated all by His death. This is our comfort, for if He died in our stead, then we shall not die for our sins; our transgression is put away, and our iniquity is pardoned. If the sacrifice had never been slain, we might despair; but since the spear-wound proves that the great Sacrifice really died, despair is slain, hope revives, and confidence rejoices.

The wounds of Jesus, next, are *the marks of identity*. By these we identify His blessed person after His resurrection. The very Christ that died has risen again. There is no illusion: there could be no mistake. It is not somebody else foisted upon us in His place; but Jesus who died has left the dead, for there are the marks of the crucifixion in His hands and in His feet, and there is the spear-thrust still. It is Jesus: this same Jesus. This is a matter of great comfort to a Christian—this indisputably proven doctrine of the resurrection of our Lord. It is the keystone of the gospel arch. Take that away, or doubt it, and there remains nothing to console you. But because Jesus died and in the selfsame person rose again, and ever lives, therefore does our heart sweetly rest, believing that "them also which sleep in Jesus will God bring with Him"; and also that the whole of the work of Jesus is true, is completed, and is accepted of God.

Again, those wounds, those scars of our Lord, were *the memorials of His love to His people*. They set forth His love so that His chosen can see the tokens; but they are also memorials to Himself. He condescendingly bears these as His reminders. In Heaven, at this moment, upon the person of our blessed Lord, there are the scars of His crucifixion. Centuries have gone by, and yet He looks like a Lamb that has been slain. Our first glance will assure us that this is He of whom they said, "Crucify him; crucify him." Steadily look with the eyes of your faith into the glory, and see your Master's wounds, and say within yourself, "He has compassion upon us still: He bears the marks of His passion." Look up, poor sufferer! Jesus knows what physical pain means. Look up, poor depressed one! He knows what a broken heart means. Canst thou not perceive this? Those prints upon His hands, these sacred stigmata, declare that He has not forgotten what He underwent for us, but still has a fellow-feeling for us.

Once again, these wounds may comfort us because in Heaven they are, before God and the holy angels, *the perpetual ensigns of His finished work*. That passion of His can never be repeated, and never needs to be: "After He had offered one sacrifice for sins forever, He sat down on the right hand of God." But the memorials are always being presented before the infinite mind of God. Those memorials are, in part, the wounds in our Lord's blessed person. Glorified spirits can never cease to sing, "Worthy is the Lamb that was slain"; for every time they gaze upon Him they perceive His scars. How resplendent shine the nail-prints! No jewels that ever gemmed a king can look one-half so lustrous as these. Though He be God over all blessed forever, yet to us, at least, His brightest splendor comes from His death.

My hearer, whensoever thy soul is clouded, turn thou to these wounds which shine like a constellation of five bright stars. Look not to thine own wounds, nor to thine own pains, or sins, or prayers, or tears, but remember that "with His stripes we are healed." Gaze, then; intently gaze, upon thy Redeemer's wounds if thou wouldest find comfort.

III. This brings me to my third point: whenever faith is staggered at all, seek such helps for your faith as you may.

Though we cannot literally put our finger into the print of the nails, and may not wish to do so, yet let us use such modes of recognition as we do possess. Let us put these to their utmost use; and we shall no longer desire to put our hand into the Savior's side. We shall be perfectly satisfied without that. Ye that are troubled with doubts and fears, I give you these recommendations.

First, if you would have your faith made vivid and strong, *study much the story of your Savior's death*. Read it: read it: read it: read it. *"Tolle: lege,"* said the voice to Augustine, "Take it: read it." So say I. Take the four evangelists; take the fifty-third chapter of Isaiah; take the twenty-second psalm; take all other parts of Scripture that relate to our suffering Substitute, and read them by day and by night, till you familiarize yourself with the whole story of His griefs and sin-bearing. Keep your mind intently fixed upon it; not sometimes, but continually. *Crux lux:* the cross is light. Thou shalt see it by its own light. The study of the narrative, if thou pray the Holy Ghost to enlighten thee, will beget faith in thee; and thou wilt, by its means, be very greatly helped, till, at last, thou wilt say, "I cannot doubt. The truth of the atonement is impressed upon my memory, my heart, my understanding. The record has convinced me."

Next, if this suffice not, *frequently contemplate the sufferings of Jesus*. I mean by that, when you have read the story, sit down, and try and picture it. Let your mind conceive it as passing before you. Put yourself into the position of the apostles who saw Him die. No employment will so greatly strengthen faith, and certainly none will be more enjoyable!

> *Sweet the moments, rich in blessing,*
> *Which before the cross I spend,*
> *Life and health and peace possessing*
> *From the sinner's dying Friend.*

An hour would be grandly spent if occupied in turning over each little detail, item, and incident in the marvelous death by which you are redeemed from death and Hell. You will be surprised to find how this familiarizing of yourself with it, by the help of the Holy Spirit, will make it as vivid to you as if you saw it; and it will have a better effect upon your mind than the sight of it would have done; for probably the actual sight would have passed away from your mind, and have been forgotten, while the contemplation of the sorrowful scene will sink deep into your soul, and leave eternal lines! You will do well, first, to read and know the narrative, and then to contemplate it carefully and earnestly—I mean, not to think of it for a minute or two at chance times, but to take an hour or two that you can specially set apart on purpose to consider the story of your Savior's death. I am persuaded, if you do this, it will be more helpful to you than putting his finger into the print of the nails was to Thomas.

What next? Why, dear friends, the Lord has a way of *giving His people wonderful realizations.* I hope I shall not say anything incorrect when I remark that there are times with us when the Lord is present with us, and we are strongly impressed with that fact, and therefore we act under a sense of that presence as if the divine glory were actually visible. Do you know what it is to write a letter to a friend feeling as if the Lord Jesus were looking over your shoulder? I know what it is at times to stand here and preach, and feel my Lord so near me that if I had literally seen Him it would not have surprised me. Have you never, in the watches of the night, lain quiet when there was no sound but the ticking of the watch, and thought of your Lord till, though you knew there was no form before you, you were just as certain that He was there as if you could see His sorrowful countenance? In quiet places all alone—you scarcely like to tell the story—in the lone wood, and in the upper chamber—you have said, "If He spake I should not be more certain of His presence; and if He smiled upon me I should not be surer of His love." These realizations have sometimes been so joyfully overwhelming that for years you have been lifted by them beyond all power of doubt. These holy summer days banish the frosts of the soul. Whenever a doubt is suggested to me about the existence of my Lord and Master, I feel that I can laugh the tempter to scorn, for I have seen Him, and spoken with Him. Not with these eyes, but with the eyes of my inner life, I have beheld my Lord, and communed with Him. Wonder not that I am not among the crew of the black, piratical ship of "Modern Thought."

Nor is it merely in seasons of enjoyment that we get these helps, but in times of *deep distress*. Prostrate with pain, unable to enjoy any comfort, unable even to sleep, I have seen the soul of the believer as happy as if all sounds were marriage peals. Some of us know what it is to be right gleesome, glad, and joyous in hours of fierce trial, because Christ has been so near. In times of losses and bereavements, when the sorrow stung you to the quick, and you thought, before it came, that you never could bear it, yet have you been so sustained by a sight of the sacred head once wounded, and by fellowship with Him in His sufferings, that you have said, "What are my griefs compared with His?" You have forgotten your sorrows and sung for joy of heart, as those that make merry. If you have been helped in this way, it will have all the effect upon you that ever could have come of putting your finger into the print of the nails. If, perchance, you have been given up to die, and have, mentally, gone through the whole process of dying, expecting soon to stand before the bar of God, and have been happy, and even exultant, then you could not doubt the reality of a religion that bore you up above the surging billows. Now that you are again restored to life for a little longer time, the recollection of your buoyant spirits, in what you thought to be your dying hours, will answer all the purpose to you, I think, of putting your finger into the nail-prints.

Sometimes the strengthening influence may be afforded under the stress of *temptation*. If ever, young man, you have had a strong temptation hurling itself against you, and your feet have almost gone—aye, let me not say "young man"; but if ever a man or a woman of any age has had to cry out, "God, help me: how shall I escape out of this?" and you have turned your eyes and seen your Lord and beheld His wounds; and if you have felt at that moment that the temptation had lost all power—you have had a seal from the Lord, and your faith has been confirmed. If at the sight of your Lord you have exclaimed, in presence of the temptation, "How can I do this great wickedness, and sin against God?" after that, you have had the best proof of your Redeemer's power to save. What better or more practical proof could you desire?

In these times, when the foundations of our faith are constantly being undermined, one is sometimes driven to say to himself, "Suppose it is not true." As I stood, the other night, beneath the sky, and watched the stars, I felt my heart going up to the great Maker with all the love that I was capable of. I said to myself, "What made me love God as I know I do? What made me feel an anxiety to be like Him in purity? Whatever made me long to obey my God cannot be a lie." I know that it was the love of Jesus for me that changed my heart, and made me, though once careless and indifferent to Him, now to pant with strong desires to honor Him. What has done this? Not a lie, surely. A truth, then, has done it. I know it by its fruits. If this Bible were to turn out untrue, and if I died and went before my Maker, could I not say to Him, "I believed great things of thee, great God; if it be not so, yet did I honor thee by the faith I had concerning thy wondrous goodness, and thy power to forgive"? and I would cast myself upon His mercy without fear. But we do not entertain such doubts; for those dear wounds continually prove the truth of the gospel, and the truth of our salvation by it. Incarnate Deity is a thought that was never invented by poet's mind, nor reasoned out by philosopher's skill. Incarnate Deity, the notion of the God that lived, and bled, and died in human form, instead of guilty man: it is itself its own best witness. The wounds are the infallible witness of the gospel of Christ.

Have you not felt those wounds very powerful to you in the form of *assistance in times of duty?* You said, "I cannot do it, it is too hard for me." You looked to Jesus wounded, and you could do anything. A sight of the bleeding Christ has often filled us with enthusiasms, and so with power: it has rendered us mighty with the omnipotence of God. Look at the church of Christ in all ages. Kings and princes did not know what to do with her. They vowed that they would destroy her. Their persecuting edicts went forth, and they put to death thousands upon thousands of the followers of Christ. But what happened? The death of Jesus made men willing to die for Him. No pain, no torture, could keep back the believing host. They loved Jesus so that though their leaders fell by bloody deaths, another rank came on, and yet another, and another, till despots saw that neither dungeon, nor rack, nor fire could stop the march of the army of Christ. It is so now. Christ's wounds pour life into the church by transfusion: the life-blood of the church of God is from Jesus' wounds. Let us know its power and feel it working within us to will and to do of His good pleasure.

And as for those who do not trust Him, what shall I say? The Lord help you to do so at once; for as long as you do not trust Him, you are under an awful curse, for it is written, "If any man love not the Lord Jesus, let Him be *Anathema Maranatha*"—cursed at the coming of the Lord. May it not be so with you! Amen.

The Resurrection

I Know That My Redeemer Liveth

"For I know that my redeemer liveth, and that he shall stand at the latter day upon the earth: and though after my skin, worms destroy this body, yet in my flesh shall I see God: whom I shall see for myself, and mine eyes shall behold, and not another; though my reins [kidneys and back] be consumed within me."—Job 19:25-27.

Our text deserves our profound attention; its preface would hardly have been written had not the matter been of the utmost importance in the judgment of the patriarch who uttered it. Listen to Job's remarkable desire: "Oh that my words were now written! oh that they were printed in a book! That they were graven with an iron pen and lead in the rock forever!" Perhaps, hardly aware of the full meaning of the words he was uttering, yet his holy soul was impressed with a sense of some weighty revelation concealed within his words; he therefore desired that it might be recorded in a book; he has had his desire: the Book of books embalms the words of Job. He wished to have them graven on a rock; cut deep into it with an iron pen, and then the lines inlaid with lead; or he would have them engraven, according to the custom of the ancients, upon a sheet of metal, so that time might not be able to eat out the inscription. He has not had his desire in that respect, save only that upon many and many a sepulcher those words of Job stand recorded, "I know that my redeemer liveth."

It is the opinion of some commentators that Job, in speaking of the rock here, intended his own rock-hewn sepulcher, and desired that this might be his epitaph; that it might be cut deep, so that ages should not wear it out; that when any asked, "Where does Job sleep?" as soon as they saw the sepulcher of the patriarch of Uz, they might learn that he died in hope of resurrection, resting upon a living Redeemer. Whether such a sentence adorned the portals of Job's last

441

sleeping-place we know not; but certainly no words could have been more fitly chosen. Should not the man of patience, the mirror of endurance, the pattern of trust, bear as his memorial this golden line, which is as full of all the patience of hope, and hope of patience, as mortal language can be? Who among us could select a more glorious motto for his last escutcheon?

In discoursing upon these words I shall speak upon three things. First, *let us, with the patriarch, descend into the grave and behold the ravages of death.* Then, with him, *let us look up on high for present consolation.* And, still in his admirable company, let us, in the third place, *anticipate future delights.*

I. First of all then, with the patriarch of Uz, let us descend into the sepulcher.

The body has just been divorced from the soul. Friends who loved most tenderly have said—"Bury my dead out of my sight." The body is borne upon the bier and consigned to the silent earth; it is surrounded by the earthworks of death. Death has a host of troops. If the locusts and the caterpillars be God's army, the worms are the army of death. These hungry warriors begin to attack the city of man. They commence with the outworks; they storm the munition, and overturn the walls. The skin, the city wall of manhood, is utterly broken down, and the towers of its glory covered with confusion. How speedily the cruel invaders deface all beauty. The face gathers blackness; the countenance is defiled with corruption. Those cheeks once fair with youth, and ruddy with health, have fallen in, even as a bowing wall and a tottering fence, those eyes, the windows of the mind whence joy and sorrow looked forth by turns, are now filled up with the dust of death; those lips, the doors of the soul, the gates of Mansoul, are carried away, and the bars thereof are broken. Alas, ye windows of agates and gates of carbuncle, where are ye now? How shall I mourn for thee, O thou captive city, for the mighty men have utterly spoiled thee! Thy neck, once like a tower of ivory, has become as a fallen column; thy nose, so lately comparable to "the tower of Lebanon, which looketh toward Damascus," is as a ruined hovel; and thy head, which towered like Carmel, lies low as the clods of the valley. Where is beauty now? The most lovely cannot be known from the most deformed.

Cruel have ye been, ye warriors of death. The skin is gone. The troops have entered into the town of Mansoul. And now they pursue their work of devastation; the pitiless marauders fall upon the body itself. There are those noble aqueducts, the veins through which the streams of life were wont to flow, these, instead of being rivers of life, have become blocked up with the soil and wastes of death, and now they must be pulled to pieces; not a single relic of them shall be spared.

Dear friends, why should we wish to have it otherwise? Why should we desire to preserve the body when the soul has gone?

Do not seek to avoid what God has purposed; do not look upon it as a gloomy thing. Regard it as a necessity; nay more, view it as the platform of a miracle, the lofty stage of resurrection, since Jesus shall surely raise again from the dead the particles of this body, however divided from one another. We have heard of miracles, but what a miracle is the resurrection! All the miracles of Scripture, yea even those wrought by Christ, are small compared with this. The philosopher says, "How is it possible that God shall hunt out every particle of the human frame?" He can do it: He has but to speak the word, and every single atom, though it may have traveled thousands of leagues, though it may have been blown as dust across the desert, and anon have fallen upon the bosom of the sea, and then have descended into the depths thereof to be cast up on a desolate shore, sucked up by plants, fed on again by beasts, or passed into the fabric of another man—I say that individual atom shall find its fellows, and the whole company of particles at the trump of the archangel shall travel to their appointed place, and the body, the very body which was laid in the ground, shall rise again.

When the fabric has been absolutely broken up, the tenement all pulled down, ground to pieces, and flung in handfuls to the wind, so that no relic of it is left, yet when Christ stands in the latter days upon the earth, all the structure shall be brought together, bone to his bone—then shall the might of Omnipotence be seen. This is the doctrine of the resurrection, and happy is he who finds no difficulty here, who looks at it as being an impossibility with man but a possibility with God, and lays hold upon the omnipotence of the Most High and says, "Thou sayest it, and it shall be done"! I comprehend Thee not great God; I marvel at Thy purpose to raise my mouldering bones; but I know that Thou dost great wonders, and I am not surprised that Thou shouldst conclude the great drama of Thy creating works here on Earth by re-creating the human frame by the same power by which Thou didst bring from the dead the body of Thy Son Jesus Christ, and by that same divine energy which has regenerated human souls in Thine own image.

II. *Now, having thus descended into the grave, and seen nothing there but what is loathsome, let us look up with the patriarch and behold a sun shining with present comfort.*

"I know," said he, "that my Redeemer liveth." The word "Redeemer" here used, is in the original "goel"—kinsman. The duty of the kinsman, or goel, was this: suppose an Israelite had alienated his estate, as in the case of Naomi and Ruth; suppose a patrimony which had belonged to a family, passed away through poverty, it was the goel's business, the redeemer's business to pay the price as the next of kin, and to buy back the heritage. Boaz stood in that relation to Ruth.

Now, the body may be looked upon as the heritage of the soul—the soul's small farm, that little plot of Earth in which the soul has been wont to walk and delight, as a man walketh in his garden or dwelleth in his house. Now, that becomes alienated. Death, like Ahab, takes away the vineyard from us who are as Naboth; we lose our patrimonial estate; Death sends his troops to take our vineyard and to spoil the vines thereof and ruin it. But we turn round to Death and say, "I know that my Goel liveth, and He will redeem this heritage; I have lost it; thou takest it from me lawfully, Death, because my sin hath forfeited my right; I have lost my heritage through my own offence, and through that of my first parent Adam; but there lives One who will buy this back."

Brethren, Job could say this of Christ long before He had descended upon earth, "I know that he liveth"; and now that He has ascended up on high, and led captivity captive, surely we may with double emphasis say, "I know that my Goel, my Kinsman liveth, and that he hath paid the price, that I should have back my patrimony, so that in my flesh I shall see God." Yes, my hands, ye are redeemed with blood; bought not with corruptible things, as with silver and gold, but with the precious blood of Christ. Yes, heaving lungs and palpitating heart, ye have been redeemed! He that redeemed the soul to be His altar has also redeemed the body, that it may be a temple for the Holy Ghost. Not even the bones of Joseph can remain in the house of bondage. No smell of the fire of death may pass upon the garments which His holy children have worn in the furnace.

Remember, too, that it was always considered to be the duty of the goel, not merely to redeem by price, but where that failed, to redeem by power. Hence, when Lot was carried away captive by the four kings, Abraham summoned his own hired servants, and the servants of all his friends, and went out against the kings of the East, and brought back Lot and the captives of Sodom. Now, our Lord Jesus Christ, who once has played the kinsman's part by paying the price for us, liveth, and He will redeem us by power. O Death, thou tremblest at this Name! Thou knowest the might of our Kinsman! Against His arm thou canst not stand! Thou didst once meet Him foot to foot in stern battle, and O Death, thou didst indeed tread upon His heel. He voluntarily submitted to this, or else, O Death, thou hadst no power against Him. But He slew thee, Death, He slew thee! He rifled all thy caskets, took from thee the key of thy castle, burst open the door of thy dungeon; and now, thou had knowest, Death, thou hast no power to hold my body; thou mayst set thy slaves to devour it, but thou shalt give it up, and all their spoil must be restored.

Insatiable Death, from thy greedy maw yet shall return the multitudes whom thou hast devoured. Thou shalt be compelled by the Savior to restore thy captives to the light of day. I think I see Jesus coming with His Father's servants. The chariots of the Lord are twenty thousand, even thousands of angels. Blow ye the trumpet! blow ye the trumpet! Immanuel rides to battle! The Most Mighty in majesty girds on His sword. He comes! He comes to snatch by power, His people's lands from those who have invaded their portion. Oh, how glorious victory! No battle shall there be. He comes, He sees, He conquers. The sound of the trumpet shall be enough; Death shall fly affrighted; and at once from beds of dust and silent clay, to realms of everlasting day the righteous shall arise.

To linger here a moment, there was yet, very conspicuously in the Old Testament, we are informed, a third duty of the goel, which was to avenge the death of his friend. If a person had been slain, the Goel was the avenger of blood; snatching up his sword, he at once pursued the person who had been guilty of bloodshed. So now, let us picture ourselves as being smitten by Death. His arrow has just pierced us to the heart, but in the act of expiring, our lips are able to boast of vengeance, and in the face of the monster we cry, "I know that my Goel liveth." Thou mayst fly, O Death, as rapidly as thou wilt, but no city of refuge can hide thee from him; he will overtake thee; he will lay hold upon thee, O thou skeleton monarch, and he will avenge my blood on thee. I would that I had powers of eloquence to work out this magnificent thought. Chrysostom, or Christmas Evans could picture the flight of the King of Terrors, the pursuit by the Redeemer, the overtaking of the foe, and the slaying of the destroyer. Christ shall certainly avenge Himself on Death for all the injury which Death hath done to His beloved kinsmen. Comfort thyself then, O Christian; thou hast ever living, even when thou diest, One who avenges thee, One who has paid the price for thee, and One whose strong arms shall yet set thee free.

Passing on in our text to notice the next word, it seems that Job found consolation not only in the fact that he had a Goel, a Redeemer, but that this Redeemer liveth. He does not say, "I know that my Goel *shall live*, but that he *lives*,"—having a clear view of the self-existence of the Lord Jesus Christ, the same yesterday, today, and forever. And you and I looking back do not say, "I know that He *did live*, but He *lives* today." This very day you that mourn and sorrow for venerated friends, your prop and pillar in years gone by, you may go to Christ with confidence, because He not only lives, but He is the source of life; and you therefore believe that He can give forth out of Himself life to those whom you have committed to the tomb. He is the Lord and giver of life originally, and He shall be specially declared to be the resurrection and the life, when the legions of His redeemed shall be glorified with Him. If I saw no fountain from which life could stream to the dead, I would yet believe the promise when God said that the dead shall live; but when I see the fountain provided, and know that it is full to the brim and that it runneth over, I can rejoice without trembling. Since there is one who can say, "I am the resurrection and the life," it is a blessed thing to see the means already before us in the person of our Lord Jesus Christ. Let us look up to our Goel then who liveth at this very time.

Still the marrow of Job's comfort it seems to me lay in that little word "my." "I know that today *my* Redeemer liveth." Oh, to get hold of Christ! I know that in His offices He is precious. But, dear friends, we must get a property in Him before we can really enjoy Him. What is honey in the wood to me, if like the fainting Israelites, I dare not eat? It is honey in my hand, honey on my lip, which enlightens mine eyes like those of Jonathan. What is gold in the mine to me? Men are beggars in Peru, and beg their bread in California. It is gold in my purse which will satisfy my necessities, purchasing the bread I need. So, what is a Kinsman if He be not a Kinsman to me? A Redeemer that does not redeem me, an avenger who will never stand up for my blood, of what avail were such? But Job's faith was strong and firm in the conviction that the Redeemer was his.

Dear friends, dear friends, can all of you say, "I know that my redeemer liveth." The question is simple and simply put; but oh, what solemn things hang upon your answer, "Is it today *my* Redeemer?" I charge you rest not, be not content until by faith you can say, "Yes, I cast myself upon Him; I am His, and therefore He is mine." I know that full many of you, while you look upon all else that you have as not being yours, yet can say, "*My* Redeemer is mine." He is the only piece of property which is really ours. We borrow all else, the house, the children; nay, our very body we must return to the Great Lender. But Jesus, we can never leave, for even when we are absent from the body we are present with the Lord, and I know that even death cannot separate us from Him, so that body and soul are with Jesus truly even in the dark hours of death, in the long night of the sepulcher, and in the separate state of spiritual existence. Beloved, have you Christ? It may be you hold Him with a feeble hand, you half think it is presumption to say, "He is my Redeemer"; yet remember, if you have but faith as a grain of mustard seed, that little faith entitles you to say, and say now, "I know that my Redeemer liveth."

There is another word in this consoling sentence which no doubt served to give a zest to the comfort of Job. It was that he could say, "I *know*"—"I *know* that my Redeemer liveth." To say, "I hope so, I trust so," is comfortable; and there are thousands in the fold of Jesus who hardly ever get much further. But to reach the marrow of consolation you *must* say, "I *know*." Ifs, buts, and perhapses, are sure murderers of peace and comfort. Doubts are dreary things in times of sorrow. Like wasps they sting the soul! If I have any suspicion that Christ is not mine, then there is vinegar mingled with the gall of death. But if I know that Jesus is mine, then darkness is not dark; even the night is light about me. Out of the lion cometh honey; out of the eater cometh forth sweetness. "I know that my Redeemer liveth." This is a brightly burning lamp cheering the damps of the sepulchral vault, but a feeble hope is like a flickering smoking flax, just making darkness visible, but nothing more. I would not like to die with a mere hope mingled with suspicion. I might be safe with this but hardly happy; but oh, to go down into the river knowing that all is well, confident that as a guilty, weak, and helpless worm I have fallen into the arms of Jesus, and believing that He is able to keep that which I have committed to Him.

I would have you, dear Christian friends, never look upon the full assurance of faith as a thing impossible to you. Say not "It is too high; I cannot attain unto it." I have known one or two saints of God who have rarely doubted their interest at all. There are many of us who do not often enjoy any ravishing ecstasies, but on the other hand we generally maintain the even tenor of our way, simply hanging upon Christ, feeling that His promise is true, that His merits are sufficient, and that we are safe. Assurance is a jewel for worth but not for rarity. It is the common privilege of all the saints if they have but the grace to attain unto it, and this grace the Holy Spirit gives freely. Surely if Job in Arabia, in those dark misty ages when there was only the morning star and not the sun, when they saw but little, when life and immortality had not been brought to light—if Job before the coming and advent still could say, "*I know*," you and I should not speak less positively. God forbid that our positiveness should be presumption.

Let us try ourselves, and see that our marks and evidences are right, lest we form an ungrounded hope; for nothing can be more destructive than to say, "Peace, peace, where there is no peace." But oh, let us build for eternity, and build solidly.

Let us not be satisfied with the mere foundation, for it is from the upper rooms that we get the widest prospect. Let us pray the Lord to help us to pile stone on stone, until we are able to say as we look at it, "Yes, I *know*, I *know* that my Redeemer liveth." This, then, for present comfort today in the prospect of departure.

III. And now, in the third and last place, as the anticipation of future delight, let me call to your remembrance the other part of the text.

Job not only knew that the Redeemer lived, but he anticipated the time when He should *stand in the latter day upon the earth.* No doubt Job referred here to our Savior's first advent, to the time when Jesus Christ, "the goel," the Kinsman, should stand upon the Earth to pay in the blood of His veins the ransom price, which had, indeed, in bond and stipulation been paid before the foundation of the world in promise. But I cannot think that Job's vision stayed there; he was looking forward to the second advent of Christ as being the period of the resurrection. We cannot endorse the theory that Job arose from the dead when our Lord died, although certain Jewish believers held this idea very firmly at one time. We are persuaded that "the latter day" refers to the advent of glory rather than to that of shame. Our hope is that the Lord shall come to reign in glory where He once died in agony.

The bright and hallowed doctrine of the second advent has been greatly revived in our churches in these latter days, and I look for the best results in consequence. There is always a danger lest it be perverted and turned by fanatical minds, by prophetic speculations, into an abuse; but the doctrine in itself is one of the most consoling, and, at the same time, one of the most practical, tending to keep the Christian awake, because the Bridegroom cometh at such an hour as we think not. Beloved, we believe that the same Jesus who ascended from Olivet shall so come in like manner as He ascended up into Heaven. We believe in His personal advent and reign. We believe and expect that when both wise and foolish virgins shall slumber; in the night when sleep is heavy upon the saints; when men shall be eating and drinking as in the days of Noah, that suddenly as the lightning flasheth from Heaven, so Christ shall descend with a shout, and the dead in Christ shall rise and reign with Him. We are looking forward to the literal, personal, and actual standing of Christ upon Earth as the time when creation's groans shall be silenced forever, and the earnest expectation of the creature shall be fulfilled.

Mark, that Job describes Christ as *standing.* Some interpreters have read the passage, "he shall stand in the latter days against the earth; "that as the earth has covered up the slain, as the earth has become the charnel-house of the dead, Jesus shall arise to the contest and say, "Earth, I am against thee; give up thy dead! Ye clods of the valley cease to be custodians of my people's bodies! Silent deeps, and you, ye caverns of the earth, deliver, once for all, those whom ye have imprisoned!" Macphelah shall give up its precious treasure, cemeteries and graveyards shall release their captives, and all the deep places of the earth shall resign the bodies of the faithful. Well, whether that be so or no, the posture of Christ, in standing upon the earth, is significant. It shows His triumph. He has triumphed over sin, which once like a serpent in its coils had bound the earth. He has defeated Satan. On the very spot where Satan gained his power Christ has gained the victory. Earth, which was a scene of defeated goodness, whence mercy once was all but driven [out], where virtue died, where everything heavenly and pure, like flowers blasted by pestilential winds, hung down their heads, withered and blighted—on this very earth everything that is glorious shall blow and blossom in perfection; and Christ Himself, once despised and rejected of men, fairest of all the sons of men, shall come in the midst of a crowd of courtiers, while kings and princes shall do Him homage, and all the nations shall call Him blessed. "He shall stand in the latter day upon the earth."

Then, at that auspicious hour, says Job, "In my flesh I shall see God." Oh, blessed anticipation!—"I shall see God." He does not say, "I shall see the saints"—doubtless we shall see them all in Heaven—but, "I shall see *God*." Note he does not say, "I shall see the pearly gates, I shall see the walls of jasper, I shall see the crowns of gold and the harps of harmony," but "I shall see God"; as if that were the sum and substance of Heaven. "In my flesh shall I see *God*." The pure in heart shall see God. It was their delight to see Him in the ordinances by faith. They delighted to behold Him in communion and in prayer. There in Heaven they shall have a vision of another sort. We shall see God in Heaven, and be made completely like Him; the divine character shall be stamped upon us; and being made like to Him we shall be perfectly satisfied and content. Likeness to God, what can we wish for more? And a sight of God, what can we desire better? We shall see God, and so there shall be perfect contentment to the soul and a satisfaction of all the faculties.

Some read the passage, "Yet, I shall see God in my flesh," and hence think that there is here an allusion to Christ, our Lord Jesus Christ, as the Word made flesh. Well, be it so, or be it not so, it is certain that we shall see Christ, and He, as the divine Redeemer, shall be the subject of our eternal vision. Nor shall we ever want any joy beyond simply that of seeing Him. Think not, dear friend, that this will be a narrow sphere for your mind to dwell in. It is but one source of delight, "I shall see God," but that source is infinite. His wisdom, His love, His power, all His attributes shall be subjects for your eternal contemplation, and as He is infinite under each aspect, there is no fear of exhaustion. His works, His purposes, His gifts, His love to you, and His glory in all His purposes, and in all His deeds of love—why, these shall make a theme that never can be exhausted. You may with divine delight anticipate the time when in your flesh you shall see God.

But I must have you observe how Job has expressly made us note that it is in the same body. "Yet, *in my flesh* shall I see God"; and then he says again, "whom I shall see for myself, and mine eye shall behold and not another." Yes, it is true that I, the very man standing here, though I must go down to die, yet I shall as the same man most certainly arise and shall behold my God. Not part of myself, though the soul alone shall have some view of God, but the whole of myself, my flesh, my soul, my body, my spirit shall gaze on God. We shall not enter Heaven, dear friends, as a dismasted vessel is tugged into harbor; we shall not get to glory some on boards, and some on broken pieces of the ship, but the whole ship shall be floated safely into the haven, body and soul both being safe. Christ shall be able to say, "*All* that the Father giveth to me shall come to me," not only all the persons, but all of the persons—each man in his perfection. There shall not be found in Heaven one imperfect saint. There shall not be a saint without an eye, much less a saint without a body. No member of the body shall have perished; nor shall the body have lost any of its natural beauty. All the saints shall be all there, and all of all; the same persons precisely, only that they shall have risen from a state of grace to a state of glory. They shall be ripened; they shall be no more the green blades, but the full corn in the ear; no more buds but flowers; not babes but men.

Please to notice, and then I shall conclude, how the patriarch puts it as being a real personal enjoyment. "Whom mine eye shall behold, and not another." They shall not bring me a report as they did the Queen of Sheba, but I shall see Solomon the King for myself. I shall be able to say, as they did who spake to the woman of Samaria, "Now I believe, not because of thy word who did bring me a report, but I have seen him for myself." There shall be personal intercourse with God; not through the Book, which is but as a glass; not through the ordinances; but directly, in the person of our Lord Jesus Christ, we shall be able to commune with the Deity as a man talketh with his friend. "Not another." If I could be a changeling and could be altered, that would mar my comfort. Or if my Heaven must be enjoyed by proxy, if draughts of bliss must be drunk for me, where were the hope? Oh, no; for myself, and not through another, shall I see God.

Have we not told you a hundred times that nothing but personal religion will do, and is not this another argument for it, because resurrection and glory are personal things? "Not another." If you could have sponsors to repent for you, then, depend upon it, you would have sponsors to be glorified for you. But as there is not another to see God for you, so you must yourself see and yourself find an interest in the Lord Jesus Christ.

In closing let me observe how foolish have you and I been when we have looked forward to death with shudders, with doubts, with loathings. After all, what is it? Worms! Do ye tremble at those base crawling things? Scattered particles! Shall we be alarmed at these? To meet the worms we have the angels; and to gather the scattered particles we have the voice of God. I am sure the gloom of death is altogether gone now that the lamp of resurrection burns. Disrobing is nothing now that better garments await us. We may long for evening to undress, that we may rise with God. I am sure my venerable friends now present, in coming so near as they do now to the time of the departure, must have some visions of the glory on the other side of the stream. Bunyan was not wrong, my dear brethren, when he put the land Beulah at the close of the pilgrimage. Is not my text a telescope which will enable you to see across the Jordan; may it not be as hands of angels to bring you bundles of myrrh and frankincense? You can say, "I know that my Redeemer liveth." You cannot want more; you were not satisfied with less in your youth, you will not be content with less now.

Those of us who are young, are comforted by the thought that we may soon depart. I say comforted, not alarmed by it; and we almost envy those whose race is nearly run, because we fear—and yet we must not speak thus, for the Lord's will be done—I was about to say, we fear that our battle may last long, and that mayhap our feet may slip; only He that keepeth Israel does not slumber nor sleep. So since we know that our Redeemer liveth, this shall be our comfort in life, that though we fall we shall not be utterly cast down; and since our Redeemer liveth, this shall be our comfort in death, that though worms destroy this body, yet in our flesh we shall see God.

May the Lord add His blessing on the feeble words of this morning, and to Him be glory forever. Amen.

> *Grave, the guardian of our dust!*
> *Grave, the treasury of the skies!*
> *Every atom of thy trust*
> *Rests in hope again to rise.*
> *Hark! the judgment trumpet calls;*
> *Soul, rebuild thy house of clay,*
> *Immortality thy walls,*
> *And Eternity thy day."*

Resurrection with Christ

"But God, who is rich in mercy, for his great love wherewith
he loved us, even when we were dead in sins, hath
quickened us together with Christ (by grace ye are saved)."
—*Ephesians 2:4, 5.*

There have been conferences of late of all sorts of people upon all kinds of subjects, but what a remarkable thing a conference would be if it were possible of persons who have been raised from the dead! If you could somehow or other get together the daughter of the Shunammite, the daughter of Jairus, the son of the widow at the gates of Nain, Lazarus, and Eutychus, what strange communings they might have one with another! what singular enquiries they might make, and what remarkable disclosures might they present to us! The thing is not possible, and yet a better and more remarkable assembly may be readily gathered on the same conditions, and more important information may be obtained from the confessions of its members.

This morning we have a conference of that very character gathered in this house; for many of us were dead in trespasses and sins, even as others, but we hope that through the divine energy we have been quickened from that spiritual death, and are now the living to praise God. It will be well for us to walk together, to review the past, to rejoice in the present, to look forward to the future. "You hath he quickened who were dead in trespasses and sins"; and as ye sit together, an assembly of men possessed of resurrection life, ye are a more notable conclave than if merely your bodies and not your spirits had been quickened.

The first part of this morning's discourse will be occupied with *a solemnity in which we shall take you into the charnel house;* secondly, we shall spend a while in *reviewing a miracle,* and *we shall observe dead men living;* we shall then turn aside to observe *a sympathy* indicated in the test; and we shall close with a song, for the text reads somewhat like music—it is full of thankfulness, and thankfulness is the essence of true song; it is full of holy and adoring wonder; it is evermore true poetry even though expressed in prose.

I. Celebrate first a great solemnity, and descend into the charnel house of our poor humanity.

According to the teaching of sacred Scripture, men are dead, spiritually dead. Certain vain men would make it out that men are only a little disordered and bruised by the fall, wounded in a few delicate members, but not mortally injured. However, the word of God is very express upon the matter, and declares our race to be not wounded, not hurt merely, but slain outright, and left as dead in trespasses and sin. There are those who fancy that fallen human nature is only in a sort of syncope or fainting fit, and only needs a process of reviving to set it right. You have only, by education and by other manipulations, to set its life-floods in motion, and to excite within it some degree of action, and then life will speedily be developed. There is much good in every man, they say, and you have only to bring it out by training and example.

This fiction is exactly opposite to the teaching of sacred Scripture. Within these truthful pages, we read of no fainting fit, no temporary paralysis, but death is the name for nature's condition, and quickening is its great necessity. Man is not partly dead, like the half drowned mariner, in whom some spark of life may yet remain, if it be but fondly tendered, and wisely nurtured. There is not a spark of spiritual life left in man—manhood is to all spiritual things an absolute corpse. "In the day thou eatest thereof thou shalt surely die," said God to our first parents, and die they did—a spiritual death; and all their children alike by nature lie in this spiritual death, not a sham death, or a metaphorical one, but a real, absolute, spiritual death.

Yet it will be said, "Are they not alive?" Truly so, but not spiritually. There are grades of life. You come first upon the vegetable life; but the vegetable is a dead thing as to the vitality of the animal. Above the animal life rises the mental life, a vastly superior life; the creature, which is only an animal, is dead to either the joys or the sorrows of mental life. Then, high above the mental, as much as the mental is above the animal, rises what Scripture calls the spiritual life—the life in Christ Jesus. All men have more or less of the mental life, and it is well that they should cultivate it—get as much as they can of it, that they should put it to the best uses, and make it subserve the highest ends.

If you could conceive a man in all respects like yourselves, with this one difference, that his soul had died out of him, that he only possessed his animal faculties, but had no intellectual faculties, so that he could breathe and walk, sleep and eat, and drink, and make a noise, but all mental power was gone, you would then speak of him as being entirely dead to mental pursuits. He might be a most vigorous and well developed animal, but his manhood would be dead. It would be of no use explaining a proposition to him, or working out a problem on the black board for his instruction, or offering him even the simplest school book, for if he had no mind to receive, how could you impart?

Now, spiritually, this is the condition of every unregenerate man. It is of no use whatever, apart from the Spirit of God, to hope to make the man understand spiritual things, for they are spiritually discerned, says the apostle. The carnal mind cannot understand the things which be of God—when best trained it has no glimmering of the inward sense of spiritual things; it stumbles over the letter and loses the real meaning, not from want of mental capacity, but from the absence of spiritual life. O sons of men, if ye would know God, "Ye must be born again"; "Except a man be born again, he *cannot* see the kingdom of God," he cannot understand it, he cannot know it. The carnal man cannot understand the things which are of God, which are eternal and invisible, any more than an ox can understand astronomy, or a fish can admire the classics. Not in a moral sense, nor a mental sense, but in a spiritual sense, poor humanity is dead, and so the word of God again and again most positively describes it.

Step with me, then, into the sepulcher-house, and what do you observe of yonder bodies which are slumbering there? They are quite unconscious. Whatever goes on around them, neither occasions them joy nor causes them grief. The dead in their graves may be marched over by triumphant armies, but they shout not with them that triumph. Or, friends they have left behind may sit there, and water the grass upon the green mound with their tears, but no sigh responsive comes from the gloomy cavern of the tomb.

It is thus with men spiritually dead: they are unaffected by spiritual things. A dying Savior, whose groans might move the very adamant, and make the rocks dissolve, they can hear of all unmoved. Even the all present Spirit is undiscerned by them, and His power unrecognized. Angels, holy men, godly exercises, devout aspirations, all these are beyond and above their world. The pangs of Hell do not alarm them, and the joys of Heaven do not entice them. They hear after a sort mentally, but the spirit-ear is fast shut up, and they do not hear.

A man totally deaf is not startled by thunder claps; if totally blind, he is not alarmed by the flashing of the lightning, he fears not the tempest which he does not discern. Even thus is it with you who are at ease in your sins, you cannot discern the danger of your sin, you do not perceive the terror that rises out of it, else let me tell you there were no sleep to those wanton eyes, no rest to those giddy spirits; you would cry out in grief the very moment you received life, nor would you rest till delivered from those evils which now ensure for you a sure damnation. Oh! were you but alive, you would never be quiet till you were saved from the wrath to come. Man remains unconscious of spiritual things and unmoved by them because, in a spiritual sense, he is dead.

Invite yonder corpse to assist you in the most necessary works of philanthropy. The pestilence is abroad: ask the buried one to kneel with you and invoke the power of Heaven to recall the direful messenger; or, if he prefers it, ask him to assist you in purifying the air and attending to sanitary arrangements. You ask in vain, however needful or simple the act he cannot help you in it. And in spiritual things, it is even so with the graceless. The carnal man can put himself into the posture of prayer, but he cannot pray; he can open his mouth and make sweet sounds in earth-born music, but the true praise he is an utter stranger to. Even repentance, that soft and gentle grace which ought to be natural to the sinful, is quite beyond his reach. How shall he repent of a sin the weight of which he cannot feel? How shall he pray for a blessing, the value of which he has no power to perceive? How shall he praise a God in whom he feels no interest, and in whose existence he takes no delight? I say that to all spiritual things the man is quite as unable as the dead are unable to the natural works and services of daily life.

"And yet," says one, "we heard you last Lord's-day tell these dead people to repent and be converted." I know you did, and you shall hear me yet again do the like. But why speak I to the dead thus, and tell them to perform actions which they cannot do? Because my Master bids me, and as I obey my Master's errand, a power goes forth with the word spoken, and the dead start in their sleep, and they wake through the quickening power of the Holy Spirit, and they who naturally cannot repent and believe, *do* repent and believe in Jesus, and escape from their former sins and live; yet, believe me, it is no power of theirs which makes them thus start from their death-sleep, and no power of mine which arrests the guilty, slumbering conscience—it is a power of divine which God has yoked with the word which He has given forth when it is fully and faithfully preached.

Therefore have we exercised ourselves in our daily calling of bidding dead men live, because life comes at the divine bidding. But dead they are, most thoroughly so, and the longer we live the more we feel it to be so; and the more closely we review our own condition before conversion, and the more studiously we look into our own condition even now, the more fully do we know that man is dead in sin, and life is a gift, a gift from Heaven, a gift of undeserved love and sovereign grace, so that the living must, every one of them, praise God and not themselves.

One of the saddest reflections about poor dead human nature is what it will be. Death in itself, though a solemn matter, is not so dreadful as that which comes of it. Many a time when that dear corpse has first been forsaken of the soul, those who have lost a dear one have been fain to imprint that cold brow with kisses still. The countenance has looked even more lovely than in life, and when friends have taken the last glimpse, there has been nothing revolting, but much that was attractive. Our dead ones have smiled like sleeping angels, even when we were about to commit them to the grave. Ah! but we cannot shake from us a wretched sense of what is sure to be revealed before long. It is only a matter of time, and corruption must set in. So it is with us all. "When lust hath conceived, it bringeth forth sin: and sin, when it is finished, bringeth forth death"; and this, dear hearer, do we solemnly remind you will be your portion forever and ever, unless God be pleased to quicken you. Unless you be made to live together with Christ you will be in this world dead, perhaps in this world corrupt, but certainly so in the next world, where all the dreadful influences of sin will be developed and discovered to the very full, and you shall be cast away from the presence of God and the glory of His power.

II. We now change the subject for something more pleasant, and observe a miracle, or dead men made alive.

The great object of the gospel of Christ is to create men anew in Christ Jesus. It aims at resurrection, and accomplishes it. The gospel did not come into this world merely to restrain the passions or educate the principles of men, but to infuse into them a new life which, as fallen men, they did not possess. I saw yesterday what seemed to me a picture of those preachers whose sole end and aim is the moralizing of their hearers, but who have not learned the need of supernatural life.

Not very far from the shore were a dozen or more boats at sea dragging for two dead bodies. They were using their lines and grappling irons, and what with hard rowing and industrious sailing, were doing their best most commendably to fish up the lost ones from the pitiless sea. I do not know if they were successful but if so, what further could they do with them but decently to commit them to their mother earth? The process of education and everything else, apart from the Holy Spirit, is a dragging for dead men, to lay them out decently, side by side, in the order and decency of death, but nothing more can man do for man.

The gospel of Jesus Christ has a far other and higher task: it does not deny the value of the moralist's efforts, or decry the results of education, but it asks what more can you do, and the response is, "Nothing." Then it bids the bearers of the bier stand away and make room for Jesus, at whose voice the dead arise. The preacher of the gospel cannot be satisfied with what is done in drawing men out of the sea of outward sin, he longs to see the lost life restored, he desires to have breathed into them a new and superior life to what they have possessed before. Go your way, education, do your best, you are useful in your sphere; go your way, teacher of morality, do your best, you too are useful in your own manner; but if it comes to what man really needs for eternity, you, all put together, are little worth—the gospel, and the gospel alone, answers to men's requirements: man must be regenerated, quickened, made anew, have fresh breath from Heaven breathed into him, or the work of saving him is not begun. The text tells us that God has done this for His people, for those who trust in Him. Let us observe the dry bones as they stir and stand before the Lord, and observing, let us praise the Lord, that according to His great love wherewith He loved us, He hath quickened us together with Christ.

In this idea of quickening, there is *a mystery*. What is that invisible something which quickens a man? Who can unveil the secret? Who can track life to its hidden fountain? Brother, you are a living child of God: what made you live? You know that it was by the power of the Holy Spirit. In the language of the text, you trace it to God, you believe your new life to be of divine implantation. You are a believer in the supernatural; you believe that God has visited you as He has not visited other men, and has breathed into you life. You believe rightly, but you cannot explain it. We know not of the wind, whence it cometh or whither it goeth: so is every one that is born of the Spirit. He that should sit down deliberately and attempt to explain regeneration, and the source of it, might sit there till he grew into a marble statue before he would accomplish the task. The Holy Spirit enters into us, and we who were dead before to spiritual things, begin to live by His power and in-dwelling. He is the great worker, but how the Holy Spirit works is a secret that must be reserved for God Himself. We need not wish to understand the mode; it is enough for us if we partake of the result.

It is a great mystery then, but while it is a mystery it is a great *reality*. We know and do testify, and we have a right to be believed, for we trust we have not forfeited our characters, we know and do testify that we are now possessors of a life which we knew nothing of some years ago, that we have come to exist in a new world, and that the appearance of all things outside of us is totally changed from what it used to be. "Old things have passed away, behold all things are become new." I bear witness that I am this day the subject of sorrows which were no sorrows to me before I knew the Lord, and that I am uplifted with joys which I should have laughed at the very thought of if any one had whispered the name of them in my ears before the life divine had quickened me.

This is the witness of hundreds of us, and although others disbelieve us, they have no right to deny our consciousness because they have not partaken of the like. If they have never tried it, what should they know about it? If there should be an assembly of blind men, and one of them should have his eyes opened, and begin to talk of what he saw, I can imagine the blind ones all saying, "What a fool that man is! There are no such things." "Here I have lived in this world seventy years," says one,

> and I never saw that thing which he calls a color, and I do not believe in his absurd nonsense about scarlet and violet, and black and white; it is all foolery together.

Another wiseacre declares,

> I have been up and down the world, and all over it, for forty years, and I declare I never had the remotest conception of blue or green, nor had my father before me. He was a right good soul, and always stood up for the grand old darkness. "Give me," said he, "a good stick and a sensible dog, and all your nonsensical notions about stars, and suns, and moons, I leave to fools who like them."

The blind man has not come into the world of light and color, and the unregenerate man has not come into that world of spirit, and hence neither of them is capable of judging correctly.

I sat one day, at a public dinner, opposite a gentleman of the gourmand species, who seemed a man of vast erudition as to wines and spirits, and all the viands of the table; he judged and criticized at such a rate that I thought he ought to have been employed by our provision merchants as taster in general. He had finely developed lips, and he smacked them frequently. His palate was in a fine critical condition. He was also as proficient in the quantity as in the quality, and disposed of meats and drinks in a most wholesale manner. His retreating forehead, empurpled nose, and protruding lips, made him, while eating at least, more like an animal than a man. At last, hearing a little conversation around him upon religious matters, he opened his small eyes and his great mouth, and delivered himself of this sage utterance, "I have lived sixty years in this world, and I never felt or believed in anything spiritual in all my life." The speech was a needless diversion of his energies from the roast duck. We did not want him to tell us that. I, for one, was quite clear about it before he spoke. If the cat under the table had suddenly jumped on a chair and said the same thing, I should have attached as much importance to the utterance of the one as to the declaration of the other; and so, by one sin in one man and another in another man, they betray their spiritual death. Until a man has received the divine life, his remarks thereon, even if he be an archbishop, go for nothing. He knows nothing about it according to his own testimony.

This life brings with it the *exercise of renewed faculties*. The man who begins to live unto God has powers now which he never had before: the power really to pray, the power heartily to praise, the power actually to commune with God, the power to see God, to talk with God, the power to receive tidings from the invisible world, and the power to send messages up through the veil which hides the unseen up to the very throne of God.

Suppose a man to have been dead, and to have been buried like others in some great necropolis, some city of the dead, in the catacombs. An angel visits him, and by mercy's touch he lives. Now, can you conceive that man's first emotion when he begins to breathe? There he is in the coffin—he feels stifled, pent up. He had been there twenty years, but he never felt inconvenienced until now. He was easy enough, in his narrow cell, if ease can be where life is not. The moment he lives he feels a horrible sense of suffocation, life will not endure to be so hideously compressed, and he begins to struggle for release. He lifts with all his might that dreadful coffin lid! What a relief when the decaying plank yields to his pressure!

So the ungodly man is content enough in his sin, his Sabbath breaking, his covetousness, his worldliness, but the moment God quickens him his sin is as a sepulcher to the living, he feels unutterably wretched, he is not in a congenial position, and he struggles to escape. Often at the first effort the great black lid of blasphemy flies off, never to be replaced. Satan thought it was screwed down fast enough, and so it was for a dead man, but life makes short work of it, and many other iniquities follow. But to return to our resurrection in the vault: the man gasps a minute, and feels refreshed with such air as the catacomb affords him; but soon he has a sense of clammy damp about him, and feels faint and ready to expire. So the renewed man at first feels little but his inability, and groans after power, he cries, "I want to repent; I want to believe in Jesus; I want to be saved." Poor wretch! he never felt that before—of course he did not—he was dead; now he is alive, and hence he longs for the tokens, signs, fruits and refreshments of life.

That giddy ball-room—why, it was well enough for one who knew no better. That ale-bench was suitable for an unregenerate soul—but what can an heir of Heaven do in such places? Lord, deliver me. Give me light and liberty. Bring my soul out of prison, that I may live and praise thy name. The man pines for liberty, and if, at last, he stumbles to the door of the vault and reaches the open air, methinks he drinks deep draughts of the blessed oxygen! How glad he is to look upon the green fields and the fresh flowers. You do not imagine that he will wish to return to the vaults again; he will utterly forsake those gloomy abodes; he shudders at the remembrance of the past, and would not for all the world undergo again what he has once passed through; he is tenderly affected at every remembrance of the past, and is especially fearful lest there should be others like himself newly quickened, who may need a brother's hand to set them at liberty; he loathes the place where once he slept so quietly.

So the converted man dreads the thought of going back to the joys which once so thoroughly fascinated him. "No," saith he, "they are no joys to me. They were joys well enough for my old state of existence, but now, having entered into a new life, a new world, they are no more joys to me than the spade and shroud are joys to a living man, and I can only think of them with grief, and of my deliverance with gratitude."

III. I must pass on very briefly to the third point. The text indicates a sympathy: "He hath quickened us together with Christ."

What does that mean? It means that the life which lives in a saved man is the same life which dwells in Christ. To put it simply—when Elisha had been buried for some years, we read that they threw a man who was dead into the tomb where the bones of Elisha were, and no sooner did the corpse touch the prophet's bones than it lived at once. Yonder is the cross of Christ, and no sooner does the soul touch the crucified Savior than it lives at once, for the Father hath given to Him to have life in Himself, and life to communicate to others. Whosoever trusts Christ has touched Him, and by touching Him he has received the virtue of eternal life: to trust in the Savior of the world is be quickened through Him.

We are quickened together with Christ in three senses: First, *representatively*. Christ represents us before the eternal throne; He is the second Adam to His people. So long as the first Adam lived the race lived, and so long as the second Adam lives the race represented by Him lives before God. Christ is accepted, believers are accepted; Christ is justified, the saints are justified; Christ lives, and the saints enjoy a life which is hid with Christ in God.

Next we live by *union* with Christ. So long as the head is alive the members have life. Unless a member can be served from the head, and the body maimed, it must live so long as there is life in the head. So long as Jesus lives, every soul that is vitally united to Him, and is a member of His body, lives according to our Lord's own word, "Because I live ye shall live also." Poor Martha was much surprised that Christ should raise her brother from the dead, but He said, as if to surprise her still more, "Whosoever liveth and believeth in me shall never die. Believest thou this?" This is one of the things we are to believe, that when we have received the spiritual life, it is in union with the life of Christ, and consequently can never die; because Christ lives, our life must abide in us forever.

Then we also live together with Christ as to *likeness*. We are quickened together with Christ, that is, in the same manner. Now, Christ's quickening was in this wise. He was dead through the law, but the law has no more dominion over Him now that He lives again. So you, Christian, you are cursed by the old law of Sinai, but it has no power to curse you now, for you are risen in Christ. You are not under the law; its terrors and threatenings have nought to do with you. Of our Lord it is written, "In that he liveth," it is said, "he liveth unto God." Christ's life is a life unto God. Such is yours. You are not henceforth to live unto the flesh to mind the things of it; but God who gave you life is to be the great object of your life; *in* Him you live, and *for* Him you live. Moreover, it is said, "Christ being raised from the dead dieth no more; death hath no more dominion over him." In that same way the Christian lives; he shall never go back to his spiritual death—having once received divine life, he shall never lose it. God plays not fast and loose with His chosen; He does not save today, and damn tomorrow. He does not quicken us with the inward life, and then leave us to perish; grace is a living, incorruptible seed, which liveth and abideth forever. "The water that I shall give him," saith Jesus, "shall be in him a well of water springing up unto everlasting life." Glory be to God, then, you who live by faith in Christ live an immortal life, a life dedicated to God, a life of deliverance from the bondage of the law; rejoice in it, and give your God all the praise!

IV. And this brings us to the last word, which was a song.

We have not time to sing it, we will just write the score before your eyes, and ask you to sing it at your leisure, your hearts making melody to God. Brethren and sisters, if you have indeed been thus made alive as others are not, you have first of all, in the language of the test, to praise *the great love* of God, great beyond all precedent. It was love which made Him breathe into Adam the breath of life, and make poor clay to walk and speak; but it is far greater love which makes Him now after the fall has defiled us, renew us with a second and yet higher life.

He might have made new creatures by millions out of nothing. He had but to speak, and angels would have thronged the air, or, beings like ourselves, only pure and unfallen, would have been multiplied by myriads upon the greensward. If He had left us to sink to Hell as fallen angels had done before us, who could have impugned His justice? But His great love would not let Him leave His elect to perish. He loved His people, and therefore He would cause them to be born again, His great love wherewith He loved us, defied death, and Hell, and sin. Dwell on the theme you who have partaken of this love! He loved *us,* the most unworthy, who had no right to such love: there was nothing in us to love, and yet He loved us, when we were dead. Here His great love seems to swell and rise to mountainous dimensions: love to miserable sinners, love to loathsome sinners, love to the dead and to the corrupt. Oh, heights and depths of sovereign grace, where are the notes which can sufficiently sound forth your praise? Sing, O ye redeemed, of His great love wherewith He loved us, even when we were dead in sins.

And cease not ye to praise God, as ye think of the riches of His mercy, for we are told that He is rich in mercy, rich in His nature as to mercy, rich in His covenant as to treasured mercy, rich in the person of His dear Son as to purchased mercy, rich in providential mercy, but richest of all in the mercy which saves the soul. Friends, explore the mines of Jehovah's wealth if you can. Take the key and open the granaries of your God and see the stores of love which He has laid up for you. Strike your sweetest notes to the praise of God, who is rich in mercy, for His great love wherewith He hath loved us.

And let the last note and the highest and the loudest of your song be that with which the text concludes, "By grace are ye saved." O never stammer there; brethren and sisters, whatever you do, hold or do not hold, never be slow to say this, "If saved at all, I am saved by grace; grace in contradistinction to human merit, for I have no merit; grace in contradistinction to my own free will, for my own free will would have led me further and further from God. Preventing grace brought me near to Him." Do bless and magnify the grace of God, and as you owe all to it cry, "Perish each thought of pride," consecrate yourself entirely to the God to whom you owe everything. Desire to help to spread the Savior of that grace which has brought such good things to you, and vow in the name of the quickening Spirit, that He who has made you live by faith shall, from this day till you enter into Heaven, have the best of your thoughts, and your words, and your actions, for you are not your own; you have been quickened from the dead, and you must live in newness of life.

The Lord bless you, dear friends; if you have never spiritually lived, may He give you grace to believe in Jesus this morning, and then you are alive from the dead; and if you are alive already, may He quicken you yet more and more by his eternal Spirit, till He brings you to the land of the living on the other side of the Jordan. Amen.

The Stone Rolled Away

"The angel of the Lord descended from Heaven, and came and rolled back the stone from the door, and sat upon it."—Matthew 28:2.

As the holy women went towards the sepulcher in the twilight of the morning, desirous to embalm the body of Jesus, they recollected that the huge stone at the door of the tomb would be a great impediment in their way, and they said one to another, "Who shall roll us away the stone?" That question gathers up the mournful enquiry of the whole universe. They seem to have put into language the great sigh of universal manhood, "Who shall roll us away the stone?" In man's path of happiness lies a huge rock, which completely blocks up the road. Who among the mighty shall remove the barrier? Philosophy attempted the task, but miserably failed. In the ascent to immortality the stone of doubt, uncertainty, and unbelief, stopped all progress. Who could upheave the awful mass, and bring life and immortality to light?

Men, generation after generation, buried their fellows; the all devouring sepulcher swallowed its myriads. Who could stay the daily slaughter, or give a hope beyond the grave? There was a whisper of resurrection, but men could not believe in it. Some dreamed of a future state, and talked of it in mysterious poetry, as though it were all imagination and nothing more. In darkness and in twilight, with many fears and few guesses at the truth, men continued to enquire, "Who shall roll us away the stone?"

To the women there were three difficulties. The stone of itself was huge; it was stamped with the seal of the law; it was guarded by the representatives of power. To mankind there were the same three difficulties. Death itself was a huge stone not to be moved by any strength known to mortals: that death was evidently sent of God as a penalty for offences against His law—how could it therefore be averted, how removed? The red seal of God's vengeance was set upon that sepulcher's mouth—how should that seal be broken? Who could roll the stone away?

No answer was given to sages and kings, but the women who loved the Savior found an answer. They came to the tomb of Christ, but it was empty, for Jesus had risen. Here is the answer to the world's enquiry—there is another life; bodies will live again, for Jesus lives. Sorrow no longer, ye mourners, around the grave, as those that are without hope; for since Jesus Christ is risen, the dead in Christ shall rise also. Wipe away those tears, for the believer's grave is no longer the place for lamentations, it is but the passage to immortality.

I purpose, this morning, to talk a little concerning the resurrection of our exalted Lord Jesus; and that the subject may the more readily interest you, I shall, first of all, *bid this stone which was rolled away, preach to you;* and then shall invite you *to hear the angel's homily from his pulpit of stone.*

I. First, let the stone preach.

It is not at all an uncommon thing to find in Scripture stones bidden to speak. Great stones have been rolled as witnesses against the people; stones and beams out of the wall have been called upon to testify to sin. I shall call this stone as a witness to valuable truths of which it was the symbol. The river of our thought divides into six streams.

- *First, the stone rolled must evidently be regarded as the door of the sepulcher removed.*

Death's house was firmly secured by a huge stone; the angel removed it, and the living Christ came forth. The massive door, you will observe, was taken away from the grave—not merely opened, but unhinged, flung aside, rolled away; and henceforth death's ancient prison house is without a door. The saints shall pass in, but they shall not be shut in. They shall tarry there as in an open cavern, but there is nothing to prevent their coming forth from it in due time.

As Samson, when he slept in Gaza, and was beset by foes, arose early in the morning, and took up upon his shoulders the gates of Gaza—post, and bar, and all—and carried all away, and left the Philistine stronghold open and exposed, so has it been done unto the grave by our Master, Who, having slept out His three days and nights, according to the divine decree, arose in the greatness of His strength, and bore away the iron gates of the sepulcher, tearing every bar from its place. The removal of the imprisoning stone was the outward type of our Lord's having plucked up the gates of the grave—post, bar, and all—thus exposing that old fortress of death and Hell, and leaving it as a city stormed and taken, and henceforth bereft of power.

Remember that our Lord was committed to the grave as a hostage. "He died for our sins." Like a debt they were imputed to Him. He discharged the debt of obligation due from us to God, on the tree; He suffered to the full, the great substitutionary equivalent for our suffering, and then He was confined in the tomb as a hostage until His work should be fully accepted. That acceptance would be notified by His coming forth from durance vile; and that coming forth would become our justification—"He rose again for our justification." If He had not fully paid the debt He would have remained in the grave. If Jesus had not made effectual, total, final atonement, He must have continued a captive. But He had done it all. The "It is finished," which came from His own lips, was established by the verdict of Jehovah, and Jesus was set free.

Come, brethren, let us rejoice in this. In the empty tomb of Christ, we see sin forever put away: we see, therefore, death most effectually destroyed. Our sins were the great stone which shut the mouth of the sepulcher, and held us captives in death, and darkness, and despair. Our sins are now forever rolled away, and hence death is no longer a dungeon dark and drear, the ante-chamber of Hell, but the rather it is a perfumed bedchamber, a withdrawing room, the vestibule of Heaven. For as surely as Jesus rose, so must His people leave the dead: there is nothing to prevent the resurrection of the saints. The stone which could keep us in the prison has been rolled away. Who can bar us in when the door itself is gone? Who can confine us when every barricade is taken away?

> *Who shall rebuild for the tyrant his prison?*
> *The scepter lies broken that fell from his hands;*
> *The stone is removed; the Lord is arisen:*
> *The helpless shall soon be released from their bands.*

- *In the second place, regard the stone as a trophy set-up.*

As men of old set up memorial stones, and as at this day we erect columns to tell of great deeds of prowess, so that stone rolled away was, as it were, before the eyes of our faith consecrated that day as a memorial of Christ's eternal victory over the powers of death and Hell. They thought that they had vanquished Him; they deemed that the Crucified was overcome. Grimly did they smile as they saw His motionless body wrapped in the winding sheet and put away in Joseph's new tomb; but their joy was fleeting; their boasting were but brief, for at the appointed moment He who could not see corruption rose and came forth from beneath their power. His heel was bruised by the old serpent, but on the resurrection morning He crushed the dragon's head.

> *Vain the stone, the watch, the seal,*
> *Christ has burst the gates of Hell;*
> *Death in vain forbids His rise,*
> *Christ hath open'd Paradise.*
>
> *Lives again our glorious King!*
> *"Where, O death, is now thy sting?"*
> *Once He died our souls to save;*
> *"Where's thy victory, boasting grave?"*

Brethren beloved in Christ, as we look at yonder stone, with the angel seated upon it, it rises before us as a monument of Christ's victory over death and Hell, and it becomes us to remember that His victory was achieved for us, and the fruits of it are all ours. We have to fight with sin, but Christ has overcome it. We are tempted by Satan: Christ has given Satan a defeat. We by-and-by shall leave this body; unless the Lord come speedily, we may expect to gather up our feet like our fathers, and go to meet our God; but death is vanquished for us, and we can have no cause to fear. Courage, Christian soldiers, you are encountering a vanquished enemy: remember that the Lord's victory is a guarantee for yours. If the Head conquers, the members shall not be defeated. Let not sorrow dim your eye; let no fears trouble your spirit; you must conquer, for Christ has conquered. Awaken all your powers to the conflict, and nerve them with the hope of victory. Set up that stone before your faith's eye this morning, and say, "Here my Master conquered Hell and death, and in His name and by His strength I shall be crowned, too, when the last enemy is destroyed."

- *For a third use of this stone, observe that here is a foundation laid.*

That stone rolled away from the sepulcher, typifying and certifying as it does the resurrection of Jesus Christ, is a foundation stone for Christian faith. The fact of the resurrection is the key-stone of Christianity. Disprove the resurrection of our Lord, and our holy faith would be a mere fable; there would be nothing for faith to rest upon if He who died upon the tree did not also rise again from the tomb; then "your faith is vain;" said the apostle, "ye are yet in your sins," while "they also which are fallen asleep in Christ are perished." All the great doctrines of our divine religion fall asunder like the stones of an arch when the key-stone is dislodged, in a common ruin they are all overthrown, for all our hope hinges upon that great fact. If Jesus rose, then is this gospel what it professes to be; if He rose not from the dead, then is it all deceit and delusion.

But, brethren, that Jesus rose from the dead is a fact better established than almost any other in history. The witnesses were many: they were men of all classes and conditions. None of them ever confessed himself mistaken or deceptive. They were so persuaded that it was the fact, that the most of them suffered death for bearing witness to it. They had nothing to gain by such a witnessing; they did not rise in power, nor gain honor or wealth; they, were truthful, simple minded men who testified what they had seen and bore witness to that which they had beheld.

The resurrection is a fact better attested than any event recorded in any history whether ancient or modern. Here is the confidence of the saints; our Lord Jesus Christ, who witnessed a good confession before Pontius Pilate, and was crucified, dead, and buried, rose again from the dead, and after forty days ascended to the throne of God. We rest in Him; we believe in Him. If He had not risen, we had been of all men most miserable to have been His followers. If He had not risen, His atonement would not have been proved sufficient. If He had not risen, His blood would not have been to us proven to be efficacious for the taking away of sin; but as He has risen, we build upon this truth; all our confidence we rest upon it, and we are persuaded that

> *Raised from the dead, He goes before;*
> *He opens Heaven's eternal door;*
> *To give His saints a blest abode,*
> *Near their Redeemer and their God.*

My dear hearers, are you resting your everlasting hopes upon the resurrection of Jesus Christ from the dead? Do you trust in Him, believing that He both died and rose again for you? Do you place your entire dependence upon the merit of His blood certified by the fact of His rising again?

If so, you have a foundation of fact and truth, a foundation against which the gates of Hell shall not prevail; but if you are building upon anything that you have done, or anything that priestly hands can do for you, you are building upon the sands which shall be swept away by the all devouring flood, and you and your hopes too shall go down into the fathomless abyss wrapped in the darkness of despair. Oh, to build upon the living stone of Christ Jesus! Oh, to rest on Him who is a tried cornerstone, elect, precious! This is to build safely, eternally, and blessedly.

- *A fourth voice from the stone is this: here is rest provided.*

The angel seemed to teach us that as he sat down upon the stone. How leisurely the whole resurrection was effected! How noiselessly, too! What an absence of pomp and parade! The angel descended, the stone was rolled away, Christ rose, and then the angel sat down on the stone. He sat there silently and gracefully, breathing defiance to the Jews and to their seal, to the Roman legionaries and their spears, to death, to earth, to Hell. He did as good as say, "Come and roll that stone back again, ye enemies of the risen One. All ye infernal powers, who thought to prevail against our ever-living Prince, roll back that stone again, if so ye dare or can!" The angel said not this in words, but his stately and quiet sitting upon the stone meant all that and more. The Master's work is done, and done forever, and this stone, no more to be used, this unhinged door, no more employed to shut in the charnel house, is the type that "it is finished"—finished so as never to be undone, finished so as to last eternally. Yon resting angel softly whispers to us, "Come hither, and rest also." There is no fuller, better, surer, safer rest for the soul than in the fact that the Savior in whom we trust has risen from the dead.

Do you mourn departed friends today? O come and sit upon this stone, which tells you they shall rise again. Do you soon expect to die? Is the worm at the root? Have you the flush of consumption on your cheek? O come and sit you down upon this stone, and bethink you that death has lost its terror now, for Jesus has risen from the tomb. Come you, too, ye feeble and trembling ones, and breathe defiance to death and Hell. The angel will vacate his seat for you, and let you sit down in the face of the enemy. Though you be but a humble woman, or a man broken down, and wan, and languid with long years of weary sickness, yet may you well defy the hosts of Hell, while resting down upon this precious truth, "He is not here, but He is risen: He has left the dead, no more to die."

> Every note with wonders swell,
> Sin o'erthrown, and captived Hell;
> Where is Hell's once dreaded king?
> Where, O death, thy mortal sting?
> Hallelujah.

- *In the fifth place, that stone was a boundary appointed.*

Do you not see it so? Behold it then, there it lies, and the angel sits upon it. On that side see what you? The guards affrighted, stiffened with fear, like dead men. On this side what see you? The timid trembling women, to whom the angel softly speaks, "Fear not ye: for I know that ye seek Jesus." You see, then, that stone became the boundary between the living and the dead, between the seekers and the haters, between the friends and the foes of Christ. To His enemies His resurrection is "a stone of stumbling, and a rock of offence"; as of old on Mar's Hill, when the sages heard of the resurrection, they mocked. But to His own people, the resurrection is the headstone of the corner. Our Lord's resurrection is our triumph and delight.

The resurrection acts much in the same manner as the pillar which Jehovah placed between Israel and Egypt: it was darkness to Egypt, but it gave light to Israel. All was dark amidst Egypt's hosts, but all was brightness and comfort amongst Israel's tribes. So the resurrection is a doctrine full of horror to those who know not Christ, and trust Him not. What have they to gain by resurrection? Oh, the horrors of that tremendous morning, when every sinner shall rise, and the risen Savior shall come in the clouds of Heaven, and all the holy angels with Him! Truly there is nothing but dismay for those who are on the evil side of that resurrection stone.

But how great the joy which the resurrection brings to those who are on the right side of that stone! How they look for His is appearing with daily growing transport! How they build upon the sweet truth that they shall arise, and with these eyes their Savior see! I would have you ask yourselves, this morning, on which side you are of that boundary stone now. Have you life in Christ? Are you risen with Christ? Do you trust alone in Him who rose from the dead? If so, fear not ye: the angel comforts you, and Jesus cheers you; but oh! if you have no life in Christ, but are dead while you live, let the very thought that Jesus is risen, strike you with fear, and make you tremble, for tremble well you may, at that which awaits you.

- *Sixthly, I conceive that this stone may be used, and properly too, as foreshadowing ruin.*

Our Lord came into this world to destroy all the works of the devil. Behold before you the works of the devil pictured as a grim and horrible castle, massive and terrible, overgrown with the moss of ages, colossal, stupendous, cemented with blood of men, ramparted by mischief and craft, surrounded with deep trenches, and garrisoned with fiends. A structure dread enough to cause despair to every one who goeth round about it to count its towers and mark its bulwarks. In the fullness of time our Champion came into the world to destroy the works of the devil. During His life He sounded an alarm at the great castle, and dislodged here and there a stone, for the sick were healed, the dead were raised, and the poor had the gospel preached unto them. But on the resurrection morning the huge fortress trembled from top to bottom; huge rifts were in its walls; and tottering were all its strongholds. A stronger than the master of that citadel had evidently entered it and was beginning to overturn, overturn, overturn, from pinnacle to basement. One huge stone, upon which the building much depended, a cornerstone which knit the whole fabric together, was lifted bodily from its bed and hurled to the ground. Jesus tore the huge granite stone of death from its position, and so gave a sure token that every other would follow. When that stone was rolled away from Jesus' sepulcher, it was a prophecy that every stone of Satan's building should come down, and not one should rest upon another of all that the powers of darkness had ever piled up, from the days of their first apostasy even unto the end.

Brethren, that stone rolled away from the door of the sepulcher gives me glorious hope. Evil is still mighty, but evil will come down. Spiritual wickedness reigns in high places; the multitude still clamor after evil; the nations still sit in thick darkness; many worship the scarlet woman of Babylon, others bow before the crescent of Mohammed, and millions bend themselves before blocks of wood and stone; the dark places and habitations of the Earth are full of cruelty still; but Christ has given such a shiver to the whole fabric of evil that, depend upon it, every stone will be certain to fall. We have but to work on, use the battering-ram of the gospel, continue each one to keep in his place, and like the hosts around Jericho, to sound the trumpet still, and the day must come when every hoary evil, every colossal superstition, shall be laid low, even with the ground, and the prophecy shall be fulfilled, "Overturn, overturn, overturn it; and it shall be no more, until he come whose right it is; and I will give it him." That loosened stone on which the angel sits is the sure prognostic of the coming doom of everything that is base and vile. Rejoice, ye sons of God, for Babylon's fall draweth near. Sing, O Heavens, and rejoice, O earth, for there shall not an evil be spared. Verily, I say unto you, there shall not be one stone left upon another, which shall not be cast down.

Thus has the stone preached to us; we will pause awhile and hear what the angel has to say.

II. The angel preached two ways: he preached in symbol, and he preached in words.

Preaching *in symbol* is very popular with a certain party nowadays. The gospel is to be seen by the eye, they tell us, and the people are to learn from the change of colors, at various seasons, such as blue, and green, and violet, exhibited on the priest and the altar, and by lace and by candles, and by banners, and by cruets, and shells full of water; they are even to be taught or led by the nose, which is to be indulged with smoke of incense; and drawn by the ears, which are to listen to hideous intonings or to dainty canticles. Now, mark well that the angel was a symbolical preacher, with his brow of lightning and his robe of snow; but you will please to notice for whom the symbols were reserved. He did not say a word to the keepers—not a word. He gave them the symbolical gospel, that is to say, he looked upon them—and his glance was lightning; he revealed himself to them in his snow-white garments, and no more. Mark how they quake and tremble! That is the gospel of symbols; and wherever it comes it condemns. It can do no other. Why, the old Mosaic law of symbols, where did it end? How few ever reached its inner meaning! The mass of Israel fell into idolatry, and the symbolic system became death to them. The gospel message is, "Hear, and your soul shall live"; "Incline your ear, and come unto me." This is the life-giving message, "Believe in the Lord Jesus Christ, and thou shalt be saved." But, O perverse generation, if ye look for symbols and signs, ye shall be deluded with the devil's gospel, and fall a prey to the destroyer.

Now we will listen to the angel's sermon *in words.* Thus only is a true gospel to be delivered. Christ is the Word, and the gospel is a gospel of words and thoughts. It does not appeal to the eye; it appeals to the ear, and to the intellect, and to the heart. It is a spiritual thing, and can only be learned by those whose spirits are awakened to grasp at spiritual truth. The first thing the angel said was, "Fear not ye." Oh! this is the very genius of our risen Savior's gospel—"Fear not ye." Ye who would be saved, ye who would follow Christ, ye need not fear. Did the Earth quake? Fear not ye: God can preserve you though the Earth be burned with fire. Did the angel descend in terrors? Fear not ye: there are no terrors in Heaven for the child of God who comes to Jesus' cross, and trusts his soul to Him who bled thereon. Poor women, is it the dark that alarms you? Fear not ye: God sees and loves you in the dark, and there is nothing in the dark or in the light beyond His control.

Are you afraid to come to a tomb? Does a sepulcher alarm you? Fear not ye: you cannot die. Since Christ has risen, though you were dead yet should you live. Oh, the comfort of the gospel! Permit me to say there is nothing in the Bible to make any man fear who puts his trust in Jesus. Nothing in the Bible, did I say? There is nothing in Heaven, nothing on earth, nothing in Hell, that need make you fear who trust in Jesus. "Fear not ye." The past you need not fear, it is forgiven you; the present you need not fear, it is provided for; the future also is secured by the living power of Jesus. "Because I live," saith He, "ye shall live also." Fear! Why, that [fear] were comely and seemly when Christ was dead, but now that He lives there remains no space for it? Do you fear your sins? They are all gone, for Christ had not risen if He had not put them all away. What is it you fear? If an angel bids you "Fear not," why will you fear? If every wound of the risen Savior, and every act of your reigning Lord consoles you, why are you still dismayed? To be doubting, and fearing, and trembling, now that Jesus has risen, is an inconsistent thing in any believer. Jesus is able to succor you in all your temptations; seeing He ever liveth to make intercession for you, He is able to save you to the uttermost: therefore, do not fear.

Notice the next words, "Fear not ye: for I know." What! does an angel know the women's hearts? Did the angel know what Magdalene was about? Do spirits read our spirits? 'Tis well. But oh! 'tis better to remember that our heavenly Father knows. Fear not ye, for God knows what is in your heart. You have never made an avowal of anxiety about your soul, you are too bashful even for that; you have not even proceeded so far as to dare to say that you hope you love Jesus; but God knows your desires. Poor heart, you feel as if you could not trust, and could not do anything that is good; but you do at least desire, you do at least seek. All this God knows; with pleasure he spies out your desires. "Fear not ye," for your heavenly Father knows. Lie still, poor patient, for the surgeon knows where the wound is, and what it is that ails thee. Hush, my child, be still upon thy great Parent's bosom, for He knows all; and ought not that content thee, for His care is as infinite as His knowledge?

Then the angel went on to say, "Fear not ye: for I know that ye seek Jesus, which was crucified." There was room for comfort here. They were seeking Jesus, though the world had crucified Him. Though the many had turned aside and left Him, they were clinging to Him in loving loyalty. Now, is there any one here who can say,

> Though I am unworthy to be a follower of Christ, and often think that He will
> reject me, yet there is one thing I am sure of—I would not be afraid of the fear of

man for His sake. My sins make me fear, but no man could do it. I would stand at His side if all the world were against Him. I would count it my highest honor that the crucified One of the world should be the adored One of my heart. Let all the world cast Him out, if He would but take me in, poor unworthy worm as I am, I would never be ashamed to own His blessed and gracious Name.

Ah! then, do not fear, for if that is how you feel towards Christ, He will own you in the last great day. If you are willing to own Him now, "Fear not ye."

Then he adds, "He is not here, for he is risen." Here is the instruction which the angel gives. After giving comfort, he gives instruction. Your great ground and reason for consolation, seeker, is that you do not seek a dead Christ, and you do not pray to a buried Savior; He is really alive. Today He is as able to relieve you, if you go to your closet and pray to Him, as He was to help the poor blind man when He was on earth. He is as willing today to accept and bless you as He was to bless the leper, or to heal the paralytic. Go to Him then at once, poor seeker; go to Him with holy confidence, for He is not here, He would be dead if He were—He is risen, living, and reigning, to answer your request.

The angel bade the holy women investigate the empty tomb, but, almost immediately after, he gave them a commission to perform on their Lord's behalf. Now, if any seeker here has been comforted by the thought that Christ lives to save, let him do as the angel said, let him go and tell to others of the good news that he has heard. O you who have learned of Jesus, keep not the blessed secret to yourselves. Today, in some way or other, I pray you make known that Jesus Christ is risen. Pass the watchword round, as the ancient Christians did. On the first day of the week they said to one another, "The Lord is risen indeed."

If any ask you what you mean by it, you will then be able to tell them the whole of the gospel, for this is the essence of the gospel, that Jesus Christ died for our sins, and rose again the third day, according to the Scriptures—died the substitute for us criminals, rose the representative of us pardoned sinners—died that our sins might die, and lives again that our souls may live. Diligently invite others to come and trust Jesus. Tell them that there is life for the dead in a look at Jesus crucified; tell them that that look is a matter of the soul, it is a simple confidence; tell them that none ever did confide in Christ and were cast away; tell them what you have felt as the result of your trusting Jesus, and who can tell, many disciples will be added to His church, a risen Savior will be glorified, and you will be comforted by what you have seen! The Lord follow these feeble words with His own blessing, for Christ's sake. Amen.

The Coming Resurrection

"Marvel not at this: for the hour is coming, in the which all that are in the graves shall hear his voice, and shall come forth; they that have done good, unto the resurrection of life; and they that have done evil, unto the resurrection of damnation."—John 5:28, 29.

The doctrine of the resurrection of the dead is peculiarly a Christian belief. With natural reason, assisted by some little light lingering in tradition, or borrowed from the Jews, a few philosophers spelled out the immortality of the soul; but that the body should rise again, that there should be another life for this corporeal frame, was a hope which is brought to light by the revelation of Christ Jesus. Men could not have imagined so great a wonder, and they prove their powerlessness to have invented it, by the fact, that still, as at Athens, when they hear of it for the first time, they fall to mocking. "Can these dry bones live?" is still the unbeliever's sneer.

The doctrine of the resurrection is a lamp kindled by the hand which once was pierced. It is indeed in some respects the key-stone of the Christian arch. It is linked in our holy faith with the person of Jesus Christ, and is one of the brightest gems in His crown. What if I call it the signet on His finger, the seal by which He hath proven to a demonstration, that He hath the king's authority, and hath come forth from God? The doctrine of resurrection ought to be preached much more commonly than it is, as vital to the gospel. Listen to the apostle Paul as he describes the gospel which he preached, and by which true believers were saved: "I delivered unto you," saith he, "first of all that which I received, how that Christ died for our sins according to the Scriptures; and that he was buried, and that he rose again the third day according to the Scriptures."

From the resurrection of Christ, he argues that of all the dead, and insists upon it, that if Christ be not risen, both their faith and his preaching were vain. The doctrine of the resurrection in the early church was the main battle-axe and weapon of war of the preacher. Wherever the first missionaries went they made this prominent, that there would be a judgment, and that the dead should rise again to be judged by the Man Christ Jesus, according to their gospel. If we would honor Christ Jesus the Risen One, we must give prominence to this truth.

Moreover, the doctrine is continually blessed of God to arouse the minds of men. When we fancy that our actions are confined to this present life, we are careless of them, but when we discover that they are far-reaching, and that they cast influences for good or evil athwart an eternal destiny, then we regard them more seriously. What trumpet call can be more startling, what arousing voice can be more awakening than this news to the careless sinner that there is a life hereafter, that men must stand before the judgment seat of Christ to receive for the things done in their bodies whether they be good or evil? Such doctrine I shall try to preach this morning for just such ends, for the honoring of Christ, for the awakening of the careless. God send us good speed and abundance of the desired results.

We shall first *expound the text*, and then secondly, *endeavor to learn its lessons*.

I. *First we shall expound the text. No exposition will be more instructive than a verbal one. We will take each word and weigh its meaning.*

Observe then, first, in the text there is a forbidding to marvel. "Marvel not at this." Our Savior had been speaking of two forms of life-giving which belonged to Himself as the Son of Man. The first was the power to raise the dead from their graves to a renewed natural life. He proved this on one or two occasions in His lifetime, at the gates of Nain, in the chamber of the daughter of Jairus, and again at the tomb of the almost rotting Lazarus. Jesus had power when He was on Earth and has power still, if so He should will it, to speak to those who have departed, and bid them return again to this mortal state and reassume the joys and sorrows and duties of life. "As the Father raiseth up the dead, and quickeneth them; even so the Son quickeneth whom he will."

After our Lord had dwelt for a moment upon that form of His life-giving prerogative, He passed on to a second display of it, and testified that the time was then present when His voice was heard to the quickening of the spiritually dead. The spiritually dead—the men who are dead to holiness and dead to faith, dead to God and dead to grace; the men that lie enshrouded in the grave clothes of evil habits, rotting in the coffins of their depravity, deep down in the graves of their transgressions—these men, when Jesus speaks in the gospel, are made to live; a spiritual life is given to them, their dead souls are raised out of their long and horrible sleep, and they are enlivened with the life of God.

Now, both of these forms of quickening are worthy to be marveled at. The resurrection of the natural man to natural life is a great wonder; who would not go a thousand miles to see such a thing performed? The raising up of the dead spirit to spiritual life, this is a greater wonder by far.

To you, dear brethren in the faith, the quickening of the dead is not so great a marvel as the saving of dead souls; and, indeed, the raising of a corpse from the grave is by no means so great a marvel as the raising up of a dead soul from the sleep of sin. For in the raising up of a dead body there is no opposition to the fiat of Omnipotence. God speaketh, and it is done; but in the saving of a dead soul, the elements of death within are potent, and these resist the life-giving power of grace, so that regeneration is a victory as well as a creation, a complicated miracle, a glorious display both of grace and power.

Beloved, let us humbly learn one lesson from this. We are ourselves by nature very like the Jews; we wonder mistrustfully, we unbelievingly wonder when we see or hear of fresh displays of the greatness of our Lord Jesus Christ. So narrow are our hearts, that we cannot receive His glory in its fullness. Ah, we love Him, and we trust Him, and we believe Him to be the fairest, and the greatest, and the best, and the mightiest, but if we had a fuller view of what He can do, the probabilities are that our amazement would be mingled with no small portion of doubt. As yet we have but slender ideas of our Lord's glory and power. We hold the doctrine of His deity, we are orthodox enough, but we have not thoroughly realized the fact that He is Lord God Almighty. Does not it sometimes seem to you to be impossible that such-and-such a grievously ungodly man could be converted? But why impossible with Him who can raise the dead? Does it not seem impossible that you could ever be supported through your present trouble? But how impossible with Him who shall make the dry bones live, and cause the sepulcher to disgorge? It appears improbable at times that your corruptions should ever be cleansed away, and that you should be perfect and without spot. But why so? He who is able to present tens of thousands of bodies before His throne, who long have slept in the sepulcher, and moldered into dust, what can He not accomplish within His people?

O doubt no more, and let not even the greatest wonders of His love, His grace, His power, or His glory, cause you to marvel unbelievingly, but rather say as each new prodigy of His divine power rises before you,

> I expected this of such a one as He is. I gathered that He could achieve this, for I understood that He was able to subdue all things to Himself. I knew that He fashioned the worlds, and built the Heavens, and guided the stars, and that by Him all things consist, I am not therefore astounded though I behold the greatest marvels of His power.

The first words of the text, then, urge us to faith, and rebuke all unbelieving amazement.

To the second sentence I now call your attention. The coming hour. *"The hour cometh,"* saith Christ. I suppose He calls it an hour, to intimate how very near it is in His esteem, since we do not begin to look at the exact hour of an event when it is extremely remote. An event which will not occur for hundreds of years is at first looked for and noted by the year, and only when we are reasonably near it do men talk of the day of the month, and we are coming very near it when we look for the precise hour. Christ intimates to us, that whether we think so or not, in God's thought the day of resurrection is very near; and though it may be a thousand years off even now, yet still to God it is but one day, and He would have us endeavor to think God's thought about it, not reckon any time to be long, since if it be time at all it must be short, and will be so regarded by us when it is past, and the day has arrived. This is practical wisdom, to bring close up to us that which is inevitable, and to act towards it as though it were but tomorrow morning when the trump should sound, and we should be judged.

"The hour is coming," saith the Savior. He here teaches us the certainty of that judgment. The hour cometh; it assuredly cometh. In the divine decree this is the day for which all other days were made; and if it were possible that any determination of the Almighty could be changed, yet this never shall be, for "He hath appointed a day, in the which he will judge the world in righteousness by that man whom he hath ordained; whereof he hath given assurance unto all men, in that he hath raised him from the dead." "The hour cometh." Reflect, my brethren, that most solemn hour cometh every moment. Every second brings it nearer. While you have been sitting still in this house, you have been borne onwards towards that great event. As the pendulum of yonder clock continues unceasingly to beat like the heart of time, as morning dawn gives place to evening shade, and the seasons follow in constant cycle, we are drifted along the river of time nearer to the ocean of eternity. Borne as on the wings of some mighty angel who never pauses in his matchless flight, I onward journey towards the judgment bar of God. My brethren, by that self-same flight are you also hurried on. Look to the resurrection, then, as a thing that ever cometh, silently drawing nearer and nearer hour by hour. Such contemplations will be of the utmost service to you.

Our Lord's words read as if the one hour of which He spake completely drove into the shade all other events; as if the hour, the one hour, the last hour, *the* hour par excellence, the master hour, the royal hour, was of all hours the only hour that was coming that was worth mentioning as being inevitable and important. Like Aaron's rod, the judgment hour swallows up every other hour. We hear of hours that have been big with the fate of nations, hours in which the welfare of millions trembled in the balances, hours in which for peace or war the die must be cast, hours that have been called crises of history; and we are apt to think that frequently periods such as this occur in the world's history: but here is the culminating crisis of all, here is the iron hour of severity, the golden hour of truth, the clear sapphire hour of manifestations.

In that August hour there shall be proclamation made of the impartial decisions of the Lord Christ with regard to all the souls and bodies of men. Oh, what an hour is this which cometh on apace! My dear brethren, now and then I covet the tongue of the eloquent, and now I do so that I might on such a theme as this, fire your imaginations and inflame your hearts; but let me pray you assist me now for a moment, and since this hour cometh, try to think it very, very near. Suppose it should come *now* while we are here assembled; suppose that even now the dead should rise, that in an instant this assembly should be melted into the infinitely greater one, and that no eye should be fixed upon the forgotten preacher, but all fixed upon the great descending Judge, sitting in majesty upon His great white throne, I pray you bethink yourselves as though the curtain were uplifted, at this moment; anticipate the sentence which will come forth to you from the throne of righteousness, consider as though at this precise moment it were pronounced upon you! Oh now, pray you examine yourselves as though the testing days were come, for such an examination will be to your souls' benefit if you be saved, and they may be to your souls' arousing if you be unconverted.

But we must pass on. "Marvel not at this: the hour is coming when all that are in the graves." Notice this very carefully, *"all that are in the graves,"* by which term is meant, not only all whose bodies are actually in the grave at this time, but all who ever were buried even though they may have been disinterred, and their bones may have mingled with the elements, been scattered by the winds, dissolved in the waves, or merged into vegetable forms. All who have lived and died shall certainly rise again. All! Compute then the numberless number! Count ye now the countless! How many lived before the deluge? It has been believed, and I think accurately, that the inhabitants of this world, were more numerous at the time of the deluge than they probably are now, owing to the enormous length of human life; men's numbers were not so terribly thinned by death as they are now.

Think if you will from the times of the deluge onward, of all Adam's progeny. From Tarshish to Sinim men covered the lands. Nineveh, Babylon, Chaldea, Persia, Greece, Rome, these were vast empires of men. The Parthians, Scythians, and Tartar hordes, who shall reckon up? As for those northern swarms of Goths and Huns and Vandals, these were continually streaming as from a teeming hive, in the middle ages, and Frank and Saxon and Celt multiplied in their measure. Yet these nations were but types of a numerous band of nations even more multitudinous. Think of Ethiopia and the whole continent of Africa; remember India and Japan, and the land of the setting sun; in all lands great tribes of men have come and have gone to rest in their sepulchers. What millions upon millions must lie buried in China and Burmah! What innumerable hosts are slumbering in the land of the pyramids and the mummy pits! Every one, both great and small, embalmed of old in Egypt, who shall compute the number?

Hear ye then and believe—out of all who have ever lived of woman born, not one shall be left in the tomb; all, all shall rise. I may well say as the psalmist did of another matter, "Such knowledge is too wonderful for me; it is high, I cannot attain unto it." How hath God marked all these bodies, how hath He tracked the form of each corporeal frame? How shall Jesus Christ be able to raise all these? I know not, but He shall do it, for so He declareth and so hath God purposed. "All that are in their graves shall hear his voice." All the righteous, all the wicked, all that were engulfed in the sea, all that slumber on the lap of earth; all the great ones, all the multitudes of the sons of toil; all the wise and all the foolish, all the beloved and all the despised: there shall not be one single individual omitted.

My dear friend, it may be best for you to look at the question in a more personal light: *you* will not be forgotten; your separated spirit shall have its appointed place, and that body which once contained it shall have its watcher to guard it, till by the power of God it shall be restored to your spirit again, at the sounding of the last trump. You, my hearer, shall rise again. As surely as you sit here this morning, you shall stand before the once crucified Son of Man. It is not possible that you should be forgotten; you shall not be permitted to rot away into annihilation, to be left in the darkness of obscurity; you must, you shall rise, each and every one without a solitary exception. It is a wondrous truth, and yet we may not marvel at it so as to doubt it, though we may marvel at it and admire the Lord who shall bring it to pass.

Pass on. "All that are in the grave *shall hear his voice.*" Hear! Why, the ear has gone! A thousand years ago a man was buried, and his ear—there is not the slightest relic of it left—all has vanished; shall that ear ever hear? Yes, for he that made it hear at the first, wrought as great a wonder then as when he shall make it hear a second time. It needed a God to make the hearing ear of the newborn babe; it shall need no more to renew the hearing ear the second time. Yes, the ear so long lost in silence shall hear! And what shall be the sound that shall startle that newly awakened and fresh fashioned ear? It shall be the voice of the Son of God; the voice of Jesus Christ Himself.

Ah, my brethren, while this teaches us the stolidity of human nature and how depraved the heart is, it also reminds you who are careless that there is no escape for you; if you will not hear the voice of Jesus now, you *must* hear it then. You may thrust those fingers into your ears today, but there will be no doing that in the day of the last trump, you must hear then; O that you would hear now! You must hear the summons to judgment; God grant that you may hear the summons to mercy, and become obedient to it and live. "All that are in their graves *shall* hear his voice"; whoever they may have been, they shall become subject to the power of His omnipotent command, and appear before His sovereign judgment seat.

Note the next words, *"and shall come forth."* That is to say, of course, that their bodies shall come out of the grave, out of the earth, or the water, or the air, or wherever else those bodies may be. But I think there is more than that intended by the words, "shall come forth." It seems to imply manifestation, as though all the while men were here, and when in their graves they were hidden and concealed, but as the voice of God in the thunder discovereth the forests and maketh the hinds to calve, so the voice of God in resurrection shall discover the secrets of men, and make them to bring forth their truest self into the light, to be revealed to all. The hypocrite, masked villain as he is, is not discovered now, but when the voice of Christ soundeth he shall come forth in a sense that will be horrible to him, deprived of all the ornaments of his masquerade, the vizard of his profession torn away, he shall stand before men and angels with the leprosy upon his brow, an object of universal derision, abhorred of God and despised of men.

Ah! dear hearers, are you ready to come forth even now? Would you be willing to have your hearts read out? Would you wear them on your sleeve for all to see? Is not there much about you that would not bear the light of the sun? How much more will it not bear the light of Him whose eyes are as a flame of fire, seeing all and testing all by trial which cannot err! Your coming forth on that day will be not only a reappearance from amidst the shadows of the sepulcher, but a coming forth into the light of Heaven's truth which shall reveal you in meridian clearness.

And then the text goes on to say that they shall come forth as *those who have done good* and those who have done evil. From which we must gather the next truth, that death makes no change in man's character, and that after death we must not expect improvements to occur. He that is holy, is holy still, and he that is filthy, is filthy still. They were, when they were put into the grave, men who had done good, they rise as men who have done good; or they were, when they were interred, men who had done evil, they rise as those that have done evil. Expect, therefore, no place for repentance after this life, no opportunities for reformation, no further proclamations of mercy, or doors of hope. It is now or never with you, remember that.

Note, again, that *only two characters rise,* for indeed there are only two characters who ever lived, and, therefore, two to bury and two to rise again—those who had done good and those who had done evil. Where were those of mingled character, whose conduct was neither good nor evil, or both? There were none such. You say, do not the good do evil? May not some who are evil still do good? I answer, he that doeth good is a man who, having believed in Jesus Christ, and received the new life, doeth good in his new nature, and with his newborn spirit, with all the intensity of his heart. As for his sins and infirmities, into which by reason of his old nature he falleth, these being washed away by the precious blood of Jesus, are not mentioned in the day of account, and he rises up as a man who hath done good, his good remembered, but the evil washed away.

As for the evil, of whom it is asserted that they may do good, we answer, so they may do good in the judgment of their fellow men, and as towards their fellow mortals, but good towards God from an evil heart cannot proceed. If the fountain be defiled, every stream must be polluted also. Good is a word that may be measured according to those who use it. The evil man's good is good to you, his child, his wife, his friend, but he hath no care for God, no reverence, no esteem for the great Lawgiver. Therefore, that which may be good to you may be ill to God, because done for no right motive, even perhaps done with a wrong motive; so that the man is dishonoring God while he was helping his friend. God shall judge men by their works, but there shall be but two characters, the good and the evil; and this makes it solemn work for each man to know where he will be, and what has been the general tenor of his life, and what is a true verdict upon the whole of it.

O sirs, there are some of you, who with all your excellences and moralities, have never done good as God measures good, for you have never thought of God to honor Him, you have never even confessed that you had dishonored Him, in fact, you have remained proudly indifferent to God's judgment of you as a sinner, and you have set yourself up as being all you should be. How shall it be possible, while you disbelieve your God, that you could do anything that can please Him? Your whole life is evil in God's sight—only evil. And as for you who fear His name, or trust you do, take heed unto your actions, I pray you, seeing that there are only those that have done good, and those that have done evil. Make it clear to your conscience, make it clear to the judgment of those who watch you (though this is of less importance), and make it clear before God, that your works are good, that your heart is right, because your outward conduct is conformed unto the law of God.

I shall not keep you much longer in the exposition, except to notice that the mode of judging is remarkable. Those who search the Scriptures know that the mode of judging at the last day will be entirely according to works. Will men be saved then for their works? No, by no means. Salvation is in every case the work and gift of grace. But the judgment will be guided by our works. It is due to those to be judged, that they should all be tried by the same rule. Now, no rule can be common to saints and sinners, except the rule of their moral conduct, and by this rule shall all men be judged. If God finds not in thee, my friend, any holiness of life whatever, neither will He accept thee. "What," saith one, "of the dying thief then?" There was the righteousness of faith in him, and it produced all the holy acts which circumstances allowed; the very moment he believed in Christ, he avowed Christ, and spoke for Christ, and that one act stood as evidence of his being a friend of God, while all his sins were washed away. May God grant you grace so to confess your sins, and believe in Jesus, that all your transgression may be forgiven you.

There must be some evidence of your faith. Before the assembled host of men there shall be no evidence given of your faith fetched from your inward feelings, but the evidence shall be found in your outward actions. It will still be, "I was hungered, and ye gave me meat: I was thirsty, and ye gave me drink: I was a stranger, and ye took me in: naked, and ye clothed me: I was sick, and ye visited me: I was in prison, and ye came unto me." Take heed, then, as to practical godliness, and abhor all preaching which would make sanctity of life to be a secondary thing. We are justified by faith, but not by a dead faith; the faith which justifies is that which produces holiness, and "without holiness no man shall see the Lord." See ye then the two classes into which men are divided, and the stern rule by which God shall judge them, and judge yourselves that ye be not condemned with the wicked.

The different dooms of the two classes are mentioned in the text. One shall rise to *the resurrection of life.* This does not mean mere existence; they shall both exist—both exist forever—but "life" means, when properly understood, happiness, power, activity, privilege, capacity, in fact, it is a term so comprehensive that I should need no small time to expound all it means. There is a death in life which the ungodly shall have, but ours shall be a life in life—a true life; not existence merely, but existence in energy, existence in honor, existence in peace, existence in blessedness, existence in perfection. This is the resurrection unto life.

As for the ungodly, there is a resurrection to damnation, by which their bodies and souls shall come manifestly under the condemnation of God; to use our Savior's word, shall be *damned.* Oh, what a resurrection! and yet we cannot escape from it if we neglect the great salvation. If we could lay us down and sleep, and never wake again, oh, what a blessing it were for an ungodly man! if that grave could be the last of him, and like a dog he should never start again from slumber, what a blessing! But it is a blessing that is not yours, and never can be. Your souls must live, and your body must live. "O fear Him, I pray you, who is able to destroy both soul and body in Hell. Yea, I say unto you, fear him."

II. Our time is almost spent, but I must occupy the remaining minutes in drawing lessons from the text.

The first is the lesson of *adoring reverence.* If it be so, that all the dead shall rise at the voice of Christ, let us worship Him. What a Savior was He who bled upon the tree! How gloriously is He who was despised and rejected, now exalted! O brethren, if we could even get but to see the skirts of this truth, that He shall raise all the dead out of their graves, if we did but begin to perceive its grandeur of meaning, methinks we should fall at the Savior's feet as John did when he said, "I fell at his feet as dead." Oh, what amazing power is Thine, my Lord and Master! What homage must be due to Thee! All hail, Immanuel! Thou hast the keys of death and of Hell. My soul loves and adores Thee, Thou ever great enthroned Prince, the Wonderful, the Counselor, King of kings, and Lord of lords.

The next lesson is *consolation* for our wounded spirits concerning our departed friends. We never mourn with regard to the souls of the righteous, they are forever with the Lord. The only mourning that we permit among Christians concerns the body, which is blighted like a withered flower. When we read at funerals that famous chapter in the epistle to the Corinthians, we find in it no comfort concerning the immortal spirit, for it is not required, but we find much consolation with regard to that which is "sown in dishonor," but shall be "raised in glory." Thy dead men shall live; that decaying dust shall live again. Weep not as though thou hadst cast thy treasure into the sea, where thou couldst never find it; thou hast only laid it by in a casket, whence thou shalt receive it again brighter than before. Thou shalt look again with thine own eyes into those eyes which have spoken love to thee so often, but which are now closed in sepulchral darkness. Thy child shall see thee yet again; thou shalt know thy child; the selfsame form shall rise. Thy departed friend shall come back to thee, and having loved his Lord as thou dost, thou shalt rejoice with him in the land where they die no more. It is but a short parting, it will be an eternal meeting. Forever with the Lord, we shall also be forever with each other. Let us comfort one another, then, with these words.

The last lesson is that of *self-examination*. If we are to rise, some to rewards and some to punishments, what shall be my position? "What shall be my position?" let each conscience ask. How do you feel, my hearers, in the prospect of rising again? Does the thought give you any gleam of joy? Does it not create a measure of alarm? If your heart trembles at the tidings, how will you bear it when the real fact is before you, and not the thought merely? What has your life been? If by that life you shall be judged, what has it been? What has been its prevailing principle up till now? Have you believed God? Do you live by faith upon the Son of God? I know you are imperfect, but are you struggling after holiness? Do you desire to honor God? This shall rule the judgment of your life; what was its end, and aim, and bent, and object? Imperfection there has been, but has there been sincerity? Has grace, divine grace, that washes sinners in the blood of Christ, proved itself to be in you by alienating you from the sins you loved, and leading you to the duties that you once neglected?

I will ask you another question: if you do not feel happy at the thought of yourself, are you quite peaceful concerning the raising of all others? Are you prepared to meet before God those whom you have sinned with among men? It is a question worthy of the sinner's thought, of what must be the terrors of men and women who will have to meet the companions of their sins! Was not this at the bottom of Dives wishing Lazarus to be sent back to the world to warn his five brethren lest they should come into the place of torment? Was not he afraid to see them there, because their recriminations would increase his misery? It will be a horrible thing for a man who has been a debauched villain to rise again and confront his victims whom his lusts dragged down to Hell! How will he quail as he hears them lay their damnation at his door, and curse him for his lasciviousness! O man, your sin is not dead and buried, and the sinner whom you joined hands with in iniquity shall rise to witness against you. The crime, the guilt, the punishment, and the guilty one, shall alike live again, and you shall live forever in remorse to rue the day in which you thus transgressed.

Another question, if it will be terrible to many to see the dead rise again, how will they endure to see Him, the Judge Himself, the Savior? Of all men that ever lived, He is the one that you have need to be the most afraid of, because it is he whom this day you ought most to love, but whom you forget. How many times from this pulpit have I pleaded with you to yield yourselves to Jesus Christ, and how frequently have you given Him a flat denial! It may be, some of you have not quite done that, but you have postponed your decision, and said, "When I have a more convenient season I will send for thee." When He cometh, how will you answer Him? Man, how will you answer Him? How will you excuse yourselves? You would not have Him as a Savior, but you must have Him as your Judge, to pronounce your sentence. You despised His grace, but you cannot escape His wrath. If you will but look to Jesus now, you shall find salvation in that glance, but in refusing so to do you heap up for yourself wrath when that terrible but inevitable glance shall be yours, of which the prophet says, "All the kindreds of the Earth shall wail because of him." O spurn Him not, then! Despise not the Crucified! I pray you trample not upon His blood, but come to Him, that so, when you see Him on His throne you may not be afraid.

Beloved, I might have continued to ask more questions, but I shall close with these two. One of the best ways by which to learn what will be our portion in the future, is to enquire what is our portion in the present. Have you life now, I mean spiritual life—the life that grieves for sin, the life that trusts a Savior? If so, you shall certainly have the resurrection to life. On the other hand, have you condemnation now? for he that believeth not is condemned already. Are you an unbeliever? Then you are condemned now, you shall suffer the resurrection to damnation. How can it be otherwise? Seek, then, that you may possess the life of God now by faith, and you shall have it forever in fruition. Escape from condemnation now, and you shall escape from damnation hereafter.

God bless you all with the abundance of His salvation, for Christ's sake. Amen.

The Power of Christ
Illustrated by the Resurrection

*"For our conversation is in Heaven; from whence also we look
for the Savior, the Lord Jesus Christ: who shall change our vile
body, that it may be fashioned like unto his glorious body,
according to the working whereby he is able even to subdue
all things unto himself."—Philippians 3:20, 21.*

I should mislead you if I called these verses my text, for I intend only to lay stress upon the closing expression, and I read the two verses because they are needful for its explanation. It would require several discourses to expound the whole of so rich a passage as this.

Beloved, how intimately is the whole of our life interwoven with the life of Christ! His first coming has been to us salvation, and we are delivered from the wrath of God through Him. We live still because He lives, and never is our life more joyous than when we look most steadily to Him. The completion of our salvation in the deliverance of our body from the bondage of corruption, in the raising of our dust to a glorious immortality, that also is wrapped up with the personal resurrection and quickening power of the Lord Jesus Christ. As His first advent has been our salvation from sin, so His second advent shall be our salvation from the grave. He is in Heaven, but, as the apostle saith, "We look for the Savior, the Lord Jesus Christ: who shall change our vile body, that it may be fashioned like unto his glorious body."

We have nothing, we are nothing, apart from Him. The past, the present, and the future are only bright as He shines upon them. Every consolation, every hope, every enjoyment we possess, we have received, and still retain because of our connection with Jesus Christ our Lord. Apart from Him we are naked, and poor, and miserable. I desire to impress upon your minds, and especially upon my own, the need of our abiding in Him. As zealous laborers for the glory of God I am peculiarly anxious that you may maintain daily communion with Jesus, for as it is with our covenant blessings, so is it with our work of faith and labor of love, everything depends upon Him. All our fruit is found in Jesus. Remember His own words, "Without me ye can do nothing." *Our* power to work comes wholly from *His* power. If we work effectually it must always be according to the effectual working of His power in us and through us.

In the text, notice, first of all, *the marvel to be wrought by our Lord at His coming;* and then gather from it, in the second place, helps to the consideration of *the power which is now at this time proceeding from Him and treasured in Him;* and then, thirdly, *contemplate the work which we desire to see accomplished,* and which we believe will be accomplished on the ground of the power resident in our Lord.

I. First, we have to ask you to consider believingly the marvel which is to be wrought by Our Lord at His coming.

When He shall come a second time He will change our vile body and fashion it like unto His glorious body. What a marvelous change! How great the transformation! How high the ascent! Our body in its present state is called in our translation a "vile body," but if we translate the Greek more literally it is much more expressive, for there we find this corporeal frame called "the body of our humiliation." Not "this humble body," that is hardly the meaning, but the body in which our humiliation is manifested and enclosed. This body of our humiliation our Lord will transform until it is like unto His own. Here read not alone "his glorious body," for that is not the most literal translation, but "the body of his glory"; the body in which He enjoys and reveals His glory. Our Savior had a body here in humiliation; that body was like ours in all respects except that it could see no corruption, for it was undefiled with sin; that body in which our Lord wept, and sweat great drops of blood, and yielded up His spirit, was the body of His humiliation. He rose again from the dead, and He rose in the same body which ascended up into Heaven, but He concealed its glory to a very great extent, else had He been too bright to be seen of mortal eyes. Only when He passed the cloud, and was received out of sight, did the full glory of His body shine forth to ravish the eyes of angels and of glorified spirits. Then was it that His countenance became as the sun shining in its strength.

Now, beloved, whatever the body of Jesus may be in His glory, our present body which is now in its humiliation is to be conformed unto it; Jesus is the standard of man in glory. "We shall be like him, for we shall see him as he is." Here we dwell in this body of our humiliation, but it shall undergo a change, "in a moment, in the twinkling of an eye, at the last trump: for the trumpet shall sound, and the dead shall be raised incorruptible, and we shall be changed." Then shall we come into our glory, and our body being made suitable to the glory state, shall be fitly called the body of glory. We need not curiously pry into the details of the change, nor attempt to define all the differences between the two estates of our body; for "it doth not yet appear what we shall be," and we may be content to leave much to be made known to us hereafter. Yet though we see through a glass darkly, we nevertheless do see something, and would not shut our eyes to that little. We know not yet as we are known, but we do know in part, and that part knowledge is precious.

The gates have been ajar at times, and men have looked awhile, and beheld and wondered. Three times, at least, human eyes have seen something of the body of glory. The face of Moses, when he came down from the mount, shone so that those who gathered around him could not look thereon, and he had to cover it with a veil. In that lustrous face of the man who had been forty days in high communion with God, you behold some gleams of the brightness of glorified manhood. Our Lord made a yet clearer manifestation of the glorious body when He was transfigured in the presence of the three disciples. When His garments became bright and glistering, whiter than any fuller could make them, and He Himself was all aglow with glory, His disciples saw and marveled. The face of Stephen is a third window as it were through which we may look at the glory to be revealed, for even His enemies as they gazed upon the martyr in his confession of Christ, saw his face as it had been the face of an angel. Those three transient gleams of the morning light may serve as tokens to us to help us to form some faint idea of what the body of the glory of Christ and the body of our own glory will be.

Turning to that marvelous passage in the Corinthians, wherein the veil seems to be more uplifted than it ever had been before or since, we learn a few particulars worthy to be rehearsed. The body while here below, is corruptible, subject to decay; it gradually becomes weak through old age, at last it yields to the blows of death, falls into the ground, and becomes the food of worms. But the new body shall be incorruptible, it shall not be subject to any process of disease, decay, or decline, and it shall never, through the lapse of ages, yield to the force of death. For the immortal spirit it shall be the immortal companion. There are no graves in Heaven, no knell ever saddened the New Jerusalem. The body here is weak, the apostle says "it is sown in weakness"; it is subject to all sorts of infirmities in life, and in death loses all strength. It is weak to perform our own will, weaker still to perform the heavenly will; it is weak to do and weak to suffer: but it is to be "raised in power, all infirmity being completely removed." How far this power will be physical and how far spiritual we need not speculate; where the material ends and the spiritual begins we need not define; we shall be as the angels, and we have found no difficulty in believing that these pure spirits "excel in strength," nor in understanding Peter when he says that angels are "greater in power and might." Our body shall be "raised in power."

Here, too, the body is a natural or soulish body—a body fit for the soul, for the lowest faculties of our mental nature; but according to the apostle in the Corinthians, it is to be raised a spiritual body, adapted to the noblest portion of our nature, suitable to be the dwelling place and the instrument of our newborn grace-given life. This body at present is no assistance to the spirit of prayer or praise; it rather hinders than helps us in spiritual exercises. Often the spirit truly is willing, but the flesh is weak. We sleep when we ought to watch, and faint when we should pursue. Even its joys as well as its sorrows tend to distract devotion: but when this body shall be transformed, it shall be a body suitable for the highest aspirations of our perfected and glorified humanity—a spiritual body like unto the body of the glory of Christ.

Being sinless, the body when it shall be raised again shall be painless. Who shall count the number of our pains while in this present house of clay? Truly we that are in this tabernacle do groan. Does it not sometimes appear to the children of sickness as if this body were fashioned with a view to suffering; as if all its nerves, sinews, veins, pulses, vessels, and valves, were parts of a curious instrument upon which every note of the entire gamut of pain might be produced? Patience, ye who linger in this shattered tenement, a house not made with hands awaits you. Up yonder no sorrow and sighing are met with; the chastising rod shall fall no longer when the faultiness is altogether removed. As the new body will be without pain, so will it be superior to weariness. The glory-body will not yield to faintness, nor fail through languor. Is it not implied that the spiritual body does not need to sleep, when we read that they serve God day and night in His temple?

In a word, the bodies of the saints, like the body of Christ, will be perfect; there shall be nothing lacking and nothing faulty. If saints die in the feebleness of age they shall not rise thus; or if they have lost a sense or a limb or are halt or maimed, they shall not be so in Heaven, for as to body and soul "they are without fault before the throne of God." "We shall be like him," is true of all the saints, and hence none will be otherwise than fair, and beautiful, and perfect. The righteous shall be like Christ. My imagination is not able to give you a picture of the transformation; but those who will be alive and remain at the coming of the Son of God will undergo it, and so enter glory without death. "For this corruptible must put on incorruption, and this mortal must put on immortality," and therefore the bodies of living believers shall in the twinkling of an eye pass from the one state into the other; they shall be transformed from the vile to the glorious, from the state of humiliation into the state of glory, by the power of the coming Savior.

The miracle is amazing, if you view it as occurring to those who shall be alive when Christ comes. Reflect, however, that a very large number of the saints when the Lord shall appear a second time will already be in their graves. Some of these will have been buried long enough to have become corrupt. If you could remove the mold and break open the coffin-lid, what would you find but foulness and putrefaction? But those moldering relics are the body of the saint's humiliation, and that very body is to be transformed into the likeness of Christ's glorious body. Admire the miracle as you survey the mighty change! Look down into the loathsome tomb, and, if you can endure it, gaze upon the putrid mass; this, even this, is to be transformed into Christ's likeness. What a work is this! And what a Savior is He who shall achieve it!

Go a little further. Many of those whom Christ will thus raise will have been buried so long that all trace of them will have disappeared; they will have melted back into the common dust of earth, so that if their bones were searched for not a vestige of them could be found, nor could the keenest searcher after human remains detect a single particle. They have slept in quiet through long ages in their lonely graves, till they have become absorbed into the soil as part and parcel of mother earth. No, there is not a bone, nor a piece of a bone left; their bodies are as much one with Earth as the drop of rain which fell upon the wave is one with the sea: yet shall they be raised. The trumpet call shall fetch them back from the dust with which they have mingled, and dust to dust, bone to bone, the anatomy shall be rebuilt and then refashioned. Does your wonder grow? does not your faith accept with joy the marvel, and yet feel it to be a marvel none the less?

Son of man, I will lead thee into an inner chamber more full of wonder yet. There are many thousands of God's people to whom a quiet slumber in the grave was denied; they were cut off by martyrdom, were sawn asunder, or cast to the dogs. Tens of thousands of the precious bodies of the saints have perished by fire, their limbs have been blown in clouds of smoke to the four winds of Heaven, and even the handful of ashes which remained at the foot of the stake their relentless persecutors have thrown into rivers to be carried to the ocean, and divided to every shore. Some of the children of the resurrection were devoured by wild beasts in the Roman amphitheaters, or left a prey to kites and ravens on the gibbet. In all sorts of ways have the saints' bodies been hacked and hewn, and, as a consequence, the particles of those bodies have no doubt been absorbed into various vegetable growths, and having been eaten by animals have mingled with the flesh of beasts; but what of that?

"What of that?" say you, how can these bodies be refashioned? By what possibility can the selfsame bodies be raised again? I answer it needs a miracle to make any of these dry bones live, and a miracle being granted, impossibility vanishes. He who formed each atom from nothing can gather each particle again from confusion. The omniscient Lord of providence tracks each molecule of matter, and knows its position and history as a shepherd knows his sheep; and if it be needful to constitute the identity of the body, to regather every atom, he can do it. It may not, however, be needful at all, and I do not assert that it will be, for there may be a true identity without sameness of material; even as this my body is the same as that in which I lived twenty years ago, and yet in all probability there is not a grain of the same matter in it. God is able then to cause that the same body which on Earth we wear in our humiliation, which we call a vile body, shall be fashioned like unto Christ's body. No difficulties, however stern, that can be suggested from science or physical law, shall for a single instant stand in the way of the accomplishment of this transformation by Christ the King.

What marvels rise before me! indeed, it needs faith, and we thank God we have it. The resurrection of Christ has forever settled in our minds, beyond all controversy, the resurrection of all who are in Him; "For if we believe that Jesus died and rose again, even so them also which sleep in Jesus will God bring with him." Still it is a marvel of marvels, a miracle which needs the fullness of the deity. Of whom but God, very God of very God, could it be said that He shall change our bodies, and make them like unto His glorious body?

II. We will now pass on. Here is the point we aim at. Consider, in the second place, that this power which is to raise the dead is resident in Christ at this moment.

So saith the text, "according to the working whereby *he is able* to subdue all things unto himself." It is not some new power which Christ will take to Himself in the latter days and then for the first time display, but the power which will arouse the dead is the same power which is in Him at this moment, which is going forth from Him at this instant in the midst of His church and among the sons of men. I call your attention to this, and invite you to follow the track of the text.

First notice that all the power by which the last transformation will be wrought is ascribed to our Lord Jesus Christ now *as the Savior.* "We look for the Savior, the Lord Jesus." When Christ raises the dead it will be as a Savior, and it is precisely in that capacity that we need the exercise of His power at this moment. Fix this, my brethren, in your hearts; we are seeking the salvation of men, and we are not seeking a hopeless thing, for Jesus Christ is able as a Savior, to subdue all things, to Himself; so the text expressly tells us. It doth not merely say that as a raiser of the dead He is able to subdue all things, but as the Savior, the Lord Jesus Christ. His titles are expressly given, He is set forth to us as the Lord, the Savior, the Anointed and in that capacity is said to be able to subdue all things to Himself. Happy tidings for us! My brethren, how large may our prayers be for the conversion of the sons of men, how great our expectations, how confident our efforts! Nothing is too hard for our Lord Jesus Christ: nothing in the way of saving work is beyond His power. If as a Savior He wakes the dead in the years to come, He can quicken the spiritually dead even now.

The power of the resurrection is being put forth today, it is pulsing through the quickened portion of this audience, it is heaving with life each bosom that beats with love to God, it is preserving the life-courses in the souls of all the spiritual, so that they go not back to their former death in sin. The power which will work the resurrection will be wonderful, but it will be no new thing. It is everywhere to be beheld in operation in the church of God at this very moment by those who have eyes to see it; and herein I join with the apostle in his prayer:

> that the God of our Lord Jesus Christ, the Father of glory may give unto you the spirit of wisdom and revelation in the knowledge of him: the eyes of your understanding being enlightened; that ye may know what is the hope of his calling, and what the riches of the glory of his inheritance in the saints, and what is the exceeding greatness of his power to us-ward who believe, according to the working of his mighty power, which he wrought in Christ, when he raised him from the dead, and set him at his own right hand in the heavenly places, far above all principality, and power, and might, and dominion, and every name that is named, not only in this world, but also in that which is to come: and hath put all things under his feet, and gave him to be the head over all things to the church, which is his body, the fullness of him that filleth all in all.

Note next that the terms of our text imply *that opposition may be expected to this power,* but that all resistance will be overcome. That word "subdue" supposes a force to be conquered and brought into subjection. "He is able even to subdue all things unto Himself." Herein is a great wonder! There will be no opposition to the resurrection. The trumpet sound shall bring the dead from their graves, and no particle shall disobey the summons; but to spiritual resurrection there is resistance—resistance which only omnipotence can vanquish. In the conversion of sinners natural depravity is an opposing force; for men are set upon their sins, and love not the things of God, neither will they hearken to the voice of mercy.

My brethren, to remove all our fears concerning our Lord's ability to save, the word is here used, "He is able," not only to raise all things from the dead, but *"to subdue* all things to Himself." Here again I would bid you take the encouragement the text presents you. If there be opposition to the gospel, He is able to subdue it. If in one man there is a prejudice, if in another man the heart is darkened with error, if one man hates the very name of Jesus, if another is so wedded to his sins that he cannot part from them, if opposition has assumed in some a very determined character, does not the text meet every case? "He is able to subdue all things," to conquer them, to break down the barriers that interpose to prevent the display of

His power, and to make those very barriers the means of setting forth that power the more gloriously. "He is able even to subdue all things."

Note next, that the language of our text *includes all supposable cases.* He is able to "subdue *all* things unto Himself," not here and there one, but "*all* things." Brethren, there is no man in this world so fallen, debased, depraved, and willfully wicked, that Jesus cannot save him—not even among those who live beyond the reach of ordinary ministry. He can bring the heathen to the gospel, or the gospel to them. The wheels of providence can be so arranged that salvation shall be brought to the outcasts; even war, famine, and plague, may become messengers for Christ, for He, too, rides upon the wings of the wind.

There lived some few years ago in Perugia, in Italy, a man of the loosest morals and the worst conceivable disposition. He had given up all religion, he loathed God, and had arrived at such a desperate state of mind that he had conceived an affection for the devil, and endeavored to worship the evil one. Imagining Satan to be the image and embodiment of all rebellion, free thinking, and lawlessness, he deified him in his own mind, and desired nothing better than to be a devil himself. On one occasion, when a Protestant missionary had been in Perugia preaching, a priest happened to say in this man's hearing, that there were Protestants in Perugia, the city was being defiled by heretics. "And who do you think Protestants are?" said he. "They are men who have renounced Christ and worship the devil." A gross and outrageous lie was this, but it answered far other ends than its author meant. The man hearing this, thought, "Oh, then, I will go and meet with them, for I am much of their mind"; and away he went to the Protestant meeting, in the hope of finding an assembly who propagated lawlessness and worshiped the devil. He there heard the gospel, and was saved.

Behold in this and in ten thousand cases equally remarkable, the ability of our King to subdue all things unto Himself. How can any man whom God ordains to save, escape from that eternal love which is as omnipresent as the deity itself? "He is able to subdue all things to Himself." If His sword cannot reach the far off ones His arrows can, and even at this hour they are sharp in His enemy's hearts. No boastful Goliath can stand before our David; though the weapon which He uses today be but a stone from the brook, yet shall the Philistine be subdued. If there should be in this place a Deist, an Atheist, A Romanist, or even a lover of the devil, if he be but a man, mercy yet can come to him. Jesus Christ is able to subdue him unto Himself. None have gone too far, and none are too hardened. While the Christ lives in Heaven we need never despair of any that are still in this mortal life—"He is able to subdue all things unto Himself."

You will observe, in the text that *nothing is said concerning the unfitness of the means*. My fears often are lest souls should not be saved by our instrumentality because of faultiness in us; we fear lest we should not be prayerful enough or energetic or earnest enough; or that it should be said, "He could not do many mighty works there because of their unbelief." But the text seems to obliterate man altogether—"He is able to subdue all things unto Himself"—that is to say, *Jesus* does it, *Jesus* can do it, will do it all. By the feeblest means He can work mightily, can take hold of us, unfit as we are for service, and make us fit, can grasp us in our folly and teach us wisdom, take us in our weakness and make us strong. My brethren, if we had to find resources for ourselves, and to rely upon ourselves, our enterprise might well be renounced, but since He is able, we will cast the burden of this work on Him, and go to Him in believing prayer, asking Him to work mightily through us to the praise of His glory, for "He is able even to subdue all things unto Himself."

Note that *the ability* is said in the text to be *present* with the Savior now. I have already pointed that out to you, but I refer to it again. The resurrection is a matter of the future, but the working which shall accomplish the resurrection is a matter of the present. "According to the working whereby He *is* able even to subdue all things unto Himself," Jesus is as strong now as He ever will be, for He changes not. At this moment He is as able to convert souls as at the period of the brightest revival, or at Pentecost itself. There are no ebbs and flows with Christ's power. Omnipotence is in the hand that once was pierced, permanently abiding there. Oh, if we could but rouse it; if we could but bring the Captain of the host to the field again, to fight for His church, to work by His servants! What marvels should we see, for He is able. We are not straitened in Him, we are straitened in ourselves if straitened at all.

Let us cry unto our Lord, for He has but to will it and thousands of sinners will be saved; let us lift up our hearts to Him who has but to speak the word and whole nations shall be born unto Him. The resurrection will not be a work occupying centuries, it will be accomplished at once; and so it may be in this house of prayer, and throughout London, and throughout the world, Christ will do a great and speedy work to the amazement of all beholders. He will send forth the rod of His strength out of Zion, and rule in the midst of His enemies. He will unmask His batteries, He will spring His mines, He will advance His outworks, He will subdue the city of His adversaries, and ride victoriously through the Bozrah of His foes. Who shall stay His hand? Who shall say unto Him, "What doest thou?"

I wish we had time to work out the parallel which our text suggests, between the resurrection and the subduing of all things. The resurrection will be worked by the divine power, and the subduing of sinners is a precisely similar instance of salvation. All men are dead in sin, but He can raise them. Many of them are corrupt with vice, but He can transform them. Some of them are, as it were, lost to all hope, like the dead body scattered to the winds, desperate cases for whom even pity seems to waste her sighs; but He who raises the dead of all sorts, with a word can raise sinners of all sorts by the selfsame power. And as the dead when raised are made like to Christ, so the wicked when converted are made like to Jesus too. Brilliant examples of virtue shall be found in those who were terrible instances of vice; the most depraved and dissolute shall become the most devout and earnest. From the vile body to the glory-body, what a leap, and from the sinner damnable in lust to the saint bright with the radiance of sanctity, what a space! The leap seems very far, but omnipotence can bridge the chasm. The Savior, the Lord Jesus Christ is able to do it; He is able to do it in ten thousand thousand cases, able to do it at this very moment.

III. *I said I would ask you to consider, in the third place, the work which we desire to see accomplished. I will not detain you however, with that consideration further than this.*

Brethren, we long to see the Savior subduing souls *unto Himself.* Not to our way of thinking, not to our church, not to the honor of our powers of persuasion, but *"unto Himself."* "He is able even to subdue all things unto himself." O sinner, how I wish thou wert subdued to Jesus, to kiss those dear feet that were nailed for thee, to love in life Him Who loved thee to the death. Ah! soul, it were a blessed subjection for thee. Never subject of earthly monarch so happy in his king as thou wouldst be. God is our witness, we who preach the gospel, we do not want to subdue you to ourselves, as though we would rule you and be lords over your spirits. It is to Jesus, to Jesus only that we would have you subdued. O that you desired this subjection, it would be liberty, and peace, and joy to you!

Notice that this subjection is eminently to be desired, since it consists in transformation. Catch the thought of the text. He transforms the vile body into His glorious body, and this is a part of the subjection of all things unto Himself. But do you call that subjection? Is it not a subjection to be longed after with an insatiable desire, to be so subdued to Christ that I, a poor, vile sinner, may become like Him: holy, harmless, undefiled? This is the subjection that we wish for you, O unconverted ones. We trust we have felt it ourselves, we pray you may feel it too. He is able to give it to you. Ask it of Him at once. Now breathe the prayer, now believe that the Savior can work the transformation even in you, in you at this very moment. And, O my brethren in the faith, have faith for sinners now. While they are pleading, plead for them that this subjection which is an uplifting, this conquering which is a liberating, may be accomplished in them.

For, remember again, that to be subjected to Christ is, according to our text, to be fitted for Heaven. He will change our vile body and make it like the body of His glory. The body of the glory is a body fitted for glory, a body which participates in glory. The Lord Jesus can make you, sinner, though now fitted for Hell, fitted for Heaven, fitted for glory, and breathe into you now an anticipation of that glory, in the joy and peace of mind which His pardon will bring to you. It must be a very sad thing to be a soldier under any circumstances; to have to cut and hack and kill and subdue, even in a righteous cause, is cruel work; but to be a soldier of King Jesus is an honor and a joy. The service of Jesus is a grand service.

Brethren, we have been earnestly seeking to capture some hearts that are here present, to capture them for Jesus. It has been a long and weary siege up till this hour. We have summoned them to surrender, and opened fire upon them with the gospel, but as yet in vain. I have striven to throw a few live shells into the very heart of their city, in the form of warning and threatening and exhortation. But oh! how I wish I could burst open the gates of a sinner's heart today, for the Prince Emmanuel to come in. He who is at your gates is not an alien monarch, He is your rightful Prince, He is your Friend and Lover. It will not be a strange face that you will see, when Jesus comes to reign in you. When the King in His beauty wins your soul, you will think yourselves a thousand fools that you did not receive Him before. Instead of fearing that He will ransack your soul, you will open all its doors and invite Him to search each room. You will cry, "Take all, Thou blessed monarch, it shall be most mine when it is Thine. Take all, and reign and rule."

I propound terms of capitulation to you, O sinner. They are but these: yield up yourself to Christ, give up your works and ways, both good and bad, and trust in Him to save you, and be His servant henceforth and forever. While I thus invite you, I trust He will speak through me to you and win you to Himself. I shall not plead in vain, the word shall not fall to the ground. I fall back upon the delightful consolation of our text, "He is able to subdue all things unto himself." May He prove His power this morning. Amen and Amen.

The Resurrection Credible

"Why should it be thought a thing incredible with you,
that God should raise the dead?"—Acts 26:8.

Concerning the souls of our believing friends who have departed this life we suffer no distress, we feel sure that they are where Jesus is, and behold His glory, according to our Lord's own memorable prayer. We know but very little of the disembodied state, but we know quite enough to rest certain beyond all doubt that

> *They are supremely blest,*
> *Have done with sin, and care, and woe,*
> *And with their Savior rest.*

Our main trouble is about their bodies, which we have committed to the dark and lonesome grave. We cannot reconcile ourselves to the fact that their dear faces are being stripped of all their beauty by the fingers of decay, and that all the insignia of their manhood should be fading into corruption. It seems hard that the hands and feet, and all the goodly fabric of their noble forms, should be dissolved into dust, and broken into an utter ruin. We cannot stand at the grave without tears; even the perfect Man could not restrain His weeping at Lazarus' tomb. It is a sorrowful thought that our friends are dead, nor can we ever regard the grave with love. We cannot say that we take pleasure in the catacomb and the vault. We still regret, and feel it natural to do so, that so dreadful a ban has fallen upon our race as that it should be "appointed unto all men once to die." God sent it as a penalty, and we cannot rejoice in it.

The glorious doctrine of the resurrection is intended to take away this cause of sorrow. We need have no trouble about the body, any more than we have concerning the soul. Faith being exercised upon immortality relieves us of all trembling as to the spirits of the just; and the same faith, if exercised upon resurrection, will with equal certainty efface all hopeless grief with regard to the body; for, though apparently destroyed, the body will live again—it has not gone to annihilation. That very frame which we lay in the dust shall but sleep there for a while, and, at the trump of the archangel, it shall awaken in superior beauty, clothed with attributes unknown to it while here. The Lord's love to His people is a love towards their entire manhood, He chose them not as disembodied spirits, but as men and women arrayed in flesh and blood. The love of Jesus Christ towards His chosen is not an affection for their better nature merely, but towards that also which we are wont to think their inferior part; for in His book all their members were written, He keepeth all their bones, and the very hairs of their head are all numbered.

Did He not assume our perfect manhood? He took into union with His Deity a human soul, but He also assumed a human body; and in that fact He gave us evidence of His affinity to our perfect manhood, to our flesh, and to our blood, as well as to our mind and to our spirit. Moreover, our Redeemer has perfectly ransomed both soul and body. It was not partial redemption which our Kinsman effected for us. We know that our Redeemer liveth, not only with respect to our spirit, but with regard to our body; so that though the worm shall devour its skin and flesh, yet shall it rise again because He has redeemed it from the power of death, and ransomed it from the prison of the grave.

It is a joy to think that, as Christ has redeemed the entire man, and sanctified the entire man, and will be honored in the salvation of the entire man, so our complete manhood shall have it in its power to glorify Him. The hands with which we sinned shall be lifted in eternal adoration; the eyes which have gazed on evil shall behold the King in His beauty. Not merely shall the mind which now loves the Lord be perpetually knit to Him, and the spirit which contemplates Him will delight forever in Him, and be in communion with Him; but this very body which has been a clog and hindrance to the spirit, and been an arch rebel against the sovereignty of Christ, shall yield Him homage with voice, and hand, and brain, and ear, and eye. We look to the time of resurrection for the accomplishment of our adoption, to wit, the redemption of the body.

Now, this being our hope, though we believe and rejoice in it in a measure, we have, nevertheless, to confess that, sometimes, questions suggest themselves, and the evil heart of unbelief cries, "Can it be true? Is it possible?" At such times the question of our text is exceedingly needful, "Why should it be thought a thing incredible with you that God should raise the dead?"

This morning, I shall *first* ask you, dear brethren, to *look the difficulty in the face;* and, then, *secondly, we will endeavor to remove the difficulty,*—there is but one way of doing so, and that a very simple one; and then, *thirdly, we* shall have a word or two say to about *our relation to this truth.*

I. First, then, let us look this difficulty in the face.

We shall not, for a moment, flinch from the boldest and most plain assertion of our belief in the resurrection, but will let its difficulties appear upon the surface. Attempts have been made at different times by misguided Christians, to tone down or explain away the doctrine of the resurrection and kindred truths, in order to make them more acceptable to skeptical or philosophical minds, but this has never succeeded. No man has ever been convinced of a truth by discovering that those who profess to believe it are half ashamed of it, and adopt the tone of apology. How can a man be convinced by one who does not himself believe, for that, in plain English, is what it comes to. When we modify, qualify, and attenuate our doctrinal statements, we make concessions which will never be reciprocated, and are only received as admissions that we do not believe ourselves what we assert. By this cutting and trimming policy we shear away the locks of our strength, and break our own arm. Nothing of that kind affects me, either now or any time.

We do then really in very truth believe that the very body which is put into the grave will rise again, and we mean this literally, and as we utter it. We are not using the language of metaphor, or talking of a myth; we believe that, in actual fact, the bodies of the dead will rise again from the tomb. We admit, and rejoice in the fact, that there will be a great change in the body of the righteous man; that its materialism will have lost all the grossness and tendency to corruption which now surrounds it; that it will be adapted for higher purposes; for, whereas, it is now only a tenement fit for the soul or the lower intellectual faculties, it will then be adapted for the spirit or the higher part of our nature: we rejoice that though sown in weakness it will be raised in glory; but we nevertheless know that it will be the same body. The selfsame body which is put into the grave shall rise again; there shall be an absolute identity between the body in which we die and the body in which we rise again from the dust.

But, let it be remembered that identity is not the same thing as absolute sameness of substance and continuance of atoms. We do not mention this qualification at all by way of taking off the edge from our statement, but simply because it is true. We are conscious, as a matter of fact, that we are living in the same bodies which we possessed twenty years ago; yet we are told, and we have no reason to doubt it, that perhaps not one single particle of the matter which constitutes our body now was in it twenty years ago. The changes our physical forms have undergone from infancy to manhood are very great, yet have we the same bodies. Admit the like identity in the resurrection, and it is all we ask. The body in which we die will be the same body in which we were born—everybody admits that, though it is certainly not the same as in all its particles; nay, every particle may have been exchanged, and yet it will remain the same. So the body in which we rise will be the same body in which we die; it will be greatly changed, but those changes will not be such as to affect its identity.

Now this hope is naturally surrounded with many difficulties, because, first of all, in the great mass of the dead decay has taken place. The large majority of dead bodies have rotted and been utterly dissolved, and the larger proportion of all other bodies will probably follow them. When we see bodies that have been petrified, or mummies which have been embalmed, we think that if all bodies were preserved in that way it were easier to believe in their restoration to life; but when we break open some ancient sarcophagus, and find nothing there but a little impalpable brown powder, when we open a grave in the churchyard and find only a few crumbled pieces of bone, and when we think of ancient battlefields where thousands have fallen, where, notwithstanding, through the lapse of years there remains not a trace of man, since the bones have so completely melted back into earth, and in some cases have been sucked up by the roots and plants, and have passed into other organizations [organisms], it certainly does seem a thing incredible that the dead should be raised.

The wonder increases when we remember in what strange places many of these bodies now may be. For the bodies of some have been left in deep mines where they will never be reached again; they have been carried by the wash and swell of tides into deep caverns of the ancient main; there they lie, far away on the pathless desert where only the vulture's eye can see them, or buried beneath mountains of fallen rock. In fact, where are not man's remains? Who shall point out a spot of Earth where the crumbling dust of Adam's sons is not? Blows there a single summer wind down our streets without whirling along particles of what once was man? Is there a single wave that breaks upon any shore which holds not in solution some relic of what was once human? They lie beneath each tree, they enrich the fields, they pollute the brooks, they hide beneath the meadow grass; yet surely from anywhere, from everywhere, the scattered bodies shall return, like Israel from captivity. As certainly as God is God, our dead men shall live, and stand upon their feet, an exceedingly great army.

And, moreover, to make the wonder extraordinary beyond conception, they will rise at once, or perhaps in two great divisions. There is a passage (Rev. 20:5, 6) which apparently teaches us that between the resurrection of the righteous and the resurrection of the wicked there will be an interval of a thousand years. Many think that the passage intends a spiritual resurrection, but I am unable to think so; assuredly the words must have a literal meaning. Hear them and judge for yourself. "But the rest of the dead lived not again until the thousand years were finished. This is the first resurrection. Blessed and holy is he that hath part in the first resurrection: on such the second death hath no power, but they shall be priests of God and of Christ, and shall reign with him a thousand years." Yet, granted that there may be this great interval, yet what a mass will be seen when the righteous rise, a "multitude that no man can number"; an inconceivable company only known to God's enumeration shall suddenly start up from "beds of dust and silent clay."

The break of a thousand years shall be as nothing in the sight of God, and shall soon be over, and then shall rise the unjust also. What teeming multitudes! where shall they stand? What plains of Earth shall hold them? Shall they not cover all the solid Earth even to the mountaintops? Shall they not need to use the sea itself as a level floor for God's great assize? Before God in a moment shall they stand when the trump of the archangel shall ring out clear and shrill the summons for the last assize!

And then, bethink you, that this resurrection will not be a mere restoration of what was there, but the resurrection in the case of the saints will involve a remarkable advance upon anything we now observe. We put into the ground a bulb, and it rises as a golden lily; we drop into the mold a seed, and it comes forth an exquisite flower, resplendent with brilliant colors;—these are the same which we put into the earth, the same identically, but oh, how different; even thus, the bodies, which are sown in burial, are so many seeds, and they shall spring up by divine power into outgrowths, surpassing all imagination in beauty. This increases the wonder, for the Lord Jesus not only snatches the prey from between the teeth of the destroyer, but that which had become worm's meat, ashes, dust, He raises in His own sacred image. It is as though a tattered and moth-eaten garment were rent to shreds, and then by a divine word restored to its perfectness, and in addition made whiter than any fuller on Earth could make it, and adorned with costly fringes and embroideries unknown to it before, and all this in a moment of time. Let it stand as a world of wonders, marvelous beyond all things: we will not, for a moment, attempt to explain it away, or pare down the angles of the truth.

One of the difficulties of believing it is this, that there are positively no full analogies in nature by which to support it. There are phenomena around us somewhat like it so that we can compare, but I believe that there is no analogy in nature upon which it would be at all fair to found an argument. For instance, some have said that sleep is the analogy of death, and that our awaking is a sort of resurrection. The figure is admirable, but the analogy is very far from perfect, since in sleep there is still life. A continuance of life is manifest to the man himself in his dreams, and to all onlookers who choose to watch the sleeper, to hear him breathe, or to watch his heart beat. But in death the body has no pulses or other signs of life left in it; it does not even remain entire as the body of the sleeper does. Imagine that the slumberer should be torn limb from limb, pounded in a mortar, and reduced to powder, and that powder mixed up with clay and mold, and then see him awaken at your call, and you would have something worth calling an analogy; but a mere sleep from which a man is startled, while it is an excellent comparison, is far enough from being the counterpart or prophecy of resurrection.

More frequently we hear mentioned the development of insects as a striking analogy. The larva is man in his present condition, the chrysalis is a type of man in his death, and the imago or perfect insect is the representation of man in his resurrection. An admirable simile, certainly, but no more, for there is life in the chrysalis; there is organization, there is, in fact, the entire fly. No observer can mistake the chrysalis for a dead thing; take it up and you shall find everything in it that will come out of it; the perfect creature is evidently dormant there. If you could crush the chrysalis, dry up all its life juices, bruise it into dust, pass it through chemical processes, utterly dissolve it, and then afterwards call it back into a butterfly, you would have seen an analogy of the resurrection; but this is unknown to nature as yet. I find no fault with the picture, it is most instructive and interesting; but to argue from it would be childish to the last degree.

Nor is the analogy of the seed much more conclusive. The seed when put into the ground dies, and yet rises again in due season, hence the apostle uses it as the apt type and emblem of death. He tells us that the seed is not quickened except it die. What is death? Death is the resolution of an organization into its original particles, and so the seed begins to separate into its elements, to fall back from the organization of life into the inorganic state; but still a life germ always remains, and the crumbling organization becomes its food from which it builds itself up again.

Is it so with dead bodies, of which not even a trace remains? Who shall discover a life germ in the putrid corpse? I shall not say there may not be some essential nucleus which better instructed beings might perceive, but I would demand where in the corrupted body it can be supposed to dwell. Is it in the brain? The brain is among the first things to disappear. The skull is empty and void. Is it in the heart? That also has a very brief duration, far briefer than the bones. Nowhere could a microscope discover any vital principle in bodies disinterred from the sod. Turn up the soil wherein the seed is buried, at anytime you will, and you will find it where you placed it, if indeed it will ever rise from the ground; but such is not the case with the man who has been buried a few hundred years; of him the last relic has probably passed beyond all recognition.

The generations to come are not more undiscoverable than those which have gone. Think of those who were buried before the flood, or drowned in that general deluge, where, I ask, have we the smallest remnant of them? Grind your corn or wheat to fine flour, and throw it to the winds, and behold corn fields rising from it, and then you will have a perfect analogy; but as yet I do not think that nature contains a parallel case. The resurrection stands alone; and, concerning it the Lord might well say, "Behold, I do a new thing in the earth." With the exception of the resurrection of our Lord, and those granted to a few persons by miracle, we have nothing in history that can be brought to bear upon the point; nor need we look there for evidence, we have a far surer ground to go upon. Here, then, is the difficulty, and a notable one it is. Can these dry bones live? Is it a credible thing that the dead should be raised?

II. *How are we to meet the demands of the case? We said that in the second place we would remove the difficulty.*

We made no empty boast, the matter is simple. Read the text again with due emphasis, and it is done. "Why should it be thought a thing incredible with you *that* God *should raise the dead*"? It might seem incredible that the dead should be raised, but why should it seem incredible that *God*, the Almighty, the Infinite, should raise the dead? Grant a God, and no difficulties remain. Grant that God is, and that He is omnipotent: grant that He has said the dead shall be raised, and belief is no longer hard but inevitable. Impossibility and incredulity—both vanish in the presence of God. I believe this is the only way in which the difficulties of faith should be met: it is of no use to run to reason for weapons against unbelief, the Word of God is the true defense of faith. It is foolish to build with wood and hay when solid stones may be had. Our logic is, "God has said it," and this is our rhetoric too. If God declares that the dead shall be raised, it is not a thing incredible to us. Difficulty is not in the dictionary of the Godhead. Is anything too hard for the Lord? Heap up the difficulties, if you like, make the doctrine more and more hard for reason to compass, so long as it contains no self-evident contradiction and inconsistency, we rejoice in the opportunity to believe great things concerning a Great God.

When Paul uttered our text he was speaking to a Jew, he was addressing Agrippa, one to whom he could say, "King Agrippa, believest thou the prophets? I know that thou believest!" It was, therefore, good reasoning to use with Agrippa, to say, "Why should it be thought a thing incredible with you that God should raise the dead?" For first, as a Jew, Agrippa had the testimony of Job—

> For I know that my Redeemer liveth, and that he shall stand at the latter day upon the earth: And though after my skin worms destroy this body, yet in my flesh shall I see God: whom I shall see for myself, and mine eyes shall behold, and not another; though my reins be consumed within me.

He had, also, the testimony of David, who, in the sixteenth Psalm, says, "My flesh also shall rest in hope." He had the testimony of Isaiah in the twenty-sixth chapter and the nineteenth verse,

> Thy dead men shall live, together with my dead body shall they arise. Awake and sing, ye that dwell in dust: for thy dew is as the dew of herbs, and the Earth shall cast out the dead.

He had the testimony of Daniel in his twelfth chapter, second and third verses, where the prophet says,

> And many of them that sleep in the dust of the Earth shall awake, some to everlasting life, and some to shame and everlasting contempt. And they that be wise shall shine as the brightness of the firmament; and they that turn many to righteousness as the stars forever and ever.

And then again, in Hosea 13:14, Agrippa had another testimony where the Lord declares,

> I will ransom them from the power of the grave; I will redeem them from death: O death, I will be thy plagues; O grave, I will be thy destruction: repentance shall be hid from mine eyes.

Thus God had plainly promised resurrection in the Old Testament Scriptures, and that fact should be quite enough for Agrippa. If the Lord has said it, it is no longer doubtful.

To us as Christians there has been granted yet fuller evidence. Remember how our Lord has spoken concerning resurrection: with no bated breath has He declared His intention to raise the dead. Remarkable is that passage in John 5:28,

> Marvel not at this: for the hour is coming, in the which all that are in the graves shall hear his voice, and shall come forth; they that have done good, unto the resurrection of life; and they that have done evil, unto the resurrection of damnation.

And so in Chapter 6:40,

> And this is the will of him that sent me, that every one which seeth the Son, and believeth on him, may have everlasting life: and I will raise him up at the last day.

The Holy Ghost has spoken the same truth by the apostles. In that precious and most blessed eighth chapter of the Romans, we have a testimony in the eleventh verse,

> But if the Spirit of him that raised up Jesus from the dead dwell in you, he that raised up Christ from the dead shall also quicken your mortal bodies by his Spirit that dwelleth in you.

I read you just now the passage from the first of Thessalonians, which is very full indeed, where we are bidden not to sorrow as those that are without hope; and you have in the Phillippians the third chapter and twenty-first verse, another proof,

> Who shall change our vile body, that it may be fashioned like unto his glorious body, according to the working whereby he is able even to subdue all things unto himself.

I scarcely need remind you of that grand chapter of massive argument, Corinthians the fifteenth. Beyond all doubt the testimony of the Holy Ghost is that the dead shall rise; and granted that there is an Almighty God, we find no difficulty in accepting the doctrine and entertaining the blessed hope.

At the same time it may be well to look around us, and note what helps the Lord has appointed for our faith. I am quite certain, dear friends, that there are many wonders in the world which we should not have believed by mere report, if we had not come across them by experience and observation. The electric telegraph, though it be but an invention of man, would have been as hard to believe in a thousand years ago as the resurrection of the dead is now. Who in the days of packhorses would have believed in flashing a message from England to America? When our missionaries in tropical countries have told the natives of the formation of ice, and that persons could walk across frozen water, and of ships that have been surrounded by mountains of ice in the open sea, the water becoming solid and hard as a rock all around them, the natives have refused to believe such absurd reports. Everything is wonderful till we are used to it, and resurrection owes the incredible portion of its marvel to the fact of our never having come across it in our observation—that is all. After the resurrection we shall regard it as a divine display of power as familiar to us as creation and providence now are.

Will resurrection be a greater wonder than creation? You believe that God spoke the world out of nothing. He said, "Let it be," and the world was. To create out of nothing is quite as marvelous as to call together scattered particles and refashion them into what they were before. Either work requires omnipotence, but if there be any choice between them, the resurrection is the easier work of the two. If it did not happen so often, the birth of every child into the world would astound us; we should consider a birth to be, as indeed it is, a most transcendent manifestation of divine power. It is only because we know it and see it so commonly that we do not behold the wonder working hand of God in human births and in our continued existence. The thing, I say, only staggers us because we have not become familiar with it as yet: there are other deeds of God which are quite as marvelous.

Remember, too, that there is one thing which, though you have not seen, you have received on credible evidence, which is a part of historic truth, namely, that Jesus Christ rose again from the dead. He is to you the cause of your resurrection, the type of it, the foretaste of it, the guarantee of it. As surely as He rose you shall rise. He proved the resurrection possible by rising, nay, He proved it certain because He is the representative man; and, in rising, He rose for all who are represented by Him. "As in Adam all die, even so in Christ shall all be made alive." The rising of our Lord from the tomb should forever sweep away every doubt as to the rising of His people. "For if the dead rise not, then is Christ not raised," but because He lives, we shall live also.

Remember also, my brethren and sisters, that you who are Christians have already experienced within yourselves as great a work as the resurrection, for you have risen from the dead as to your innermost nature. You were dead in trespasses and sins, and you have been quickened into newness of life. Of course the unconverted here will see nothing in this. The unregenerate man will even ask me what this means, and to him it can be no argument, for it is a matter of experience which one man cannot explain to his fellow. To know it ye must yourselves be born again. But, believers, ye have already passed through a resurrection from the grave of sin, and from the rottenness and corruption of evil passions and impure desires, and this resurrection God has wrought in you by a power equal to that which He wrought in Christ when He raised Him from the dead, and set Him at His own right hand in the heavenly places. To you the quickening of your spiritual nature is an assured proof that the Lord will also quicken your mortal bodies.

The whole matter is this, that our persuasion of the certainty of the general resurrection rests upon faith in God and His word. It is both idle and needless to look elsewhere. If men will not believe the declaration of God, they must be left to give an account to Him of their unbelief. My hearer, if thou art one of God's elect, thou wilt believe thy God, for God gives faith to all His chosen. If thou dost reject the divine testimony, thou givest evidence that thou art in the gall of bitterness, and thou wilt perish in it unless grace prevents. The gospel and the doctrine of the resurrection were opened up to men in all their glory to put a division between the precious and the vile. "He that is of God," saith the apostle, "heareth God's words." True faith is the visible mark of secret election. He that believeth in Christ gives evidence of God's grace towards him, but he that believes not gives sure proof that he has not received the grace of God. "But ye believe not," said Christ, "because ye are not of my sheep, as I said unto you. My sheep hear my voice, and I know them, and they follow me." Therefore this truth and other Christian truths are to be held up, maintained, and delivered fully to the whole of mankind to put a division between them, to separate the Israelites from the Egyptians, the seed of the woman from the seed of the serpent. Those whom God has chosen are known by their believing in what God has said; while those who remain unbelieving perish in their sin, condemned by the truth which they willfully reject.

III. Thus much upon these points. Now let us consider, lastly, our relation to this truth.

Our first relation to this truth is this: Children of God, comfort one another with these words. You have lost those dear to you;—amend the statement—they have passed into a better land, and the body which remains behind is not lost, but put out to blessed interest. Sorrow ye must, but sorrow not as those that are without hope. I do not know why we always sing dirges at the funerals of the saints, and drape ourselves in black. I would desire, if I might have my way, to be drawn to my grave by white horses, or to be carried on the shoulders of men who would express joy as well as sorrow in their habiliments, for why should we sorrow over those who have gone to glory, and inherited immortality?

I like the old Puritan plan of carrying the coffin on the shoulders of the saints, and singing a psalm as they walked to the grave. Why not? What is there, after all, to weep about concerning the glorified? Sound the gladsome trumpet! Let the shrill clarion peal out the joyous note of victory! The conqueror has won the battle; the king has climbed to His throne. "Rejoice," say our brethren from above, "rejoice with us, for we have entered into our rest." "Blessed are the dead which die in the Lord from henceforth: yea, saith the Spirit, that they may rest from their labors and their works do follow them." If we must keep up the signs of woe, for this is natural, yet let not your hearts be troubled, for that were unspiritual. Bless God evermore that over the pious dead we sing His living promises.

Let us, in the next place, cheer our hearts in prospect of our own departure. We shall soon pass away. My brethren, we too must die; there is no discharge in this war. There is an arrow and there is an archer; the arrow is meant for my heart, and the archer will take deadly aim. There is a place where you shall sleep, perhaps in a lone grave in a foreign land; or, perhaps, in a niche where your bones shall lie side by side with those of your ancestors; but to the dust return you must. Well, let us not repine, it is but for a little, it is but a rest on the way to immortality. Death is a passing incident between this life and the next—let us meet it not only with equanimity, but with expectation, since it is not death now but resurrection to which we aspire.

Then again: are we expecting a blessed resurrection? Let us respect our bodies. Let not our members become instruments of evil, let them not be defiled with sin. The Christian man must neither by gluttony nor drunkenness, nor by acts of uncleanness, in any way whatever defile his body, for our bodies are the temples of the Holy Ghost. "If any man defile that temple of God, him will God destroy." Be ye pure. In your baptism, your bodies were washed with pure water to teach you that henceforth ye must be clean from all defilement. Put away from you every evil thing. Bodies that are to dwell forever in Heaven, should not be subjected to pollution here below.

Lastly, and this is a very solemn thought, the ungodly are to rise again, but it will be to a resurrection of woe. Their bodies sinned and their bodies will be punished. "Fear him," says Christ, "who is able to destroy both soul and body in Hell." He will cast both of them into a suffering which shall cause perpetually enduring destruction to them; this is terrible indeed. To slumber in the grave would be infinitely preferable to such a resurrection—"the resurrection of damnation," so the Scripture calls it; a rising "to shame and everlasting contempt," so Daniel styles it. That is a dreadful resurrection, indeed; you might be glad to escape from it. Surely it were dreadful enough for your soul to suffer the wrath of God eternally without the body having to be its companion, but so it must be; if body and soul sin, body and soul must suffer, and that forever.

Jeremy Taylor tells us of a certain Acilius Aviola who was seized with an apoplexy, and his friends conceiving him to be dead carried him to his funeral pile, but, when the heat had warmed his body, he awoke to find himself hopelessly encircled with funeral flames. In vain he called for deliverance, he could not be rescued, but passed from torpor into intolerable torment. Such will be the dreadful awakening of every sinful body when it shall be aroused from its slumber in the grave. The body will start up to be judged, condemned, and driven from God's presence into everlasting punishment. May God grant that it may never be your case or mine, but may we believe in Christ Jesus now, and so obtain a resurrection to life eternal. Amen.

A Visit to the Tomb

"He is not here: for he is risen, as he said. Come see
the place where the Lord lay."—Matthew 28:6.

The holy women, Mary Magdalene and the other Mary, came to the sepulcher, hoping to find there the body of their Lord, which they intended to embalm. Their intention was good; their will was accepted before God; but, for all that, their desire was not gratified, for the simple reason that it was contrary to God's design: it was at variance with even what Christ had foretold and plainly declared to them. "He is not here; for he is risen, *as he said.*" I gather from this, that there may be good desires in our hearts as believers, and we may earnestly try to carry them out, and yet we may never succeed in them, because through our ignorance we have not understood, or through our obliviousness we have happened to forget, some word of Christ that stands in our way.

I have known this to be the case in prayer. We have prayed, and we have not received, because we had no warrant in the word of God to ask the thing we did. Peradventure there was some prohibition in the Scriptures, which ought to have restrained us from offering the prayer. We have thought in our daily life, amidst the pursuits of business, that if we could gain such and such a position, then we should honor God; yet though we have sought it vigorously, and prayed about it earnestly, we have never gained it. God had never intended that we should; and, had we succeeded in compassing our own project, it might have been evil rather than advantageous, an entail of trouble instead of a heritage of joy. We were seeking great things for ourselves, we forgot that expostulation of the Lord, "Seekest thou great things for thyself? Seek them not." Do not, therefore, expect to realize all those desires which seem to you to be pure and proper. They may not happen to run in the right channel. It may be that there is a word from the Lord that forbids your ever seeing them brought to pass.

These good women found that they had lost the presence of Him Who had been their greatest delight. "He is not here," must have sounded like a funeral knell to them. They expected to find Him: He was gone. But then the grief must have been taken out of their hearts when it was added, "He is risen." I gather from this, that if God takes away from me any one good thing, He will be sure to justify Himself in having so done, and that very frequently He will magnify His grace by giving me something infinitely better. Did Mary think it would be a good thing to find the dead body of her Lord? Perhaps it would have given her a kind of melancholy satisfaction. So she thought, according to her poor judgment. The Lord took that good thing away. But then Christ was risen, and now to hear of Him, then presently to see Him, was not that an infinitely better thing?

Hast thou lost anything of late around which thy heart had intertwisted all its tendrils? Thou shalt find that there is good cause for the privation. The Lord never takes away a silver blessing without intending to confer on us a golden gain. Depend upon it, for wood He will give iron, and for iron He will give brass, and for brass He will give silver, and for silver He will give gold. All His takings are but preliminaries to larger giving. Hast thou lost thy child? What if thou find thy Lord more dear than ever? One smile of thy Lord will be better to thee than all the cheerful frolics of thy child. Is He not better to thee than ten sons? Hast thou lost the familiar companion who once cheered thee along the vale of life? Thou shalt now by that loss be driven closer to thy Savior; His promises shall be more sweet to thee, and the Blessed Spirit shall reveal His truth more clearly to thee. Thou shalt be a gainer by thy loss.

"He is not here"—that is sorrowful. But, "He is risen"—this is gladsome. Christ, the dead one, thou canst not see. Thou canst not tenderly embalm that blessed body. But Christ, the living one, thou shalt see; and at His feet thou shalt be able to prostrate thyself; and from His lips thou shalt hear the gladsome words, "Go, tell my brethren that I am risen from the dead." That lesson may be worth your remembering. If God apply it to your soul it may yield you rich comfort. Should the Lord take away one joy from you, He will give you another and a better one. "He doth not afflict willingly, nor grieve the children of men." You never deny your children any pure gratification, I am sure, without intending their real good. How many of you have a way, when you put your child to a little self-denial, of making it up to him again so that he is no loser by it. And your heavenly Father will deal quite as gently and tenderly with you his children.

The text contains, first, *an assurance;* and secondly, *an invitation.* First, an assurance: "He is not here, for he is risen;" secondly, an invitation: "Come, see the place where the Lord lay."

I. The assurance: "He is not here, for he is risen."

Jesus Christ has really *risen from the dead.* There is, probably, no fact in history which is so fully proven and corroborated as the fact that Jesus of Nazareth, who was nailed to the cross, and died, and was buried, did rise again. As we believe the histories of Julius Caesar—as we accept the statements of Tacitus—we are bound on the same grounds, even as historical documents, to accept the testimony of Matthew, and Mark, and Luke, and John, and of those persons who were eye witnesses of His death, and who saw Him after He had risen from the dead.

That Jesus Christ rose from the dead is not an allegory and a symbol, but it is a reality. There He lay dead, friend or foe to witness—a corpse fit to be committed to the grave. Handle Him, and see. It is the very Christ you knew in life. It is the very same. Look into those eyes. Were there ever such eyes in any other human form? Behold Him! You can see the impress of sorrow on His face. Was there ever any visage so marred as His, any sorrow so real in its effects? That is the Emperor of Misery, the Prince of all Mourners, the King of Sorrow! There He lies, unmistakably the same. Now, mark the nail prints. There went the iron through those blessed hands; and there His feet were pierced; and there is the gash that found out the pericardium, and divided the heart, and brought forth the marvelous blood and water from His side. It is He, the selfsame Christ! And the holy women lift limb by limb, and wrap Him in linen, and put the spices about Him, such as they had brought in their haste, and they lay Him down in that place—in that new tomb.

Now, let it be known and understood that our faith is that those very limbs that lay stiff and cold in death became warm with life again—that the very body which lay there, became again instinct with life, and came forth into a glorious existence. Those hands broke the piece of honeycomb and the fish in the presence of the disciples; and those lips partook thereof; and He held out those wounds and said, "Reach hither thy finger, and put it into the print of the nails"; and He bared His side, the selfsame side, and said, "Reach hither thy hand, and thrust it into my side; and be not faithless, but believing." He was no phantom, no specter. As He Himself said, "A spirit hath not flesh and bones as ye see me have." He was real man, as much after the resurrection as He had been before;

and He is real man in glory now, even as He was when here below. He has gone up: the cloud has received Him out of our sight.

The selfsame Christ who said unto Peter, "Lovest thou me?"—the self-same Jesus who said to His disciples, "Come and dine,"—a real man has really risen from a real death into a real life. Now, we always want to have that doctrine stated to us plainly, for though we believe it we do not always realize it; and even if we have realized it, it is good to hear it again, so as to let our minds be confirmed about it. The resurrection is as literal a fact as any other fact stated in history, and is so to be believed among us. "He is not here: for he has risen."

Pursue the narrative, beloved, and you will see that when our Lord Jesus Christ had risen on that occasion, being quickened from the slumbers of death, it was not only true that He had really risen from the sepulcher, but He had risen in order to ascend to a higher place. He now possesses that position of glory at the right hand of the Father. When He had burst the iron bonds of the grave, the disciples had this for their consolation—that He was now beyond the reach of His enemies. They could hurt Him no more. And it is so now.

He is not here, in another sense; and He is now beyond the reach of all His malignant adversaries. Does not this cheer you? It does me. No Judas can betray the Master now to be seized by Roman guards. No Pilate can now take Him and suborn justice and give Him over to be crucified, though he knows Him to be innocent. No Herod can now mock Him with his men of war: no soldiery can now spit in His dear face. Now none can buffet Him, or blindfold Him, and say unto Him, "Prophesy who it is that smote thee." The head, the dear majestic head, of Jesus can never now be crowned with thorns again, and the busy feet that ran on errands of mercy can never be pierced by the nails any more. Men shall no longer strip Him naked, and stand and exult over His agonies. He is gone beyond their reach.

Now they may rail and seek to spite Him through His people, who are the members of His body. Now they may rage; but God has set Him at His own right hand, and He is inaccessible to their malice. Oh, blessed are those words, and blessed was the pen that wrote them, and blessed was the Spirit who dictated them—

> Wherefore God also hath highly exalted him, and given him a name which is above every name; that at the name of Jesus every knee should bow, of things in Heaven, and things in earth, and things under the earth; and that every tongue should confess that Jesus is Lord to the glory of God the Father.

With regard to our Lord's not being here, but having risen, it should console us to think that He is now beyond all pain, as well as beyond all personal attack. Oh, can you bear to think of Him, that He had no where to lay His head? Who among us would not have left his couch to give Him a night's rest?—aye, and have forsworn the bed forever if we might have given Him soft repose. Would we not ourselves have taken to the hillside, and been there all night, till our head was wet with dew, if we might have gained rest for Him? He is worth ten thousand of us; and did it not seem as if it were too much for Him to have to suffer—to be homeless and houseless? He hungered, brethren; He was athirst; He was weary; he was faint. He suffered our sicknesses: we are told that He took them upon Himself. Often had He the heartache. He knew what "cold mountains and the midnight air" were to chill the body; and He knew what the bleak atmosphere and bitter privation were to freeze the soul. He passed through innumerable griefs and woes.

From the first blood-shedding at His birth, down to the last blood-shedding at His death, it seemed as if sorrow had marked Him as her peculiar child. Always was He troubled, tempted, vexed, assailed, assaulted, molested, by Satan, by wicked men, and by the evils that are without! Now there is no more of that for Him; and we are glad that He is not here for that reason. He is no child of poverty now; no carpenter's shop for Him now; no smockfrock of the peasant, woven from the top throughout, now; no mountain-side and heather for His resting place now; no jeering crowds around Him now; no stones taken up to stone Him now; no sitting on the well, weary, and saying, "Give me to drink"; no needing that He should be supplied with food when He is hungry. Now no more can there be any scourgings and flagellations. No more will He give "his back to the smiters, and his cheeks to them that plucked off the hair." No piercing His hands and His feet now; no burning thirst upon the bloody tree; no cry of *"Eloi, Eloi, lama sabacthani."*

God's waves and billows went over Him once, but no more can they assail Him. He was brought into the dust of death, and His soul was exceeding sorrowful once. He is beyond all that. The sea is passed, and He has come to the Fair Havens, where no storms can beat upon Him. He has reached His joy; He has entered into His rest; and He has received His reward. Brethren and sisters, let us be glad about this. Let us enter into the joy of our Lord. Let us be glad, because He is glad—happy, because He is happy. Oh, that we might feel our hearts leaping within us, though we for a little while longer are on the field of battle, because He is clean gone from it, and now is acknowledged and adored King of kings and Lord of lords.

The fact that our Lord has risen has not only these consoling elements about it, with reference to Him, but we must remember that it is the guarantee, to every one of us who believe in Him, of our own resurrection. The apostle, in the first epistle to the Corinthians, makes the whole argument for the resurrection of the body hinge upon this one question—did Christ rise from the dead? If He did, then all His people must rise with Him. He was a representative man, and as the Lord the Savior rose, so all His followers must. Settle the question that Christ rose, and you have settled the question that all who are in Him, and conformed to His image, must rise too.

That body of the dear child of God to which you bade farewell some years ago, shall rise again. Those eyes that you closed—those very eyes—shall see the King in His beauty in the land that is very far off. Those ears that could not hear you when you spoke the last tender word—those ears shall hear the eternal melodies. That heart that grew stone cold and still, when death laid his cold hand upon the bosom, shall beat again with newness of life, and leap with joy amidst the festivities of the home-bringing, when Christ the Bridegroom shall be married to His church, the bride.

That selfsame body!—Was it not the temple of the Holy Ghost? Was it not redeemed with blood? Surely it shall rise at the trump of the arch-angel and at the voice of God! Be thou sure of this: be thou sure of it—sure for thy friend and sure for thyself. And fear not death. What is it? The grave is but a bath wherein our body, like Esther, buries itself in spices to make it sweet and fresh for the embrace of the glorious King in immortality. It is but the wardrobe where we lay aside the garment for a while. It shall come forth cleansed and purified, with many a golden spangle on it which was not there before. It was a work-day dress when we put it off; it will be a Sabbath robe when we put it on, and it will be fit for Sabbath wear. We may even long for evening to undress, if there is to be such a waking and such a putting on of garments in the presence of the King.

Further—not to linger too long on any one thought—let us remember that our Lord's not being here, but having risen, has in it this consolatory thought, that He has gone where He can best protect our interests. He is an advocate for us. Where should the advocate be but in the King's court? He is preparing a place for us. Where should He be who is preparing a place, but there—making it ready? We have a very active adversary, who is busy accusing us. Is it not well that we have one who can meet him face to face, and put the accuser of the brethren to silence? He would be precious here, but He is more precious there. He is doing more for us in Heaven, than it could have been possible for Him to do for us here below, as far as our finite intelligence can judge, and as truly as His infinite wisdom can pronounce. Meanwhile His absence is well compensated by the presence of His own Spirit; and His presence there is well consecrated by His personal administration of sacred service for our sake. All is well in Heaven, for Jesus is there. The crown is safe, and the harp is secure, and the blessed heritage of each tribe of Israel all secure, for Christ is keeping it. He is, to the glory of God, the representative and preserver of His saints.

And does not this truth, that Christ is not here, but is gone, fall upon our ears with a sweet force as it constrains us to feel that this is the reason why our heart should not be here? "He is not here": then our heart should not be here. When this text, "He is not here," was first spoken, it meant that He was not in the grave. He was somewhere on Earth then. But now He is not here at all. Suppose you are very rich, and Satan whispers to you, "These are delightful gardens; this is a noble mansion; take thine ease"—reply to him, "But *He* is not here; He is not here, He is risen; therefore I dare not put my heart where my Lord is not." Or, suppose thy family make thee very happy, and, as the little ones cluster around thee and sit around the fireside, thy heart is very glad; and though thou hast not much of this world's goods, yet thou hast enough, and thou hast a contented mind. Well, if Satan should say to thee, "Be well content, and make thy rest here," say to him, "No, *He* is not here; and I cannot feel that this is to be my abiding place. Only where Jesus is can my spirit rest." And have you lately started in life? Has the marriage day scarcely passed over? Are you just now beginning the merry days of youth, the sweet enchantment of this life's purest joy? Well, delight thyself therein, but still remember that *He* is not here, and therefore thou hast no right to say, "Soul, take thine ease!" Nowhere on Earth is Christ, and therefore nowhere on Earth may our heart build her nest. Oh, get thee up, my soul; get thee up, and let all thy sweetest incense go towards Him who "is not here, for He is risen."

II. I must leave that point, and come with a few words to speak upon the second point, which is an invitation. "Come, see the place where the Lord lay."

Not, beloved, that I am going to take you to Joseph of Arimathea's tomb. About that I shall not speak much. But I think any tomb might suffice to point the same sacred moral. In the little town of Campodolcini I once realized the tomb of Christ very vividly, in an affair which had been built for Catholic pilgrims. I was up on the hillside, and I saw written upon a wall these words, "And there was a garden." It was written in Latin. I pushed open the door of this garden. It was like any other garden; but the moment I entered there was a hand, with the words, "And in the garden there was a new tomb." Then I saw a tomb which had been newly painted, and when I came up to it I read thereon, "A new tomb wherein never man lay." I then stooped down to look inside the tomb, and I read in Latin the inscription, "Stooping down, he looked, yet went he not in." But there were the words written, "Come, see the place where the Lord lay." I went in, and I saw there, graven in stone, the napkin and the linen clothes laid by themselves. I was all alone, and I read the words, "He is not here, for he is risen," graven on the floor of the tomb. Though I dread anything scenic and histrionic and popish, yet certainly I realized very much the reality of the scene. I felt that Jesus Christ was really buried, really laid in the earth, and has really gone out of it, and it is good for us to come and see the place where Jesus lay.

Why should we see it?

Well, first, that we may see how condescending He was that ever He should lay in the grave. He that made Heaven and earth, lay in the grave. He who gave light to angels' eyes, lay in the darkness three days. He slept in the darkness there. He without whom was not anything made that was made, was given up to death, and lay a victim of death there. Oh, wonder of wonders! Marvel of marvels! He, who had immortality and life within Himself, yields Himself up to the place of death!

"Come, see the place where the Lord lay," in the next place, to see how we ought to weep over the sin that laid Him there. Did I make the Savior lie in the grave? Was it needful that before my sin could be put away, my sweet Prince, whose beauties enchant all Heaven, must be chill and cold in death, and actually be laid in the tomb? Must it be so? O ye murderous sins! Ye murderous sins! Ye cruel and cursed sins! Did ye slay my Savior? Did ye find out that tender heart? Could ye never be content until you had led Him to His death, and laid Him there? Oh, come and weep, as you see the place where the Lord lay.

"Come, see the place where the Lord lay," that you may see where you will have to lie, unless the Lord should come on a sudden. You may take the measure of that tomb, for that is where you will have to repose. It does us good to recollect, if we have great landed estates, that six feet of Earth is all that will ever be our permanent freehold. We shall have to come to it—that solitary mound, with two spears length of level ground:

> *Princes, this clay must be your bed,*
> *In spite of all your towers;*
> *The tall, the wise, the reverent head*
> *Must lie as low as ours.*

There is no discharge in this war. To the dust return we must. So "Come, see the place where the Lord lay"; to see that, thou must lie there too.

But then, "Come, see the place where the Lord lay," to see what good company thou wilt have there. That is where Jesus lay: doth not that comfort thee?

Why should the Christian fear the day
That lands him in the tomb;
There the dear flesh of Jesus lay,
And left a long perfume.

What more appropriate chamber for a prince's son to go to sleep in than the prince's own tomb? There slept Emmanuel. There, my body, thou mayest be well content to sleep too! What more royal couch canst thou desire than the bosom of that same mother earth, whereon the Savior was laid to rest awhile? Think, beloved, of the ten thousand saints that have gone that way to Heaven. Who shall dread to go where all the flock have gone? Thou one poor timid sheep, if thou alone hadst to go through this dark valley, thou mightest well be afraid; but, oh, in addition to thy Shepherd, who marches at the head of all the flock, listen to the footsteps of the innumerable sheep that follow Him. And some were very dear to thee, and fed in the same pasture with thee. Dost thou dread to go where they have gone? No; see the place where Jesus lay, to see what good company is to be had, though it may seem to be in a dark chamber.

"Come, see the place where the Lord lay," to see that thou canst not lie there long. It is not the place where Jesus *is.* He is gone, and thou art to be with Him where He is. Come and look at this tomb. There is no door to it. There *was* one; it was a huge rock, a monstrous stone, and none could move it. It was sealed. Seest thou not how they have set the stamp of the Sanhedrim, the stamp of the law, upon the seal, to make it sure, that none should move it?

But now, if thou wilt go to the place where Jesus lay, the seal is broken, the guards are fled, the stone is gone. Such will thy tomb be. It is true they will cover thee up, and lay on the sods of green turf. If thou art wise thou wilt prefer these things to the heavy slabs of stone they sometimes lay upon the dead. That sweet mound, with here and there a daisy, like the eye of Earth looking up to Heaven asking mercy, or smiling in joy of expectation—there, there wilt thou sleep; but just as in the morning thou dost but open thine eyes and the curtains are updrawn, and thou comest forth, none standing in thy way, to do the labor of the day, so, when the trump of the resurrection sounds, thou wilt rise out of thy bed in perfect liberty, none hindering thee, to see the light of the day that shall go no more down forever. You have nothing to confine you. Bolt and bar there are none: guard and watchman none; stone and seal none. "Come, see the place where Jesus lay." I would not care to go to bed in a prison, where there stood a turnkey with his iron key to fasten me in. But I am not afraid to go to sleep in the chamber out of which I can come at the morning's call a perfectly free man! And such art thou, beloved, if thou be a believer. Thou comest to lie in a place that is open and free—a fit slumbering-place for the Lord's free men.

"Come, see the place where the Lord lay," in order to celebrate the triumph over death. If Miriam sang at the Red Sea we also may sing at Jesus' tomb. If she said, "Sing unto the Lord, for he hath triumphed gloriously," shall not we say the same? If all the hosts of Israel went out with her, the women with dances, and the strong men with their voices, in the song, so let all Israel go forth this day, and bless and praise the Lord, saying, "O death, where is thy sting? O grave, where is thy victory?" The place where Jesus lay has told us that

> Vain the watch, the stone, the seal!
> Christ hath burst the gates of Hell.

Now let us sing unto Him, and give Him all the praise.

I was thinking to say to you, beloved, let us come and see the place where Jesus lay, to weep there for our sins; let us come and see the place where Jesus lay, to die there to our sins; let us come and see the place where Jesus lay, to be buried there with Him; let us come and see the place where Jesus lay, to rise from that place to newness of life, and find our way through resurrection-life into the ascension-life in which we shall sit in the heavenly place, and look down upon the things of Earth with joyous contempt, knowing that He hath lifted us up far above them, and made us to be partakers of brighter bliss than this Earth can ever know. But I will forbear.

I have done. I would to God that all here present had some share in this. You all have a share in dying. There is a tree growing out of which your coffin will be made; or perhaps it is already cut down and seasoning against the time when it shall make you a timber-suit—the last suit that you shall ever need. There is a spot of Earth that must be shoveled out for you to be laid into to fill up the vacuum. And your soul shall live: your soul shall never die. Let not those who tell you of annihilation be believed for a moment. It must exist. Put it to yourself whether it shall be with the worm that never dieth and the fire that never shall be quenched, or with Christ who liveth in His glory, and who shall come a second time to give glory to His people and raise their bodies like His own. Oh, it will all hinge on this—"Dost thou believe in Jesus?" If thou dost, thou mayest welcome life and welcome death, and welcome resurrection, and welcome immortality. But if thou believest not, then a blast has come upon thee, and to thee it is terrible to die. It is terrible even to live; more terrible to die; it will be terrible to rise again; it will be terrible to be damned, and that forever! God save thee from it, for Christ's sake! Amen.

"The Lord Is Risen Indeed"

"Why seek ye the living among the dead? He is not here, but is risen: remember how he spake unto you when he was yet in Galilee."—Luke 24:5, 6.

The first day of the week commemorates the resurrection of Christ, and, following apostolical example, we have made the first day of the week to be our Sabbath. Does not this intimate to us that the rest of our souls is to be found in the resurrection of our Savior? Is it not true that a clear understanding of the rising again of our Lord is, through the power of the Holy Spirit, the very surest means of bringing our minds into peace? To have a part in the resurrection of Christ is to enjoy that Sabbath which remaineth for the people of God. We who have believed in the risen Lord do enter into rest, even as He also Himself is resting at the right hand of the Father. In Him we rest because His work is finished, His resurrection being the pledge that He has perfected all that is needful for the salvation of His people, and we are complete in Him. I trust this morning that some restful thoughts may, by the power of the Holy Spirit, be sown in the minds of believers while we make a pilgrimage to the new tomb of Joseph of Arimathea, and see the place where the Lord lay.

I. And, first, this morning I will speak to you upon certain instructive memories which gather around the place where Jesus slept "with the rich in his death."

Though He is not there, He assuredly once was there: for "He was crucified, dead, and buried." He was as dead as the dead now are, and though He could see no corruption, nor could be holden by the bands of death beyond the predestined time, yet He was in very deed most assuredly dead. No light remained in His eye, no life in His heart; thought had fled from His thorn-crowned brow, and speech from His golden mouth;

He was not in mere appearance, but in reality dead—the spear-thrust decided that question once for all; therefore in the sepulcher they laid Him, a dead man, fit occupant of the silent tomb. Yet as He is not there now, but is risen, it is for us to search for memorials of His having been there. Not for the "holy sepulcher" will we contend with superstitious sectaries [religious non-conformists], but in spirit we will gather up the precious relics of the risen Redeemer.

First, He has left in the grave *the spices*. When He rose He did not bring away the costly aromatics in which His body had been wrapped, but He left them there. Joseph brought about one hundred pounds weight of myrrh and aloes, and the odor remaineth still. In the sweetest spiritual sense, our Lord Jesus has filled the grave with fragrance. It no longer smells of corruption and foul decay, but we can sing with the poet of the sanctuary

> *Why should we tremble to convey*
> *These bodies to the tomb?*
> *There the dear flesh of Jesus lay,*
> *And left a long perfume.*

Yonder lowly bed in the Earth is now perfumed with costly spices and decked with sweet flowers, for on its pillow the truest Friend we have once laid His holy head. We will not start back with horror from the chambers of the dead, for the Lord Himself has traversed them, and where He goes no terror abides.

The Master also left His *grave-clothes* behind Him. He did not come from the tomb wrapped about with a winding-sheet; He did not wear the cerements of the tomb as the habiliments of life, but when Peter went into the sepulcher he saw the grave-clothes lying carefully folded by themselves. What if I say He left them to be the hangings of the royal bed-chamber wherein His saints fall asleep? See how He has curtained our last bed! Our dormitory is no longer bare and drear, like a prison cell, but hung around with fair white linen and comely arras—a chamber fit for the repose of princes of the blood! We will go to our last bed-chamber in peace, because Christ has furnished it for us. Or if we change the metaphor, I may say that our Lord has left those grave-clothes for us to look upon as pledges of His fellowship with us in our low estate, and reminders that as He has cast aside the death garments, even so shall we. He has risen from His couch and left His sleeping robes behind Him, in token that at our waking there are other vestures ready for us also.

What if I again change the figure, and say that as we have seen old tattered flags hung up in cathedrals and other national buildings, as the memorials of defeated enemies and victories won, so in the crypt where Jesus vanquished death His grave clothes are hung up as the trophies of His victory over death, and as assurances to us that all His people shall be more than conquerors through Him that hath loved them. "O death, where is thy sting? O grave, where is thy victory?"

Then, carefully folded up and laid by itself, our Lord left *the napkin* that was about His head. Yonder lies that napkin now. The Lord wanted it not when He came forth to life. Ye who mourn may use it as a handkerchief with which to dry your eyes. Ye widows and ye fatherless children—ye mourning brothers and ye weeping sisters—and you, ye Rachels, who will not be comforted because your children are not; here, take you this which wrapped your Savior's face, and wipe your tears away forever. The Lord is risen indeed, and therefore thus saith the Lord, "Refrain thy voice from weeping, and thine eyes from tears, for they shall come again from the land of the enemy," "Thy dead men shall live," O mourner—together, with the Lord's dead body, shall they arise; wherefore, sorrow not as they that are without hope, for if ye believe that Jesus died and rose again, even so them also, which sleep in Jesus, will the Lord bring with Him.

What else has the risen Savior left behind Him? Our faith has learned to gather up memorials sweet from the couch of our Lord's tranquil slumber. Well, beloved, He left *angels* behind Him, and thus made the grave

> *A cell where angels use*
> *To come and go with heavenly news.*

Angels were not in the tomb before, but, at His resurrection, they descended; one rolled away the stone, and others sat where the body of Jesus had lain. They were the personal attendants and bodyguard of the Great Prince, and therefore they attended Him at His rising, keeping the doorway, and answering the enquiries of His friends. Angels are full of life and vigor, but they did not hesitate to assemble at the grave, gracing the resurrection even as flowers adorn the spring. I read not that our Master has ever recalled the angels from the sepulcher of His saints; and now, if believers die as poor as Lazarus, and as sick and as despised as he, angels shall convey their souls into the bosom of their Lord, and their bodies, too, shall be watched by guardian spirits, as surely as Michael kept the body of Moses and contended for it with the foe. Angels are both the servitors of living saints and the custodians of their dust.

What else did our Well-beloved leave behind Him? He left *an open passage* from the tomb, for the stone was rolled away; doorless is that house of death. We shall, in our turn, if the Master come not speedily, descend into the prison-house of the grave. What did I say?—I called it a "prison-house," but how a prison-house, that hath no bolts or bars?—how a prison-house, that hath not even a door to close upon its occupants? Our Samson has pulled up the posts and carried away the gates of the grave with all their bars. The key is taken from the girdle of death and is held in the hand of the Prince of Life. The broken signal and the fainting watchmen are tokens that the dungeons of death can no more confine their captives. As Peter, when he was visited by the angel, found his chains fall from off him, while iron gates opened to him of their own accord, so shall the saints find ready escape at the resurrection morning. They shall sleep awhile, each one in his resting-place, but they shall rise readily, for the stone is rolled away. A mighty angel rolled away the stone, for it was very great, and when he had done the deed he sat down upon the stone. His garment was white as snow, and his face like lightning, and as he sat on the stone he seemed to say to death and Hell, "Roll it back again if you can."

> *Who shall rebuild for the tyrant his prison!*
> *The scepter lies broken that fell from his hands;*
> *His dominion is ended, the Lord is arisen;*
> *The helpless shall soon be released from their bands.*

One thing else I venture to mention as left by my Lord in His forsaken tomb. I visited some few months ago several of the large columbaria which are to be found outside the gates of Rome. You enter a large square building, sunk in the earth, and descend by many steps, and as you descend you observe on the four sides of the great chamber, innumerable little pigeon-holes, in which are the ashes of tens of thousands of departed persons. Usually in front of each compartment prepared for the reception of the ashes stands *a lamp*. I have seen hundreds, if not thousands, of these lamps, but they are all unlit, and indeed do not appear ever to have carried light: they shed no ray upon the darkness of death. But now our Lord has gone into the tomb and illuminated it with His presence, "the lamp of His love is our guide through the gloom." Jesus has brought life and immortality to light by the gospel; and now in the dove-cotes where Christians nestle, there is light; yea, in every cemetery there is a light which shall burn through the watches of earth's night till the day break and the shadows flee away, and the resurrection morn shall dawn.

So then the empty tomb of the Savior leaves us many sweet reflections, which we will treasure up for our instruction.

II. Our text expressly speaks of vain searches: "Why seek ye the living among the dead? He is not here, but is risen."

There are places where seekers after Jesus should not expect to find Him, however diligent may be their search, however sincere their desire. You cannot find a man where he is not, and there are some spots where Christ never will be discovered.

At this present moment I see many searching for Christ among the monuments of *ceremonialism,* or what Paul called "the weak and beggarly elements," for they "observe days and months and times and years." Ever since our Lord arose, Judaism and every form of symbolic ceremony have become nothing better than sepulchers. The types were of God's own ordaining, but when the substance had come, the types became empty sepulchers and nothing more. Since that time men have invented other symbols, which have not even the sanction of Divine authority, and are only dead men's graves. He Himself declared, "Neither in this mountain nor yet at Jerusalem shall men worship the Father, but the hour cometh, and now is, when the true worshipers shall worship the Father in spirit and in truth, for the Father seeketh such to worship him." Jesus has rent the veil and abolished ceremonial worship, and yet men seek to revive it, building up the sepulchers which the Lord has broken down.

Alas! there are many others who are seeking Christ as their Savior among the tombs of *moral reformation.* Our Lord likened the Pharisees to white-washed sepulchers; inwardly they were full of dead men's bones, but outwardly they were fairly garnished. Oh, the way in which men, when they get uneasy about their souls, try to white-wash themselves. Some one gross sin is given up, not in heart, but only in appearance, and a certain virtue is cultivated not in the soul, but only in the outward act, and thus they hope to be saved, though they still remain enemies to God, lovers of sin, and greedy seekers after the wages of unrighteousness. They hope that the clean outside of the cup and the platter will satisfy the Most High, and that He will not be so severe as to look within and try their hearts.

O, Sirs, why seek ye the living among the dead? Many have sought peace for their consciences by their moral reforms, but if the Holy Spirit has truly convinced them of sin, they have soon found that they were looking for a living Christ amidst the tombs. He is not here, for He is risen. If Christ were dead, we might well say to you, "Go and do your best to be your own Saviors," but while Christ is alive, He wants no help of yours—He will save you from top to bottom, or not at all. He will be Alpha and Omega to you, and if you put your hand upon His work, and think in any way that you can help Him, you have dishonored His holy name, and He will have nothing to do with you. Seek not a living salvation amongst the sepulchers of outward formality.

Too many also are struggling to find the living Christ amidst the tombs which cluster so thickly at the foot of Sinai; they look for life to *the law,* whose ministry is death. Men think that they are to be saved by keeping God's commandments. They are to do their best, and they conceive that their sincere endeavors will be accepted, and they will thus save themselves. This self-righteous idea is diametrically opposed to the whole spirit of the gospel. The gospel is not for you who can save yourselves, but for those who are lost. If you can save yourselves, go and do it, and do not mock the Savior with your hypocritical prayers. Go and stumble among the tombs of ancient Israel, and perish as they did in the wilderness, for into rest Moses and the law can never lead you. The gospel is for sinners who cannot keep the law for themselves, who have broken it, and incurred its penalty, who know that they have done so, and confess it. For such, a living Savior has come that He may blot out their transgressions. Seek not salvation by the works of the law, for by them shall no flesh living be justified. By the law is the knowledge of sin, and nothing more; but righteousness, peace, life, salvation, come by faith in the living Lord Jesus Christ, and by no other means. "Believe in the Lord Jesus Christ, and thou shalt be saved"; but if thou goest about to establish thine own righteousness, thou shalt surely perish, because thou hast rejected the righteousness of Christ.

Others there are who seek the living Jesus among the tombs, by looking for something good in *human nature,* in their own natural hearts and dispositions. I can see you now, for I have known you long, and this has always been your folly, you will go into the charnel-house of your own nature, and say, "Is Jesus here?" Beloved, you are sad and depressed, and I do not wonder. Look at yonder dry bones and bleaching skeletons. See that heap of rottenness, that mass of corruption, that body of death—can you bear it? "Ah," say you, "I am a wretched man indeed, but I long to find some good thing in my flesh!" O beloved, you sigh in vain, you might as well rake Hell over to find Heaven in it, as look into your own carnal nature to find consolation. Behold ye this day, God has abandoned the old nature, and given it up to death.

Under the old law, circumcision was the putting away of the filth of the flesh, as though after this filth were gone the flesh might perhaps be bettered, but now, under the new covenant, we have a far deeper symbol, for "know ye not, that so many of us as were baptized into Jesus Christ were baptized into his death? Therefore we are buried with him by baptism into death: that like as Christ was raised up from the dead by the glory of the Father, even so we also should walk in newness of life." The old man is buried, as a dead thing out of which no good can come. "Knowing this, that our old man is crucified with him, that the body of sin might be destroyed, that henceforth we should not serve sin." God does not attempt to renew the old carnal mind, but to make us new creatures in Christ Jesus.

Yet again, too many have tried to find Christ amidst the gloomy catacombs of the world's *philosophy*. For instance, on the Sabbath day they like to have a sermon full of thought—thought being in the modern meaning of it something beyond, if not opposite to, the simple teaching of the Bible. If a man tells his people what he finds in the Scriptures he is said to "talk platitudes"; but if a man amuses his people with his own dreams, however opposed they may be to God's thoughts, he is a "thinking man," a "highly intellectual preacher." There be some who love above all things the maunderings of day-dreamers, and the crudities of skeptics. If they can hear what an infidel professor [of Christianity] has said against inspiration, if they can be indulged with the last new blasphemy, some hearers feel that they are making advances in that higher culture, which is so much vaunted now-a-days. But, believe me, the bat-haunted caves of false philosophy and pretended science have been searched again and again, but salvation dwells not in them. In Paul's day there were Gnostics who tracked all the winding passages of vainglorious learning, but they only discovered "another gospel which was not another."

The world by wisdom knew not God. After roaming amid the dreary catacombs of philosophy, we come back to breathe the fresh air of the living Word, and concerning the mazes of science, we gasp out the sentence—"He is not there." Reason has not found Him in her deepest mining, not speculation in her highest soaring, though indeed He is not far from any one of us. Athens has her unknown God, but in the simple gospel God is known in the person of Jesus. Socrates and Plato hold up their candles, but Jesus is the sun. Our moderns cavil and dispute, and yet a living Christ is among us converting sinners, cheering saints, and glorifying God.

How anxiously do I wish that you who have been searching for salvation in any of these directions would give up the hopeless task, and understand that Christ is nigh you, and if you with the heart believe on Him, and with the mouth confess Him, you shall be saved. "Look unto me and be ye saved, all the ends of the earth; for I am God, and beside me there is none else": this is His cry to you. "Faith cometh by hearing, and hearing by the word of God." "Believe in the Lord Jesus Christ and thou shalt be saved." Jesus is living still, and able to save to the uttermost. All you have to do is simply to turn the glance of your faith towards Him: by that faith He becomes yours, and you are saved, but oh, seek not the living among the dead, for He is risen.

III. We will again change our strain and consider, in the third place, unsuitable abodes.

The angels said to the women, "He is not here, but is risen." As much as to say—since He is alive He does not abide here. The living Christ might have sat down in the tomb—He might have made the sepulcher His resting place, but it would not have been appropriate; and so He teaches us today that Christians should dwell in places appropriate to them. Ye are risen in Christ, ye ought not to dwell in the grave. I shall now speak to those who, to all intents and purposes, live in the sepulcher, though they are risen from the dead.

Some of these are excellent people, but their temperament, and perhaps their mistaken convictions of duty, lead them to be perpetually *gloomy and desponding*. They hope they have believed in Christ, but they are not sure; they trust that they are saved, but they would not be presumptuous enough to say so. They do not dare to be happy in the conviction that they are accepted in the Beloved. They love the mournful string of the harp, they mourn an absent God. They hope that the divine promises will be fulfilled: they trust that, perhaps, one of these days they may come forth into light, and see a little of the brightness of the Lord's love, but now they are ready to halt, they dwell in the valley of the shadow of death, and their soul is sore burdened.

Dear friend, do you think this is a proper condition for a Christian to be in? I am not going to deny your Christianity for a moment, for I have not half so much doubt about that as you have; I have a better opinion of you than you have of yourself. The most trembling believer in Jesus is saved, and your little faith will save you; but do you really think that Christ meant you to stay where you are, sitting in the cold and silent tomb, amid the dust and ashes? Why keep underground? Why not come into the Master's garden where the flowers are breathing perfume? Why not enjoy the fresh light of full assurance, and the sweet breath of the Spirit's comforting influences? It was a madman who dwelt among the tombs, do not imitate him. Do not say, "I have been such a sinner, that this is all I deserve to enjoy"; for if you talk of deserving, you have left the gospel altogether. I know you believe in Jesus, and you would not give up your hope for all the world: you feel after all that He is a precious Christ to you; come, then, rejoice in Him, though you cannot rejoice in yourself.

Come, beloved, come out of this dreary vault, leave it at once! Though you have lien [lain] among the pots, yet now shall ye be as the wings of a dove covered with silver, and her feathers with yellow gold. Your Master comes to you now, and says,

> O my dove, that art in the clefts of the rocks, in the secret places of the stairs, let me see thy countenance, let me hear thy voice; for sweet is thy voice, and thy countenance is comely.

Members of the body of a risen Savior, will ye lie in the grave still? Arise ye, and come away! Doubt no longer. O believer, what cause hast thou to doubt thy God? Has he ever lied unto thee? Question no longer the power of the precious blood. Why shouldst thou doubt it? Is it not able to cleanse thee from sin? No longer enquire as to whether thou art saved or can be—if thou believest thou art as safe as Christ is. Thou canst no more perish than Christ can if thou art resting in Him—His word has pledged it, His honor is involved in it, He will surely bring thee unto the promised rest; therefore be glad.

Another sort of people seem to dwell among the tombs: I mean Christians—and I trust real Christians—who are very, very *worldly*. It is no sin for a man to be diligent in business, but it is a grievous fault when diligence in business destroys fervency in spirit, and when there is no serving of God in daily life. A Christian man should be diligent so as to provide things honest in the sight of all men, but there be some who are not content with this. They have enough, but they covet more, and when they have more, they still stretch their arms like seas to grasp in all the shore, and their main thought is not God, but gold; not Christ, but wealth. O brethren, brethren, permit me earnestly to rebuke you, lest you receive a severe rebuke in providence in your own souls. Christ is not here! He dwells not in piles of silver. You may be very rich, and yet not find Christ in it all; and you might be poor, and yet if Christ were with you, you would be happy as the angels. He is not here, He is risen! A marble tomb could not hold Him, nor could a golden tomb have contained Him. Let it not contain you. Unwrap the cerements [burial garments] of your heart; cast all your care on God who careth for you. Let your conversation be in Heaven. Set not your affection on things on the earth, but set it upon things above, where Christ sitteth at the right hand of God.

Once more on this point, a subject more grievous still, there are some professors [Christians] who live in the dead-house of *sin*. Yet they say that they are Christ's people. Nay, I will not say they live in it, but they do what, perhaps, is worse—they go to sin to find their pleasures. I suppose we may judge of a man more by that wherein he finds his pleasure than by almost anything else. A man may say, "I do not habitually frequent the gaieties of the world; I am not always found where sin is mixed with mirth, and where worldlings dance upon the verge of Hell, but I go there now and then for a special treat."

I cannot help quoting the remark of Rowland Hill, who, when he met with a professor who went to the theater, a member of his church, said to him, "I understand you attend the theater." "No," he said, "I only go for a treat now and then." "Ah," said Mr. Hill,

> that makes it all the worse. Suppose that somebody said, "Mr. Hill is a strange being, he eats carrion." I am asked, "Is it true, Mr. Hill, that you live on carrion?" "No, I do not habitually eat carrion, but I have a dish of it now and then just for a treat." Why, you would think I was nastier than I should have been if I had eaten it ordinarily.

There is much force in the remark. If anything that verges on the unclean and lascivious is a treat to you, why then your very heart is unclean, and you are seeking your pleasure and comfort among the dead.

There are some things that men take pleasure in now-a-days that are only fit to make idiots laugh, or else to cause angels to weep. Do be choice, Christian men and women, in your company. You are brothers to Christ; will you consort with the sons of Belial? You are heirs of perfection in Christ, you are even now arrayed in spotless linen, and you are fair and lovely in the sight of God; you are a royal priesthood, you are the elect of mankind; will you trail your garments in the mire and make yourselves the sport of the Philistines? Will you consort with the beggarly children of the world? No; act according to your pedigree and your newborn nature, and never seek the living among the dead. Jesus was never there—go not there yourselves. He loved not the noise and turmoil of the world's pleasures; He had meat to eat of another kind. God grant you to feel the resurrection life strong within your spirits.

IV. But I pass on from that. In the fourth place, I want to warn you against unreasonable services.

Those good people to whom the angels said, "He is not here, but is risen," were bearing a load, and what were they carrying? What is Joanna carrying, and her servants, and Mary, what are they carrying? Why, white linen, and what else? Pounds of spices, the most precious they could buy. What are they going to do? Ah, if an angel could laugh, I should think he must have smiled as he found they were coming to embalm Christ. "Why he is not here: and, what is more, he is not dead, he does not want any embalming, he is alive."

You might have seen all over England on Good Friday, and also on this Easter Sunday, crowds of people, I have no doubt very sincere people, coming to embalm Christ. They tolled a bell because He was dead, and they hung crepe over what they call their altars because He was dead, and they fasted and sung sad hymns over their dead Savior. I bless the Lord my Redeemer is not dead, and I have no bells to toll for Him either. He is risen, He is not here! Here they come, crowds of them with their white linen, and their precious spices to wrap a dead Christ up in. Are the men mad? But say they, we were only acting it over again. Oh, was that it? Practical charades was it? Acting the glorious atonement of Calvary as a play! Then I accuse the performers of blasphemy before the throne of the eternal God who hears my words; I charge them with profanity in daring to rehearse in mimicry that which was once done and done forever, and is never to be repeated.

No, I cannot suppose they meant to mimic the great sacrifice, and, therefore, I conclude that they thought their Savior to be dead, and so they said, "Toll the bell for Him! Kneel down and weep before His image on a cross." If I believed Jesus Christ died on Good Friday, I would feast all day long because His death is over; as He has ordained the high festival of the Lord's Supper to be His commemoration, I would follow His bidding, and keep no fast. Who would sit down and whine over a friend once dead if you knew Him to be restored to life and exalted in power? Why toll a bell for a living friend? However, I condemn not the good people any more than the angels condemned those holy women, only they may take their spices home and their white linen too, for Jesus is alive, and does not want them.

In other ways a great many fussy people do the same thing. See how they come forward in defense of the gospel. It has been discovered by geology and by arithmetic, that Moses was wrong. Straightway many go out to defend Jesus Christ. They argue for the gospel, and apologize for it, as if it were now a little out of date, and we must try to bring it round to suit modern discoveries and the philosophies of the present. That seems to me exactly like coming up with your linen and precious spices to wrap Him in. Take them away. I question whether Butler and Paley have not both of them created more infidels than they ever cured, and whether most of the defenses of the gospel are not sheer impertinences. The gospel does not want defending. If Jesus Christ is not alive, and cannot fight His own battles, then Christianity is in an evil case. But He is, and we have only to preach His gospel in all its naked simplicity, and the power that goes with it will be the evidence of its divinity. No other evidence will ever convince mankind. Apologies and defenses are well intended no doubt, so was the embalming well intended by these good women, but they are of small value. Give Christ room, give His preachers space and opportunities to preach the gospel, and let the truth be brought out in simple language, and you will soon hear the Master say, "Take away the spices, take away the linen! I am alive, I do not want these."

We see the same kind of thing in other good people who are sticklers for old-fashioned, stereotyped ways—they must have everything conducted exactly as it used to be conducted one hundred or two hundred years ago. Puritanic order must be maintained, and there must be no divergence, and the way of putting the gospel must be exactly the same way in which it was put by good old Dr. So-and-so, and in the pulpit there must be the most awful dreariness that can possibly be compassed, and the preacher must be devoutly dull, and all the worship must be serenely proper—lots of spices and fine linen to wrap a dead Christ up in. I delight to break down conventional proprieties. It is a grand thing to put one's foot right through merely human regulations, because life cannot be strapped down by regulations fit only for the dead. Mr. Hill went to Scotland to preach the gospel, and they said he rode on the back of all order and decorum. Then said he, "I will call my pair of horses by those names, and make it true." It was true; no doubt, he did ride on the back of order and decorum, but then he drew souls to Christ with those two strange steeds, and his breaking through rules enabled him to get at men and women who never would have been got at in any other way. Be ready to set Christ at liberty, and give His servants liberty to serve Him as the Spirit of God shall guide them.

V. I wanted to speak, last of all, upon the amazing news which these good women received—"He is not here, but he is risen."

This was amazing news to His enemies. They said, "We have killed Him—we have put Him in the tomb; it is all over with Him." A-ha! Scribe, Pharisee, Priest, what have you done? Your work is all undone, for He is risen! It was amazing news for Satan. He no doubt dreamed that he had destroyed the Savior, but He is risen! What a thrill went through all the regions of Hell! What news it was for the grave! Now was it utterly destroyed, and death had lost his sting! What news it was for trembling saints. "He is risen indeed." They plucked up courage, and they said, "The good cause is the right one still, and it will conquer, for our Christ is still alive at its head." It was good news for sinners. Aye, it is good news for every sinner here. Christ is alive; if you seek Him He will be found of you.

He is not a dead Christ to whom I point you today. He is risen; and He is able to save to the uttermost them that come unto God by Him. There is no better news for sad men, for distressed, desponding, and despairing men, than this—the Savior lives, able still to save and willing to receive you to His tender heart. This was glad news, beloved, for all the angels and all the spirits in Heaven, glad news indeed for them. And this day it shall be glad news to us, and we will live in the power of it by the help of His Spirit, and we will tell it to our brethren that they may rejoice with us, and we will not despair any longer. We will give way no more to doubts and fears, but we will say to one another, "He is risen indeed; therefore let our hearts be glad." The Lord bless you, and in coming to His table, as I trust many of His people will come, let us meet our risen Master. Amen.

The Power of the Risen Savior

"And Jesus came and spake unto them, saying, 'All power is given unto me in Heaven and in earth. Go ye therefore, and teach all nations, baptizing them in the name of the Father, and of the Son, and of the Holy Ghost: teaching them to observe all things whatsoever I have commanded you: and, lo, I am with you alway, even unto the end of the world. Amen.'"—Matthew 28:18-20.

T he change from "the man of sorrows" before His crucifixion to the "Lord over all" after His resurrection is very striking. Before His passion He was well known by His disciples, and appeared only in one form, as the Son of man, clad in the common peasant's garment without seam, woven from the top throughout; but after He had risen from the dead He was on several occasions unrecognized by those who loved Him best, and is once at least described as having appeared to certain of them "under another form." He was the same person, for they saw His hands and His feet, and Thomas even handled Him, and placed his finger in the print of the nails; but yet it would seem that some gleams of His glory were at times manifested to them, a glory which had been hidden during His previous life, save only when He stood on the Mount of Transfiguration.

Before His death, His appearances were to the general public—He stood in the midst of Scribes and Pharisees and publicans and sinners, and preached the glad tidings; but now He appeared only to His disciples, sometimes to one, at another time to two, on one occasion to about five hundred brethren at once, but always to His disciples, and to them only. Before His death His preaching was full of parable, plain to those who had understanding, but often dark and mysterious even to His own followers, for it was a judgment from the Lord upon that evil generation that seeing they should not see, and hearing they should not perceive. Yet with equal truth we may say that our Lord before His death brought down His teaching to the comprehension of the uninstructed minds which listened to it, so that many of the deeper truths were slightly touched upon because they were not able to bear them as yet.

Till His crucifixion He veiled the effulgence of many truths, but after His resurrection He spake no more in parables, but introduced His disciples into the inner circle of the great doctrines of the kingdom, and as it were showed Himself face to face to them. Before His death the Lord Jesus was ever with His followers, and even the secret places of His retirement were known to them, but after He had risen He came and went among them at irregular intervals. Where He was during many of those forty days, who among us can tell? He was seen in the garden upon Olivet, He walked to Emmaus, He comforted the assembly at Jerusalem, He showed Himself again to the disciples at the Sea of Tiberias, but where went He when, after the various interviews, He vanished out of their sight?

They were in the room alone, the doors were shut, and suddenly He stood in the midst of them; again He called to them from the sea-beach, and on landing they found a fire of coals kindled, and fish laid thereon, and bread; His appearings were strange, and His disappearings equally so. Everything betokened that, after He had risen from the dead, He had undergone some marvelous change, which had revealed in Him that which had been concealed before, though still His identity was indisputable.

It was no small honor to have seen our risen Lord while yet He lingered here below. What must it be to see Jesus as He is now! He is the same Jesus as when He was here; yonder memorials as of a lamb that has been slain assure us that He is the same man. Glorified in Heaven His real manhood sits, and it is capable of being beheld by the eye, and heard by the ear, but yet how different. Had we seen Him in His agony, we should all the more admire His glory. Dwell with your hearts very much upon Christ crucified, but indulge yourselves full often with a sight of Christ glorified. Delight to think that He is not here, for He is risen; He is not here, for He has ascended; He is not here, for He sits at the right hand of God, and maketh intercession for us. Let your souls travel frequently the blessed highway from the sepulcher to the throne. As in Rome there was a *Via Sacra* along which returning conquerors went from the gates of the city up to the heights of the Capitol, so is there another *Via Sacra* which you ought often to survey, for along it the risen Savior went in glorious majesty from the tomb of Joseph of Arimathea up to the eternal dignities of his Father's right hand. Your soul will do well to see her dawn of hope in His death, and her full assurance of hope in His risen life.

Today my business is to show, as far as God the Spirit may help me, first, *Our Lord's resurrection power!* and secondly, *Our Lord's mode of exercising the spiritual part of that power so far as we are concerned.*

I. Our Lord's resurrection power.

"All power is given unto me in Heaven and in earth." At the risk of repeating myself, I should like to begin this head by asking you to remember last Sabbath morning's sermon, when we went to Gethsemane, and bowed our spirits in the shade of those grey olives, at the sight of the bloody sweat. What a contrast between that and this! There you saw the weakness of man, the bowing, the prostrating, the crushing of the manhood of the Mediator; but here you see the strength of the God-man—He is girt with omnipotence, though still on Earth when He spoke these words He had received a privilege, honor, glory, fullness and power which lifted Him far above the sons of men. He was, as Mediator, no more a sufferer, but a sovereign; no more a victim, but a victor; no more a servant, but the monarch of Earth and Heaven. Yet He had never received such power if He had not endured such weakness. All power had never been given to the Mediator if all comfort had not been taken away. He stooped to conquer. The way to His throne was downward. Mounting upon steps of ivory, Solomon ascended to his throne of gold; but Our Lord and Master descended that He might ascend, and went down into the awful deeps of agony unutterable that all power in Heaven and Earth might belong to Him as our Redeemer and Covenant Head.

Now think a moment of these words, *"All power."* Jesus Christ has given to Him by His Father, as a consequence of is death, "all power." It is but another way of saying that the Mediator possesses omnipotence, for omnipotence is but the Latin of "all power." What mind shall conceive, what tongue shall set in order before you, the meaning of all power? We cannot grasp it; it is high, we cannot attain unto it. Such knowledge is too wonderful for us. The power of self-existence, the power of creation, the power of sustaining that which is made, the power of fashioning and destroying, the power of opening and shutting, of overthrowing or establishing, of killing and making alive, the power to pardon and to condemn, to give and to withhold, to decree and to fulfill, to be, in a word, "head over all things to his church,"—all this is vested in Jesus Christ our Lord. We might as well attempt to describe infinity, or map the boundless as to tell what "all power" must mean; but whatever it is, it is all *given* to our Lord, all lodged in those hands which once were fastened to the wood of shame, all left with that heart which was pierced with the spear, all placed as a crown upon that head which was sur-rounded with a coronet of thorns.

"All power *in Heaven*" is His. Observe that! Then He has the power of God, for God is in Heaven, and the power of God emanates from that cen-tral throne. Jesus, then, has divine power. Whatever Jehovah can do Jesus can do. If it were His will to speak another world into existence, we should see tonight a fresh star adorning the brow of night. Were it His will at once to fold up creation like a worn-out vesture, lo the elements would pass away, and yonder Heavens would be shriveled like a scroll. The power which binds the sweet influences of the Pleiades and looses the bands of Orion is with the Nazarene, the Crucified leads forth Arcturus with his sons. Angelic bands are waiting on the wing to do the bidding of Jesus of Nazareth, and cherubim and seraphim and the four living crea-tures before the throne unceasingly obey Him. He Who was despised and rejected of men now commands the homage of all Heaven, as "God over all, blessed forever."

"All power in Heaven" relates to the providential skill and might with which God rules everything in the universe. He holds the reins of all created forces, and impels or restrains them at His will, giving force to law, and life to all existence. The old heathen dreamed of Apollo as driving the chariot of the sun and guiding its fiery steeds in their daily course, but it is not so: Jesus is Lord of all. He harnesses the winds to His chariot, and thrusts a bit into the mouth of the tempest, doing as He wills among the armies of Heaven and the inhabitants of this lower world. From Him in Heaven emanates the power which sustains and governs this globe, for the Father hath committed all things into His hands. "By him all things consist."

"All power" must include—and this is a practical point to us—all the power of the Holy Ghost. In the work which lies nearest our heart the Holy Spirit is the great force. It is He that convinces men of sin, and leads them to a Savior, gives them new hearts and right spirits, and plants them in the church, and then causes them to grow and become fruitful. The power of the Holy Ghost goes forth among the sons of men according to the will of our Lord. As the anointing oil poured upon Aaron's head ran down his beard, and bedewed the skirts of his garments, so the Spirit which has been granted to him without measure flows from Him to us. He hath the residue of the Spirit, and according to His will the Holy Ghost goeth forth into the church, and from the church into the world, to the ac-complishment of the purposes of saving grace. It is not possible that the church should fail for want of spiritual gifts or influence while her heavenly Bridegroom has such overflowing stores of both.

All the power of the sacred Trinity, Father, Son, and Spirit, is at the command of Jesus, who is exalted far above all principality, and power, and might, and dominion, and every name that is named, not only in this world, but in that which is to come.

Our Lord also claimed that all power had been given to him *on earth*. This is more than could be truly said by any mere man; none of mortal race may claim all power in Heaven, and when they aspire to all power on Earth it is but a dream. Universal monarchy has been strained after; it has seldom, if ever, been attained; and when it seemed within the clutch of ambition it has melted away like a snowflake before the sun. Indeed, if men could rule all their fellows, yet they would not have all power on earth, for there are other forces which scorn their control. Fell diseases laugh at the power of men. The King of Israel, when Naaman came to him to be recovered of his leprosy, cried, "Am I God, to kill and to make alive, that this man doth send unto me to recover a man of his leprosy?" He had not all power. Winds and waves, moreover, scorn mortal rule. It is not true that even Britannia rules the waves. The proudest princes have been made to feel by sickness, and pain, and death that after all they were but men; and oftentimes their weaknesses have been such as to make the more apparent the truth that power belongeth unto God, and unto God alone, so that when He entrusts a little of it to the sons of men, it is so little that they are fools if they boast thereof. See ye, then, before us a wonder. A man who has power over all things on Earth without exception, and is obeyed by all creatures, great and small, because the Lord Jehovah has put all things under His feet.

For our purposes it will be most important for us to remember that our Lord has "all power" over the minds of men, both good and bad. He calleth whomsoever He pleaseth into His fellowship, and they obey. Having called them, He is able to sanctify them to the highest point of holiness, working in them all the good pleasure of His will with power. The saints can be so influenced by our Lord, through the Holy Ghost, that they can be impelled to the divinest ardors, and elevated to the sublimest frames of mind. Often do I pray, and I doubt not the prayer has come from you too, that God would raise up leaders in the church, men full of faith and of the Holy Ghost, standard-bearers in the day of battle. The preachers of the gospel who preach with any power are few; still might John say, "Ye have not many fathers." More precious than the gold of Ophir are men who stand out as pillars of the

Lord's house, bulwarks of the truth, champions in the camp of Israel. How few are our apostolic men! We want again Luthers, Calvins, Bunyans, Whitfields, men fit to mark eras, whose names breathe terror in our foemen's ears. We have dire need of such. Where are they? Whence will they come to us? We cannot tell in what farmhouse or village smithy, or school house such men may be, but our Lord has them in store. They are the gifts of Jesus Christ to the church, and will come in due time. Let us believe in the power of Jesus to give us valiant men and men of renown, and we little know how soon He will supply them.

Since all power on Earth is lodged in Christ's hands, He can also clothe any and all of His servants with a sacred might, by which their hands shall be sufficient for them in their high calling. Without bringing them forth into the front ranks He can make them occupy their appointed stations till He comes, girt with a power which shall make them useful. My brother, the Lord Jesus can make you eminently prosperous in the sphere in which He has placed you; my sister, your Lord can bless the little children who gather at your knee through your means. You are very feeble, and you know it, but there is no reason why you should not be strong in Him. If you look to the strong for strength, He can endue you with power from on high, and say to you as to Gideon, "Go in this thy might." Your slowness of speech need not disqualify you, for He will be with your mouth as with Moses. Your want of culture need not hinder you, for Shamgar with his oxgoad smote the Philistines, and Amos, the prophet, was a herdsman.

Like Paul, your personal presence may be despised as weak, and your speech as contemptible, but yet like him you may learn to glory in infirmity, because the power of God doth rest upon you. Ye are not straitened in the Lord, but in yourselves, if straitened at all. You may be as dry as Aaron's rod, but He can make you bud and blossom, and bring forth fruit. You may be as nearly empty as the widow's cruse, yet will He cause you still to overflow towards His saints. You may feel yourself to be as near sinking as Peter amid the waves, yet will He keep you from your fears. You may be as unsuccessful as the disciples who had toiled all night and taken nothing, yet He can fill your boat till it can hold no more. No man knows what the Lord can make of him, nor what He may do by him, only this we do know assuredly that "all power" is with Him by whom we were redeemed, and to whom we belong.

Oh, believers, resort ye to your Lord, to receive out of His fullness grace for grace. Because of this power we believe that if Jesus willed He could stir the whole church at once to the utmost energy. Does she sleep?

His voice can awaken her. Does she restrain prayer? His grace can stimulate her to devotion. Has she grown unbelieving? He can restore her ancient faith. Does she turn her back in the day of battle, troubled with skepticisms and doubts? He can restore her unwavering confidence in the gospel, and make her valiant till all her sons shall be heroes of faith and put to flight the armies of the aliens.

Let us believe, and we shall see the glory of God. Let us believe, I say, and once again our conquering days shall come, when one shall chase a thousand, and two shall put ten thousand to flight. Never despair for the church; be anxious for her, and turn your anxiety into prayer, but be hopeful evermore, for her Redeemer is mighty and will stir up His strength. "The Lord of Hosts is with us; the God of Jacob is our refuge." Degenerate as we are, there standeth one among us whom the world seeth not, whose shoe's latchet we are not worthy to unloose: He shall again baptize us with the Holy Ghost and with fire, for "all power is given unto him."

It is equally true that all power is given unto our Lord over the whole of mankind, even over that part of the race which rejects and continues in willful rebellion. He can use the ungodly for his purposes. We have it on inspired authority that Herod and Pilate, with the Gentiles and the people of Israel, were gathered together to do whatsoever the Lord's hand and counsel determined before to be done. Their utmost wickedness did but fulfill the determinate counsel of God. Thus doth He make wrath of man to praise Him, and the most rebellious wills to be subservient to His sacred purposes. Jesus' kingdom ruleth over all. The powers of Hell and all their hosts, with the kings of the earth, and the rulers set themselves and take counsel together, and all the while their rage is working out His designs. Little do they know that they are but drudges to the King of Kings, scullions in the kitchen of His imperial palace. All things do His bidding, His will is not thwarted, His resolves are not defeated; the pleasure of the Lord prospers in His hands.

By faith I see Him ruling and overruling on land and sea, and in all deep places. Guiding the decisions of parliaments, dictating to dictators, commanding princes, and ruling emperors. Let Him but arise, and they that hate Him shall flee before Him; as smoke is driven, so will He drive them away; as wax melteth before the fire, so shall all His enemies perish at His presence.

As to *sinful men* in general, the Redeemer has power over their minds in a manner wonderful to contemplate. At the present moment we very much deplore the fact that the current of public thought runs strongly to-wards Popery, which is the alias of idolatry. Just as, in Old Testament history, the people of Israel were always breaking away after their idols, so is it with this nation. The Israelites were cured of their sin for a little while, so long as some great teacher or judge had power among them, but at his death they turned aside to worship the queen of Heaven or the calves of Bethel, or some other visible symbols. So it is now. Men are mad after the idols of old Rome. Well, what next? Are we despairing? God forbid that we should ever despond while all power is in the hand of Jesus.

A great philosopher has told us that it is absurd to suppose that prayer can have any effect upon the events of life; but God has only to visit the nation with some judgment severely felt by all and your philosopher will become as quiet as a mouse. The current of thought can readily be turned by our Lord; He can as easily manage it as the miller controls the stream which flows over His wheel, or rushes past it. The times are safe in our Redeemer's management, He is mightier than the devil, the Pope, the infidel, and the ritualist, all put together. All glory be to Him who has all power in Earth and Heaven.

So too, our Lord can give, and He does give to the people an inclination to hear the gospel. Never be afraid of getting a congregation when the gospel is your theme. Jesus, who gives you a consecrated tongue, will find willing ears to listen to you. At His bidding deserted sanctuaries grow crowded, and the people throng to hear the joyful sound. Aye, and He can do more than that, for He can make the word powerful to the conversion of thousands. He can constrain the frivolous to think, the obstinately heretical to accept the truth, and those who set their faces like a flint to yield to His gracious sway. He has the key of every human heart; He openeth, and no man shutteth; He shutteth, and no man openeth. He will clothe His word with power and subdue the nations thereby. It is ours to proclaim the gospel, and to believe that no man is beyond the saving power of Jesus Christ. Doubly dyed, yea, sevenfold steeped in the scarlet dye of vice, the sinner may be cleansed, and the ringleader in vice may become a pattern of holiness. The Pharisee can be converted—was not Paul? Even priests may be saved, for did not a great multitude of the priests believe? There is no man in any conceivable position of sin, who is beyond the power of Christ. He may be gone to the uttermost in sin, so as to stand on the verge of Hell, but if Jesus stretch out His pierced hand, he will be plucked like a brand out of the burning.

Brethren, we have no doubts, we entertain no fears, for every moment of time is bringing on the grand display of the power of Jesus. We preach today, and some of you despise the gospel; we bring Christ before you, and you reject Him; but God will change His hand with you before long, and your despisings and your rejectings will then come to an end, for that same Jesus who went from Olivet, and ascended into Heaven, will so come in like manner as He was seen to go up into Heaven. He will descend with matchless pomp and power, and this astonished world which saw Him crucified shall see Him enthroned; and in the selfsame place where men dogged His heels and persecuted Him, they shall crowd around Him to pay Him homage, for He must reign, and put His enemies under His feet. This same Earth shall be gladdened by His triumphs which once was troubled with His griefs.

And more. You may be dead before the Lord shall come, but you will know that all power is His, for at the blast of His trumpet your bodies shall rise again to stand before His terrible judgment seat. You may have resisted Him here, but you will be unable to oppose Him then; you may despise Him now, but then you must tremble before Him. "Depart ye cursed," will be to you a terrible proof that He has "all power," if you will not now accept another and a sweeter proof of it by coming unto Him who bids the laboring and heavy laden partake of His rest. "Kiss the Son, lest he be angry, and ye perish from the way, when his wrath is kindled but a little. Blessed are all they that put their trust in him."

II. I have, secondly, by your patience, to show our Lord's usual mode of exercising his great spiritual power.

Brethren, the Lord Jesus might have said, "All power is given to Me in Heaven and earth; take ye then your swords and slay all these My enemies who crucified Me." But He had no thoughts of revenge. He might have said, "These Jews put Me to death, therefore go ye straightway to the Isles and to Tarshish and preach, for these men shall never taste of My grace," but no, He expressly said, "beginning at Jerusalem," and bade His disciples first preach the Gospel to His murderers. In consequence of His having "all power" His servants were bidden to disciple all nations. My brethren, the method by which Jesus proposes to subdue all things unto Himself appears to be utterly inadequate. To teach, to make disciples, to baptize these disciples, and to instruct them further in the faith! Good Master, are these the weapons of our warfare? Are these thy battle-axe and weapons of war? Not thus do the princes of this world contemplate conquest, for they rely on monster guns, ironclads, and engines of death-doing power. Yet what are these but proofs of their weakness? Had they all power in themselves they would not need such instruments. Only He who has all power can work His bidding by a word, and dispense with all force but that of love.

Mark that *teaching and preaching are the Lord's way of displaying His power.* Today they tell us that the way to save souls is to rig out an altar with different colored silks and satins, variable according to the almanac, and to array priests in garments of diverse colors, "of diverse colors of needlework, on both sides, meet for the necks of them that take the spoil," and to make men wear petticoats, dishonorable to their sex. With these ribbons and embroideries, joined with incense burning, posturing, and incantations, souls are to be saved! "Not so," saith the Master, but "Go ye into all the world, and preach the gospel to every creature." Preaching and teaching and baptizing the disciples are Christ's way, and priestcraft is not Christ's way. If Christ had ordained sacramental efficacy it would succeed, but He has ordained nothing of the kind; His mandate is—All power is given unto Me in Heaven and earth, go ye, therefore, disciple, baptize, and then still further instruct in the name of the Triune God.

My brethren, remember who the men were who were sent on this errand. The eleven who were foremost were mostly fishermen. Does the omnipotent Jesus choose fishermen to subdue the world? He does, because He needs no help from them; all power is His. We must have an educated ministry, they tell us; and by "an educated ministry" they mean, not the ministry of a man of common sense, clear head and warm heart, deep experience, and large acquaintance with human nature, but the ministry of mere classical and mathematical students, theorists, and novices, more learned in modern infidelities than in the truth of God. Our Lord, if he had wished to employ the worldly-wise, might certainly have chosen an eleven in Corinth or in Athens who would have commanded general respect for their attainments, or He could have found eleven learned rabbis near at home; but He did not want such men: their vaunted attainments were of no value in His eyes. He chose honest, hearty men who were childlike enough to learn the truth, and bold enough to speak it when they knew it.

The church must get rid of her notion that she must depend on the learning of this world. Against a sound education we cannot have a word to say, especially an education in the Scriptures, but to place learned degrees in the place of the gift of the Holy Spirit, or to value the present style of so-called culture above the spiritual edification of our manhood, is to set up an idol in the house of the living God. The Lord can as well use the most illiterate man as the most learned, if so it pleaseth Him. "Go ye," he said, "ye fishermen, go ye, and teach all nations." Carnal reason's criticism on this is—a feeble method to be worked out by feebler instruments!

Now let it be noted here that the work of preaching the gospel, which is Christ's way of using His power among men, is based only upon His having that power. Hearken to some of my brethren; they say, "You must not preach the gospel to a dead sinner, because the sinner has no power." Just so, but our reason for preaching to him is that all power is given unto Jesus, and He bids us preach the gospel to every creature. I tell you this, if my Lord and Master should bid me go tomorrow to Norwood cemetery and bid the dead to rise I would do it with as much pleasure as I now preach the gospel to this congregation; and I would do it for the same reason which now leads me to urge the unregenerate to repent and be converted; for I regard men as being dead in sin, and yet I tell them to live, because my Master commands me do so: that I am right in thus acting is proved by the fact that while I am preaching sinners do live; blessed be His name, thousands of them have been quickened into life.

Ezekiel had to cry, "Ye dry bones, live." What a foolish thing to say! But God justified His servant in it, and an exceeding great army stood upon their feet in what was once a large charnel house. Joshua's men were bidden to blow their trumpets around Jericho—a most absurd thing to blow a trumpet to fetch city walls down—but they came down for all that. Gideon's men were bidden simply to carry lamps within their pitchers, and to break their pitchers, and stand still and cry aloud, "The sword of the Lord and of Gideon,"—a most ridiculous thing to hope by this means to smite the Midianites—but they were smitten, for God never sends His servants on a fool's errand. It pleases God by the foolishness of preaching to accomplish His divine purpose, not because of the power of preaching, nor the power of the preacher, nor any power in those preached to, but because "all power" is given unto Christ "in Heaven and in earth," and He chooses to work by the teaching of the Word.

Our business, then, is just this. We are to teach, or as the Greek word has it, to make disciples. Our business is, each one according to the grace given, to tell our fellow men the gospel, and to try and disciple them to Jesus. When they become disciples, our next duty is to give them the sign of discipleship, by "baptizing them." That symbolic burial sets forth their death in Jesus to their former selves and their resurrection to newness of life through Him. Baptism enrolls and seals the disciples, and we must not omit or misplace it.

When the disciple is enrolled, the missionary is to become the pastor, "teaching them to observe all things whatsoever I have commanded you."

The disciple is admitted into the school by obeying the Savior's command as to baptism, and then he goes on to learn, and as he learns he teaches others also. He is taught obedience, not to some things, but to all things which Christ has commanded. He is put into the church not to become a legislator or a deviser of new doctrines and ceremonies, but to believe what Christ tells him, and to do what Christ bids him.

I would close this sermon very practically. The greater part of my congregation at this time consists of persons who have believed in Jesus, who have been baptized, and have been further instructed. You believe that Jesus has all power, and that He works through the teaching and preaching of the gospel, and therefore I wish to press you with a home question. How much are you doing as to teaching all nations? This charge is committed to you as well as to me; for this purpose are we sent into the world; ourselves receivers that we may be afterwards distributors. How much have you distributed?

Dear brother, dear sister, to how many have you told the story of redemption by the blood of Jesus? You have been a convert now for some time: to whom have you spoken of Jesus, or to whom have you written? Are you distributing as best you can the words of others if you are not capable of putting words together yourself? Do not reply, "I belong to a church which is doing much." That is not to the point. I am speaking of that which you are personally doing. Jesus did not die for us by proxy, but He bore our sins in His own body on the tree. I ask then, what are you personally doing? Are you doing anything at all? "But I cannot go for a missionary," says one. Are you sure you cannot? I have been long looking for a time when numbers of you will feel that you must go to preach the gospel abroad, and will relinquish comforts and emoluments for the Lord's sake. There can be no greater honor to a church than to have many sons and daughters bearing the brunt of the battle for the Lord.

Lo, I set up a standard among you this day, let those whose hearts God has touched rally to it without delay. The heathen are perishing; they are dying by millions without Christ, and Christ's last command to us is "Go ye, teach all nations:" are you obeying it? "I cannot go," says one, "I have a family and many ties to bind me at home." My dear brother, then, I ask you, are you going as far as you can? Do you travel to the utmost length of the providential tether which has fastened you where you are? Can you say "Yes." Then, what are you doing to help others to go? As I was thinking over this discourse, I reflected how very little we were most of us doing towards sending the gospel abroad.

We are, as a church, doing a fair share for our heathen at home, and I rejoice at the thought of it; but how much a year do you each give to foreign missions? I wish you would put down in your pocket-book how much you give per annum for missions, and then calculate how much per cent it is of your income. There let it stand—"Item: Gave to the collection last April. . .1 shilling." One shilling a year towards the salvation of the world. Perhaps it will run thus—"Item: Income £5,000; annual subscription to mission £1." How does that look? I cannot read your hearts, but I could read your pocket-books and work a sum in proportion. I suggest that you do it yourselves, while I also take a look at my own expenditure. Let us all see what more can be done for the spread of the Redeemer's kingdom, for all power is with Him; and when His people shall be stirred up to believe in that power, and to use the simple but potent machinery of the preaching of the Gospel to all nations, then God, even our own God shall bless us, and all the ends of the Earth shall fear Him. Amen.

Christ The Destroyer of Death

"The last enemy that shall be destroyed is death."—I Cor. 15:26.

During four previous Sabbaths we have been following our Lord and Master through His great achievements: we have seen Him as the end of the law, as the conqueror of Satan, as the overcomer of the world, as the creator of all things new, and now we behold Him as the destroyer of death. In this and in all His other glorious deeds let us worship Him with all our hearts.

May the Spirit of God lead us into the full meaning of this, which is one of the Redeemer's grandest characters.

To the text itself then: *death is an enemy: death is an enemy to be destroyed: death is an enemy to be destroyed last:* —"the last enemy that shall be destroyed is death."

I. Death an enemy.

It was so born, even as Haman the Agagite was the enemy of Israel by his descent. Death is the child of our direst foe, for "sin when it is finished bringeth forth death." "Sin entered into the world and death by sin." Now, that which is distinctly the fruit of transgression cannot be other than an enemy of man. Death was introduced into the world on that gloomy day which saw our fall, and he that had the power of it is our arch enemy and betrayer, the devil: from both of which facts we must regard it as the manifest enemy of man. Death is an alien in this world, it did not enter into original design of the unfallen creation, but its intrusion mars and spoils the whole. It is no part of the Great Shepherd's flock, but it is a wolf which cometh to kill and to destroy.

Geology tells us that there was death among the various forms of life from the first ages of the globe's history, even when as yet the world was not fitted up as the dwelling of man. This I can believe and still regard death as the result of sin. If it can be proved that there is such an organic unity between man and the lower animals that they would not have died if Adam had not sinned, then I see in those deaths before Adam the antecedent consequences of a sin which was then uncommitted. If by the merits of Jesus there was salvation before He had offered his atoning sacrifice I do not find it hard to conceive that the foreseen demerits of sin may have cast the shadow of death over the long ages which came before man's transgression. Of that we know little, nor is it important that we should, but certain is it that as far as this present creation is concerned death is not God's invited guest, but an intruder whose presence mars the feast. Man in his folly welcomed Satan and sin when they forced their way into the high festival of Paradise, but he never welcomed death: even his blind eyes could see in that skeleton form a cruel foe. As the lion to the herds of the plain, as the scythe to the flowers of the field, as the wind to the sere leaves of the forest, such is death to the sons of men. They fear it by an inward instinct because their conscience tells them what it is: the child of their sin.

Death is well called an enemy for *it does an enemy's work* towards us. For what purpose doth an enemy come but to root up, and to pull down, and to destroy? Death tears in pieces that comely handiwork of God, the fabric of the human body, so marvelously wrought by the fingers of divine skill. Casting this rich embroidery into the grave among the armies of the worm, to its fierce soldiery death divideth "to every one a prey of diverse colors, of diverse colors of needlework"; and they ruthlessly rend in pieces the spoil. This building of our manhood is a house fair to look upon, but death the destroyer darkens its windows, shakes its pillars, closes its doors and causes the sound of the grinding to cease. Then the daughters of music are brought low, and the strong men bow themselves. This Vandal spares no work of life, however full of wisdom, or beauty, for it looseth the silver cord and breaketh the golden bowl. Lo, at the fountain the costly pitcher is utterly broken, and at the cistern the well-wrought wheel is dashed in pieces. Death is a fierce invader of the realms of life, and where it comes it fells every good tree, stops all wells of water, and mars every good piece of land with stones. See you a man when death has wrought his will upon him, what a ruin he is! How is his beauty turned to ashes, and his comeliness to corruption. Surely an enemy hath done this.

Look, my brethren, at the course of death throughout all ages and in all lands. What field is there without its grave? What city without its cemetery? Whither can we go to find no sepulchers? As the sandy shore is covered with the up-castings of the worm, so art thou, O earth, covered with those grass-grown hillocks beneath which sleep the departed generations of men. And thou, O sea, even thou, art not without thy dead! As if the Earth were all too full of corpses and they jostled each other in their crowded sepulchers, even into thy caverns, O mighty main, the bodies of the dead are cast. Thy waves must become defiled with the carcasses of men, and on thy floor must lie the bones of the slain! Our enemy, death, has marched as it were with sword and fire ravaging the human race. Neither Goth, nor Hun, nor Tartar could have slain so universally all that breathed, for death has suffered none to escape. Everywhere it has withered household joys and created sorrow and sighing; in all lands where the sun is seen it hath blinded men's eyes with weeping. The tear of the bereaved, the wail of the widow, and the moan of the orphan—these have been death's war music, and he has found therein a song of victory.

The greatest conquerors have only been death's slaughtermen, journeymen butchers working in his shambles. War is nothing better than death holding carnival, and devouring his prey a little more in haste than is his common wont.

Death has done the work of an enemy to those of us who have as yet escaped his arrows. Those who have lately stood around a new-made grave and buried half their hearts can tell you what an enemy death is. It takes the friend from our side, and the child from our bosom, neither does it care for our crying. He has fallen who was the pillar of the household; she has been snatched away who was the brightness of the hearth. The little one is torn out of its mother's bosom though its loss almost breaks her heartstrings; and the blooming youth is taken from his father's side though the parent's fondest hopes are thereby crushed. Death has no pity for the young and no mercy for the old; he pays no regard to the good or to the beautiful. His scythe cuts down sweet flowers and noxious weeds with equal readiness. He cometh into our garden, trampleth down our lilies and scattereth our roses on the ground; yea, and even the most modest flowers planted in the corner, and hiding their beauty beneath the leaves that they may blush unseen, death spieth out even these, and cares nothing for their fragrance, but withers them with his burning breath. He is thine enemy indeed, thou fatherless child, left for the pitiless storm of a cruel world to beat upon, with none to shelter thee. He is thine enemy, O widow, for the light of thy life is gone, and the desire of thine eyes has been removed with a stroke. He is thine enemy, husband, for thy house is desolate and thy little children cry for their mother of whom death has robbed thee.

Even *those who die* may well count death to be their enemy: I mean not now that they have risen to their seats, and, as disembodied spirits, behold the King in His beauty, but aforetime while death was approaching them. He seemed to their trembling flesh to be a foe, for it is not in nature, except in moments of extreme pain or aberration of mind, or of excessive expectation of glory, for us to be in love with death. It was wise of our Creator so to constitute us that the soul loves the body and the body loves the soul, and they desire to dwell together as long as they may, else had there been no care of self-preservation, and suicide would have destroyed the race.

When death cometh even to the good man he cometh as an enemy, for he is attended by such terrible heralds and grim outriders as do greatly scare us.

> *Fever with brow of fire;*
> *Consumption wan; palsy, half-warmed with life,*
> *And half a clay-cold lump; joint-torturing gout,*
> *And ever-gnawing rheum; convulsion wild;*
> *Swollen dropsy; panting asthma; apoplexy*
> *Full forged.*

None of these add to the aspect of death a particle of beauty. He comes with pains and griefs; he comes with sighs and tears. Clouds and darkness are round about him, an atmosphere laden with dust oppresses those whom he approaches, and a cold wind chills them even to the marrow. He rides on the pale horse, and where his steed sets its foot the land becomes a desert. By the footfall of that terrible steed the worm is awakened to gnaw the slain. When we forget other grand truths and only remember these dreadful things, death is the king of terrors to us. Hearts are sickened and reins are loosened, because of him.

If you think for a few moments of this enemy, you will observe some of his points of character. He is the *common* foe of all God's people, and the enemy of all men: for however some have been persuaded that they should not die, yet is there no discharge in this war; and if in this conscription a man escapes the ballot many and many a year till his grey beard seems to defy the winter's hardest frost, yet must the man of iron yield at last. It is appointed unto all men once to die. The strongest man has no elixir of eternal life wherewith to renew his youth amid the decays of age: nor has the wealthiest prince a price where-with to bribe destruction. To the grave must thou descend, O crowned monarch, for scepters and shovels are akin. To the sepulcher must thou go down, O mighty man of valor, for sword and spade are of like metal. The prince is brother to the worm, and must dwell in the same house. Of our whole race it is true, "Dust thou art, and unto dust shalt thou return."

Death is also a *subtle* foe, lurking everywhere, even in the most harmless things. Who can tell where death has not prepared his ambuscades? He meets us both at home and abroad; at the table he assails men in their food, and at the fountain he poisons their drink. He waylayeth us in the streets, and he seizeth us in our beds; he rideth on the storm at sea, and he walks with us when we are on our way upon the solid land. Whither can we fly to escape from thee, O death, for from the summit of the Alps men have fallen to their graves, and in the deep places of the Earth where the miner goeth down to find the precious ore, there hast thou sacrificed many a hecatomb [large scale slaughter] of precious lives. Death is a subtle foe, and with noiseless footfalls follows close at our heels when least we think of him.

He is an enemy *none of us will be able to avoid*, take what by-paths we may, nor can we escape from him when our hour is come. Into this fowler's nets, like the birds, we shall all fly; in his great seine [net] must all the fishes of the great sea of life be taken when their day is come. As surely as sets the sun, or as the midnight stars at length descend beneath the horizon, or as the waves sink back into the sea, or as the bubble bursts, so must we all early or late come to our end, and disappear from Earth to be known no more among the living.

Sudden too, full often, are the assaults of this enemy.

> *Leaves have their time to fall,*
> *And flowers to wither at the north wind's breath,*
> *And stars to set—but all,*
> *Thou hast all seasons for thine own, O Death!*

Such things have happened as for men to die without an instant's notice; with a psalm upon their lips they have passed away; or engaged in the daily business they have been summoned to give in their account. We have heard of one who, when the morning paper brought him news that a friend in business had died, was drawing on his boots to go to his counting-house, and observed with a laugh that as far as he was concerned, he was so busy he had no time to die. Yet, ere the words were finished, he fell forward and was a corpse. Sudden deaths are not so uncommon as to be marvels if we dwell in the center of a large circle of mankind. Thus is death a foe not to be despised or trifled with. Let us remember all his characteristics, and we shall not be inclined to think lightly of the grim enemy whom our glorious Redeemer has destroyed.

II. Secondly, let us remember that death is an enemy to be destroyed.

Remember that our Lord Jesus Christ has already wrought a great victory upon death so that He has delivered us from life-long bondage through its fear. He has not yet *destroyed death,* but He has gone very near to it, for we are told that He has "abolished death and hath brought life and immortality to light through the gospel." This surely must come very near to having destroyed death altogether.

In the first place, our Lord has subdued death in the very worst sense by having delivered His people from spiritual death. "And you hath he quickened who were dead in trespasses and sins." Once you had no divine life whatever, but the death of original depravity remained upon you, and so you were dead to all divine and spiritual things; but now, beloved, the Spirit of God, even He that raised up Jesus Christ from the dead, has raised you up into newness of life, and you have become new creatures in Christ Jesus. In this sense death has been subdued.

Our Lord in His lifetime also conquered death by restoring certain individuals to life. There were three memorable cases in which at His bidding the last enemy resigned his prey. Our Lord went into the ruler's house, and saw the little girl who had lately fallen asleep in death, around whom they wept and lamented: He heard their scornful laughter, when He said, "She is not dead but sleepeth," and He put them all out and said to her, "Maid, arise!" Then was the spoiler spoiled, and the dungeon door set open. He stopped the funeral procession at the gates of Nain, whence they were carrying forth a young man, "the only son of his mother, and she was a widow," and he said, "Young man, I say unto thee arise." When that young man sat up and our Lord delivered him to his mother, then again was the prey taken from the mighty. Chief of all when Lazarus had laid in the grave so long that his sister said, "Lord, by this time he stinketh," when, in obedience to the words, "Lazarus come forth!" forth came the raised one with his grave clothes still about him, but yet really quickened, then was death seen to be subservient to the Son of man. "Loose him and let him go," said the conquering Christ, and death's bonds were removed, for the lawful captive was delivered. When at the Redeemer's resurrection many of the saints arose and came out of their graves into the holy city then was the crucified Lord proclaimed to be victorious over death and the grave.

Still, brethren, these were but preliminary skirmishes and mere foreshadowings of the grand victory by which death was overthrown. The real triumph was achieved upon the cross—

> He Hell in Hell laid low;
> Made sin, He sin o'erthrew:
> Bow'd to the grave, destroy'd it so,
> And death, by dying, slew.

When Christ died He suffered the penalty of death on the behalf of all His people, and therefore no believer now dies by way of punishment for sin, since we cannot dream that a righteous God would twice exact the penalty for one offence. Death since Jesus died is not a penal infliction upon the children of God: as such He has abolished it, and it can never be enforced. Why die the saints then? Why, because their bodies must be changed ere they can enter Heaven. "Flesh and blood" as they are "cannot inherit the kingdom of God." A divine change must take place upon the body before it will be fit for incorruption and glory; and death and the grave are, as it were, the refining pot and the furnace by means of which the body is made ready for its future bliss. Death, it is true thou art not yet destroyed, but our living Redeemer has so changed thee that thou art no longer death, but something other than thy name! Saints die not now, but they are dissolved and depart. Death is the loosing of the cable that the bark [ship] may freely sail to the fair havens. Death is the fiery chariot in which we ascend to God: it is the gentle voice of the Great King, who cometh into his banqueting hall, and saith, "Friend, come up higher." Behold, on eagle's wings we mount, we fly, far from this land of mist and cloud, into the eternal serenity and brilliance of God's own house above. Yes, our Lord has abolished death. The sting of death is sin, and our great Substitute has taken that sting away by His great sacrifice. Stingless, death abides among the people of God, but it so little harms them that to them "it is not death to die."

Further, Christ vanquished death and thoroughly overcame him when He rose. What a temptation one has to paint a picture of the resurrection, but I will not be led aside to attempt more than a few touches. When our great Champion awoke from His brief sleep of death and found Himself in the withdrawing-room of the grave, He quietly proceeded to put off the garments of the tomb. How leisurely He proceeded! He folded up the napkin and placed it by itself, that those who lose their friends might wipe their eyes therewith; and then He took off the winding sheet and laid the grave clothes by themselves that they might be there when His saints come thither, so that the chamber might be well furnished, and the bed ready sheeted and prepared for their rest. The sepulcher is no longer an empty vault, a dreary charnel, but a chamber of rest, a dormitory furnished and prepared, hung with the arras which Christ Himself has bequeathed. It is now no more a damp, dark, dreary prison: Jesus has changed all that.

> 'Tis now a cell where angels use
> To come and go with Heavenly news.

The angel from Heaven rolled away the stone from our Lord's sepulcher and let in the fresh air and light again upon our Lord, and He stepped out more than a conqueror. Death had fled. The grave had capitulated.

> Lives again our glorious King!
> "Where, O death, is now thy sting?"
> Once He died our souls to save;
> "Where's thy victory, boasting grave?"

Well, brethren, as surely as Christ rose so did He guarantee as an absolute certainty the resurrection of all His saints into a glorious life for their bodies, the life of their souls never having paused even for a moment. In this He conquered death; and since that memorable victory, every day Christ is overcoming death, for He gives His Spirit to His saints, and having that Spirit within them they meet the last enemy without alarm: often they confront Him with songs, perhaps more frequently they face him with calm countenance, and fall asleep with peace. I will not fear thee, death, why should I? Thou lookest like a dragon, but thy sting is gone. Thy teeth are broken, oh old lion, wherefore should I fear thee? I know thou art no more able to destroy me, but thou art sent as a messenger to conduct me to the golden gate wherein I shall enter and see my Savior's unveiled face forever. Expiring saints have often said that their last beds have been the best they have ever slept upon. Many of them have enquired,

Tell me, my soul, can this be death?

To die has been so different a thing from what they expected it to be, so lightsome, and so joyous; they have been so unloaded of all care, have felt so relieved instead of burdened, that they have wondered whether this could be the monster they had been so afraid of all their days. They find it a pin's prick, whereas they feared it would prove a sword-thrust: it is the shutting of the eye on Earth and the opening of it in Heaven, whereas they thought it would have been a stretching upon the rack, or a dreary passage through a dismal region of gloom and dread. Beloved, our exalted Lord has overcome death in all these ways.

But now, observe, that this is not the text:—the text speaks of something yet to be done. The last enemy that *shall be* destroyed is death, so that death in the sense meant by the text is not destroyed yet. He is to be destroyed, and how will that be?

Well, I take it death will be destroyed in the sense first that, at the coming of Christ, *those who are alive and remain shall not see death.* They shall be changed; there must be a change even to the living before they can inherit eternal life, but they shall not actually die. Do not envy them, for they will have no preference beyond those that sleep; rather do I think theirs to be the inferior lot of the two in some respects. But they will not know death: the multitude of the Lord's own who will be alive at His coming will pass into the glory without needing to die. Thus death, as far as they are concerned, will be destroyed.

But the sleeping ones, the myriads who have left their flesh and bones to molder back to earth, death shall be destroyed even as to them, for when the trumpet sounds they shall rise from the tomb. *The resurrection is the destruction of death.* We never taught, nor believed, nor thought that every particle of every body that was put into the grave would come to its fellow, and that the absolutely identical material would rise; but we do say that the identical body will be raised, and that as surely as there cometh out of the ground the seed that was put into it, though in very different guise, for it cometh not forth as a seed but as a flower, so surely shall the same body rise again. The same material is not necessary, but there shall come out of the grave, aye, come out of the earth, if it never saw a grave, or come out of the sea if devoured by monsters, that selfsame body for true identity which was inhabited by the soul while here below. Was it not so with our Lord? Even so shall it be with His own people, and then shall be brought to pass the saying that is written, "Death is swallowed up in victory. O death, where is thy sting! O grave where is thy victory!"

There will be this feature in our Lord's victory, that death will be fully destroyed because *those who rise will not be one whit the worse for having died.* I believe concerning those new bodies that there will he no trace upon them of the feebleness of old age, none of the marks of long and wearying sickness, none of the scars of martyrdom. Death shall not have left his mark upon them at all, except it be some glory mark which shall be to their honor, like the scars in the flesh of the Well beloved, which are His chief beauty even now in the eyes of those for whom His hands and feet were pierced. In this sense death shall be destroyed because he shall have done no damage to the saints at all, the very trace of decay shall have been swept away from the redeemed.

And then, finally, there shall, after this trumpet of the Lord, be no *more death,* neither sorrow, nor crying, for the former things have passed away. "Christ being raised from the dead dieth no more, death hath no more dominion over him"; and so also the quickened ones, His own redeemed, they too shall die no more. Oh dreadful, dreadful supposition, that they should ever have to undergo temptation or pain, or death a second time. It cannot be. "Because I live," says Christ, "they shall live also." Yet the doctrine of the natural immortality of the soul having been given up by some, certain of them have felt obliged to give up with the eternity of future punishment the eternity of future bliss, and assuredly as far as some great proof texts are concerned, they stand or fall together. "These shall go away into everlasting punishment, and the righteous into life eternal"; if the one state be short, so must the other be: whatever the adjective means in the one case it means in the other. To us the word means endless duration in both cases, and we look forward to a bliss which shall never know end or duration. Then in the tearless, sorrowless, graveless country, death shall be utterly destroyed.

III. And now last of all, (and the word "last" sounds fitly in this case), death is to be destroyed last.

Because he came in last he must go out last. Death was not the first of our foes: first came the devil, then sin, then death. Death is not the worst of enemies; death is an enemy, but he is much to be preferred to our other adversaries. It were better to die a thousand times than to sin. To be tried by death is nothing compared with being tempted by the devil. The mere physical pains connected with dissolution are comparative trifles compared with the hideous grief which is caused by sin and the burden which a sense of guilt causes to the soul. No, death is but a secondary mischief compared with the defilement of sin. Let the great enemies go down first; smite the shepherd and the sheep will be scattered; let sin, and Satan, the lord of all these evils, be smitten first, and death may well be left to the last.

Notice, that death is the last enemy to each individual Christian and the last to be destroyed. Well now, if the word of God says it is the last I want to remind you of a little piece of practical wisdom—leave him to be the last. Brother, do not dispute the appointed order, but let the last be last. I have known a brother wanting to vanquish death long before he died. But, brother, you do not want dying grace till dying moments. What would be the good of dying grace while you are yet alive? A boat will only be needful when you reach a river. Ask for living grace, and glorify Christ thereby, and then you shall have dying grace when dying time comes. Your enemy is going to be destroyed, but not today. There is a great host of enemies to be fought today, and you may be content to let this one alone for a while. This enemy will be destroyed, but of the times and the seasons we are in ignorance; our wisdom is to be good soldiers of Jesus Christ as the duty of every day requires. Take your trials as they come, brother! God will in due time help you to overcome your last enemy, but meanwhile see to it that you overcome the world, the flesh, and the devil. If you live well you will die well. That same covenant in which the Lord Jesus gave you life contains also the grant of death, for "All things are yours, whether things present or things to come, or life or death, all are yours, and ye are Christ's, and Christ is God's."

Why is death left to the last? Well, I think it is because Christ can make much use of him. The last enemy that shall be destroyed is death, because death is of great service before he is destroyed. Oh, what lessons some of us have learned from death! There are, perhaps, no sermons like the deaths which have happened in our households; the departure of our beloved friends have been to us solemn discourses of divine wisdom, which our heart could not help hearing. So Christ has spared death to make him a preacher to his saints. Brethren, if I may die as I have seen some of our church members die, I court the grand occasion. I would not wish to escape death by some by-road if I may sing as they sang. If I may have such hosannas and hallelujahs beaming in my very eyes as I have seen as well as heard from them, it were a blessed thing to die. Yes, as a supreme test of love and faith, death is well respited awhile to let the saints glorify their Master.

Besides, brethren, without death we should not be so conformed to Christ as we shall be if we fall asleep in Him. If there could be any jealousies in Heaven among the saints, I think that any saint who does not die, but is changed when Christ comes, could almost meet me and you, who probably will die, and say, "My brother, there is one thing I have missed, I never lay in the grave, I never had the chill hand of death laid on me, and so in that I was not conformed to my Lord. But *you* know what it is to have fellowship with Him, even in His death." Did I not well say that they that were alive and remain should have no preference over them that are asleep? I think the preference if anything shall belong to us who sleep in Jesus, and wake up in His likeness.

Death, dear friends, is not yet destroyed, because he brings the saints home. He does but come to them and whisper his message, and in a moment they are supremely blessed.

> *Have done with sin and care and woe,*
> *And with the Savior rest.*

And so death is not destroyed yet, for he answers useful purposes.

But, beloved, he is going to be destroyed. He is the last enemy of the church collectively. The church as a body has had a mass of foes to contend with, but after the resurrection we shall say, "This is the last enemy. Not another foe is left." Eternity shall roll on in ceaseless bliss. There may be changes, bringing new delights; perhaps in the eternity to come there may be eras and ages of yet more amazing bliss, and still more superlative ecstasy; but there shall be

> *No rude alarm of raging foes,*
> *No cares to break the last repose.*

The last enemy that shall be destroyed is death, and if the last be slain there can be no future foe. The battle is fought and the victory is won forever. And who hath won it? Who but the Lamb that sitteth on the throne, to Whom let us all ascribe honor, and glory, and majesty, and power, and dominion, and might, forever and ever. The Lord help us in our solemn adoration. Amen.

Following the Risen Christ

"If ye then be risen with Christ, seek those things which are above, where Christ sitteth on the right hand of God. Set your affection on things above, not on things on the earth."—Colossians 3:1, 2.

The resurrection of our divine Lord from the dead is the corner-stone of Christian doctrine. Perhaps I might more accurately call it the key-stone of the arch of Christianity, for if that fact could be disproved the whole fabric of the gospel would fall to the ground. If Jesus Christ be not risen then is our preaching vain, and your faith is also vain; ye are yet in your sins. If Christ be not risen, then they which have fallen asleep in Christ have perished, and we ourselves, in missing so glorious a hope as that of resurrection, are of all men the most miserable.

Because of the great importance of His resurrection, our Lord was pleased to give many infallible proofs of it, by appearing again and again in the midst of His followers. It would be interesting to search out how many times He appeared; I think we have mention of some sixteen manifestations. He showed Himself openly before His disciples, and did eat and drink with them. They touched His hands and His side, and heard His voice, and knew that it was the same Jesus that was crucified. He was not content with giving evidence to the ears and to the eyes, but even to the sense of touch He proved the reality of His resurrection.

These appearances were very varied. Sometimes He gave an interview to one alone, either to a man, as to Cephas, or to a woman, as to Magdalene. He conversed with two of His followers as they went to Emmaus, and with the company of the apostles by the sea. We find Him at one moment amongst the eleven when the doors were shut for fear of the Jews, and at another time in the midst of an assembly of more than five hundred brethren, who years after were most of them living witnesses to the fact. They could not all have been deceived. It is not possible that any historical fact could have been placed upon a better basis of credibility than the resurrection of our Lord from the dead. This is put beyond all dispute and question, and of purpose is it so done, because it is essential to the whole Christian system.

For this same cause the resurrection of Christ is commemorated frequently. There is no ordinance in Scripture of any one Lord's-day in the year being set apart to commemorate the rising of Christ from the dead, for this reason, that every Lord's-day is the memorial of our Lord's resurrection. Wake up any Lord's-day you please, whether in the depth of winter, or in the warmth of summer, and you may sing:

> Today He rose and left the dead,
> And Satan's empire fell;
> Today the saints His triumph spread,
> And all His wonders tell.

To set apart an Easter Sunday for special memory of the resurrection is a human device, for which there is no Scriptural command, but to make every Lord's-day an Easter Sunday is due to Him Who rose early on the first day of the week. We gather together on the first rather than upon the seventh day of the week, because redemption is even a greater work than creation, and more worthy of commemoration, and because the rest which followed creation is far outdone by that which ensues upon the completion of redemption. Like the apostles, we meet on the first day of the week, and hope that Jesus may stand in our midst, and say, "Peace be unto you." Our Lord has lifted the Sabbath from the old and rusted hinges whereon the law had placed it long before, and set it on the new golden hinges which His love has fashioned. He hath placed our rest-day, not at the end of a week of toil, but at the beginning of the rest which remaineth for the people of God. Every first day of the week we should meditate upon the rising of our Lord, and seek to enter into fellowship with Him in His risen life.

Never let us forget that all who are in Him rose from the dead in His rising. Next in importance to the fact of the resurrection is the doctrine of the federal headship of Christ, and the unity of all His people with Him. It is because we are in Christ that we become partakers of everything that Christ did—we are circumcised with Him, dead with Him, buried with Him, risen with Him, because we cannot be separated from Him. We are members of His body, and not a bone of Him can be broken. Because that union is most intimate, continuous, and indissoluble, therefore all that concerns Him concerns us, and as He rose so all His people have arisen in Him.

They are risen in two ways. First, representatively. All the elect rose in Christ in the day when He quitted the tomb. He was justified, or declared to be clear of all liabilities on account of our sins, by being set free from the prison-house of the tomb. There was no reason for detaining Him in the sepulcher, for He had discharged the debts of His people by dying "unto sin once." He was our hostage and our representative, and when He came forth from His bonds we came forth in Him. We have endured the sentence of the law in our Substitute, we have lain in its prison, and even died under its death-warrant, and now we are no longer under its curse. "Now if we be dead with Christ, we believe that we shall also live with him: knowing that Christ being raised from the dead dieth no more; death hath no more dominion over him. For in that he died, he died unto sin once; but in that he liveth, he liveth unto God."

Next to this representative resurrection comes our spiritual resurrection, which is ours as soon as we are led by faith to believe in Jesus Christ. Then it may be said of us, "And you hath he quickened who were dead in trespasses and sins."

The resurrection blessing is to be perfected by-and-by at the appearing of our Lord and Savior, for then our bodies shall rise again, if we fall asleep before His coming. He redeemed our manhood in its entirety, spirit, soul, and body, and He will not be content until the resurrection which has passed upon our spirit shall pass upon our body too. These dry bones shall live; together with His dead body they shall rise.

> When He arose ascending high,
> He showed our feet the way;
> Up to the Lord our flesh shall fly
> At the great rising day.

Then shall we know in the perfection of our resurrection beauty that we are indeed completely risen in Christ, and "as in Adam all die, so in Christ shall all be made alive."

This morning we shall only speak of our fellowship with Christ in His resurrection as to our own spiritual resurrection. Do not misunderstand me as if I thought the resurrection to be only spiritual, for a literal rising from the dead is yet to come; but our text speaks of spiritual resurrection, and I shall therefore endeavor to set it before you.

I. First, then, let us consider our spiritual rising with Christ: "If ye then be risen with Christ."

Though the words look like a supposition they are not meant to be so. The apostle casts no doubt, and raises no question, but merely puts it thus for argument's sake. It might just as well be read, "Since ye then are risen in Christ." The "if" is used logically, not theologically: by way of argument, and not by way of doubt. All who believe in Christ are risen with Christ. Let us meditate on this truth.

For, first, we were "dead in trespasses and sins," but having believed in Christ *we have been quickened by the Holy Ghost,* and we are dead no longer. There we lay in the tomb, ready to become corrupt. We lay in our death quite unable to raise ourselves there from; ours were eyes that could not see, and ears that could not hear; a heart that could not love; and a withered hand that could not be stretched out to give the touch of faith. We were as guilty as if we had power, for the loss of moral power is not the loss of moral responsibility: we were, therefore, in a state of spiritual death of the most fearful kind. The Holy Spirit visited us and made us live.

We remember the first sensation of life, some of us—how it seemed to tingle in our soul's veins with pain sharp and bitter; just as drowning persons when life is coming back to them suffer great pain; so did we. Conviction was wrought in us and confession of sin, a dread of judgment to come and a sense of present condemnation; but these were tokens of life, and that life gradually deepened and opened up until the eye was opened—we could see Christ, the hand ceased to be withered, and we stretched it out and touched His garment's hem; the feet began to move in the way of obedience, and the heart felt the sweet glow of love within. Then the eyes, not content with seeing, fell to weeping; and afterwards, when the tears were wiped away, they flashed and sparkled with delight.

Oh, my brethren, believers in Jesus, you are not spiritually dead any longer; on Christ you have believed, and that grand act proves that you are no more dead. You have been quickened by God according to the working of His mighty power, which He wrought in Christ when He raised Him from the dead, and set Him at His own right hand in the Heavenlies. Now, beloved, you are new creatures, the produce of a second birth, begotten again in Christ Jesus unto newness of life. Christ is your life; such a life as you never knew before, nor could have known apart from Him. If ye then be risen with Christ ye walk in newness of life, while the world abideth in death.

Let us advance another step: we are risen with Christ, and therefore *there has been wrought in us a wonderful change.* When the dead shall rise they will not appear as they now are. The buried seed rises from the ground, but not as a seed, for it puts forth green leaf, and bud, and stem, and gradually develops expanding flower and fruit, and even so we wear a new form, for we are renewed after the image of Him that created us in righteousness and holiness.

I ask you to consider the change which the Spirit of God has wrought in the believer: a wonderful change indeed! Before regeneration our soul was as our body will be when it dies; and we read that "it is sown in corruption." There was corruption in our mind and it was working irresistibly towards every evil and offensive thing. In many the corruption did not appear upon the surface, but it worked within; in others it was conspicuous and fearful to look upon. How great the change! For now the power of corruption within us is broken, the new life has overcome it, for it is a living and incorruptible seed which liveth and abideth forever. Corruption is upon the old nature, but it cannot touch the new, which is our true and real self. Is it not a great thing to be purged of the filthiness which would have ultimately brought us down to Tophet where the fire unquenchable burns, and the worm undying feeds upon the corrupt?

When a body is buried, we are told by the apostle again that it is "sown in weakness." The poor dead frame cannot lay itself down in its last bed, friendly hands must place it there; even so we were utter weakness towards all good. When we were the captives of sin we could do nothing good, even as our Lord said, "Without me ye can do nothing." We were incapable of even a good thought apart from Him. But "when we were yet without strength, in due time Christ died for the ungodly"; and now we know Him and the power of His resurrection. God hath given us the spirit of power and of love; is it not written, "As many as received him, to them gave he power to become the sons of God, even to them that believe on his name"? This change from the natural to the spiritual is such as only God Himself could have wrought, and yet we have experienced it. To God be the glory. So that by virtue of our rising in Christ we have received life and have become the subjects of a wondrous change—"old things are passed away; behold, all things are become new."

In consequence of our receiving this life and undergoing this change *the things of the world and sin become a tomb to us.* To a dead man a sepulcher is as good a dwelling as he can want. You may call it his bedchamber, if you will; for he lies within it as unconscious as if he were in slumber. But the moment the dead man lives, he will not endure such a bedchamber; he calls it a dreary vault, a loathsome dungeon, an unbearable charnel, and he must leave it at once. So when you and I were natural men, and had no spiritual life, the things of this life contented us; but it is far otherwise now. A merely outward religion was all that we desired; a dead form suited a dead soul. Judaism pleased those who were under its yoke, in the very beginning of the gospel; new moons and holy days and traditional ordinances, and fasting and feasting were great things with those who forgot their resurrection with Christ. All those things make pretty furniture for a dead man's chamber; but when the eternal life enters the soul these outward ordinances are flung off, the living man rends off his grave clothes, tears away his cerements, and demands such garments as are suitable for life. So the apostle in the chapter before our text tells us to let no man spoil us by the traditions of men and the inventions of a dead ritualism, for these things are not the portion of renewed and spiritual men.

So, too, all merely carnal objects become as a grave to us, whether they be sinful pleasures or selfish gains. For the dead man the shroud, the coffin, and the vault are suitable enough; but make the corpse alive again, and he cannot rest in the coffin; He makes desperate struggles to break it up. See how by main force he dashes up the lid, rends off his bandages, and leaps from the bier. So the man renewed by grace cannot abide sin, it is a coffin to him: he cannot bear evil pleasures, they are as a shroud; he cries for liberty. When resurrection comes the man uplifts the hillock above his grave, and scatters monument and headstone, if these are raised above him. Some souls are buried under a mass of self-righteousness, like wealthy men on whom shrines of marble have been heaped; but all these the believer shakes off, he must have them away, he cannot bear these dead works. He cannot live otherwise than by faith; all other life is death to him. He must get out of his former state; for as a tomb is not a fit place for a living man, so when we are quickened by grace the things of sin, and self, and carnal sense become dreary catacombs to us, wherein our soul feels buried, and out of which we must arise. How can we that are raised out of the death of sin live any longer therein?

And, now, beloved, *we are at this time wholly raised from the dead* in a spiritual sense. Let us think of this, for our Lord did not have His head quickened while His feet remained in the sepulcher; but He rose a perfect and entire Man, alive throughout. Even so have we been renewed in every part. We have received, though it be but in its infancy, a perfect spiritual life: we are perfect in Christ Jesus. In our inner man our eye is opened, our ear is awakened, our hand is active, our foot is nimble: our every faculty is there, though as yet immature, and needing development, and having the old dead nature to contend with.

Moreover, and best of all, we are so raised that *we shall die no more.* Oh, tell me no more the dreary tale that a man who has received the divine life may yet lose grace and perish. With our Bibles in our hands we know better. "Christ being raised from the dead dieth no more, death hath no more dominion over him," and therefore he that hath received Christ's life in him shall never die. Hath He not said, "He that believeth in me, though he were dead yet shall he live; and whosoever liveth and believeth in me shall never die"? This life which He has given us shall be in us "a well of water, springing up unto everlasting life." He has Himself said, "I give unto my sheep eternal life, and they shall never perish, neither shall any pluck them out of my hand." On the day of our quickening we bid farewell to spiritual death, and to the sepulcher wherein we slept under sin's dominion. Farewell, thou deadly love of sin; we have done with thee! Farewell, dead world, corrupt world; we have done with thee! Christ has raised us. Christ has given us eternal life. We forsake forever the dreary abodes of death, and seek the heavenly places. Our Jesus lives, and because He lives we shall live also, world without end.

Thus I have tried to work out the metaphor of resurrection, by which our spiritual renewal is so well set forth.

II. *We are urged by the apostle to use the life which we have received, and so, secondly, let us exercise the new life in suitable pursuits.*

"If ye then be risen with Christ, seek those things which are above." Let your actions be agreeable to your new life.

First, then, *let us leave the sepulcher.* If we are quickened, our first act should be to leave the region of death. Let us quit the vault of a merely outward religion, and let us worship God in spirit and in truth. Let us have done with priestcraft, and all the black business of spiritual undertaking, and let the dead bury their dead; we will have none of it. Let us have done with outward forms, and rites, and ceremonies, which are not of Christ's ordaining, and let us know nothing save Christ crucified; for that which is not of the living Lord is a mere piece of funeral pomp, fit for the cemeteries of formalists, whose whole religion is a shoveling in of dust on coffin lids. "Earth to earth, ashes to ashes, dust to dust." "That which is born of the flesh is flesh."

Let us also quit the vault of carnal enjoyments, wherein men seek to satisfy themselves with provision for the flesh. Let us not live by the sight of the eye, nor by the hearing of the ear. Let us not live for the amassing of wealth, or the gaining of fame, for these ought to be as dead things to the man who is risen in Christ. Let us not live for the world which we see, nor after the fashion of men to whom this life is everything. Let us live as those that have come out of the world, and who, though they are in it, are no more of it. Let us be unmindful of the country from whence we came out, and leave it, as Abraham did, as though there were no such country, henceforth dwelling with our God, sojourners with Him, seeking "a city which hath foundations, whose builder and maker is God." As Jesus Christ left behind Him all the abodes of death, let us do the same.

And, then, let us *hasten to forget every evil, even as our Lord hastened to leave the tomb.* How little a time, after all, did He sojourn among the dead. He must needs lie in the heart of the Earth three days, but He made them as short as possible, so that it is difficult to make out the three days at all. They were there, for there were fragments of each period, but surely never were three days so short as Jesus made them. He cut them short in righteousness, and being loosed from the pains of death, He rose early, at the very break of day. At the first instant that it was possible for Him to get away from the sepulcher consistently with the Scriptures He left the napkin and the grave-clothes, and stood in the garden, waiting to salute His disciples. So let it be with us: there should be no lingering, no loitering, no hankering after the world, no clinging to its vanities, no making provision for the flesh. Up in the morning early, oh ye who are spiritually quickened! Up in the morning early, from your ease, your carnal pleasure, your love of wealth and self, and away out from the dark vault into a congenial sphere of action: "If ye then be risen with Christ, seek those things which are above."

To pursue the analogy: when our Lord had left the tomb thus early He spent a season on Earth among His disciples, *and we are to pass the time of our sojourning here on earth, as His was passed, and in holy service.* Our Lord reckoned that He was on the move from Earth as soon as He rose. If you remember, He said, "I ascend unto my Father, and your Father." He did not say, "I shall ascend," as though He looked at it as a future thing; but He said, "I ascend," as if it were so quickly to be done that it was already doing. Forty days He stayed, for He had forty days' work to do; but He looked upon Himself as already going up into Heaven. He had done with the world, He had done with the grave, and now He said, "I ascend to my Father, and your Father."

We also have our forty days to tarry here; the period may be longer or shorter as the providence of God ordains, but it will soon be over, and the time of our departure will come. Let us spend our risen life on Earth as Jesus spent His—in a greater seclusion from the world and in greater nearness to Heaven than ever. Our Lord occupied Himself much in testimony, manifesting Himself, as we have already seen, in diverse ways, to His friends and followers. Let us also manifest the fruits of our risen life, and bear testimony to the power of God. Let all men see that you are risen. So live that there can be no more doubt about your spiritual resurrection than there was about Christ's literal resurrection. Let us spend the time of our sojourning here in the fear of God worshiping Him, serving Him, glorifying Him, endeavoring to set everything in order for the extension of our Master's kingdom, for the comforting of His saints, for the accomplishment of His sacred purposes.

But now I have led you up so far, I want to go further and rise higher. May the Lord help us. *Let our minds ascend to Heaven in Christ.* Even while our bodies are here we are to be drawn upwards with Christ; attracted to Him, so that we can say, "He hath raised us up together and made us sit together in heavenly places in Christ Jesus." Our text saith, "Seek those things which are above where Christ sitteth on the right hand of God"; what is this but rising to heavenly pursuits? Jesus has gone up; let us go up with Him. As to these bodies, we cannot as yet ascend, for they are not fit to inherit the kingdom of God; yet let our thoughts and hearts mount up and build a happy rest on high. Let not a stray thought alone ascend like one lone bird which sings and mounts the sky; but let our whole mind, soul, spirit, heart, arise as when doves fly as a cloud.

Let us be practical, too, and in very deed seek the things that are above: seek them because we feel we need them; seek them because we greatly prize them; seek them because we hope to gain them; for a man will not heartily seek for that which he hath no hope of obtaining. The things which are above which we are even now to seek are such as these; let us seek heavenly communion, for we are no more numbered with the congregation of the dead, but we have fellowship in Christ's resurrection, and with all the risen ones. "Truly our fellowship is with the Father and with his Son Jesus Christ," and "our conversation is in Heaven." Let us seek to walk with the living God, and to know the fellowship of the Spirit.

Let us seek heavenly graces; for "every good gift and every perfect gift is from above." Let us seek more faith, more love, more patience, more zeal: let us labor after greater charity, greater brotherly kindness, greater humbleness of spirit. Let us labor after likeness to Christ, that He may be the first-born among many brethren. Seek to bear the image of the heavenly, and to wear those jewels which adorn heavenly spirits.

"Seek those things which are above," that is, heavenly joys. Oh seek to know on Earth the peace of Heaven, the rest of Heaven, the victory of Heaven, the service of Heaven, the communion of Heaven, the holiness of Heaven: you may have foretastes of all these; seek after them. Seek, in a word, to be preparing for the Heaven which Christ is preparing for you. You are soon to dwell above; robe yourselves for the great festival. Your treasure is above, let your hearts be with it. All that you are to possess in eternity is above, where Christ is; rise, then, and enjoy it. Let hope anticipate the joys which are reserved, and so let us begin our Heaven here below. If ye then be risen with Christ, live according to your risen nature, for your life is hid with Christ in God.

What a magnet to draw us towards Heaven should this fact be—that Christ sitteth at God's right hand. Where should the wife's thoughts be when her husband is away, but with the absent and beloved one? You know, brethren, it is not otherwise with us: the objects of our affection are always followed by our thoughts. Let Jesus, then, be as a great loadstone, drawing our meditations and affections towards Himself. He is *sitting,* for His work is done; as it is written, "This man, when he had offered one sacrifice for sins forever, sat down at the right hand of God." Let us rise and rest with Him. He is sitting on a throne. Observe His majesty, delight in His power, and trust in His dominion. He is sitting at the right hand of God in the place of honor and favor. This is a proof that we are beloved and favored of God, for our representative has the choicest place, at God's right hand. Let your hearts ascend and enjoy that love and favor with Him. Take wing, my thoughts, and fly away to Jesus. My soul, hast thou not often said, "Woe's me that I dwell in Meshech, and tabernacle in the tents of Kedar: oh that I had wings like a dove, that I might flee away and be at rest"? Now, then, my soul, here are wings for thee. Jesus draws thee upward. Thou hast a right to be where Jesus is, for thou art married to Him; therefore let thy thoughts abide with Him, rest in Him, delight in Him, rejoice in Him, and yet again rejoice. The sacred ladder is before us; let us climb it until by faith we sit in the Heavenlies with Him.

May the Spirit of God bless these words to you.

III. Thirdly, inasmuch as we are risen with Christ, let the new life delight itself in suitable objects.

This brings in the second verse: "Set your affection on things above, not on things on the earth." "Set your affection." These words do not quite express the meaning, though they are as near it as any one clause could well come. We might render it thus: "Have a relish for things above"; or, "study industriously things above"; or, "set your mind on things above, not on things on the earth." That which is proper enough for a dead man is quite unsuitable for a risen one. Objects of desire which might suit us when we were sinners are not legitimate nor worthy objects for us when we are made saints. As we are quickened we must exercise life, and as we have ascended we must love higher things than those of earth.

What are these "things above" which we should set our affection upon? I ask you now to lift your eyes above yon clouds and this lower firmament to the residence of God. What see you there? First, there is *God Himself.* Make Him the subject of your thoughts, your desires, your emotions, your love. "Delight thyself also in the Lord, and he will give thee the desires of thine heart." "My soul, wait thou only upon God, for my expectation is from him." Call Him "God my exceeding joy." Let nothing come between you and your heavenly Father. What is all the world if you have not God, and when you once have God, what matters it though all the world be gone? God is all things, and when thou canst say "God is mine," thou art richer than Croesus. O to say, "Whom have I in Heaven but thee? and there is none upon Earth that I desire beside thee." O to love God with all our heart, and with all our soul, and with all our mind, and with all our strength: that is what the law required, it is what the gospel enables us to render.

What see I next? I see *Jesus,* who is God, but yet is truly Man. Need I press upon you, beloved, to set your love upon the Well-beloved? Has He not won your heart, and doth He not hold it now as under a mighty spell? I know you love Him. Fix your mind on Him then. Often meditate upon His divine person, His perfect work, His mediatorial glory, His second coming, His glorious reign, His love for you, your own security in Him, your union with Him. Oh let these sweet thoughts possess your breasts, fill your mouths, and influence your lives. Let the morning break with thoughts of Christ, and let your last thought at night be sweetened with His presence. Set your affection upon Him Who has set His affection upon you.

But what next do I see above? I see *the new Jerusalem,* which is the mother of us all. I see the church of Christ triumphant in Heaven, with which the church militant is one. We do not often enough realize the fact that we are come unto the general assembly and church of the firstborn, whose names are written in Heaven. Love all the saints, but do not forget the saints above. Have fellowship with them, for we make but one communion. Remember those:

> *Who once were mourning here below,*
> *And wet their couch with tears,*
> *Who wrestled hard, as we do now,*
> *With sins, and doubts, and fears.*

Speak with the braves who have won their crowns, the heroes who have fought a good fight, and now rest from their labors, waving the palm. Let your hearts be often among the perfected, with whom you are to spend eternity.

And what else is there above that our hearts should love but *Heaven itself?* It is the place of holiness; let us so love it that we begin to be holy here. It is the place of rest; let us so delight in it that by faith we enter into that rest. O my brethren, you have vast estates which you have never seen; and methinks if I had an estate on Earth which was soon to be mine I should wish to take a peep over the hedge now and then. If I could not take possession, I should like to see what I had in reversion. I would make an excuse to pass that way and say to any who were with me, "That estate is going to be mine before long." In your present poverty console yourselves with the many mansions. In your sickness delight much in the land where the inhabitants shall no more say, "I am sick." In the midst of depression of spirit comfort your heart with the prospect of unmixed felicity.

> *No more fatigue, no more distress,*
> *Nor sin nor death shall reach the place;*
> *No groans to mingle with the songs*
> *Which warble from, immortal tongues.*

What! Are you fettered to earth? Can you not project yourself into the future? The stream of death is narrow; cannot your imagination and your faith leap over the brook to stand on the hither shore awhile and cry, "All is mine, and mine forever. Where Jesus is there shall I be; where Jesus sits there shall I rest":

> *Far from a world of grief and sin,*
> *With God eternally shut in?*

"Set your affection on things above." Oh to get away at this present time from these dull cares which like a fog envelope us! Even we that are Christ's servants, and live in His court, at times feel weary, and droop as if His service were hard. He never means it to be a bondage, and it is our fault if we make it so. Martha's service is due, but she is not called to be *cumbered* with much serving; that is her own arrangement: let us serve abundantly, and yet sit with Mary at the Master's feet.

You who are in business, and mix with the world by the necessity of your callings, must find it difficult to keep quite clear of the down-dragging influences of this poor world; it will hamper you if it can. You are like a bird, which is always in danger when it alights on the earth. There are lime-twigs, and traps, and nets, and guns, and a poor bird is never safe except upon the wing and up aloft. Yet birds must come down to feed, and they do well to gather their meal in haste, and take to their wings again. When we come down among men we must speedily be up again. When you have to mix with the world, and see its sin and evil, yet take heed that you do not light on the ground without your Father: and then, as soon as ever you have picked up your barley, rise again, away, away, for this is not your rest. You are like Noah's dove flying over the waste of waters, there is no rest for the sole of your feet but on the ark with Jesus.

On this resurrection-day fence out the world, let us chase away the wild boar of the wood, and let the vines bloom, and the tender grapes give forth their good smell, and let the Beloved come and walk in the garden of our souls, while we delight ourselves in Him and in His heavenly gifts. Let us not carry our burden of things below on this holy day, but let us keep it as a Sabbath unto the Lord. On the Sabbath we are no more to work with our minds than with our hands. Cares and anxieties of an earthly kind defile the day of sacred rest. The essence of Sabbath-breaking lies in worry, and murmuring, and unbelief, with which too many are filled. Put these away, beloved, for we are risen with Christ, and it is not meet that we should wander among the tombs. Nay, rather let us sing unto the Lord a new song, and praise Him with our whole soul.

The Resurrection of Our Lord Jesus

"Remember that Jesus Christ of the seed of David was raised from the dead according to my gospel."—II Timothy 2:8.

O ur text is found in Paul's second letter to Timothy. The venerable minister is anxious about the young man who has preached with remarkable success, and whom he regards in some respects as his successor. The old man is about to put off his tabernacle, and he is concerned that his son in the gospel, should preach the same truth as his father has preached, and should by no means adulterate the gospel. A tendency showed itself in Timothy's day, and the same tendency exists at this very hour, to try to get away from the simple matters of fact upon which our religion is built, to something more philosophical and hard to be understood. The word which the common people heard gladly is not fine enough for cultured sages, and so they must needs surround it with a mist of human thought and speculation.

Three or four plain facts constitute the gospel, even as Paul puts it in the fifteenth chapter of his first Epistle to the Corinthians: "For I delivered unto you first of all that which I also received, how that Christ died for our sins according to the Scriptures; and that he was buried, and that he rose again the third day according to the Scriptures." Upon the incarnation, life, death, and resurrection of Jesus our salvation hinges. He who believes these truths aright hath believed the gospel, and believing the gospel he shall without doubt find eternal salvation therein.

But men want novelties; they cannot endure that the trumpet should give forth the same certain sound, they crave some fresh fantasia every day. *"The gospel with variations"* is the music for them. Intellect is progressive, they say; they must, therefore, march ahead of their forefathers. Incarnate Deity, a holy life, an atoning death, and a literal resurrection—having heard these things now for nearly nineteen centuries they are just a little stale, and the cultivated mind hungers for a change from the old fashioned manna. Even in Paul's day this tendency was manifest, and so they sought to regard facts as mysteries or parables, and they labored to find a spiritual meaning in them till they went so far as to deny them as actual facts. The Apostle Paul was very anxious that Timothy at least should stand firm to the old witness, and should understand in their plain meaning his testimonies to the fact that Jesus Christ of the seed of David rose again from the dead.

Within the compass of this verse several facts are recorded: and, first, there is here the great truth that Jesus, the Son of the Highest, was anointed of God; the apostle calls Him "Jesus *Christ*," that is, the anointed One, the Messiah, the sent of God. He calls Him also *"Jesus,"* which signifies a Savior, and it is a grand truth that He Who was born of Mary, He Who was laid in the manger at Bethlehem, He Who loved and lived and died for us, is the ordained and anointed Savior of men. We have not a moment's doubt about the mission, office, and design of our Lord Jesus; in fact, we hang our soul's salvation upon His being anointed of the Lord to be the Savior of men.

This Jesus Christ was really and truly man; for Paul says He was *"of the seed of David."* True He was divine, and His birth was not after the ordinary manner of men, but still He was in all respects partaker of our human nature, and came of the stock of David. This also we do believe. We are not among those who spiritualize the incarnation, and suppose that God was here as a phantom, or that the whole story is but an instructive legend. Nay, in very flesh and blood did the Son of God abide among men: bone of our bone and flesh of our flesh: was He in the days of His sojourn here below. We know and believe that Jesus Christ has come in the flesh. We love the incarnate God and in Him we fix our trust.

It is implied, too, in the text that *Jesus died;* for He could not be raised from the dead if He had not first gone down among the dead, and been one of them. Yes, Jesus died: the crucifixion was no delusion, the piercing of His side with a spear was most clear and evident proof that He was dead: His heart was pierced, and the blood and water flowed therefrom. As a dead man He was taken down from the cross and carried by gentle hands, and laid in Joseph's virgin tomb. I think I see that pale corpse, white as a lily. Mark how it is stained with the blood of His five wounds, which make Him red as the rose. See how the holy women tenderly wrap Him in fine linen with sweet spices, and leave Him to spend His Sabbath all alone in the rock-hewn sepulcher. No man in this world was ever more surely dead than He. "He made his grave with the wicked and with the rich in his death." As dead they laid Him in the place of the dead, with napkin and grave-clothes, and habiliments fit for a grave: then they rolled the great stone at the grave's mouth and left Him, knowing that He was dead.

Then comes the grand truth, that as soon as ever the third sun commenced his shining circuit *Jesus rose again.* His body had not decayed, for it was not possible for that holy thing to see corruption; but still it had been dead; and by the power of God—by His own power, by the Father's power, by the power of the Spirit—for it is attributed to each of these in turn, before the sun had risen His dead body was quickened. The silent heart began again to beat, and through the stagnant canals of the veins the life-flood began to circulate. The soul of the Redeemer again took possession of the body, and it lived once more. There He was within the sepulcher, as truly living us to all parts of Him as He had ever been. He literally and truly, in a material body, came forth from the tomb to live among men till the hour of His ascension into Heaven. This is the truth which is still to be taught, refine it who may, spiritualize it who dare. This is the historical fact which the apostles witnessed; this is the truth for which the confessors bled and died. This is the doctrine which is the keystone of the arch of Christianity, and they that hold it not have cast aside the essential truth of God. How can they hope for salvation for their souls if they do not believe that "the Lord is risen indeed"?

This morning I wish to do three things. First, let us *consider the bearings of the resurrection of Christ upon other great truths;* secondly, let us consider *the bearings of this fact upon the gospel,* for it has such bearings, according to the text—"Jesus Christ of the seed of David was raised from the dead according to my gospel"; thirdly, let us *consider its bearings on ourselves,* which are all indicated in the word "Remember."

I. First, then, beloved, as God shall help us, let us consider the bearings of the fact that Jesus rose from the dead.

It is clear at the outset that *the resurrection of our Lord was a tangible proof that there is another life.* Have you not quoted a great many times certain lines about "That undiscovered country from whose borne no traveler returns"? It is not so. There was once a traveler who said that "I go to prepare a place for you, and if I go away I will come again and receive you unto myself; that where I am there ye may be also." He said, "A little time and ye shall see me, and again a little time and ye shall not see me, and because I go to the Father."

Do you not remember these words of His? Our divine Lord went to the undiscovered country, and He returned. He said that at the third day He would be back again, and He was true to his word.

There is no doubt that there is another state for human life, for Jesus has been in it, and has come back from it. We have no doubt as to a future existence, for Jesus existed after death. We have no doubt as to a paradise of future bliss, for Jesus went to it and returned. Though He has left us again, yet that coming back to tarry with us forty days has given us a sure pledge that He will return a second time when the hour is due, and then will be with us for a thousand years, and reign on Earth amongst His ancients gloriously. His return from among the dead is a pledge to us of existence after death, and we rejoice in it.

His resurrection is also a pledge that the body will surely live again and rise to a superior condition; for the body of our blessed Master was no phantom after death any more than before. "Handle me, and see." Oh wondrous proof! He said, "Handle me, and see"; and then to Thomas, "Reach hither thy finger, and behold my hands; and reach hither thy hand, and thrust it into my side." What deception is possible here? The risen Jesus was no mere spirit. He promptly cried, "A spirit hath not flesh and bones, as ye see me have." "Bring me," said He, "something to eat"; and as if to show how real His body was, though He did not need to eat, yet He did eat, and a piece of a broiled fish and of a honeycomb were proofs of the reality of the act.

Now, the body of our Lord in its risen state did not exhibit the whole of His glorification, for otherwise we should have seen John falling at His feet as dead, and we should have seen all His disciples overcome with the glory of the vision; but, still, in a great measure, we may call the forty days' sojourn—"The life of Jesus in his glory upon earth." He was no longer despised and rejected of men; but a glory surrounded Him. It is evident that the raised body passed from place to place in a single moment, that it appeared and vanished at will, and was superior to the laws of matter. The risen body was incapable of pain, of hunger, thirst, and weariness during the time in which it remained here below—fit representative of the bulk of which it was the first fruits. Of our body also it shall be said ere long, "It was sown in weakness, it is raised in power: it was sown in dishonor, it is raised in glory."

Secondly, *Christ's rising from the dead was the seal to all His claims.* It was true, then, that He was sent of God, for God raised Him from the dead in confirmation of His mission. He had said Himself, "Destroy this body, and in three days I will raise it up." Lo, there He is: the temple of His body is rebuilt!

He had even given this as a sign, that as Jonas was three days and three nights in the whale's belly, so should the Son of man be three days and three nights in the heart of the earth, and should then come forth to life again. Behold His own appointed sign fulfilled! Before men's eye the seal is manifest! Suppose He had never risen. You and I might have believed in the truth of a certain mission which God had given Him; but we could never have believed in the truth of such a commission as He claimed to have received—a commission to be our Redeemer from death and Hell. How could He be our ransom from the grave if He had Himself remained under the dominion of death?

Dear friends, the rising of Christ from the dead proved that this man was innocent of every sin. He could not be held by the bands of death, for there was no sin to make those bands last. Corruption could not touch His pure body, for no original sin had defiled the Holy One. Death could not keep Him a continual prisoner, because He had not actually come under sin; and though He took sin of ours, and bore it by imputation, and therefore died, yet He had no fault of His own, and must, therefore, be set free when His imputed load had been removed.

Moreover, Christ's rising from the dead proved His claim to Deity. We are told in another place that He was proved to be the Son of God with power by the resurrection from the dead. He raised Himself by His own power, and though the Father and the Holy Spirit were co-operative with Him, and hence His resurrection is ascribed to them, yet it was because the Father had given Him to have life in Himself, that therefore He arose from the dead. Oh, risen Savior, Thy rising is the seal of Thy work! We can have no doubt about Thee now that Thou hast left the tomb. Prophet of Nazareth, Thou art indeed the Christ of God, for God has loosed the bands of death for Thee! Son of David, Thou art indeed the elect and precious One, for Thou ever livest! Thy resurrection life has set the sign-manual of Heaven to all that Thou hast said and done, and for this we bless and magnify Thy name.

A third bearing of his resurrection is this, and it is a very grand one—*The resurrection of our Lord, according to Scripture, was the acceptance of His sacrifice.* By the Lord Jesus Christ rising from the dead evidence was given that He had fully endured the penalty which was due to human guilt. "The soul that sinneth, it shall die"—that is the determination of the God of Heaven. Jesus stands in the sinner's stead and dies: and when He has done *that* nothing more can be demanded of Him, for He that is dead is free from the law. You take a man who has been guilty of a capital offence: he is condemned to be hanged, he is hanged by the neck till he is dead—what more has the law to do with him? It has done with him, for it has executed its sentence upon him; if he can be brought back to life again he is clear from the law; no writ that runs in Her Majesty's dominions can touch him—he has suffered the penalty.

So when our Lord Jesus rose from the dead, after having died, He had fully paid the penalty that was due to justice for the sin of His people, and His new life was a life clear of penalty, free from liability. You and I are clear from the claims of the law because Jesus stood in our stead, and God will not exact payment both from us and from our Substitute: it would be contrary to justice to sue both the Surety and those for whom He stood. And now, joy upon joy! the burden of liability which once did lie upon the Substitute is removed from Him also; seeing He has by the suffering of death vindicated justice and made satisfaction to the injured law. Now both the sinner and the Surety are free. This is a great joy, a joy for which to make the golden harps ring out a loftier style of music. He who took our debt has now delivered Himself from it by dying on the cross. His new life, now that He has risen from the dead, is a life free from legal claim, and it is the token to us that we whom He represented are free also.

Listen! "Who shall lay anything to the charge of God's elect? It is God that justifieth, who is he that condemneth? It is Christ that died, yea rather, that is risen again." It is a knock-down blow to fear when the apostle says that we cannot be condemned because Christ has died in our stead, but he puts a double force into it when he cries, "Yea rather, that is risen again." If Satan, therefore, shall come to any believer and say, "What about your sin?" tell him Jesus died for it, and your sin is put away. If he come a second time, and say to you, "What about your sin?" answer him, "Jesus lives, and His life is the assurance of our justification; for if our Surety had not paid the debt He would still be under the power of death." Inasmuch as Jesus has discharged all our liabilities, and left not one farthing due to God's justice from one of His people, He lives and is clear, and we live in Him, and are clear also by virtue of our union with Him. Is not this a glorious doctrine, this doctrine of the resurrection, in its bearing upon the justification of the saints? The Lord Jesus gave Himself for our sins, but He rose again for our justification.

Bear with me while I notice, next, another bearing of this resurrection of Christ. *It was a guarantee of His people's resurrection.* There is a great truth that never is to be forgotten, namely, that Christ and His people are one just as Adam and all his seed are one. That which Adam did He did as a head for a body, and as our Lord Jesus and all believers are one, so that which Jesus did He did as a head for a body. We were crucified together with Christ, we were buried with Christ, and we are risen together with Him; yea, He hath raised us up together and made us sit together in the heavenly places in Christ Jesus. He says, "Because I live ye shall live also." If Christ be not raised from the dead your faith is vain, and our preaching is vain, and ye are yet in your sins, and those that have fallen asleep in Christ have perished, and you will perish too; but if Christ has been raised from the dead then all His people must be raised also; it is a matter of gospel necessity. There is no logic more imperative than the argument drawn from union with Christ. God has made the saints one with Christ, and if Christ has risen all the saints must rise too. My soul takes firm hold on this and as she strengthens her grasp she loses all fear of death. Now we bear our dear ones to the cemetery and leave them each one in his narrow cell, calmly bidding him farewell and saying—

> *So Jesus slept: God's dying Son*
> *Pass'd through the grave, and blest the bed;*
> *Rest here, dear saint, till from His throne*
> *The morning break, and pierce the shade.*

It is not merely ours to know that our brethren are living in Heaven, but also that their mortal parts are in divine custody, securely kept till the appointed hour when the body shall be reanimated, and the perfect man shall enjoy the adoption of God. We are sure that our dead men shall live; together with Christ's dead body they shall rise. No power can hold in durance the redeemed of the Lord. "Let my people go" shall be a command as much obeyed by death as once by the humbled Pharaoh who could not hold a single Israelite in bonds. The day of deliverance cometh on apace.

> *Break from His throne, illustrious morn!*
> *Attend, O earth, His sovereign word;*
> *Restore thy trust, a glorious form:*
> *He must ascend to meet his Lord.*

Once more, *our Lord's rising from the dead is a fair picture of the new life which all believers already enjoy.* Beloved, though this body is still subject to bondage like the rest of the visible creation, according to the law stated in Scripture, "the body is dead because of sin," yet "the spirit is life because of righteousness." The regeneration which has taken place in those who believe has changed our spirit, and given to it eternal life, but it has not affected our body further than this, that it has made it to be the temple of the Holy Ghost, and thus it is a holy thing, and cannot be obnoxious to the Lord, or swept away among unholy things; but still the body is subject to pain and weariness, and to the supreme sentence of death. Not so the spirit. There is within us already a part of the resurrection accomplished, since it is written, "And you hath he quickened who were dead in trespasses and sins." You once were like the ungodly, under the law of sin and death, but you have been brought out of the bondage of corruption into the liberty of life and grace; the Lord having wrought in you gloriously, "according to the working of his mighty power, which he wrought in Christ, when He raised Him from the dead, and set Him at His own right hand in the heavenly places."

Now, just as Jesus Christ led, after His resurrection, a life very different from that before His death, so you and I are called upon to live a high and no-ble spiritual and heavenly life, seeing that we have been raised from the dead to die no more. Let us joy and rejoice in this. Let us behave as those who are alive from the dead, the happy children of the resurrection. Do not let us be money-grubbers, or hunters after worldly fame. Let us not set our affections on the foul things of this dead and rotten world, but let our hearts fly upward, like young birds that have broken loose of their shells—upward towards our Lord and the heavenly things upon which He would have us set our minds. Living truth, living work, living faith, these are the things for living men: let us cast off the grave-clothes of our former lusts, and wear the garments of light and life. May the Spirit of God help us in further meditating upon these things at home.

II. Now, secondly, let us consider the bearings of this fact of the resurrection upon the gospel; for Paul says, "Jesus Christ was raised from the dead according to my gospel."

I always like to see what way any kind of statement bears on the gospel. I may not have many more opportunities of preaching, and I make up my mind to this one thing, that I will waste no time upon secondary themes, but when I do preach it shall be the gospel, or something very closely bearing upon it. I will endeavor each time to strike under the fifth rib, and never beat the air. Some preachers remind me of the emperor who had a wonderful skill in carving men's heads upon cherry stones. What a multitude of preachers we have who can make wonderfully fine discourses out of a mere passing thought, of no consequence to anyone. But we want the gospel. We have to live and die, and we must have the gospel. Certain of us may be cold in our graves before many weeks are over, and we cannot afford to toy and trifle: we want to see the bearings of all teachings upon our eternal destinies, and upon the gospel which sheds its light over our future.

The resurrection of Christ is vital, because first it tells us that *the gospel is the gospel of a living Savior.* We have not to send poor penitents to the crucifix, the dead image of a dead man. We say not, "These be thy gods, O Israel!" We have not to send you to a little baby Christ nursed by a woman. Nothing of the sort. Behold the Lord that liveth and was dead and is alive for evermore, and hath the keys of Hell and of death! Behold in Him a living and accessible Savior who out of the glory still cries with loving accents, "Come unto me, all ye that labor and are heavy laden, and I will give you rest." "He is able also to save them to the uttermost that come unto God by him, seeing he ever liveth to make intercession for them." I say we have a living Savior, and is not this a glorious feature of the gospel?

Notice next that *we have a powerful Savior* in connection with the gospel that we preach; for He Who had power to raise Himself from the dead, has all power now that He is raised. He Who in death vanquishes death, can much more conquer by His life. He Who being in the grave did, nevertheless, burst all its bonds, can assuredly deliver all His people. He Who, coming under the power of the law, did, nevertheless, fulfill the law, and thus set His people free from bondage, must be mighty to save. You need a Savior strong and mighty, yet you do not want one stronger than He of Whom it is written that He rose again from the dead. What a blessed gospel we have to preach—the gospel of a living Christ Who hath Himself returned from the dead, leading captivity captive.

And now notice, that we have *the gospel of complete justification* to preach to you. We do not come and say, "Brethren, Jesus Christ by His death did something by which men may be saved if they have a mind to be, and diligently carry out their good resolves." No, no; we say Jesus Christ took the sin of His people upon Himself and bore the consequences of it in His own body on the tree, so that He died; and having died, and so paid the penalty, He lives again; and now all for whom He died, all His people whose sins He bore, are free from the guilt of sin. You ask me, "Who are they?" and I reply, as many as believe on Him. Whosoever be- lieveth in Jesus Christ is as free from the guilt of sin as Christ is. Our Lord Jesus took the sin of His people, and died in the sinner's stead, and now be- ing Himself set free, all His people are set free in their Representative. He has performed the work entrusted to Him. He has finished transgression, made an end of sin, and brought in everlasting righteousness, and whoso- ever believeth in Him is not condemned, and never can be.

Once again, the connection of the resurrection and the gospel is this, *it proves the safety of the saints,* for if, when Christ rose His people rose also, they rose to a life like that of their Lord, and therefore they can never die. It is written, "Christ being raised from the dead dieth no more; death hath no more dominion over him," and it is so with the believer: if you have been dead with Christ and are risen with Christ, death has no more dominion over you; you shall never go back to the beggarly elements of sin, you shall never become what you were before your regeneration. You shall never perish, neither shall any pluck you out of Jesus' hand. He has put within you a living and incorruptible seed which liveth and abideth forever. He says Himself, "The water that I shall give him shall be in him a well of living water springing up unto everlasting life." Wherefore hold ye fast to this, and let the resurrection of your Lord be the pledge of your own final perseverance.

Brethren, I cannot stop to show you how this resurrection touches the gospel at every point, but Paul is always full of it. More than thirty times Paul talks about the resurrection, and occasionally at great length, giving whole chapters to the glorious theme. The more I think of it the more I delight to preach Jesus and the resurrection. The glad tidings that Christ has risen is as truly the gospel as the doctrine that He came among men and for men presented His blood as a ransom. If angels sang glory to God in the highest when the Lord was born, I feel impelled to repeat the note now that He is risen from the dead.

III. *And so I come to my last head, and to the practical conclusion: the bearing of this resurrection upon ourselves.*

Paul expressly bids us "Remember" it. "Why," says one, "we don't forget it." Are you sure you do not? I find myself far too forgetful of divine truths. We ought not to forget, for this first day of the week is consecrated for Sabbatic purposes to constrain us to think of the resurrection. On the seventh day men celebrated a finished creation, on the first day we celebrate a finished redemption. Bear it, then, in mind. Now, if you will remember that Jesus Christ of the seed of David rose from the dead, what will follow?

First, you will find that *most of your trials will vanish*. Are you tried by your sin? Jesus Christ rose again from the dead for your justification. Does Satan accuse? Jesus rose to be your advocate and intercessor. Do infirmities hinder? The living Christ will show Himself strong on your behalf. You have a living Christ, and in Him you have all things. Do you dread death? Jesus in rising again, has vanquished the last enemy. He will come and meet you when it is your turn to pass through the chill stream, and you shall ford it in sweet company. What is your trouble? I care not what it is, for if you will only think of Jesus as living, full of power, full of love, and full of sympathy, having experienced all your trials, even unto death, you will have such a confidence in His tender care and in His boundless ability that you will follow in His footsteps without a question. Remember Jesus, and that He rose again from the dead, and your confidence will rise as on eagles' wings.

Next remember Jesus, for then you will see how your present sufferings are as nothing compared with His sufferings, and you will learn to *expect victory over your sufferings even as He obtained victory.* Kindly look at the chapter, and you will find the apostle there saying in the third verse, "Thou therefore endure hardness, as a good soldier of Jesus Christ," and further on in the eleventh verse, "It is a faithful saying: For if we be dead in him, we shall also live in him: if we suffer, we shall also reign with him." Now, then, when you are called to suffer, think—"Jesus suffered, yet Jesus rose again from the dead; He came up out of His baptism of griefs the better and more glorious for it, and so shall I!" Wherefore go you into the furnace at the Lord's bidding, and do not fear that the smell of fire shall pass upon you. Go you even down into the grave, and do not think that the worm shall make an end of you any more than it did of Him. Behold in the risen One the type and model of what you are to be! Wherefore fear not, for He conquered! Stand not trembling, but march boldly on, for Jesus Christ of the seed of David rose from the dead, and you who are of the seed of the promise shall rise again from all your trials and afflictions and live a glorious life.

We see here, dear brethren, in being told to remember Jesus that there *is hope even in our hopelessness.* When are things most hopeless in a man? Why, when he is dead. Do you know what it is to come down to that, so far as your inward weakness is concerned? I do. We take a deal of killing, and it is by being killed that we live. Many a man will never live till his proud self is slain. Alas, how many are so good and excellent, and strong and wise, and clever, and all that, that they cannot agree to be saved by grace through faith. If they could be reduced to less than nothing it would be the finest thing that ever happened to them. Remember what Solomon said might be done with the fool, and yet it would not answer—he was to be brayed in a mortar among wheat with a pestle—pretty hard dealing that, and yet his folly would not depart from him. Not by that process alone, but through some such method, the Holy Spirit brings men away from their folly. Under His killing operations this may be their comfort that, if Jesus Christ rose literally from the dead (not from sickness, but from death), and lives again, even so will His people.

Did you ever get, where Bunyan pictures Christian as getting, right under the old dragon's foot? He is very heavy, and presses the very breath out of a fellow when he makes him his footstool. Poor Christian lay there with the dragon's foot on his breast; but he was just able to stretch out his hand and lay hold on his sword, which, by a good providence, lay within his reach. Then he gave Apollyon a deadly thrust, which made him spread his dragon wings and fly away. The poor crushed and broken pilgrim, as he gave the stab to his foe, cried, "Rejoice not over me, O mine enemy; though I fall, yet shall I rise again." Brother, do you the same. You that are near despair, let this be the strength that nerves your arm and steels your heart. "Jesus Christ of the seed of David was raised from the dead according to Paul's gospel."

Lastly, this proves *the futility of all opposition to Christ*. The learned are going to destroy the Christian religion. Already, according to their boastings, it has pretty nearly come to an end. The pulpit is effete, it cannot command public attention. We stand up and preach to empty benches! As you see—or do not see. Nothing remains for us but to die decently, so they insinuate. And what then? When our Lord was dead, when the clay-cold corpse lay, watched by the Roman soldiery, and with a seal upon the enclosing stone, was not the cause in mortal jeopardy? But how fared it? Did it die out? Every disciple that Jesus had made forsook Him, and fled, was not Christianity then destroyed? Nay, that very day our Lord won a victory which shook the gates of Hell, and caused the universe to stand astonished. Matters are not worse with Him at this hour! His affairs are not in a sadder condition today than then. Nay, see Him today and judge. On His head are many crowns, and at His feet the hosts of angels bow! Jesus is the master of legions today, while the Caesars have passed away! Here are His people—needy, obscure, despised, I grant you, still, but assuredly somewhat more numerous than they were when they laid Him in the tomb. His cause is not to be crushed, it is forever rising. Year after year, century after century, bands of true and honest hearts are marching up to the assault of the citadel of Satan.

Truly if Christ were dead I would admit our defeat, for they that are fallen asleep in Him would have perished: but as the Christ liveth so the cause liveth, and they that have fallen are not dead: they have vanished from our sight for a little, but if the curtain could be withdrawn every one of them would be seen to stand in his lot unharmed, crowned, victorious! "Who are these arrayed in white robes, and whence came they?" These are they that were defeated! Whence, then, their crowns? These are they that were dishonored! Whence then their white robes? These are they who clung to a cause which is overthrown. Whence then their long line of victors, for there is not a vanquished man among them all?

Let the truth be spoken. Defeat is not the word for the cause of Jesus, the Prince of the house of David. We have always been victorious, brethren; we are victorious now. Follow your Master on your white horses, and be not afraid! I see Him in the front with His blood-stained vesture around Him, fresh from the wine-press where He has trodden down His foes. You have not to present atoning blood, but only to conquer after your Lord. Put on your white raiment and follow Him on your white horses, conquering and to conquer. He is nearer than we think, and the end of all things may be before the next jibe shall have come forth from the mouth of the last new skeptic. Have confidence in the risen One, and live in the power of His resurrection. Amen.

Spurgeon's Sermons
on the
Death and Resurrection
of Jesus

The text of this book is set in Dante 11/14 and Delphin IA,
with Poetica SuppOrnaments.

Typeset in Corel Ventura Publisher.

Electronic text development, interior design, copyediting, and production by
Publication Resources, Inc., of Ipswich, MA.